Archaeology of Louisiana

Archaeology of Louisiana

Edited by Mark A. Rees

With a Foreword by Ian W. Brown

LOUISIANA STATE UNIVERSITY PRESS

BATON ROUGE

Publication of this book is supported by DeeDee and Kevin P. Reilly, Sr.

Published by Louisiana State University Press
Copyright © 2010 by Louisiana State University Press
All rights reserved
Manufactured in the United States of America
First printing

DESIGNER: *Mandy McDonald Scallan*
TYPEFACES: *text, Whitman; display, U 59*
PRINTER AND BINDER: *McNaughton & Gunn, Inc.*

Library of Congress Cataloging-in-Publication Data
Archaeology of Louisiana / edited by Mark A. Rees ; with a foreword by Ian W. Brown.
p. cm.
Includes bibliographical references and index.
ISBN 978-0-8071-3703-1 (cloth : alk. paper) — ISBN 978-0-8071-3705-5 (paper : alk. paper) 1. Louisiana—Antiquities. 2. Archaeology—Louisiana. 3. Indians of North America—Louisiana—Antiquities. 4. Archaeology and history—Louisiana. 5. Ethnoarchaeology—Louisiana. 6. Social archaeology—Louisiana. 7. Excavations (Archaeology)—Louisiana. 8. Historic sites—Louisiana. I. Rees, Mark A.
F371.A73 2010
976.3'01—dc22

2010020022

The paper in this book meets the guidelines for permanence and durability of the Committee on Production Guidelines for Book Longevity of the Council on Library Resources. ∞

This book is dedicated to all those

archaeologists, scholars, scientists, and shovel bums

who carried a shovel or screen, dug by trowel, or studied artifacts

and cared enough about the archaeology of Louisiana

to ask questions and patiently seek answers.

And for the future generations

who follow in their

footsteps.

Contents

Illustrations

Foreword

"Mind the gap." Anyone traveling in the London Tube system soon becomes very familiar with that phrase. At each and every station a lilting feminine voice provides this warning, a message that quickly works its way into the traveler's subconscious. Although everyone knows of the potential danger, the constant reminder is universally appreciated. The gap, of course, is the narrow space that occurs between the solid stable platforms and the fast-moving trains that come and go. Whether one enters the Tube at Covent Garden, Piccadilly Circus, or Leicester Square, each and every train is absolutely packed with humanity, a perfect mélange of multiple ethnicities, all rushing hither and yon. The gaps that separate the safe and secure landings from the speedy exciting trains are narrow, but they also run deep. Danger and uncertainty lurk within their depths.

The week before I sat down to write this foreword, I was traveling in London. Consequently, each time I heard "Mind the gap," I thought of Louisiana archaeology and my personal experiences with it. Unlike the many authors of this volume, my own contributions to the archaeology of Louisiana have been rather minimal. I have done some fieldwork in the state to be sure, but it has occurred sporadically and at wide-spaced intervals. Nevertheless, I feel an attachment to Louisiana and its rich heritage and have great respect for the state's researchers and their many contributions to its archaeological knowledge.

I first saw Louisiana from the vantage point of the Vicksburg bluffs in the summer of 1971. This was also my introduction to the Mississippi River, a wide watery gap that separated the tall solid bluffs from the flatlands that stretched out into seeming infinity. I myself come from a hilly area in upstate New York and did not travel much in my youth. Therefore, the Louisiana terrain—its mixture of fields, swamps, and curious half-moon lakes—was totally unfamiliar to me. It was wild and dangerous, a land continually being modified by the great body of water that flowed below me. Having done some readings in Fisk (1944), I knew that the Mississippi narrowed as it approached the Gulf of Mexico, but that it also got continually deeper to the south and ever more dangerous. There were currents, eddies, and other impediments in the Father of Waters that would drag you down if you did not "mind the gaps."

On the same day that I saw the Mississippi River, I met Robert S. Neitzel, also known as Stu or, more fondly, "The Great Sun." He was helping Jeff Brain, my teacher, set up operations in the Natchez Bluffs and was awaiting us at an old train stop called Cannonsburg. "He's from Louisiana," said Jeff, "and a little bit different." Different indeed! Stu was the wildest man I had ever met, and after several hours in his company I was quite anxious to go home. Within but a day's time, however, I had settled on archaeology as a career. A couple of weeks after the project started, Stu invited us all to his home at a place called Marksville, located (I was told) somewhere vaguely to the west. I had great anticipation of the type of abode that The Great Sun inhabited, but when we pulled into his driveway at 110 Joffrion Street and entered his delightful suburban ranch-style home, I immediately accused him of being a fake. "It's Miz Gwen's home," he said. "She merely lets me live here." Stu was forever wild, as was Louisiana.

Over the next day or two, Stu gave us the royal tour of Marksville and its environs. He was the shaman passing on the lore of the land to young neophytes. We drove around the state park that he once managed and climbed the mounds and embankments that Jim Ford had once dug. Stu pointed in one direction and said, "Greenhouse—that would be Troyville and Coles Creek. Dug there in '38." Then he pointed in another direction towards another site. "Baptiste—Plaquemine. Dug there in 1940," he continued, "not analyzed yet. Someone needs to do that." Another slight turn and he pronounced, "Tunica reservation. Chief Joe used to be my neighbor. Good fellow. He would love to see the Treasure once you Harvard folk are done with it." "Tunica?" I asked, "I thought they were up around Vicksburg?" "They were," said Stu, "but they moved. Read your Swanton. And while you're at it, you might read a little of Ford too." I was embarrassed, but noted that his eyes were twinkling and kind. Even still, the message was clear—there were ample gaps in my education.

We left Stu in Marksville and traveled up to Poverty Point, yet another site that Ford had worked on. He was everywhere, it seemed. Jeff explained that Poverty Point was where mound building began in Louisiana. I was amazed that anything so big could have simply started from scratch, but that was almost forty years ago. Joe Saunders has taught us since that there are much earlier mounds, much earlier indeed and impressive in their own right. Although many people have dug at Poverty Point over the years, I have a lasting image of Bill Haag and his operations there. Here was another wild character of Louisiana, one who normally managed to keep that side of his personality hidden beneath a professorial cloak. Fred Kniffen was another, but that's another story.

In 1976, I brought my crew over to Poverty Point from Fort St. Pierre, an early eighteenth-century French installation located just to the northeast of Vicksburg. My purpose was to have them view the great site. We were fortunate to discover Bill digging along the south side of the big mound's ramp, the "bird tail" if you will. I can still see him standing atop the trench, gazing down into the depths of his *sondage*. "Why so deep?" I asked. "Because it keeps going down," he responded. "This mound was a lot bigger than anyone has ever conceived." He proceeded to explain that erosion has given us a false impression of size by raising the ground surface around the mound. This was the first time that I really appreciated just how much of Louisiana's heritage lies buried at great depths. In the present work Mark Rees reminds us that if we wish to ever gain a true appreciation of the Paleoindian and Early Archaic periods in the state, we are going to have to dig very deep. Similarly, Allen Saltus and Charles Pearson reveal that much of Louisiana's early heritage lies offshore, initially covered by a rising sea and then buried by expanding deltas.

I got a personal taste of this "depth factor" when working on Avery Island in the late 1970s. Woody Gagliano had already demonstrated that the earliest occupations at the Salt Mine Valley site (16IB23) were too low to explore by conventional archaeology, but to my great horror I also discovered that much of the site's late prehistory also occurred at great depths. And this phenomenon was not confined to sites on Avery Island. I spent a good portion of the spring of 1979 following in the footsteps (or rather boat wake) of William McIntire, who, two decades earlier, had conducted a survey of Louisiana's coastline. In the intervening years much dredging had occurred as oil rigs were moved from spot to spot. In the process, deeply buried materials were thrown up onto the banks, producing an absolute paradise for surface collecting. I soon came to realize, however, that the dredging offered only very minor glimpses into this underworld. The resulting slits across the landscape were far too narrow to give a true appreciation of all that lay below.

The gaps in our knowledge have been greatly reduced in the almost four decades that have passed since my first view of Louisiana. There was no underwater archaeology in 1971, for example. Nor was there such a thing as African American archaeology. As Laurie Wilkie, Paul Farnsworth, and David Palmer remind us, there has always been a degree of racism involved in its neglect. There was no question that the rich cultural resources of St. Francisville would be preserved for posterity, but when the Corps of Engineers flooded the nearby Bayou Sara community, there was very little thought given as to all that would be lost. One was a white community, the other black.

African American archaeology has come a long way in the past forty years, as has urban archaeology. This book devotes two full chapters to investigations in New Orleans, whereas only a sentence or two would have been possible when I entered the profession. Throughout its history, New Orleans has been bombarded with change, a result of its incredibly diverse populations. It is no surprise, then, that the archaeology of this fascinating city inevitably deals with the processes of change. As Shannon Lee Dawdy and Christopher Matthews point out, "The story is not how an Indian town became an Afro-French one or how a French town became an American one. Rather, it is how everyone in New Orleans eventually becomes Creole." The story of New Orleans archaeology does not stop with creolization. Ryan Gray and Jill-Karen Yakubik show how even such complex topics as immigration and urbanization can be revealed by archaeological research. Who, for example, would have thought that anything would be left of the fabled Storyville once the Iberville Housing Project was constructed in the 1940s? There is indeed much to be told, as the reader will see. A wealth of history remains hidden beneath New Orleans's housing developments, so it is absolutely critical that such areas are not written off in the haste to renew.

The authors of this series of essays clearly demonstrate that there is far more below the ground and water than most people are aware of, but they also emphasize that cultural resources are limited and that we, the public, have a responsibility to care for them. The tragedy of Hurricane Katrina and the subsequent flooding of New Orleans have amplified the matter. As Gray and Yakubik remind us, many residents are in danger of being "separated from their past and disenfranchised in the future." Hurricanes and river flooding are natural occurrences in Louisiana. We have seen what an effect they have on contemporary peoples and must acknowledge that past populations were impacted by natural catastrophes too. The great site of Poverty Point may have been abandoned because of such forces. T. R. Kidder (2006) has pointed to climatic changes and flooding as critical factors in its demise, which may well be true, but we must also ask why Poverty Point came about in the first place. Jon Gibson, in his chapter, says that although the site was occupied for about four hundred years, "Everywhere, construction looks to have been carried out quickly and continuously." In other words, it seems there was a plan right from the beginning. The inner ring of the site was started first and the other rings were added accordingly, but the basic structure of Poverty Point existed all along. We did not know this in 1971—a gap filled.

But we must continue to "mind the gaps." As mentioned earlier, we now know that the people of Poverty Point were not the first to construct such enormous sites. Major mound-building events occurred in Louisiana since Middle Archaic times, as argued by Joe Saunders. Sites such as Watson Brake (16OU175) and Hedgepeth (16LI7) are different, very different indeed, from those that came before or after them, both in terms of mound structure and artifacts. I would feel a lot better about these sites if it could be demonstrated just why they came about, what they were used for, and why they were abandoned. We know, for example, that the people of Poverty Point were engaged in an elaborate long-distance exchange of exotic imported stones, but what were the earlier Louisiana Middle Archaic people doing with their immense mounds, and why did they stop building them?

We must ask a similar question of Tchefuncte, which is discussed here by Christopher Hays and Richard Weinstein. Did the Poverty Point people become Tchefuncte, or was there a break, biologically as well as culturally? Why did the elaborate lithic exchange system terminate and why did the age of pottery begin? Did Tchefuncte people simply copy St. Johns or Wheeler pottery traditions from the east, or were they themselves being copied? In short, what were the mechanisms involved?

Similar questions can be asked of the succeeding Marksville period. Chip McGimsey tells us, "If Marksville is defined as the time of interaction with northern-Midwestern Hopewellian cultures, it is limited to a small number of communities that may have participated in it for only a generation or two. After that, Louisiana Marksville went its own way, with little influence from cultural developments outside of the state." Once again, change seems to have come rapidly at the beginning, and the stability that followed took a long time to solidify. But, with their feet firmly planted on various metaphorical station platforms, the inhabitants of Louisiana managed to confront those fast-moving trains with a certain amount of success. Even still, the incessant refrain of "Mind the gap" must give us pause.

One gap that has filled considerably over the last several years is the Baytown period. As a result of Aubra Lee's work at the Troyville site (16CT7) and the strikingly similar McGuffee site (16CT17), we now have a much greater understanding of Troyville culture in Louisiana. Troyville is another one of those spectacular sites that was thought to have been all but destroyed. Once again, however, that which is visible on the landscape often does not reveal all that lies below. For that information we must dig deeper. As an example, we still do not understand the nature of the transition from Troyville to Coles Creek culture. I suspect that once again there is a fast-moving train behind the scenes, because it was during this transitional period that the bow and arrow first entered Louisiana. Lori Roe and Timothy Schilling tell us, "Coles Creek societies were more centralized and more focused on mound centers than previous cultures in the region," yet "Coles

Creek material culture shows that Coles Creek communities did not participate extensively in long-distance exchanges of goods." How curious. I can't help but wonder what effects warfare may have had on formulating the inward-looking nature of Coles Creek society.

Mark Rees goes on to tell us that the late prehistoric societies of Louisiana also seem to have been relatively insular. As he writes, "While Mississippian chiefdoms are associated with more elaborate, non-local artifacts made of stone, shell, and copper, often interred as burial goods at major mound centers . . . the scarcity of such items has led researchers to conclude that contemporaneous communities in Louisiana were less complex, or removed from the Mississippian 'climax.'" It bears pointing out, as Jeffrey Girard does in his essay, that although the Coles Creek and Mississippi period societies seem far more complex than their Caddo neighbors in the northwest part of the state, it was the early Caddo centers that actually maintained strong contacts with the great Cahokia site in southwestern Illinois. Why? That's another gap to be filled.

The Caddo were removed to Indian Territory, now Oklahoma, in the early nineteenth century, but Robert Cast, Bobby Gonzalez, and Timothy Perttula reveal quite clearly in their essay that Caddo interest in their homeland remains very strong. They report on a visit that the Caddo Repatriation Committee made to sites still considered to be sacred: "The committee was able to visit several important places relating to the Caddo people's long history in Louisiana. Mounds Plantation (16CD12), the Southern Compress site (16NA14), Drake's Salt Lick site (16NA11), Los Adaes (16NA16), Fort St. Jean Baptiste des Natchitoches (16NA68), and the Fish Hatchery site (16NA9) in Natchitoches were some of the places that were visited." A salt production site, a Spanish fort, and a French fort are not sites that one would necessarily consider sacred to indigenous peoples, but they were and still are sacred to the Caddo.

George Avery tells us that almost 35,000 fragments of American Indian pottery have been recovered at Los Adaes to date, comprising almost 90 percent of the total number of potsherds found there. These are not the remnants of earlier occupation; rather, the local Caddo people maintained strong economic relationships with the Spaniards who settled amongst them. Most of the ceramics the Europeans used at the site were traded to them by the Indians. Similarly, Wilkie, Farnsworth, and Palmer make very clear that African Americans were also major consumers of Indian pots, thus complicating the picture with regard to material culture and ethnicity. Sadly enough, this thought never crossed my mind in the 1970s when I was excavating the Fort St. Pierre site for my graduate work. I simply assumed that the large collection of Indian pottery found on the site related to pre- or post-French occupation. Life seemed so much simpler then.

How to get at ethnicity in the past is a very complex issue. One would think that having readily identifiable historic sites would help, but the ever-constant interaction of people—that fast-moving train—often muddles the works. For example, as Avery points out, almost two-thirds of the ninety-four gunflints and gunflint fragments found at Los Adaes, a Spanish fort, are French blonde gunflints. As long as Europeans, Indians, and Africans continued to trade among themselves, as they clearly did, materials alone will not sort out ethnic groups. Many years ago Stanley South insisted that studying behavioral patterns in the patterning of material culture would get us closer to distinguishing ethnicity among historic populations, and he was right. Avery, for example, tells us that the material remains at Los Adaes reveal that the Spaniards had a fondness for chocolate, which was native to southern Mexico. Conversely, the French at Natchitoches were consuming coffee, which was native to Africa, and the British wherever they were found seemed to prefer tea, which was native to China.

But what does that tell us with regard to prehistory? There are Natchezan pottery sherds, those good old Fatherland Incised vessels, distributed all over the Coastal Plain in late prehistoric and historic times. Are they the result of Natchez Indians moving around? Did they trade vessels? Or are we simply observing a time marker? In discussing Marksville societies, McGimsey warns us that common projectile point forms and ceramic vessel designs are no indication that the people are of the same social group (i.e., a tribe or similar organization). I believe he is correct, and because of this I do refrain from using pottery types to define such units. However, I have made great use of varieties in this manner with the hope of coming up with the magic expression, "This is *their* assemblage." Phases are often thought to be representative of social entities wherein the complex of materials is a reflection of identity (see Rees, Chapter 1 in this volume). Historical archaeology continues to challenge this view, reminding us that life is but a blend of stable platforms and fast-moving trains. If people just stayed still it would be far easier to understand what they did, but I suppose it would be far less interesting as well.

As I look at the collective bibliography of this book, I am amazed at just how much has occurred in Louisiana archaeology since I entered the field. The vast bulk of the references relate to the last thirty-five years, the time following the initiation of cultural resource management (Byrd and Neuman, Chapter 2 in this volume). This is no accident. Federal money has not only permitted some archaeological practitioners to exist, but it has also provided the means for investigation. Many gaps in our knowledge have filled in the intervening years, but just as many gaps have widened. This book not only shows how far archaeology has come in the last four decades, but also reveals just how exciting the ride has been. Yet the wary traveler must continue to "mind the gaps" to profit from the experience, because there are dangers lurking in the depths. Deep down, things occurred in the past that we cannot fully appreciate without expanding our view by excavating. The one thing this book does not do, and which ultimately cannot be done, is to post our final destination point. The stations along the way are starting to come into view, but the end of the line is nowhere in sight. Perhaps that is inevitable. I am firmly convinced there are patterns in the past that enable us to make sense of it. As for the future, I believe we are in for a wild ride.

Ian W. Brown

Preface

Contrary to popular belief, the history of the region included within the present bounds of the State of Louisiana begins not with the discovery of the Mississippi River, but long before that time, even before the dawn of the Christian Era.
—JAMES A. FORD (1935a:8)
from "An Introduction to Louisiana Archaeology"

As students of American history learn in high school, *Louisiane* formerly extended from the Gulf of Mexico beyond the Great Lakes, from the Ohio Valley westward to the Rocky Mountain headwaters of the Missouri River. Two centuries ago one of the largest river basins in the world became a real-estate sensation. When the Louisiana Purchase was made by the United States for as little as four cents an acre in 1803, the leaders of the fledgling nation hoped to establish possession of a western frontier claimed by competing European empires (Kukla 2003; Richter 2001:227–228). The celebrated Lewis and Clark expedition explored this uncharted territory, informing its native inhabitants along the way that their homeland had just been purchased in a foreign land. The rights of Native Americans—whose ancestors had lived there for thousands of years—were treated as inferior, if considered at all (Wilson 1998:162–163; Zinn 2003:126). Long after the revolutionary founding of the United States, Native Americans were unreasonably regarded as a wild and nomadic race, either incapable of the "higher attainments" of civilization or desperately in need of salvation, rehabilitation and assimilation (Berkhofer 1978; Pearce 1988).

Native American societies downriver in the Lower Mississippi Valley (LMV) had dealt with European encroachments before, since at least A.D. 1541, eventually succumbing in the eighteenth century to the combined effects of foreign diseases, enslavement, and wars of colonial expansion (Barnett 2007; Ethridge 2006; Galloway 2002; Kelton 2007). The Chitimacha Tribe of Louisiana, who endured centuries of colonialism and oppression in their homeland, exemplify the determination and dignity of a people's cultural survival and resurgence (Goldsmith 2003:7–13). Other "smaller tribes" of the LMV, such as the Bayougoula and Mugulasha, were less fortunate. The present-day State of Louisiana was carved out of the homelands of the Atakapa, Caddo, Chitimacha, and other First Americans (Gregory 1992, 2004; Kniffen et al. 1987; Swanton 1911).

Louisiana's past is more ancient and varied than commonly acknowledged. The roots extend deep—to at least ten thousand years before European exploration and colonization. As James Ford (1935a:8) noted three quarters of a century ago, Louisiana's actual history contradicts conventional beliefs concerning discovery and statehood. While archaeology has since developed as a profession, beliefs have unfortunately changed more slowly. Students do not often learn that Native Americans in the Mississippi Valley long ago established impressive civilizations truly worthy of the term, and that among these were permanent, densely populated towns, political and religious centers, productive agricultural economies, and prosperous fishing, hunting, and gathering in the original Sportsman's Paradise.

The material remnants of these societies are scattered across fields of the alluvial valley and buried within natural levees, along relict river channels abandoned long ago. Sherds of broken ceramic vessels buried in the earth are incised and engraved with their immeasurable thoughts and dreams. The proverbial arrowhead, shot from a bow centuries before any European laid eyes on the great muddy river, still glimmers in the sun following an afternoon thunderstorm. Sacred temples and houses of honored families towered over surrounding neighborhoods, casting civic shadows that modern city dwellers might recognize. Earthen monuments had been constructed for millennia in Louisiana, the earliest laid down a thousand years before construction began on the Great Pyramids of Egypt. Daily life was made possible by the labor, industry, and accomplishments of individuals and communities throughout the countryside. Their stories, mostly unrecorded and forgotten, are not entirely lost to us. Yet few students of Louisiana history are taught to appreciate the antiquity, complexity, and diversity of Native American cultures.

Indeed, there has been and remains for some today a pervasive disinterest in preserving and learning about the material remains of Louisiana's earlier, pre-colonial past. The ultimate cost of such indifference is obliteration and ignorance, of both the material record and the scarce evidence of Louisiana's unrecorded past—the very cultural resources it can least afford to lose. Berwick, Runway Mound, Teche Street, Troyville: the list of bulldozed and demolished sites is longer than anyone knows for sure, and it is still increasing. The remains of entire towns, ancient mounds and cultures have been regarded as an inconvenience, commodities to be dismantled, mined and sold, hoary obstacles to highways, suburbs, and unmitigated progress. The material record of colonial European, African, and later arrivals is obliterated as well. Progress is not always choosy in its destruction, although the favored places of privileged history are sometimes protected by popular acclamation of historical significance. Those other, "invisible" places are endangered by ongoing construction and modifications of the environment, canal digging and dredging, levees and deep plowing, subsidence and wetlands loss. Louisiana is in danger of losing what makes it most distinctive and unique; it's cultural landscape.

This is no new revelation. James Ford (1935a:11) long ago observed the consequences of such destruction. Efforts have more recently been made to recognize and conserve some of the ancient and more modern places on the landscape—historic sites that make Louisiana truly fascinating and unique not just in the United States but throughout the world (e.g., Louisiana Division of Archaeology 2000). The turning point comes with the realization that culture and history are not impediments to progress, but indispensable elements of economic development, tourism, recreation, sense of identity, and quality of life. Archaeologists engaged in cultural resource management (CRM) have only begun to document some of the irretrievable losses and to inform future planning and development (Byrd and Neuman, Chapter 2 in this volume; Smith et al. 1983). Contemporary Native American participation as cultural resource managers and archaeologists, as well as greater public involvement through collaboration, educational outreach, and Louisiana Archaeology Month, promise to advance archaeology and increase public understanding of its significance (Cast, Gonzalez, and Perttula, Chapter 12 in this volume).

The modern history of Louisiana is marked by successive migrations, interactions, conflicts, and cross-cultural connections of increasingly diverse and heterogeneous populations, beginning with the arrival of the Choctaw, Coushatta, Houma, Tunica, and other Native Americans, who were displaced or driven from their homelands (Kniffen et al. 1987:71–105; Usner 1992, 1998). As much as any other state, Louisiana has repeatedly been refashioned as a fertile homeland of the displaced, of immigrants and migrants, refugees and colonists, exiles and foreigners (both authorized and otherwise), all of whom have called it home. Africans and French, Germans and Spaniards, Irish and Isleños, Acadians, Américains, and others came to Louisiana by volition and force, swept up in the colonial transformation and creolization of what would become the eighteenth state in 1812. Historical trends persist today as Filipinos and Vietnamese, Lebanese and Pakistanis, Hondurans and Mexicans find their way to the Pelican State (Brasseaux, ed. 1996; White 1998; Wilson et al. 1979).

As in the past, diversity is both cherished and disdained. Historical narratives come to represent shared, public recollections of Louisiana's multifaceted past and, by extension, forethoughts of what it might become (Shackel 2001b). The political victories and personal foibles of successive governors and administrations may receive more attention than the soon-forgotten histories of native resistance and survival, laborers enslaved in houses and fields, indomitable sharecroppers, the urban working class, and so many unnamed and dispossessed who comprise Louisiana's heritage and lifeblood. But it does not mean their lives were inconsequential or uninteresting. Their interrelated stories, and how this broadly conceived, collective past unfolded, represent alternative histories of a socially relevant American archaeology (Pauketat and Loren 2005). The everyday, material lives of ordinary people are archaeologically accessible and counterbalance the fragmentary, biased accounts of outsiders and elites. Such an inclusive past matters because it deepens history and broadens heritage, both of which define who we are as a people, where we come from, and what the future might hold. The reassessment of Louisiana's little-known, earliest and more recent culture histories is one ambitious aim of this volume. Another is to hopefully steer archaeology into the mainstream of historical dialogue and debate. The principal aim of the present work, however, is to provide a cohesive collection of up-to-date overviews of Louisiana's long and diverse past, drawing upon recent archaeological research and earlier studies.

A genuine and urgent need for the archaeology of Louisiana is readily apparent with the recognition that Native Americans lived here many thousands of years prior to the advent of any systematic, written records. More than 98 percent of Louisiana's past consequently falls under a "silent age" in relation to standard historical sources, partly accessible only through archaeology. The oral histories of thirty consecutive generations may relate knowledge of a more timeless American heritage, yet the corresponding millennium would still leave untouched more than 90 percent of Louisiana's culture history. Much of this past remains silent, unexamined and yet to be discovered. While "pre-historic" in its absence of written documentation, the course of history was never constrained by a lack of journalist or scribe. All societies and cultures are characterized by significant events and changes, influential individuals and groups, technological innovations, economic and political trends, dominant beliefs or ideologies, and ecological relationships. Based on the systematic retrieval and cross-examination of material sources, archaeologists are well-equipped to interrogate and comprehend this "silent" past.

Historical archaeologists have extended the scope of study conspicuously forward in time, so that archaeology is today much more than the study of a preliterate or undocumented past (e.g., Hall and Silliman, ed. 2006; Hicks and Beaudry, ed. 2006; Orser, ed. 1996). Historical omissions are not limited to the absence of written sources after all, but emanate from past and present biases and predispositions (Trouillot 1995:1–30). Contemporary archaeology teaches us that historical significance must not be based on the often capricious presence or absence of incomplete and subjective written documents. Through the meticulous investigation of material traces of human behavior, artifacts, and residues known broadly as the archaeological record, scholars strive to interpret the lives of people for whom there may be little or no written documentation. These are the people for whom the usual sources are decidedly biased against. African Americans working on sugarcane plantations and Creoles living in urban neighborhoods may not be well represented in existing documents, but to the archaeologist theirs are the histories that really matter—and are significant to a truly modern and enlightened, multicultural Louisiana.

The archaeology of Louisiana consequently uncovers alternative histories and strives toward cross-cultural understanding and anthropological knowledge. The archaeological lens is telescopic—gazing into distant pasts, but focusing on comparative details, more recent times, and long-term changes. Archaeologies of Louisiana engage people of today with new and various ways of looking into the past, turning history on its side and making it seem more vulnerable and alive. The excitement of finding an unexpected arrowhead, still gleaming in the sunset, need not die in a relic hunter's odd collection of curios on a dusty shelf. The archaeological record can make a difference—and be preserved. Indifference thrives only through ignorance. As soon as questions are raised, and answers sought—concerning who made and used certain artifacts, when and how those people lived—then archaeology has just begun. Like students of history who learn that modern-day Louisiana is only the southern terminus of a vast territory once purchased by a young nation, archaeology reveals that recorded history is merely the tip of an immense iceberg. Undiscovered countries and their inhabitants, long submerged, remain to be explored.

Mark A. Rees

Acknowledgments

The origin of this book was drawn out, as was its production. The possibility of a multiauthored, accessible, and up-to-date overview of Louisiana archaeology was initially considered by the editor in 2001, upon moving back home to Lafayette. Obligations and responsibilities intervened, so the idea was shelved and not pursued for many years. The project was informally discussed with colleagues and officially organized at the 2007 meeting of the Louisiana Archaeological Society in Leesville. A tentative outline of 12 or so chapters quickly grew to 18, with 26 contributing authors. Sensible suggestions that such a tome might be best divided into two separate volumes were stubbornly resisted by the editor, who had no inclination to do twice what might be over and done with once.

It would be impossible to thank all the individuals and institutions who contributed to or played a role in this undertaking. Several people stand out, however, and their contributions should be readily acknowledged. David G. Anderson, in the Department of Anthropology at the University of Tennessee, reviewed the manuscript in its entirety and offered thoughtful comments and advice. While his balanced critique and insights about Louisiana archaeology are much appreciated, he is of course not responsible for the interpretations presented here. David's coauthored overview of archaeology at Fort Polk in west-central Louisiana is required reading for anyone interested in Louisiana archaeology, as it provides one of the most comprehensive studies of any region in the state (Anderson and Smith 2003). At Louisiana State University Press, Joseph Powell, Alisa Plant, and Neal Novak facilitated the manuscript preparation and review. The Press's director, MaryKatherine Callaway, and the entire staff deserve special thanks for their continued interest and involvement in the project, despite frequent delays.

Philip "Duke" Rivet, formerly at the Louisiana Division of Archaeology, Department of Culture, Recreation, and Tourism, assisted many of this volume's contributors with information from the division's records and site files. Duke also generously reviewed numerous chapters, providing helpful comments and careful corrections. For his dedicated, longstanding service to the archaeology of Louisiana, by no means limited to this book, the authors offer their sincere gratitude. Nancy W. Hawkins, also with the Louisiana Division of Archaeology, provided invaluable assistance and deserves thanks for her contributions and dedication to Louisiana archaeology. The authors would also like to thank Charles "Chip" McGimsey, Louisiana State Archaeologist and contributor to this volume, for help in preparing their chapters. Other individuals with the Division of Archaeology assisted directly or indirectly in this work: Jill Andrew, Dennis Jones, Stacie Palmer, Sherry Wagener, Rachel Watson, and Cheraki Williams. If a spirit of camaraderie endures in Louisiana archaeology today, as it has among the membership of the Louisiana Archaeological Society (e.g., Gibson, ed. 1984), it is embodied in the archaeologists and staff with the Louisiana Division of Archaeology and Regional Archaeology Program, many of whom generously contributed their time and effort to this book. The Regional Archaeology Program is in many ways the most visible, effective approach, and represents the best prospect for archaeology in the state.

Others who greatly improved this publication by reviewing individual chapters include the lengthy list of authors. Nearly all of the contributing authors took the time to provide a peer review of a colleague's drafts, in several instances reading and offering comments on two or more chapters. Their critical remarks and suggestions, while not always followed, reached toward the highest level of professionalism. The editor is sincerely appreciative of the diligence, persistence, and collegiality of each contributing author. Not only did they surprisingly agree to participate in such an ambitious undertaking, but each also came through in the end with a first-rate contribution. Like other collaborative works, it is no exaggeration to declare this a group effort. There would be no book without the group's collective accomplishments.

In addition to those already mentioned, the authors would like to recognize the following individuals and express appreciation for their assistance: Louis Baker, Benton, Louisiana; Velicia Bergstrom, Forest Heritage Program Manager, Kisatchie National Forest, Pineville, Louisiana; Jay C. Blaine, Volunteer Texas Archeological Steward, Allen, Texas; Anne Marie Blank, Coastal Environments, Inc., Baton Rouge; Mary Lee Eggart, Cartographic Section of the Department of Geography and Anthropology, Louisiana State University, Baton Rouge; Thomas Emerson and colleagues, Illinois Transportation Archaeological Research Program, Champaign; Gary A. Glass, Department of Physics and Director, Louisiana Accelerator Center, University of Louisiana at Lafayette; Diana Greenlee, Poverty Point State Historic Site, Epps, Louisiana; H. F. "Pete" Gregory, School of Social Sciences, Northwestern State University of Louisiana, Natchitoches; David Griffing, Poverty Point State Historic Site, Epps, Louisiana; Joel Gunn, Department of Anthropology, University of North Carolina, Greensboro; Thurston H. G. Hahn III, Coastal Environments, Inc., Baton Rouge; Jacqueline Hawkins, Watson Library, Northwestern State University of Louisiana, Natchitoches; Richard Hughes, Geochemical Research Laboratory, Portola Valley, California; Donald G. Hunter, Coastal Environments, Inc., Baton Rouge; Ned Jenkins, Fort Toulouse/Fort Jackson State Park, Wetumpka, Alabama; Alice B. Kehoe, Milwaukee, Wisconsin; Tristram R. Kidder, Department of Anthropology, Washington University in St. Louis; Dennis LaBatt, Poverty Point State Historic Site, Epps, Louisiana; Robert Murry, Corpus Christi, Texas; Melinda Parrie, Space Science Group, Northwestern State University of Louisiana, Natchitoches; Bob Patten, Lakewood, Colorado; Rebecca Saunders, Museum of Natural Science and Department of Geography and Anthropology, Louisiana State University, Baton Rouge; John Walthall, Illinois Department of Transportation, Springfield; Mary Linn Wernet, Cammie G. Henry Research Center, Watson Memorial Library, Northwestern State University of Louisiana, Natchitoches; Gregory D. Wilson, Department of Anthropology, University of California, Santa Barbara; Brent Woodfill, Department of Sociology and Anthropology, University of Louisiana at Lafayette.

The following institutions and organizations assisted directly or indirectly in this work and provided necessary and greatly appreciated support: Coastal Environments, Inc., Baton Rouge; Earth Search, Inc., New Orleans; Edith Garland Dupré Library, University of Louisiana at Lafayette; Los Adaes Foundation, Robeline, Louisiana; Louisiana Archaeological Society; Louisiana Board of Regents Support Fund, Awards to Louisiana Artists and Scholars, and Research Competitiveness Subprogram; Louisiana Department of Transportation and Development; Louisiana Education Quality Support Fund; Museum of Natural Science, Louisiana State University; Regional Archaeology Program, Louisiana Division of Archaeology, Office of Cultural Development, Department of Culture, Recreation, and Tourism, with support from Louisiana State University, Northwestern State University of Louisiana, University of Louisiana at Lafayette, University of Louisiana at Monroe, and the National Park Service, U.S. Department of the Interior.

Archaeology of Louisiana

1

Introduction

MARK A. REES

Archaeology has been called a historical science (Trigger 1985, see also 2006:519–528). Like history, it deals with the past. Unlike historians, archaeologists examine the material traces of people for whom there may be little or no written documentation. Although studies of material culture have explored common ground, archaeologists write about the past in terms of specific places, things, and residues in the earth, which are collectively referred to as the archaeological record (e.g., Glassie 1999; Lubar and Kingery, ed. 1993; cf. Wylie 2002). This book is not an introduction to archaeology, or an explanation of how archaeology is or should be done, but method and theory are implicated throughout. Instead, *Archaeology of Louisiana* is ultimately concerned with different communities, societies and cultures, dating from widely different periods of time, throughout the present-day State of Louisiana. Although archaeology is fundamentally a material science, focusing on artifacts, sites, physical remains, and the environment, it is also humanistic and anthropological in its underlying concern for past human experiences, practices, beliefs, technologies, and traditions (Deetz 1983; Rees 2001). Whether examining ancient stone tools or a historic bottle dump, archaeologists study remnants of the everyday past of humankind (Gillespie and Nichols, ed. 2003). The archaeology of the earliest Americans at the end of the last Ice Age (10,000 years ago) thus finds common ground with the historical archaeology of nineteenth-century New Orleans.

The history of archaeology in Louisiana is presented by Kathleen Byrd and Robert Neuman in the following chapter, providing an introduction to its relatively recent development. Neuman's *An Introduction to Louisiana Archaeology* (1984:6–55) provides a detailed history of early investigations and remains an essential reference in this regard (see also Neuman 2002). The present work provides updated overviews of many of the major cultures summarized in *An Introduction to Louisiana Archaeology,* along with new perspectives influenced by recent discoveries and research. The archaeology of Louisiana is a work in progress, rewritten and revised with new discoveries and additional information, as well as innovative methods and techniques. *An Introduction to Louisiana Archaeology* presented information not covered in earlier summaries (e.g., Haag 1965, 1971, 1978; Neuman and Hawkins 1982). These summaries drew on previous studies, which in turn built on earlier research (e.g., Ford 1936; Ford and Webb 1956; Ford and Willey 1941; Kniffen 1936; McIntire 1958; Walker 1936; Webb 1948). But in 1933, when James Ford, a young archaeologist recently returned from Point Barrow, Alaska, began excavating at Peck Village (16CT1), near Sicily Island in Catahoula Parish, hardly anything was known about Louisiana archaeology (Brown 1978a:4; Byrd and Neuman, Chapter 2 in this volume). The ceramic horizons and chronological sequences he laid down became the foundation for Louisiana archaeology (Ford 1935a, 1935b, 1935c, 1936, 1938).

Archaeology in Louisiana has developed and diversified since then, from being principally focused on Native American sites and artifacts, to being a more socially representative profession that draws on various material aspects of the undocumented and documented past. Since the 1970s, a wide range of new information has come from historical archaeology and investigations in cultural resource management (CRM), as reflected in the references cited throughout this book. The chapters in this volume represent current knowledge and contemporary ideas on Louisiana archaeology, summarizing the still-burgeoning literature and interpreting the archaeological data from different perspectives. As is evident from a perusal of its contents, the scope of *Archaeology of Louisiana* is intentionally broad, ranging from the Paleoindian period to historic shipwrecks. While not intended to be a comprehensive culture history of all regions or a management plan for cultural resources, it is hoped this book provides practical and easily accessible information for anyone interested in Louisiana's lengthy and multifaceted past. References cited throughout the text will guide readers to additional studies that provide more in-depth information on topics of specific interest.

The Archaeology of States

Given the relatively arbitrary demarcation of present-day state boundaries in light of the immense time span preceding European colonization, any purported state archaeology should weigh the possible disadvantages and reasons for adopting contemporary political borders. State borders are irrelevant and even problematic in understanding communities and cultures that predate the states' origins and transcend their boundaries. Most archaeologists consequently focus on geographic regions such as the Central Mississippi Valley (e.g., McNutt, ed. 1996; Morse and Morse 1983; O'Brien and Dunnell, ed. 1998), intervals of time such as the Woodland period (ca. 1000 B.C.–A.D. 1000; e.g., Anderson and Mainfort, ed. 2002), or cultures such as Poverty Point and Caddo (e.g., Gibson 2000; Perttula 1992). Imposing state boundaries on data can result in redundancies or duplicate classifications, and can even obstruct collaboration or direct it in less effective ways. State lines may result in artificial "gray zones" not conducive to understanding interregional interaction or natural regions such as the Sabine and Pearl river drainages (e.g., Ricklis 2004:202). The arbitrariness and impediment of present-day state boundaries applies even in understanding interactions during more recent colonial times (e.g., Mann, Chapter 14 in this volume).

Yet to the extent historical narratives are always produced in contemporary contexts, boundaries can be employed in the service of present-day objectives. This includes state and federal management of cultural resources, heritage conservation, and cultural tourism (e.g., Louisiana Division of Archaeology 2009; Smith et al. 1983). Archaeological research identifies historically significant properties and produces documentation in state site files; major archaeological discoveries become state historic sites, national monuments, and public memorials. Recognition of historical significance and cultural value may involve listing on, or eligibility for, the National Register of Historic Places, or even nomination as a World Heritage site (Louisiana Division of Historic Preservation 2009; UNESCO 2009). Knowledge of the antiquity and uniqueness of the archaeological record can benefit society by producing informed decisions on what might be lost, what should be further studied, and what must be preserved for future generations.

But this has not always been acknowledged, and it is often disregarded even today. The status of Poverty Point (16WC5) as a State Historic Site, National Monument, and world-renowned Native American mound site was never guaranteed, nor was its preservation. Earlier blunders, such as the demolition of the 1,400-year-old Troyville mounds (16CT7) in Jonesville, stand today as grim warnings of the cost of ignorance and indifference (Lee, Chapter 8 in this volume; Walker 1936). Of an estimated 700 sites in Louisiana with Indian mounds, less than 10 percent have been carefully or systematically studied, most are privately owned, and many are endangered by looting, recreational overuse, or obliteration through inconsiderate development (Louisiana Division of Archaeology 2000). As in other states, Louisiana stands to benefit from greater understanding and public appreciation of its archaeological sites and cultural resources. Decisions on what is (or is not) a historically significant site, and how a site should (or should not) be presented to the public are informed by contemporary social preferences, biases, and politics (e.g., Loewen 1999:206–230). The archaeology of states is accordingly carried out in modern social and political contexts, of which historical archaeologists are often even more immediately aware (Orser 2001; Shackel 2001a; see Wilkie et al., Chapter 15 in this volume). Lack of support for public archaeology also leads to further destruction of the archaeological record, the erasure of history and culture, and a loss of potential knowledge of the past, as well as unrealized opportunities such as cultural tourism and economic development.

Just as state histories can introduce and promote fundamental civic principles, the archaeology of states might perform a similarly beneficial role. The social and historical critique that anthropological archaeology offers should be incorporated into state histories, or at least achieve parity in public education. To continue otherwise is to succumb to the omissions and silences that have segregated academic disciplines and the past, omitting Native Americans and others from "mainstream" history, unintentionally acquiescing to unjust stereotypes (Lightfoot 1995; Wesson and Rees 2002). Archaeologists themselves have at times been accused of appropriating indigenous pasts in the advancement of antihistorical or ahistorical science (Biolsi and Zimmerman, ed. 1997; McNiven and Russell 2005; Trigger 2006:386–444). Excluding or minimizing the lives of subjugated peoples, ethnic diversity, and conflicts in American history is decidedly un-American. It produces simplistic myths that sustain prejudices or legitimize present-day social inequalities (Foner 2002; Raphael 2004). Collaboration, public participation, and increased dialogue are fostering shared interests and transforming archaeological practice (Cast et al., Chapter 12 in this volume; Dongoske et al., ed. 2000; Swidler et al., ed. 1997). Alongside oral history and ethnohistory, archaeology holds the potential for giving voice to alternative histories of ordinary people and shedding light on the "shadows" of American history (Conn 2004; Galloway 2006; Sturtevant 1966). What results is not social history as such, but a more inclusive, historical anthropology (Cobb 2005).

Recent studies of surrounding states have set the bar high for any state archaeology. The detailed and lavishly illustrated *Prehistory of Texas* is essential reading for those interested in archaeology west of the Mississippi River, including west and northwest Louisiana (Perttula, ed. 2004). Organized geographically or by "cultural-ecological regions," *Prehistory of Texas* is an impressive tome that synthesizes a vast amount of data from the beginning of the Paleoindian period (ca. 13,500 years before present, or B.P.) until the earliest contacts between Native Americans and Europeans. An alternative, more streamlined approach is to address successive time periods throughout an entire state, as seen in *The Prehistory of Missouri* (O'Brien and Wood 1998). One potential drawback is the dif-

Fig. 1.1. Major river drainages and physiographic regions of Louisiana.

ficulty in accounting for substantial ecological and cultural diversity within what is essentially a single culture-historical chronology. In contrast, *Arkansas Archaeology* presents regional studies focused on specific periods and cultures, balancing the pros and cons of a combined approach (Mainfort and Jeter, ed. 1999).

In preparing the present work, a definite chronological organization was anticipated. In an effort to desegregate the past, chapters on historical archaeology build on the culture history of the previous 13,000 years. Physiographic, ecological, and cultural variation within such a long time span demanded certain regions receive more or less attention. Louisiana falls within the Coastal Plain physiographic province but can be subdivided into five major natural regions: the uplands of the northwest, coastal terraces, Mississippi and Red River alluvial plains, the Mississippi Delta, and Chenier Plain (Figure 1.1; Yodis et al. 2003). Due to the overall organization, focus of research, and preferences of individual

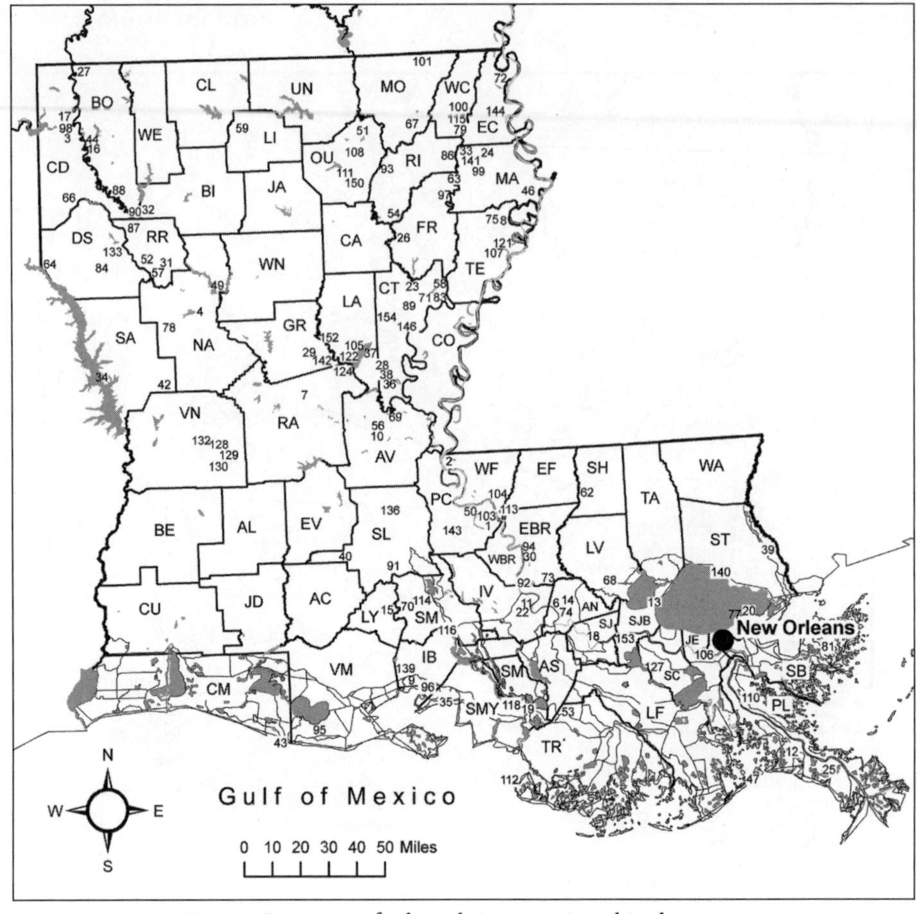

Fig. 1.2. Locations of selected sites mentioned in the text.

1. Alma Plantation (16PC76)
2. Above the Mastodon (16WF63)
3. Albany Landing (16CD2)
4. American Cemetery (16NA67)
5. Angola Farm (16WF2)—see 2
6. Ashland-Belle Helene Plantation (16AN26)
7. Bailey's Dam (16RA90)
8. Balmoral (16TE12)
9. Banana Bayou (16IB24)
10. Baptiste Place (16AV25)
11. Bayou Goula (16IV11)
12. Bayou Grande Cheniere (16PL159)
13. Bayou Jasmine (16SJB2)
14. Beau Mire (16AN17)
15. Beau Rivage (16LY5)
16. Beene (16BO19)
17. Belcher (16CD13)
18. Belmont (16SJ1)
19. Berwick (16SMY184)
20. Big Oak Island (16OR6)
21. Bloodhound Hill (16WF21)—see 2
22. Blythewood Plantation (16IV8)
23. Boothe Landing (16CT31)
24. Borrow Pit (16MA57)
25. Buras (16PL13)
26. Bush (16FR163)
27. Byram Ferry (16BO17)
28. Caney (16CT5)
29. Catahoula Cur (16GR58)
30. Catfish Town (16EBR63)
31. Charles Webb (16RR86)
32. Conly (16BI19)
33. Copes (16MA47)
34. Coral Snake Mound (16SA48)
35. Côte Blanche Island (16SMY79)
36. Cowpen Slough (16CT147)
37. Crooks (16LA3)
38. Cross Bayou (16CT365)
39. CSS Arrow (16ST99)
40. Da Dump (16SL59)

(continued on next page)

41. Dragline (16CT36)—see 36
42. Eagle Hill II (16SA50)
43. El Nuevo Constante (16CM112)
44. Festervan (16BO327)
45. Fish Hatchery (16NA9)—see 4
46. Fitzhugh (16MA1)
47. Fort Livingston (16JE49)
48. Fort St. Jean Baptiste (16NA68)—see 4
49. Fredericks (16NA2)
50. French Site 1 (16PC80)
51. Frenchman's Bend (16OU259)
52. Gahagan (16RR1)
53. Gibson (16TR5)
54. Gold Mine (16RI13)
55. Grand Terre Island (16JE128)—see 47
56. Greenhouse (16AV2)
57. Hanna (16RR4)
58. Hedgeland (16CT19)
59. Hedgepeth (16LI7)
60. Henderson (16OU303)—see 150
61. Hillman's Mound (16MA201)—see 24
62. Hornsby (16SH21)
63. Insley (16FR3)
64. James Pace (16DS268)
65. Joe Clark (16BO237)—see 90
66. John Pearce (16CD56)
67. Jordan (16MO1)
68. King George Island (16LV22)
69. Lac St. Agnes (16AV26)
70. Lafayette Mounds (16SM17)
71. Lake Louis (16CT24)
72. Lake Providence Mounds (16EC6)
73. Lee (16EBR51)
74. L'Hermitage Plantation (16AN24)
75. Lisa's Ridge (16TE144)
76. Little Oak Island (16OR7)—see 20
77. Little Woods Middens (16OR1-5)
78. Los Adaes (16NA16)
79. Lower Jackson (16WC10)
80. LSU Campus Mounds (16EBR6)—see 30
81. Magnolia Mound (16SB49)
82. Magnolia Mound Plantation (16EBR30)—see 30
83. Maitland Plantation (16CT176)
84. Mansfield (16DS187)
85. Marksville (16AV1)—see 56
86. Marsden (16RI3)
87. Marston (16RR2)
88. McDade (16BO331)
89. McGuffee (16CT17)
90. McLelland (16BO236)
91. Meche-Wilkes (16SL18)
92. Medora (16WBR1)
93. Metz Midden (16RI105)
94. Monte Sano (16EBR17)
95. Morgan (16VM9)
96. Morton Shell Mound (16IB3)
97. Mott (16FR11)
98. Mounds Plantation (16CD12)
99. Mt. Nebo (16MA18)
100. Neely Place (16WC4)
101. Neimeyer-Dare (16MO43)
102. New Orleans (see Chapters 16 and 17)
103. Nina Plantation (16PC62)
104. Oakley Plantation (16WF34)
105. Old Creek (16LA102)
106. Orange Grove Plantation (16JE141)
107. Osceola (16TE2)
108. Pargoud Landing (16OU1)
109. Peck Village (16CT1)—see 83
110. Phoenix Cemetery (16PL146)
111. Plum Creek (16OU89)
112. Point au Fer Lighthouse (16TR257)
113. Port Hudson (16EF7)
114. Portage Guidry (16SM38)
115. Poverty Point (16WC5)
116. Prairie Landing Village (16SM5)
117. Pritchard's Landing (16CT14)—see 89
118. *Qiteet kutingi namu* (16SMY10)
119. Raffman (16MA20)—see 24
120. Riverlake Plantation (16PC63)—see 1
121. Routh (16TE8)
122. Russell Landing (16LA9)
123. Salt Mine Valley (16IB23)—see 9
124. Sanson (16RA1)
125. Sarah Peralta (16EBR67)—see 73
126. Shackleford Lake (16TE1)—see 75
127. Sim's Place (16SC2)
128. Site 16VN1421
129. Site 16VN1505
130. Site 16VN2729
131. Site 16VN2730—see 130
132. Site 16VN791
133. Smithport Landing (16DS4)
134. Southern Compress (16NA14)—see 4
135. St. Mary's Mound (16MA62)—see 24
136. Stelly (16SL1)
137. Stonewall Plantation (16PC80)—see 50
138. Swan Lake (16BO11)—see 44
139. Tapir (16IB66)
140. Tchefuncte (16ST1)
141. Terral Lewis (16MA16)
142. Terry Jones #3 (16GR643)
143. Thom (16PC6)
144. Transylvania (16EC8)
145. Trappey Mastodon (16LY63)—see 15
146. Troyville (16CT7)
147. Trudeau (16WF25)—see 2
148. Vanceville Mound (16BO7)—see 44
149. Veazey (16VM7/8)—see 95
150. Watson Brake (16OU175)
151. Werner (16BO8)—see 16
152. Whatley (16LA37)
153. Whitney Plantation (16SJB11)
154. Womac (16CT312)

authors, some regions went relatively unexamined for certain time periods and represent obvious omissions. As evident from the map of site locations discussed in this book (Figure 1.2), some of this represents gaps in current knowledge, a result of uneven archaeological research, lack of systematic survey coverage, or direction of CRM archaeology. In this and previous studies, attention has often focused on those cultures, sites, and regions of greatest interest to archaeologists, which have also captured popular imagination (e.g., Neuman 1984; Neuman and Hawkins 1982). Poverty Point and Marksville (16AV1) have been joined by such notable places as Watson Brake (16OU175) and Ashland–Belle Helene Plantation (16AN26; Figure 1.2), generating increased interest in complex foraging societies of the Middle Archaic period (ca. 6000–2000 B.C.) and the lives of enslaved African Americans on an antebellum sugarcane plantation (Saunders, Chapter 4 in this volume; Yakubik and Méndez 1995).

There has been an upsurge of interest in the historical archaeology of Louisiana during the past three decades. In contrast, knowledge of Louisiana's original inhabitants during the Paleoindian and Early Archaic periods (ca. 11,500–6000 B.C.) remains conspicuously deficient (see Chapter 3 in this volume). The considerably greater time span of pre-colonial Louisiana is hardly reflected in the allotment of chapters. More than 9,000 years are covered in two chapters (3 and 4), while five chapters are devoted to the four centuries since colonial times. This should not be interpreted to mean pre-colonial Louisiana was uneventful, inconsequential, or uninteresting. If anything, it points out a crucial yet still largely unfulfilled need for more detailed, long-term archaeological investigations of the Paleoindian and Archaic periods in Louisiana. Archaeologists only recently established that Native Americans were building massive earthworks in Louisiana more than 5,000 years ago, over a thousand years earlier than previously known (Russo 1996; Saunders et al. 1997; Saunders, Chapter 4 in the volume). The unrealized potential for other startling new discoveries should alone be sufficient to attract enthusiastic young scholars. Nine thousand years of Louisiana's earliest history lies buried, yet to be discovered and written.

There are also shorter periods and smaller regions in the state still relatively unexamined by archaeologists. Some historically known groups, such as the Atakapa, have not been adequately or even systematically studied (but see Aten 1983; Newcomb 2004). While Cajun culture and cuisine are widely touted today, archaeologists have only just recently begun to look at the home sites of Acadians and other early immigrants (e.g., Hunter et al. 2003; Mann 2008b; Mann and Schilling 2004; Rees 2008). The deficits in the archaeological database are too numerous to list here. In such instances even the most rudimentary and small-scale research projects have the potential to yield extraordinary and far-reaching results. Such are the promises and shortcomings of archaeology as a cumulative, historical science. Any state archaeology that sets out on the ambitious goal of describing the past 13,000 years of human habitation in such a large, diverse area will ultimately fall short. Any apparent deficiencies and ensuing questions should hopefully spur future archaeological studies.

The State of Archaeology

Although the chapters in this volume do not directly deal with archaeological method and theory, major methodological and theoretical trends inevitably lie just beneath the surface and are necessarily intertwined throughout its pages. A brief consideration of terminology will familiarize readers with some of the underlying concepts. Those already familiar with the practice of archaeology may prefer to skip this section.

Throughout these pages, archaeologists commonly refer to sites, meaning a specific, geographic location of human activity or habitation, as represented by material remains in the landscape. Archaeological sites range from evidence for ephemeral, short-term activities to major civic centers with monumental architecture; they include seasonal hunting camps, homesteads, villages or entire communities, military fortifications, and underwater or submerged resources. Sites recorded with the Louisiana Division of Archaeology (LDA) are designated by numbers and letters corresponding to the state, parish, and site within the parish (e.g., 16OU175 refers to site number 175 in Ouachita Parish, Louisiana), allowing for accurate cataloguing and association of collections and documentation. Site numbers are provided only once for most of the sites discussed in each chapter, after which sites are generally referred to by name.

Sites are commonly identified by the presence of artifacts such as stone projectile points (which include arrowheads), ceramic sherds, bottle glass, or any other humanly modified object. Certain kinds of artifacts with similar characteristics or attributes found to occur regularly at sites have been designated specific type names, such as the San Patrice projectile point or Coles Creek Incised pottery (Ford 1954; cf. Spaulding 1953). Measurable, though at times minor, variations of types are sometimes described as *varieties*, such as San Patrice, *var. St. Johns*, and Coles Creek Incised, *var. Hardy* (Brown 1998a; Webb 1981). Some iconic or wide-ranging artifact types have become associated with distinct cultures, as in San Patrice culture and Coles Creek culture, although the original purpose was generally in constructing chronologies (e.g., Ford 1936, 1938). Other evidence of human activity includes animal bones and plant remains, suitable when preserved, for studies in zooarchaeology and archaeobotany, which allow for the reconstruction of subsistence or diet. The majority of materials normally excavated by archaeologists are not impressive or elaborate museum relics, but would be regarded by most people as garbage—the unpretentious refuse and ruins of past lives. In combination with non-artifactual residues or cultural features, such as charcoal-filled hearths, such artifacts and eco-facts comprise the archaeological record of a site.

A single episode of human activity or occupancy of a site is sometimes referred to as a component, with multiple habitations and cultural deposits through time constituting a multi-component site. The Coles Creek component of a site might represent fifty years or three hundred years of habitation during the Coles Creek period (A.D. 700–1200). If the same site was inhabited at other times by other people, with perhaps an earlier Poverty Point component, it is referred to as a multi-component site. At sites with layer upon layer of soil and cultural deposits, it is sometimes possible to interpret successive habitations or components from stratigraphy. Sites in floodplains or river valleys may conceal deeply buried archaeological deposits due to environmental conditions (such as alluvial sediments) and cultural activities. Other locations, such as exposed ridge tops, may reveal several millennia of human habitation interspersed on the ground surface, or within a few inches of it.

Archaeological phases are the next larger step, representing related components at multiple sites within a particular period and region, or interrelated in time and space (Willey and Phillips 1958:21–24). Archaeology in Louisiana and the Lower Mississippi Valley (LMV), in general, has been strongly influenced by the concept of phases (e.g., Phillips 1970; Williams and Brain 1983). While considerable disagreement persists among archaeologists as to its analytical merit and precisely what it may represent, some phases have been described as the archaeological remains of a distinct society (cf. Lyman et al. 1997:171–174; Mainfort 1999; McNutt 2008). As products of archaeological research, phases are intuitive units of study with variable boundaries, which can be adjusted or redefined by further study. Some of the phases mentioned in this book may serve effectively as models for the approximate geographic extent and time span of undocumented societies. Others probably do not.

"Culture" has become so ubiquitous a term that it seemingly needs no further clarification. Archaeological cultures however, are fashioned in the present-day to reflect shared artifact types, technologies, behaviors, and beliefs for a large area and period of time in the past, often encompassing numerous phases. Cultural traditions, as intended here, are consequently archaeological, and therefore coupled to observable, material evidence in (or on) the ground, which is the cumulative archaeological record. The time span of a culture is sometimes referred to as a period, as in the Poverty Point culture and period (ca. 1700–800 B.C.). The geographic extent may in other instances be referred to as a culture area. The integration of all these units of study constitutes a culture-historical chronology or synthesis (Willey and Sabloff 1993:188–288), often described in years before present (B.P.) or radiocarbon years (RCY) before present. Archaeologists acknowledge that some well-defined cultures such as Poverty Point existed independently of archaeological investigation, but that they are knowable only in present circumstances.

The preceding descriptive and chronological focus has come to be called the culture historical approach in archaeology, distinguished since the 1960s from an overriding interest in cultural ecology and the evolution of complex societies, which is generally known as processual archaeology (Binford 1965, 1968). Claims of scientific objectivity regarding the function of cultural systems and the nature of culture change by processualists led other archaeologists beginning in the 1980s to propose a post-processual archaeology, aimed toward alternative interpretations, historical context, and meaning (Hodder 1985, 1986, 1991). Archaeologists have more recently suggested that a combination or synthesis of these approaches is not only feasible, but beneficial (Hegmon 2003; Pauketat 2001b; VanPool and VanPool 1999). The methods and perspectives of culture history are not only applicable today, but are being transformed in view of new data, techniques, and theories. As an early source of culture history, Louisiana archaeology is ideally situated to advance such an innovative, historical approach (e.g., Ford 1935b, 1936; Pauketat 2001a).

Louisiana's ancient, pre-colonial past has previously been characterized in terms of three wide ranging and protracted eras or periods: Paleo-Indian (ca. 10,000–6000 B.C.), Meso-Indian (6000–2000 B.C.), and Neo-Indian (2000 B.C.–A.D. 1600). While the first two have generally been described as 8,000 years of gradual environmental changes and associated cultural adjustments, the latter has undergone considerable chronological refinement and is typically subdivided into at least eight major cultures (Neuman 1984; Neuman and Hawkins 1982; Williams and Brain 1983:394–420). Culture histories of Louisiana have included terms such as Burial Mound, Temple Mound, Formative, Lithic, Archaic, and Woodland, with at times the nearly interchangeable use of "culture" and "period" in referring to Poverty Point, Tchefuncte, Marksville, Troyville, Coles Creek, Caddo, Plaquemine, and Mississippian (e.g., Griffin 1967; Haag 1971,

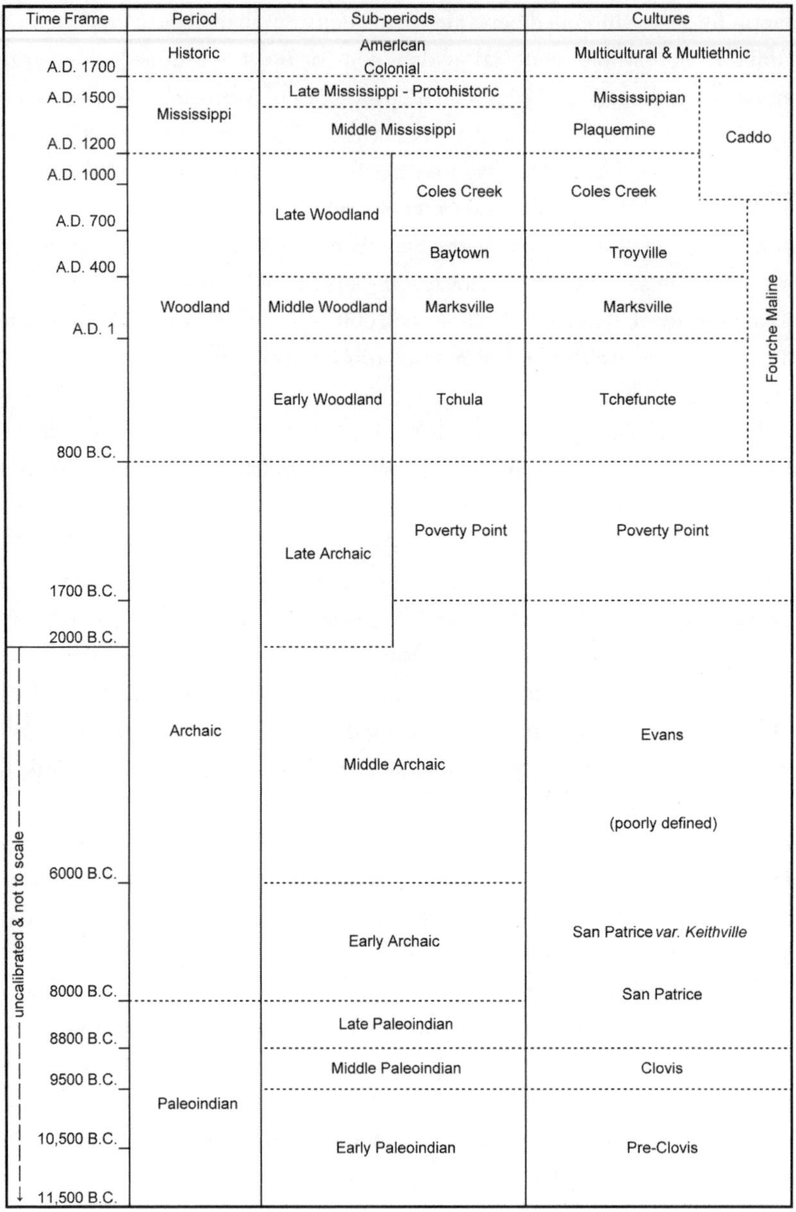

Time Frame	Period	Sub-periods		Cultures	
A.D. 1700	Historic	American Colonial		Multicultural & Multiethnic	
A.D. 1500	Mississippi	Late Mississippi - Protohistoric		Mississippian	Caddo
A.D. 1200	Mississippi	Middle Mississippi		Plaquemine	Caddo
A.D. 1000	Woodland	Late Woodland	Coles Creek	Coles Creek	Caddo
A.D. 700	Woodland	Late Woodland	Baytown	Troyville	Fourche Maline
A.D. 400	Woodland	Middle Woodland	Marksville	Marksville	Fourche Maline
A.D. 1	Woodland	Early Woodland	Tchula	Tchefuncte	Fourche Maline
800 B.C.	Archaic	Late Archaic	Poverty Point	Poverty Point	
1700 B.C.	Archaic	Late Archaic			
2000 B.C.	Archaic	Middle Archaic		Evans (poorly defined)	
6000 B.C.	Archaic	Early Archaic		San Patrice *var. Keithville*; San Patrice	
8000 B.C.	Paleoindian	Late Paleoindian			
8800 B.C.	Paleoindian	Middle Paleoindian		Clovis	
9500 B.C.	Paleoindian	Early Paleoindian		Pre-Clovis	
10,500 B.C.					
11,500 B.C.					

uncalibrated & not to scale

Fig. 1.3. Culture chronology for Louisiana.

1978; Willey 1966:246–341; Williams 1956). The lasting influence of Harvard University's Lower Mississippi Survey (LMS) in Louisiana and throughout the LMV has resulted in numerous phases and periods, such as Issaquena, Troyville, and Baytown (e.g., Phillips 1970; Phillips et al. 1951:436–445).

Although useful in classifying and describing sites and material culture through time and space, the profusion of varying culture-historical terminologies risks creating confusion rather than clarification (e.g., Gibson 1984b). During the past few decades many archaeologists working in the southeastern United States have adopted a more or less standardized culture-historical nomenclature, beginning with the Paleoindian period and followed by the Archaic, Woodland, Mississippian, and historic stages or periods (e.g., Bense 1994; Griffin 1967; Steponaitis 1986). These are each in turn subdivided into periods or sub-periods, such as Early, Middle, and Late Archaic. The general chronology adopted here, as shown in Figure 1.3, represents a simplified overview of Louisiana's culture history. The chapters in this book are organized for the most part according to this scheme, recognizing that regional coverage is at times positively and negatively influenced by periods with wide-ranging cultural associations.

Louisiana's Historical Ecology

Before proceeding, it is worthwhile to consider briefly how the unique landscape and environments of Louisiana have influenced and been transformed by human actions over the past millennia. Such relationships have been, and continue to be, widely influential in the archaeology of Louisiana (e.g., Gagliano 1984; Haag 1978; Kidder 1996, 1998c; Kniffen 1936; Saucier 1981). Interactions between humans and the environment are a defining characteristic of culture and not unique to modern societies increasingly concerned with global warming and coastal erosion. The relationship commenced when humans first arrived on the continent some 15,000 or more years ago (Meltzer 2009). The changing panorama of physical geography, climate, plant and animal communities, and how human societies prospered and interacted, is the subject matter of historical ecology, or long-term relationships with the landscape (Crumley 1994:9; Kidder 1998c). The five natural regions mentioned earlier encompass considerable physiographic and ecological variation within the Coastal Plain province: the Tertiary Uplands and hills of the northwest, Pleistocene terraces of the southwest and southeast, alluvial plains of the Mississippi and Red rivers, Deltaic Plain, and Chenier Plain on the southwest coast (Figure 1.1). Environments within each of these regions have not been constant, but have varied through time.

The story begins with paleoenvironmental reconstruction, which, simply put, is the description of landscapes during the last Ice Age, or earlier than 10,000 years ago (Dincauze 2000:20–24; Rapp and Hill 2006:165–168). As described in Chapter 3, Louisiana was a different place then, and would be unrecognizable to its twenty-first-century residents. The central and southern half of the state were formed during and after the Pleistocene Epoch (2 million to 10,000 years ago), as Coastal Plain and river valleys filled with sand and gravels deposited by southerly flowing streams. During the peak of the last Ice Age (Wisconsin glaciation), the receding Gulf of Mexico exposed a vast expanse of the continental shelf and the shoreline extended farther south. The end of the Pleistocene brought a deluge of glacial runoff and rising sea levels, as precursors of the modern Red and Mississippi rivers laid down thick layers of sediments (Walker and Coleman 1987). Both streams flowed in more dynamic and deeply entrenched channels that shifted east and west over the millennia, leaving behind Pleistocene-age terraces, channel deposits and scars, natural levees, and braided-stream terraces or valley trains such as Maçon Ridge (Saucier 1974, 1994a).

This foreign landscape was the setting for the initial arrival of Paleoindian hunter-gatherers, followed by successive habitation, abandonment, and resettlement (Anderson 1990, 1996:34–39). The geomorphology or geological history of northwest Louisiana is among the most ancient in the state, including rock formations that date from the Tertiary period (65 to 2 million years ago). These geological formations also comprise the highest elevations in Louisiana, from approximately 400 to 535 feet (122 to 163 m) above sea level. The Tertiary Uplands are bisected by the Red River Valley and drained by smaller tributaries of the Ouachita, Red, and Sabine rivers. The landscape is consequently deeply dissected, hilly, and characterized in places by steep slopes prone to severe erosion (Yodis et al. 2003).

Beginning in the Paleoindian period (11,500–8,000 B.C.), Native Americans utilized exposed gravels and bedrock outcrops to fashion stone tools (e.g., Anderson and Smith 2003:41–47, 350–352). Sites on upland ridges thus have the potential to provide a record of the earliest human presence in Louisiana, although these exposed surfaces are susceptible to weathering, subsequent human impacts, and erosion. The extinction of Pleistocene megafauna (such as Mastodon) was likely related to progressively altered climate and vegetation rather than just human predation, especially in locally varied environments such as the LMV (Kelly and Prasciunas 2007; Meltzer 2004:550–552; see Chapter 3 in this volume). The modern (Holocene) vegetation of northwest Louisiana, once characterized by vast expanses of Longleaf and Loblolly Pine forest, further distinguishes it from the rest of the state. Deforestation by the lumber industry during the late nineteenth and early twentieth centuries deteriorated ecosystems and accelerated erosion. Floodplains and adjacent Pleistocene terraces have been impacted by subsequent deposition of sediments (Girard 2007:5–7).

The coastal prairies of southwest and southeast Louisiana are Pleistocene terraces dissected by the Calcasieu, Mermentau, Pontchartrain, and Pearl drainage basins. Thick deposits of loess, or wind-blown (aeolian) unconsolidated silt, blanket the eastern escarpment of the Mississippi alluvial valley from Baton Rouge northward, along large portions of Maçon Ridge, and the edges of the prairie terrace (Saucier 1974, 1994a). Avery Island, the largest of five prominent salt domes in south-central Louisiana, is covered in loess, and at 150 feet (46 m) in elevation, it stands out from the surrounding marsh. Maçon Ridge and the salt domes may be culturally as well as geologically unique within the alluvial valley in preserving an archaeological record of concerted human-environmental relationships stretching from present-day far back into the Late Pleistocene. Humans impacted and transformed these landscapes from the very beginning through clearing, burning, resource extraction, and construction (Kidder 1998c:148–157; Walker and Coleman 1987:101–102). The coastal tallgrass prairie that once covered huge expanses of southwest Louisiana supported incredible ecological diversity, including bison, antelope, and wild plants that Native Americans harvested for food and medicine (Allain et al. 1999:9, 21).

The Mississippi Delta, alluvial plains of the Mississippi and Red rivers, and Chenier Plain of southwest Louisiana are more recent, Holocene-age formations that continue to undergo profound alterations (Autin et al. 1991; Pearson and Hunter 1993; Saucier 1994a; Yodis et al. 2003). The Chenier Plain consists of low-lying, relict beach ridges, mudflats, and marsh that have formed progressively southward from the prairie terrace, west of the Deltaic Plain, as a result of delta formation, shoreline currents, and tidal action. Archaeological sites on the Chenier Plain consequently postdate its formation 3,000 to 4,000 years ago and in some instances have been successively impacted and redeposited (Saucier 1994a:159). The cheniers or ridges where live oaks and other vegetation were concentrated provided outstanding habitations for coastal communities. Archaeological sites in the Chenier Plain and Delta represent evidence for long-term coastal adaptations that varied in response to a dynamic environment but were not determined by it (Gagliano 1984; McIntire 1958; Neuman 1977a). Human impacts have not been limited to modern degradation of the environment, such as canal construction or the introduction of invasive species, but include selective burning, land clearing, and the production of shell middens by earlier Native Americans (Kidder 1998c:148–157).

The typically slow-moving, meandering rivers, oxbow lakes, backwaters, bayous, and deltas of Louisiana are a relatively late development, as sea levels and river channels stabilized between 7,000 and 2,000 years ago (Saucier 1994a:50,

328–329). The progression of the Mississippi Delta over the past 7,000 years has reworked a series of lobes and associated deltaic and estuarine environments such as the Maringouin, Teche, and Lafourche complexes (Saucier 1994a:276–286). Archaeological sites must accordingly be examined in the context of continuously altered landscapes, as suggested a half century ago by Phillips, Ford, and Griffin (1951:295–306; cf. Saucier 1981, 1994a:13–16; Smith et al. 1986:72–78). Flora and fauna of the Mississippi alluvial plain and coastal wetlands have been extremely productive for fishing, hunting, and gathering, offering an abundance of resources and considerable potential for subsistence surpluses. Indigenous agriculture does not appear to have become significant until around A.D. 1200, and even then maize was grown primarily on terraces and levees of the Red and Mississippi alluvial valleys (Kidder 1992b). The subtropical, coastal climate of Louisiana would subsequently make the terraces, alluvial valleys, and Delta ideal environments for the historical production of cotton, rice, and sugarcane.

The clearing of rafts or immense series of log jams on the Red and Atchafalaya rivers during the 1830s and 1850s drained previously inundated lands and transformed entire drainage patterns in the LMV. As a result of catastrophic floods during the twentieth century, the Mississippi River Commission and U.S. Army Corps of Engineers became increasingly involved in levee construction and flood-control projects (Barry 1997; Reuss 2004). Anthropogenic or human-created changes, both intentional and otherwise, have drawn recent attention due to increased coastal erosion and the hurricane seasons of 2005 and 2008. The devastation wrought by Hurricanes Katrina, Rita, and Ike can only be understood in relation to canal and levee construction, dredging, floodway engineering, related modifications to wetlands, and urbanization in the coastal zone (Freudenburg et al. 2009; Hartman and Squires, ed. 2006; Van Heerden and Bryan 2006). Combined with accelerated coastal erosion and subsidence, the prospect of rising sea levels from human-induced global warming further raises the likelihood of severe impacts to densely populated south Louisiana.

Such ecological relationships are not entirely new. Indeed, Louisiana's residents have modified and been influenced by the environment for millennia. People living along the Gulf Coast learned long ago how to navigate and surmount long-term and more immediate environmental risks (Lewis 2000). Terminal Pleistocene adjustments to a more modern or Holocene environment entailed changes in subsistence, residential mobility, domestic economy, and social relations (Anderson 1996; Ricklis and Weinstein 2005; Walker and Driskell, ed. 2007). T. R. Kidder (2006) associates evidence for climate change between 3000 and 2600 cal. B.P. with more frequent and intensified flooding throughout the Mississippi drainage during the Late Archaic–Early Woodland transition. Human responses may have included alteration of subsistence economies, settlement shifts, and realignment of existing social interactions and exchange. Decreased mound construction 1,800 years earlier may have likewise coincided with ecologically related social reorganization (Kidder 2006:218–221; Saunders, Chapter 4 in this volume). On a broader, continent-wide scale, the Medieval Warm Period (ca. A.D. 800–1300) and subsequent "Little Ice Age" (ca. A.D. 1300–1850) have been linked to culture changes in the northern hemisphere, from colonization and regional abandonments to the rise and fall of civilizations (e.g., Fagan 2000, 2004).

What *is* radically new is the degree and extent of human modifications to the environment and the concomitant severity of potential repercussions on society (e.g., Freudenburg et al. 2009). Archaeology fortunately provides the long time frames and information needed to place human history and historical ecology in context (Trigger 2006:539). Regrettably, the archaeological record is endangered by the same historical and ecological processes. Fort Livingston (16JE49), Magnolia Mound (16SB49), the Bayou Grande Cheniere mounds (16PL159), and the Toncrey site (16PL7) are among the many places that may be lost not simply to natural processes, but to cultural modifications of coastal environments (Gagliano 1984; Jones et al. 2009; Mann 2002:48–60; Saucier 1994a:53–54; Schilling 2004; Wiseman et al. 1979:6.1–6.32). Robert Neuman (1977a:31) raised this very issue over thirty years ago, but adverse impacts have since accelerated and intensified (see also Tidwell 2003).

Humans are not hapless victims of the environment, nor have they entirely mastered or detached themselves from the forces of nature, even at the beginning of the twenty-first century. Human-environmental interactions, adaptations, traditions, and beliefs are intertwined as an ecological, historical process (Patterson 1994; Trigger 1991). Knowledge of how this process occurred in the past may well assist in planning for the future.

Conclusion

If archaeology is regarded as an applied, historical science, it is worth reflecting on the potential benefits. The archaeological record provides evidence of human interactions and historical ecology from the Late Pleistocene to present day, offering the only means of systematically examining reciprocal changes as they relate to the environment. Accordingly, studies have shown connections between subsistence changes, political and economic organization, settlement patterns, and social relations (e.g., Jackson 1989, 1991a; Kidder 1992a). Greater knowledge of human settlement in the Delta and coastal zone over thousands of years can inform future decisions concerning development, resource use, and sustainability. But the archaeological record is finite and endangered by coastal erosion and unmitigated development. Sites and cultural resources throughout the state should be systematically recorded, evaluated, and whenever appropriate or possible, preserved. Otherwise, we will not know what we have lost until it is too late. As Bruce Trigger (2006:548) concluded in *A History of Archaeological Thought*, knowledge of previous human failures and success may prove more effective than continued "trial and error." In an age of such technological sophistication and progress, it is imperative to learn from the past.

Archaeology also offers vital lessons concerning social change and the history of Louisiana. History in this sense is not merely written documentation or chronological description of particular events and cultures, but refers to representations of the past (Taylor 1983:25–36; cf. Trouillot 1995:1–30). Louisiana history customarily deals with only a portion of the last three centuries—a miniscule fraction of its actual, 13,000-year-long past. The pre-colonial histories of the Atakapa, Caddo, Chitimacha, other First Americans, and their ancestors are not well known and have yet to be fully integrated into Louisiana history. The lives of African Americans and Creoles have likewise been disregarded or misrepresented in popular historical narratives. Yet much of what is regarded today as uniquely Louisianan is drawn from the intermingling of the traditions and experiences of these and other peoples. Archaeology can provide a "deeper historical anthropology" not constrained by the presence or absence of the written word and its usual biases, dismantling the artificial barriers between history and prehistory, colonists and the colonized, the empowered and oppressed (Cobb 2005:569–572; Wolf 1982).

For Louisiana truly to realize the multicultural society it promotes and celebrates, its residents must have some understanding of its multifaceted and lengthy past. Archaeology redresses major historical omissions and can provide useful social critiques. Archaeologists strive toward a comparative and more inclusive study of cultural diversity and change. While the authors of the following chapters write from different theoretical perspectives, they share an abiding interest in the interpretation and preservation of the archaeological record. It is hoped that this volume contributes in some way to the greater pursuit and broader understanding of Louisiana's archaeological past.

2

A History of Archaeology in Louisiana

KATHLEEN M. BYRD AND ROBERT W. NEUMAN

Louisiana has an incredibly rich archaeological heritage (Neuman and Simmons 1969). But it is not the purpose of this chapter to delve into the details of this heritage. That is the task for others in this volume. Instead, this chapter attempts to provide an overview of the individuals in the nineteenth and twentieth centuries who contributed to the discovery and recording of the archaeological sites, of the watershed events of the Great Depression and its effect on archaeology, of the development of cultural resource management (CRM) and its impact on Louisiana's archaeology, and, finally, of some of the challenges facing archaeologists in the twenty-first century.

The Nineteenth and Early Twentieth Centuries

The nineteenth century can be considered Louisiana's descriptive period. Soon after the Louisiana Purchase, Thomas Jefferson sent surveyors, cartographers, naturalists, geologists, and soldiers to explore and describe the new territory. Jefferson chose William Dunbar to lead an expedition to investigate the newly acquired territory of the lower Red and Ouachita rivers. While surveying parts of the Ouachita River basin, Dunbar came upon the extensive earthworks of the Troyville site (16CT7), in present-day Catahoula Parish (Lee, Chapter 8 in this volume). Dunbar returned to the site in 1805 and composed the first detailed description of the mounds and earthworks: "There is an embankment . . . about 10 ft. high and 10 ft. broad. This surrounds 4 large mounds . . . each of which may be 100 x 300 ft. at the top, and 20 ft. high, besides a stupendous turret . . . whose base covers about an acre of ground, rising by 2 steps or stories tapering in the ascent, the whole surmounted by a great cone with its top cut off. This tower of earth on measurement proved to be about 80 feet perpendicular" (in Walker 1936:5–6). Jefferson, who had excavated a burial mound on his property in Virginia, was so impressed with Dunbar's findings that he mentioned them in an address to Congress along with a description of the site (Walker 1936). This

Fig. 2.1. Influential individuals in Louisiana archaeology: a. Caleb Goldsmith Forshey (from Jewell, ed. 1873:232); b. George Beyer; c. Clarence Bloomfield Moore (Harvard University Archives, call # HUP Moore, Clarence B.); d. Frank Setzler; e. James A. Ford; f. Roger T. Saucier; g. Clarence H. Webb; h. Reca B. Jones. Photos b, d, e, and g courtesy of the Museum of Natural Science, Louisiana State University.

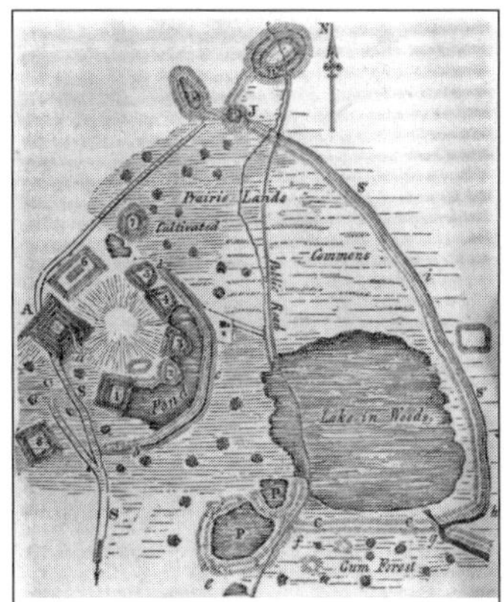

a.

b.

c.

d.

Fig. 2.2. Scenes in the historical development of Louisiana archaeology: a. Forshey's (1845, Figure 1) map of the site on Prairie Jefferson in Morehouse Parish; b. C. B. Moore's paddle-wheeled quarter boat the *Gopher* during the winter of 1900–1901. Courtesy of Bob Murry, Baton Rouge, Louisiana, 1976; c. Mining clam shells from the archaeological site Little Temple (16JE19). Illustration by James E. Taylor for *Frank Leslie's Illustrated Newspaper*, October 17, 1868 (Swanson 1991); d. Excavations into Mound A at the Crooks site (16LA3), LaSalle Parish, January 31, 1939. Photo courtesy of the Museum of Natural Science, Louisiana State University.

is probably the first written description of an archaeological site in what is now the State of Louisiana.

Caleb Goldsmith Forshey (Figure 2.1a), an engineer and military officer, is credited with publishing the first detailed map of a site in Louisiana. His 1845 drawing recorded the dimensions of the mounds and embankments at the Jordan site (16MO1) in Morehouse Parish (Figure 2.2a; Forshey 1845, Figure 1). Forshey recognized the value of recording archaeological sites but lamented that "the leveling hand of American Industry is fast obliterating these dumb, yet eloquent records of the past; and hence the necessity of early attention and accurate description" (Forshey 1845:39). Forshey's map would be reproduced three years later by Ephraim G. Squier and Edward Hamilton Davis (1848) in their classic work, *Ancient Monuments of the Mississippi Valley*, the first volume of the Smithsonian Contributions to Knowledge series of the newly formed Smithsonian Institution.

Numerous accounts of prehistoric sites appeared over the next fifty years (Neuman 1984: 6–52). For example, in 1898 and 1899 the geologist Arthur Clifford Veatch, working for the experiment stations of Louisiana State University (LSU), reported a number of archaeological sites while conducting his geological surveys. He described human burials from Caddo Parish, several shell mounds and middens on the salt domes in Iberia and St. Mary parishes—including the 600-foot-long Morton Shell Mound (16IB3) on Weeks Island—and fossil bones recovered from Avery Island. He also examined the Drake's Salt Works in Bienville Parish and during the fall of 1899 described archaeological sites in Caldwell, Catahoula, and Ouachita parishes (Veatch 1899a, 1899b, 1902a, 1902b).

Many naturalists and geologists noted the presence of large prehistoric mound sites and shell middens, collecting the artifacts that they found as curiosities. But it wasn't until George Eugene Beyer that anyone was funded specifically to undertake detailed archaeological investigations. George Beyer was born in Germany in 1861, studied biology at the University of Berlin, and settled in New Orleans in 1891, becoming a professor of entomology and curator for Tulane's Museum of Natural History in 1893 (Figure 2.1b). In 1896, he presented a report on mounds in Catahoula Parish at a meeting of the Louisiana Historical Society. At the meeting he admonished the society for not supporting archaeological investigations into the state's prehistoric past, and he was successful in convincing the Louisiana Historical Society to support his fieldwork, which continued until the end of the century. Beginning in 1896, Beyer investigated sites in Calcasieu, Catahoula, Franklin, Iberia, Natchitoches, Orleans, St. Charles, and West Feliciana parishes (Neuman 1984). His articles can be considered Louisiana's first site reports. These reports included site maps, profiles, and plans, as well as drawings of some of the artifacts recovered. His interest was not simply to collect artifacts but also to investigate methods of mound construction and document their multistage structure. He examined shell middens as well, observing various layers and features, such as fire pits, and his reports described the various burial patterns and practices (Beyer 1896, 1899). Although not up to today's standards, Beyer's work foreshadowed developments in scientific investigations.

Probably the most talked about discovery in nineteenth-century Louisiana archaeology was the split-cane basketry purportedly found with the bones of extinct fauna on Avery Island in Iberia Parish. This find brought to the forefront of nineteenth-century scholarship the question of human contemporaneity with Pleistocene fauna. As reported by Dr. Joseph Leidy in 1866, the fragments of cane matting were said to be found beneath the bones of mastodon, mylodon, and horse (Leidy 1866). In 1890, the salt mining operations revealed additional artifacts and fossil bone, but these archaeological remains, including pottery, were found above the layer containing the fossil bones. Mine workers unearthed matting again in 1898, and this time George Eugene Beyer (1899) traveled to Avery Island to examine the find and the locale from which it was discovered. The matting had been located two feet above the salt and sixteen feet below the ground surface. A fossil horse tooth was reported to have been found, partially covered by the matting. In all cases, there were questions of wall slumping and wash contaminating the deposits (Neuman 1984:26–34, 61–65). Interest in these finds continued well into the 1960s. Eventually the original matting, which had been donated to the Smithsonian Institution, was radiocarbon dated to 4260 B.P. (years before present; Gagliano 1967:43).

There is no question that the most important effort at site investigations during the first two decades of the twentieth century was that of Clarence Bloomfield Moore (Figure 2.1c). Moore was born in Philadelphia and received his A.B. from Harvard University. He traveled extensively in Europe, the Middle East, Egypt, and South America, where he crossed over the Andes and down the Amazon River to its mouth. Starting in the early 1890s under the auspice of the Academy of Natural Sciences of Philadelphia, although funded by Moore himself, he began his archaeological explorations of the Southeast. He would eventually work in Alabama, Arkansas, Florida, Georgia, Kentucky, Louisiana, Mississippi, South Carolina, and Tennessee. Between 1908 and 1917, Moore traveled in his steamboat, the *Gopher*, up and down the rivers and bayous of Louisiana (Figure 2.2b). Eventually he would visit 104 sites in 27 of the state's parishes. Although Moore often omitted site maps or excavation dimensions for the sites he visited, he did include soil descriptions. He employed trenching and troweling methods, occasional screening the soil that came from his tests, and he provided detailed drawings of key artifacts, especially beautifully illustrated ceramic vessels. Moore was also the first to involve other scientists in his research projects, including the physical anthropologist Aleš Hrdlička of the Smithsonian Institution. Hrdlička analyzed the human skeletal remains from Moore's work at six sites in Caldwell, Franklin, Morehouse, and Ouachita parishes, recording the sex of the individuals and various cranial and postcranial measurements. Hrdlička also described artificial cranial deformation and pathologies such as arthritis and bone lesions. Moore (1909, 1912, 1913) routinely published his results with uncommon speed, usually within a year of completing his fieldwork (see also Hrdlička 1909; Weinstein et al., ed. 2003).

The Smithsonian Institution was also interested in the archaeological sites of Louisiana, and it sent Gerard Fowke, Henry B. Collins, Jr., and Winslow M. Walker to Louisiana's rivers and bayous. Fowke arrived in Louisiana in 1926. He was assigned the task of exploring the Red River Valley from its mouth to the Arkansas border. Fowke reported a number of sites and spent three months excavating six mounds located in and around the Marksville site (16AV1) in Avoyelles Parish (McGimsey, Chapter 7 in this volume). He produced the first detailed map of the mounds and encircling earthworks at the Marksville site (Fowke 1927, 1928). Also in 1926, the Smithsonian sent Henry Collins to Louisiana to gather data on archaeological remains on the coast. Collins concluded that Louisiana's coastal sites were the furthest south and west extent of the mound cultures of the Mississippi Valley. He also noted the presence of certain distinctive pottery styles that were similar to those from Florida (Collins 1927a).

In 1931, Winslow Walker arrived in Louisiana and during a four-week period attempted to locate historic Caddo sites in the Natchitoches area, including remnants of a burial ground of the historic Natchitoches Indians (16NA9) that had recently been heavily impacted by the construction of a fish hatchery (Walker 1932, 1934, 1935). From there Walker traveled to the Marksville area, where he learned of the destruction at the Troyville site in present-day Jonesville, Louisiana. Arriving at Troyville, he discovered that the largest mound at the site had been leveled by a construction company that used the dirt as fill material for the approach to a new highway bridge being built nearby over the Black River. Walker (1933, 1936) stated that this was the first time such an enormous mound had ever been so thoroughly destroyed (but see Lee, Chapter 8 in this volume).

Prior to this, the stock market crash in October 1929 began the spiraling panic of the Great Depression. By 1933, 13 million Americans were unemployed, about one-fourth of the workforce. The overall economic collapse, coupled with falling cotton prices, resulted in widespread unemployment in the South. When President Franklin D. Roosevelt took office in March 1933, he immediately began his relief programs. Some of these relief programs were to have a monumental impact on archaeology, ushering in excavation on a scale unimaginable in the past.

One of the first relief agencies was the Federal Emergency Relief Administration (FERA), begun in May 1933. FERA provided the funding for the first large-scale archaeological project of the New Deal: the excavation at the Marksville site in Avoyelles Parish (Lyon 1996:28). The city council of Marksville had purchased much of the Marksville site for development as a park, and the council and FERA officials requested that the Smithsonian send someone to oversee the park's development. The Smithsonian selected its own curator of archaeology, Frank Setzler, for the task (Figure 2.1d). From August 22 to December 1, 1933, Setzler excavated mounds and village areas at the site with the assistance of young James A. Ford and a crew of one hundred men. In addition to answering questions about the important archaeological deposits, the project demonstrated that with proper supervision, unskilled workers could provide the labor for controlled, scientific archaeological excavations. This had a major impact on the development of federally funded archaeological relief projects. Setzler went on to serve as a major advisor for the program (Lyon 1996:66).

There were other relief projects as well, such as the Civil Works Administration (CWA), but it wasn't until the Emergency Relief Appropriation Act of 1935 that the Works Progress Administration (WPA) was born. Although not without its problems, the WPA was to have a major impact on archaeology in the southeastern United States. James A. Ford was the driving force behind WPA archaeology in Louisiana (Lyon 1996:63).

James A. Ford was born in Water Valley, Mississippi, on February 12, 1911 (Figure 2.1e). His father died while Ford was young, and he was raised by his mother. In 1927, the Mississippi Department of Archives and History employed Ford, along with his friend Moreau B. Chambers, to collect artifacts in the counties around Jackson. Fieldwork continued in 1928 and 1929 (Lyons 1996:79). Ford enrolled at Mississippi College, but in 1930 an opportunity to accompany Henry Collins to Alaska to excavate Eskimo sites interrupted his formal education. Ford returned to Alaska in 1931–1932. In the summer of 1933, a grant from the National Research Council provided him with the funds to continue his survey work in Mississippi and adjoining northern Louisiana (Willey 1969). He assisted Frank Setzler with the excavations at the Marksville site and then worked under A. R. Kelly at a site near Macon, Georgia. At the urging of the geographer Fred B. Kniffen, Ford returned to Louisiana and entered LSU in the fall of 1934 on a fellowship to study and report on the survey work he conducted in 1927–1929 and 1933. This research would be published as the classic *Analysis of Indian Village Site Collections from Louisiana and Mississippi* (Ford 1936). Ford's work established an outline of the ceramic chronology for the Lower Mississippi Valley. He received a B.A. from LSU in 1936 and remained a research archaeologist for the institution until 1946 (Evans 1968:1162). In 1937, Ford was involved in two small WPA projects in Concordia Parish. With the support and participation of LSU and while working on his graduate degree at the University of Michigan, Ford organized the WPA program for Louisiana, receiving final approval for it in September 1938 (Lyon 1996).

With $112,000 in federal funds and $12,852 from LSU, Ford was able to hire two hundred workers, as well as a staff including archaeologists Gordon R. Willey, William T. Mulloy, R. Stuart Neitzel, Arden D. King, and geographer Edwin B. Doran. In subsequent years, George I. Quimby, Preston Holder, Walter Beecher, Carlyle Smith, and ethnohistorian Andrew Albrecht would join the team (Willey 1969). Ford had carefully designed the research project to answer major questions about the Lower Mississippi Valley's cultural sequence. He set up a laboratory first in New Orleans and later in Baton Rouge, as well as two field units, one in Avoyelles Parish and another in LaSalle Parish. Initially, Gordon Willey supervised the laboratory, which included a catalog division, a preparation division, an analysis division, a statistical section, an engineering division, a photography unit, archives and records, a dendrochronology unit, and various administrative sections. Stuart Neitzel managed the Avoyelles unit with the assistance of Edwin Doran. In October 1938, Neitzel began excavation at the Greenhouse site (16AV2), continuing work there until spring floods forced the crew to move to higher ground, where they conducted additional excavations at the Marksville site. In 1940, Neitzel supervised excavation of the Marksville period Martin Baptiste Place (16AV25), and in 1941 he worked at the Nick Place (16AV22) (Lyon 1996). The LaSalle unit, under the direction of William Mulloy with Arden King as his assistant, began excavation on the Crooks Mound (16LA3) in October 1938, continuing until April 1939 (Figure 2.2d).

Members of the LSU–WPA program also worked in the New Orleans area. Previously as part of a CWA project, in 1934 Maurice Weil and then J. Richard Czajkowski excavated into shell deposits known as the Little Woods Middens (16OR1–5). An LSU–WPA team under the direction of Preston Holder returned to the area in 1939, and excavations resumed for four months. Edwin Doran spent two weeks excavating at Big Oak Island (16OR6) and then in January and February 1941 moved to the Tchefuncte site (16ST1) in St. Tammany Parish. These sites were to form the basis for the description of the newly defined Tchefuncte culture (Hays and Weinstein, Chapter 6 in this volume). From November 1939 until April 1940, Doran worked at the Medora site (16WBR1), a predominantly late prehistoric Plaquemine culture site in West Baton Rouge Parish, where geomorphology helped to date the archaeological remains. Doran and then Carlyle Smith supervised excavation at the Bayou Goula site (16IV11) in Iberville Parish, which, based on the historical research of Andrew Albrecht, was the village of the Bayougoula, Mugulasha, Acolapissa, and other tribes during the period from 1699 to 1758. Excavations here were directed toward understanding the little-known historic contact period archaeology (Lyon 1996).

Nationwide, by early 1939, 24 archaeological projects costing $2.3 million and employing 2,000 workers and 100 scientists were underway. Almost every presentation at the 1938 Society for American Archaeology meeting was based on WPA projects (Lyon 1996:67). The start of World War II in Europe in September 1939, however, saw the beginning of the end of WPA archaeology. As the months passed, the government directed more funds to projects that contributed to national defense. But in three short years WPA archaeology in Louisiana had accomplished much. The cultural sequence Ford had developed for the Lower Mississippi Valley was confirmed and expanded, a number of large mound sites had been extensively excavated, and a new culture, the Tchefuncte, had been added to the beginning of the prehistoric chronology, resulting in the sequence of Tchefuncte–Marksville–Troyville–Coles Creek–Plaquemine–Natchez/Caddoan. Major reports on many of the excavations were published in the 1940s and 1950s (e.g., Ford 1951; Ford and Quimby 1945; Ford and Willey 1940). In 1952, 1953, and 1955, Ford returned to Louisiana to conduct further surveys and excavate at the Poverty Point site (16WC5) in West Carroll Parish (Ford and Webb 1956).

Concern for archaeological resources went into a hiatus during World War II. After the war, the U.S. economy boomed and major new federally funded projects got underway. Some of these, particularly the reservoir projects, the federal highway program and the development of the interstate highway system, and various urban renewal efforts, would radically change the physical landscape. Thousands of archaeological sites and historic structures were standing in the way of "progress" and were at risk of being destroyed. The information about the past that they contained would then be irretrievably lost.

CRM and the State

By the late 1950s and early 1960s, momentum was building for federal legislative action to protect the nation's patrimony. The historic preservation community, led by the National Trust for Historic Preservation and Colonial Williamsburg, sponsored a conference, and eventually the U.S. Conference of Mayors formed a committee to review national preservation in eight different countries. The resulting report contained a number of recommendations, including the enactment of federal legislation (National Trust for Historic Preservation 1999, original 1966). In October 1966, President Lyndon B. Johnson signed into law the National Historic Preservation Act (NHPA) (Public Law 89–665, 16 U.S.C. 470 et seq.) as part of his Great Society legislative efforts. This legislation required federal agencies to develop preservation programs. It also established the framework for state historic preservation programs.

At first, archaeologists were not enthusiastic about this new law. As originally written, only sites that were listed on the National Register would be protected under Section 106 of the law, and few archaeological sites were so listed. It would not be until the law was amended in 1980 and the words "or eligible for nomination to" were added to Section 106 that most archaeological sites received any type of protection under the NHPA. The relatively short Section 106 of the NHPA was to have a major impact on archaeological research and investigation throughout the United States.

In the meantime, archaeologists had been engaged in their own legislative efforts. The Committee for the Recovery of Archaeological Remains (CRAR) lobbied both Congress and the executive branch to expand federal support for archaeological investigations in riverine areas that were slated to be dammed to create reservoirs. This resulted in the Reservoir Salvage Act of 1960 (Fowler 2000). This act was further amended in 1974 as the Archaeological and Historic Preservation Act, also known as the "Moss-Bennett Act" (P.L. 86–523, 16 U.S.C. 469–469 c-2). The Moss-Bennett Act extended the previous legislation to include all federally funded, licensed, or assisted projects and authorized agencies to expend funds on archaeological investigations (King 1987). Additional important legislation for archaeological site protection included the National Environmental Policy Act of 1969 (NEPA) (P.L. 91–190; 42 U.S.C. 4321 and 4331–4335) which required that environmental impact assessments address project impact on archaeological resources; the Archaeological Resources Protection Act of 1979 (ARPA) (P.L. 96–95; 16 U.S.C. 470aa-mm), which was designed to discourage looting of archaeological sites on federal lands; the Abandoned Shipwreck Act of 1987 (P.L. 100–298; 43 U.S.C. 2101–2106), which stated that historic shipwrecks could not be subjected to the law of salvage or the law of find; and the Native American Graves Protection and Repatriation Act (NAGPRA), passed in 1990 (P.L. 101–601; 25 U.S.C. 3001 et seq.), which addressed Native American graves and funerary remains (Cast et al., Chapter 12 in this volume).

These various pieces of legislation, with their associated rules and regulations (e.g., 36CFR800), provided an arsenal of legal tools to protect archaeological sites. Along with the legislation came the need for a framework to administer the various programs. In time, federal agencies hired archaeologists in Washington, D.C., as well as regional offices, to direct the federal agencies' archaeological efforts. State governments added archaeologists to administer the archaeological portions of the National Historic Preservation Act at the state level, especially Section 106. Initially university-based archaeologists but in time an ever-increasing number of contract archaeologists would conduct the archaeological surveys and excavations made necessary under these laws. These developments spawned the cultural resource management (CRM) movement, which was to define archaeology in the later decades of the twentieth century until the present day.

In Louisiana, concern for archaeological resources resulted in the passage of the Archaeological Treasure Act (R.S. 41:1601–1613) in 1974. This act established Louisiana's state archaeology program under the administration of the Louisiana Archaeological Survey and Antiquities Commission (LASAC). Margaret D. Drew was appointed the first chair and William G. Haag was named Louisiana's first state archaeologist. Under the new law, the LASAC promulgated rules and regulations concerning the recovery and study of archaeological remains on state lands; maintained the state archaeological site files; functioned as legal custodian of artifacts recovered from state lands or donated to the state from private lands; implemented a public outreach program; and advised state agencies relative to archaeological resources. In 1976, as part of Governor Edwin Edwards's reorganization of state government, the state archaeology program was combined with the state preservation program and became the Division of Archaeology and Historic Preservation under the Department of Culture, Recreation, and Tourism. The LASAC became an advisory body to the governor, and the state program assumed additional responsibilities as defined by federal law, foremost of which included the administration of the archaeological portion of Section 106 of the NHPA. The Division of Archaeology was separated from Historic Preservation in 1989, but it continues to work closely with its sister agency. The Louisiana Unmarked Human Burial Sites Preservation Act was passed in 1991, providing legal protections over human skeletal remains and artifacts at unmarked burial sites.

On the academic front, in 1952 LSU became the first state institution to hire an archaeologist (William G. Haag) onto its faculty. By the early 1970s, Northwestern State University (Hiram F. Gregory), the University of New Orleans (R. Richard Shenkel), the University of Louisiana at Lafayette (Jon L. Gibson), the University of Louisiana at Monroe (Glen S. Greene), and Louisiana Tech University (C. Wade Meade) all had archaeologists, most of whom were actively engaged in archaeological research in Louisiana. Tulane University archaeologists also occasionally conducted research projects within the state. Moreover, Louisiana drew researchers from outside its boundaries. Foremost among these have been archaeologists with Harvard University's Lower Mississippi Valley Survey, which conducted summer projects in Louisiana or neighboring Mississippi for a number of years. Many of these university-based archaeologists, including the Division of Archaeology's regional and station archaeologists who work at universities, continue to make major contributions toward understanding the state's past.

During the late 1960s and throughout the 1980s and 1990s, many of the university-based archaeologists conducted surveys that were required by federal legislation, but today environmental companies perform most of the federal-based archaeological investigations in the state. The large cultural resource management firms—such as Coastal Environments, Inc., Earth Search, Inc., Heartfield, Price, and Greene, Inc., Prentice Thomas and Associates, Inc., and R. Christopher Goodwin and Associates, Inc.—all have contributed in substantially increasing knowledge of Louisiana's archaeological past, not only in recording new sites but also through excavations. The impact of these various firms is evident in the references cited in subsequent chapters of this volume.

Not all efforts to protect and preserve Louisiana's archaeological resources are the results of federal legislation. The Louisiana Office of State Parks has some of the state's most important archaeological sites under its management, including some of the type sites for major cultures. These include Poverty Point (West Carroll Parish), Tchefuncte (St. Tammany Parish), and Marksville (Avoyelles Parish). Both Poverty Point and Marksville have interpretive programs and displays that narrate the story of the past residents at these two significant sites. Other important sites managed by State Parks include Los Adaes (16NA16), an early Spanish mission and *presidio* in Natchitoches Parish; the Civil War battlefields of Port Hudson (16EF7) in East Feliciana Parish and Mansfield (16DS187) in DeSoto Parish; and several historic sites, such as the Oakley Plantation (16WF34; West Feliciana Parish), with substantially intact archaeological deposits.

Avocational Archaeology and the LAS

The Louisiana Archaeological Society (LAS) has been a major player in the investigation, interpretation, and preservation of archaeological sites in Louisiana (Neuman 2002). As early as 1961, there had been efforts to form a statewide archaeological organization, but it wasn't until a 1974 meeting in Jonesville, not far from the Troyville site, that the LAS was founded. The purpose of the LAS is to unite individuals, both professional and amateur archaeologists, who have a deep and enduring interest in the state's past. Its stated aims are "to foster the scientific recovery, analysis and interpretation of Louisiana's archaeological resources; to initiate and support preservation policies and non-offensive displays of archaeological materials; to publish and disperse information on Louisiana archaeology; and to encourage a greater public awareness of and interest in the cultural heritage of Louisiana" (Webb and Duhe 1984:65). For over thirty years the LAS has done just that. Today the LAS has over three hundred members with five chapters around the state that hold regular meetings. The organization's newsletter provides notes on ongoing research and activities of the regional and station archaeologists, as well as the societies' local chapters. *Louisiana Archaeology,* the LAS bulletin, is a major venue for current research into Louisiana's archaeology.

Many of those who earn their livelihood outside of archaeology have made substantial contributions to understanding Louisiana's past. Roger T. Saucier, a member of the LAS and professional geomorphologist, applied interdisciplinary studies toward the comprehension of relationships between the location of archaeological site deposits and geological phenomena in the Lower Mississippi River Valley (Figure 2.1f). For his dedicated efforts, Saucier was presented with the prestigious Fryxell Award for Interdisciplinary Research by the Society of American Archaeology. Two other LAS members have been honored by the Society for American Archaeology. In 1985, Clarence H. Webb (Figure 2.1g) became the first recipient of the Crabtree Award, which is presented to an outstanding amateur archaeologist by the Society for American Archaeology. Reca B. Jones received the Crabtree Award in 1998 for her tireless and sustained endeavors in enhancing knowledge of Louisiana's past (Figure 2.1h).

No review of Louisiana's archaeology would be complete without mentioning the contributions of Clarence H. Webb (Figure 2.1g). Webb was an amateur in the truest sense of the word. He engaged in archaeology for love of it rather than for financial benefit or professional motives, often using his own funds to support his projects. Born on August 25, 1902, in Shreveport, Webb grew up on farms in DeSoto and Caddo parishes. He received his bachelor's and medical degrees from Tulane University in 1923 and 1925 respectively. After receiving a pediatrics degree from the University of Chicago in 1931, Webb returned to Shreveport, where he set up a private practice. He went on to jointly establish the Well Baby Clinic in Shreveport's Public Health Department, would publish over fifty articles in medical journals and receive numerous awards from the medical profession.

Webb's interest in archaeology began by collecting artifacts during a Boy Scout camping trip with his sons. This quickly developed into a passion for unraveling the human past. When Webb learned that a property owner had discovered burials while tearing down a mound, Webb and friends began to excavate the site, which became known as the Belcher Mound (16CD13). With advice from James Ford, working on weekends at the site with volunteers, over many years, Webb uncovered the remains of eight prehistoric structures and twenty-six human burials. The results were published as a memoir of the Society for American Archaeology (Webb 1959). In time, Webb excavated more than a dozen sites, including major excavations at the Belcher Mound, Mounds Plantation (16CD12), Resch (41HS16), and John Pearce (16CD56) sites. His work provided the basis for the formulations of the Belcher, Bossier, Glendora, and Bellevue foci (Gibson 1992). Webb was also fascinated with the Poverty Point site and spent over fifty years researching this culture. Finding a cache of steatite vessel fragments in 1935, he returned often to the site. He analyzed the material excavated by Ford during the 1952, 1953, and 1955 excavations and traveled throughout the Southeast examining collections as he worked on unraveling the enigma that was the Poverty Point culture (Ford and Webb 1956; Webb 1968, 1982a).

It has been over two hundred years since Thomas Jefferson presented William Dunbar's findings on the Troyville site to Congress. Today, federal agencies routinely evaluate the impact of their projects on archaeological resources. Federal land-managing agencies, such as the U.S. Army and the U.S. Forest Service, have surveyed extensive tracts of their lands and have in place management plans to avoid impacting significant sites (e.g., Anderson and Smith 2003). University and CRM archaeologists are active in surveying, excavating, reporting and disseminating the results of their findings to both the professional archaeological community and the general public. As of July 2009, the Louisiana Division of Archaeology's records contained information on over 18,000 sites and some 3,300 survey and excavation reports (Philip G. Rivet, personal communication July 14, 2009). Several public educational programs, such as Louisiana Archaeology Month, and various educational resources, such as publications, classroom activity guides, and exhibits, bring Louisiana archaeology to the public (Neuman 2002). Louisiana's archaeological community continues to make major contributions to protecting the past. But challenges still exist.

Present and Future Challenges

One of the most immediate difficulties facing Louisiana's archaeologists is how to deal effectively with the havoc resulting from Hurricanes Katrina and Rita, which struck Louisiana on August 29 and September 24, 2005, respectively. The massive rebuilding efforts, largely financed with federal funds and therefore subject to Section 106 of the NHPA, are providing unimaginable opportunities to delve into New Orleans's rich archaeological heritage. The challenge is to assist efficiently and effectively in the rebuilding of New Orleans, putting people back into homes and rebuilding communities, while maximizing the recovery of significant archaeological and scientific data in a complex urban landscape undergoing rapid construction. New Orleans's recovery efforts are expected to continue over the next ten years. Also as a result of Katrina, the north shore of Lake Pontchartrain is experiencing rapid population growth as people from New Orleans relocate, spawning new subdivisions and urban expansion with the concomitant effects on archaeological deposits (Charles R. McGimsey, personal communication September 11, 2007, and July 16, 2009).

One of the long-term challenges facing Louisiana archaeology is the need to investigate Louisiana's past through targeted excavations that answer major research questions. Although there has been a tremendous amount of archaeological investigation conducted in Louisiana in recent years, most of it has been the result of federally mandated projects and thus area-specific. Few archaeological programs have been designed specifically to address wide-ranging research questions. Methods must be found to support and encourage researchers to take on these critical research areas (Charles R. McGimsey, personal communication September 11, 2007, and July 16, 2009).

Lastly, and probably most importantly, efforts must continue and expand to make the results of archaeological discoveries available to the public and thereby engender an appreciation for the past and feelings of stewardship among Louisiana's residents. It is mainly through the support of the public that both archaeological research and site preservation will continue. The readers of the following chapters will be impressed with Louisiana's rich archaeological past. They hopefully will be enthusiastic to learn more and interested in protecting Louisiana's endangered archaeological sites.

3

Paleoindian and Early Archaic

MARK A. REES

The Paleoindian and Early Archaic periods encompass the earliest known presence of humans in North America and span the formidable ecological changes of the Late Pleistocene–Early Holocene transition, from approximately 11,500 to 6000 B.C. or 13,500 to 8,000 years before present (B.P.). This coincides with the end of the Wisconsin glaciation or last Ice Age, around 10,000 years ago, and the onset of the modern climate and environment of the Holocene. Although Louisiana and the surrounding Gulf Coastal Plain were not directly impacted by the advance and retreat of glaciers prior to and following the Last Glacial Maximum (LGM), the overall effect was profound in terms of geomorphology (the geologic formation and modification of landforms), plant and animal communities, human habitation, and documentation of these earliest Native American sites (Autin et al. 1991; Hill 2006a, 2006b; Lepper and Funk 2006:171; Saucier 1994a:36–41; Simms et al. 2007). Variations in sea level and alteration of the Lower Mississippi Valley (LMV) transformed much of the landscape, to the point that it would be hardly recognizable today.

This chapter summarizes what is presently known about Paleoindian and Early Archaic cultures in Louisiana based on previous investigations. Paleoindian and Early Archaic sites in the state, though generally sparse, are likely more common than previously reported. The distribution of Paleoindian and Early Archaic sites must be understood in relation to geomorphic processes and the constraints of previous investigations, as well as cultural behavior, particularly in comparison to the number of sites known for the same time periods in surrounding states (e.g., Bousman et al. 2004; Jeter and Williams 1989c; McGahey 1996). Potential difficulties sometimes arise in working across modern-day state borders. For example, many early diagnostic artifacts found in Louisiana have names borrowed from Texas and other states. Terminology has sometimes been applied differently in various states (Jeter and Williams 1989c:73–91; McGahey

2000:1–87; Neuman 1984:56–85; Webb 1981). The use of terms such as "Coastview" for Plainview, "Epipaleoindian" for transitional Late Paleoindian–Early Archaic, and "Meso-Indian" for Early and Middle Archaic can be confusing (see Anderson and Smith 2003:246, 254; Gunn 1984:145; Hillman 1990a:205; Neuman 1984:75). The earliest cultures recognized in Louisiana existed across modern state boundaries and need to be dealt with over their actual distributions in order to make sense of the archaeological record (e.g., Jennings 2008a). This is especially true of mobile communities of hunter-gatherers, who regularly moved great distances across the landscape.

In comparison to later periods, particularly the Late Archaic and Woodland, research on the Paleoindian and Early Archaic in Louisiana seems to have advanced little in the past few decades. The greatest strides have invariably been made by state- and federally-funded research geared toward cultural resource management (CRM), along with the work of a few interested individuals (e.g., Campbell and Weed 1986; Hillman 1990a; Morehead et al. 2002; Saucier 1994b). Yet in contrast to adjacent states, Louisiana archaeology might seem to have less to offer in understanding Paleoindian and Early Archaic cultures. Louisiana is hardly mentioned in Anderson and Sassaman's (ed. 1996) *The Paleoindian and Early Archaic Southeast*, reflecting the relative dearth of recent studies in the state. It is noteworthy only for "an absence of well-dated deeply stratified sites" that might contribute to the dating of diagnostic projectile point forms (Anderson et al. 1996:15). Current knowledge of Paleoindian and Early Archaic cultures is consequently also drawn from outside of the state, from the Great Plains to the Atlantic Coast.

But this state of affairs need not persist. Indeed, Louisiana has considerable untapped potential for archaeological research on the earliest inhabitants of North America. One of the most crucial yet unmet needs is a systematic, statewide survey of Paleoindian projectile point distributions. As yet undiscovered, stratified sites with Paleoindian and Early Archaic components undoubtedly exist, especially in deeply buried and submerged landforms along the edges of the alluvial valley and coast. Of the sites that have already been recorded, well-planned and focused investigations might transform current understanding of Louisiana's first inhabitants. The potential for additional research on previously investigated early sites and collections should be considered (e.g., Cotter 1991). A more detailed and nuanced understanding of technological innovations and adaptations, subsistence practices, site distributions, and resource and landscape use will depend on such studies. A more thorough knowledge of geomorphology and paleoenvironments represents an important step in that direction. It will also be necessary to emphasize the significance of Louisiana's most ancient sites and to foster greater interest in research.

Geomorphology and Paleoenvironments

Locating and studying Paleoindian and Early Archaic sites in Louisiana require knowledge of geomorphology, as well as the reconstruction of the paleoenvironments in which the first Americans lived. The differences between Pleistocene and Holocene landscapes of Louisiana are as dramatic as anywhere in North America, particularly in the LMV and along the Gulf Coast. The surfaces of the alluvial valley and entire Deltaic and Chenier plains are Holocene-age formations, meaning that associated archaeological sites date from this period and were impacted by geomorphic processes such as meander belt and distributary formation and abandonment, mudflat progradation (seaward expansion), subsidence (decreasing surface elevation), and shoreline erosion (Autin et al. 1991:563; Kidder et al. 2008; Saucier 1994a:13–16, 41). Aggradation, or the infilling of the alluvial valley, and the inundation of ancient shorelines due to rising sea level are two of the greatest hurdles in identifying sites of human habitation dating prior to 8,000 years ago (Gagliano 1977, 1984; Gagliano et al. 1982:3–10; Saucier 1994a:35–54). The low archaeological visibility of deeply buried and inundated sites is compounded by the relative unobtrusiveness of cultural deposits from the Paleoindian period, making such sites even more difficult to locate and study. Where Pleistocene-age or more ancient, Tertiary period (65–2 million years ago) landforms are accessible, as in parts of northwest Louisiana, millennia of exposure, inhabitation, and erosion have often repositioned, redeposited, or conflated Paleoindian and Archaic materials with later deposits. Surmounting these challenges requires a combined knowledge of geomorphology, regional paleoenvironments, and archaeological formation processes, in order to examine and understand the earliest human presence in Louisiana (Kidder 1996; e.g., Saucier 1981, 1994b).

During the LGM of the Wisconsin glaciation, around 22,000 years ago, vast quantities of water were frozen in glaciers and the sea level was approximately 125 meters (410 ft) lower than today. Pleistocene shorelines of the northern Gulf of Mexico were as much as 200 kilometers (124 mi) farther south, exposing large expanses of the Outer Continental Shelf (OCS) to human habitation (Gagliano et al. 1982:7–10; Saucier 1994a:49–50, Figure 5; Walker and Coleman 1987:65–66). By the end of the Younger Dryas, or last millennium-long cold cycle of the Late Pleistocene around 10,000 B.P., a warming hemispheric climate resulted in deglaciation and retreat of the Cordilleran and Laurentide ice sheets (Hill 2006a, 2006b, 2006c; Simms et al. 2007). The first Americans to enter the Gulf Coastal Plain around 13,500 to 12,500 years ago encountered an environment colder than today, with greater seasonal extremes, but far removed from the frigid tundra just south of the glaciers. Oak-hickory forest was increasingly predominant after this time, with diminishing spruce forest in the uplands and mixed hardwoods in the river valleys (Anderson et al. 1996; Delcourt and Delcourt 1987; Wright 2006). People hunted Pleistocene megafauna, such as mastodon, but smaller mammals, aquatic and migratory birds, fish, reptiles, and wild plant foods were also utilized and increased in importance as growing populations moved into new and different environments (Collins 2007; Dunbar and Vojnovski 2007; Fiedel 2007; Hollenbach 2007; Walker 2007).

Paleoindian foraging groups may have practiced more variable and generalized subsistence than previously recognized, especially in coastal regions (Cannon and Meltzer 2004; Kelly and Todd 1988; Lapham 2006; Rick et al. 2001; Walker and Driskell, ed. 2007). Characterization of Paleoindian Clovis culture as expert big-game hunters has fueled conjectures concerning megafauna overkill and extinction (Martin 1967, 1984), despite the lack of substantiating evidence and ample support to the contrary (Grayson and Meltzer 2002, 2003, 2004). At present there is no unequivocal evidence from Louisiana that Paleoindians hunted Pleistocene megafauna. But the remains of Pleistocene fauna have long been recovered throughout the state, and based on analogies with other regions, the first people to arrive in Louisiana hunted mastodon and possibly *Bison antiquus*, an enormous and now extinct species of bison (Carpenter 1838; Domning 1969; Rice 1981). Among the archaeological sites that have produced remains of megafauna are Salt Mine Valley (16IB23) and the Tapir site (16IB66) in Iberia Parish, Côte Blanche Island (16SMY79) in St. Mary Parish, Trappey Mastodon (16LY63) in Lafayette Parish, and the vicinity of Above the Mastodon (16WF63) in West Feliciana Parish (Gagliano 1967; Gibson and Miller 1973; Marckese 1993). Three of these five sites are located on salt domes along the south-central coast, and all are located on Pleistocene-age land surfaces in the south half of the state.

One of the most prominent sites in the search for early humans was discovered at Avery Island in Iberia Parish in south-central Louisiana (Figure 1.2). Bones of extinct Pleistocene fauna have been found there since the 1860s (Gagliano 1967:7–8; see Neuman 1984:24–34, 61–65). Investigation by Gagliano (1967:39–41, Table III, 92–100, 1970) at Salt Mine Valley on Avery Island identified deeply buried Paleoindian, Early Archaic, and later components, along with the fossilized remains of mastodon, mammoth, horse, bison, ground sloth, and other extinct megafauna. Radiocarbon analysis produced dates of 10,995 B.C. and 12,115 B.C. for an organic stratum 4.9 to 5.5 meters (16 to 18 ft) below surface (cal. median dates from McGimsey and van der Koogh 2001:28–29, Table 2). The recovery of Late Pleistocene faunal remains, split-cane matting, plant fiber, and bipolar pebble tools from deeper levels led Gagliano (1967:92–102, 1970:6–20) to propose a lithic component contemporaneous with Paleoindian or transitional Paleoindian–Early Archaic. Yet the association of faunal remains and artifacts was unclear and the scarcity of diagnostic Paleoindian artifacts was regarded as problematic (Neuman 1984:61–65).

A single Clovis point was found on the shore at Côte Blanche Island, presumed to have eroded from the same deposit that contained remains of mastodon, horse, and other Pleistocene fauna (Marckese 1993). Mastodon remains from the Trappey Mastodon site were recovered from 4 meters (13 ft) below the surface of a Pleistocene terrace, along with two unassociated Marcos projectile points thought to date no earlier than the Late Archaic (2000–800 B.C.). A single Clovis point on the same landform 5 kilometers (3 mi) downstream, at Site 16LY68, places Paleoindian hunters in the region at the end of the Pleistocene era, perhaps around the time the Trappey mastodon was grazing along the banks of the Vermilion River (Gibson 1976:76–77; Gibson and Miller 1973). The extinction of Pleistocene megafauna, including mammoth, mastodon, and *Bison antiquus*, was part of the widespread ecological transformation that characterized terminal Pleistocene–Early Holocene climate change and rearrangement of plant and animal communities, although the possibility of later survivals in parts of Louisiana has been proposed (Gagliano 1967:39–41; Wright 2006). Numerous species of Pleistocene mammals, for which there is little or no evidence of human hunting, went extinct in North America by the Early Holocene (Meltzer 2009:44–48, Table 2, 255–267).

Deglaciation during the end of the Pleistocene was accompanied by stream entrenchment, as well as the broadening and degradation of the alluvial Mississippi Valley, which eroded Pleistocene landforms and potentially associated sites (Autin et al. 1991:550–552). Increased melt water and glacial outwash in the Mississippi River reshaped earlier valley train (braided stream) surfaces, such as Maçon Ridge in northeast Louisiana, eroding some deposits and burying others in alluvium. More extensive seasonal flooding of the alluvial valley may have made ridges and higher terraces more suitable for habitation and perhaps even more advantageous for hunting (Saucier 1994b:137–143). Terminal and post-

Pleistocene processes of degradation and deposition occurred at different scales and rates in tributaries and smaller drainages throughout the state. Dissected uplands of the Tertiary period in the northwest, Pleistocene terraces along major drainages, and prairie terraces of southwest and southeast Louisiana were modified by erosion and redeposition, potentially conflating or mixing archaeological deposits dating from the Paleoindian and Early Archaic periods (Autin et al. 1991:556–559).

Sea level approached its modern level by the Middle Archaic period (6000–2000 B.C.), submerging abandoned distributaries and deltaic lobes, some Pleistocene surfaces (such as natural levees and shorelines), and associated Paleoindian and Early Archaic sites (Autin et al. 1991; Gagliano et al. 1982; Saucier 1994a:50). Rising sea level and valley entrenchment produced a lower gradient and meandering river courses, with associated abandoned channels, natural levees, backswamps, and overbank deposits characteristic of the modern LMV (Saucier 1994a:87–129). Cypress-gum wetlands and mixed hardwood forests proliferated with the establishment of a more modern, temperate climate during the Early Holocene era, which is generally associated with the Early Archaic period. A warming interval known as the Hypsithermal during the mid-Holocene supported the further development of modern vegetation, including cypress and mixed-hardwood bottomlands, southern pine forests throughout the Tertiary Uplands, and prairie grasslands on Pleistocene terraces (Anderson and Sassaman 2004:87; Anderson et al. 1996:4–6, 14–15; Gremillion 1996, 2006; Saucier 1994a:260; Schuldenrein 1996). Woodland fauna were well established by this time, with white-tailed deer, fish, and aquatic resources increasingly important in Archaic period subsistence (Jackson and Scott 2001; Lapham 2006:398–399).

Channel movement and distributary formation continually reshaped the alluvial valley and Deltaic Plain during the Early and mid-Holocene, eroding some Pleistocene surfaces and leaving others on abandoned channels or levees (Kidder et al. 2008; Saucier 1994a; Smith et al. 1986). The Teche and St. Bernard deltas formed as the sea level stabilized, as indicated by the presence of sites associated with Poverty Point and later cultures. Distributary abandonment and subsidence in the Deltaic Plain produced extensive marsh, estuarine, and marine environments that characterize Louisiana's coastal wetlands. The Chenier Plain developed as delta complexes distributed sediment westward along the coast. Successive mudflat formation and erosion produced ridges or cheniers ideal for coastal inhabitation, with the oldest cheniers farthest inland dating from less than 4,000 years ago (Autin et al. 1991; Saucier 1994a:29–30, 136–161, 283–284). Modern-day subsidence and wetlands loss, while not entirely new, are nonetheless unprecedented in the accelerating rate and anthropogenic (humanly produced) source.

GEOARCHAEOLOGY

As should be clear from the preceding overview, knowledge of the geologic history of meander belts, deltaic distributaries, and other geomorphic processes is essential to Louisiana archaeology, employing the concepts and techniques of geoarchaeology (Gagliano 1984; Kidder 1996). Archaeological sites in some instances can provide an estimate for the minimum age of a landform (Saucier 1994a:14, 280–282). Processes of erosion and deposition on Pleistocene landforms throughout the state have obliterated or buried some sites, while other surfaces have been modified but essentially preserved. Buried sites with potentially intact stratigraphy are most likely so deeply buried that archaeological discovery and investigation are infrequent and problematic, even with the most advanced remote-sensing technologies (Smith et al. 1986). Paleoindian and Early Archaic sites with broad surface exposure along ridge tops, or at higher elevations between river drainages, may be immediately accessible, but they often lack stratigraphic deposits or have been impacted by erosion and subsequently disturbed (Hillman 1990a).

Among the most visible and best-known Paleoindian and Early Archaic sites are those recorded on the Tertiary Uplands and dissected hills in the northwest and west-central parts of the state (Anderson and Smith 2003:11–13; Girard 2007:5). While erosion and alluvial deposition have obscured, redeposited, and in some instances obliterated sites, the same processes have also exposed artifacts and worked in favor of site discovery. More than half of all currently recorded sites with Paleoindian components are located in northwest Louisiana, or what is known as Management Unit II (Smith et al. 1983). Maçon Ridge in northeast Louisiana has also demonstrated good potential for the discovery of intact Paleoindian and Early Archaic sites in the LMV, despite considerable erosion and alluvial deposition. Some sites along Maçon Ridge may be buried and preserved by thick deposits of loess or wind-blown silt, yet within the reach of archaeologists (Hillman 1990a:210; Saucier 1994a:131–133; 1994b:139). The same may apply to the peripheries of the LMV, on the rolling prairies of southwest and southeast Louisiana, especially the higher terraces of drainages, such as the Calcasieu, Mermentau, Vermilion, Amite, and Tangipahoa. On the south-central coast, the diverse ecotones and higher elevations offered at Avery Island, Côte Blanche Island, and Jefferson Island salt domes have demonstrated potential for Paleoindian and Early Archaic sites (Gagliano 1967; Marckese 1993; Russo 1993:13).

Some landforms and potentially associated sites present exceptional difficulties, such as low-lying portions of the LMV and OCS. In some areas of the Atchafalaya Basin, it is estimated that archaeological deposits predating 3500 B.C. may lie beneath as much as 9 to 40 meters (30–131 ft) of sediment (Smith et al. 1986:79). Where Pleistocene surfaces, such as natural levees, are deeply buried but still intact, archaeological survey and site discovery through coring and remote sensing are haphazard and time consuming, even for the most focused CRM research. Large-scale excavation would be even more problematic due to the potential depth of deposits, especially for Early Paleoindian sites. The continued subsidence and erosion of some coastal landforms, such as deltaic lobes, and the obliteration of any associated sites, make it practically impossible to study associated human inhabitation or land use prior to the Late Archaic period in those areas (Kidder et al. 2008).

Pleistocene landforms and an unknown number of potentially associated sites also lie submerged offshore (see Saltus and Pearson, Chapter 18 in this volume). The potential for underwater archaeology of these early periods is still being explored, as the technological capability to effectively and efficiently do so has only recently been developed (e.g., Evans et al. 2007; Gagliano 1977; Pearson et al. 1986; Stright 1986). Ongoing research on the OCS by Patrick Hesp, Amanda Evans, and colleagues with the Coastal Marine Institute at Louisiana State University (LSU) has identified a possible prehistoric midden on a submerged alluvial terrace (Evans et al. 2007). Since coastal routes have been proposed as among the earliest pathways of initial human settlement, the investigation of Pleistocene shorelines and paleochannels holds tremendous potential for informing current understanding of migrations into the continent and early coastal adaptations (Anderson and Gillam 2000; Faught 2004). Due to the logistical constraints of locating and excavating deeply buried sites in the LMV, the future of Paleoindian and Early Archaic research may lie offshore.

McFaddin Beach (41JF50) in Jefferson County, Texas, provides a compelling example of the unrealized research potential of submerged coastal sites. Located only 19 kilometers (12 mi) west of Sabine Pass, McFaddin Beach has produced hundreds of artifacts 8,000 years old or older, representing Clovis through Early Archaic and later components. In the collections studied by Stright (1999:43–46), artifacts diagnostic of the Middle and Late Paleoindian periods are the most common, comprising approximately 43 percent of the total sample. Recovered materials include Clovis, Dalton, Scottsbluff, and San Patrice points, as well as Pleistocene fauna (Bousman et al. 2004:78, Table 2.5; Hester et al. 1992; Stright 1999:32, 44). These materials were redeposited by erosion of a now submerged, relict Pleistocene shoreline. Based on her comparative study of the collections, Stright (1999:46–47) suggests the McFaddin Beach Paleoindian assemblage shares greater similarities with the Eastern Woodlands than with Southern Great Plains cultures to the west (also Stright et al. 1999). Yet considerably less is known about any potentially contemporaneous components across the Sabine River to the east, where Paleoindian projectile point distributions have not been recorded (see Anderson and Gillam 2000:59, Figure 9). Geomorphic processes of the Chenier Plain have undoubtedly impacted site integrity and visibility along the modern, Holocene-age shoreline. Future geoarchaeological studies in the region must consequently begin with paleoenvironmental reconstruction and the identification of buried or submerged Pleistocene landforms (e.g., Evans et al. 2007; Pearson et al. 1986; Saltus and Pearson, Chapter 18 in this volume).

Paleoindian and Early Archaic Periods

For the purposes of this volume, the Paleoindian period dates from approximately 11,500 to 8000 B.C. The Early Archaic period in Louisiana might then be placed at 8000 to 6000 B.C. (Figure 1.3). The culture chronology for these earliest of periods varies by region in southeastern North America, but it corresponds more or less with the terminal Pleistocene and Early Holocene (Anderson and Sassaman 2004:87; Anderson et al. 1996:14). Archaeologists now distinguish calibrated radiocarbon years before present (cal. B.P.) from years before present (B.P.), correcting for the effects of environmental fluctuations in radiocarbon dating techniques (e.g., Anderson 2004; Meltzer 2009:6–10). In general, calibration of radiocarbon years farther back in time produces successively earlier calendar dates, such that 10,000 radiocarbon years B.P. is calibrated at 11,450 B.P. (Anderson and Smith 2003:331; Struiver et al. 1998).

There are unfortunately very few accurate radiocarbon (^{14}C), oxidizable carbon ratio (OCR), or thermoluminescence (TL) dates for Paleoindian and Early Archaic components in Louisiana (McGimsey and van der Koogh 2001:3), and most come from relatively few sites in west-central Louisiana (Anderson and Smith 2003:340–345, Table 6.2). The 5,500-year-long time span of 11,500–6000 B.C. thus represents at best a loose approximation based on available radiocarbon dates and cultural horizons in Louisiana and the Southeast as a whole (Anderson and Smith 2003:349–369; Jeter and Williams 1989c:71–89). Except where specific radiometric dates are noted as cal. B.P. or cal. B.C., the chronology presented here represents uncalibrated calendar ages (for a general Southeast chronology in cal. B.P., see Anderson 2004; cf. Meltzer 2009:10). Further refinement of a Paleoindian and Early Archaic culture chronology for Louisiana will require careful excavation of stratified deposits and the collection of a well-defined series of calibrated radiometric dates.

Moreover, it is important to recognize the somewhat arbitrary demarcation of the Paleoindian and Early Archaic periods, a distinction drawn from long-term ecological trends and diagnostic artifact types, such as Clovis and San Patrice projectile points (e.g., Anderson et al. 1996:14). Based on recent evidence from far beyond present-day Louisiana, the first Americans arrived on the continent by 11,500 B.C. (median cal. 16,040 B.P.), although it is not yet known exactly how much earlier (Anderson 2004:119–120; Goodyear 2006; Lepper and Funk 2006:174–176; Meltzer 2009:9, Table 1, 131–134; OxCal 3.10 2009). Until convincing evidence has been collected and presented for sites throughout the state, 11,500 B.C. represents a reasonable estimate for Louisiana. Paleoindian can be subdivided into Early, Middle, and Late periods based largely on stratigraphic associations of diagnostic lithic (stone) artifacts that do not necessarily represent completely different cultural adaptations (e.g., Anderson and Smith 2003:348–360). Since organic artifacts are only rarely preserved from these pre-ceramic periods, lithic technology is the primary evidence of human inhabitation and cultural practices. Moving forward in time, there was no abrupt cultural break at 8000 B.C. The Paleoindian and Early Archaic periods instead represent more than five millennia of cultural developments and associated ecological changes during the end of the last Ice Age and onset of a modern, Holocene climate. This becomes apparent in considering the archaeological manifestations of Native American cultures dating from the Early Paleoindian through the Early Archaic periods.

EARLY AND MIDDLE PALEOINDIAN (CA. 11,500–8800 B.C.)

The Early Paleoindian period (ca. 11,500–9500 B.C.) can be distinguished from Middle Paleoindian (ca. 9500–8800 B.C.) based on relatively recent discoveries of pre-Clovis components (Goodyear 2006; Meltzer 2006:122–128, 2009:95–135). Modern Paleoindian research began during the early twentieth century with discoveries of artifacts associated with extinct Pleistocene megafauna, confirming that humans had reached the Americas before the end of the last Ice Age. Clovis culture, named after the lanceolate-shaped, fluted projectile points found near Clovis, New Mexico, was subsequently identified as the earliest widespread culture in the Americas. Clovis peoples were thought to be the first Americans, having entered the continent by way of Beringia, a land mass exposed during the LGM connecting Siberia and Alaska, and an ice-free corridor that opened after 10,000 B.C. (Meltzer 2009:34–37). The "Clovis first" scenario stood practically unchallenged for six decades, until recent recognition of indisputable evidence for pre-Clovis sites (e.g., Bonnichsen et al., ed. 2006; Dillehay 1989, 1997, 2000; Meltzer 2004, 2005; but see Adovasio et al. 1978). Previous chronologies equating Clovis culture with Early Paleoindian are consequently being revised to allow a millennium or more for a poorly understood and still-to-be-defined pre-Clovis occupation (e.g., Anderson 2004:119–120).

Given what little is presently known, the pre-Clovis presence of humans in North America should not be considered a defining characteristic of Early Paleoindian. Pre-Clovis components are currently differentiated from later components based on age, stratigraphy (lying beneath Clovis) and what appears to be a more limited or rudimentary lithic technology. Pre-Clovis in eastern North America has been regarded in this respect as "consistent with a general Eurasiatic Upper Paleolithic technology" (Lepper and Funk 2006:175). There is otherwise insufficient data to move beyond such generalizations and describe uniformity or variation in distinct assemblages. Pre-Clovis is unlikely to represent a single Early Paleoindian culture, just as Clovis is no longer thought of as an unvarying Paleoindian cultural adaptation (Cannon and Meltzer 2004:1981–1982; Walker and Driskell, ed. 2007). In distinguishing pre-Clovis from Clovis and later regional cultures, it will be necessary to first identify and describe numerous pre-Clovis components in detail, amending more than seventy years of research and accumulated knowledge.

The number of pre-Clovis sites in the New World that stand up to scrutiny is growing and will likely continue to increase with additional research. Monte Verde in Chile, Meadowcroft in Pennsylvania, and Cactus Hill in Virginia were among the first recognized sites and are the most well known (Adovasio et al. 1978; Dillehay 1989, 1997; McAvoy and McAvoy 1997). Others include Big Eddy in Missouri, Page/Ladson and Little Salt Spring in Florida, and Topper in South Carolina (Clausen et al. 1979; Dunbar et al. 1988; Goodyear 2006; Lopinot et al., ed. 1998, 2000; see also Leper and Funk 2006:174–176). Although there are presently no known or confirmed pre-Clovis sites in Louisiana, discoveries of Late Pleistocene fauna and potentially associated artifacts merit further study. Based on geomorphology and previously discussed investigations at Salt Mine Valley, Avery Island is among the best candidates for locating a pre-Clovis site (Gagliano 1967:92–99, 1970). The scant evidence of pre-Clovis components in the state, usually consisting of non-diagnostic lithics, has otherwise remained unconvincing (Campbell and Weed 1986:9.5). Considering the relatively ephemeral evidence for Clovis in Louisiana, it is expected that pre-Clovis components may be even harder to find. Whether or not Louisiana's salt domes, buried and submerged Pleistocene landforms, or Tertiary Uplands contain evidence of pre-Clovis inhabitation remains a provocative yet unanswered question.

The archaeological record of North America indicates people arrived on the continent before the appearance of Clovis and Clovis-like lanceolate projectile point forms. By the time culturally diagnostic Clovis artifacts are recognizable across the continent, it is clear that people were already familiar with the Pleistocene landscape, including numerous wide-ranging sources of high-quality stone for the production of tools (Bousman et al. 2004:93–95; Ferring 2001). This applies to sites in Louisiana as well. Clovis artifacts found in Louisiana were often made out of stone from sources in central Texas and Arkansas or Missouri, sometimes hundreds of kilometers from where the artifacts were found (Gagliano and Gregory 1965:66; Hillman 1990a:206; Webb et al. 1971:17–19). The majority of these are isolated finds, meaning that a single artifact dropped thousands of years ago was fortuitously discovered on the surface (Neuman 1984:66).

The dates for Clovis culture vary across the continent, but generally fall within the range of 9500 to 8800 B.C. (13,500–12,750 cal. B.P.) in the Southeast, corresponding with the Middle Paleoindian period as it is proposed here (Anderson 2004:121; Meltzer 2004:539). The dates for the occurrence of Clovis culture are not yet well established for Louisiana. As characterized by the manufacture and use of lanceolate, fluted projectile points, Clovis culture lasted no more than 1,000 years, spreading across the continent perhaps in as little as two or three centuries between ca. 9000–8800 B.C. (Waters and Stafford 2007). Association of Clovis with the Middle Paleoindian period is a new development (Anderson 2004:119–120). Just as there is no known pre-Clovis culture characteristic of Early Paleoindian, the Middle Paleoindian period refers only to a chronological unit of study and should not be inexorably equated with Clovis culture in Louisiana. Nonetheless, the argument to do so is compelling. Clovis is without a doubt the best known and widest occurring Paleoindian culture of North America. It is thought to represent a relatively rapid radiation of lithic technology across the continent in the centuries before and during the beginning of the Younger Dryas, representing either the movement of people or the spread of ideas (Meltzer 2004:552–553). Considering the earlier dates for pre-Clovis, the apparent familiarity of Clovis peoples with the landscape, and the lack of Clovis artifacts at sites in what was formerly Beringia (Siberia and Alaska), it has been proposed that Clovis was not introduced into North America but was an entirely indigenous innovation or home-grown technology that spread rapidly among existing populations (Anderson 2004:124; Waters and Stafford 2007; see also Gagliano 1967:95). While this may be so, the source and direction of initial movements are still unclear. Although fluted point distributions are concentrated in the Eastern Woodlands, suggesting Clovis may have originated there, the earliest dated Clovis sites are in the Great Plains and Southwest, as well as at components such as Aubrey (41DN479) in Texas (Anderson 1991:2–7, 2004:123; Anderson and Faught 1998, 2000; Ferring 2001; Meltzer 2009:254).

Paleoindian projectile points, including Clovis, have been reported in Louisiana from the 1930s to the present (e.g., Gagliano and Gregory 1965; Marckese 1995; Neuman 1984:66–74). In 1935, David Bushnell (1935:36) described Folsom points from northwest Louisiana, which at the time might have referred to Clovis or another early fluted point. Clarence Webb (1946, 1948:230–231, 1965) was instrumental in establishing the presence of Paleoindian and Early Archaic cultures in Louisiana, including sites and collections with Clovis, Scottsbluff, Plainview, and San Patrice points (see also Webb et al. 1971). His research continues to influence present understanding of the Paleoindian and Early Archaic periods in the state (Neuman 1984:70–74). Webb's (2000:2–7) classification and description of lithics in northwest Louisiana is still a standard reference, along with more recent regional reports and guides from other states (e.g., Anderson and Smith 2003:241–296; Campbell et al. 1990:47–77; McGahey 2000:3–87; Morehead, Thomas et al. 1995:33–55; Turner and Hester 1999).

Very few sites with Middle Paleoindian period or Clovis components have been systematically excavated in Louisiana. Gagliano (1967:61–62; 71–72, Figure 25) identified an unfluted "lanceolate-type" projectile point in the Bradford collection from Avery Island. The early stone tools and Late Pleistocene faunal remains from Salt Mine Valley were not associated with Clovis points or similar artifacts diagnostic of the Middle Paleoindian period (Gagliano 1967:98). Subsequent analysis of organic artifacts from Salt Mine Valley produced a series of radiocarbon dates with a calibrated calendar range of 2460 to 2900 B.C. for split-cane and textile fragments (McGimsey and van der Koogh 2001:28–29, Table 2; Strickland-Olsen et al. 1999:103–104, Table 2). While these are among the oldest known basketry and textile fragments in the Southeast, the Middle to Late Archaic dates for materials recovered at considerable depth (23.4 to 29.4 feet below surface) raises questions concerning the age of the artifacts and their possible association with Late Pleistocene fauna (see also Gagliano 1967:43). Nonetheless, the unique geomorphology and well-preserved, deeply stratified deposits at Avery Island increase the likelihood for future identification of undisturbed Paleoindian components in association with Late Pleistocene fauna at salt domes in south-central Louisiana (Autin et al. 1986; Marckese 1993; Russo 1993:13).

One of the best-known Paleoindian sites in the state lies far to the northwest, on a terrace overlooking Cypress Bayou in Caddo Parish. Three Clovis points were recovered from excavations at the John Pearce site (16CD56), along with 19 other lanceolate-shaped points or point fragments (Webb et al. 1971). These included 6 Pelican points, 2 Meserve (possibly Dalton or San Patrice, *var. Hope*) points, and 11 "untyped" lanceolate points. Two of the Clovis points, one described as "possibly of Clovis type," were recovered from the bottom of a pit protruding at least 36 centimeters (14 in) into the subsoil and approximately 1.5 meters (5 ft) in diameter (Webb et al. 1971:7). The third was collected in or near the sandy surface. Neuman (1984:66) referred to these more than a decade later as the only early Paleoindian artifacts in the state known to have been recovered by archaeological excavation.

While a majority of the projectile points and point fragments from two excavated assemblages at the John Pearce site were made of local pebble chert or petrified wood (76 percent; n=60; total=79), more than half of the Clovis and lanceolate points (63 percent; n=5; total=8) from these assemblages were described as non-local or "exotic" material, likely from central Texas (Webb et al. 1971:25, Table III). A majority of the San Patrice projectile points, which comprised nearly half of the projectile points in the two assemblages (49 percent; n=39), were in contrast made mostly from local chert. The investigators were uncertain as to whether the Clovis artifacts represented a separate Clovis component or were part of the more extensive, Late Paleoindian–Early Archaic San Patrice assemblages (Webb et al. 1971:10, 17–19, 27–29, 39–41). Considering the differences in sources of raw materials and the pit feature that produced two Clovis points, it is plausible that the site was first inhabited by Clovis peoples around the end of the Middle Paleoindian period.

One of the most intensively studied Paleoindian sites in the state is located in the Peason Ridge area of the Fort Polk U.S. military installation in western Louisiana. Eagle Hill II (16SA50) is located on an eroded ridge slope near the hill for which it was named (Servello and Bianchi 1983:404). This was an ideal locale to obtain local Eagle Hill chert, petrified wood, chert gravel, sandstone, and other raw materials for tools (Brassieur 1983:246–254; Heinrich 1983, 1987; Servello and Bianchi 1983:383–444). Excavations by researchers from the University of Southwestern Louisiana produced evidence of an undisturbed Paleoindian component, including a Clovis point recovered from a test unit at a depth of 40 to 50 centimeters (16 to 20 in) below surface. Associated biface fragments, tools, and flakes represent a Clovis or Middle Paleoindian lithic industry (Servello and Bianchi 1983:404–444).

Further investigations by researchers from the University of Texas at San Antonio produced detailed information on lithic procurement and settlement at Eagle Hill II (Gunn and Brown 1982; Gunn and Kerr 1984). A "Folsom-like" lanceolate point recovered during excavation of a Paleoindian stratum (90 to 100 cm below surface), subsequently referred to by Gunn (1984:145) as a Coastview, might otherwise be described as a Plainview point (Anderson and Smith 2003:254; Campbell and Weed 1986:4.8–4.9). However, flaking techniques and fluting also suggest possible classification as a Clovis (Gunn and Brown 1982:233, 236). Chemical analysis of chert artifacts from Eagle Hill II indicated local and non-local sources of raw materials, including western Louisiana, and central and east Texas (Brown 1982:173–179). Late Archaic and Woodland components were also identified in the upper levels at the site. A series of radiocarbon and TL dates subsequently confirmed the Paleoindian, Archaic, and Woodland age of the deposits (Anderson and Smith 2003:42, 342, Table 6.2; McGimsey and van der Koogh 2001:12–13, 137).

At least three Clovis points, including two point base fragments, another similar lanceolate point, and a large number of unifacial tools and debitage (lithic debris) have been recovered from excavations at Eagle Hill II (Anderson and Smith 2003:41–47, 351; Gunn and Brown 1982:233, 236; Servello and Bianchi 1983:432). The Eagle Hill II Clovis component demonstrates the largely unrealized potential for the investigation of Paleoindian sites in Louisiana. CRM archaeology on Fort Polk has since recorded numerous sites with Late Paleoindian and Early Archaic components, with a notably high concentration in the vicinity of Eagle Hill. A Clovis projectile point and lanceolate-shaped point were recovered from excavations at sites 16VN1505 and 16VN2730 (Abrams et al. 1995; Louisiana Division of Archaeology Site Files; Meyer, Morehead, Mathews et al. 1996; Morehead et al. 2002). The latter was recovered in association with a San Patrice, *var. Keithville*, made out of local Citronelle gravel chert, and described as an unfinished preform (Morehead et al. 2002:106-107, 153). To date, no other Clovis components in the state have been as intensively studied as Eagle Hill II. Subsequent damage to the site from military vehicles, erosion, and looting has unfortunately reduced its future research potential (Anderson and Smith 2003:29; Gunn and Kerr 1984:46).

Sites with Middle Paleoindian components are not confined to Fort Polk but are scattered far and wide in the state, from the uplands in the northwest to the Gulf Coast. Other sites that have produced Clovis or potentially early, lanceolate-shaped points include Albany Landing (16CD2) in Caddo Parish, Catahoula Cur (16GR58) in Grant Parish, Da Dump (16SL59) in St. Landry Parish, and Côte Blanche Island in St. Mary Parish (Keller 1981:23; Louisiana Division of Archaeology Site Files; Marckese 1993; Smith et al. 1983:137; Webb et al. 1971:43–44). Besides the frequent use of non-local stone, two further generalizations might be drawn from excavated contexts and surface collections. Clovis-like and similar lanceolate-shaped points are often unfluted and frequently occur in association with Late Paleoindian San Patrice components (Campbell and Weed 1986:9–10; Gunn and Brown 1982:229–233; Servello and Bianchi 1983:432–436). Webb et al. (1971:42–44) described "untyped" lanceolate points in collections from five of the six San Patrice sites they compared with the John Pearce site assemblages. Whether these represent separate Clovis and San Patrice components has yet to be determined.

Since so few sites with Middle Paleoindian components have been systematically investigated in the state, the distribution of Clovis culture must be pieced together through isolated surface finds. Isolated finds throughout the state, usually the result of unsystematic surface collection, provide general information on the distribution of diagnostic artifacts but usually lack clear association and context. Gagliano and Gregory's (1965) preliminary survey of Paleoindian projectile points from Louisiana, although published more than forty years ago, remains relevant today. It has yet to be followed up with a more systematic, statewide comprehensive survey (see Anderson and Smith 2003:351). Of the eighteen Clovis points identified in the collections they studied, 77 percent were made of non-local lithic material most likely from Texas, Arkansas, and Missouri. Most were found in the Tertiary Uplands of northwest Louisiana, although a few came from the Pleistocene Terrace in the southwest and southeast (Gagliano and Gregory 1965:66).

Mitchell Hillman's (1990a) study of collections from Maçon Ridge identified sites with Clovis and later Dalton, Pelican, and Scottsbluff projectile points, with an especially high concentration of San Patrice points. Hillman (1990a:206) reported 15 Clovis points from Maçon Ridge, along with 8 other lanceolate forms, over half of which were made of non-local gray chert thought to be from central Texas (Figure 3.1). Drawing on Hillman's study, Saucier (1994b:132–134) noted that of the 90 sites in northeastern Louisiana with Clovis, Folsom, or Plainview points, 77 (86 percent) were found on Maçon Ridge. Most were located on the edges of floodplains, concentrated on the east side of Maçon Ridge. The other 13

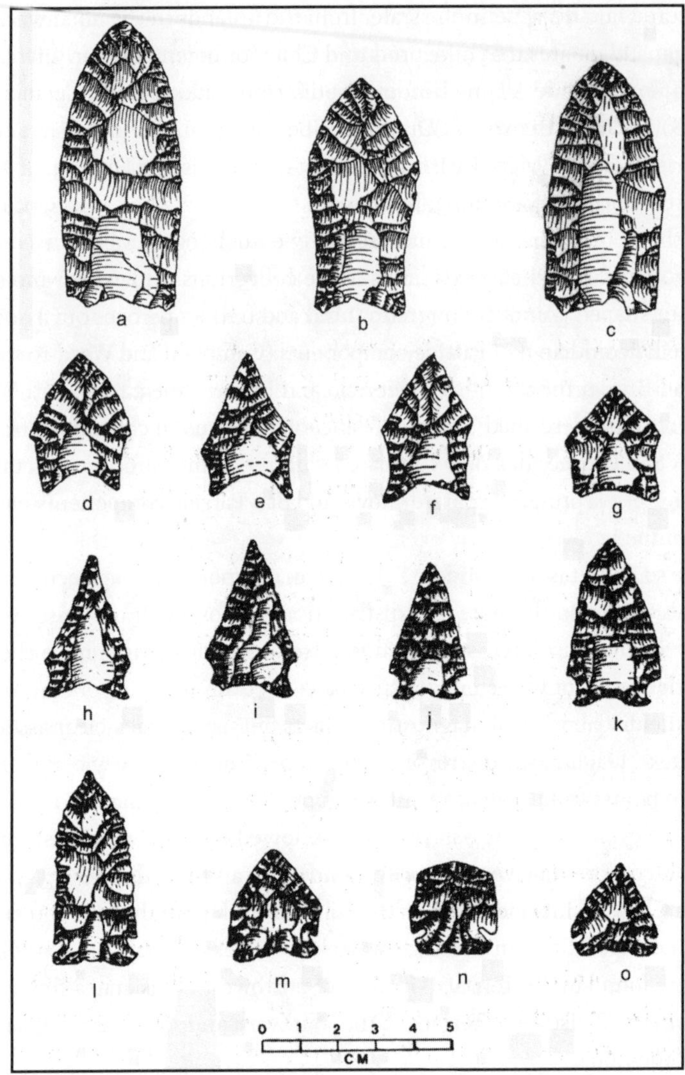

Fig. 3.1. Paleoindian and Early Archaic projectile points: a–c. Fluted lanceolate or Clovis; d–g. San Patrice, *var. Hope*; h–k. San Patrice, *var. St. Johns*; l–o. San Patrice, *var. Keithville* (from Hillman 1990:216, 218, Figures 1 and 3).

were located on the Tertiary Uplands or Pleistocene Terrace along the alluvial valley. Regional archaeologists with the Louisiana Division of Archaeology (LDA) have subsequently reported isolated finds of Paleoindian points in surface collections, primarily in the northwest and northeast (e.g., Girard 2007:8–9; Saunders et al. 2007:6–7).

The statewide distribution of Paleoindian sites is not well understood and is based mostly on surface collections and isolated finds. The LDA site records provide only a general impression of site distribution, consisting primarily of Late Paleoindian components but also including an unknown number of possibly related Middle Paleoindian components. Out of a total sample of 232 recorded sites with Paleoindian components, 54 percent (n=126) are located in the northwest (Management Unit I) and 28 percent (n=65) are located in the northeast (Management Unit II), mostly in the Tertiary Uplands or on Maçon Ridge (see Smith et al. 1983). Together this represents 82 percent of all recorded Paleoindian components in Louisiana. The other Paleoindian components are distributed across the Pleistocene Terrace in the southwest and southeast, or they are located on the salt domes of the south-central coast (Management Units III and IV). This provides only a general idea of the distribution of all known sites, which is constrained by the limited extent of previous investigations. Further examination would likely exclude some of the sites from this sample and reduce the number of recorded Paleoindian components. For example, one site with a dubious Paleoindian component consists of a now-destroyed shell midden along Lake Pontchartrain in Orleans Parish (16OR34), with more plausible late prehistoric and historic components.

Although our knowledge of site distribution is affected by sampling bias, Paleoindian sites are not restricted to the older land surfaces in the northern half of the state (cf. Gagliano and Gregory 1965:63; Neuman 1984:68; Webb et al. 1971:44–45). Distributions and higher concentrations of Clovis points in neighboring states suggest that the scarcity of these artifacts in Louisiana may result from a combination of the lack of systematic survey and geomorphic processes affecting discovery, rather than prehistoric absence. It is likely that the sampling bias of surface collections has been disproportionately influenced by site visibility, in which case deeply buried and submerged sites in the alluvial valley, tributary drainages, and the coastal region have simply escaped detection. Whether or not the lower-lying drainages and alluvial valley were inhabited and utilized, surface visibility is generally poorer and discovery of intact sites may require remote sensing and deep testing.

If Clovis sites are in fact more common on Pleistocene terraces, Maçon Ridge, and higher elevations of the Tertiary Uplands, this may indicate a preference for hunting game in these environments. A related possibility is that fauna were periodically more abundant or concentrated on elevated landforms due to extensive seasonal flooding of the LMV during the Late Pleistocene (Saucier 1994b). This might also account for Paleoindian presence on the salt domes in south-central

Louisiana. Large mammals hunted by Paleoindians would have been drawn to the salt, as well as higher ground. Foraging societies might have accordingly taken advantage of different ecotones with a wider diversity of fauna and flora. Recent studies have likewise indicated greater subsistence variability during the Paleoindian period, including more generalized foraging with greater reliance on small mammals, birds, aquatic resources, and wild plant foods (e.g., Walker and Driskell, ed. 2007). Clovis and even pre-Clovis groups from the mid-continent may have used the Mississippi Valley as an effective route for colonization of present-day Louisiana (Anderson 1996:32–39; Anderson and Gillam 2000:48). If so, increased subsistence variability might well predate the Archaic period.

Another possibility is that Clovis groups regularly moved great distances in pursuit not only of game but of high-quality lithic sources, as indicated by the high percentage of Clovis points made from non-local stone (Anderson and Sassaman 1996:23–27). Given that the source of much lithic material was from Texas, it is plausible that Clovis peoples moved eastward out of central Texas or northeastward along the coast. The Gault site (41BL323) in central Texas and McFaddin Beach are two proposed "staging areas" for the movement of groups into western Louisiana (Anderson and Smith 2003:351). In such a case, groups inhabited strategic locations in a landscape oriented on access to the best-known, highest-quality sources of stone, whether near or far. Moving in and out of these locations, game could be hunted and wild plant foods collected. This seems to fit the description of Eagle Hill II. Besides the nearby source of chert for tools, promontories and ridge tops—such as Eagle Hill—may have served as ideal gathering places for interactions among widely dispersed foraging groups (Anderson and Smith 2003:51, 352). Such portrayal of Clovis in western Louisiana is sketched with very limited evidence, however, and may not be an accurate representation of other regions in the state.

LATE PALEOINDIAN AND EARLY ARCHAIC (8800–6000 B.C.)

Discussion of the Late Paleoindian period is combined here with the Early Archaic based on the evidence for cultural continuity (Anderson and Smith 2003:352–369; Morehead, Thomas et al. 1995:13–16). This may seem counterintuitive, considering the previously described ecological changes associated with the terminal Pleistocene–Early Holocene transition. The Early Archaic dates from roughly 8000 B.C., coinciding with the onset of a warmer, Holocene climate (Anderson and Smith 2003:365). It ends around 6000 B.C. with the beginning of the mid-Holocene and associated increased temperature fluctuations of the

Altithermal or Hypsithermal Interval (Anderson et al. 1996:15; Anderson and Sassaman 2004:94; Schuldenrein 1996:4). Distinguishing the Late Paleoindian and Early Archaic periods based on material culture is nonetheless problematic across much of the Southeast. It is particularly challenging in Louisiana, where a more gradual cultural transition appears to have occurred (Anderson et al. 1996; Ellis et al. 1998; Morse et al. 1996).

The Late Paleoindian period spans the Younger Dryas, the last cold cycle of the Wisconsin glaciation. The last remaining species of Pleistocene megafauna became extinct around this time, perhaps as early as 8800 B.C. (Meltzer 2009:254, 265; cf. Waters and Stafford 2007). It has recently been proposed that the Younger Dryas was triggered by the catastrophic impact of an asteroid or comet, perhaps even related to the extinction of megafauna and the demise of Clovis culture in North America (Firestone et al. 2007). While there is presently only limited evidence and considerable uncertainty remains (Meltzer 2009:55–58), the ensuing cultural demise and postulated population collapse are not at all evident in Louisiana. To the contrary, the Late Paleoindian period coincides with archaeological evidence for the first dramatic indigenous population *increase* in Louisiana—the appearance of San Patrice sites and material culture.

In contrast to the "Clovis comet" hypothesis, there have been suggestions that some species of megafauna may have survived much later, perhaps well into the Early Holocene. Environments where these animals are supposed to have survived are called *refugia* (Rogers et al. 1991). Holocene ages for a few Late Pleistocene fossils from Louisiana, including mastodon and an extinct species of horse, were produced by radiocarbon dating of associated wood samples (Gagliano 1963:110–114, 1967:39–41). In such instances of indirect dating, it may be unclear what has been dated, since samples were not obtained directly from the faunal specimens. Error can also be introduced by bulk bone dating and the potential contamination of samples from collections taken out of context long ago (Stafford et al. 2005). Despite its enduring appeal, the idea of Ice Age *refugia* is presently unsubstantiated. Climate change and related ecological adjustments, particularly the onset of the Younger Dryas, offer a convincing scenario for the demise of the remaining species of Late Pleistocene fauna and related cultural developments (Grayson 2006:218; Haynes, ed. 2009; Meltzer 2009:255, 266–267).

The Late Paleoindian period is characterized by the proliferation of post-Clovis cultures in Texas and the Southeast, with evidence for population increase and decreased mobility of groups in many regions (Anderson 2004:122; Bousman et al. 2004:22–34, 116–119). This is indicated by increased numbers of site components dating from this period and a shift toward more localized use of raw materials in lithic technology. Higher levels of residential mobility associated with Clovis are thought to have been replaced with more restricted mobility, as reflected in a reduction of non-local stone acquired from distant sources (Gagliano and Gregory 1965:66, 73). The regional diversification of projectile point forms, including more variable types and varieties, is another indication of less wide-ranging movements of groups (Anderson and Smith 2003:353). Related changes in subsistence emphasized deer, small mammals, fish, and seasonally available resources in river drainages and woodland environments (Jennings 2008a:555).

Late Paleoindian components are identified by a profusion of new types of projectile points across Texas and the Southeast, beginning with lanceolate forms such as Beaver Lake, Coldwater, Cumberland, Dalton, Folsom, Greenbrier, Midland, Pelican, Plainview, San Patrice, Simpson, Suwannee, and Quad (Bousman et al. 2004:16–26; McGahey 2000:11–21). These are followed by a variety of early side- and corner-notched types generally associated with the Early Archaic period: Big Sandy, Bolen, Cache River, Kirk, Keithville, Martindale, and Palmer; stemmed types, such as Hardin; and bifurcate-base forms, such as LeCroy and St. Albans (Anderson and Sassaman 2004:88–90; Anderson et al. 1996:14–15; Anderson and Smith 2003:350–369; McGahey 2000:26–87; Turner and Hester 1999:50–63). Some of these represent subtle typological distinctions that grade into one another, making classification of individual specimens difficult. The Pelican point in Louisiana, for example, is very similar to the Hinds point in Mississippi. Both are commonly made of locally available stone (McGahey 2000:23–24). There is further difficulty in classifying and assessing stylistic variation in assemblages that include unused, resharpened, reworked and exhausted points, as is often the case with Dalton points, which are among the best-known Late Paleoindian point types in the Mississippi Valley and mid-South (Goodyear 1974, 1982; Morse 1997).

Regional diversification is initially represented at sites in Louisiana in the occurrence of Pelican and San Patrice projectile point types (Figure 3.1; Webb 1946, 1948, 2000:3–4; Webb et al. 1971:11–15, 27–29). Angostura, Folsom, Meserve, Midland, Plainview (or Coastview), Quad, Scottsbluff, and other lanceolate-shaped points have been recovered in smaller numbers, often in association with San Patrice. These are generally regarded as evidence of Plains influence, interactions through Texas, or wide-ranging Woodland-Plains adaptations. Classification of types such as Angostura, Coastview, and Scottsbluff is less certain and may unrealistically emphasize local distinctions or similarities across vast distances and among diverse cultures (Anderson and Smith 2003:246, 254, 278, 282–283, 360–362; Campbell and Weed 1986:4–8, 4–9, 9–7, 9–8; Gagliano and Gregory 1965:68–73; Servello et al. 2004:28-29; Webb 2000:2–6). Some varieties of San Patrice resemble Hardaway Side Notched or Dalton, of which San Patrice has been regarded as a regional variant (Anderson and Smith 2003:279; Justice 1987:40–44; cf. Redfield 1971).

Based on the distribution of points classified as San Patrice, a San Patrice horizon or culture covers the LMV and trans-Mississippi south, from southern Missouri and eastern Oklahoma to Mississippi (Jennings 2008a:540, 2008b). San Patrice is by far the most numerous and intensively studied Late Paleoindian and Early Archaic point type in the region (Jeter and Williams 1989c:81–84). Redfield (1971:98–99) described Dalton and San Patrice points from the LMV, based on surface collections from Maçon Ridge in northeast Louisiana. As previously mentioned, Hillman (1990a) identified a high concentration of San Patrice sites along Maçon Ridge (see also Saucier 1994b). However, the highest distribution of points in the so-called San Patrice "heartland" lies in western Louisiana and eastern Texas (Bousman et al. 2004:74; Jennings 2008a:540).

The dating of San Patrice has been more challenging, alternatively associated with the Late Paleoindian–Early Archaic transition and Early Archaic period (Girard 2007:8–9; Guderjan and Morehead 1981:26; Saunders and Allen 1997:3–4; Saunders et al. 2007:7–8). Clarence Webb (1946, 1948:230) first described San Patrice in north Louisiana as a relatively "late survival" of fluted types such as Clovis and Folsom, possibly dating from the Late Archaic (see also Duffield 1963). As previously mentioned, Webb's later work with Joel Shiner and Wayne Roberts at the John Pearce site further defined the San Patrice lithic assemblage as a "socio-cultural unit" or complex, with similarities to Plains Paleoindian yet transitional to the Early Archaic (Webb et al. 1971:47). By considering Clovis and other lanceolate points as part of the San Patrice assemblages, they implied some overlap or association, rather than two separate or distinct components. San Patrice has subsequently been regarded as a regional culture and point type, with varieties dating from the Late Paleoindian and Early Archaic periods (Neuman 1984:69–74).

Knowledge of San Patrice culture in Louisiana has been advanced since the 1970s by the work of Janice Campbell, James Morehead, Prentice Thomas, and others (e.g., Campbell and Weed 1986; Campbell et al. 1990; Morehead et al. 2002; Thomas and Campbell 1978). Among the most productive research has been CRM archaeology at Fort Polk in western Louisiana, where extensive surveys and test excavations provide the basis for current understanding of San

Patrice (Anderson and Smith 2003; Anderson et al. 1997). While Middle Paleoindian components are relatively rare, San Patrice components are widespread and among the most common at Fort Polk (Anderson and Smith 2003:349–369). At many sites with more substantial later components, such as 16VN791, there is also ephemeral evidence of San Patrice (Campbell et al. 1990:88). Numerous sites with well-defined San Patrice components have been systematically excavated in Vernon Parish, providing the basis for understanding Late Paleoindian and Early Archaic settlement and mobility, subsistence, and technology (e.g., Mathews et al. 1997; Meyer, Morehead, Campbell et al. 1996; Morehead, Campbell et al. 1995, 1996; see Anderson and Smith 2003:357–360).

A regional chronology for the Late Paleoindian and Early Archaic periods is based on excavations at these and other well-stratified San Patrice sites at Fort Polk. A series of OCR dates from sites 16VN2729 and 16VN2730 has further refined the regional chronology and confirmed a Late Paleoindian and Early Archaic association (McGimsey and van der Koogh 2001; Morehead et al. 2002:123–124, Table 16; see also Anderson and Smith 2003:343–344, Table 6.2). Prentice Thomas and Associates have defined three successive phases (Anacoco I–III) dating from the Late Paleoindian, transitional Late Paleoindian–Early Archaic, and Early Archaic (Morehead et al. 2002:25–31; Morehead, Mathews et al. 2007:19-33). Recovery of San Patrice points in stratigraphic contexts indicates a general time frame of 8800 B.C. to 6500 B.C. for western Louisiana, although estimates vary from 9000 to 6000 B.C. (Anderson and Smith 2003:357–358, 366–368; Jennings 2008a:540; Saunders et al. 2007:7).

Varieties of San Patrice projectile points represent differences in shape, notching, and proportions, with related chronological, functional, and geographic variations. San Patrice, *vars. Hope* and *St. Johns* are the earliest, associated with the Anacoco I phase. Side-notched forms, such as San Patrice, *var. Dixon,* appear to be transitional Late Paleoindian–Early Archaic and have been found with stone tools described by Webb (1948:230) as Albany scrapers. Corner-notched points, like San Patrice, *var. Keithville,* date from the Early Archaic period, along with occasional ground stone tools such as abraders, manos, and metates. Other varieties of San Patrice less common to sites in Louisiana include *Brazos* and *Leaf River.* Those with similarities to the Coldwater point type are recognized as San Patrice, *var. Coldwater.* Besides diagnostic projectile points, the San Patrice lithic assemblage includes reworked points, Albany tools (such as scrapers), bifacial reduction, utilized flakes, and small amounts of ground stone (Anderson and Smith 2003: 279–282, 333, 352–367; Morehead et al. 2002:19–31, Figure 5; Morehead, Campbell et al. 2007:19–33; Morehead, Thomas et al. 1995:43–48).

The diversification of point forms during this time has been attributed to functional variation related to changes in hafting technology, or how projectile points were fastened and used (Morse et al. 1996:331; O'Brien and Wood 1998:112–117). Thomas Jennings (2008a:544–549) analyzed a large sample of San Patrice points and demonstrated decreased hafting area from *vars. Hope* to *St. Johns*, suggesting a rapid shift from lanceolate to notched hafting techniques. His analysis also suggested that the use of different varieties overlapped for some time (see also Jennings 2007, 2008b). Technological changes in hafting, as indicated by notches, may have been related to the points' use as knives for cutting or the adoption of the atlatl (Jennings 2008a:548). The latter argument suggests a major revolution in hunting technology, ostensibly related to broader changes in subsistence and characterized by the pursuit of deer and smaller game (Anderson and Smith 2003:353).

The atlatl or spear thrower is thought to have been a technological innovation that diffused into Louisiana by the Early or Middle Archaic, based largely on changes in projectile point forms (e.g., Neuman 1984:79; Vasbinder 2005:21). According to this argument, stemmed and perhaps earlier notched points were modifications in hafting design that allowed stone-tipped darts to be thrown with greater velocity than hand-held spears. Side and corner-notched varieties of San Patrice (e.g., *vars. St. Johns, Dixon*, and *Keithville*) and later stemmed point types (such as Sinner and Yarbrough) likely correspond with the use of the atlatl. But there is some evidence that atlatls may date even earlier in North America, perhaps as early as Clovis (Hutchings 1997:134–136; cf. Meltzer 2009:187, 296–297). Replication experiments have suggested that fluted Paleoindian points were propelled with atlatls (Hutchings 1997). Atlatl hooks have been found in association with bison kills dating from ca. 9,000 years ago, and they were made from the bone of extinct Pleistocene mammals at sites in Florida (Hemmings 2004:141, Table 3.2; Johnson 1987; Wheat 1979). While notching was probably related to changes in hafting technology, the connection to the atlatl remains uncertain. In any case, the atlatl appears to have been used in some places by the Late Paleoindian period, and it became widespread across the continent during the Early to Middle Archaic.

A related explanation for the appearance of different point forms underscores increased stylistic variation through time and space, as represented in the regional development of San Patrice culture. This would suggest related changes in group mobility, long-distance interactions, subsistence, and lithic technology. The concentration of San Patrice sites in the vicinity of Eagle Hill in western Louisiana has been attributed to chert outcrops as a source of high-quality lithic raw material, the prominent position offered by higher elevation, and its strategic location between the Sabine, Calcasieu, and Red River drainages (Anderson and Smith 2003:363–364). Building on the concept of band and macroband territories along the Atlantic Coast, Anderson and Smith (2003:364) suggest that San Patrice bands in western Louisiana may have gathered periodically at such prominent locations or "aggregation loci" (as macrobands) to exchange information and engage in social relations, such as marriages (see also Anderson 1996; Anderson and Hanson 1988). Similar models have been considered for contemporaneous Dalton settlement in the Central Mississippi Valley, where foraging societies lived in large base camps and established short-term camps and special activity stations in surrounding territories (Gillam 1999:103–117; Morse 1997:125–132).

While this would explain the existence of both large San Patrice sites and numerous smaller sites in the vicinity of Eagle Hill, it has also been suggested that lithic procurement played a major role in site location and distribution (Daniel 2001). Jennings (2008a, 2008b) examined contrasting models of San Patrice settlement and resource use across the Woodland-Plains border based on projectile point distributions, raw materials, and hafting technologies. As suggested by Webb, Shiner, and Roberts (1971), Jennings found a clear preference for the use of local stone sources in the Woodlands, including projectile points from sites in northern Louisiana and eastern Texas (see also Hillman 1990a:209). In a sample of sixty-nine San Patrice points from nine parishes in Louisiana, Jennings (2007) identified 91 percent (n=63) as local gravel chert. The remainder appear to have been from sources in the Ouachita and Ozark Mountains rather than central Texas. Based on this information and on comparative data from Oklahoma, Missouri, and Texas, San Patrice groups in Louisiana and east Texas appear to have been less mobile than those in the Plains. They relied more on local lithic sources and tended to orient their movements north and south (Jennings 2008a:553–555). In contrast to the Middle Paleoindian period in Louisiana, San Patrice peoples were more regionally focused on lithic sources and Woodland subsistence. Plains interactions and influences may have become less significant, although Midland, Plainview, and Scottsbluff points have been found in association with Late Paleoindian San Patrice (Morehead, Campbell et al. 2007:30–32).

The decreased mobility and generalized subsistence strategies of San Patrice groups in Louisiana correspond with a still poorly defined Early Holocene, Archaic pattern (e.g., Girard 2007:8–10; Saunders et al. 2007:6–9). Although deer were regularly hunted, San Patrice subsistence appears to have increasingly focused on small mammals, fish and other aquatic resources, wild plant foods, and seasonally available bottomland resources (Jennings 2008a:555). Since plant and animal remains are rarely preserved, changes in subsistence are inferred from settlement patterns and lithic technology. San Patrice sites are located in a variety of environments, including the edges of floodplains (Saucier 1994b). The locations of Early Archaic components at Fort Polk appear more focused on drainages, such as the Calcasieu, rather than higher elevations like Eagle Hill (Anderson and Smith 2003:367). Recovery of artifacts such as manos and metates, ground stone abraders, pitted stones, and grinding tools from Early Archaic components suggests an increased emphasis on plant processing and woodworking (Anderson et al. 1997:146–147). The San Patrice tool complex has been described as well-suited to hide preparation and working with bone, antler, and wood (Webb et al. 1971:42). The latter may have included manufacture of small bone and wood tools for fishing.

Although a scarcity of ground stone artifacts was initially noted in San Patrice contexts, subsequent investigations have revealed a variety of ground stone tools at sites such as Catahoula Cur in Grant Parish, 16VN1421 in Vernon Parish, and Whatley (16LA37) in LaSalle Parish (Keller 1981; Mathews et al. 1997; Thomas and Campbell 1978). Abraders, a mortar and pestle, and other ground stone artifacts were recovered in association with a San Patrice, *var. Keithville*, projectile point at 16VN1421 (Mathews et al. 1997, in Anderson and Smith 2003:367–368). While 16VN1421 lies on the edge of a Pleistocene landform overlooking a creek, the other two sites are located on lower-lying terraces. Catahoula Cur is located on a Pleistocene terrace near the confluence of two small streams, with stratigraphically mixed Clovis and San Patrice components (Keller 1981:46–48, 1983:51). At the multi-component Whatley site on the Little River, a small San Patrice component with ground stone artifacts was identified beneath later Archaic and Woodland deposits (Thomas and Campbell 1978:195–206). Site locations and tool assemblages thus generally support increased variability in San Patrice settlement and subsistence, especially by the Early Archaic (Jennings 2008a:555).

With the end of the Younger Dryas, the subsistence practices of San Patrice peoples likely became increasingly modern. These trends continued well into the Archaic period and are related to the broader ecological changes associated with the onset of the Holocene (Jackson and Scott 2001; Morse et al. 1996). Exploitation of fauna and flora during the greater part of the Early Archaic was probably more similar to the Middle Archaic than the Late Paleoindian period. Excavations at the Conly site (16BI19) on Loggy Bayou in Bienville Parish indicate the likely direction of these trends. Analyses of well-preserved faunal and plant remains from a deeply buried Middle Archaic component indicate intensive use of fish and abundant aquatic resources, as well as deer, small mammals, and wild plant foods, such as hickory nuts (Girard 2000a; Jackson and Scott 2001:194–195; Scott and Jackson 2000). A continued trend toward plant processing and sedentism among Archaic foraging societies is suggested by increased numbers of ground stone tools, dense midden deposits, and human burials (see Saunders, Chapter 4 in this volume).

Conclusions and Future Research Potential

As should be obvious from this overview, there is an urgent yet largely unaddressed need for more systematic and detailed studies of Paleoindian and Early Archaic sites in Louisiana. Discoveries during the nineteenth and early twentieth centuries—particularly the remains of extinct Pleistocene megafauna and potentially associated Paleoindian artifacts—established Louisiana as a promising place for such research (e.g., Carpenter 1838; Neuman 1983:6–61). These early investigations played an important role in understanding the landforms, geomorphic processes, and environmental adjustments of the Late Pleistocene–Early Holocene transition. Since the 1940s, the more ancient, exposed and often heavily eroded surfaces in the state have drawn the most attention in Paleoindian research. For this reason, it is important to reiterate that some of the sites identified early on, such as Salt Mine Valley on Avery Island, are very deeply buried and may lie 7 meters (23 ft) or more beneath the ground surface. Research initiated more than a century ago has seen only incremental advancement in most areas of the state, or it has been hindered by geomorphology, formation processes, and poor site visibility. Unknown numbers of sites may lie submerged beneath the Gulf of Mexico. As argued here, further knowledge of the first inhabitants of Louisiana will require a more detailed understanding of geomorphology and paleoenvironments.

In comparison to later periods, there are relatively few sites older than 8,000 years that have been systematically investigated in the state, and even fewer dating from the Middle Paleoindian period. Most of these are known simply as isolated finds or from surface collections. Other than general information on site distributions, lithic technology, and raw material procurement, these finds offer little in the way of cultural associations, chronology, or context. Still, the lack of a comprehensive survey of Paleoindian projectile points in Louisiana represents a serious and lingering deficiency in research (see Anderson and Smith 2003:351). Gagliano and Gregory (1965:62) noted the urgent need for such a study more than forty years ago. They prefaced their work "in the hope of encouraging a statewide survey," but their brief study remains to this day one of the most current sources of information on the subject.

Since the 1970s, the most substantive contributions to understanding the Paleoindian and Early Archaic periods in the state have been from CRM investigations and the work of a few inspired individuals (e.g., Anderson and Smith 2003; Hillman 1990a; Saucier 1994b; Webb et al. 1971). Much of the information presented here represents the results of nearly four decades of research at Fort Polk and a few other regions (e.g., Campbell and Weed 1986; Morehead et al. 2002; Thomas and Campbell 1978). In contrast to the relatively sparse and ephemeral evidence for Clovis culture, a growing database has been compiled on Late Paleoindian and Early Archaic components. Such information has finally begun to transform current understanding of San Patrice culture, perceived by Webb (1946, 1948) more than six decades ago as a transitional culture dating sometime between Clovis and the Late Archaic.

Painstaking excavations and increased chronological refinement have been accompanied by studies of lithic technology, mobility patterns, and subsistence practices, to the point where San Patrice foraging societies now seem less like Clovis or Plains Paleoindian cultures and are thought to encompass considerable cultural variability (e.g., Jennings 2008a). The content and extent of this variability have yet to be fully explored. The Late Paleoindian and Early Archaic periods are understood today primarily based on research in the San Patrice "heartland" of eastern Texas and western Louisiana. As variations likely existed in different environments, the temptation to apply models of Paleoindian and Early Archaic cultures from distant regions should be tempered with systematic surveys and controlled excavations. The knowledge of well-preserved and stratified sites with San Patrice and potential Clovis components should attract any curious scholar interested in knowing more about the lives of Native Americans 8,000 to more than 11,000 years ago. Knowing that some of these sites have already been destroyed and others are in imminent danger of destruction should compel anyone interested in Louisiana's past to a greater involvement in archaeology.

There is considerable unrealized potential for research on the Paleoindian and Early Archaic periods in Louisiana. The current relevance of themes and related goals laid out a quarter of a century ago in *Louisiana's Comprehensive Archaeological Plan* underlines the slow pace of research and how much has yet to be methodically addressed (Smith et al. 1983:131–150). Among the outstanding goals that need to be accomplished are analyses of spatial distributions and relationships among sites representing various activities, cultures, time periods and environments, both within and outside of the state. Completion of a systematic and comprehensive Paleoindian projectile point survey for Louisiana, including at the very least provenience, physical attributes, and raw material sources, would serve as a baseline for future research in the state and would generate immediately useful comparative information for the Paleoindian Database of the Americas (http://pidba.tennessee.edu/).

As mentioned here and in the state plan (Smith et al. 1983:138–139), the reanalysis and comparative analysis of collections from sites such as Salt Mine Valley and John Pearce might resolve problematic issues regarding cultural associations and chronology. The more precise chronological refinement of Paleoindian and Early Archaic components is still high on this list, but it will require the excavation of deeply stratified deposits with diagnostic artifacts and radiometric dates from sites in different areas of the state. San Patrice components at Fort Polk have already demonstrated considerable potential in this regard (Anderson and Smith 2003:364). This research should be planned and conducted not only on the Tertiary Uplands and Pleistocene Terrace, but also on Pleistocene landforms along the edges of the alluvial valley and Gulf Coastal Plain. Such investigations might produce greatly needed information on regional and temporal variations in subsistence and resource use, lithic technology, group mobility, long-distance interactions, the acquisition of non-local resources, and social relations among local groups. Nearly all of these issues were set forth three decades ago as research goals in the state plan (Smith et al. 1983:134–145).

Discoveries at Salt Mine Valley and other salt domes along the coast offer excellent opportunities for research. The OCS, the coastal region, and the alluvial valley hold unrealized potential for the discovery of submerged and deeply buried relict Pleistocene shorelines, landforms, and associated sites with evidence for early human occupation. While such sites might have seemed beyond reach only a few decades ago, recent advances in geophysical remote sensing and geoarchaeology have expanded the possibilities for underwater archaeology, site identification, deep coring, and testing (Evans et al. 2007; Gagliano et al. 1982; Pearson et al. 1986). Such investigations may revolutionize present understanding of Paleoindian cultures and the peopling of the Americas. As demonstrated by decades of research at Fort Polk, progress will require meticulous, long-term studies by dedicated scholars, adequate funding, and support. Such important research should be actively pursued in Louisiana and not depend on analogies from distant regions or dissimilar environments. Nor should it rely any longer on fortuitous discoveries, haphazard collections, or be solely confined to the requirements and objectives of CRM. In closing, the Paleoindian and Early Archaic periods in Louisiana are still largely unexplored eras that await more focused research.

4

Middle Archaic and Watson Brake

JOE W. SAUNDERS

Over the past thirty years, the Middle Archaic (ca. 6000–2000 B.C.) has been transformed from a nebulous gray period, defined by projectile point styles that fell between Early Archaic and Poverty Point periods, to a well-defined and remarkable period of Louisiana prehistory—although there still is a little quibbling as to when it began and when it ended. The Middle Archaic marks the beginning of riverine adaptation for fishing, hunting, and gathering people, a shift toward sedentism, the first construction of earthen mounds, the demise of mound construction,and an elaborate material culture unique to the Lower Mississippi Valley and Louisiana (Anderson et al. 2007). The florescence by these precocious people transformed the Archaic period, but it also challenged traditional models of Archaic culture, hunters and gatherers, egalitarian societies and social evolution.

The Beginning (6000 B.C.)

The first evidence in Louisiana of a shift from the presumably mobile, generalized exploitation strategy of the Early Archaic (8000–6000 B.C.) to a more sedentary, selective exploitation strategy of the Middle Archaic is the Conly site (16BI19) in northwest Louisiana (Figure 1.2). The Conly site is located in the floodplain of the Red River, with Tertiary Uplands to the east and relict channels of the Red River to the west (Girard 2000a, 2002). The deposition of 3 meters (9.8 ft) of fluvial sediments over the past 7,500 years has protected the site from disturbance and promoted the preservation of the animal and plant remains. This provides unique evidence of the animals and plants the Native Americans had captured and collected while living at the site.

The soil development in the riverbank/lakeside of the Conly site shows that the area was accessible to the natives for hundreds of years. Nine radiocarbon assays suggest that the occupation spanned about five hundred years. Consequently the site contains a series of encampments by different groups of hunter-fisher-gatherers. Girard's (2000a) careful excavations isolated a number of large pit features and a midden deposit, making it possible to examine the activities and foods from the different occupations at the site (see also Girard 2002).

Scott and Jackson (2000) analyzed bone fragments recovered at the site. They identified 5,805 individual specimens (NISP) and 42 taxonomic categories (Jackson and Scott 2001:189). The fauna were from the surface midden, pit features 1, 3, and 7 (subdivided into upper and lower levels), representing a total of five samples. By percentage of weight, the fauna indicate that deer and fish were the focus of procurement activities at the site. A comparison of the five samples by NISP shows that twelve taxa are common in each sample and that seven taxa are present in four of the five samples. Conversely, sixteen taxa are unique and occur in only one sample, but this appears to be a function of sample size. The common taxa are: opossum, cottontail and swamp rabbit, gray squirrel, white-tailed deer, box turtle, bowfin, gar, largemouth buffalo, channel catfish, blue catfish, and finfish. Shared taxa (four of five samples) are: fox squirrel, raccoon, soft-shell turtle, bullhead, flathead catfish, freshwater drum, and sunfish. Mussels and aquatic snails were common. Flora were dominated by hickory nuts and acorns, suggesting the exploitation of mast crops in the adjoining uplands and surrounding floodplain. Seasonal indicators in the fauna and flora suggest year-round usage of the site. A diet of fish, deer, small mammals, and mast crops was consumed by sequential occupants of the Conly site.

Fire-cracked rock was the most abundant artifact class, attesting to the processing of foods at the site. Evidence of stone tool manufacturing was sparse. Apparently complete and broken bifaces/projectile points were transported to the site and refurbished or discarded. Only 12 dart points, 3 scrapers, 6 grinding stones, 1 pitted stone, 1 grooved-ax, 2 abrading stones, and 3 hammerstones were recovered. Modified bone and antler tools, of which 29 were recovered, made up part of the tool industry.

The remains of five people were recovered from site excavations, but the exact number of individuals found at the site is unknown (Girard 2000a, 2001; Raisor and Steele 2001). Four individuals were placed in shallow pits excavated into the midden surface. Three were adults, one was a child, and one was a fetus. Two burials were supine (lying on the back) and one was in a flexed position. The radiocarbon dates from Burial 1 (5843 ± 76 cal. B.C.) and Burial 3 (ca. 5600 ± 33 cal. B.C.) do not overlap at the calibrated two-sigma range, suggesting that the two burials were associated with separate site occupations. The remains were analyzed and subsequently reburied in consultation with the Caddo Nation (see Cast et al., Chapter 12 in this volume).

By 5500 B.C., native populations in northwest Louisiana had established an economy centered on the procurement of riparian (riverbank) resources. Furthermore, the data from Conly suggest that residential sites were being established—as indicated by multiple burials, large pit features, and extensive midden deposits. This adaptive strategy of hunter-fisher-gatherers established an economic foundation for the construction of earthen mounds not only in the Middle Archaic period, but also well into the Woodland period. Additional data are necessary to determine whether or not this riverine adaptive strategy was triggered by environmental change (Anderson et al. 2007; Bense 1994; Girard 2000a; Kidder 2006; Scott and Jackson 2000; Smith 1986; Styles and Klippel 1996).

The Evans Projectile Point Horizon (ca. 3400 B.C.)

Although it is not well understood, a uniquely styled projectile point, the Evans (Figure 4.1a), appears on the west side of the Mississippi River in Louisiana, southern Arkansas, and northeast Texas (Jeter et al. 1989; Prewitt 1995; Saunders and Allen 1997; Schambach 1970). Its distinguishing attribute is a pair of notches in the blade of the point, above a corner-notched base (Ford and Webb 1956; Turner and Hester 1999:116). A variant of the Evans point, Tangipahoa (Figure 4.1b) occurs in western Mississippi (McGahey 2000:148–152).

An Archaic origin (ca. 4000–2000 B.C.) of the Evans point was postulated by Schambach (1970) as a consequence of his research at the Cooper site (3HS1) in southwest Arkansas (Klinger et al. 1992). Later, Schambach and Early (1982) defined the Evans point as a diagnostic artifact of the Middle to Late Archaic (Jeter et al. 1989). Recent excavations in northeast Louisiana have defined a ca. 3400–3000 B.C. time span or horizon for the Evans point. Associated projectile points include Sinner (Figure 4.1c) and the straight-stemmed type Bulverde (Figure 4.1d).

Throughout the Evans point horizon, local raw materials were selected for projectile point and lithic-tool manufacturing. Evidence of trade for non-local raw material is limited (Fogleman 1991:93; Girard 2000a; Schambach 1970; Webb 1981). Recent excavations of Middle Archaic sites suggest that localization, or the use of local raw materials, continued until the end of the Middle Archaic. The subsequent emergence of trade is one of the criteria used to distinguish the Late Archaic period (see Gibson, Chapter 5 in this volume; Jackson and Jeter 1991; Jeter and Jackson 1994).

Middle Archaic Mounds (ca. 3900–2800 B.C.)

The startling realization that mound construction began in the Middle Archaic had incipient evidence as early as 1962 (Gagliano 1963, 1967). Over the next thirty years, data supporting their existence accumulated until only one con-

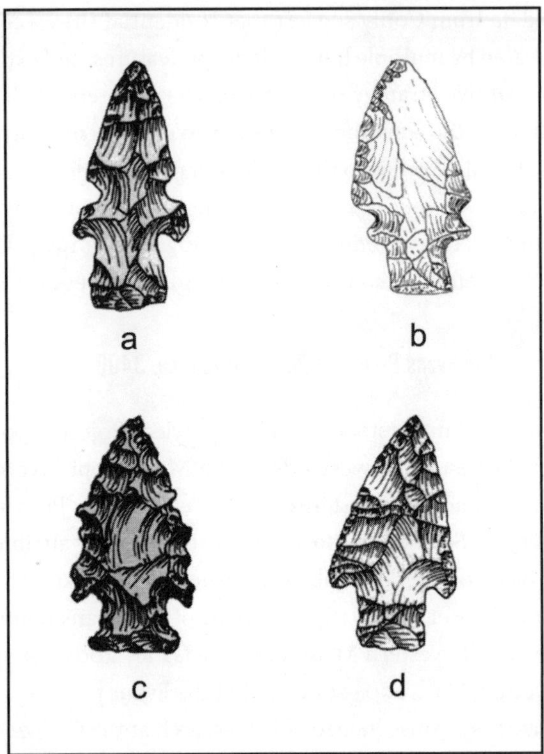

Fig. 4.1. Projectile points from the Middle Archaic period: a. Evans from Mound A, Watson Brake (16OU175). Illustration by David Griffing; b. Tangipahoa (McGahey 2000:149, Figure 137a); c. Sinner from the Resch site (41HS16; Turner and Hester 1999:187); d. Bulverde from Frenchman's Bend Mounds (16OU259) surface collection. Illustration by David Griffing.

clusion could be reached: that earthen mounds were built during the Middle Archaic. The frequent occurrence of Evans points on Middle Archaic mounds suggested that the two were associated, especially since both seem to disappear after 2800 B.C. In fact, a 1,000-year mound-building hiatus appears to have taken place in Louisiana during the final centuries of the Middle Archaic, before the beginning of the Poverty Point period (see Gibson, Chapter 5 in this volume).

To date, thirteen mound sites in Louisiana have been radiocarbon dated to between 3700 and 2800 B.C. Six are in the northeast part of the state, and seven are in the southeast (Figure 1.2). Two have been identified in west Mississippi. Many other potential Archaic mound sites have been recorded in central and southeast Louisiana, especially among the Florida Parishes, but confirmation of their age is lacking (Gagliano and Webb 1970; Gibson 1991; R. Saunders 1994).

The first mound to be tested and dated was Banana Bayou Mound (16IB24) on Avery Island, in 1962 (Figure 4.1). Gagliano's (1963, 1967) excavations in the 2 meter (6.6 ft) tall and 30 meter (98 ft) diameter mound revealed two episodes of mound construction. Charcoal from the surface of the first stage dated to 3260 cal. B.C. Subsequent testing by Brown and Lambert-Brown (1978) refined the two episodes of mound building. A charcoal sample from substage 1 of the primary mound returned an assay of cal. A.D. 1515, placing the earlier date in doubt.

Perhaps the most controversial excavation took place in 1967, at Monte Sano Bayou (16EBR17). Archaeologists James A. Ford and William G. Haag were notified that two mounds near Baton Rouge were scheduled for demolition. Salvage excavations were conducted for three days. Parallel trenching through Mound A exposed a small earthen platform in the center of the mound and a square post hole pattern under the mound. A layer of charcoal on the earthen platform was determined to be over 5000 B.C. in age, as was a later sample of charcoal. However, a third charcoal sample from Mound B with an unknown provenience had an age of 3050 B.C., which falls in line with radiocarbon dates from other Middle Archaic mounds. Projectile points and an effigy bead from the mound fill support an Archaic age for the mounds. Disagreement as to the age of Monte Sano persists to this day. Although the earlier (pre-5000 B.C.) dates may represent intrusive material, this author accepts the 3050 B.C. date for the age of mound construction.

Limited testing of the LSU Campus Mounds (16EBR6) and Hornsby (16SH21) produced additional data, suggesting mound construction earlier than 3000 B.C., but the research was generally regarded as inconclusive (Homburg 1992; Manuel 1979; Neuman 1985). Beginning in the 1990s, investigations verified the Middle Archaic age of several mounds, including Stelly Mounds (16SL1; Russo and Fogleman 1996), Belmont Mounds (16SJ1; Saunders 2000; Saunders et al. 2009), and King George Island Mounds (16LV22; Vasbinder 2005).

Hedgepeth Mounds (16LI7) was the first verified Archaic mound site in northeast Louisiana (Saunders and Allen 1994). Five other mound sites were added to the list in rapid succession: Frenchman's Bend Mounds (16OU259; J. Saunders 1994; Saunders et al. 1994); Watson Brake (16OU175; Jones 1985; Saunders et al. 1997; Saunders et al. 2005); Caney Mounds (16CT5; Gibson 1991; Gregory et al. 1987; Saunders et al. 2000); Lower Jackson (16WC10; Gibson 1989; Saunders et al. 2001), and Hillman's Mound/Nolan (16MA201; Arco et al. 2006; Saunders et al. 1994). Denton (22QU522) is one of the two verified

Archaic mound sites in Mississippi (Connaway, Brookes, and McGahey 1977). The other site is 22LI504 (Peacock et al. 2010).

The Middle Archaic mound sites vary in the number of mounds, site layout, sub-mound architecture, lithic technology, and material culture. Banana Bayou, Lower Jackson, and Belmont are single mound sites. Monte Sano, the LSU Campus Mounds, and Hornsby have two mounds. Stelly and Nolan have three or more. Frenchman's Bend Mounds and King George Island Mounds have five. Caney Mounds and Hedgepeth Mounds have six mounds. Watson Brake has eleven, or possibly twelve, earthen mounds. Many of the mounds at Watson Brake are connected by ridges. Frenchman's Bend Mounds, Nolan, Stelly, Caney, and King George Island Mounds may also have ridge architecture.

Although the number of mounds at various sites varies considerably, Sassaman and Heckenberger (2004) have offered insight into the layout of the larger mound groups. They noticed that a line of mounds, with the largest mound in the central position, was usually built along a terrace edge. The second largest mound (the "backset" mound) is on a line perpendicular from the largest mound at a distance 1.4 times the length of the terrace line mounds. The perpendicular line from the largest mound to the backset mound is within 10 degrees of a right angle. Alternative models have been proposed, such as Clark's (2004a) analysis, which is based on the Toltec unit of measurement. The Sassaman and Heckenberger model seems to apply to Watson Brake and Caney Mounds. At Watson Brake, the calibrated intercepts for sub-mound charcoal under Mound A (the largest) and Mound E (the backset mound) fall within one standard deviation of one another. This indicates that the layout of the mounds was not accretional, but deliberate from the inception of the earthworks. Testing at Insley (16FR3), however, one of the sites mentioned by Sassaman and Heckenberger (2004:224), revealed that the large mound was built during the late Woodland period. So before any model is applied to a site, it is necessary to establish the age of all of its earthen architecture.

Only two sites have been found to have evidence of aboveground architecture: the square post hole pattern under Mound A at Monte Sano, and a line of post holes and floor (along one side of the post line) under Mound A at Frenchman's Bend Mounds. Three successive floors, and a hearth excavated through the floors, were found under Mound C. It is not known if the sub-mound floors at Frenchman's Bend Mounds were associated with standing structures (Saunders et al. 1994). A post hole was found under Mound C at Stelly Mounds, but insufficient data exist to determine if it was part of a structure (Russo and Fogleman 1996). Unexpectedly, there was no evidence of aboveground structures or floors under any of the mounds at Watson Brake.

Watson Brake

Watson Brake (16OU175) is a spectacular Middle Archaic mound group. It also is the most securely dated early mound site in North America (Saunders et al. 1997, 2005). The mound site is constructed along the edge of the Pleistocene terrace, on the east foot of the uplands to the west of what was at that time the Arkansas and is now the Ouachita River. Watson Brake swamp to the west is the source of an intermittent stream that runs east along the base of the terrace and into the Ouachita River.

A combination of eleven mounds and connecting ridges form an oval more than 300 meters (984 ft) in diameter (Figure 4.2). A possible twelfth mound is located outside of the oval. Thirty radiocarbon dates place the occupation of the mound complex between 3500 and 2800 cal. B.C. Radiometric assays, optically stimulated luminescence (OSL) data, and the extensive soil development in the mound and ridge fill strongly indicate that the mounds and ridges are contemporaneous. Test unit excavations and soil cores have demonstrated that many of the mounds and ridges were constructed in sequential stages. Sand and gravel were the construction fill for the mounds and ridges along the escarpment (mounds A, B, C, D, I, J, and K). Interestingly, except for Mound K, all of these mounds were built in multiple stages. The mounds and ridges farthest away from the terrace edge were built with sediments from outside of the enclosure, and all of these mounds (E, F, G, and H) and ridges were built in one episode, with the possible exception of Mound F.

Mound A (Gentry Mound) is the largest. It is a 7.5 meter (25 ft) tall conical mound that appears to have been built in seven episodes. Mound E is the second largest. It is dome-shaped and was built in a single episode of construction. The height of the other mounds ranges between 3.5 meters (11 ft, Mound J) and 0.5 meters (1.6 ft, Mound K). The ridges are less than 2 meters (6.6 ft) tall and approximately 20 meters (66 ft) in width. The recovery of fire-cracked rock, earthen blocks, stone flakes, and tools from the surface of the sequential stages of the mounds and ridges indicates that these earthen features were lived on and that daily activities took place in these locations. Auger tests in the plaza/enclosure conclusively demonstrated that daily activities did not take place there, with the exception of a large natural rise (not a mound) toward the center of the enclosure.

Test unit excavations identified a lithic workshop between Mounds A and K at Watson Brake. It contained a number of projectile point preforms that were broken in varying stages of production. A stone bead workshop with 154 microdrills, each about the size of a grain of rice, was found on Mound D. Unfortunately, only one complete barrel-shaped stone bead and a few broken beads were

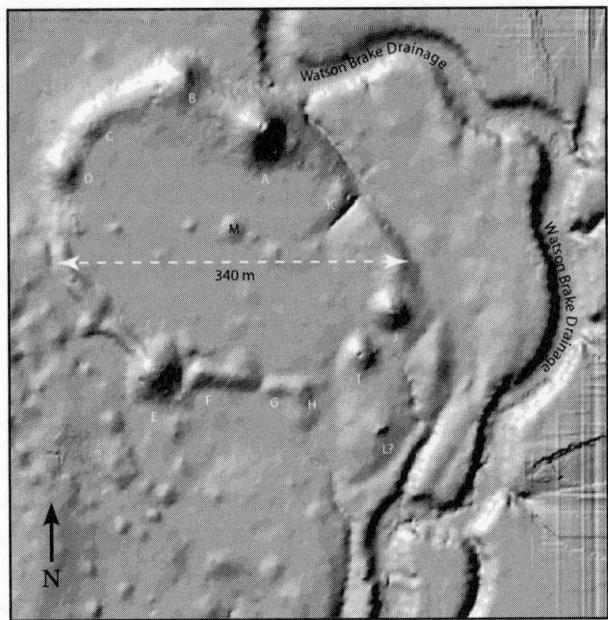

Fig. 4.2. Light Detection and Ranging (LIDAR) image of the Watson Brake site (16OU175). White letters designate mounds. Black letter *M* is a natural mound.

recovered from the site (Johnson 2000). Complete projectile points and beads, once produced, were apparently removed from the site. Both the lithic tools and stone beads were made of local raw material. One bone bead, five bead blanks, and eleven bone tools were recovered from the midden.

Fire-cracked rock is the most common artifact at Watson Brake and other Middle Archaic mound sites. People did not have ceramic or stone vessels for cooking during the Middle Archaic period. Instead, they heated rocks (usually cobbles and gravel) to bake, steam, and boil food. Heating caused the gravel to break into jagged rock fragments, making it very easy to identify fire-cracked rock. Stone used only for roasting (dry heat) can be distinguished from stone used for steaming or boiling (wet heat). Both fracture patterns were identified at Watson Brake. Small pits in the mounds and ridges show evidence of heating. This may indicate that the pits had been lined with skins for steaming and boiling food.

Among the most peculiar artifacts recovered at Watson Brake are small, fired-earthen geometric objects or blocks (Figure 4.3). These have only been found on Middle Archaic sites in northeast Louisiana. Blocks are the most common form of the objects, measuring approximately 5.5 by 4.5 by 3.5 centimeters (2.2 by 1.8 by 1.4 in) (Saunders et al. 2000). Their function is presently unknown.

Fig. 4.3. Fired-earthen geometrics from Frenchman's Bend Mounds (16OU259).

Perhaps these objects were for heat-treating stone used to make projectile points. Heat-treating improves the flint-knapping quality of stone, and it was a common practice among Archaic cultures. Or perhaps the blocks were a substitute for heating stones, as clay cooking balls were for the later Poverty Point culture (Gibson, Chapter 5 in this volume). The contemporaneous Metz Midden site (16RI105) had a high concentration of broken blocks and cubes, which is best described as a "burned block midden" (Saunders 2001).

The faunal preservation at Watson Brake was excellent. A thick midden deposit in Mound B contained over 185,000 bone fragments. Jackson and Scott (2001) identified 9,224 fragments according to taxonomic category, including 58 mutually-exclusive taxa. The ecotonal setting of the site is reflected in the composition of the fauna: main channel fish (drum, buffalo, channel, and blue catfish) from the Arkansas River, backwater species (bass, crappie, and bream) from the Watson Brake swamp, small mammals and waterfowl (beaver, raccoon, muskrat, otter, gray squirrel, swamp rabbit, duck, and geese) from the floodplain, and upland species (fox squirrel, cottontail, turkey, ruffed grouse, and deer) from the prairie terrace. But the lynchpin of the Watson Brake economy was fish, which comprised 60 percent of the fauna by weight (Jackson and Scott 2001:190). Deer were second in importance. Mussels and snails were components in the local diet, as were hickory, acorn, goosefoot, and marshelder (Saunders et al. 2005).

Settlement Pattern

Seasonal indicators in the fauna and flora suggest year-round usage of the Watson Brake site. This is not to be confused with year-round site occupation (Jackson and Scott 2001; Stringer, in Saunders et al. 2005). The high density of artifacts associated with many of the Middle Archaic mounds suggests that they were residential sites. Surveys in the adjacent uplands and shores of Watson Brake swamp have recorded ninety-two sites, but only one site (Plum Creek, 16OU89) matches the Watson Brake artifact density. Two possibly smaller camps have been identified but not yet evaluated. The remaining sites are ephemeral in size and artifact density, representing a veneer of isolated finds rather than limited artifact scatters across the landscape. These sites are interpreted as the remains of plant and animal procurement activities. It appears that food procurement took place in fairly close proximity to the earthworks. Small and large game and waterfowl were hunted, mollusks collected, fish trapped and caught, and plants and mast crops gathered and transported to the mounds for processing and consuming.

Plum Creek is a non-mound residential campsite approximately 6 kilometers (3.7 mi) north of Watson Brake (Saunders 1998). The site is on the edge of the Pleistocene terrace between Cheniere Brake and a paleochannel of the Arkansas River. Sheffield (2003:69) examined 64,769 bone fragments and identified 26,138 pieces to some taxonomic category. Although the taxa from the two sites are almost identical, fish make up approximately 84 percent of the sample by weight at Plum Creek, compared to 60 percent at Watson Brake. Plum Creek has a virtual absence of waterfowl and a total absence of winter-captured fish. Other than the non-winter use of the site, the density of bone, fire-cracked rock, lithic tools, bone tools, and fired-earthen geometric objects are remarkably the same.

Limited excavations at Frenchman's Bend, Hedgepeth Mounds, Caney Mounds, Lower Jackson, Stelly Mounds, Banana Bayou, Hornsby Mounds, and King George Island Mounds seem to indicate some of the same attributes observed at Watson Brake and Plum Creek. Principal among these is high artifact density, suggesting that these other mound sites too were residential encampments where everyday activities took place. This does not exclude ceremonialism associated with the mounds, as the two are not mutually exclusive. Sub-mound structures at Monte Sano, Frenchman's Bend Mounds, and Stelly Mounds seem to be more than domestic. Small earthen platforms in the center of Mound A at Monte Sano and Mound A at Hedgepeth may be ceremonial as well. Human remains have been recovered at Watson Brake, but not from burials. Seven bone fragments of at least three individuals were recovered from the midden fill in Mound B.

Excavations by Ramenofsky encountered twenty-eight burials and cremations at Cowpen Slough (16CT147), a Middle Archaic site in Catahoula Parish (Ramenofsky and Mires 1985). She identified Middle and Late Archaic/Poverty

Point components at the site, but concluded that the cemetery was only associated with the Middle Archaic component (ca. 3500–3000 B.C., dates calibrated by the author). Her analysis of the associated artifacts, fauna and flora, and cultural features suggest that the site had been occupied intermittently as a residential camp (Debusschere et al. 1989; Ramenofsky 1991; Ramenofsky and Mires 1985). So from the beginning of the Middle Archaic to its end, it appears that mortuary customs prevailed, but apparently not in mounds.

Localization

Middle Archaic mound building does not appear to have required the adoption of a unified cultural tradition. The variability in the expression of the mounds and associated material culture suggests instead that autonomous groups opted to build mounds.

Each group combined an array of mound-building traits to create earthworks that were unique in mound number, architecture, configuration, ridges, enclosure, sub-mound architecture, and sub-mound platforms. Even fired-earthen geometric objects were a sub-regional phenomenon. Evans points had a pan-regional distribution among the mound-building folk. Effigy beads were found at Monte Sano, Stelly Mounds, and Lower Jackson. The lapidary technology occurs at Watson Brake, but both the effigy beads and their associated technology occur throughout the southeast—mounds or no mounds (Connaway 1982; Crawford 2003; Gibson 1968a). Otherwise, except for a possible trend toward larger and more complex mound groups in the northeast (R. Saunders 1994), as the Sassaman and Heckenberger (2004) model may indicate, localism superseded regionalism. What is even more remarkable is that the localization transcends what appears to be a fairly uniform economic strategy of the mound builders. Their propensity to occupy ecotonal settings, centered on aquatic resources, is well documented (Gibson 1996b; Russo 1994b), and appears to be a variant of Taylor's (1964) tethered nomadism-riparian sedentism. The off-site data from Watson Brake seem to fit a forager settlement pattern, one that is tethered to the riparian resources along the rivers, bayous, and backswamps during the pre-mound and mound occupations. However, the apparent lack of residential mobility is not tied to one particular resource necessary for survival, as postulated by Binford (1980) and Taylor. Instead, the opposite seems to apply. The diversity and abundance of resources available to the community appear to be what promote residential stability and autonomy.

Perhaps the absence of trade best personifies these peoples' autonomy. Local raw material was sufficient for their lithic industry. It was not until the Late Archaic that trade became a significant component of the native economy. And coupled with the advent of trade was the emergence of a regional cultural entity that reintroduced mound building on a colossal scale—the Poverty Point culture.

The End (2800 B.C.)

The end of Middle Archaic mound building was as sudden and mysterious as its beginning. There is mounting evidence of a cessation of mound construction at approximately 2800 B.C., a hiatus that lasted until the emergence of Poverty Point over 1,000 years later. The evidence is marginal and unfortunately the assertion is based on negative evidence—a precarious way to conduct scientific inquiry. But it is testable, and the assertion can be falsified. Simply stated, if mound sites are identified dating from 1800 cal. B.C. to 2800 cal. B.C., then the hiatus did not occur.

The last stage of Mound A at Watson Brake was constructed after ca. 2800 cal. B.C. The last stage of Mound C dates to ca. 2800 cal. B.C. and the last stage of Mound J postdates ca. 3000 cal. B.C. (Saunders et al. 2005). At Hedgepeth Mounds, Mounds A, D, and E postdate ca. 2900 cal. B.C. The last stage of Mound E dates to ca. 2750 cal. B.C. The youngest radiocarbon date from Frenchman's Bend Mounds is approximately 2800 cal. B.C. Recently, Arco et al. (2006) have determined that the Nolan site dates to between ca. 3200 and 2800 cal. B.C.

A review of 1,050 radiocarbon dates from Louisiana (McGimsey and van der Koogh 2001; Saunders 2010), Mississippi (Sims and Connaway 2000), and Arkansas (Marvin Jeter, personal communication 2007) identified fifty-six radiocarbon assays, in which the midpoint of the calibrated range (with the highest p. value) fell between 2800 cal. B.C. and 1700 cal. B.C. The latter coincides with the beginning of the Poverty Point period (see Gibson, Chapter 5 in this volume). Four assays were excluded from the sample (bone and shell dates as well as standard deviations >200 were categorically excluded). There were a total of seventeen radiocarbon dates from mound sites. Ten of the calibrated dates are earlier than 2750 cal. B.C. Six of the dates fall between 1790 cal. B.C. and 2750 cal. B.C.: one each from the Claiborne site (22HA501) and Jaketown site (22HU505) in Mississippi, two from Poverty Point (16WC5), and two from Watson Brake. One Watson Brake assay has previously been rejected, since a stratigraphically higher date was determined to be older. The second outlier is from humates, which average 280 years younger than charcoal assays. The corrected age is ca 2850 cal. B.C. This leaves four radiocarbon dates from two mound sites in a span of approximately 1,000 years.

So there does appear to be a sudden end of mound building. The cause is unknown, but environmental change has been mentioned (Hamilton 1999; Sampson, in Saunders et al. 2005). Kidder (2006) has proposed that the end of the Poverty Point culture and an abandonment of northeast Louisiana were brought about by climate change between 1000–600 B.C. Perhaps similar events contributed to the Middle Archaic hiatus. Roger Saucier (in Saunders et al. 1994) suggested that the formation of a natural levee at the confluence of the Ouachita River and the Watson Brake drainage changed the free-flowing Watson Brake drainage near the mounds into a backwater swamp. He speculated that this might have contributed to either the occupation or abandonment of the site. Mississippi alluvium covers the base of Belmont Mound in southeast Louisiana. The age of the depositional event is undetermined, so it is not known if the site was abandoned in response to flooding. Equivalent evidence for environmental change at other Middle Archaic mound sites is marginal. If environmental change ended the Middle Archaic, then the change must have been catastrophic to cause a cessation of mound building throughout the eastern half of Louisiana. It would have been more than a local event. Perhaps the localization or autonomy of the Middle Archaic mound builders made them more susceptible to local environmental change. But this still would have required synchronous change and site abandonment throughout the area, which seems very unlikely.

Inadequate data exist for offering social causes of the Middle Archaic mound building hiatus. Since trade was negligible, the most common means of examining the extent of social interaction among communities, societies, and cultures is not available. Speculation without evidence generally fails to increase our understanding of an issue. So until new and relevant data are acquired, knowledge of potential social factors will remain sparse.

At this incipient stage of research, any conjecture as to the cause of the demise of mound building is equally plausible. A change in the natural environment, social entropy, or a combination of the two should be investigated. Additional data, especially from known Middle Archaic mound sites, are desirable. The pursuit of buried Middle to Late Archaic sites will be necessary in order to distinguish between an end of mound building only, or a depopulation/abandonment of the region. The latter seems to be very unlikely, given that significant, buried non-mound sites are known to date to the mound-building hiatus: Cowpen Slough, Dragline (16CT36), McGuffee (16CT17, pre-mound component), Bush (16FR163, pre-mound component), Terry Jones #3 (16GR643), Henderson (16OU303), Womac (16CT312), and Copes (16MA47). Buried Archaic sites occur in the Catahoula Basin (Gibson 1991) for miles along the cut banks of Little River (Saunders 1999), in and under natural levee deposits in northeast

Louisiana, and conceivably in the Florida Parishes (Gagliano and Webb 1970; R. Saunders 1994). With better data from a wider area, it should be possible to determine what happened among the Middle Archaic cultures in Louisiana to produce a cessation of mound construction.

The Middle Archaic Review

Confirmed evidence for mound building during the Middle Archaic requires archaeologists to rethink models of social evolution. Prior to this discovery, the discipline had become complacent about the trajectory of social evolution, particularly in the Southeast. Mound building, especially the building of mound complexes, fell under the domain of complex societies. Planning, building, and sustaining a labor force required leadership. A simple equation explained it all: complex sites = complex societies. This simple equation even accommodated Poverty Point; the extensive trade network, elaborate material culture, and unique configuration of earthworks indicated social complexity.

Gradually, evidence of mounds earlier than Poverty Point accumulated (Gibson and Shenkel 1988), but most of these were simple affairs—a small conical mound or two, nothing beyond the means of mobile hunter-gatherers. But larger mounds and more complex mound groups were soon discovered to date from the Middle Archaic, until eventually their existence became commonplace and it became necessary to rethink progressive models for the evolution of social complexity (Russo 1994b; Gibson and Carr, ed. 2004). Egalitarian societies apparently did build complex earthworks. Middle Archaic mounds have also led archaeologists to reconceptualize mound building itself. The traditional view of earthworks was that their construction required a ranked or stratified polity sustained by horticulture. Today, we now know that mound building persisted for over five thousand years, and that up until the last five hundred years, the societies could sustain themselves by hunting, fishing, and foraging.

Finally, in terms of progress, it is too often tacitly assumed that once an innovation such as pottery is introduced, it becomes a permanent component of material culture for future generations. This clearly was not the case with mound building. Apparently it came and went on at least two occasions: the Middle Archaic hiatus and the Late Archaic hiatus (Kidder 2006). So the question that must be addressed is not just why the mounds were built, but why mound building ceased.

5

Poverty Point Redux

JON L. GIBSON

Hugging the high eastern rim of the Maçon Ridge overlooking the Lower Mississippi River swamplands are the ruins of Poverty Point (16WC5; Ford and Webb 1956; Webb 1982a), ancient earthworks built and occupied by Archaic fisher-hunter-gatherers between 1730 and 1250 cal. B.C. Although not the earliest, Poverty Point is nonetheless the largest and most complex of the Archaic earthworks in North America (Figure 5.1). The name Poverty Point is also given to the artifact complex associated with the site and, in a broader sense, to contemporary assemblages throughout the Lower Mississippi Valley (LMV) and the Gulf South, which feature earthenware cooking objects and several other diagnostic artifact classes (Webb 1968, 1982a). It is in this broad taxonomic sense that Poverty Point *culture* finds articulation (Webb 1968), but Poverty Point culture construed in a social sense is a different matter. Few investigators agree on its nature or even if there was *a* Poverty Point culture—that is, a communal group of people.

Archaeological Profile

Clarence Webb (1968:Table 2, 1982a:Table 18) found that a handful of artifact types and other material classes were suitable for identifying Poverty Point cultural components. The most revealing items included, first and foremost, hand-molded earthenware objects or Poverty Point objects (PPOs; Figure 5.2), followed by tubular pipes, terracotta human figurines, stone vessels, microflints, rough greenstone hoes and celts, hematite and magnetite plummets, and jasper beads and ornaments. Other commonly associated but less diagnostic materials included morphologically and stylistically consistent chipped-stone implements and polished-stone items. Finally, there was a group of not-as-diagnostic materials: galena, quartz, plummets made of rock other than iron ores, fiber-tempered pottery, grinding stones, and ground stone celts. Webb (1982a:Table 18) rounded out this list by adding semicircular and linear settlements, conical mounds, and

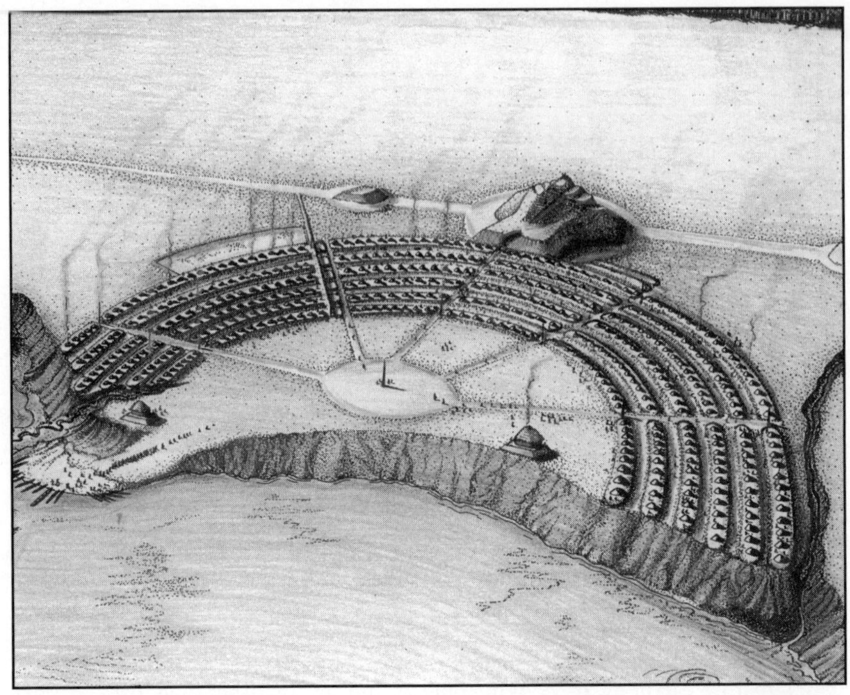

Fig. 5.1. Poverty Point (16WC5) central earthwork precinct, ca. 1500 B.C. Illustration by Jon Gibson.

monumental construction. Essentially, these traits were a distillation of the materiality found at the Poverty Point site.

The relative number of diagnostic traits represented at a component configured its degree of Poverty "Pointness." Thus, definite Poverty Point components had several PPO types and other diagnostic traits; possible Poverty Point components had few PPO types and other consistent, though not always diagnostic traits; and related components either lacked PPOs or yielded aberrant PPO forms and did not have other typical artifacts (Webb 1968:304–306).

Using this cultural-taxonomic gauge, Webb (1968, 1970, 1982a) identified Poverty Point components throughout the LMV from just south of the latitude of Memphis to the Gulf of Mexico, as well as related sites across the coast from Mississippi Sound to Choctawhatchee Bay (Webb 1968:Figure 1). Poverty Point sites clustered along relict Mississippi and Arkansas river courses, especially where paralleled by valley-rim bluffs or elevated edges of older surfaces down in the floodplain (Gibson 1973:366–379; Webb 1970). The most prominent clusters or the geographic phases of Phillips (1970:869–876) surrounded the Poverty

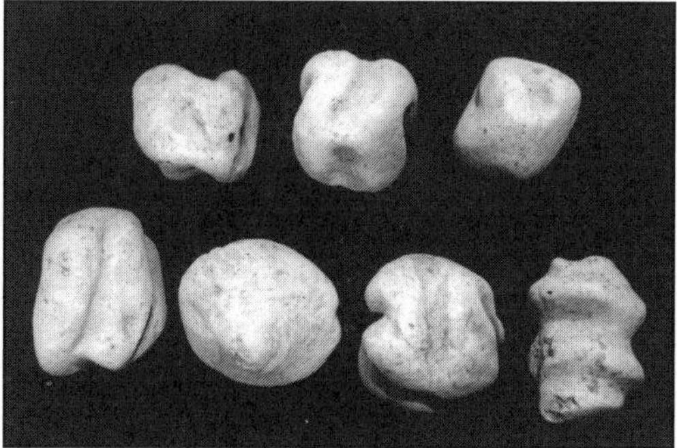

Fig. 5.2. Poverty Point objects.

Point site (Gibson 1993, 1996c, 1998a; Gregory et al. 1970; see Griffing 1990; Jackson 1986; Webb 1982a:5–6, 24–30), Jaketown in the Yazoo Basin (Connaway, McGahey, et al. 1977; Ford et al. 1955; Johnson 1980; Lehmann 1982; Webb 1982a:19–24), Calion in the Grand Marais lowlands (Hemmings 1982; Jeter and Jackson 1994:151), Neimeyer-Dare on Bayou Bartholomew (Jackson and Jeter 1994; Kidder 1991:35–40; Webb 1968:302), Claiborne on the Pearl River estuary (Bruseth 1980, 1991; Gagliano and Webb 1970; Webb 1982a:34–36), and Beau Rivage on the Vermilion River (Gibson 1976:66–73, Figures 6–7, Table 20, 1979, 1990:Table 26, 29). These clusters extend 450 kilometers (280 mi) along the Mississippi axis, and their assemblages are all materially variable (see Gibson 2000:232–265).

For example, Beau Rivage (16LY5), located more than 275 kilometers (171 mi) south of Poverty Point, on the western edge of the alluvial valley near the point where dry land meets the coastal marsh, has typical Poverty Point–type PPO forms—cylindrical grooved, biconical, and cross-grooved—but the majority types are flattened ellipsoidal, trianguloid, and sub-spheroidal forms, many of which are "decorated" with finger fluting or irregular slashes (Gibson 1976:Figures 6–7, 1979:Table 1). These atypical forms are more reminiscent of earthenware objects from Elliott's Point sites around Choctawhatchee Bay in Florida, which lies more than 230 kilometers (143 mi) east along the littoral (Small 1966:65–67; Thomas and Campbell 1991:108, Figure 6). Claiborne (22HC30), located on the eastern edge of the Mississippi Valley also at the dry land-marsh contact, has PPOs that superficially look like typical forms from Poverty Point, but differ in their details (Gibson 2007:511–512). Claiborne's melon-shaped PPOs normally have one end groove; Poverty Point's melons have two. Claiborne's melons usually have three body grooves; Poverty Point's have four. Proportions of the major types, bicones, melons, and cylinders differ widely. Perforated PPOs are three times more common at Claiborne, while miniature, tool-decorated objects are sixteen times more common at Poverty Point.

From locality to locality, general (compositional, class-level, and type-level) material similarities lose themselves among the attributes. Being close to Poverty Point is not a sure sign of material similarity. For instance, assemblages from the Turkey Creek and Big Creek site clusters, which have components within 35 kilometers (22 mi) south and southwest of the Poverty Point enclosure, have comparatively few PPOs and very few of the typical finger-grooved forms (Gibson 2000:238). Of the six most common projectile point types at Poverty Point, only the Gary type is abundant, and exotic lithics are scarce (Gibson 2000:238). In contrast, the site cluster around Neimeyer-Dare (16MO43), located about the same distance west of Poverty Point, has component assemblages more reminiscent of Poverty Point's, but they are nonetheless distinctive. PPOs are infrequent, especially finger-grooved forms. Gary points predominate, but Motleys, Delhis, and Epps occur. Exotic materials, particularly Ouachita novaculite, are more common than in Turkey Creek and Big Creek components (Gibson 2000:235).

Actually, site clusters closest to the Poverty Point site are not as compositionally similar as more distant clusters, such as around Jaketown (22HU505) and Claiborne, which do have the finger-grooved PPOs, the Motleys and other narrow-necked projectile points, and the heavy representation of exotic materials. Differences between Poverty Point and far-off clusters show up chiefly in artifact attributes. Distance is not the key to the resemblances, nor is time to blame for the differences. Although all components are unlikely to be contemporary—and there are an insufficient number of radiocarbon dates to tell which were and which were not—it is probable that some components in each cluster overlapped sufficiently in time that history can be ascribed the major role in shaping the material resemblances. To me, this means that human agents, directly or indirectly, through their actions or inactions, were responsible for the material resemblances or differences.

Mound building is another trait ascribed to Poverty Point culture, although it is by no means universal. Small conical mounds occur on only a handful of components other than Poverty Point itself (Webb 1982a:11–12), most notably at Jaketown (Ford et al. 1955:25), Lake Enterprise (3AS379; Jackson and Jeter 1994:153–162), Marksville Mound 10 (16AV1; Fowke 1928b; Gibson 2000:250–251), and Meche-Wilkes (16SL18; Gibson 1990:Tables 26–27; 2000:251–156, Figure 13.4), where excavations provide ample evidence that construction was carried out during Poverty Point times. Only at Poverty Point can construction be truly called monumental, encompassing between two-thirds and three-quarters of a million cubic meters of artificial fill in the various structures (Gibson 1987:17). The two largest mounds at Poverty Point contain 238,000 and 99,000 cubic meters of dirt (Kidder et al. 2008:10; Shenkel 1986:Table 1), which is more fill than all the rest of the proven and suspected Poverty Point mounds combined. Mound building was prosecuted more commonly and extensively between the fourth and third millennium B.C., over thirteen hundred years before the start of Poverty Point's building program (Saunders 2010, Chapter 4 in this volume). Yet, none of this earlier construction approached the massiveness of Poverty Point's construction. Kidder and colleagues dub Poverty Point a singularity (Kidder et al. 2008). For Ford (1955), it was an enigma.

Another material feature of Poverty Point culture is the presence of exotic rock (Brasher 1973; Conn 1976; Ford and Webb 1956:125–127; Gibson 1994b, 1999; Webb 1982a:Table 17). Exotics are ubiquitous, making up minor to dominant fractions of assemblages everywhere. The list is long: novaculite, hematite, magnetite, quartz crystal, greenstone, slate, shale, nepheline syenite, bauxite, some quartzites, and possibly Pitkin chert from the Ouachita Mountains in central Arkansas; galena, Crescent Hills chert, and possibly hematite, magnetite, and fluorite from the Ozark Rim in eastern Missouri; galena from the Upper Mississippi region; fluorite and various cherts, including Mill Creek, Dongola/Cobden, and others from the Shawnee Hills in southern Illinois; Harrison County and Harrodsburg flints from the Knobs region of northern Kentucky and southeastern Indiana; blue-gray Dover and Fort Payne, Camden, and Pickwick cherts, as well as phyllite, schist, and dark-gray quartzite from the bedrock zones lining the Tennessee River upstream from the Ohio River junction; Tallahatta quartzite and chalcedony from the Lower Tombigbee or Alabama River valleys in southeastern Mississippi and southwestern Alabama; soapstone and greenstone from the piedmont province of east-central Alabama and western Georgia; and copper, presumably from the Great Lakes region (Gibson 1994c:258–261). There is even a piece of obsidian from an undisclosed source in the Rockies (analyzed by Richard Hughes, see White 2005:21). Sources of dozens of other materials remain unconfirmed: talc, feldspar, channel coal, amethyst, kaolinite, calcite, mica, hornblende basalt porphyry, granite, basalt, dorite, pyrite, tuff, and many types of cherts. Most of these materials have been linked to sources by expert witness, but a few have been traced by chemical analyses: galena (Walthall et al. 1982), magnetite (Lasley 1983), soapstone (Smith 1981), and Dover flint (analyzed by Gary Glass, personal communication 2000).

Most chipped-stone materials seem to have arrived at the Poverty Point site as prepared blanks or preforms, after having undergone initial trimming at the rock outcrops or deposits (Baker 1982; Jeter and Jackson 1994:164; Walthall et al. 1982). Materials used for ground stone objects were probably also preformed at the outcrops or were selected for sizes and shapes. Although commonly assumed to have involved long-distance exchange (Ford and Webb 1956:125; Gibson 1994b) or direct acquisition (Carr and Stewart 2004:136–138; Ford and Webb 1956:125; Williams and Brain 1983:399), the actual means by which foreign materials came to Poverty Point and other interacting villages are debatable (but see Carr and Stewart 2004; cf. Sassaman 2005:355–359), as are the enabling domestic and political economies and motives. One thing is certain. Arriving materials had to be boated in (Gibson 1999). Distances involved and tonnage transported were simply too enormous for foot traffic and overland trails. Besides, practically all source areas were on or accessible to the Mississippi River.

Close to Home: Core and Periphery

There is no question that the Poverty Point site and surrounding site nexus are the geographic and cultural heart of Poverty Point culture—taxonomically, socially, and spiritually. The earthworks at Poverty Point dominate the landscape (Figure 5.3; Kidder 2002a; Ford and Webb 1956:14–19, Figures 2–4), their raised construction and extensive land-leveling reaching across three square kilometers (1.2 square mi). A set of six concentric earthen rings commands the arrangement and encloses a 14-hectare (35 acre) central area or plaza. Five aisles crosscut the ringed enclosure, dividing it into six compartments (Figure 5.3). Six earthen mounds mark primary alignments (Clark 2004a:171–183). Four of the mounds, including the two massive structures—the cruciform-shaped Mound A and the ellipsoidal Motley Mound—lie outside the ringed enclosure to the west and the north respectively, and two small platforms lie on the inside. One of the small platforms reposes on the southeastern end of the interior ring, overlooking the bluff-lined Bayou Maçon. Because it does not seem to fit into any of the mound alignments and later Baytown pottery has been found in superficial levels, its Poverty Point origin is periodically questioned (Connolly 2003:2; Ortmann 2010). Three of the western mounds fall in a straight line, running north-south, a line that originates at a fourth mound, the Lower Jackson Mound (16WC10), located 2.8 kilometers (1.7 mi) south of the cruciform mound. Lower Jackson was built at least thirteen centuries before Poverty Point's construction (Saunders et al. 2001).

Not all of the individual mounds or compartmentalized segments of the elliptical rings have been excavated or securely radiocarbon dated. This, coupled

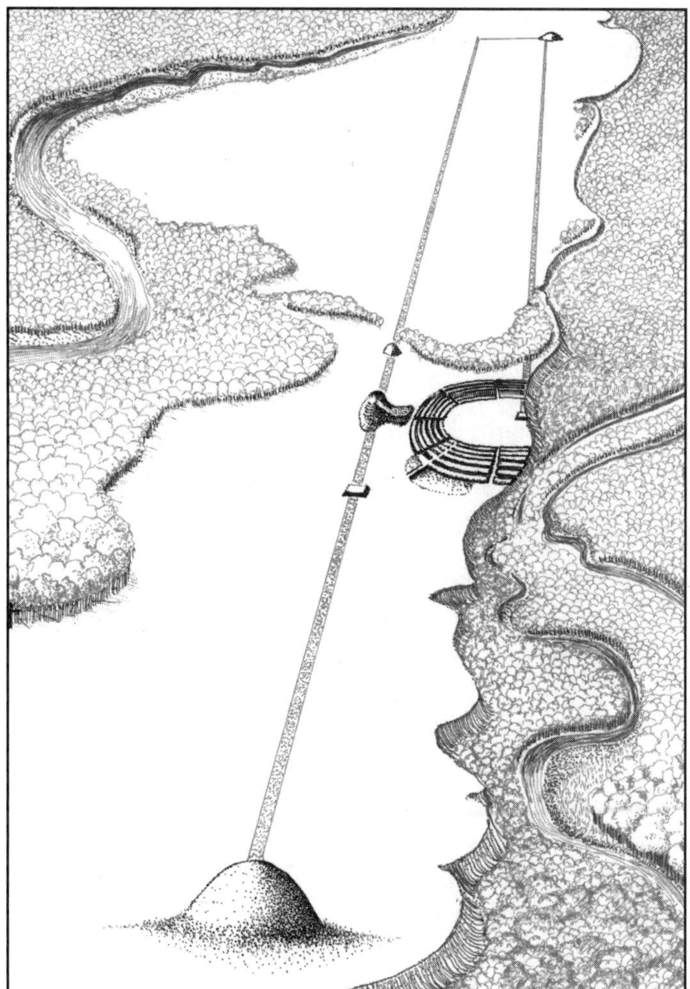

Fig. 5.3. Alignment of Poverty Point earthworks.
Illustration by Jon Gibson.

with concern over the long-held presumption that Poverty Point's features form a unitary complex, has led some investigators to question the representativeness of previous descriptions (Kidder 2002a). Based on laser mapping, Kidder (2002a) proposes that previous interpretations of the site overemphasize the symmetry of the site and portray an unproven image of it as a "great town." Yet laser mapping is not so efficacious that it can overturn previous interpretations, especially when ruins, not active dwellings, are being mapped.

Seventeen Poverty Point components and nine additional spots yielding a few Poverty Point artifacts are known within easy walking distance (3.5 km or 2.2 mi radius) of the central ringed enclosure (Gibson 1993, 1998a:299; Thomas and Campbell, ed. 1978; Webb 1944). Twenty-nine additional Poverty Point components are known outside this core area, up to 30 kilometers (19 mi) distant (Gibson 1998a:308). These peripheral components occur upon the high ground of Maçon Ridge, as well as down in the adjoining Tensas lowlands. No taxonomically identifiable Poverty Point components are known outside of this peripheral zone, until reaching one of the distant, surrounding site clusters.

Comparisons show that the most productive of these components are divisible into two assemblage classes, arguably attributable to villages and field camps (Gibson 1998a:320–324:Table 1, Figure 4; Gibson and Griffing 1994). Village assemblages are characterized by large percentages of PPOs and small percentages of projectile points and microliths, whereas field-camp assemblages show just the opposite. Five of the six core components with collections suitable for analysis fit a village profile: Alexander Point, Ballcourt Field, Locality 2, Motley East, and Steatite Field (Gibson 1993, 1998a; Thomas and Campbell, ed. 1978; Webb 1944). But only three of the suitable assemblages from the periphery fit a village profile: J. W. Copes (16MA47; Jackson 1986; Webb 1982a:25–29), Stockland Plantation (Gibson 1998a:318–319), and Terral Lewis (16MA16; Gregory 1991; Gregory et al. 1970; Webb 1982a:24–25).

Assemblage similarities and complements across this 1,800-km^2 (695-mi^2) locality suggest levels of stylistic, technological, and economic familiarity that befits a corporate body of people, a socially interacting community. Assemblage divisions and the way they map onto the landscape intimates a communal pattern of logistical mobility, with relatively sedentary villages surrounded by temporary field camps (Gibson 2006). Stirring spiritual and momentous social or political goings-on likely transpired on the high places at Poverty Point, where personages and spirit beings massed (Gibson 2007:516). The remainder of this chapter is devoted to reconstructing the lifeways of the people who dwelled at the Poverty Point site and in the surrounding countryside.

Birth of the Tamaroha

> Soon after the earth (yahne) was made, men and grasshoppers came to the surface through a long passageway that led from a large cavern, in the interior of the earth, to the summit of a high hill.
>
> —DAVID BUSHNELL, in Swanton (1931:37), "Source Material for the Social and Ceremonial Life of the Choctaw Indians"

Thus do the Choctaw tell how the Great Spirit created people. As unlikely as it seems, versions of this story are told by Indian peoples from Canada to South America, suggesting a common source, possibly an ancient, ancestral population. The Aztecs called their cities and pyramids "water mountains" and believed that a cave filled with sacred water lay beneath them, a cave where the first people issued forth to populate the earth above (Heyden 1981). During its peak, Poverty Point was the largest town in native North America above Mexico (Clark et al. 2010), and, like the Aztec towns and cities twenty-five centuries later, it too had great mounds. In keeping with the widespread native creation story and the Aztec name for city, we named the ancient inhabitants of Poverty Point, "Mound Cave People," or Tamaroha (Clark et al. 2010; Gibson 2006, 2007), in the old Tunica dialect they probably spoke (Gibson 2000:8).

Why make up a tribal name? A name, especially one that embodies the creation story of mound-building peoples, keeps our attention focused on the people who called Poverty Point home. Though we study the things they left behind—discarded tools, ruined buildings, food residues, and other physical remains—we do so in order to learn about the people themselves. The Tamaroha are best envisaged as a people, not as what they produced. So why not simply call the inhabitants Poverty Point people? Using the term Tamaroha avoids the thorny issue of conflating Poverty Point archaeological culture with a social culture. Tamaroha refers specifically to the people who resided at the town of Poverty Point and in the outlying community. The distinction allows us to speak of Poverty Point culture—an archaeological taxon predicated on artifacts and physical traits—and Tamaroha culture—a social grouping or corporate nexus integrated by common traditions, beliefs, and practices; kinship, marriage, and associations; and shared technology, styles, and material forms. Though there is no absolute assurance that the Tamaroha constituted a unitary group (see Kidder and Sassaman 2009; Sassaman 2005), I believe the case for nativistic communalism (Gibson 2007) is much stronger than a ritually forged, multi-ethnic coalition (Sassaman 2005). My exposition is based on that premise.

Tamaroha roots are usually sought in earlier mound-builder cultures in the LMV. Indeed, there are threads of continuity in the practice of mound building and a few areas of technology (Gibson 2007:513–514; Saunders and Allen 1997), but the Tamaroha were some fifty generations removed from the earlier mound-builders. There may have been biological ties, but genetics cannot account for Tamaroha origins any more than a contemporary son of the South can attribute his culture to distant Scottish or Choctaw ancestors.

Poverty Point was not merely a political-economic or ritual event periodically staged by unrelated opportunists from foreign lands (Jackson 1991b; Kidder and Sassaman 2009; Sassaman 2005). Poverty Point was a town (Clark et al. 2010); it was the heart of an extensive community. Evidences for communalism lie in local artifact styles, a logistically mobile economy, mound building, and cosmic-based mensuration (Gibson 2007).

So, from whence did the Tamaroha come? Where are the homes of their forefathers? Why did they establish themselves at Poverty Point? The answer to these questions is disarmingly simple: the Tamaroha created themselves (Gibson 2007:514–519). In this regard, they are no different than the rest of us, a consequence of engaging history and tradition, nature and cosmos, work and play, ideas and feelings, family, friends, and strangers. They did not exist before their time, so we need not look for them before they created, and were created by, their great town (cf. Kidder 2007a; Kidder and Sassaman 2009). But why at Poverty Point? That mystical place of giant mounds and earthen rings is their Mound Cave, their Navel of the Earth (see Swanton 1928:63–64). The Tamaroha were born there, made "from the same earth they used to create their great buildings" (Gibson 2007:515). Building gave them their identity and endowed them with a complex social structure that was capable of handling burgeoning actions and factions, a mutable structure that kept pace with gathering monumentality.

Mound Building

Poverty Point was not a product of sprawl and haphazard building. The earthworks were carefully planned, laid off, and executed (Clark 2004a; Gibson 1987:19–22; Kidder 2002a; Sassaman 2005). One theory maintains that it was a model of the cosmos in mounded earth, which precisely depicted the cycles of the sun, moon, and Venus by means of a standard measure (an arm span) and celestial geometry (Clark 2004a; Patten 2007a, 2007b, personal communication 2007, 2008). When converted to integers by the standard measure, inter-mound distances and lengths of chords created by relative mound positioning reveal a fascinating series of numbers: 13, 20, 52, 260, 360, 584, and 949—the day counts of the Mesoamerican calendar (Patten 2007b). Yet the Tamaroha were not the first to use the cosmic calendar. Middle Archaic sky watchers used the same heavenly cycle day counts to lay off their own mound centers two thousand years earlier (Clark 2004a). Calendar history gets even more interesting. Poverty Point and Mesoamerica share day counts too, but the geometry responsible for some counts is based on celestial cycles observable only at latitude 32.6° North, a narrow north-south viewing angle in north Louisiana (Patten 2007a, 2007b). Because these counts are preserved in the Mesoamerican calendar, it is conceivable that the calendar had been carried south by a visiting Tamaroha delegation, or perhaps by their Middle Archaic mentors (Patten 2007b:12).

On the eve of Poverty Point's construction, people were living in a level ring-and-plaza village, which followed the same tract as the mounded village they would shortly erect over it. Judging from the thinness of the pre-construction midden, they did not dwell there long before initiating construction. One thing is clear. Pre-construction inhabitants were Tamaroha. Their artifacts show it, the exotic raw materials they were importing show it, and their pre-construction village arrangement shows it. Once building began, working families moved off the construction site into nearby barrios until work was completed, returning afterwards and putting up new homes on the broad ring tops. Returning villagers would not have needed to wait until the entire earthwork was finished but could have moved in several families at a time, as soon as individual ring sections were available.

The Poverty Point earthworks were the largest building project undertaken in Archaic North America. Labor costs, including manpower, time, and coordination, were enormous. Compared with construction estimates for Nanih Waiya, the sacred mound of the Choctaw in east-central Mississippi, Poverty Point's labor pool required the equivalent of a staggering 700 to 800 workers drawn from a village population of around 2,000 to 2,600 (Gibson 2004a:266–267). There are simply too many uncontrolled variables for these numbers to be considered accurate estimates, but they do project a sense of just how much labor would have been required.

Everywhere, construction looks to have been carried out quickly and continuously (Gibson 1987, 2000:96, 2006:321–322; Kidder 2007a; Kidder et al. 2008; Ortmann 2005). Still, I remind myself that Poverty Point consists of many separate elements. Most are components for the rings, and, despite forming larger composite structures, each could have been erected swiftly and without interruption by relatively small work parties (Gibson 2006). Nonetheless, the earthworks in their entirety are so colossal that even thousands of workers could not have built it all at once. Where there is passage of time, there is succession in building. Although we do not know how much of Poverty Point's 400-year occupation span was devoted to construction, I would not be surprised to find that the major part of the earthworks were raised by first generation Tamaroha, when esprit de corps and passions were fresh.

Based on the relative stratigraphic depth of many kinds of artifacts, I suggested that the Tamaroha raised the innermost ring first and continued to add

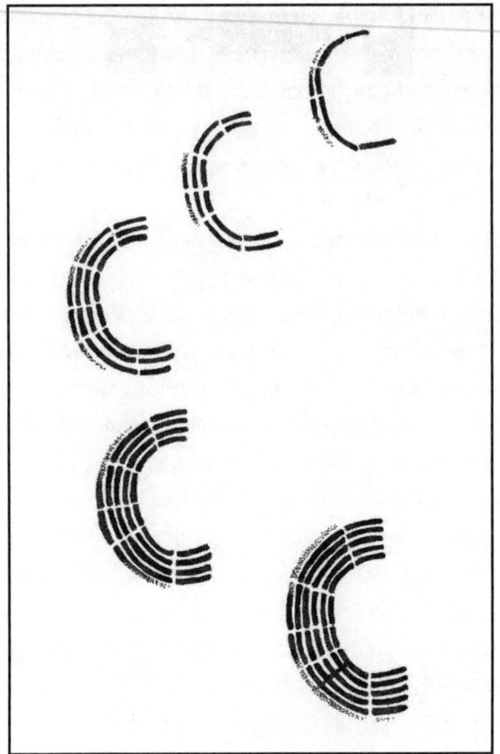

Fig. 5.4. Proposed Poverty Point ring-building succession.
Illustration by Jon Gibson.

rings outwardly until all six were installed (Gibson 2001, 2002). Preliminary evidence suggests they initialized each ring at its midpoint in the west and simultaneously advanced clockwise and counterclockwise around the ring axis until reaching the eastern ends (Figure 5.4). Due to inherent statistical uncertainty, radiocarbon dating offers no greater support for this model of ring succession than any other possible alternative. The construction order of the mounds is also controvertible. Anthony Ortmann (2010) suggests that Mound B was built first, followed in order by Ballcourt Mound (Mound E), Dunbar Mound (Mound C), and lastly, by the giant edifices Mound A and Motley Mound. His proposal privileges the upper bound (oldest) limits of the one-standard-error ranges of relevant radiocarbon ages, as well as morphological resemblances among mounds. Yet mound dates are not any different than ring dates in that true ages cannot be reconciled more precisely than standard errors permit (cf. Kidder 2006).

All mounds fall at or halfway between points marked by an imaginary series of equilateral triangles projected northward from Lower Jackson Mound. The height of these triangles (600 meters or 1,969 feet) is equal to the perpendicular distance between Poverty Point's two principal axes (Figure 5.3; Clark 2004a:172–173). As far as I can tell, this arrangement connotes no necessary chronological order, only some undisclosed cosmic divination.

Domestic Economy

The Tamaroha made a living by fishing, hunting, and collecting. They did not farm. Even the squash they collected was an inedible, wild variety suitable only for containers (Ward 1998). Unlike their contemporaries farther up the Mississippi Valley, they eschewed the starchy-oily annuals and their tiny seeds. They fine-tuned their food pursuits according to season and place, but they also developed technology that enabled them to circumvent seasonal constraints and deliver food "on demand."

Although they hunted game and collected nuts and acorns on Maçon Ridge, they devoted most of their attention to the rich river swamp, with its endless supply of fish and aquatic plants (Byrd and Neuman 1978:Table 3; Cummings 2006; Jackson 1991a; Ward 1998). They extended fishing past the warm-water season by using nets with plummet-weighted mudlines, which caught fish when waters were rimmed with ice and swollen by flood. They streamlined grubbing for roots by designing an efficient, durable, and maintainable hand size hoe for pulling lotus and cattail rhizomes out of the soft mud, lining shallow lake bottoms and bayou banks (Gibson 1998a:324). Technological tinkering is obvious in the atlatl-dart delivery system. A new oven design, coupled with thermal controls in the form of variously shaped PPOs, revolutionized cooking and freed cooks from having to stand over the fire turning the spit or picking exploded bits of rock out of the mulligan. Thermal-shock resistant soapstone pots even caught on as heavy-duty cookware, but local clay/loess copies failed to achieve similar popularity, probably because of their relative fragility and secularity.

While technological acuity revamped the cutting edge of domestic economy, it was a change in logistics that streamlined food delivery. For centuries, practical Archaic hunter-gatherers followed a seasonal round, living most of the year in one place and then scattering throughout nearby woods for the remainder. When the group was together, provisioning fell to individuals or parties who went out, collected food and supplies, and then brought their bounty back to share with the others. Sometimes, suppliers ranged too far from home and wound up having to camp overnight. Logistics varied from group to group and may have even experienced a complete reversal after some groups shifted from generalized hunting and nut harvesting to focused fishing and aquatic root digging. The first appearance of Middle Archaic multiple-mound ritual centers, such as Watson Brake (16OU175), Frenchman's Bend (16OU259), Hillman's Mound (16MA201), and Caney Mounds (16CT5), brought further changes in logistics, as groups who lived most of the year apart congregated at these sacred places, temporarily consuming larger than usual amounts of food (Arco et al. 2006; Saunders, Chapter 4 in this volume; Saunders and Allen 1997; Saunders et al. 1994, 2000, 2001, 2005). No wonder all these centers lay alongside vast stretches of river swamp where intensification could be absorbed and sustained. Yet having access to a limitless aquatic storehouse is just part of the story. Food still had to be gathered, prepared, and distributed, and this was feasible only through inter-group cooperation and feasting (see Hayden 2001). Staging these gatherings at the same place year after year became possible when participating groups began subscribing to a common set of beliefs and observances, thus ensuring multiple-group bonding and corporate action. I suspect mound building was the central cause and consequence of this engagement.

Tamaroha domestic economy was not merely more of the same. It was something new and different in the swamp. Poverty Point was not a temporary meeting ground. The Tamaroha lived there permanently (Gibson 2006:321–322), as well as in several villages along Joes Bayou, south of town (Jackson 1991a). While there was logistical movement between villages and field camps, the Tamaroha all over the great swamp were organically sedentary.

The Tamaroha focused on sustainable, high-yield foods, such as fish and aquatic roots, and they developed the essential technology to ensure mass production. They technologically leveled out seasonal abundance and shortfall, turning domestic economy into steady, year-round, "on-demand" economy. The consequences were profound. Production engaged fewer people, or required less time for the many. Storage was practically eliminated, as fish were simply left in the bayou and roots in the mud until needed.

Political Economy

Technological advances were directly responsible for the intensification in the Tamaroha's domestic economy, but they also intensified the political economy. Many technological improvements were based on foreign raw materials, which brought distant mountains and hard-rock plateaus within reach of the Tamaroha. Tons of rock were delivered. This contributed to the making of the Tamaroha persona and body politic, but three materials stand out among those that were technologically indispensable to the surging political economy: iron ore, soapstone, and Dover flint.

The Tamaroha added heavy hematite and magnetite weights to fish netting, converting it into all-weather webbing. Particle-induced x-ray emission analysis (PIXE) shows that these iron ores came from the Ouachita Mountains around Hot Springs, Arkansas (Lasley 1983). Neutron activation analysis (Smith 1981) and reflectance infrared spectroscopy (PIMA) (Emerson et al. 2006) reveal that soapstone vessels, which economized cooking time with their durability, were cut from outcrops on Soapstone Ridge, Georgia, and other mountain sides in eastern Alabama. A third material, blue-gray Dover flint, which was used to make the big hoes that enhanced aquatic root production, came from the highlands along the Tennessee River in Stewart County, Tennessee. The match between Poverty Point hoes and highland sources was confirmed by PIXE analysis (Gary Glass, personal communication 2000).

No matter how exotic substances arrived, the simple truth is that the Tamaroha dealt directly or indirectly with foreigners from many lands (cf. Sassaman 2005). Trafficking was so far-reaching and involved such massive quantities of materials that local politics must have energized the process. Yet centralized control by tribal leaders was not necessarily required. Informal management, such as negotiation among cooperating or competing family stewards, probably would have sufficed. Without some measure of management, overproduction of nonessential materials, stepping on each other's toes, and even duplicity would have been unavoidable. The bigger the enterprise, the greater the likelihood that "control" was formalized, possibly institutionalized. No matter who was responsible, it is difficult not to envision political and social importance accruing to those individuals in the process. If such prominence did attach to specific families or factions, it undoubtedly was inheritable, because management of exotics persisted for at least a dozen generations. Whether corporate or familial, management was rife with inequality—the social and political cornerstone of ranked society (Gibson 1974a, 1998a).

It is reasonable to view relative importance, absolute volume, and transactional complexity of various exotics as bases for bestowing sociopolitical importance, but we have no scale that measures the importance of one domestic material against another or of a domestic versus a ritual material. For example, did importers of ten tons of Dover flint receive greater recognition, power, and privilege than importers of a hundred pounds of galena, a face and body paint? Did suppliers of soapstone vessels rank above the family that brought in ten quartz crystals used in divining? Relative value is not something that comes from counting or weighing. The Tamaroha made those judgments by their own standards.

Iron ore, soapstone, and Dover flint lay on the leading edge of daily matters of life and limb, a vitality that undoubtedly conferred recognition on local Tamaroha suppliers. Prominence ostensibly accruing to local providers did not spill over into the workaday domain. Providers of iron ore, for example, did not restrict their supplies to certain consumer groups. I found no difference in the inter-ring distribution of magnetite versus hematite plummets, which we would have expected if different factions had been supplying independent groups (Gibson 2004b). At Poverty Point and throughout the remainder of the Tamaroha community, access to exotic materials, at least the most abundant ones, was free and open: "Findings point to the same conclusion—that the distribution of foreign exchange material in Poverty Point's hinterland was strongly influenced by functional circumstances. . . . Local exchange would appear to have had a relatively simple organization and mission—to get the exchange items directly into the hands of workers and out into the work areas. In this context, exchange patterns should be a near mirror of the distribution of base and work camps, and, to some extent, this is what our findings indicate" (Gibson and Griffing 1994:243). Open access does not, in and of itself, mean the Tamaroha were egalitarian. It simply means that daily chores of fishing, digging roots, and cooking were done by everyone, using widely available tools best suited for the task.

Open access to materials used for domestic tools leads me to wonder if the Tamaroha had open access to materials used for fine items, such as hard-stone owl carvings and beads (Webb 1982a:58–60, Figure 29). Or was access denied to everybody except powerful families, community leaders, and artisans attached to them? Was craft specialization an integral facet of Tamaroha political economy, or were makers of fine items simply talented individuals who neither influenced nor were influenced by partisanship or social standing (Gibson 2004b)?

Stone owls represent the apogee of Tamaroha craftsmanship (Figure 5.5), but not even these meet expectations of specialized production (see Costin 2001; Schortman and Urban 2004). There are too few that are too individually distinctive, and too widespread to have been the handiwork of a lapidary specialist or craft guild. These owls occur in villages and field camps, at Poverty Point and hundreds of miles away in contexts that are culturally non-Tamaroha, suggesting their magical power as charms or fetishes (Connaway, Brookes, and McGahey 1977:118–129). Even if most statuettes originated at Poverty Point, which I doubt, who in town could or would have afforded to sponsor their production in

Fig. 5.5. Stone owl effigy bead. Photograph by Steven Carricut.

face of such obviously low demand? Such low-level production would have certainly fallen far short of what was needed to have fed and clothed independent specialists and their brood. I cannot imagine a situation where elite sponsorship of lapidary services managed to leverage material or political gain or fame from such a widely dispersed clientele from so many different walks of life. But the most direct argument against carved owls being made by craft specialists lies in their stylistic individuality and lack of standardization. I think I can see as many different hands in their crafting as there are statuettes. They were masterpieces all, but masters separate.

Theocracy from the Heavens

Poverty Point was destined to be different from the very beginning, and the Tamaroha were special under the sun. Tradition passed down from as far back as Middle Archaic times seems to have glorified movements of the sun, moon, and Venus (Clark 2004a; Patten 2007a, 2007b). How ancient astrologers managed to figure out such complex cycles and incorporate them into construction were really simple matters. They watched the paths of these celestial orbs along the horizon and knew the width of their arm span, the standard measure (see Clark 2004a). That northeastern Louisiana natives six millennia ago chose to scale off their mound villages after these cycles underscores one very important fact: the keepers of cosmic knowledge parlayed heavenly cycles and earthly creation into a symbolic manifesto for tribal consolidation and corporate undertaking. From the outset, Lower Mississippi mound builders were brought together and held together by sky-watching shaman priests, whose authority came from understanding and explaining the great mysteries. The mysteries were always the heart and mind of mound-building groups, but somewhere along the line, these shaman priests became the Great Spirit's earthbound agents, even children of the Great Spirit, imbued with awesome supernatural powers. The Tamaroha constituted a theocracy run by heads whose authority was heaven-sent.

Fascination with the cosmos and portraying it in mounded earth culminated at Poverty Point, where massiveness commanded awe and reverential homage. Yet the giant earthwork told another story too—the story of creation. By tying their own birth navel directly to the navel of the ancients (Lower Jackson Mound), the Tamaroha through their shaman priests established an ancestral basis for their dynasty, legitimizing their rights to the land, as well as proprietary claims to the ancient cosmic knowledge (Figure 5.3). Not only do the earthworks symbolically incorporate cosmic cycles, but Poverty Point also has many features that can be interpreted as sacred and magical embodiments (Gibson 1998b:22–26), which lend further credibility to its fundamentally theocratic character. The east side opening, concentricity of the rings, and repetitious use of the number six all have a bearing on matters of world portrayal and supernatural protection. Not to be forgotten are symbolic artifact forms and glyphs depicting birds, beasts, and human-animal chimeras. This rich symbolism is represented in the sacred and just-so stories of many historic Gulf language–linked tribes, so many that a common source in deep antiquity must be responsible (Gibson 1998b:26–30).

The earthworks embedded the power of theocratic leadership by formalizing private and public space (Gibson 2007:516). Laity had free access practically everywhere except mound summits, which were arguably for clergy only: "Hierarchy is built into mounded earth—commonness on the ground level, privilege on the mound tops; ordinariness for passive participants in spectator events and perhaps in construction, high status for those staging those events, performing in them, and acting as fiduciaries" (Gibson 2007:516).

Nonetheless, power and prestige seem to have been shared with secular personages. The two inner, residential rings were set apart from the outer four by a wider space and were raised higher than the others, ostensibly to house prominent families. In addition, a platform mound—the only mound not incorporated in one of the two principal mound axes—was built atop the innermost ring, precisely where the ring terminated at the steep eastern bluff. Not only did this artificially exaggerate the height of the mound when viewed from the bayou below, but the mound abutted a gently sloped section of the bluff, the only such section for miles around. Although it is unclear whether or not the

Tamaroha intentionally graded the area, they did add a broad earthen façade across its front. The area has been colloquially called the Dock (Gibson 1989:3; Hillman 1990b:133), but in light of the enormity of water-borne commerce (Gibson 1994b:160, 1999:59–60), an unloading wharf would have been infinitely practical and an elevated residence of a "dock boss," a reasonable addition.

Secular power-sharing does not diminish the theocratic legitimacy of governance; the enormity of the earthworks aggrandizes heavenly-decreed authority. Still, the mix of secular and sacred authority does have practical repercussions for Tamaroha society and history. Supernaturally empowered, shaman priests were shielded from blame when individuals or community experienced runs of bad luck, sickness, or other malaise. Then again, secular leaders, who were made by their actions or those of their fathers, could be unmade when their actions went awry (see Clark 2004b). I suspect that evidence for both kinds of leaders means that Tamaroha society was hierarchical, divided into ranks of civil and ritual leaders and their families, and commoners whose social standing was determined less by genealogy than by effort, personality, age, and gender.

Absence of the usual accouterments of office, status, and privilege does not make the Tamaroha any less socially and politically complex than societies with such trappings. Their complexity is incorporated in the massive construction and mastery of cosmic design. Until the great Mississippian polity at Cahokia two thousand years later, no other Native American group came close to unleashing the amount of labor expended on Poverty Point.

The End of Days

The Tamaroha abandoned their town sometime shortly after 3300 B.P. No local polity arose to fill the void. There were no nearby towns, villages, or vestiges of Tamaroha material traditions. As was the case during the preceding Middle Archaic period, people seem to have disappeared into the wilderness, taking their traditions with them (Gibson 1996a:44–47; Saunders 2010, Chapter 4 in this volume). The ensuing Tchefuncte culture did not appear until many long centuries later (Ford and Quimby 1945; Gibson 1996a:47–49, 1998c:831–832; Kidder 2002b:69–72, 2006; Kidder and Roe 2007; Hays and Weinstein, Chapter 6 in this volume).

Was the Tamaroha legacy left elsewhere, perhaps on a distant shore? John Clark (2006:5) thinks that the Olmecs at San Lorenzo Tenochtitlán, Mesoamerica's first city and capital of the Olmec state, adopted building principles and the standard measure from the Tamaroha. It is conceivable that the Tamaroha also tutored the Olmec in other cosmological matters (Patten 2007b), theocratic labor management, and social skills of town living.

San Lorenzo Tenochtitlán founded Mesoamerican civilization (Clark 2006). Maybe Poverty Point's fate was indeed lost in the swamps, only in Vera Cruz and not the Lower Mississippi Valley. Poverty Point, co-founder of Mesoamerican civilization—somehow the irony seems fitting.

6

Tchefuncte and Early Woodland

CHRISTOPHER T. HAYS AND RICHARD A. WEINSTEIN

Tchefuncte is one of the best-known cultures of the Early Woodland period, a segment of time that is identified in the Lower Mississippi Valley (LMV) as the Tchula period (Figure 1.3). Tchefuncte's fame comes in large part from an early classic archaeological monograph, James A. Ford and George I. Quimby's (1945) *The Tchefuncte Culture: An Early Occupation of the Lower Mississippi Valley.* The size and content of Tchefuncte sites are also a distinguishing aspect of the culture, since the large coastal Tchefuncte shell middens represent some of the most extensive occupation locales of the Early Woodland period, often containing a comparatively rich assemblage of pottery, bone artifacts, and other cultural remains. The ceramic assemblage itself is quite distinctive, as it is one of the most stylistically diverse of the period. In addition, to the authors' knowledge, pottery of the Tchefuncte series and that of the Goose Creek series of coastal Texas are the only untempered aboriginal ceramic assemblages in North America, although the two series are not closely related, if related at all.

Another important distinguishing characteristic of Tchefuncte culture is that it represents a distinct departure from its Late Archaic predecessor, the flamboyant Poverty Point culture (see Gibson, Chapter 5 in this volume). Tchefuncte lacks, for the most part, the elaborate long-distance exchange systems, large mound complexes, and lapidary or exotic stone industries characteristic of the Poverty Point culture. Accounting for these differences is one of the most vital areas of research on Tchefuncte.

This chapter will focus on new developments and research related to Tchefuncte culture, particularly work done within the last fifteen years. The theoretical and methodological focus of this new research has primarily been on the origins and chronology of Tchefuncte culture and the composition of its diagnostic pottery series (both technological and chronological/stylistic studies). In this chapter, we examine these trends and discuss new data on Tchefuncte that have been generated by field and laboratory research. Most of this current research on Tchefuncte pottery and its origins has taken place in coastal and northeast Louisiana, specifically for the latter within the Tensas Basin and at the Poverty Point site (16WC5). Since an understanding of the Tchefuncte ceramic assemblage is so important in our understanding of Tchefuncte culture as a whole, much of the research and our following discussion focus on this aspect of the culture. However, before we turn to our reporting and analysis of this new research, we begin with a synopsis of Tchefuncte culture.

A Tchefuncte Synopsis

MATERIAL CULTURE

As noted above, one of the hallmarks of Tchefuncte culture is the first widespread and intensive use of pottery in Louisiana (Jeter and Williams 1989a:111–112, Figure 10; Toth 1988:19). The chronology of the Tchefuncte culture will be discussed in more detail later in this chapter, but most archaeologists would agree that it begins at least by about 800 B.C. and ends around A.D. 1 with the beginning of the Marksville culture (Fullen 2005; Gibson 2000; Hays and Weinstein 1999:50, 61; Kidder 2006; McGimsey, Chapter 7 in this volume).

Pottery of the Tchefuncte series is quite distinctive in appearance, primarily because the paste is relatively crude, poorly wedged, and lacks any intentionally added tempering particles (Phillips 1970:173; Shenkel 1980:74; Toth 1988:25; Weaver 1963:53–56; Weinstein and Rivet 1978:26–30). In cross section, it is characteristically laminated and contorted. Some researchers have suggested that pottery of the Tchefuncte series is clay- or sand-tempered (e.g., Gibson 2000; Neuman 1984; Rivet 1973), but as just noted, the vast majority (if not all) of Tchefuncte ware has no intentional inclusions in the paste. Specks of shell, fired clay, sand, bone, hematite, and even fiber are sometimes found in Tchefuncte ware, but these items were natural inclusions in the original clay and clearly were not added and worked into the paste in any systematic fashion.

It is worth noting here that the type Mandeville Plain, which was established by Ford and Quimby (1945) and used by Shenkel (1980, 1984b) to denote Tchefuncte sherds with sandy paste, is not a type recognized by the majority of archaeologists in the LMV and surrounding regions (Aten and Bollich 2002; Blitz and Mann 2000; Phillips 1970; Rivet 1973; Weinstein and Rivet 1978). Phillips (1970) and later Rivet (1973) argued quite convincingly that Mandeville Plain sherds should be designated as Tchefuncte Plain, *var. Mandeville,* since they have typical contorted and laminated Tchefuncte paste with the simple addition of more sand in the body fabric. The sand does not appear to have been systematically added as temper when compared to truly sand-tempered wares such as O'Neal Plain and other elements of the Alexander series (to be discussed below). Unfortunately, Shenkel's (1980, 1984b) placement of sherds with Mandeville paste into what he termed the "Mandeville series" has resulted in undue confusion among later investigators. For example, Weinstein and Rivet (1978) established Orleans Punctated, *var. Chappapeela,* and Lake Borgne Incised, *var. Ponchitolawa,* as sandy-paste counterparts to the typical non-sandy varieties of *Orleans* and *Lake Borgne.* Shenkel (1980, 1984b) assigned these varieties to his Mandeville series and this ultimately led Blitz and Mann (2000:23, 110, Table 3.2) to move them (incorrectly) into the Alexander series after they decided (correctly) that Shenkel's Mandeville series was untenable. Weinstein and Rivet (1978) never intended for either of these two varieties to be included in the Alexander series. They are simply sandy-paste (not sand-tempered) varieties of typical laminated Tchefuncte ware.

Several decades ago, Doyle Gertjejansen, a professional ceramicist, attempted to replicate pots of the Tchefuncte series. After numerous experiments, he reached the conclusion that Tchefuncte potters did very little to prepare the clay before they made their pots. For example, they did not remove much of the natural debris in the clay. Nor did they knead or work the clay, which is why the paste is typically laminated and contorted (Gertjejansen and Shenkel 1983:45, 60). Interestingly, this is virtually the same conclusion reached by Ford and Quimby (1945:67) almost forty years earlier, although they did not conduct replication experiments. When Gertjejansen fired replica Tchefuncte pots, many of them failed or broke because of the lack of temper and clay preparation. This may account, in part, for the large number of sherds (e.g., ca. 50,000) at some Tchefuncte sites. One interesting exception to typical Tchefuncte pottery is the type Chene Blanc Plain, which is non-laminated and contains flecks of bone and/or hematite (Hays and Weinstein 2004). This type was defined very recently and will be discussed in more detail below.

In addition to Chene Blanc Plain, other non-Tchefuncte series pottery can be found in small quantities at Tchefuncte sites. Specifically, one sometimes finds a few sherds of fiber-tempered Wheeler series pottery and a slightly larger sample of the sand-tempered Alexander series pottery. For example, the Alexander series at the Tchefuncte type site (16ST1) included 671 sherds of O'Neal Plain, 56 sherds of Alexander Incised, 69 sherds of Alexander Pinched, 23 sherds of Chinchuba Brushed, 21 sherds of Mandeville Stamped, and 5 sherds of Smithsonia Zone Stamped, but these represented only 1.7 percent of the total Tchefuncte culture assemblage of 49,989 sherds (Ford and Quimby 1945:Table I). At the Bayou Jasmine site (16SJB2), we found only 13 Alexander sherds amidst an assemblage of over 15,000 Tchefuncte sherds (Hays and Weinstein 1999:Table 2), while the Beau Mire site (16AN17) produced none (Weinstein and Rivet 1978). Alexander sherds are also present in very small numbers at Tchefuncte sites in northeastern Louisiana, where they are considered intrusive items from the east (Kidder 2007b:20, 36, Tables 2–4). The only Tchula period site with substantial numbers of Alexander sherds (ca. 35 percent of the assemblage) is the Norman site (22QU518) in northwest Mississippi (Phillips 1970:879–880; Toth 1988:23–26), but that site is now considered to be part of the Lake Cormorant culture rather than Tchefuncte culture (Weinstein 1995:166). It is interesting to note that the Tchefuncte component at the Jaketown site (22HU505), located in west-central Mississippi, contained only a few Alexander sherds: 2 Alexander Incised, 12 Alexander Pinched, 1 rim of the rare type Mandeville Stamped, and at least 5 of O'Neal Plain (Ford et al. 1955:74–75, Table 5, Figure 26). Like the few Alexander sherds in the Tensas Basin, those at Jaketown were considered by the authors to be the remains of intrusive trade items in what was otherwise a very vibrant Tchefuncte occupation (Ford et al. 1955:75). In summary, the typical Tchefuncte component is dominated by Tchefuncte wares, suggesting that the culture was fairly homogeneous and possibly somewhat parochial, but the presence of these other wares indicates that Tchefuncte folks did not live in true cultural isolation.

Although the paste of Tchefuncte ware pottery is comparatively crude, the surface treatments and resulting decorations are surprisingly varied and relatively sophisticated. They include incising (with straight and curved lines, wiggled lines, and drag-and-jab lines), rocker stamping, simple stamping, punctations, and, infrequently, cord impressing (Burke 2002; Ford and Quimby 1945; Hays and Weinstein 1999; Phillips 1970; Shenkel 1980; Weinstein and Rivet 1978). Generally, incised decorations consist of rectilinear patterns that include nested diamonds, alternating decorated and non-decorated bands (particularly evident in certain varieties of Lake Borgne Incised), line-filled triangles, herringbones, and crosshatching (Weinstein and Rivet 1978:36–37), while stamped decorations include unzoned dentate and non-dentate rocker stamping (usually arranged in horizontal rows around a vessel) and close-spaced, haphazard simple stamping (Weinstein and Rivet 1978:45–47, 76). Punctations occur as either random or neatly aligned rows of fingernail punctations, hollow circular punctations formed by the end of a piece of cane, pointed and wedge-shaped punctations created by a cut stick or bone, and bands of punctations zoned by incised lines that alternate with non-decorated bands (Weinstein and Rivet 1978:51–53, 71–72). Cord-impressed decoration usually occurs in simple linear

Fig. 6.1. Tchefuncte ceramics: a–d. Tchefuncte Plain, *var. Tchefuncte* (a, plain rim; b, flattened podal support; c, fluted base; d, wedge-shaped podal support); e–f. Tchefuncte Plain, *var. Mandeville* (e, plain rim; f, teat-shaped podal support); g–i. Tchefuncte Incised, *var. Tchefuncte* (g, plain rim; h–i, notched rims); j–k. Tchefuncte Incised, *var. Bogue Falaya* (plain rims); l. Tchefuncte Stamped, *var. Tchefuncte;* m–n. Tchefuncte Stamped, *var. Vermilion* (plain rims); o. Tchefuncte Stamped, *var. Lewisburg;* p–q. Orleans Punctated, *var. Orleans;* r. Orleans Punctated, *var. Chappepeela;* s–t. Sherds from vessel decorated with both Orleans Punctated, *var. Orleans* and Tchefuncte Stamped, *var. Vermilion* (plain rims); u. Tchefuncte Red, *var. Tchefuncte;* v–x. Lake Borgne Incised, *var. Lake Borgne* (v–w, plain rims; x, incised rim); y–z. Tammany Punctated, *var. Tammany* (y, notched rim; z, plain rim); aa. Alexander Incised, *var. Green Point;* bb–cc. Chinchuba Brushed, *var. Chinchuba* (plain rims). All sherds from the Tchefuncte site (16ST1) save for c, d, and g from Little Woods Midden No. 1 (16OR1), and m from an unknown site within the Pontchartrain Basin of southeastern Louisiana. Note that m was illustrated previously by Saucier (1963:Figure 36d). Photographs by Anne Marie Blank. Arranged by Thurston H. G. Hahn III.

patterns, particularly on vessel rims, where it forms herringbone and triangular designs (Kidder 2007b). Typical examples of some of these decorations are shown in Figure 6.1. Sometimes a single vessel exhibits a combination of different decorative techniques. Indeed, Tchefuncte ware has one of the most diverse set of surface treatments in the Early Woodland of eastern North America, with seven distinct common types (Jenkins et al. 1986). The variety of such decorative treatments is believed to be the result of influences primarily from the east, specifically the Wheeler, Alexander, and St. Johns pottery series, which were all part of a pan-Gulf pottery tradition (Jenkins and Krause 1986). Initially, these ceramic influences entered Louisiana during the Poverty Point period, when exotic exchange items were still being brought into the region in large numbers (Gibson, Chapter 5 in this volume; Hays and Weinstein 2004:166–167; Jenkins et al. 1986:560; Jeter and Williams 1989a; Sassaman 1993:26, 2004; Shenkel 1984b).

Tchefuncte vessel types include globular pots with shoulders, simple bowls, and jars with slightly constricted necks and flaring rims (Shenkel 1984b:50). The latter is one of the most recognizable of all Tchefuncte vessel forms (see Shenkel 1974:Figure 4c and Weinstein 1995:Figure 7 for illustrations). Rim sherds are incurvate, straight, and often thickened by an exterior strap. Sometimes the lips are notched, and exterior rim nodes are often present, having been punched outward from the interior of the pot. The exterior color of Tchefuncte pottery is often grey, but sherds with oxidized surfaces are also common (Hays and Weinstein 2004:159). The bases of Tchefuncte pots are distinctive, since they often have teat- or wedge-shaped podal supports. Annular and flattened bases are also found (Shenkel 1984b:50).

In his analysis of the Big Oak Island (16OR6) and Little Oak Island (16OR7) assemblages, Shenkel (1984b: 51) divided Tchefuncte vessels into small, medium, and large sizes. He found that the earth midden at Little Oak Island, which he considered to be a village site, had larger vessels than those at the shell midden site of Big Oak Island, which he considered to be a specialized food-processing area. He also noted that Big Oak Island had fewer decorated sherds.

Other common Tchefuncte artifacts include tubular ceramic pipes, both plain and decorated with incising or punctating, bone tools that are typically geared to hunting and fishing technologies (e.g., fishhooks or socketed bone points), shell tools (e.g., adzes and chisels), and pendants (Figure 6.2; see Ford and Quimby 1945:29–31, 43–51, Figures 7, 12, 13, 15; Weinstein 1986:Figures 9.5 and 9.6). Lewis (1997:56) identified a wide range of bone tools at the Tchefuncte site, and she suggests that some animal species were selected for use because they were unusual or exotic (e.g., golden or bald eagle, shark, or otter). She also argues for

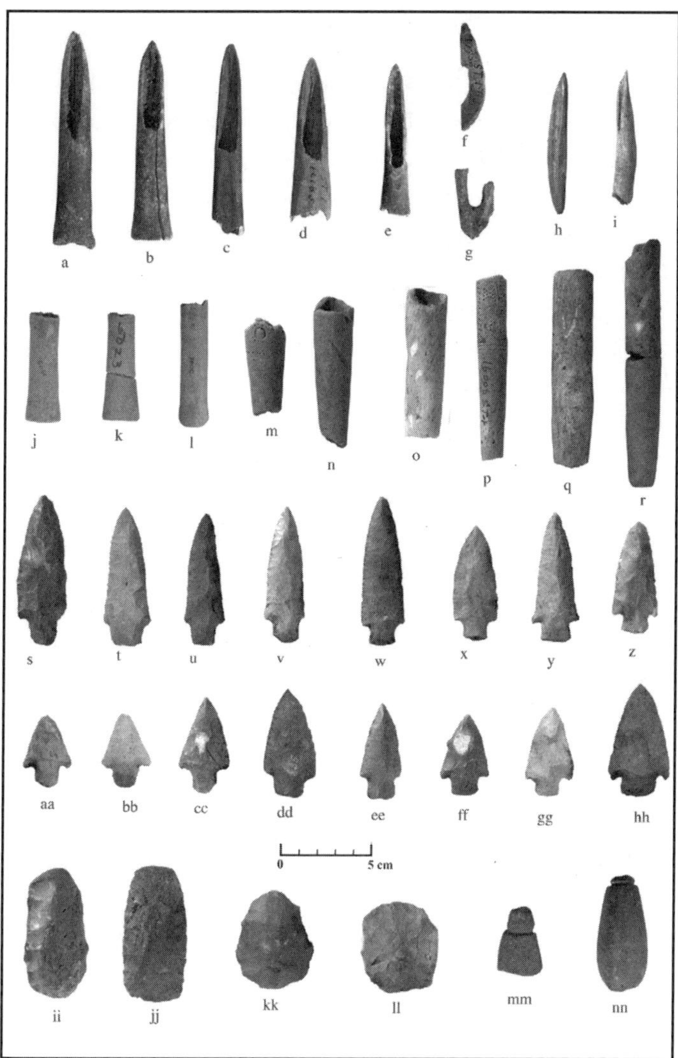

Fig. 6.2. Additional Tchefuncte artifacts: a–e. Bone points fashioned from deer long bones; f–g. Bone fishhook blank fragments; h. Possible bone fishing gorge; i. Bone point or perforator; j–r. Tubular ceramic pipe fragments (m and p are decorated with incised lines and tiny punctations); s–hh. Stone projectile points; ii–jj. Rectangular adzes or celts; kk–ll. Probable cores; mm–nn. Plummets. All from the Tchefuncte site (16ST1). Note that a, c, e, h–m, p, r, aa–bb, mm–nn were previously illustrated by Ford and Quimby (1945) as Figures 7a–b, h, n, p–q, 8h, j–k, 10a, f, 12e–f, m–o, t; g–h, j, p–q, w, y, mm–nn were previously illustrated by Neuman (1984) as Plates 19i, k, m, 20c, e, 22h, j, 23e, l; and a–b, e, m–p, t–u, w, y were previously illustrated by Weinstein (1986) as Figures 9.5A, C–D, 9.6B–E, 9.7A–B, F, J. Printed from 1940s negatives on file at the Museum of Natural Science, Louisiana State University. Photographs courtesy of Rebecca Saunders. Arranged by Donald G. Hunter.

a ceremonial or ritual use of some bone elements (e.g., deer antler still attached to the crania for use in masks and turtle-shell rattles; Lewis 1997:62–63).

Lithic artifacts are much less common than ceramics at most Tchefuncte sites (Figure 6.2). In Jim Morehead's analysis of the Big Oak and Little Oak Island assemblages, the most common projectile point types included Pontchartrain and Ellis, and in lesser numbers Kents, Maçons, and Garys (Morehead 1980; Shenkel 1984b:57–58; see also Ford and Quimby 1945:32–36, Figure 8; Weinstein 1986:Figure 9.7). Kidder (2007b:21) notes a consistent association of Kent points with components of the Panther Lake phase of Tchefuncte culture in northeast Louisiana. Debitage, burins, notched pieces, and denticulates were also found. Tchefuncte sites also contain ground stone tools, including plummets, hammerstones, bar weights, mortars, and occasionally soapstone fragments (Ford and Quimby 1945:37–41; Shenkel 1984b). Small numbers of baked-clay Poverty Point objects (PPOs) are sometimes found on Tchefuncte sites. For example, the Tchefuncte site contained only four PPOs, which is about .0001 percent of the ceramic total. By contrast, even a relatively small Poverty Point site such as Terral Lewis (16MA16) contained around five hundred PPOs (Ford and Quimby 1945: 14–15; Webb 1977:25).

SETTLEMENT PATTERNS AND PHASES

Tchefuncte folk were hunters, fishers, and gatherers who lived in small hamlets primarily in eastern Louisiana and all along its coast, with some sites in western Mississippi and southeast Texas. The seasonal range represented by the animal and fish bones in Tchefuncte middens indicates that the Tchefuncte were a relatively sedentary people who lived in these camps or villages nearly year-round. Another indication that at least some of these camps were occupied almost year-round is that a few sites (e.g., the Tchefuncte site, Big and Little Oak Islands) contain upwards of 50,000 sherds, numerous burials, and a wide variety of bone implements.

Tchefuncte sites have been found as far north as southeastern Arkansas and west-central Mississippi, but most are concentrated in eastern Louisiana. In fact, in northern Louisiana, Tchefuncte sites are generally not found west of the Ouachita River basin (Jeter and Williams 1989a:118). Tchefuncte groups appear to have lived in relatively autonomous and isolated communities. Even the largest sites typically have only a few long-distance exchange items, such as steatite, quartz crystals, and orthoquartzite (Shenkel 1984b; Weinstein and Rivet 1978). The presence of Alexander series pottery in small numbers at a few Tchefuncte sites, as mentioned earlier, indicates some type of contact with groups east of the LMV.

Toth (1988: 21–23) notes that Tchefuncte sites are typically situated near slow-moving, secondary streams, such as Bayou Maçon or Bayou Teche, in a "slack-water environment." They are rarely found along the Mississippi River and its more active tributaries and distributaries (e.g., the Atchafalaya and Red rivers). Gibson (1974b:85, 1976; Gibson and Shenkel 1988:13–14) and Kidder (2007b:24) argue that non-coastal Tchefuncte settlement in both south-central and northeast Louisiana consisted of residential sites of various sizes grouped around a ceremonial mound site that included at least one probable mortuary structure. Gibson (1974b:85) regarded the residential sites as seasonal base camps or semi-permanent villages that occupied relatively high ground on the natural levees of the ancient Teche-Mississippi or the edge of the Pleistocene Terrace that flanked the Mississippi floodplain to the west. Kidder (2007b:24) suggested a community in the Tensas Basin that extended outward from the central mound site for a distance of about 10 kilometers (6.2 mi).

Shenkel (1984b) noted two principal site types in the eastern Mississippi Delta area. One type consisted of massive shell middens (e.g., Big Oak Island and Bayou Jasmine). As noted, these appear to be specialized hunting and fishing locales. The other site type was a village/base camp (e.g., Little Oak Island), with an extensive earthen midden containing dense artifact and faunal concentrations and post holes indicative of some type of structure. The post holes at Little Oak Island evince no clear structural patterns, but Shenkel and Holley (1975:232–233) have suggested that they might have represented a shed-like structure. The only other known Tchefuncte site with definite post holes is the Lafayette Mounds (16SM17), which had post holes on a pre-mound floor that included an arc, suggestive of a circular structure (Ford and Quimby 1945:21–22). It should be noted that Greenwell (1984:141, Figure 5.8) reported finding "portions of house patterns" at two sites in the Biloxi area of coastal Mississippi, which he considered to be associated with Tchefuncte culture. However, only one of these locales (Harvey, 22HA534) was identified by name or site number, and more recent and reliable research by Blitz and Mann (2000:32–34, 178) indicates that the site did not have a substantial Tchefuncte occupation, if one at all.

Over a decade ago, Weinstein (1995:166–169, Figure 5) identified twelve named Tchefuncte phases and at least three areas of Tchefuncte site groups that had not received phase designations. This is still the situation today (Figure 6.3), although we now know that the eastern portion of one of the unnamed areas (the Mississippi coast) can be placed in the Apple Street phase, a cultural manifestation marked by a mixture of Bayou La Batre, Alexander, and Tchefuncte series ceramics, with the first two predominating (Blitz and Mann 2000:22–25, 98,

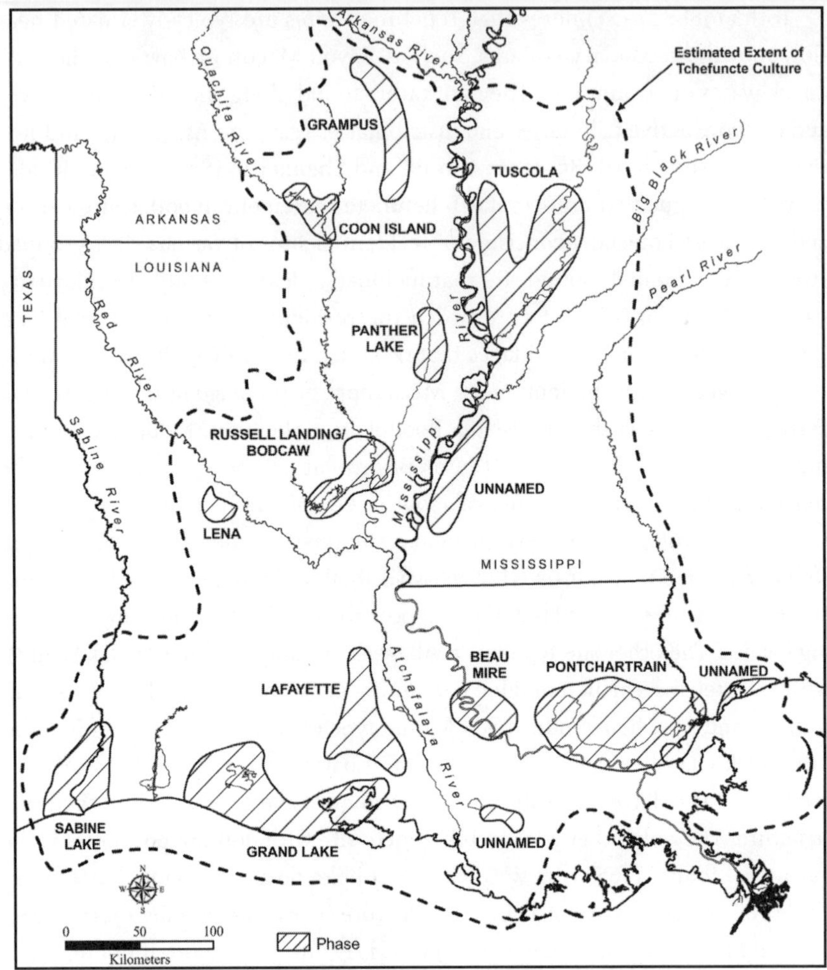

Fig. 6.3. Locations of phases associated with Tchefuncte culture.
Map by Thurston H. G. Hahn III.

Figure 3.6). The western portion of the Mississippi coast still remains unnamed and virtually unknown today. Regardless, all Tchefuncte phases and site clusters are marked by a very homogeneous set of pottery types, which are the principal means used in identifying a Tchefuncte occupation. The presence or absence of specific types, or any of their related varieties, is the primary factor utilized in distinguishing one phase from another. Diagnostic ceramic markers consist of the types Tchefuncte Plain, Tchefuncte Incised, Tchefuncte Stamped, Lake Borgne Incised, Tammany Punctated, Orleans Punctated, and Jaketown Simple Stamped. Alexander series pottery is found primarily in the eastern phases and includes O'Neal Plain, Alexander Incised, Alexander Pinched, Smithsonia Zone Stamped, Mandeville Stamped, and probably Chinchuba Brushed.

SUBSISTENCE

Since most of what we know about Tchefuncte is based on coastal sites, it is not surprising that the available subsistence data indicate a strong dependence on riverine and coastal flora and fauna. Coastal sites typically contain abundant amounts of shellfish, most commonly the brackish-water clam *Rangia cuneata*, but remains of oysters (*Crassostrea virginica*) also have been recovered (e.g., from the Tchefuncte site). Apparently, Tchefuncte people also used a wide variety of mammalian taxa (deer, otter, wolf, bear, fox, cougar, and raccoon), birds (duck, geese, eagle, goose, swan, and crane), reptiles (turtle, snake, and alligator), amphibians (frogs), and fish (sheepshead, gar, shark, and drum) (Byrd 1974, 1994; Lewis 1997). In the Tchefuncte component at Morton Shell Mound (16IB3) in Iberia Parish, Byrd (1974, 1994) found several types of plant remains, including squash, bottle gourd, greenbrier, persimmon, knotweed, wild plum, grape, and haws. The squash remains are the earliest found on the Gulf Coast (Neuman 1984:160).

MOUNDS

The question of whether Tchefuncte people constructed mounds of any type is somewhat contentious. Late Tchula period burial mounds are unquestionable elements of the Lake Cormorant culture located in northwest Mississippi (Ford 1990; Rafferty 2002). There also is good evidence that Lake Cormorant folks built flat-topped, pyramidal mounds (Holland-Lilly 1996; Johnson et al. 2002). Therefore, it should come as no surprise to find mounds in similar late Tchefuncte contexts. Nevertheless, the presence of mounds at sites with Tchefuncte components has long been a topic of discussion and moderate skepticism (see Ford 1990; Gibson 1974b, 1976; Neuman 1984:134–135; Toth 1988; Weinstein 1986).

Some of the clearest evidence in favor of Tchefuncte mounds comes from the Lafayette Mounds site (Ford and Quimby 1945). A review of the site was presented previously by Weinstein (1986:115–117, Figures 9.9–9.10), but it is worth repeating because of the importance of the locale:

> Located along the natural levee of the ancient Teche-Mississippi channel, the site consisted of three low, circular mounds. . . . These measured

> 5 feet high by 60 feet in diameter, 4 feet high by 50 feet in diameter and one foot high by 40 feet in diameter (Ford and Quimby 1945:21). Only one of the mounds, the tallest, was excavated. . . .
>
> The premound surface consisted of a shallow, irregular depression apparently scooped out of the natural levee deposits, and upon which several structures were built and burials laid. An arc of post molds suggests that at least one of the premound structures was circular. All of the approximately 30 burials were placed either on the premound floor or on one or two earthen levels piled atop the floor. All were then covered by a thick mantle of soil creating a primary mound. Of the 30 burials, eight were flexed . . . and 12 were bundled or reburials. Ten burials could not be interpreted adequately. No burial furniture was found. All of the ceramics incorporated within the primary mantle were Tchefuncte types.
>
> A secondary mantle, which lacked burials, was constructed upon the primary mantle. Sherds in the secondary mantle consisted of Tchefuncte, Marksville, and Plaquemine types. [Weinstein 1986:115–117]

Previously, Weinstein (1986:117) made the argument that, since Tchefuncte materials dominated the mound assemblage at the site, with the only non-Tchefuncte material (a few late prehistoric sherds) coming from a shallow pit at the top of the mound, the mound is Tchefuncte in origin. It should be noted, furthermore, that Ford, Quimby, and the mound's excavators (Doran and Neitzel) also thought that the Lafayette Mounds were part of the Tchefuncte culture. Most recently, Melançon (1999) seriated the Tchefuncte ceramics from the locale, and this placed the occupation midway in his chronological sequence of several Lafayette phase sites.

In addition to the Lafayette Mounds, test excavations at the Meche-Wilkes Mound (16SL18) on Coulee de Marks in St. Landry Parish (Gibson 1990:117; Gibson and Shenkel 1988:12) recorded only Tchefuncte and Wheeler series ceramics, a few baked-clay Poverty Point–like objects, and scattered dart points and flakes. No post-Tchefuncte material reportedly came from the mound fill. When Melançon (1999) seriated the Tchefuncte assemblage, he found that the occupation occurred early within the Lafayette phase. Overall, when these Lafayette phase data are coupled with evidence of earlier Archaic and Poverty Point period mounds, as summarized by Gibson (1994a), Gibson and Shenkel (1988), Russo (1994a, 1994b; Russo and Fogleman 1996), R. Saunders (1994), Saunders and Allen (1997), and Saunders et al. (1994, 1997, 2005), the case for Tchefuncte burial mounds becomes ever more convincing.

Perhaps the best recent evidence in favor of Tchefuncte mounds comes from four test units dug to subsoil in the flanks of the five-meter-tall conical mound at the St. Mary's Mound site (16MA62) in Madison Parish (Kidder 2007b). These revealed a rich but thin (10- to 15-cm thick) pre-mound Tchefuncte midden capped by mound fill. The presence of a very sharp contact between the midden and the mound fill, and a clear continuity in ceramics between the two, suggest that there was very little time separating the end of midden creation and the beginning of mound construction (Kidder 2007b:10). Most compelling of all was the discovery of a trash pit (Feature 7) positioned about midway up the south flank of the mound. Clearly dug after the mound had been built, this pit contained a pure Tchefuncte assemblage of 97 sherds and yielded a calibrated 2-sigma ^{14}C date range of ca. 390 to 90 B.C. (Kidder 2007b:Tables 2, 5). This matched very well four of the five calibrated ^{14}C 2-sigma date ranges from the pre-mound midden at the site: ca. 385 to 185 B.C., ca. 395 to 205 B.C., ca. 360 B.C. to A.D. 80, and ca. 405 to 210 B.C. (Kidder 2007b:Table 5). One other date from the pre-mound midden was a bit earlier, yielding a calibrated 2-sigma range of ca. 760 to 410 B.C. (Kidder 2007b:Table 5). Not enough of the mound was investigated to determine if it contains burials, although Kidder (2007b:34) suggests this is likely. Lastly, Ford and Quimby (1945:21–24) have argued that mounds at the Lake Louis (16CT24) and Boothe Landing (16CT31) sites (both in Catahoula Parish) were also Tchefuncte mounds, but the evidence for these is equivocal and no recent work has been conducted at either site to address this issue.

MORTUARY DATA

Typically the Tchefuncte buried their dead in shallow, unadorned graves in midden deposits (Ford and Quimby 1945:25–26; Jeter and Williams 1989a). The bodies are often flexed, and sometimes the leg bones are broken, which may be the only direct physical evidence for any ritualized behavior in their mortuary treatments (Lewis 1991). Secondary bundle burials are also found and sometimes the bones are scattered in the midden. The burials typically contain no grave goods; the only exception is a grave at one of the Little Woods Middens (16OR1–5) that contained two quartz crystals (Ford and Quimby 1945). Since the bones typically are poorly preserved, we have no systematic overview of the health of the population (see the discussion on the bioarchaeology of the Tchefuncte in Rose and Harmon 1989:340–341). In one of the more recent studies of Tchefuncte skeletal remains, Lewis (1994) found evidence for extensive treponemal infection in the Tchefuncte site population. This bacterial infection causes conditions such as yaws and syphilis. The only data on mound burials come from the Lafayette Mounds. There, 26.7 percent of the 30 burials uncovered were flexed, 40 percent were bundled, and the remaining 33.3 percent were of unknown position. None contained any grave goods.

Recent Research on Tchefuncte

TCHEFUNCTE ORIGINS

As noted above, Tchefuncte culture was definitely in existence and relatively widespread in Louisiana by about 800 B.C. There are Tchefuncte sites in both northern Louisiana and coastal Louisiana with radiocarbon dates around that time. However, recent research at Poverty Point indicates that Tchefuncte pottery was present in relatively small numbers by at least the end of the Poverty Point period, possibly several hundred years prior to 800 B.C. Our analysis of early pottery sherds at the Poverty Point site found 153 Tchefuncte sherds, including the types Tchefuncte Plain, Tchefuncte Incised, Tchefuncte Stamped, and Tammany Punctated (Hays and Weinstein 2004). Ortman's (2003) recent work at Poverty Point also found a relatively small number of Tchefuncte sherds and a similar range of types.

It is worth noting that this is a relatively non-diverse assemblage when compared to the varied suite of types and varieties that one sees at classic Tchefuncte sites, such as the Tchefuncte site itself, Bayou Jasmine, and Big Oak Island. For example, the Poverty Point assemblage lacks any clear examples of the common types Orleans Punctated and Lake Borgne Incised, and the range of varieties of the existing types is also very limited. Jaketown Simple Stamped, which was abundant in the Tchefuncte levels at the Jaketown site, is also uncommon at Poverty Point. Our analysis of 642 sherds from Poverty Point produced only two of this type (Hays and Weinstein 2004:157).

One important research question concerning the Tchefuncte pottery at Poverty Point is whether or not it was locally manufactured. Gibson (1995:70–72, Figure 4, 2000:117–119, Figure 6.4, 2007:512) has conjectured that Poverty Point was a largely independent center of early southeastern pottery manufacture, producing a pottery series that he labeled "Old Floyd" Tchefuncte. Specifically, he suggested that "the early age of 'Old Floyd' Tchefuncte at Poverty Point means that the Tchefuncte decoration complex arose in the Lower Mississippi Valley, possibly at or around the Poverty Point site" (Gibson 1995:70). We, however, see no substantial difference between the manufacturing techniques used to create Tchefuncte vessels at Poverty Point and those employed at other sites, such as

Bayou Jasmine (Hays and Weinstein 2004:225–226). Therefore, we argue that the term "Old Floyd" is not typologically meaningful. We maintain, furthermore, that it is much more likely that most, if not all, of the Tchefuncte pottery at Poverty Point was not manufactured at the site but possibly was transported to the locale through the same or similar exchange networks that brought in other exotic goods (Hays and Weinstein 2004:163). Stoltman's (2004) petrographic analysis of Tchefuncte sherds from Poverty Point also indicates that they were not manufactured from local clay sources, or at least not from the sources used by Poverty Point residents to manufacture their ubiquitous PPOs. This raises the question, then—where did the Tchefuncte pottery originate?

Elsewhere, we consider this question in more detail (Hays and Weinstein 2004). We noted that there were four possibilities: (1) the Catahoula Basin, which has an early dated Tchefuncte component; (2) sites of the Pontchartrain phase in coastal Louisiana, such as Bayou Jasmine, with its deep, thick, and relatively early Tchefuncte deposits, which have produced calibrated radiocarbon dates between 3370 and 2730 B.P. (1420 and 780 B.C.); (3) sites of the McGary phase in the Yazoo Basin (Williams and Brain 1983:355); and (4) sites of the so-called "Teche cluster" (Weinstein 1995) in south-central Louisiana. Any one of these four areas may provide the key to understanding the development of Tchefuncte pottery.

Furthermore, we suggest that Tchefuncte pottery most likely developed out of ceramic types that originated east of the LMV and most probably in a coastal region. Most scholars agree that the varied surface treatments found on Tchefuncte pottery (i.e., combinations of incising, cordmarking, rocker stamping, and punctating) are the result of an amalgamation of influences of earlier pottery series that began east of the LMV, including St. Johns, Wheeler, Bayou La Batre, Stallings, Thoms Creek, and Refuge (e.g., Blitz and Mann 2000; Jenkins and Krause 1986; Jenkins et al. 1986). Indeed, some southeastern archaeologists prefer the term "Gulf Formational" period when discussing archaeological cultures along or near the Gulf and South Atlantic coasts that developed early ceramics that were quite different from contemporary pottery assemblages manufactured north of the Fall Line (Saunders and Hays 2004). In this sequence, Tchefuncte culture is considered to be part of the Late Gulf Formational period (Jenkins and Krause 1986).

Several researchers (Blitz and Mann 2000:20; Jenkins et al. 1986:550; Webb 1977) have suggested that the Poverty Point–age Claiborne site (22HA501) near the mouth of the Pearl River may have served as a conduit for dispersing valued goods from the Mississippi coast to the LMV. This seems to be a reasonable route for St. Johns pottery to have traveled, given that it is the only other known Poverty Point–age site (besides Poverty Point itself) with true St. Johns pottery (Gagliano and Webb 1970). We have examined some of the St. Johns sherds from the Claiborne site that are housed at Coastal Environments, Inc., in Baton Rouge, and they appear macroscopically and microscopically identical to the St. Johns sherds found at the Poverty Point site.

In fact, we argue that the importation of the St. Johns series pottery into the LMV may have been a very crucial impetus for the development of Tchefuncte pottery (see also Jenkins et al. 1986; Shenkel 1984b:47, 62). Elsewhere, we have established that the earliest dated pottery in the LMV is St. Johns pottery, which was concentrated in the lowest levels of the Poverty Point site and radiocarbon dated to between 3160 and 3040 B.P. (1210 and 1090 B.C.) (Hays and Weinstein 2004:159). The vast majority of Tchefuncte pottery appears stratigraphically above the St. Johns pottery at Poverty Point and continues to the top of the stratigraphic sequence. Therefore, it appears that Tchefuncte ceramics were developed subsequent to the importation of St. Johns pottery. But what relationship, if any, did these two series have to each other?

Over thirty years ago, Bullen (1972, 1974) observed that in many respects Tchefuncte pottery appeared to copy St. Johns pottery (see also Shenkel 1984b:62). For example, Bullen (1974:83) noted, "Tchefuncte pottery used a paste like St. Johns Plain but added lumps of clay. Some Tchefuncte Incised vessels clearly used Orange or St. Johns Incised designs." Likewise he noted that "examination of the Tchefuncte Plain (cat. no. 103296) sherds in the Poverty Point collection [at the Florida State Museum] shows a similar situation. All appear chalky and many are identical to early St. Johns Plain pottery from Florida" (Bullen 1974:80). Indeed both series typically have a chalky paste, are low-fired, and have similar incised and punctated designs. One primary difference between the two pottery series not noted by Bullen, however, is that St. Johns is tempered with sponge spicules while, notwithstanding Bullen's quotation above, Tchefuncte is not tempered. The chalky feel to St. Johns pottery is due to the sloughing of the sponge spicules (Borremans and Shaak 1986:127–128), whereas the chalky feel characteristic of some Tchefuncte pottery is due primarily to its high silt content.

For many years, however, archaeologists referred to St. Johns pottery as temperless, since the spicules are invisible in the paste unless you examine a sherd with at least a 60x level of magnification. It is only since about the mid-1980s that archaeologists examined St. Johns pottery at magnification levels sufficient to observe the spicules (e.g., Borremans and Shaak 1986; Haag 1990). Even today, archaeologists refer to a temperless pottery in the Gulf Coastal region (e.g., Blitz and

Mann 2000), which we suspect may be St. Johns spiculate-tempered pottery but which has not been examined at sufficient magnification to observe the spicules.

In sum, we suggest that, following Bullen and Shenkel, local LMV people may have first created Tchefuncte pottery as an attempt at copying the earliest ceramics—St. Johns pottery—then being imported into the region. These early LMV potters created the distinctive and virtually unique temperless Tchefuncte paste, since they could not see with the naked eye the temper in the St. Johns pottery any more than the archaeologists. When they made local copies of the St. Johns series, they thus replicated the vessel shapes and design elements and even the chalky texture of the paste (although probably accidentally), but, because they could not see the spiculate temper, they did not exactly replicate the paste.

While characteristics of Tchefuncte ceramics may have been primarily influenced by St. Johns pottery, it is clear that the varied array of Tchefuncte surface treatments reflect the influence of several other pottery series (St. Johns, Bayou La Batre, and Wheeler) that also developed east of the LMV. Wheeler decorative treatments appear to have been the most influential. Both Ford et al. (1955) and Jenkins et al. (1986) have noted that several of the classic Tchefuncte types at the Jaketown site had surface treatments (e.g., Tammany Punctated, Jaketown Simple Stamped) that were nearly identical to those found in preceding fiber-tempered Wheeler types. Elsewhere, Weinstein (1995:160–161) makes this argument in more detail.

In several respects, however, the assemblage of Tchefuncte pottery at Poverty Point is quite unlike that associated with later, classic Tchefuncte sites. As noted above, the Tchefuncte pottery at Poverty Point is comparatively non-diverse in decorative styles, and there is only a relatively small amount of the ware at the site. In fact, the paucity of all pottery types at Poverty Point is relatively difficult to explain. If the Poverty Point people knew of pottery, why didn't they produce it in large quantities for use in cooking and other utilitarian tasks? They certainly knew how to make thousands upon thousands of PPOs. For now, the only viable proposition is Sassaman's (1993) hypothesis that Poverty Point leaders in control of the steatite trade may have actively suppressed the manufacturing of pottery in their communities. Therefore, while Tchefuncte pottery may have had its origins in late Poverty Point, the Tchefuncte culture, as defined above, did not begin in earnest until about several hundred years after the Poverty Point culture collapsed. But what would have caused this hiatus between the cultures?

Kidder (2006) has recently proposed that the Poverty Point–Tchefuncte disjuncture is due primarily to widespread climate change. He develops this argument by first noting that a disjuncture between Late Archaic and Early Woodland is actually a widespread trend in areas with large rivers in the eastern woodlands. In several large riverine areas there is evidence for a temporal hiatus of a couple hundred years between Late Archaic and Early Woodland cultures, and often the Woodland cultures are quite distinct from the preceding cultures. For example, Emerson and McElrath (2001) assert that Early Woodland immigrants replaced local Archaic populations in the American Bottom. Kidder (2006:212) argues that "there is no unambiguous evidence of temporal continuity from Late Archaic to Early Woodland in any region of Mississippi River basin where there are good data." The most relevant illustration of this pattern comes from Kidder's analysis of radiocarbon dates from Poverty Point and Tchefuncte sites. This analysis revealed a gap of several hundred years (from 3100 to 2700 B.P,) between the cultures (Kidder 2006:203).

Kidder proposes that this widespread cultural and temporal disjuncture was due primarily to climatic change. Specifically, he cites abundant geomorphological data indicating that between 3000 and 2600 B.P. (1050 and 650 B.C.), the climate became cooler and wetter, resulting in massive flooding in the Mississippi River basin. He argues that the floodplain sites favored by Late Archaic cultures, such as Poverty Point, would have become uninhabitable during much of this period, which would account very nicely for the Poverty Point–Tchefuncte cultural disjuncture. He notes in support of his argument that the Late Archaic–Early Woodland disjuncture did not occur in upland regions away from the major river bottoms. Kidder's hypothesis is both provocative and testable, and it should spur very productive research on the Late Archaic–Early Woodland transition throughout eastern North America.

RESEARCH ON STYLISTIC AND CHRONOLOGICAL ISSUES OF TCHEFUNCTE POTTERY

In our analysis of the pottery assemblage from Bayou Jasmine, we were hoping to find evidence for the transition between the Poverty Point and Tchefuncte cultures, mainly since earlier collections obtained from dredge material at the site included abundant evidence of both cultures (Hays and Weinstein 1999). Unfortunately, the 1975 LSU excavations did not reach the Poverty Point levels because of time and monetary constraints. Our analysis of the assemblage, however, produced a substantial body of data about Tchefuncte culture, since it is the largest Tchefuncte pottery assemblage (over 15,000 sherds) from a stratified site (2.2 m or 7.2 ft in depth). In addition, we ran ten radiocarbon assays to get some chronological control. For various reasons, however, these assays yielded some contradictory dates (one of the dates from the middle of the midden was later than those above it), which made interpreting them problematic (Hays and Weinstein 1999:57–65). Nevertheless, the average of the intercepts from the six assays associated with sealed archaeological features yielded a date of 797 B.C., which is consistent with the approximately 800 B.C. date from the Tchefuncte component at the Cross Bayou site (16CT365) in Catahoula Parish (Gibson 1991). It is also worth noting that the early end of the two-sigma range for some of the samples from Bayou Jasmine was ca. 1000–1200 B.C., and this may indicate an even earlier starting date for Tchefuncte.

Our analysis of the pottery revealed some interesting patterns, allowing us to establish a new Tchefuncte type and several new varieties. The most striking pattern was that all of the basic types and most of the varieties of Tchefuncte pottery were present in the lowest and earliest part of the midden. This same pattern was found in the earliest Tchefuncte levels at both Big Oak Island and Jaketown (Ford et al. 1955; Shenkel 1980). Indeed, Ford et al. (1955:62) state that "there is every indication that pottery appeared at Jaketown as a fully developed complex." One other interesting general trend was that there was more decorated pottery in the bottom half of the midden than in the top half. When we looked for changes in the specific types and varieties, no particularly strong trends emerged; all types were present throughout the entire midden deposit. Earlier in this chapter, we noted that the types and varieties of Tchefuncte pottery at Poverty Point are noticeably less diverse than those at Jaketown, Bayou Jasmine, and Big Oak Island. Perhaps the Tchefuncte assemblage at Poverty Point is less varied than the Tchefuncte assemblages at the other sites because it predates them, but frankly we consider this to be an open question.

Although most of the assemblage easily fits into established types and varieties, we found it necessary to define a new variety of Orleans Punctated (*var. Jasmine*), as well as a completely new type—Chene Blanc Plain. The first simply reflects a decorative motif that was found only in the deepest levels analyzed and may represent an early Tchefuncte variety (Hays and Weinstein 1999:70–73). The latter includes two varieties, one (*var. Chene Blanc*) consisting of relatively thick sherds with a non-laminated, reduced paste that contained specks of hematite, bone, and possibly shell, and another (*var. Fountain*) that had the same basic paste, but was highly oxidized and included small fragments of grog temper (Hays and Weinstein 1999:66–69). Both varieties exhibited typical Tchefuncte vessel attributes, such as teat- and wedge-shaped podal supports and notched rims. However, while *var. Chene Blanc* occurred throughout all of the analyzed levels (thus suggesting that it was a minor but consistent element during the entire Tchefuncte sequence at Bayou Jasmine), *var. Fountain* was found only in the very uppermost levels at the site, which also contained early Marksville period ceramics. Given the fact that other examples of *var. Fountain* have been found at the Lee (16EBR51) and Sarah Peralta (16EBR67) sites in East Baton Rouge Parish in contexts that also contained early Marksville ceramics (Perrault and Weinstein 1994; Weinstein 1996), this variety most likely represents an early Marksville period ware that retained many characteristics typical of Tchefuncte vessels (Hays and Weinstein 1999:69).

Ford and Willey (1940:Figure 22b) illustrated a vessel from Mound A at the Crooks site (16LA3), an early Marksville period burial mound in LaSalle Parish, which might be similar to *var. Fountain*. That vessel, identified as Marksville Plain (now Baytown Plain, *var. Marksville*), exhibits four nub-like feet reminiscent of Tchefuncte podal supports, and it undoubtedly shows a continuation into the Marksville period of this typical Tchefuncte vessel trait. Even more obvious of a late Tchefuncte/early Marksville continuum are two vessels unearthed in Mound C at Helena Crossing (3PH11), also an early Marksville period burial mound located in east-central Arkansas (Ford 1963). The vessels were discovered in two different "pottery deposits" that were thought to represent the remains of vessels scooped up with general soil in basket loads that were used to build the mound. One is a probable vessel of Indian Bay Stamped, which exhibits four classic teat-shaped podal supports around the base of what appears to be a typical Tchefuncte jar (Ford 1963:32–33, Figure 30a). The other also exhibits four teat-shaped podal supports on a jar that is divided into four lobes by raised ridges that seem to extend upward from each of the supports (Ford 1963:37, Figure 32f). Of particular interest is the fact that this second vessel had been decorated with a cord-wrapped paddle, thus classifying it today as an example of Mulberry Creek Cord Marked.

Perhaps most interesting in regard to the Tchefuncte/Marksville transition is an ossuary unearthed by Shenkel (1984a) in the upper levels of the northern end of the Big Oak Island site that dated to the last century B.C. In addition to the recovery of numerous disarticulated human remains from several bone concentrations, one of which, at least, included bodies possibly removed from a charnel house and buried during a single event (Shenkel 1984a:116–117), the excavations also uncovered several vessels with classic Marksville designs and decorative techniques (raptorial bird motifs, hemiconical punctations, and zoned dentate stamping) on typical contorted and laminated Tchefuncte paste. Included were portions of vessels identified as Mabin Stamped, *vars. Crooks* and *Point Lake*, and Marksville Incised, *var. unspecified* (Shenkel 1984a:110–111, 113, Figures 7–9). Also present was a sherd with a Tchefuncte-like design (Tammany Punctated, *var. Dutch Town*) on a non-laminated paste typical of most Marksville pottery (Shenkel 1984a:113, Figure 10c). Unfortunately, Shenkel did not specify whether the paste of the Mabin Stamped and Marksville Incised vessels also contained grog, a necessity in sorting true Tchefuncte ware from later Marksville-related pastes. Weinstein has noted that very early Marksville ceramics often have a contorted and laminated paste similar to Tchefuncte, although they invariably contain grog. Slightly later Marksville ceramics have more abundant grog and are not contorted or laminated. Regardless, the ceramics from the Big Oak ossuary clearly show a continuation of late Tchefuncte ceramic technology into early Marksville pottery.

Recently, Fullen (2005) conducted an interesting and innovative study of the Tchefuncte pottery at the Sarah Peralta and Bayou Jasmine sites. He measured the numbers and types of contortions and laminations in Tchefuncte pottery and hypothesized that there would be fewer of both over time as Tchefuncte potters became better at their craft. The assemblage at Sarah Peralta confirmed his hypothesis, as there was a gradual progression of fewer laminations and contortions from the bottom to the top of the site. The Bayou Jasmine assemblage, however, had relatively few laminations and contortions on the whole, and there was no progressive trend (Fullen 2005:107). Fullen (2005:108–109) argued that this was due to two factors. First, he suggested that the entire Bayou Jasmine midden accumulated relatively quickly, around 800 B.C., and thus one would not expect to see much change in the assemblage. Second, he argued that even though the Bayou Jasmine assemblage is very early in the Tchefuncte cultural sequence, the pottery was relatively refined because it was on the coast and therefore subject to influences from several other pottery traditions. He also suggested that Bayou Jasmine may have been the site of elite feasting, so the pottery would be comparatively refined (Fullen 2005:108).

While Fullen's study is to be applauded for its innovative methods, we offer two caveats. First, we think that it would be difficult to consistently measure the presence and type of contortions and laminations in Tchefuncte pottery. Second, while our analysis of Bayou Jasmine acknowledged the possibility that the midden accumulated rapidly around 800 B.C., we considered it unlikely since the upper levels contained both Marksville sherds and the transitional *Fountain* variety of Chene Blanc Plain. The site also was occupied during late Tchula/early Marksville times (Hays and Weinstein 1999:61).

In another recent study, Melançon (1999) used Ford's seriation method to monitor five Tchefuncte ceramic decoration styles at seven sites in south-central Louisiana. In this region, he found that Tchefuncte Stamped was the most popular style, followed by Lake Borgne Incised, Tchefuncte Incised, Orleans Punctated, and Tammany Punctated. Moreover, the data indicated that Tchefuncte Stamped was popular right up to Marksville times, Tchefuncte Incised lost popularity in late Tchula times, and Tammany Punctated was popular in early Tchefuncte times but gradually became less so. It should be noted that these data are in contrast to those from the Beau Mire site, where Weinstein and Rivet (1978) recorded relatively large percentages of Tchefuncte Incised, Tammany Punctated, and Lake Borgne Incised, as well as minor amounts of Tchefuncte Stamped in what was considered to be a late Tchula period assemblage. These patterns suggest regional variability in the popularity of Tchefuncte pottery stylistic motifs.

Finally, recent field and laboratory research has taken place in numerous locales in Louisiana. McGimsey (2001, 2003a) has reported on Tchefuncte components at the Marksville site (16AV1) and Morton Shell Mound, but the most intensive recent work on Tchefuncte has taken place in northeast Louisiana. Primarily, this research has focused on the poorly understood Panther Lake phase of the Tensas Basin. Kidder (2007b) and his students have conducted recent investigations at several sites with Tchefuncte components in Madison Parish: Raffman (16MA20), St. Mary's Mound, and Borrow Pit (16MA57). Burke (2002) has argued that Tchefuncte Cord Impressed, *var. St. Mary,* is the decorated ceramic marker of the Panther Lake phase, since it is found at all of these sites. Other decorated types common to the phase are Tchefuncte Incised, and, in small quantities (less than 1 percent), Jaketown Simple Stamped. Most of the radiocarbon dates from these sites overlap within a calibrated range of 400 B.C. to A.D. 85 (Burke 2002:9). As noted previously, the St. Mary's Mound site contains what is unquestionably a Tchefuncte mound, but its function is unknown.

Besides the presence of at least one Tchefuncte mound, the most interesting aspect of the Panther Lake phase is the Tchefuncte Cord Impressed pottery, as that type is virtually absent at other Tchefuncte sites. It is not present at Gold Mine Plantation (16RI13), Russell Landing (16LA9), or Cross Bayou, which are all in east-central or northeast Louisiana (Gibson 1968b, 1991; McGimsey 2004). Shenkel (1980) reported finding some Tchefuncte Cord Impressed sherds at Big Oak Island, but it was not present at Bayou Jasmine, Beau Mire, or the Tchefuncte site (Ford and Quimby 1945; Hays and Weinstein 1999; Weinstein and Rivet 1978). Burke (2002:6) has asserted that the type may be more widespread than is apparent, since she believes that Tchefuncte Cord Impressed sherds have been misidentified either as Tchefuncte Incised, *var. Bogue Falaya,* or *var. Joe's Bayou.*

Summary and Conclusions

Ford and Quimby's (1945) classic monograph established the basic characteristics of Tchefuncte culture. Their descriptions of Tchefuncte artifacts, subsistence, burial patterns, site types, and site structure continue to be a very important baseline of information on the culture. Nonetheless, research on Tchefuncte remains a vital area in Louisiana archaeology and in the archaeology of the southeastern woodlands, mainly because Tchefuncte flourished during the important but still poorly understood Early Woodland period. The richness and size of Tchefuncte sites enable archaeologists to begin to address some of the most interesting and important questions of the period. As we have seen, archaeologists are examining Tchefuncte data to address questions on: (1) the timing and origin of mortuary mound building in the Southeast; (2) the development and spread of ceramics; (3) subsistence economics and health in the Early Woodland period; (4) the effects of climatic change on site settlement; and (5) in general, the transition between the Archaic and the Woodland periods. We fully expect to see continued research on Tchefuncte provide new and exciting data in the quest to understand this very important part of Louisiana's prehistoric past.

7

Marksville and Middle Woodland

CHARLES R. MCGIMSEY

Marksville. In Louisiana archaeology, the word has many meanings. The three most important are a place (the Marksville site), a time period (the Middle Woodland, Marksville period), and an archaeological culture (Marksville). Archaeologists have long assumed these concepts are all part of the same cultural expression (Neuman 1984; Toth 1979a, 1988), but as new information accumulates, the relationship between the site, the time period, and the culture is becoming more complex.

The term Marksville comes from the town of that name in Avoyelles Parish (Figure 1.2). In 1926, Gerard Fowke (1928) explored a set of mounds and earthworks just east of town. The ceramic vessels he found there were immediately recognized as stylistically similar to those found in mounds in Ohio and identified as part of the Hopewell culture (Setzler 1933a, 1933b). Thus the Marksville site, and by extension the Marksville time period and culture, became associated with the Hopewell culture of the Midwestern United States (Ford 1936).

Hopewell is a remarkable cultural expression, archaeologically recognizable for its elaborate earthworks, raw material exchange, distinctive artifact styles, and burial of honored dead within discrete tombs. Variations of these material traits can be found from Florida to Kansas City and from New York to Louisiana. Extensive investigations in the Midwest place Hopewell within the interval of A.D. 1–350 or 400. Several sites in Louisiana, including Marksville, exhibit some of these Hopewellian traits. Consequently, these traits have been used to define Marksville culture as the local version of a broader Hopewell expression that is contemporary with Hopewellian sites in the Midwest (Kidder 2002b:72–79; Toth 1974, 1979a, 1988). Over the last thirty years, however, excavations at numerous sites indicate some of these defining traits are either rare or persist well beyond the presumed end of the period at ca. A.D. 400. In this sense, the archaeological definitions of the Marksville period and Marksville culture are open to interpretation. For this book, the Marksville period is arbitrarily defined as the period between A.D. 1 and 400 (Figure 1.3). An examination of selected sites dating to this interval illustrates what is known and not known about the people who lived in Louisiana during this period, and also illuminates important yet unresolved issues about how and when the Marksville culture is defined.

Key Sites

Archaeologists recognize Marksville period sites in Louisiana almost entirely on the basis of the distinctive ceramic decorative styles, including incised geometric and zoned rocker-stamped designs. Sherds with these designs can be found across the state, although their frequency varies considerably. Sites with the greatest concentration of Marksville sherds tend to lie within the Mississippi Valley and adjoining uplands, while sites across the southwestern part of the state and in the Florida Parishes north of Lake Pontchartrain yield only a very few sherds. Marksville sherds are rare in the Kisatchie Hills and the piney hills north of Alexandria. Some sites are known along the Red River, but north of Shreveport they are generally included within the Fourche Maline culture of southwestern Arkansas (Schambach 1982a, 1998). Before further discussion of Marksville artifacts, it is worthwhile to consider what is known about some of the key sites.

MARKSVILLE (16AV1)

The Marksville site is the most important site of this period. Its core consists of a C-shaped earthen embankment enclosing forty acres and six earthen mounds (Figure 7.1). The site lies on a high bluff overlooking an abandoned channel of the Mississippi River, with the river forming the eastern margin of the site. The site plan was based on a geometric grid, with alignments to the sun, certain stars, and constellations (Davis 2005), indicating that at minimum the core or central area was a carefully planned construction.

The 950-meter-long (3,117 ft) C-shaped embankment encircling the site core is open to the east, with both ends of the embankment reaching the bluff edge. It is constructed of earth borrowed from the immediately adjacent area along the exterior edge of the embankment. The borrow area forms a shallow ditch paralleling the embankment along most of its length. The embankment presently varies in height from 0.5 to 2.5 meters (1.6 to 8.2 ft). It is lowest at the north

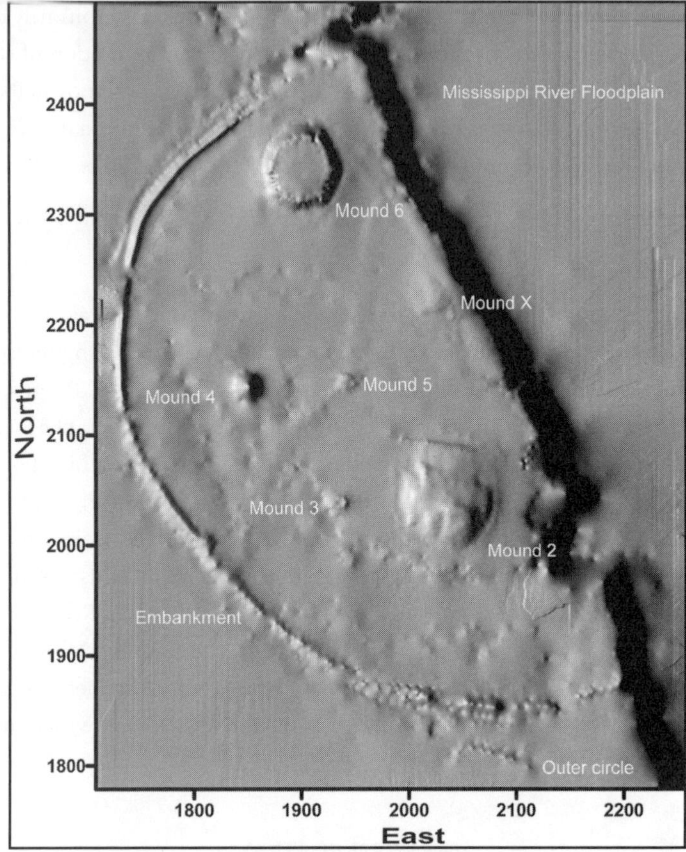

Fig. 7.1. Light Detection and Ranging (LIDAR) image of the Marksville site (16AV1).

end and slowly rises in height moving southward. This change in height compensates for the land surface slope across the site, with the absolute elevation of the embankment crest being nearly level (± 25 cm or 10 in) across its entire length. The nearly level embankment may have been constructed in this fashion to create an artificial western horizon for astronomical observations. There is no evidence that the embankment and ditch is a fortification. Rather, it defines a sacred space within.

On the south side of the embankment lies a relatively small, circular earthwork. This earthwork is approximately 100 meters (328 ft) in diameter, with walls 1 meter (3.3 ft) or less in height. It is connected to the main site area by a 2-meter-wide (6.6 ft) raised causeway built across the ditch. The causeway meets the main embankment at a double gateway, with an entrance to the main site area passing through the embankment around either side of a low mound. The purpose and function of this circular earthwork are unknown.

The six mounds within the C-shaped embankment at Marksville are variable in shape and size. The two smallest mounds, Mounds 3 and 5, are low domes 20 meters (66 ft) in diameter and approximately 1 meter (3.3 ft) high (Figure 7.1). Each is constructed entirely of white-colored earth. Mound 4 is a large conical mound 30 meters (98 ft) in diameter and 7 meters (23 ft) high. It was initially constructed as a 1.5-meter-high (5 ft) rectangular platform, upon which a series of tombs were constructed. Then the conical mound was built up over the platform, with additional burials placed in the fill as it was constructed. This is the only cemetery mound at the site. Mound 6 is a two-stage, circular platform mound approximately 95 meters (312 ft) in diameter and 4 meters (13 ft) high. Mound 2 is an irregular shaped mound, perhaps substantially altered by historic activities. It is presently 90 meters by 80 meters (295 by 263 ft) at its base and 4 meters (13 ft) tall. It is the only mound with black-colored earth included in its fill. Mound X has been significantly modified by historic activities and its original size and shape are unknown. Today it is roughly triangular in shape and 1 meter (3.3 ft) high. Other than the cemetery in Mound 4, the purpose and function of the remaining mounds are unknown. Nor is it known what the inclusion of specific colors of earth may have meant to the builders of Marksville.

The Marksville site also includes a series of small circular earthworks that vary in size from 10 to 30 meters (33 to 98 ft) in diameter. Only one was situated inside the C-shaped embankment, while at least seven others lie outside the embankment. Each has a low earthen wall, less than 1 meter (3.3 ft) high, with a shallow ditch paralleling the exterior of the wall. The interior is occupied by a semi-subterranean basin up to 1 meter (3.3 ft) deep below the ground surface. In the center of the basin is a deep pit, as much as 3 meters (9.8 ft) in diameter and 2 meters (6.6 ft) deep. Excavations have revealed that fires were repeatedly ignited within these deep pits, which were cleaned out after each use. After the last use, the pits were intentionally filled with earth, but the embankment and ditch were left to mark the location of the basin and pit. The purpose and function of these ring earthworks is unknown (McGimsey 2003b).

The Marksville site originally may have been much larger than the central, core area. Several hundred meters to the north, a second small embankment closes off a finger-like protrusion in the bluff and encloses one mound. Aerial photographs from the 1930s suggest that three other semi-circular embankments may have been present, two to the south of the main site area and one to the north, before being plowed down in the nineteenth and early twentieth centuries. These same aerial photographs also indicate that several dozen of the small ring earthworks were at one time located around and among all of these other embankments. If all of these features of the landscape were part of the Marksville site, it would have covered nearly 162 hectares (400 acres) and included up to five semi-circular embankments, seven mounds, and dozens of the smaller, circular ring earthworks.

Major excavations were undertaken at the Marksville site in 1926, 1933, 1939, and 1993, with numerous smaller projects over the last thirty years (Fowke 1928; Jones and Kuttruff 1998; Kuttruff et al. 1997; McGimsey et al. 1999, 2000, 2005; McGimsey 2001; Ryan 1975; Toth 1974; Vescelius 1957). These efforts have explored Mounds 3, 4, 5, and 6, with extensive investigations of non-mound areas around Mound 2 and along the bluff edge. Mound 4 was completely excavated in 1926 and 1933. It is consequently known to have served as a cemetery that contained the remains of at least thirty-six individuals and two dogs, buried in a series of Hopewell-like tombs. Ceramic vessels in these tombs are stylistically identical to vessels found in Hopewell tombs in Illinois and Ohio. Excavations into the other mounds at Marksville have produced no evidence of their purpose, although they were clearly not cemeteries. Beyond the mounds, artifacts and features are concentrated along the bluff edge, with material concentrated in occasional refuse piles that spill over the bluff edge. No evidence of domestic structures has been found, although two non-domestic structures have been exposed (Toth 1974). There is little evidence people lived inside the embankment. Much of the refuse may be from ceremonial activities and feasts. Radiocarbon dates indicate construction of the core site area began sometime between 50 B.C. and A.D. 1. The Marksville site was abandoned sometime after A.D. 350.

VEAZEY (16VM7/8)

Located on the Gulf Coast in Vermilion Parish (Figure 1.2), the Veazey site originally included at least fourteen mounds, but only one has produced Marksville artifacts (McGimsey 2005). Many of the other mounds may date to a subsequent Plaquemine occupation of the site (Brown 1999a). Limited test excavations by Henry Collins, Jr., into one of the mounds produced numerous human skeletal remains and several Hopewell-style artifacts; these included propeller-shaped ear spools (worn in the earlobes), bear canines with drilled holes, copper, and galena (Collins 1927a; McGimsey 2005). Test excavations in the adjoining village site produced Marksville sherds, although the associated radiocarbon date of A.D. 625 is too late for the Marksville period (Brown 1999a). The nature and extent of the Marksville presence at this site are uncertain, although the Hopewell-style artifacts found in the mound indicate that it dates to the Marksville period. Perhaps the mound explored by Collins was a Marksville period cemetery, similar to the mound at the Crooks site.

CROOKS (16LA3)

The Crooks site in LaSalle Parish was excavated by the Works Progress Administration (WPA) in 1938–1939 (Ford and Willey 1940). The larger of the two mounds at the site incorporated an earthen platform on which 382 individuals had been placed. As the mound was built up over this platform, an additional 773 people were placed in the mound. A few individuals were buried with classic Marksville or Hopewell-style artifacts, including decorated ceramic vessels, effigy and platform pipes, galena beads, and copper ear spools and beads. The smaller mound contained only fourteen individuals and no artifacts indicating the age of the mound burials. There are no radiocarbon dates from this site to further define its chronological position within the Marksville period. Nevertheless, the mounds at the Crooks site were a Marksville period ossuary (a collection of skeletal remains) where a large number of individuals were buried together, rather than in individual tombs or pits, as in Mound 4 at the Marksville site.

CORAL SNAKE MOUND (16SA48)

Coral Snake Mound lies on the western border of Louisiana in Sabine Parish and consists of a single mound excavated in 1966–1967 (Jensen 1968b). The mound has two stages overlying an initial basin. This is the only known Marksville cemetery to have included cremated burials along with bundle burials, which were placed in shallow pits. Due to poor preservation, the exact number of individuals interred in the mound is uncertain. Among the diagnostic Marksville or Hopewell-style artifacts that appear to have been placed as caches within the mound were ceramic vessels, copper ear spools, beads, a pendant, and non-local chert points. Three of the five radiocarbon dates from this site place the mound within the early to middle part of the Marksville period.

BIG OAK ISLAND (16OR6)

Lying on the south shore of Lake Pontchartrain in Orleans Parish, this site is an arcuate-shaped shell midden constructed primarily during the Tchula period (Shenkel 1984a). A low-lying knoll, or what might be an earthen mound, is located on the crest of the midden at the north end of the arc. The shell midden served as a cemetery or ossuary, which contained at least fifty individuals interred as bundle burials in a dense scatter within the knoll. Diagnostic artifacts include ceramic vessels, shell cups, one copper bead, and one tubular pipe. The ceramic vessels exhibit Marksville designs on ceramic pastes more typical of earlier, Tchula period ceramic technology (see Hays and Weinstein, Chapter 6 in this volume). Radiocarbon dates and grave goods place this ossuary in the early part of the Marksville period.

ASSESSMENT AND OTHER SITES

All but one of the sites described thus far are mound sites, and most of them are cemetery mounds. At Marksville, only one of the mounds inside the embankment served as a cemetery. The remaining mounds had different, presently unknown functions. The McGuffee site (16CT17) in Catahoula Parish has multiple mounds and an earthen embankment similar to Marksville, although McGuffee appears to be a multi-component site and the age of earthwork construction is presently uncertain (see Lee, Chapter 8 in this volume). If it is Middle Woodland in age, McGuffee would be the only other Marksville period site in Louisiana with an earthen embankment and multiple mounds.

The remaining sites described above are single or double-mound sites, or, in the case of Big Oak Island, a raised knoll on a midden, where each mound (or midden knoll) functioned as a cemetery. In addition to these sites, additional mounds for which we have limited information probably date to the Marksville period (Gibson and Shenkel 1988; Weinstein et al., ed. 2003). These investigations indicate the potential for other mounded cemeteries similar to Crooks. Most of these sites lie in the eastern part of the state within the Mississippi River Valley.

Outside of the Mississippi and Red River valleys, mounds dating to the Marksville period are extremely rare (Coral Snake Mound in the Sabine River Valley being an obvious exception). Across the southwestern one-third of the state, the northern piney hills and Florida Parishes, Marksville mounds are absent or were destroyed by modern activities before any could be recorded. Within known Marksville cemeteries, there is considerable variation in burial practices, from mass ossuaries (Big Oak Island), to single interments (Marksville Mound 4), to cremations (Coral Snake Mound, some mounds in northeastern Louisiana [Weinstein et al., ed. 2003], and Mound 8 just north of the Marksville site core [Fowke 1928]). From the perspective of the entire state, there is considerable variability in Marksville period burial traditions. This suggests similar variability in other, less well-known social patterns and cultural traditions.

The list of key sites discussed above is notable for its absence of village sites, although there were many. To date, only limited test excavations have been conducted at the numerous Marksville period village sites located across the state (Beavers 1979; Brown 1999a; Girard 1994b; Kidder 1986; Lamb 1983; McGimsey et al. 2000; Ring 1986). While these efforts have provided information on artifact assemblages and some data on subsistence, there is almost no information on structures or buildings, site organization, or the length of time villages were inhabited.

Diagnostic Artifacts and Material Exchange

Marksville sites are identified almost exclusively by the presence of incised and zoned rocker-stamped ceramics. These styles are distinctive for this period, although all of them persist well beyond the arbitrary end of the period as defined here. Complete vessels showing the entire design layout have only been recovered from burial contexts, and these vessels may reflect only a portion of the overall stylistic range. The burial vessels are notably smaller than those recovered from domestic contexts and clearly reflect a distinctive mortuary assemblage (Gibson et al. 2003). Zoned rocker-stamped vessels from mounds often exhibit one of two bird zoomorphic designs (Figure 7.2): a raptor or vulture, or a roseate spoonbill (more likely) or shoveler duck (less likely). These two birds are the only two animals found on vessels across the Hopewellian world and must represent important spirit beings within the Hopewellian cosmology. It is possible that these two bird-motif designs were produced only during the interval of exchange between Hopewell centers, and they do not appear on vessels later in the Marksville period (Gibson 1970). There is presently insufficient data on vessel design and not enough site chronology to adequately assess this inference.

The Marksville period does not have a distinctive lithic assemblage. Among the common projectile points are the Kent and Gary styles or types. Both were made well before the Marksville period and continued to be made for some time afterwards. Stone tool production emphasizes the use of local gravel cherts for points and bifaces, with very few other tool types present. There is virtually no evidence for a systematic flake-tool industry, although some larger flakes exhibit minor use-wear, reflecting opportunistic use of available pieces.

Other than the few non-local exotic materials (copper, galena) found in burial contexts, there is very little evidence that Marksville people participated in the Hopewell exchange system that was so prevalent in the Midwest. Long-distance

Fig. 7.2. Bird motif design on a Marksville period vessel from the Crooks site (16LA3). Photograph by Kevin Duffy.

exchange of some materials, especially chert, occurred occasionally in Louisiana since at least Middle Archaic times. The small amounts of materials appearing at Marksville sites may be a continuation of these long-established networks. The relatively small quantities of foreign materials indicate that long-distance trade was an uncommon, ephemeral event. It may have been limited to the onset of the Marksville period, when some communities initially adopted Hopewellian customs (Gibson 1970).

Social Organization

The great majority of Marksville period habitation sites are small artifact scatters of less than one acre in size. The few sites investigated so far do not provide any evidence of hierarchical structure between them, based on differences in site size, complexity, or proximity to mounds. Similarly, several of the known cemeteries (Big Oak Island, Crooks, and perhaps Veazey) represent mass interments, where everyone received more or less the same level of ceremony in mortuary treatment. Even those few individuals accompanied by grave goods were buried in the same manner as everyone else. The cemetery at the Morton Shell Mound site (16IB3) is of uncertain age but may represent a late Marksville or early Baytown period ossuary, since it exhibits the same burial treatment for several hundred individuals (McGimsey 2003a). These sites and cemeteries suggest Marksville society was largely egalitarian, with little class differentiation between individuals. This certainly seems to be the case for the many villages scattered across southwestern Louisiana, the piney hills, and the Florida Parishes, where there is very little evidence for mound burial or other means of distinguishing individuals or communities.

For the Crooks cemetery, however, Jon Gibson (1969, 1970) has suggested that an individual's burial treatment and position within a given mound strata may have reflected their social rank. This is not applicable to the other three sites discussed here, as those mounds lacked evidence of strata relating to their construction or the interment of remains.

The cemeteries at Marksville and Coral Snake Mound, however, do clearly indicate social segregation within those communities. At both sites, only a small number of individuals were placed within the mound. At Marksville, the thirty-six individuals present in Mound 4 represent only a small proportion of the community that built and used the site over a span of 300 to 400 years. Mound 4 included the burials of numerous children and infants. This indicates that burial within the mound and inside the embankment was restricted to members of a specific social group, such as a clan or family, within the larger Marksville site community. There appears to be a clear social difference between those members of the community buried inside the sacred precinct at Marksville and those not buried there. Perhaps the people not buried within the Marksville enclosure were interred in a mass ossuary, as at Crooks or Big Oak Island.

Most of the individuals buried at Marksville were not accompanied by artifacts or preserved burial goods. Interestingly, two dogs were also interred in Mound 4, one of which was accompanied by two ceramic vessels. This only serves to emphasize how poorly we understand the rules or customs that governed who got buried in this mound. Nor is it clear to what degree the role that time might have played in these different burial traditions. Perhaps Mound 4 represents an extended family or lineage that first introduced Hopewellian concepts to the local Marksville community, and, with the passing of its members, the larger community returned to the more egalitarian social relations evident in the preceding Tchula period (see Hays and Weinstein, Chapter 6 in this volume). At present, we do not have sufficient dates from the various Marksville cemeteries to assess the role that time and space may have played in determining a particular community's burial practices. Similarly, the available data indicate considerable variability in local community and regional social organization across the state during this period. Understanding that variability will require analysis of numerous well-dated collections from all parts of the state.

Subsistence

Long-term subsistence patterns, dating from at least the Middle Archaic period, reflect the hunting and gathering of locally available foods. This trend continued through the Marksville period and until at least the Coles Creek period. From the perspective of available subsistence data, the Marksville period cannot be distinguished from earlier or later periods, reflecting the continuation of long-standing food-gathering patterns across the state. In the Midwest, contemporaneous Hopewell communities used several domesticated native seed plants. There is no evidence that domesticated versions of these same varieties were used by people living in Louisiana (Jackson and Scott 2002; Kidder and Fritz 1993; McGimsey and Roberts 2000; Roberts 1999, 2006).

There are few Marksville period sites with subsistence data from Louisiana (Jackson 1999; Jackson and Scott 2000, 2002; Lamb 1983; McGimsey and Roberts 2000; Mariaca 1988; Roberts 1999, 2000). Even so, differential preservation of animal remains may provide a limited view of the actual procurement strategies. The faunal data exhibit considerable variability between sites, indicating that food collection was dependent on the local environment around each site. Interesting, the available data indicate a relatively lower frequency of fish in Marksville assemblages compared with earlier or later sites (McGimsey et al. 2005; Jackson and Scott 2002). It is not known whether this represents relatively less consumption of fish, differential preservation, or sampling differences. At the Marksville site, the meatier elements of deer are overrepresented in the assemblage. This suggests that feasting or other related community events and ceremonies were held at the site.

Subsistence practices remain one of the least-documented aspects of the archaeological record of the Marksville period. This reflects, in part, a lack of emphasis on subsistence data during earlier excavations, but it also indicates the paucity of sites excavated in recent years with unmixed Marksville components and good faunal or botanical preservation. The available data indicate that people throughout the Marksville period were hunters and gatherers, as their ancestors had been for generations.

Discussion

Beginning with the discovery of the Marksville site in the 1920s, the term "Marksville" has meant a number of things in Louisiana archaeology: a time period (Middle Woodland), a phase within that time period (early Middle Woodland and/or the interval of Hopewell interaction), an archaeological culture, a mortuary tradition, a series of ceramic styles, and a particular site. All of these meanings overlap to a large degree and refer to elements of the same cultural expression, yet each also represents a different aspect of the archaeological record. Disentangling all of these meanings is difficult and does not necessarily lead to greater understanding.

For this book, Marksville has been defined as a somewhat arbitrary time period: the interval between A.D. 1 and 400, give or take fifty to a hundred years earlier or later. Across the state during this interval, people were living in a wide variety of environments. Most of these communities were small villages, usually near a bayou or stream, lacking thick deposits of refuse. These data suggest to archaeologists that people did not stay in a given village for more than a few years before moving to another location. In some areas, or at some times of the year, some groups may have moved more frequently to take advantage of seasonally available resources (such as nuts, spawning fish, or clams). The people in these communities lived by hunting and gathering wild plants and animals, and they shared a common set of stone tools and ceramics. These include Gary and Kent projectile points, stone knives and scrapers, and ceramic vessels, including small cups, bowls, and larger storage jars. If one were to look only at the archaeological evidence of people's daily lives across the state during the A.D. 1–400 interval, it would be easy to conclude that everyone in Louisiana shared the same basic culture. Given that many cultural traditions have very old roots in the state, it might also be argued that this same basic cultural pattern had persisted since at least the Middle Archaic period, with a few exceptions such as the Poverty Point site (16WC5) during the Late Archaic period (Gibson, Chapter 5 in this volume). Looking at the settlement and subsistence data, there is little to distinguish the Marksville period from earlier periods, or even from the immediately succeeding periods (Baytown and Coles Creek).

Many sites lack radiocarbon dates to place them in time, so archaeologists use the presence of distinctive ceramic vessel designs (including broad-line incising and zoned rocker-stamping) to identify Marksville period sites. Since their first recognition at the Marksville site, these ceramic styles have become the defining criteria for the period. Sites with these distinctive sherds can be found all across the state, suggesting at least some sense of a shared identity between these widespread communities. What is still not clear is whether the use of common ceramic vessel designs and projectile point forms means that everyone thought of themselves as part of the same social group, such as a tribe or similar organization. The similarity in designs across the state may reflect the degree and frequency of exchange between various groups, as ideas were spread by traders, travelers, or explorers. Perhaps these designs were not actually markers of social identity, such as membership in a common tribe, but rather reflect the functional or aesthetic popularity of certain designs. The same might be said for Americans' present-day enjoyment of many artistic designs from around the world, without being part of Japanese, German, or Chinese culture.

An additional problem with the use of ceramic designs to define the Marksville period is their persistence through time. The initial definitions of the Marksville period laid out a chronology whereby certain designs—such as the bird motifs, the finer examples of rocker-stamping, and certain versions of the broad-line incising—were thought to characterize the early part of the Marksville period (i.e., A.D. 1–200; Phillips 1970; Ford 1936; Toth 1974, 1979a, 1988). Other variants of these same designs were thought to characterize the later part of the period (A.D. 200–400). Subsequent research and numerous radiocarbon dates now demonstrate very little support for this design chronology (Lee, Chapter 8 in this volume; McGimsey 2004; McGimsey et al. 2005). Ceramic sherds exhibiting the classic "early" Marksville designs have been found in contexts dating well into the A.D. 600–700 range and may even persist as late as A.D. 800 in some areas. The present evidence suggests that some communities continued to make pots with "early" and "late" Marksville-style designs well beyond the arbitrary end of this period. It is equally clear that many other communities had adopted new ceramic styles by A.D. 400. The areas where these changes occurred, or did not occur, may be a more accurate reflection of social group boundaries. But this differential persistence of ceramic styles across the state makes it difficult to use ceramic designs alone as the defining criteria for sites belonging to the Marksville period. Radiocarbon dates, or other independent dating results, may be the only reliable way of assigning a site to the Marksville period. In addition, attribute level analyses of design elements, as well as ceramic pastes, may identify chronological variation in these aspects of ceramic technology.

Overlying the basic Marksville period settlement and subsistence patterns are the Hopewell-influenced mortuary and exchange traditions. As evident in the previous discussion, sites with Hopewell-related earthworks, burial mounds, and foreign materials are few in number and widely dispersed across the state. Most communities, particularly those outside the Mississippi River Valley, appear to have been aware of the Hopewell tradition, but there is little archaeological evidence they chose to participate in the new cultural processes and beliefs. Only a few communities accepted the Hopewell expression as their own and participated in it to a significant degree. These communities include those at Marksville and Crooks, as well as smaller communities around the sites of Coral

Snake, Veazey, and Big Oak Island. At these sites, local communities chose which Hopewell ideas to accept and interpreted them in the context of their own experiences, resulting in locally distinct versions of a Louisiana-Hopewellian expression. The dispersed and locally variable appearance of Hopewell traits across the state suggests that it may be a mistake to try and define a statewide Hopewell or Marksville culture (Gibson 1969).

Some archaeologists have suggested that the ceramic designs present on vessels at Marksville and other Hopewell sites are markers of Hopewell influence on that particular group (Toth 1979a, 1988). The bird motifs on small mortuary vessels may be one example of a Hopewellian pottery assemblage. But given the widespread distribution of the incised and zoned rocker-stamped decorations at sites with no other evidence of Hopewell influence, it is more likely that these were simply the popular styles during this period. They were probably influenced by the Hopewell mortuary wares, but they are not by themselves markers of participation in the Hopewell system.

If Marksville is defined as the time of interaction with northern-Midwestern Hopewellian cultures, it is limited to a small number of communities that may have participated in it for only a generation or two. After that, Louisiana Marksville went its own way, with little influence from cultural developments outside of the state.

So in the end, what is Marksville? At least three different definitions can be offered, none of which is completely satisfactory. First, it can be defined as an arbitrary interval of time, with the beginning of this interval marked by the appearance of a distinctive set of ceramic designs. But these designs persist well beyond the defined end of the period, and they do not serve as a reliable marker for the latter half of the period. Similarly, other artifactual, settlement, and subsistence patterns reflect long-standing trends across the state and do not serve to identify a uniquely Marksville system. Second, Marksville can be defined as a distinctive set of artifact styles, primarily ceramic designs, which first appeared at approximately A.D. 1. In this definition, Marksville persisted for different lengths of time in different parts of the state and in some areas may have lasted as long as 700 to 800 years. In this sense, some communities continued to make Marksville-style ceramics long after their neighbors had adopted newer styles. And third, if Marksville is defined by participation in the Hopewell system, then it was present in only a few areas of the state and may have lasted for only a generation or two in those areas.

At the Marksville site itself, the available radiocarbon dates suggest occupation continued throughout nearly the entire A.D. 1–400 interval. At this one site, at least, some elements of a Hopewellian ceremonial system appear to have persisted as long as it did in the Midwestern United States. But, like Poverty Point, the Marksville site is an isolated example of this trend, and interest in things Hopewellian is not so evident across a majority of the state. These three definitions provide contrasting views of what Marksville culture was and what the Marksville period means today in Louisiana history. Each is probably correct, but to an unknown degree, and it will require more excavation and analysis before a more comprehensive understanding of Marksville can be developed.

8

Troyville and the Baytown Period

AUBRA L. LEE

The Late Woodland period in the Lower Mississippi Valley (LMV) is subdivided into two major culture-historical units: Baytown and Coles Creek. Baytown and Coles Creek consequently refer to sub-periods as well as archaeological cultures (see Roe and Schilling, Chapter 9 in this volume). The Baytown period and culture were named after the multi-mound Baytown site located in east-central Arkansas, as was the ubiquitous and long-standing pottery type, Baytown Plain (Phillips 1970:17–18, 47–48, 903–904; Phillips et al. 1951:76–82). Sites associated with Baytown culture are found in the northern LMV from the Yazoo Basin northward, while Baytown period sites to the south and west in present-day Louisiana are generally associated with Troyville culture (Gibson 1984b; cf. Jeter and Williams 1989a:147–152; Kidder 2004b:552–554). The Baytown period was initially regarded as a time of cultural decline, to the extent that it was characterized as a nadir between the Middle Woodland Marksville and subsequent Mississippian cultures (Griffin 1967; Phillips 1970; Williams and Brain 1983:403–405). Baytown was memorably described as a somewhat unremarkable, "good gray culture" of the LMV (Williams 1963:297).

Archaeological investigations have subsequently called into question these characterizations of cultural decline and have begun to transform our understanding of the Baytown period (Kidder 1998a:128–129, 2002b:79–85). Baytown is now regarded as a time of population growth and culture change, with related socioeconomic and political developments that provided a foundation for the later development of more complex Coles Creek societies (Cusick et al. 1995; Kidder and Wells 1994; Roe and Schilling, Chapter 9 in this volume). This is especially true of Troyville culture. The Baytown period begins as early as A.D. 300 in some cultural chronologies and ends at late as A.D. 900 in others. This chapter focuses on Troyville culture of the Baytown period, generally thought to date from A.D. 400 to 700 (Jeter and Williams 1989a:141–143).

Troyville (16CT7) is the type site for Troyville culture and the largest mound site of the Baytown period in the southern LMV. It is located on the west bank of the Black River, below the confluence of the Little, Ouachita and Tensas rivers, at present-day Jonesville, Louisiana, in Catahoula Parish (Figure 1.2). Troyville is one of the most written about, yet least understood sites of the entire Late Woodland period in the LMV. Based on work at Troyville and other mound complexes, James A. Ford (1951) originally conceived of Troyville as a culture-historical construct, which he inserted between the Marksville and Coles Creek periods in his Lower Red River chronology (see also Ford and Willey 1940:Figure 2, 1941:344–346). Troyville and Baytown were viewed as contemporary culture-historical units for some time, but Troyville was later recast as a one of several regional archaeological cultures within the Baytown period (Belmont 1984; Gibson 1984b; Jeter and Williams 1989a:147–152; Kidder 2002b:79–85).

Archaeologists have long regarded the Troyville site as a unique and even enigmatic mound complex (Gibson 1996a:55–58; Kidder 2002b:85). Recent research at Troyville has produced a wealth of new information about the site, including mound construction, residential areas, and material culture (Handley et al. 2006; Lee 2006a, 2006b, 2007; Lee et al. 2010; Saunders and Jones 2003, 2004; Saunders et al. 2006). This information expands considerably on earlier studies of mounds and mortuary practices (e.g., Walker 1936). Troyville is also the key to understanding the Baytown period throughout the southern LMV, especially since the site lies well outside of the Baytown region of east-central Arkansas and northwest Mississippi. Sites associated with Troyville culture are found throughout the Lower Red River region and Boeuf-Tensas river basins. Related sites and material culture in the Mississippi Delta and along the coast have been described as Coastal Troyville–Coles Creek culture (Jeter and Williams 1989a:144, Figure 14, 148, Table 2, 152–153).

The principal goal of this chapter is to present the results of recent research on the Baytown period in the southern LMV. To begin with, a brief overview of the Baytown period is provided, describing sociopolitical organization, settlement, subsistence, and mortuary practices. This is followed by short descriptions of some of the better-known Baytown period sites in Louisiana, in order to illustrate regional similarities and differences. New data from the Troyville site are then presented, followed by a summary of the site's significance and recommendations for future research.

Baytown Period Overview

Baytown was a time when populations in the southern LMV became increasingly regionally differentiated and adopted cultural practices and strategies that ultimately contributed to the development of more complex societies of later periods (Belmont 1984:76–78; Bitgood 1989:137; Cusick et al. 1995:4.6–4.8; Jeter and Williams 1989a:147–150; Kidder 1992a:151–152, 2002b:89–90; Kidder and Wells 1994:4, 24; Ryan, ed. 2004:17–21). People of the Baytown period continued long-standing traditions of building earthen mounds for public ceremonies, civic events, and interment of the dead (Belmont 1984:81–83; Gibson 1996a:59; Kidder 1992a:152; Williams and Brain 1983:403–405). Long-distance trade with other Gulf Coastal Plain groups to the east is reflected in *Busycon* shell artifacts, sharks' teeth, and ceramics with similar decorations, indicating that Baytown people participated on some level in trade networks that also existed during much earlier times (Belmont 1980; Davis et al. 1982; House 1982; Kidder 2002b; McGimsey 2004; Williams and Brain 1983). The bow and arrow, introduced sometime between A.D. 600 and 700, was first extensively used in the LMV during the Baytown period. This new technology is reflected in different projectile point types and likely involved changes in hunting as well as in warfare (Jeter and Williams 1989a:148; Kidder 2002b:80; Nassaney and Pyle 1999:248, 253, 260, Table 4; Rolingson 1990:34–35, 2002:56).

Pottery vessels decorated with bi-chrome and polychrome painted designs are another innovation introduced during the Baytown period (Belmont and Williams 1981). A growing body of evidence indicates that the ceramics associated with the early and late divisions of the Baytown period do not correspond well with the dated deposits from which they were recovered (Cusick et al. 1995:10–23; Lee and Yakubik 2003:8; McGimsey 2004:75–77, 194–207; Saunders and Jones 2004:24–26; cf. Bitgood 1989:132–136). Either the cultural chronology is inaccurate by as much as two centuries, or the ceramic suites may not be truly representative of the internal divisions of this period. Additional investigation will be required to resolve this problem, in which diagnostic ceramics from well-dated, stratigraphic contexts allow for the further refinement of a regional chronology.

Baytown societies are thought to correspond with a tribal or local level of sociopolitical organization. Leadership positions were achieved by individuals rather than ascribed or inherited, and power was only temporarily vested in these individuals. Communal civic rituals and ceremonies were performed at mound sites and on mound summits (Gibson 1996a:54–60). Mound construction, once believed to be the result of intensive labor supplied by the entire population, may have been less intensive or time-consuming. Some estimates indicate that large mounds could have been built in a much shorter time span than previously imagined (Muller 1997:271–275). Mound building during the

Baytown period was likely characterized by some form of ideological influence and ritual engagement of local societies and the surrounding population, rather than economic control (Cobb and Nassaney 2002:531).

Baytown people appear to have periodically held large, communal feasts. Large bathtub-shaped pits are the primary evidence for communal feasting. These pits have been associated with food preparation during civic ceremonies and burial rituals (Belmont 1967, 1984; Bitgood 1989; Ford 1951; Kidder 2002b; McGimsey 2004). Several of these pits were located in the vicinity of mounds or along the peripheries of mound sites. The high incidence of bathtub-shaped pits, or at least the pits discovered thus far, in proximity to mortuary mounds and other burial areas suggests a relationship with funerary rites (Belmont 1984:88–90; Kidder 1992a:152). Bathtub-shaped pits dating from the Baytown period have been excavated at the Greenhouse site (16AV2) in Avoyelles Parish, the Gold Mine (16RI13) and Marsden (16RI3) sites in Richland Parish, and the Neely site (16WC4) in West Carroll Parish. The large pits at the Gold Mine site have upper and lower chambers, while the pits at the other three sites have a single chamber (McGimsey 2004:109–110).

Most people during the Baytown period probably resided in small, dispersed hamlets, although the number of excavated non-mound sites in Louisiana is quite small (Jeter and Williams 1989a:147–156; Kidder 2002b:85). There is consequently little available information on domestic structures, other than those that appear to have been oval in plan and without evidence of prepared floors. Structural remains have been discovered at the Gold Mine site, the Mount Nebo site (16MA18) in Madison Parish, the Fredericks site (16NA2) in Natchitoches Parish, and possibly at the Hedgeland site (16CT19) in Catahoula Parish (Belmont 1980; Girard 2000b; McGimsey 2004; Neuman 1984:169–214; Ryan, ed. 2004). Structural data collected thus far, however, are not sufficient to determine if these buildings represent domestic contexts or special-purpose buildings that were used for brief periods during ceremonial events, such as burial rituals (Girard 2000b:12). There is little data with which to ascertain consistent site or community planning. Although settlement appears to have been highly variable, the beginning of a hierarchical settlement pattern has been inferred (Kidder 1993a:18, 1998a:134–136, 2002b:81; cf. Belmont 1984:88–89).

Subsistence data from previously excavated Baytown sites in Louisiana are heavily weighted toward mammals, reptiles, fish, and birds. Faunal remains indicate a broad-based diet of fish, deer, and smaller mammals (Girard 2000b; Hunter et al. 1995; Jackson and Scott 2002; Kelley 1992; Lee et al. 1997). Deer were most likely hunted during the summer, fall, and winter. Small mammals included raccoon, beaver, opossum, swamp and cottontail rabbit, and gray and fox squirrel (Kelley 1992:233–234). Important species of fish included gar, freshwater drum, bowfin, and catfish. Among the plants harvested were goosefoot (chenopod), knotweed, maygrass, little barley, marshelder, sunflower, and gourd, although Baytown populations in the southern LMV do not appear to have domesticated these plants. Seasonally collected fleshy fruits included persimmon, grapes, and berries. Acorns, hickory nuts, and pecans were the most commonly collected types of nuts from mast-producing trees (Fritz 1994, 1997; Girard 2000b; Gremillion 2004; Kidder and Fritz 1993; Ryan, ed. 2004).

Mortuary practices also appear to have varied, as there was not a consistent method of burial during the Baytown period. Some individuals were buried immediately after death, some were entombed in charnel buildings, and others were cremated (Belmont 1967; Gibson 1984a; Kidder 2002b; McGimsey 2004). Burial goods are generally rare, but they were sometimes elaborate and finely crafted, as with the two polychrome painted human effigy figurines from the Gold Mine site (McGimsey 2004). In most instances, objects accompanying the deceased were not placed with specific individuals but with groups interred at the same time. Two exceptions to this trend should be noted. Pottery vessels were placed directly with some of the deceased at the Old Creek site (16LA102) in LaSalle Parish, and more mundane items, such as pebbles, were buried with specific individuals at the Gold Mine site (Gibson 1984a; McGimsey 2004). Mortuary facilities were widely spaced, serving different segments of the population (Kidder 2002b:85). Overall, the egalitarian nature of Baytown mortuary practices suggests little to no individual status differentiation (Belmont 1984:85–86; Kidder 1992a:152, 1993a:18).

Baytown Period Sites

The Greenhouse site is located just north of the Marksville site (16AV1) in Avoyelles Parish. Greenhouse consists of seven mounds around an oval plaza. Extensive excavations were conducted by the Works Progress Administration (WPA) in 1938 and subsequently reported by Ford (1951:12). Ford's analysis and interpretation formed the basis of what came to be known as the Troyville–Coles Creek culture and period (e.g., Neuman 1984:169–214). John Belmont (1967) later reanalyzed the collection from the Greenhouse excavation and concluded that the mounds were affiliated with the Coles Creek period but that the midden ridges discovered beneath the mounds dated from the earlier Baytown period.

A cemetery containing eighty-four individuals and nine dogs was recorded at Greenhouse. It is still a matter of debate whether this cemetery was located in a low mound or represented a series of burials excavated into a midden ridge covered with clay (Ford 1951:42 cf. Greengo 1964:97–97; see also McGimsey 2004 for comparative discussion). Ten bathtub-shaped pits were dug into the terrace and located in a line between Mounds A and E (Ford 1951:Figure 3). The pit walls and floors were heavily fired, with thick layers of ash on the bottom, along with animal bone. The intensity of firing in these pits suggests each was used multiple times and cleaned out between uses (Ford 1951). As described previously, the size and function of these pits has been interpreted as evidence of communal feasts.

The Lac St. Agnes site (16AV26) is located in the Lower Red River Valley approximately 18 kilometers (11 mi) north of the Greenhouse site. One low, dome-shaped mound and a village midden have been found at the site. Test units in the midden yielded material culture representing successive Marksville, Baytown, Coles Creek, and Plaquemine components. The southwest quarter of the mound was mechanically excavated, exposing a 3.7-meter-deep (12 ft) profile, but the excavation did not reach beneath the mound (Toth 1979b:Figure 6). Interpretation of the profile suggests the initial construction stage was a low platform upon which seven burials were placed during the late Marksville period. Additional stages were added during the Baytown, Coles Creek, and Mississippi periods. Lastly, a burial pit was placed in the crest of the mound during the Mississippi period (Neuman 1984:265; Toth 1979b).

Archaeologists with the Louisiana Regional Archaeology Program subsequently placed a single core in the center of the mound at Lac St. Agnes. This core revealed that the pre-mound ground surface had been stripped away before construction and that the mound was built in a single stage of basket-loaded sandy loam. A sample of charred wood and cane from one of the burials (Feature 5) on the initial construction stage returned a median date of cal. A.D. 775, with a two sigma range of cal. A.D. 680–885, indicating that the mound dates to either the late Baytown or early Coles Creek period (McGimsey 2003c:12–13, 2004:214, Table 13.10; see also Kidder 2002b:85).

The Mount Nebo site has a single flat-topped mound located on the natural levee of the Tensas River near Tallulah, Louisiana (Giardino 1984b; McGimsey 2004:215; Neuman 1984:204–207). Most of the eight construction stages of the mound were mechanically excavated until burials were encountered. The remains of nearly one hundred individuals were recovered from the mound (Neuman 1984:204–207). Forty individuals from Stage F were interred during either the late Baytown or early Coles Creek period (Giardino 1984b). The problem of assigning these individuals to a single component stems from the fact that only a single radiocarbon date of cal. A.D. 875 was obtained from the lower part of the mound, and it came from Stage E, overlying Stage F (McGimsey 2004:215).

Sixteen mortuary facilities, primarily circular pits, had been dug into Stage F of the mound at Mount Nebo. These pits contained one to eight individuals and were excavated at different times, since some pits intruded into others (Neuman 1984:205). Twelve of the forty individuals were interred as bundle burials, representing secondary processing of the deceased. Fifteen individuals were buried in an extended, prone (face down) position, two were buried in an extended supine (face up) position, two were placed in a flexed position, five were represented only by crania, and no additional data are available on the remaining four individuals (Giardino 1984b:Table 2). No burial goods appear to have been placed with the interments in Stage F, although red ochre was noted on the teeth of three individuals.

One of the most extensively documented Baytown period mortuary mounds is found at the Gold Mine site in Richland Parish. A low, dome-shaped mound was built near Big Creek, a tributary of the Boeuf River. Excavations at the site uncovered sub-mound midden deposits, representing occupations that began during the Tchula period and continued into the Baytown period (McGimsey 2004:188–218).

Excavations revealed that the area beneath the mound had been cleared in preparation for mound construction. Three stages were documented in hand-excavated units and backhoe-excavated trenches. The first stage was a low, flat-topped dome approximately 70 centimeters (27 in) high. The second stage increased the height of the mound by 50 centimeters (20 in), producing a broad but low, flat-topped mound. A similar amount of soil was placed on the existing mound in the third stage, creating a dome-shaped mound approximately 2 meters (6.5 ft) high. The lack of eroded surfaces, intrusive pits, and absence of slope wash indicated that the mound was built quickly, probably within the span of a month. Three overlapping radiometric assays place mound construction between cal. A.D. 775 and 874 (McGimsey 2004:211–212).

The Fredericks site is located in the Red River Valley north of Natchitoches, Louisiana. Recent investigations have provided important comparative data for understanding the Baytown period (Girard 2000b). The site contains two midden ridges like those at Greenhouse. Mound A is a conical mound located at the west end of the complex. Mound D, a rectangular platform made of red clay, lies at the opposite end. Three low mounds, designated B, C, and D, are located within the midden ridges. Fine sandy loam was laid down beneath each of the mounds and then red clay was loaded on top of the sand to form the mounds. Burials were encountered on top of the clay in the mounds in the ridges. Burials had also been placed in the intervening midden deposits between the mounds, which is once again very similar to the Baytown mortuary practices documented at Greenhouse. Burials were also placed in Mound A (Girard 2000b).

Most of the decorated ceramics from the ridge mounds and midden at the Fredericks site have been classified as Marksville Incised, *vars. Yokena, Spanish Fort, Steele Bayou,* and *Leist,* Marksville Stamped, *vars. Mabin, Manny,* and *Troyville,* Alligator Incised, Churupa Punctated, and Larto Red. This ceramic assemblage would be relegated to the late Marksville period according to Bitgood's (1989) interpretation. However, eight radiocarbon dates clearly indicate that this ceramic assemblage falls between cal. A.D. 400 and 650, or within the Baytown period (Girard 2000b).

The McGuffee site (16CT17), formerly known as the Taylor Mounds, is located 19 kilometers (12 mi) north of Jonesville on the Ouachita River at Harrisonburg, Louisiana. Investigations at this site have recovered evidence of at least three components dating from the Poverty Point, Marksville, and Baytown periods (Saunders et al. 2005; Shuman et al. 1999; see also McGimsey, Chapter 7 in this volume). Six mounds and possibly a seventh are located within a C-shaped embankment. Mounds C, D, and E form a north-south line along the west bank of the river. Mounds B and F are set back, away from the river and are located respectively on the north and south sides of the site. A small rise northwest of Mound F might represent a seventh mound (Saunders et al. 2005:Table 6). Mound A is the largest mound at McGuffee and is located on the west side of the site. Mound A is a large, rectangular flat-topped mound, with the remnants of a conical mound at the center of the mound summit. A causeway is located on the east side of Mound A and extends eastward toward Mound D (Saunders et al. 2005:Figure 10; Shuman et al. 1999:Figure 2).

The C-shaped embankment at McGuffee runs from the north side of the site near Mound C, southwest to Mound A, then southeastward to the riverbank. Systematic soil coring of the mounds and embankment documented a single construction stage in each, with the exception of Mounds A and C, where several construction stages were evident (Saunders et al. 2005:40–44). Radiocarbon dating of a construction stage near the base of Mound C suggests construction began sometime between cal. A.D. 615 and 690 (Shuman et al. 1999:16). Charcoal and sediments collected from a sub-mound deposit below Mound A produced two radiocarbon dates that do not overlap. The charcoal sample returned a two sigma range of cal. A.D. 433–551, while the sediments yielded an earlier two sigma range of cal. A.D. 257–388 (Saunders et al. 2005:52). Radiocarbon dating of a sediment sample from beneath the southern portion of the embankment produced a two sigma range of cal. A.D. 258–404 (Saunders et al. 2005:52). The radiocarbon dates from McGuffee consequently indicate that Mound C was under construction during the late Baytown period, while Mound A and the embankment were probably built sometime earlier during the Baytown period.

The Troyville Site

Troyville sits on a natural levee on the west side of the Black River in the town of Jonesville, Louisiana (Figure 8.1). Work at Troyville during the nineteenth century produced maps and site descriptions that were at times contradictory, especially as to the number of mounds, which were variously enumerated from a minimum of six to a maximum of thirteen (Squire and Davis 1856; Thomas 1894). Nine mounds have been most consistently associated with the Troyville site since the late nineteenth century (Beyer 1896; Walker 1936). Eight of these mounds are located within an enclosure or embankment (Cusick et al. 1995:6–2; Gibson 1996a:55; Hunter and Baker 1979:26; Neuman 1984:170–177; Saunders and Jones 2003:Figures 21–22; Saunders et al. 2006:Figure 9; Thomas 1894:250–252; Walker 1936:7–9). Much of what is currently known about Troyville is based on WPA salvage excavations carried out by Winslow Walker (1936), at a time when many of the mounds and portions of the embankment had already been severely impacted by road construction, urbanization, and looting. Damage to the site, recounted in Walker's report, was perceived to be catastrophic, leading to the prevailing opinion that Troyville had been totally or mostly destroyed and was therefore unlikely to yield further data pertinent to understanding this period (Gibson 1996a:58; Girard 2000b:13; Haag 1971:22; Neuman 1984:170).

MOUNDS

Systematic soil coring, site mapping, and excavation by the Louisiana Regional Archaeology Program have provided new details on the initial occupation of Troyville, its monumental construction, and communal activities at the site (Saunders and Jones 2003; Saunders et al. 2006). Soil cores were collected from five of the eight identifiable mounds at the site (Figure 8.1). Mound 1 is 2.4 meters (8 ft) high, 60 meters (200 ft) long, and 27 meters (90 ft) wide. It has a historic cemetery on its east side. Approximately one meter of soil has been

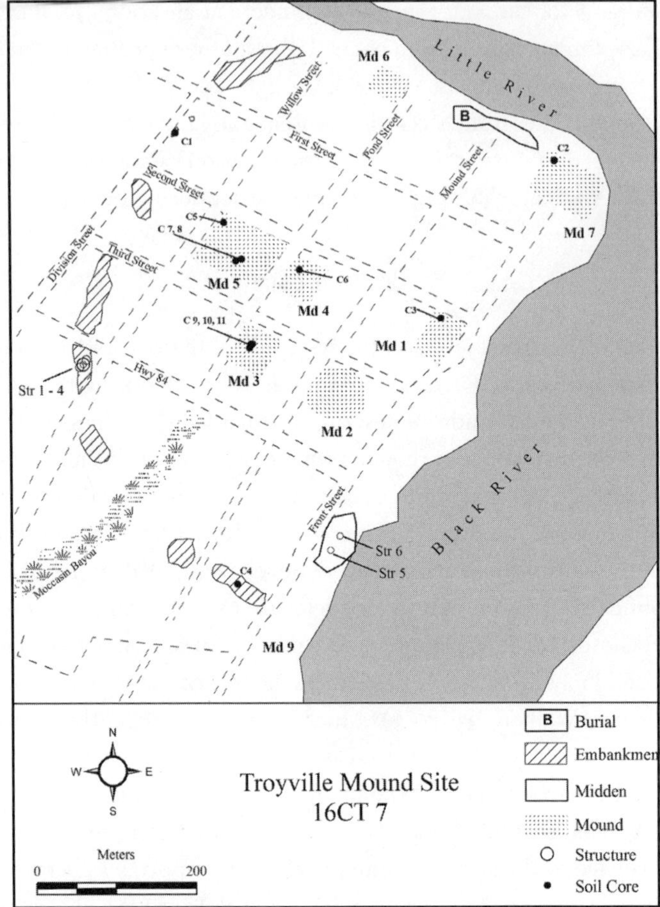

Fig. 8.1. Map of the Troyville site (16CT7).

removed from the west side of Mound 1. Coring data provide evidence that one construction stage remains in the damaged section of Mound 1 (Saunders and Jones 2003:64, Appendix II). More construction stages are likely preserved in Mound 1, since the historic cemetery has prevented further damage to this portion of the mound. Prehistoric burials were encountered when graves were dug in the cemetery area, suggesting that Mound 1 was built specifically for mortuary purposes.

In 1896, Mound 2 was described as 4.5 meters (15 ft) high, 27 meters (90 ft) long, 23 meters (75 ft) wide, and dome-shaped (Beyer 1896; cf. Thomas 1894: Figure 156). Excavation revealed that the mound was comprised of clay, loaded onto a layer of sand. A single human burial had been placed on the sand with at least one pottery vessel, and it was covered with mound fill (Beyer 1896:23–33). Road and commercial building construction have severely damaged Mound 2, leaving a barely perceptible, low circular rise. Very little information from the early work at Troyville was collected for Mound 3, other than that it was "largely destroyed" (Thomas 1894:251). Mound 3 was in fact damaged by residential construction. Data from three soil cores near what had been the center of Mound 3, however, indicate that approximately 75 centimeters (30 in) of mound fill remains intact, with a possible feature in the top of the fill (Saunders and Jones 2003:66, Appendix II).

Mound 4 was 50 meters (164 ft) square, and by the late nineteenth century it was also described as largely destroyed (Beyer 1896; Thomas 1894). Coring and excavation data confirm that four construction stages are preserved in Mound 4, as are pit features. Pottery and a radiocarbon date indicate the mound was constructed during the Marksville period, while a post on the north flank suggests a wooden palisade may have surrounded the mound (Saunders and Jones 2003:64; Saunders et al. 2006). A small pit, 50 centimeters (20 in) in diameter and 50 centimeters deep, and located near the center of Mound 4, was filled with pottery sherds representing at least thirty different vessels. Vessel forms include deep bowls, beakers, large jars and pots, cauldrons, and large shallow bowls and platters (Saunders et al. 2006:Table 9). Size and form indicate some of the vessels were used for cooking, while the most abundant forms (platters and shallow bowls) were used for serving. The context suggests these vessels were deliberately discarded after communal feasting (Saunders et al. 2006:61–62). A median date of cal. A.D. 650 from charcoal in the pit demonstrates that Mound 4 continued to be a focal point of communal activities at Troyville well into the Baytown period (Saunders et al. 2006:Table 7).

Mound 5 was described as just over 24 meters (80 ft) in height and as being the largest mound at Troyville. In fact, the height and size of Mound 5 ranks it as the second tallest mound in eastern North American and possibly third largest by volume (Gibson 1996a:54–60; Walker 1936:4–16). It was further distinguished in terms of its unique construction, as it was comprised of a lower platform 55 meters (180 ft) square, a smaller upper platform, and a conical mound in the center of the upper platform. Destruction of Mound 5 began as early as the Civil War, when the placement of a rifle pit damaged much of the upper-most conical section. More soil from Mound 5 was removed to partially fill four borrow pits that were created when the mound was built, destroying the remainder of the conical section and much of the upper platform by 1882 (Walker 1936). In 1931, the remainder of the upper platform and the top of the lower platform were utilized as material to build an approach ramp for the Long-Allen bridge over the Black River. Approximately 16,055 cubic meters (21,000 cubic yards) of soil were stripped from Mound 5 to build the approach ramp.

Winslow Walker's (1936) excavations in 1931 and 1932 revealed that the lower platform of Mound 5 was built with alternating layers of clay and river cane. Layers of river cane, some nearly one meter (3.3 ft) thick, were held in place with stakes. Wooden boards covered some of the river cane layers. Ramps had been constructed at the four corners of Mound 5, and a series of posts formed a palisade-like screen on the south side of the mound. A causeway connected Mound 5 to Mound 4. An extensive burned area beneath Mound 5 suggested the area had been cleared before construction began.

Recent coring in the location of Mound 5 recovered evidence that between one meter (3.3 ft) and up to 1.8 meters (6 ft) of stratified deposits remain intact beneath a church and houses that presently cover most of the mound (Saunders and Jones 2003). A post was uncovered on the north side of Mound 5 in 2006, when a new fire suppression system was installed in Jonesville (Handley et al. 2006:Figure 11-11). A river cane sample collected by Walker from the lower platform of Mound 5 was radiocarbon dated to cal. A.D. 679–778 (two sigma range), placing the construction of the mound during the late Baytown period (Saunders et al. 2005:Table 5; Saunders et al. 2006:62).

Mound 6 was 40 meters (131 ft) long and 30 meters (98 ft) wide. This mound was also almost totally destroyed by the end of the nineteenth century. One or possibly two construction stages remain from Mound 6, but its date of construction and function have not been established (Walker 1936:32). Mound 7 was nearly 6 meters (20 ft) tall, 75 meters (246 ft) long, and 55 meters (180 ft) wide. Most of Mound 7 was leveled to provide access to a boat landing at the junction of the Black and Little rivers. One construction level, with domestic refuse middens on top and below the mound fill, is still present at Mound 7 (Saunders and Jones 2003:64). The lower midden dates from the Baytown period, while the upper midden dates from the Coles Creek period. The cultural affiliation of the single remaining construction stage has not been established.

Little information has been recorded for Mound 8, which is thought to have been located west of the embankment on Little River, although a historic cemetery was noted on top of the mound. Mound 8 is presumed to have been either totally or partially destroyed and is not depicted in Figure 8.1. Mound 9 was nearly 40 meters (131 ft) square and was located near the southeastern terminus of the embankment. Beyer (1896) recovered modern pottery and a clay effigy pipe from this mound, but he did not provide additional description of the extent of his investigations or the soils used in the construction of the mound. A small house is currently located on the remains of Mound 9.

EMBANKMENT AND MIDDEN DEPOSITS

Embankments at Woodland period sites were interpreted as defensive barriers during the nineteenth century but are now generally viewed as highly visible delimiters of ceremonial precincts and burial areas (Cobb and Nassaney 2002:529–535; Jones and Kuttruff 1994:3, Neuman 1984:170). Embankments investigated thus far in Louisiana were built in single construction episodes and share a common arcuate or semi-circular shape, as seen at Marksville, McGuffee, and Troyville (Jones and Kuttruff 1994:3, 35, Figure 4; Williams and Brain 1983:397). No evidence in previous excavations has suggested any form of habitation on the top of embankments (Jones and Kuttruff 1994:1–8). Maps of Troyville depict the embankment first as semicircular in form, then more linear, as well as rectangular in overall form (Beyer 1896; Hunter and Baker 1979:26; Thomas 1894:Figure 155; Walker 1936:11). Coring in two of the remaining sections of the embankment at Troyville and fine-scale mapping demonstrate the embankment was originally D-shaped. Profiles from the cores also demonstrate that the extant portions of the embankment contain two construction stages, with a midden deposit of varying thickness between the stages (Saunders and Jones 2003: Appendix II).

In 2005, the author directed excavations at the section of the embankment sampled earlier by Cusick and colleagues (Cusick et al. 1995). Additional excavations were carried out on the west bank of the Black River in 2006 (Lee 2006a, 2006b, 2007; Lee et al. 2010). Two hand-excavated trenches 1 by 25 meters (3.3 by 82 ft) long were completed, followed by mechanized stripping of a 15 by 20 meter (49 by 65 ft) area. These excavations revealed that the lower, first-construction stage of the embankment was intact and that the top was covered with occupational debris, structures, and a variety of pits. Midden, structures, and numerous pit features associated with another segment of the Late Woodland period inhabitation were uncovered on the riverbank.

Construction of the D-shape embankment, or at least the section at Willow Street, began around cal. A.D. 540 (Lee 2006b:Table 1; Lee et al. 2010:Table 6.4; Saunders and Jones 2003:Figures 21–22). This section was 15 meters (49 ft) wide and nearly one meter (3.3 ft) high. It was built with basket loads of clay, silt, and sandy loam from a borrow area paralleling the outside of the embankment. The method of construction was not simply the dumping of loads of soil in a heap, but the creation of a complex series of thin, clay layers interspersed between thicker layers of silt and sand. Apparently, this portion of the site was previously unoccupied, since only a natural A-horizon was discovered beneath the embankment (cf. Cusick et al. 1995:10-22, Figures 10-8 and 10-9).

Alternating layers of midden and clay were located along the east flank of the embankment. The lowest known deposit is a 20 centimeter (7.8 in) thick midden that began to develop very soon after work on this section of the embankment was finished. A thick deposit of gray clay was placed over the midden, sealing off most of the occupational debris sometime around A.D. 620 or 630. A second midden developed on top of the gray clay; later, sometime between cal. A.D. 720 and 760, it was partially sealed with a layer of red clay (Cusick et al. 1995:Table 10-2; Lee 2006b:Table 1; Lee et al. 2010:Table 6.4). A third midden deposit, the last intact deposit documented in the embankment, accumulated on top of the red clay.

Midden not associated with mounds or the embankment is located along the Little and Black rivers (Figure 8.1). The Little River midden is west of Mound 7 and contains domestic or residential refuse from the manufacture of stone tools, broken pottery vessels, and bones of deer and turtle. A single trash pit is associated with the early development of the midden, while a cooking pit and a third pit of undetermined function date later in the use life of the midden. Sixty-one pottery vessels, most represented by a single sherd, were found in midden soil used to fill the early trash pit. Undecorated vessels forms were limited to shallow bowls, deep bowls, shallow bowls with lugs on the rim, and jars (Hunter and Baker 1979:33). Most decorated sherds from all three features were too small to determine vessel shape, but at least small bowls and large jars were present. Lithic raw material used for stone tools was almost exclusively comprised of small pebbles or cobbles. Fragments of a diorite celt and ochre were also discarded in the midden (Hunter and Baker 1979:44).

Three burials containing twelve individuals were placed in the Little River midden (Walker 1936:32). Individuals of both sexes were buried immediately after death and placed in an extended supine position. Two celts and mussel shells were recovered near the burials, but no artifacts were recovered in direct association with the deceased, making it difficult to determine the age of the burials. However, looters had disturbed the burials at night when work had ceased, so it is unknown whether or not any offerings had actually been placed with the deceased (Walker 1936:32–35).

Additional excavations in 2006 along the Black River, north of Mound 9, sampled an extensive, 30 centimeters (11.8 in) thick midden deposit (Figure 8.1).

This midden was comprised of a silty clay deposit at the top, which graded into silt loam near the bottom. Twenty-five pit features and posts from two structures were discovered on the riverbank after it was mechanically stripped. Radiometric assays from the midden, various pit features, and midden indicate that occupation began around cal. A.D. 650 and continued through the Coles Creek and Mississippi periods (Lee 2006a, 2006b, 2007).

STRUCTURES

Six structures were discovered during the 2005 and 2006 investigations. Structures 1 through 4 were located on the top of the first construction stage of the embankment (Figure 8.1). Structures 5 and 6 were located on the west bank of the Black River. Structures 1 and 2 were nearly identical in terms of construction and size (Figure 8.2). These buildings were 7 meters (23 ft) and 8 meters (26 ft) in diameter respectively, with outer walls of single-set posts and a central interior support post surrounded by four additional posts, which formed a rectangle. Only two features could be confidently associated with Structure 1: a circular trash pit on the interior, just north of the central post, and a large cooking pit southwest of the building. The large exterior pit was connected to the structure by a covered pathway. No features were discovered on the interior of Structure 2, but only the northern half of the building was uncovered during excavation. Three small pits were located in the narrow space between the two buildings. Two pits were filled with a combination of cane and wood, and the third contained midden deposit. Structures 1 and 2, and the associated features date to cal. A.D. 770 (Lee 2006b:Table 1; Lee et al. 2010:Table 6.4).

Structure 3 was 11 meters (36 ft) in diameter, with an outer wall formed of individually set, paired posts and a line of single posts arranged along the structure's east-west axis to provide internal support (Lee 2006b). A large pit was situated inside the building near the east wall, while a second large circular cooking pit was located just outside the northwest quadrant of the wall (Figure 8.3). A cluster of small, shallow pits was found just south of the building, and other small pits were located along the exterior of the southern wall. Structure 3 dates between cal A.D. 620 and 650 (Lee 2006b:Table 1; Lee et al. 2010:Table 6.4). Structure 4 was built over the remains of Structure 3. Structure 4 was 12 meters (39 ft) in diameter and nearly identical in most respects to Structure 3, except that four small interior support posts were placed at cardinal directions nearly equidistant from the outer wall (Figure 8.3). Structure 4 and the associated pit features were utilized primarily between A.D. 660 and 700 (Lee 2006b:Table 1).

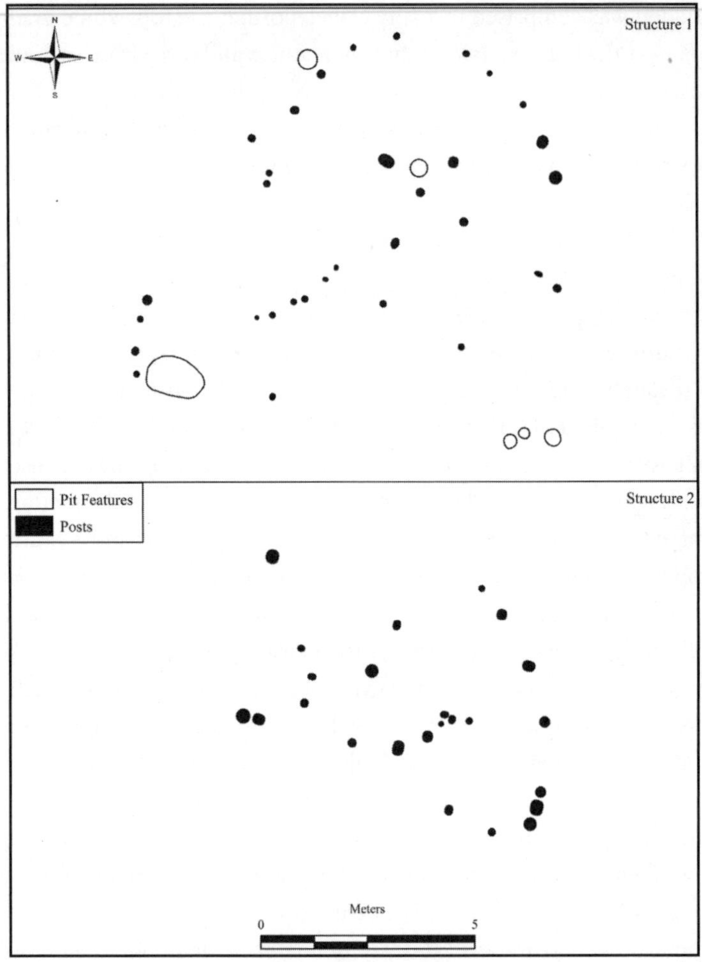

Fig. 8.2. Structures 1 and 2 on the embankment at the Troyville site (16CT7).

Structure 5 was oval in plan, with a maximum east-west diameter of 8.5 meters (27 ft). The outer wall was formed by irregularly spaced, single set posts with an east-west line of interior supports (Figure 8.4). Two large circular pits were located in the central area of the building. Both contained a wide range of artifacts, both had posts within their respective matrices, and both were disturbed by a rectangular pit placed between them. Smaller pits, some cane-lined, were placed between the outer wall posts. Structure 6 was located 20 meters (65 ft) northeast of Structure 5 (Figure 8.1). Structure 6 was circular in plan and 9 meters (29 ft) in diameter (Figure 8.4). The outer wall of the structure was formed by large and deeply set single posts. An oval cooking pit or hearth, several trash

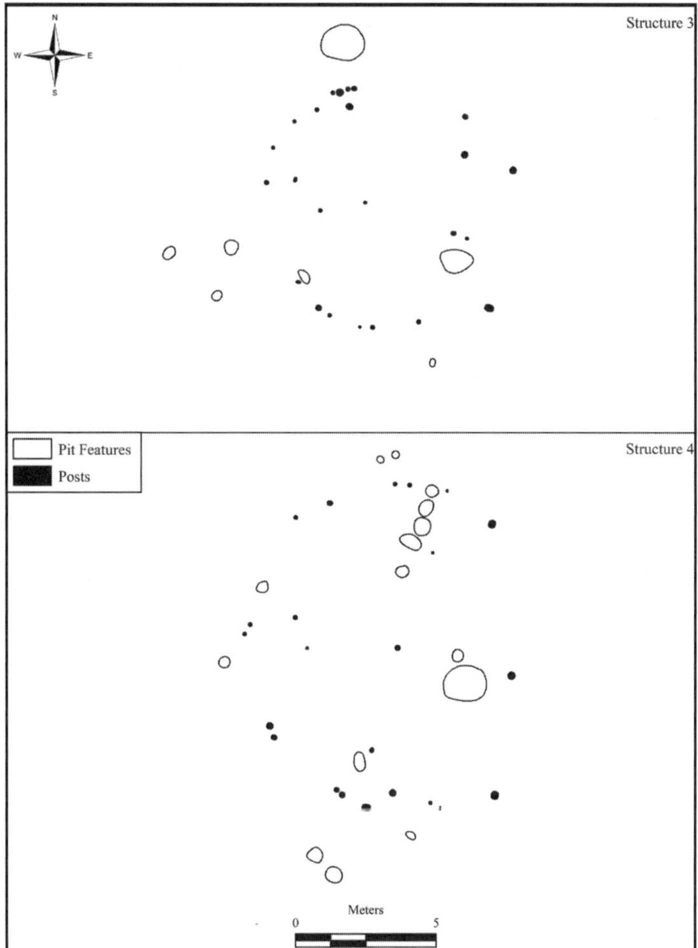

Fig. 8.3. Structures 3 and 4 on the embankment at the Troyville site (16CT7).

pits, and two bell-shaped pits were among the features located on the interior of Structure 6. Like Structures 1 and 2 from the embankment, internal support of Structure 6 consisted of a central post surrounded by four other posts set in a rectangle. Additional interior support posts were set approximately one meter (3.3 ft) from the outer wall. Four posts were set on the north side of the building to produce an extended entranceway. Radiometric assays from posts and pit features associated with Structures 5 and 6 returned fairly consistent median dates of cal. A.D. 780, indicating that both buildings were built and utilized either at the end of the Baytown period or during the early Coles Creek period (Lee 2006b; Lee et al. 2010).

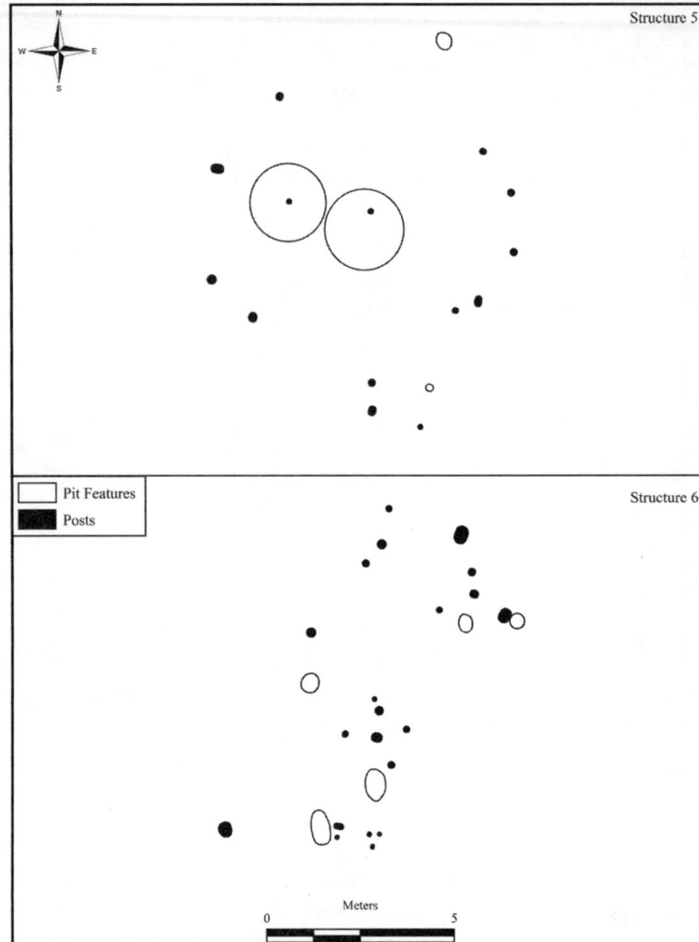

Fig. 8.4. Structures 5 and 6 on the riverbank at the Troyville site (16CT7).

MATERIAL CULTURE

Pottery used and discarded in the embankment and riverbank contexts included square/rectangular bowls, beakers, plates/platters, simple bowls, subglobular pots, restricted jars, necked jars, caldrons, and miniature pots (Figure 8.5). Marksville Incised, *vars. Goose Lake* and *Steel Bayou*, Marksville Stamped, *var. Manny*, and Churupa Punctated, *var. Churupa* ceramics were recovered from contexts dating between A.D. 570 and 650. These varieties are normally associated with the later part of the Middle Woodland period rather than with the Late Woodland (Jeter and Williams 1989a; Ryan, ed. 2004). The remaining decorated ceramic types are predominately late varieties of Marksville Incised, such as *vars.*

Fig. 8.5. Small-necked jar from Feature 49, Troyville (16CT7) 2005 embankment excavations.

Anglim and *Scott*, Marksville Stamped, *vars. Cummins, Troyville*, and *Bayou Rouge*, Churupa Punctated, *vars. Thornton* and *Watson*, Alligator Incised, Mulberry Creek Cord Marked, and Larto Red. These types and varieties are securely dated and occur after cal. A.D. 650. Although the overall Baytown cultural chronology is not in error, the clear temporal associations of these two suites of decorative ceramic types corroborate the findings from other sites, indicating that the early and late portions of the chronology are in need of reevaluation and reformulation.

Very few faunal remains were recovered from the embankment and riverbank excavations. These were highly fragmented and identifiable only as large and medium mammal. A small but diverse assemblage of plant remains was recovered from excavations at Troyville during 2005 and 2006. It included chenopod, pigweed, smartweed/knotweed, carpetweed, sunflower, purselane, spurge, passionflower, two unidentified grasses, an unidentified bean, dewberry or blackberry, grape, and persimmon. Most of the plant remains were recovered from the two pit clusters and midden south of the embankment structures. All of these starchy or oily seeds and sunflowers represented non-domesticated forms, thus substantiating earlier studies that indicated Baytown people were not actively domesticating these species.

The lithic raw material for arrow and dart points, boatstones, and drills from the 2005 and 2006 excavations included Citronelle gravel as well as novaculite. Large Citronelle cobbles with slightly concave upper surfaces and flattened lower surfaces were probably used to process seeds. Several small pieces of mica were recovered from the first midden, along the east flank of the embankment, and from the midden south of Structures 3 and 4. Although little is known about the use of mica at Troyville, it was not used as temper in pottery production. Andesite, diorite, and syenite were fashioned into celts used for heavy woodworking. White Catahoula sandstone was extensively used for abraders, grinding stones, and, in one instance, a hammerstone. Two grinding stones made of Catahoula sandstone from the pits beneath Structure 5 were encrusted with red hematite, suggesting that these tools were used to produce pigment. A small mortar of andesite that fit easily into a human fist had been discarded in one of the small interior pits in Structure 5 (see Neuman 1984:Plate 33g). Traces of pigment on the grinding surface indicate coarse pigment was further refined with these implements. Limonite, ocher, hematite, and glauconite used for pigment were more than likely used in the production of slipped and/or painted ceramics, such as Larto Red, Landon Red-on-Buff, Gold Mine Polychrome, Hewitt White-Filmed, Omega Red and Black, Quafalorma Red and White, and Woodville Zoned Red.

Citronelle gravel, hematite, and limonite are all found within 20 kilometers (12 mi) of the Troyville site (Hunter and Baker 1979; Lee et al. 1997). The most likely source of glauconite is the red ironstone deposits located along the headwaters of Bayou D'Arbonne in Lincoln and Claiborne parishes (De Hon et al. 2001:Figures 1 and 3). Bayou D'Arbonne is a major tributary of the Ouachita River and joins the river at Monroe, Louisiana.

The nearest sources of andesite, diorite, novaculite, and syenite are in the Ouachita Mountains of southern Arkansas. Specific locales where andesite, novaculite, and syenite are found in conjunction include Magnet Cove, Potash Sulphur Springs, and an unnamed dike near Hot Springs (Rolingson and Howard 1997:34–37, Figures 1 and 2). Additional locations in Arkansas include deposits in Pulaski and Saline counties, east of Hot Springs. The Hot Springs area is believed to be the likely source of the imported Arkansas material, since the Ouachita River would have been a logical and convenient transportation route. No surface or near surface deposits of mica have been identified in Louisiana (Paul Heinrich, personal communication 2007). Possible sources for mica are in Arkansas, southeast Missouri, and North Carolina (Mike Howard, personal communication 2007).

Summary and Future Research

In the overview at the beginning of this chapter, it was noted that there does not seem to be much evidence of community planning, a consistent site plan, or a hierarchical settlement pattern during the Baytown period. The information presented here suggests that there may in fact have been similarities between sites in relation to individual river drainages. The Greenhouse and Fredericks sites are located in the Lower Red River Valley and share many characteristics, such as midden ridges with mounds within them, burial within specific areas of the ridge and also in the midden, a common ceramic assemblage, and similar occupational dates. The McGuffee and Troyville sites are located in the Lower Ouachita River Valley. Both are located on natural levees on the west side of the Ouachita and Black rivers, respectively, and both have similar embankments. Troyville is only 19 kilometers (12 mi) downstream from McGuffee. The largest monuments at each site were multistage mounds with a conical mound on the summit, and both multistage mounds were connected to another mound by a causeway. Both sites have similar ranges of occupation, although there is presently insufficient data to determine whether site inhabitation was contemporaneous. The preceding, limited examples do not provide sufficient evidence for region-wide community planning at major mound sites, but they do point out striking similarities and indicate more research is needed to systematically address this issue.

Subsistence data acquired during the last twenty years have produced no evidence that Baytown populations in Louisiana had domesticated native cultigens like their contemporaries in the northern LMV. There is some evidence for long-distance trade with the eastern Gulf Coast and the upper portion of the LMV, a continuation perhaps of trade routes previously established during the Marksville period. There is also now ample evidence indicating the need to reevaluate the ceramic suites used to define the early and late divisions of the Baytown period in the southern LMV.

Despite extensive destruction, recent investigations at the Troyville site have established that some archaeological deposits remain intact. Fifty-five radiometric assays from the site document components or occupations dating from the Marksville through the Mississippi periods. Construction of the embankment began during the middle of the Baytown period, with episodic repair and reuse during the later part of the Baytown period. The embankment at Troyville seems unique in that it was built in two separate and distinct construction episodes, with structures, cultural features, and deposits placed on top of the first stage. Although its purpose is not yet fully understood, the ritual space demarcated by the embankment was created almost a century before Mound 5 was constructed. Wooden palisades likely surrounded Mounds 4 and 5 at Troyville, perhaps differentiating symbolic space, while at the same time separating these mound precincts from other site areas and the general population.

Structures 1 and 2 from the embankment were smaller than their predecessors (Structures 3 and 4) and built with different construction techniques. These differences may indicate a shift from a communal to more individualistic use of the top of the embankment. Structure 5 seems to be a multi-purpose building used for several activities, such as heat-treating lithic raw material, pigment production, and trash disposal. Structure 6 is believed to represent a domestic structure associated with the Baytown period occupation of Troyville. These structures and the presence of domestic refuse middens not associated with the mounds indicate a residential population at the site during the Baytown period. Data are not sufficient at present to determine if the residential population expanded during the Baytown or subsequent Coles Creek and Mississippi periods. Nonetheless, the Troyville mounds and embankment were clearly not part of a vacant ceremonial center.

There is an obvious need to continue research at the Troyville and McGuffee sites, both to examine mound construction and residential areas in more detail and to investigate the possible temporal and cultural relationships within and between these sites. The buildings and many of the pit features excavated at Troyville in 2005 and 2006 are the first of their kind documented in the southern LMV. Additional research will be required to elaborate on the findings presented here. Archaeological investigations of non-mound sites should also be carried out, since information from such sites is almost totally lacking for the Baytown period in the southern LMV. Only by actively pursing such research will we begin to better understand the material remains, sites, and lives of a long-ignored segment of Louisiana's prehistoric Native American population.

9

Coles Creek

LORI M. ROE AND TIMOTHY M. SCHILLING

Coles Creek culture developed in the southern Lower Mississippi Valley (LMV) around A.D. 700, and manifestations of this culture persisted until around A.D. 1200 (Figure 1.3). The Coles Creek period marks an important transition in social organization in the LMV from the relatively egalitarian cultures of the preceding Baytown period (A.D. 400–700) to the hierarchical polities that existed in Plaquemine culture of the Mississippi period (A.D. 1200–1700). Changes in settlement patterns, mortuary practices, and ceramic technology and decoration distinguish Coles Creek culture from the preceding Troyville culture (Kidder 2002b; Lee, Chapter 8 in this volume). Coles Creek culture is best known for distinctive ceremonial centers, with earthen platform mounds situated around level plazas. Numerous mound centers were constructed during the Coles Creek period, and these centers were focal points for Coles Creek communities. From early to late in the Coles Creek period, settlements became less dispersed and more aggregated around mound centers (Kidder 2002b; Wells 1997). Landscape modifications and construction efforts at some Coles Creek mound sites were tremendous, and a few Coles Creek mound sites rival later Mississippi period mound sites in size (Roe 2007).

The function of mound centers and their implications for the social and political organization of Coles Creek society have been the focus of much Coles Creek research (e.g., Barker 1999; Ford 1951; Kidder 1990a, 1992a; Roe 2007; Ryan, ed. 2004; Steponaitis 1986; Wells 1998; Wells and Weinstein 2007; Williams and Brain 1983). Mound construction techniques, cultural remains on mounds, and the plan and architecture of mound sites illustrate social change during the Coles Creek period. In the Baytown and earlier Marksville periods, most mounds were constructed to cover group burials (cf. Belmont 1984:83–86; Lee, Chapter 8 in this volume; McGimsey 2004, Chapter 7 in this volume). Mound burial practices continued in changed form during the Coles Creek period (Ford 1951; Giardino 1984b; Kassabaum 2007; Williams and Brain 1983). Mound activities expanded beyond mortuary practices, however, during the Coles Creek period. Many Coles Creek mounds were constructed primarily as platforms for activity areas and buildings that possibly served as residences, charnel (mortuary) houses, and council houses. While platform mounds were occasionally constructed in the LMV prior to the Coles Creek period (Knight 2001; Lee, Chapter 8 in this volume; Lindauer and Blitz 1997; McGimsey, Chapter 7 in this volume), they were a ubiquitous architectural feature at Coles Creek mound sites, where often the largest mound at the site was a platform mound (Kidder 2004a; Phillips 1970; Williams and Brain 1983).

The development and formalization of the mound-and-plaza ceremonial center that emphasized flat-topped, platform mounds were presumed to reflect changes in religious beliefs and institutions, as well as the increased political influence of social leaders (Jennings 1952:265; Phillips et al. 1951:441). Coles Creek mounds were first identified as "temple mounds" (Ford and Willey 1941), and they were thought to reflect a transition to public ceremonies led by high-status religious specialists with esoteric knowledge (Phillips et al. 1951:441). In addition, the remains of buildings on the summits of mounds have often been interpreted as the residences of chiefs (Kidder 1992a; Steponaitis 1986). The transformation of mounds from communal mortuary tumuli into residential and ceremonial platforms that were accessible only to a few elite may have begun during the Coles Creek period. Yet there is little clear evidence for social ranking found among the material remains of Coles Creek culture.

Coles Creek mound centers are architecturally similar to those constructed and used during the subsequent Mississippi period. Accordingly, interpretations of Coles Creek culture have been influenced by historical accounts of southeastern chiefdoms and by archaeological information about Mississippian chiefdoms. Mississippian polities were ruled by high-status chiefs and their families, who resided at mound centers and overtly displayed their wealth and social status (Cobb 2003; Rees, Chapter 10 in this volume). Archaeological data and historical accounts indicate that Mississippian societies were dependent on maize agriculture to sustain large, sedentary populations (Smith 1985, 1986:53–57).

Though Coles Creek culture has sometimes been presented as a regional variant of early or emergent Mississippian culture, Coles Creek culture did not follow the same path of development seen in Mississippian societies elsewhere in the Southeast. Maize-based agriculture and long-distance trade networks did not play significant roles in the social and ceremonial developments in the Coles Creek region (Kidder 1992a, 2004b; Kidder and Fritz 1993). Instead, Coles Creek culture apparently developed from indigenous cultural changes that were not linked to dramatic shifts in subsistence practices. Like Mississippian chiefs, high-status individuals may have resided on Coles Creek mounds. Structural remains and midden deposits indicate some type of occupation took place on the mounds. Among the archaeological remains of Coles Creek communities, though, it is difficult to find clear evidence that some community members had greater social status, wealth, or power than others. Faunal studies suggest that better cuts of meat were consumed on or near mounds compared to non-mound contexts (Belmont 1983; Brown 1984). Yet excavations at Coles Creek mound centers generally do not result in status symbols and ritual items such as those found at Mississippian mound centers. Artifact assemblages from mound and non-mound occupations are often only subtly different from one another (e.g., Roe 2008; Ryan, ed. 2004; Wells 1998). Further, differences in status and wealth are not reflected in variations in grave preparations and offerings. The vast majority of Coles Creek mound burials lack grave furniture and elaborate grave preparation (Ford 1951; Giardino 1984b; Kassabaum 2007; Williams and Brain 1983).

The social and political organization of Coles Creek society is not well understood, but polities apparently became larger, with many settlements networked together through social and ceremonial institutions. Social leaders may have gained power and influence by intensifying existing institutions of social inequality, such as those found in kinship organization (Knight 1990). Increasing population and decreased mobility would have presented new economic and social challenges, and some individuals may have capitalized on the need for greater information exchange and social interaction networks to solidify their leadership positions (Barker 1993; Kidder 1992a; Nassaney 1992). Archaeologists' perceptions of Coles Creek culture have changed markedly over several decades of research. In the following pages, the authors present an overview of Coles Creek archaeological remains and discuss related changes in perceptions, competing models of Coles Creek culture, and recent and proposed trends in Coles Creek research.

Archaeological Remains and Perceptions of Coles Creek Culture

There are widespread similarities in public architecture and other cultural remains in much of the LMV and the Louisiana coastal region during the Coles Creek period. Extensive interaction with external groups was rare in the Coles Creek world, but interaction among groups within the Coles Creek region is attested to by these widespread cultural similarities. Regional differences in ceramic assemblages and subsistence practices are also evident. These cultural variations may reflect social differences and varying strategies of internal and external group interaction within the Coles Creek world. Culture change in the Coles Creek period was not always dramatic, but there were significant indigenous social developments from early to late in the Coles Creek period. Polities became larger and more centralized, and leaders increased their power and influence. By the end of the Coles Creek period, some groups in northeast Louisiana and the Yazoo Basin began to interact and perhaps form alliances with Mississippian people from the Central Mississippi Valley to the north (Brain 1989:132; Brain and Phillips 1996:384–388; Kidder 2004b:559; Wells and Weinstein 2007; Williams and Brain 1983).

The most visible archaeological remains of Coles Creek culture are the large mound-and-plaza arrangements at major sites. Coles Creek mound centers would have required a high degree of planning and coordinated labor to construct. The mound-and-plaza precincts reflect an increased focus on mound construction and formalized site plans. Mound sites are larger and more numerous than during the Baytown period, and the general layout of mounds and plazas is similar throughout the Coles Creek region (Figure 9.1). Though there is some variability in the size and number of mounds and in the size of plazas at Coles Creek sites, Williams and Brain (1983:407) observe that Coles Creek centers appeared to have been constructed "according to rigidly considered plans that were widely disseminated." The similarity of mound sites implies widespread commonalities in the meaning and function of mound-and-plaza architecture. Most Coles Creek mound sites consist of one to several flat-topped mounds situated around a single plaza that was kept clean of debris. The plazas were constructed by flattening raised areas and filling in depressions with soil to create a level surface (Kidder 2004a). The typical Coles Creek mound site consists of two to four mounds less than 6 meters (20 ft) high, like the Balmoral site (16TE12) in the Tensas Basin (Figure 9.1; Williams and Brain 1983:405, 407). Some Coles Creek sites, such as Insley (16FR3), Mott (16FR11), Osceola (16TE2), Pritchard's Landing (16CT14), and Raffman (16MA20), were much larger and contain many more mounds (Figure 9.1, Barker 1992; Gibson 1985a, 1996a; Kidder 1998a; Roe 2007; Schilling 2006).

Excavations at mound sites such as Bayou Grande Cheniere (16PL159), Greenhouse (16AV2), Lake George (22YZ577), Mount Nebo (16MA18), Osceola, and Raffman have revealed that many Coles Creek mound sites were used and expanded over hundreds of years (Ford 1951; Kidder 2004b; Roe 2007; Saucier 1990; Schilling 2004; Williams and Brain 1983). Other mound sites had comparatively brief occupations. The Lake Providence Mounds (16EC6) were notably

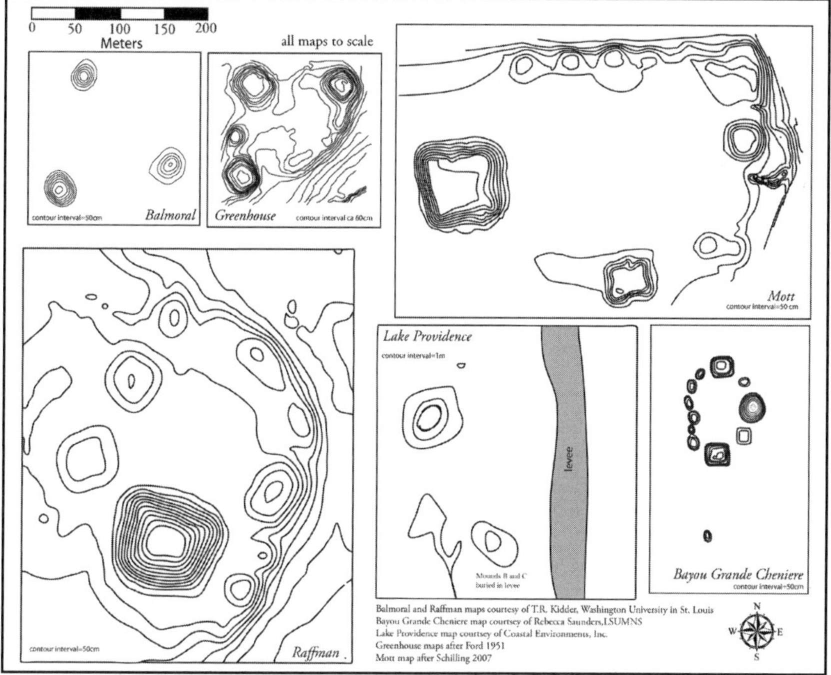

Fig. 9.1. Selected Coles Creek mound site plans.

constructed, used, and abandoned over a period of little more than one hundred years (Weinstein, ed. 2005; Wells and Weinstein 2007:45).

There is a general trend in construction through time towards more clearly delineated mound-and-plaza precincts (Kidder 1998a). Early in the Coles Creek period, many mound sites consisted of a single mound situated next to an open plaza. As new mounds were constructed and existing mounds were enlarged, the mound-and-plaza precinct became physically restricted from the surrounding area. At Raffman, an expansion of the site involved extending a natural terrace and erecting two small mounds to border the plaza on its northern edge (Kidder 2004a; Roe 2007). At Greenhouse, Coles Creek mound construction transformed an open plaza surrounded by midden into a plaza bounded by mounds (Ford 1951; Kidder 1998a). At Bayou Grande Cheniere, a ridge was constructed late in the Coles Creek period that bounded the open western portion of the plaza (Schilling 2004). This physical bounding of the mound-and-plaza precinct may indicate that access to the precinct became more restricted through time (Kidder 1998a).

In addition to the larger scale of mound construction during the Coles Creek period, settlement patterns also reflect the increased importance of mound centers. The development of multi-tiered settlement systems, with non-mound settlements surrounding mound sites, indicates that Coles Creek societies were more centralized and more focused on mound centers than previous cultures in the region. Settlement types include mound centers, small villages, and hamlets. People also lived in larger villages by the late Coles Creek period.

Settlement pattern research in the Tensas and Boeuf basins reveals that several mound centers existed at any given time (Barker 1993; Belmont 1985; Wells 1997). Early in the Coles Creek period, many small mound sites of approximately equal size were surrounded by dispersed villages and hamlets. By the late Coles Creek period, there was a significant increase in the number and size of mound centers, and non-mound settlements were more aggregated around mound sites (Wells 1997). This settlement pattern suggests both stronger ties between mound centers and surrounding settlements, and greater competition between polities. Some non-mound villages in the late Coles Creek period were larger than most. These may have served different, and perhaps more expansive, economic and social functions than smaller villages and hamlets (Wells and Weinstein 2007). Some mound centers were also larger than others, reflecting differences in labor efforts and/or duration of use. However, no single mound community appears to have been a dominant regional center, with associated influence over smaller mound communities (Kidder 2002b; Wells 1997).

Similar settlement patterns existed along the Louisiana coast, though mound sites and polities tended to be smaller than in the LMV to the north (Schilling 2004; Weinstein 1987a). Coles Creek people in the coastal region located settlements along secondary streams with easy access to both a principal waterway and the marshes lining the natural-levee systems (Kidder 1995). Researchers have argued that Coles Creek mound centers were strategically placed along natural levees and within adjacent marshes to control access to resources (Weinstein and Kelley 1992:351). Platform mounds were generally built on the natural levees of relic distributary systems or, in the western coastal region of the Chenier Plain, on remnant beach ridges. Villages were usually located at the junctures of tributaries or smaller streams. Smaller camps and resource-procurement locales were dispersed between villages.

Mound-and-plaza sites were an integral part of Coles Creek settlement systems in Louisiana, but most people lived in non-mound settlements. Coles Creek mound sites are believed to have functioned as ceremonial centers, with a small group of resident high-status individuals. The rest of the community gathered periodically for rituals and social events (Hally 1972:586; Williams and

Brain 1983:407). Relative to the overall size of mound sites, few houses and only limited areas of domestic debris have been found (Ford 1951; Phillips et al. 1951:316, 343; Williams and Brain 1983:407). It is still debated whether mound sites permanently supported larger residential populations, and, if so, what size such populations might have reached.

Few studies have been undertaken to examine the functional differences between mound and non-mound settlements. The dissertation research conducted by Douglas Wells (1998) is one notable exception. He compared artifact assemblages from Shackleford Lake (16TE1), an early Coles Creek mound site, with those from Lisa's Ridge (16TE144), a contemporary village located nearby. Artifact assemblages from the two sites were similar overall, though the mound site ceramic vessel assemblage contained a greater diversity of decorative varieties (Wells 1998:209–220). The greater diversity of ceramic decoration suggests that activities involving ceramic vessels at the mound site emphasized transmission of social information though ceramic iconography (Pauketat 1987; Wells 1998:220). Wells also found possible evidence of feasting at Shackleford Lake, in the form of large serving bowls and abundant fish remains (Wells 1998). Artifact assemblages from late Coles Creek mound and non-mound sites are also similar to one another (Roe 2008; Ryan, ed. 2004). The similarities among ceramics and lithics at mound and non-mound settlements support the idea that people lived at mound sites and conducted the same kinds of residential activities at both types of sites. Status differences between the residents of mound and non-mound settlements, however, are not evident in the artifact assemblages.

Excavations at mound sites have provided information about how these sites were used, as well as their function within the larger community. Mound sites were apparently used for a range of both residential and ceremonial activities. Coles Creek mounds often served as platforms for wooden-post structures, but the function of these structures is uncertain. At the Greenhouse, Lake George, Morgan (16VM9), and Raffman mound sites, post molds and other structural remains were discovered on the summits of some mound stages dating to the Coles Creek period (Belmont 1967; Ford 1951; Fuller and Fuller 1987; Kidder 2004a; Roe 2007; Williams and Brain 1983). On the summits of mound stages at Greenhouse, post molds formed circular patterns similar to, though larger than, non-mound wooden-post structures at the site (Belmont 1967). Structural remains on other mound stages consisted of hardened clay floors and/or post molds that formed no discernable pattern (Ford 1951). Hearths and midden deposits were associated with some mound-top structures at Greenhouse and Morgan (Belmont 1967; Fuller and Fuller 1987; Steponaitis 1986). At Lake George, burials were placed in and around mound-top structures (Williams and Brain 1983:334–335). Excavations over the last few years at the Raffman mound site have revealed remains of wooden posts and heavy midden deposits on one of the flat-topped mounds at the site (Kidder 2004a; Roe 2007). But ceramic types and forms are similar to those found in non-mound domestic contexts. Drawing on information about structural remains from Mississippian sites and ethnohistorical accounts of mound use, some scholars have interpreted those Coles Creek mound structures associated with burials as charnel houses or mortuary temples (Steponaitis 1986:385; Williams and Brain 1983:334–335). Other mound-top structural remains have generally been interpreted as residences of individuals or lineages with important social or religious roles. Structures on mounds may also have served as council houses or locations for other social gatherings.

It may be equally important that some Coles Creek flat-topped mounds did not support wooden-post buildings. For example, excavations on the largest mound at the Raffman site have uncovered no structural remains, burials, midden deposits, or other features (Kidder 2004a; Roe 2007). Lack of burials and cultural debris may attest to the social and religious importance of the mounds themselves, perhaps as markers of sacred ground or as tangible symbols of the capabilities of communities that constructed them, or the leaders that organized their construction (Knight 2001).

The existence of possible residences on the summits of Coles Creek mounds has been interpreted as marking a significant change in social organization. Steponaitis (1986) suggests that a system of rule by hereditary elites began during the Coles Creek period. He notes that during the Mississippi period, residential structures were constructed on the summits of sequential mound stages. Mississippian mound structures were often destroyed and covered with a new mound stage after the death of a chief and the ascension of an heir to power. Kidder (1998a) reasons that an emerging Coles Creek elite enhanced their social prestige by living on mounds that were often constructed over Baytown mortuary precincts. They were thereby physically linking their homes with traditional mortuary and ceremonial locations that were probably considered an integral part of the proper functioning of the community. The Coles Creek period may consequently mark a pivotal point in the development of hereditary chiefdoms in the LMV—the transformation of communal-ceremonial centers into semi-private, chiefly domains (Kidder 1998a; Steponaitis 1986).

But evidence for differences in status and wealth, which would be expected if leaders were becoming chiefs or elite, is equivocal at best in Coles Creek burials. Williams and Brain (1983:45), discussing mound burials from the Lake George site, note that "the dead seem to have been treated inconsistently and often with minimal care." Burials were generally placed on the summits and slopes of mounds and covered over with more dirt. Grave preparation was minimal, but burials were not placed haphazardly on the mound. Most Coles Creek mound burials consist of groups of primary and secondary interments, as would result from the periodic emptying of a charnel house (Kassabaum 2007:50). Mound burials include extended, bundle, and flexed burials. Many individuals are represented by partial skeletons or just a skull (Ford 1951; Giardino 1984b; Kassabaum 2007; Williams and Brain 1983). In a recent analysis of mortuary patterns at Greenhouse, Lake George, and Mount Nebo, Kassabaum (2007) found correlations between burial treatment and an individual's age. Specific mortuary practices differed between these three mound sites, but correlations were found between age groups and mortuary treatment among the burials from each site (Kassabaum 2007).

Grave offerings are extremely rare among Coles Creek burials. A few individuals, however, were buried with grave offerings or were surrounded by both primary and secondary burials of juveniles and adults (Kidder 1998a:135; Williams and Brain 1983). For example, a distinctive burial from Lake George and another from the Mount Nebo mound site were comprised of an adult male surrounded by the remains of other individuals, mostly children or adult females (Barker 1999:217–222; Giardino 1984b; Kidder 1998a:135). Burial 49 at Lake George consisted of the skeleton of an adult male surrounded by thirteen infants. The central position of the adult male may indicate he was an important person, leader, or the head of a lineage. However, the skeleton was "carelessly extended in a twisted prone position" (Williams and Brain 1983:47), suggesting that the remains were not treated with the utmost attention. At Mount Nebo, a central male individual in a mass grave was interred with deer antlers at or on his head, a deer jaw at his feet, and a human skull near his abdomen (Giardino 1984b; Kidder 2002b:86).

Barker (1999) has interpreted the central figures in mound burials as high-status individuals whose deaths warranted mass burial events and accompanying mound construction. Furthermore, Barker argues that some segments of Coles Creek communities were not buried in mounds. Based on mound burial populations at Lake George with a disproportionately high number of children, Barker (1999:219–220) states that there were two distinct groups in Coles Creek society, "a portion of the population receiving mound burial, and another (presumably commoner) portion which generally contributes only infants to mound inhumations." However, Kassabaum (2007:47) asserts that the number of infants in the Lake George mound burials fits the expected demographic profile for a prehistoric population.

Harmon and Rose (1989:337–338) examined the skeletal remains recovered from mound burials at the Mount Nebo site. They observed that the remains from early Coles Creek mound burials had typical arthritic patterns for hunter-gatherers, whereas the remains from late Coles Creek contexts showed no signs of arthritis (Harmon and Rose 1989:337). Though Harmon and Rose tested a small sample of skeletons, their research suggests that by the late Coles Creek period, the people buried in mounds were no longer undertaking workloads typical of hunter-gatherers. They may have been exempt from the normal subsistence work performed by the rest of the community.

Differences in the faunal remains between mound and non-mound contexts have been used as evidence that the activities that took place on the mounds, or the people living on the mounds, had greater social importance. Faunal assemblages from the Morgan mound site in coastal Louisiana show a marked variation among midden deposits located in non-mound and mound-top contexts. Mammals such as deer were consumed in relatively greater quantities on top of the mounds than in non-mound areas. These data may indicate elite residents on the mound were being provisioned with red meat by commoners, who themselves were eating mostly fish and turtles in non-mound locations (Brown 1984:107, 1987:163). The distribution of deer remains at the Lake George site may also indicate that the best cuts of meat were reserved for people living on mounds (Belmont 1983).

Though some degree of hierarchical organization existed in Coles Creek society, social status and wealth were apparently not displayed through possession of prestige goods and exotic trade items (Barker 1999:15–16, 175; Kidder 2002b). Coles Creek material culture shows that Coles Creek communities did not participate extensively in long-distance exchanges of goods, though ceramic decorations do show some cultural connections with areas outside of the Coles Creek region. Ceramic vessels and stone tools found in Coles Creek contexts were generally produced from local materials, and exotic special-purpose items were extremely rare for most of the Coles Creek period. Non-local lithics are uncommon, even though local lithic sources were sometimes of poor quality and the lithic material difficult to knap. Stone-tool technology was fairly simple, and formal chipped or ground stone tools are not abundant in Coles Creek contexts. Bow and arrow technology was introduced to the LMV during the Baytown period or around the transition from the Baytown to the Coles Creek period (Kidder 2004b; cf. Lee, Chapter 8 in this volume). Arrow points became the

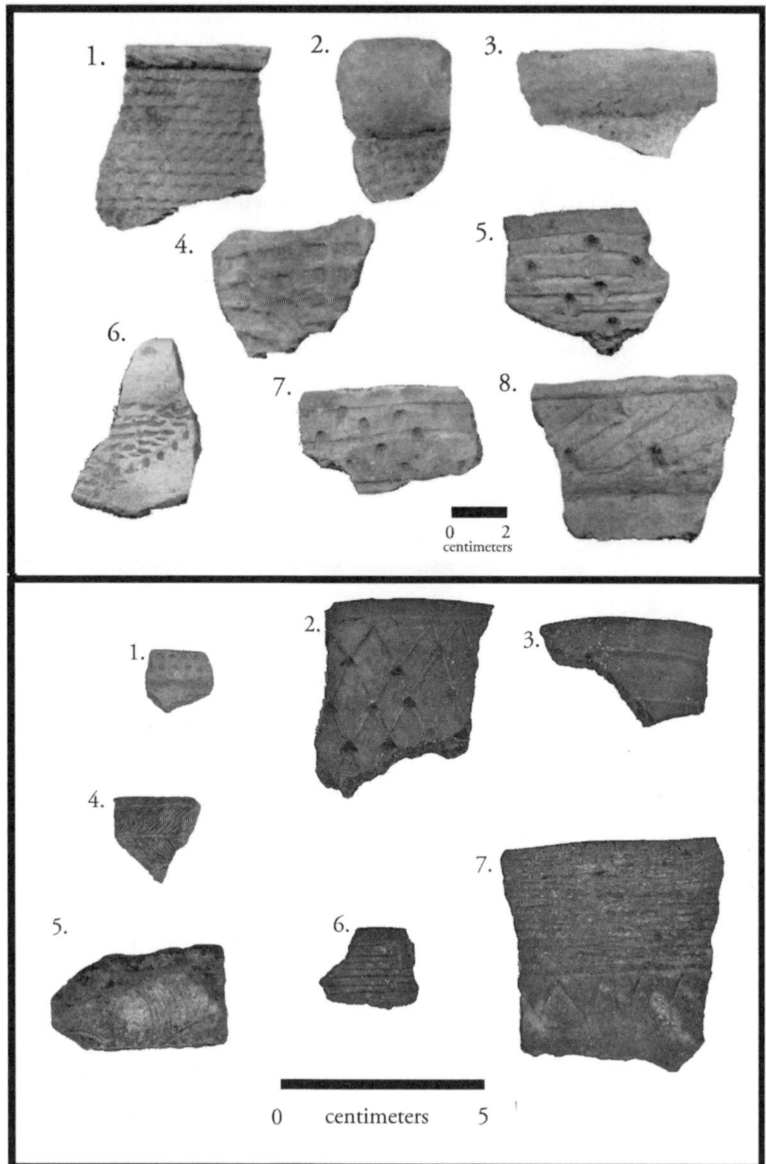

Fig. 9.2. Coles Creek decorated pottery from the eastern Delta (top) and Tensas Basin (bottom). Top: 1, 2, & 4. Pontchartrain Check Stamped, *var. Pontchartrain;* 3. Baytown Plain, *var. unspecified;* 5 & 7. Coles Creek Incised, *var. Athanasio;* 6. French Fork Incised, *var. Lafayette;* 8. Mazique Incised, *var. Back Ridge.* Bottom: 1. Evansville Punctated, *var. Evansville;* 2. Beldeau Incised, *var. unspecified;* 3. Coles Creek Incised, *var. Greenhouse;* 4. Carter Engraved, *var. Sara;* 5. French Fork Incised, *var. unspecified;* 6 & 7. Coles Creek Incised, *var. Mott.*

most common type of projectile point in Coles Creek deposits at approximately or slightly before A.D. 700.

Coles Creek ceramics tend to be hard, well-made, and tempered with grog (crushed pieces of ceramic or fired clay). Coles Creek ceramics exhibit common decorations throughout the region, although there is variation in the frequencies of different types of decorations. Rectilinear incised designs restricted to the rims of vessels are among the most common Coles Creek ceramic decoration. Curvilinear incised designs, punctations, rocker stamping, and combinations of these techniques are also found (Figure 9.2). Along the coast, paddle-stamped pottery is also common. The effigy vessels found in some Baytown period burial contexts are not found during the Coles Creek period, though a few fired-clay human figurines have been discovered in Coles Creek contexts. Decorative patterns on pottery vessels tend to be abstract, with no known anthropomorphic (human-shaped) or zoomorphic (animal-shaped) ceramic designs. Coles Creek vessel forms are fairly simple. Restricted-orifice jars, beakers, and unrestricted and globular bowls are the most common vessel forms in Coles Creek ceramic assemblages (Kidder 1993a; Lee et al. 1997; Ryan, ed. 2004).

Some Coles Creek pottery decorations show cultural connections with the Plum Bayou culture in Arkansas and cultures along the eastern Gulf Coast (Blitz and Mann 2000:41–47; Brown 1984; Fuller 1998; Jeter and Scott 2008; Phillips 1970). Decorative motifs found in both the Coles Creek and Plum Bayou areas include single-line incisions on the vessel lip (Coles Creek Incised, *var. Keo*) and parallel-line incisions on the vessel rim (Coles Creek Incised) among others (Jeter and Scott 2008).

Stylistic similarities between the coast of Louisiana and the eastern Gulf Coast have long been noted (Davis 1984). Pottery from coastal sites indicates the local residents participated in a long-standing interaction network that spanned from the Chenier Plain to at least as far east as the Apalachicola River (Saunders 1997:95). Nassaney and Cobb (1991:314) point out resemblances between Weeden Island Incised and French Fork Incised, arguing for strong cultural connections early in the Coles Creek period. One of the most ubiquitous types from the coast, Pontchartrain Check Stamped, is rarely found farther north than the Natchez Bluffs (Phillips 1970:154). Clear connections can be seen between Pontchartrain Check Stamped and Wakulla Check Stamped from Weeden Island II contexts in northwest Florida (Brown 1982a:21). At the same time, complicated paddle-stamped motifs that resemble pottery designs usually found around the Tampa Bay region are also found on the coast. Clay sourcing for complicated stamped sherds indicate local manufacture, but stylistic similarities do indicate some form of connection, either through the exchange of paddles used to produce the decorations or the movement of people (Saunders 1997; Saunders and Stoltman 1999).

Coles Creek ceramics are distinct from those produced by earlier Baytown period groups and later Plaquemine groups. Even so, ceramics show cultural continuity in the region. Late Baytown and early Coles Creek period decorative types overlap in time, and plainwares produced in the late Baytown and early Coles Creek periods are virtually indistinguishable. The transition from Coles Creek to Plaquemine culture is characterized by changes in ceramic paste composition and the introduction of new decorative patterns. Variations of Coles Creek ceramic designs continued to be applied to Plaquemine ceramic wares (Kidder 1993a; Rees, Chapter 10 in this volume; Ryan, ed. 2004; Weinstein, ed. 2005).

Coles Creek subsistence relied on wild plants and animals readily available in the areas surrounding sites. Coles Creek subsistence was once thought to be based largely on maize agriculture, much like emergent Mississippian communities in the Central Mississippi Valley. Research over the last decade and a half, however, has shown that maize played little to no role in subsistence until the very end of the Coles Creek period (Fritz 1990; Kidder and Fritz 1993). Domesticated versions of native grasses, such as maygrass, chenopod, and knotweed, have been identified at some Coles Creek sites (Roberts 2004, 2006). Grass seed remains from other Coles Creek sites appear to be wild, so cultivation was not a widespread subsistence strategy (Roberts 2004, 2006). Recent bioarchaeological analyses of human skeletons from the LMV—including examination of stable isotopes, dental pathologies, and non-specific pathologies—support the idea that Coles Creek subsistence was predominantly based on a hunting and gathering economy (Listi 2007). Consumption of starchy plants increased during the Coles Creek period, but maize remained only a minor component of Coles Creek diet (Listi 2007). Acorns and hickory nuts were staple plant foods, and berries, tubers, grass seeds, and greens played an important yet supplemental role in the diet. Along the inland river valleys, deer and fish were the main sources of animal protein (Kelley 1992; Mariaca 1988). In coastal regions, alligator and muskrat were commonly exploited, in addition to deer and fish (Smith 1996).

Research Trends

Coles Creek culture has been the focus of much research in the LMV over the past two decades. Research has focused on refining our knowledge of the material culture and subsistence strategies of the Coles Creek people, and on discovering the processes underlying the development of social and political complexity.

Perhaps the greatest challenge facing Coles Creek researchers today is to develop finer-scale chronologies. Currently, the Coles Creek period is defined through a series of archaeological phases as long as 150 years in some regions. Clearly, if we are to understand how past peoples lived, smaller temporal units are needed. This lack of chronological resolution creates interpretive problems. Although it was once thought that construction of large platform mounds was done incrementally and over a relatively long time during the Coles Creek period, data from the Tensas Basin suggest mound construction may have occurred as intense, short-term events (Kidder 2004a; Roe 2007). The lack of chronological control also hampers evaluation of settlement pattern data. Determining the occupation period of non-mound sites can be especially difficult, as chronologically diagnostic artifacts are often not found during the archaeological surveys that locate these sites. Since settlement patterns have been used as evidence for the existence of centralized polities, understanding which settlements were contemporary is important. In addition to refining chronologies, further investigations at both mound and non-mound sites are needed in order to better understand how different types of settlements functioned within Coles Creek polities. Most excavations to date have focused on mound sites. Excavations at non-mound settlements in the Tensas Basin have resulted in the recovery of intact cultural features and diagnostic artifacts (Lee et al. 1997; Kidder 1993a), demonstrating the potential of non-mound settlement research.

Geological soil-coring techniques can be useful in establishing occupation and construction chronologies at mound centers. Short of excavating and documenting numerous large and small mound sites, the best way to begin to determine individual mound construction and use histories may be through soil coring and accelerator mass spectrometry (AMS) dating of individual mounds. Multiple age determinations from individual mounds would allow researchers to establish the histories of different mound centers and to understand regional political dynamics.

Research on the possible connections between settlements is also needed. Only a few comparisons of the cultural features and artifact assemblages between mound and non-mound settlements have been conducted (e.g., Wells 1998). Artifact analyses should be geared towards deriving data on ceramic and lithic use, as well as chronological information. Studies of the form and possible function of ceramic vessels are now commonly conducted (e.g., Ryan, ed. 2004; Weinstein, ed. 2005). Continued work examining the activities that took place at different types of settlements and the material connections between these settlements will provide a much more robust understanding of the social and economic networks that held Coles Creek polities together.

In addition to improved field strategies, researchers will need to continue to develop more sophisticated interpretations of material culture. Work by Saunders (1997) may provide a model for understanding the social aspects of pottery. Understanding the source and distribution of stylistic variation should be considered vital to interpretations of social and political boundaries among Coles Creek communities. Material variation within the Coles Creek region has been used as evidence to argue that different subsistence and political strategies were practiced by different Coles Creek communities. For example, external contacts evident at some Coles Creek sites may signal political competition within the Coles Creek region and attempts by some groups to form external alliances or control trade (Wells and Weinstein 2007).

Coles Creek culture presents archaeologists with the unique challenge of understanding the organizational institutions of complex societies that were not based on more overt forms of social ranking. Examination of the material connections and variations between sites and between settlement systems should help us understand the social ties and cultural processes that led to the development of these incipiently centralized polities.

10

Plaquemine and Mississippian

MARK A. REES

Like Troyville and Coles Creek, Plaquemine and Mississippian are archaeological names for mostly undocumented Native American cultures, what Marvin Jeter (2002:184) calls "archaeo-cultures." Plaquemine and Mississippian, though, have native linguistic roots. Plaquemine culture was originally named after the city of Plaquemine in West Baton Rouge Parish. The city, bayou, and parish in southeast Louisiana in turn derive their names from the Muskogean or Mobilian "piakimin" (in Creole, "Placminier"), referring to the persimmon, an indigenous fruit tree used by Native Americans for millennia (Du Pratz 1975 [1774]; Read 1927:50–51; cf. Gatschet 1883:157). The cultural and archaeological origins of Mississippian lie upriver and outside of present-day Louisiana, buried in the vast expanse of floodplain between the Arkansas and Missouri rivers. "Mississippi" is Ojibwe or Algonquian for "great water," taught to French *coureurs des bois* in the seventeenth century (Read 1927:39; White 1991:5–6).

Geologist, anthropologist, and museum curator William Henry Holmes (1886:369–372, 1903:21, 80–81) initially described distinctive types of shell-tempered pottery from this region as the "Middle Mississippi Valley group" and "Middle Mississippi Province." By the 1930s, association of these ceramic vessels with contemporaneous earthen mounds and village sites was discussed in terms of a Middle Mississippi "phase" and a Mississippi "pattern" (Griffin 1985:44–52; e.g., Moore 1910:259; Phillips 1939:107–109). Influenced by a culture historical approach prevalent in early twentieth-century anthropology, the flat-topped pyramidal mounds and ceramics became emblematic of a prolific culture dating from the Mississippi period (ca. A.D. 1000–1700) throughout much of the southeastern United States (Griffin 1946:75–91, 1952:361–362; Phillips et al. 1951:445–451). The Mississippi period in the southern Lower Mississippi Valley (LMV), including present-day Louisiana, is now conventionally placed at A.D. 1200 to 1700 (Figure 1.3).

Plaquemine culture also emerged in this culture-historical setting. In 1939, the Louisiana State Archaeological Survey, Louisiana State University (LSU), and the federal Work Projects Administration began investigating two seemingly insignificant mounds on the west bank of the Mississippi River, south of Baton Rouge. These American Indian mounds were not the "stupendous" monuments described by Euroamerican settlers elsewhere in the Mississippi Valley (Quimby 1951:88; e.g., Brackenridge 1814:187; Shetrone 1930:39–43). Nor did they rival the much earlier, massive earthworks at Poverty Point or Troyville (see Gibson, Chapter 5 in this volume; Lee, Chapter 8 in this volume). Yet the mounds near Plaquemine, named Medora after a plantation on the river, would have a lasting influence on Louisiana archaeology. Supervised by Edwin B. Doran, Jr., the crew soon uncovered post molds and other evidence for buildings that Native Americans had constructed centuries earlier on the mounds. Although few stone artifacts were recovered from the silty clay, more than 18,500 pieces of pottery were collected. Subsequent analysis by James Ford and George Quimby (1951:85) provided the basis for what became known as the Plaquemine culture and period (Rees and Livingood 2007:3–6).

Along with Middle Mississippi, Caddoan, and south Appalachian complexes, Plaquemine soon came to be regarded as a regional variant of Mississippian culture in the LMV (e.g., Griffin 1967:190). Even so, Plaquemine artifact assemblages and sites continued to be distinguished from Mississippian assemblages and sites elsewhere in the Southeast. The appearance of non-local, Mississippian material culture after A.D. 1200 has been interpreted as evidence of generalized cultural influence, long-distance interactions, and the arrival of Mississippian people from the north and east (Brown 1979a, 1979b; Neuman 1984:258–283; Weinstein 1987a). Emphasis on these archaeological cultures has led to interpretations of late prehistoric and early historic Louisiana as characterized by fairly uniform and widespread Native American cultures: Plaquemine, Mississippian, and Caddoan. One of the greatest challenges presently facing archaeologists is to move beyond the uniformity of these archaeo-cultures—to understand regional variations in terms of historical processes and local communities.

Most research on Plaquemine and Mississippian in Louisiana has been on artifacts, especially ceramics, as well as architectural remains and sites with large earthen mounds. Archaeobotany and zooarchaeology have begun to shed light on indigenous subsistence and foodways. Additional information can be drawn from fragmentary and biased documentary sources left by the Spanish and French, allowing for circumspect analogies with historically known tribes such as the Natchez and Chitimacha (e.g., Brown 1982b, 1985a, 1990, 1998b; Giardino 1984a; Rees 2007). In tracing Plaquemine and Mississippian through time and space, regional diversity and variable social relationships become increasingly apparent. A consideration of available evidence for the economic and political aspects of local communities reveals historical variation among seemingly uniform cultural traditions. It is worthwhile to begin with a review of the manifestations and meanings of Plaquemine and Mississippian in Louisiana archaeology.

Plaquemine

In his summary of the Medora site (16WBR1) report, Quimby (1951:132) wrote that "the Plaquemine Indians were agricultural peoples who built ceremonial centers consisting of pyramidal mounds of earth surmounted by temples and built about a plaza." Quimby (1951:128–132) referred to the Plaquemine period and culture as an "outgrowth" of the earlier Coles Creek, which had previously been defined by James Ford (1936). From another perspective, Plaquemine was seen as evolving out of a combined Troyville–Coles Creek culture (Haag 1971:26). In his report on the Greenhouse site (16AV2) near Marksville, Ford (1951:129) referred to Plaquemine more conservatively as a period in his LMV chronology and suggested that "Plaquemine equates with at least the early part of the Mississippi Period" (cf. Ford and Willey 1941:Figures 2 and 6). Based on culture traits, notably certain types of decorated pottery, Plaquemine was distinguished from Late Woodland period Coles Creek and contemporaneous Mississippian culture, although it shared a number of traits with both (see Roe and Schilling, Chapter 9 in this volume).

Distinctive pottery types were identified early on, although several of these designs are continuations of earlier decorated types. Ceramic vessels with a brushed appearance are typical, appropriately known as Plaquemine Brushed (Figure 10.1). The continuation of the Coles Creek ceramic tradition includes techniques of incising around vessel rims (Brown 1998a:9, 11, 14; Phillips 1970:73–74, 129–130). Engraved and incised pottery also bear some resemblance to Caddoan and Mississippian types in the Red and Lower Mississippi River valleys, reflecting broader geographic trends (Ford 1952:348–350, 368–373; Gibson 1985b:326; cf. Kidder 1990b:65). Most ceramics were tempered with grog (fired clay or crushed pottery), and some with minor amounts of pulverized mussel shell. Ceramics with shell tempering, generally associated with Mississippian culture, are more commonly found at sites in the Tensas Basin of northeast Louisiana, in the Mississippi Delta to the southeast, in the Lower Yazoo Basin, and along the Natchez Bluffs of Mississippi (e.g., Brown 1985b:288–301; Ryan 2004:89–159; Williams and Brain 1983:117–212). The vast majority of pottery

Fig. 10.1. Plaquemine and Mississippian ceramics: a. Plaquemine Brushed; b. Mazique Incised, *var. Manchac;* c–d. Harrison Bayou Incised, all from 16SM5; Mississippi Plain (bottom), from Salt Mine Valley (16IB23).

from Plaquemine sites is an undecorated, grog-tempered type classified as Baytown Plain (Miller et al. 2000:306; Quimby 1951:125; Ryan 2004:149–151; Williams and Brain 1983:91–105). Other artifacts generally associated with Plaquemine culture include smoking pipes made of ceramic and stone, stone celts, discoidals or disks, and small, stemmed projectile points. The relative scarcity of stone arrow points and artifacts in the southern LMV suggests that bone, antler, shell, and other, less durable materials were fashioned into tools in a region with

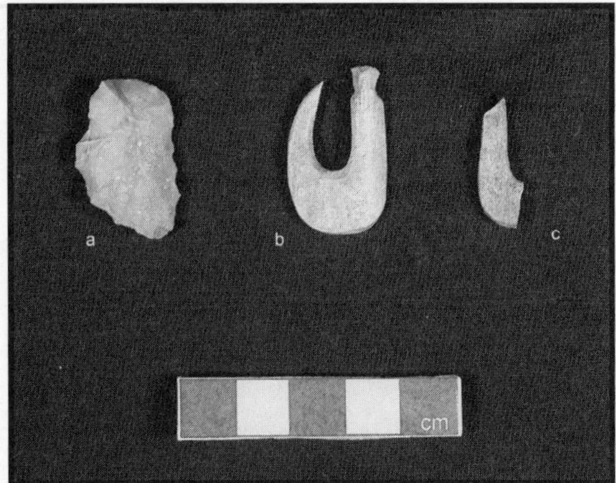

Fig. 10.2. Lithic and bone artifacts from Plaquemine mound sites: a. Scraper or bifacial tool made of gravel chert from 16SM5; b–c. Bone fish hooks from 16SMY10.

little naturally occurring rock (Figure 10.2; Hays 2000:91; Kidder and Barondess 1982:101–105; Quimby 1957:128–131).

The most visible indicators of Plaquemine culture are earthen mounds. Although a majority of people lived in small, dispersed communities without mounds, Plaquemine culture and settlement are known primarily from investigations of large sites with two or more earthen mounds (Brain 1978, 1989; Hally 1972; Kidder 1998a; Neuman 1984:258–268; Quimby 1951; Rees and Livingood, ed. 2007). The remnants of buildings on flat-topped mounds, often buried by subsequent mound construction, have been interpreted as mortuary temples and residences of chiefs. This is based on comparisons with the historically known Natchez and better-known Mississippian sites (Brown 1985b; Lorenz 1997; Neitzel 1964, 1983, 1997). As seen at the Medora site, the architecture included circular and rectangular buildings supported by posts placed individually or in wall trenches (Quimby 1951).

The temporal span and geographic extent of Plaquemine were not as great as Mississippian and were mainly defined by studies of ceramics. Plaquemine dates from the second or third century of the Mississippi period as understood for the Southeast, or around A.D. 1200, preceded by Coles Creek (see Roe and Schilling, Chapter 9 in this volume). The Plaquemine period referred to earlier by Ford (1951) and Quimby (1951) soon fell out of use, subsumed by the Mississippi period and commonly described in relation to Mississippian culture (e.g.,

Neuman and Hawkins 1993:26–28). According to this chronology, three geographically overlapping and related traditions—Coles Creek, Plaquemine, and Mississippian—fall within the first few centuries of the Mississippi period (e.g., Griffin 1990; Kidder 1998a:130–131; Steponaitis 1986:387). Others place the beginning of the Mississippi period in the southern LMV at A.D. 1200, effectively separating Coles Creek and Plaquemine, or propose a Transitional (late) Coles Creek period from A.D. 1000 to 1200 (e.g., Jeter and Williams 1989b:173; Kidder 2002b:90; Weinstein 1987a). The end of the Mississippi period elsewhere in the Southeast has been placed as early as A.D. 1500, based on the decline of major Mississippian chiefdoms prior to extensive European contacts. Late Plaquemine traditions in the LMV merge with historically known tribes such as the Natchez and Chitimacha, indicating the persistence of indigenous cultural beliefs and practices well into the eighteenth century (Brown 1985a, 1998b, 2007; Giardino 1984a; Neitzel 1964, 1997; Rees 2007).

Plaquemine sites are distributed from the vicinity of present-day Greenville, Mississippi, southward to the Gulf Coast, spanning southeast Arkansas, southwest Mississippi, and east Louisiana (Jeter and Williams 1989b:207–212; Rees and Livingood 2007). This triangular-shaped area encompasses the Mississippi River floodplain, Natchez Bluffs, and the Lower Yazoo, Tensas, Boeuf, Lower Ouachita, and Catahoula basins. It broadens south of the Red River confluence and Natchez Bluffs, across the entire Deltaic Plain, from the prairie terrace and Chenier Plain on the west to the Pontchartrain and Pearl River basins on the east (Brown 1998c:657). Clusters of site components in each of the aforementioned regions are classified as archaeological phases, sometimes named after mound sites such as Routh (16TE8), Fitzhugh (16MA1), Pargoud Landing (16OU1), and Medora. The ceramics indicate cultural connections extended upriver and across the Coastal Plain to the east. Relatively small and ephemeral Plaquemine components in west-central Louisiana may represent a marginal, short-term use of the area, or interactions with communities in the LMV (Anderson and Smith 2003:393; Morehead, Campbell et al. 2007:57-58). There is evidence for increased Plaquemine-Caddo interactions in the Boeuf and Ouachita basins after A.D. 1500, but contacts to the west appear to have otherwise remained minimal (Kidder 1998b:134–139). Plaquemine is consequently centered in the southern LMV, with roots extending back into Coles Creek.

Sites along the Natchez Bluffs and in the Lower Yazoo Basin of Mississippi fall outside of the area of immediate interest here, but these regions have contributed a wealth of information about Plaquemine culture (e.g., Brain 1969; Brown 1985b, 2007; Williams and Brain 1983). Research outside of Louisiana, particularly in the Lower Yazoo Basin, has strongly influenced current understanding of Plaquemine culture. This is largely due to the efforts of Philip Phillips (1970:950), who isolated and "reduced" Plaquemine to its "original core" in the Medora phase, in comparison to phases in the Yazoo and Tensas basins. The cultural continuum advocated by Ford (1951:12–13) was consequently subdivided, and Plaquemine was regarded as separate and distinct from Mississippian and Coles Creek (Phillips 1970:968; cf. Quimby 1951:129–131). Large mound sites, such as Lake George (22YZ557) and Winterville (22WS500), soon eclipsed Medora as characteristic of Plaquemine. Jeffrey Brain (1989) and Stephen Williams (Williams and Brain 1983:414) interpreted Plaquemine in the Lower Yazoo Basin as a result of Mississippian influence, or Coles Creek–Mississippian "hybridization" (see also Brain 1978:344–345, 1991). Contacts and interactions between Mississippian and Coles Creek communities, emanating from the major Mississippian site of Cahokia in Illinois, in effect created Plaquemine culture (Williams and Brain 1983:373–374). Plaquemine thus "owed its genesis to the Mississippian culture," instead of independently developing or evolving out of Coles Creek (Williams and Brain 1983:414). In contrast, contemporaneous sites across the Mississippi River in the Tensas Basin of Louisiana tended to support a Plaquemine-Mississippian succession, coincident with the appearance of shell-tempered pottery (Hally 1972:606). Williams and Brain (1983:413) suggested areas farther south lie "beyond strong Mississippian influence" and did not participate in the Plaquemine "grand florescence."

Plaquemine mound sites south of the Tensas Basin are in fact comparatively smaller. They are often comprised of two and sometimes three mounds arranged around a plaza, as seen at Medora (Figure 10.3; Kidder 1998a:143, 2004b:557; Rees 2007). From the perspective of "Lower Louisiana," Lake George and Winterville are outliers in terms of size, location, and non-local material culture (cf. Williams and Brain 1983:413). With as many as thirty and twenty-three mounds respectively, Lake George and Winterville are unusually large even when compared with major Mississippian mound sites (Payne 1994:78–129). The correlation of larger mound size and number with Mississippian cultural influence is conjectural, but it has generally been associated with increased political hierarchy (Blitz and Livingood 2004). Non-local Mississippian artifacts, including various types of shell-tempered pottery, are relatively less common and appear later in south Louisiana. As in northeast Louisiana, continuity is more apparent and Plaquemine might still be regarded a "logical outgrowth" of Coles Creek (Kidder 1998a:131; cf. Quimby 1951:130–131).

The hybridization theory of Plaquemine origins emphasizes Mississippian

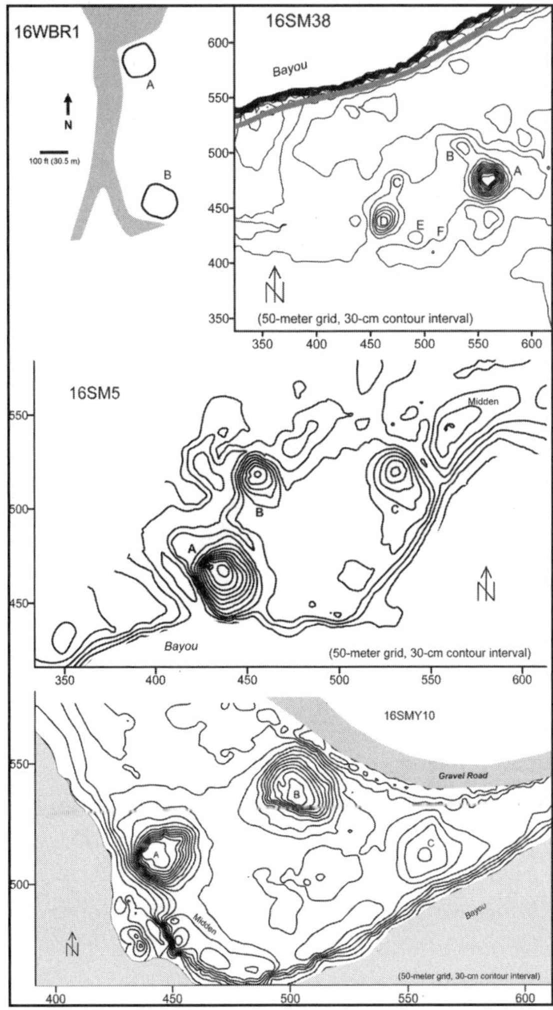

Fig. 10.3. Selected Plaquemine mound site plans: Medora (16WBR1; based on Quimby 1951:89, Figure 1), Portage Guidry (16SM38), Prairie Landing Village (16SM5), and *Qiteet kutingi namu* (16SMY10).

influence and minimizes evidence for Coles Creek–Plaquemine similarities, as seen at sites outside of the Yazoo Basin. But the Plaquemine "heartland" supposedly stretches from the Tensas Basin south of the Red River, including mound sites such as Routh, Sanson (16RA1), and Medora. Numerous Plaquemine components have been identified at sites in the Catahoula, Atchafalaya, and Terrebonne-Barataria basins, and also throughout the Delta (Gregory 1969; Gregory et al. 1987; Jeter and Williams 1989b:205–214; Miller et al. 2000; Ryan and Wells 2007; Weinstein and Kelley 1992:38–39). Coastal Plaquemine sites are found from the Chenier Plain eastward along the coast into the Pontchartrain and Pearl River basins, with Coles Creek and Plaquemine types generally comprising a majority of the ceramics (Brown 1979b, 1984; Hays 2000:10; Jeter and Williams 1989b:173–177, Figures 17–21; Kelley et al. 2000:300–304; Livingood 2007:111–112; Weinstein 1987a). Mound sites such as Gibson (16TR5), Portage Guidry (16SM38), Prairie Landing Village (*Hip-inimš namu*, 16SM5), *Qiteet kutingi namu* (16SMY10), and Thom (16PC6) have nearly indistinguishable late Coles Creek and Plaquemine components (Rees 2007:78–87). Artifact assemblages and site planning do exhibit strong continuities between Coles Creek and Plaquemine. Evidence for Mississippian culture at these and other sites appears too little and too late to have played a significant role in the formation of Plaquemine culture. So what relevance, then, is Mississippian to Louisiana archaeology?

Mississippian

Despite the broad application of the Mississippi period in Louisiana archaeology, Mississippian culture is regarded by most archaeologists as having originated well beyond the modern state boundaries (e.g., Brown 1979b; Brown and Lambert-Brown 1979; Kidder 2004b:555–559; Neuman 1984:272–283). As noted previously, Mississippian was also first recognized by distinctive types of ceramics, particularly shell-tempered wares. Other Mississippian culture traits include rectangular buildings with wall-trench architecture, platform mounds, maize agriculture, exotic or non-local items traded over long distances, and an elaborate iconography on distinctive artifacts fashioned from ceramic, stone, shell, and copper (Griffin 1985:61–63). Even more so than Plaquemine, Mississippian is characterized by large mound-and-plaza complexes that have been described as political, economic, and ceremonial centers, such as those at Moundville and Bottle Creek in Alabama, Shiloh in Tennessee, and Cahokia in Illinois (Brown, ed. 2003; Knight and Steponaitis, ed. 1998; Pauketat 2004; Welch 2006). But platform mounds and plazas predate even Coles Creek in the LMV, undercutting the argument for a distinctly Mississippian origin (Kidder 2004a, 2004b; McGimsey, Chapter 7 in this volume; Roe 2007).

Mississippian sites are found throughout the southeastern United States, from eastern Oklahoma to the Atlantic Coast and from the Midwest to the Gulf Coast. With its substantially greater distribution, Mississippian culture has received considerably more attention from archaeologists (see Peregrine 1996). Earlier assumptions about the spread of Mississippian culture through diffusion or migration from the Central Mississippi Valley also influenced interpretations of Plaquemine culture (e.g., Caldwell 1958:64–68; Phillips, et al. 1951:180, 451; Sears 1964:277; Smith 1984; Willey 1953). Some even pointed to similarities between Mississippian and Mesoamerica in relation to platform mounds, plazas, maize agriculture, and iconography, despite the differences and lack of evidence for direct or extended contacts (e.g., Griffin 1966; Willey 1966:293–294; cf. White, ed. 2005; White and Weinstein 2008). During the 1970s, Mississippian was redefined as a series of complex societies or chiefdoms, with densely inhabited settlements dependent on maize agriculture (Peebles and Kus 1977; Smith, ed. 1978). The earliest Mississippian chiefdoms evolved or "emerged" from Late Woodland societies in the Central Mississippi Valley after A.D. 900 (Smith, ed. 1990). Major mound sites such as Cahokia and Moundville were at the apex of regional hierarchies, with smaller mound sites, villages, and farmsteads located throughout the countryside (Emerson and Lewis, ed. 1991; Steponaitis 1978). An extensive body of literature has since been amassed on Mississippian polities, with an increased emphasis on variation and context (e.g., Anderson 1994; Barker and Pauketat, ed. 1992; Butler and Welch, ed. 2006; Lewis and Stout, ed. 1998; Pauketat 1998, 2004; Pauketat and Emerson, ed. 1997; Rogers and Smith, ed. 1995; Scarry, ed. 1996).

In contrast to Plaquemine, Mississippian culture is not as well represented at sites in Louisiana. Archaeological evidence for Mississippian components, characterized by definition as non-local, has been described as "meager" (Neuman 1984:280). Rectangular, wall-trench architecture has been associated with both Mississippian and Plaquemine components, although it is less well-documented south of the Natchez Bluffs and Red River (Brown 1983, 1985b:274–280; Downs 2004; Quimby 1951). The most impressive mound sites in Louisiana that date from the Mississippi period, including Routh, Fitzhugh, and Transylvania (16EC8), are in the Tensas Basin, across the river from the Lower Yazoo Basin and Natchez Bluffs (Hally 1972; Kidder 1998a:143–148). Kidder (1998a:143) notes a trend toward fewer yet larger mound sites in this region, with a concurrent proliferation of smaller, non-mound sites (cf. Brain 1978:345).

South of the Red River confluence, mound sites with Mississippian components are relatively smaller, with nothing on the scale of Lake George, Winterville, or Transylvania. Sims or Sim's Place (16SC2), one of the larger sites in the Delta with a substantial Mississippian component, had at least four and perhaps as many as six moderate-sized mounds, of which only three remain (Davis

1981:60–61, 1984:221–224; Giardino 1985; Hays 1995:16–17; Mann 2006:44–49, 2007:72–74). The Thom site had six or seven mounds, with late Coles Creek, Plaquemine, and Mississippian ceramics (Jones and Shuman 1987:150–156; Wells 2001:181–184). Other mound sites with Mississippian components, such as Buras (16PL13), Magnolia Mound (16SB49), and Toncrey (16PL7) are not as well known and are subsiding or endangered by coastal erosion (Gagliano et al. 1982:20–22; Gagliano and Weinstein 1979; Jones et al. 2009). The Berwick mound site (16SMY184) was unfortunately leveled long ago, and it is not known for certain whether it was a major regional center or if it had a Mississippian component (Rees 2007:71; Weinstein and Kelley 1992:356). Most mound sites dating from the Mississippi period in south-central Louisiana are comparatively smaller and associated with Plaquemine culture, with few characteristically Mississippian artifacts (Gibson 1990; Jones and Shuman 1987; Kelley et al. 2000; Neuman and Servello 1976; Rees 2007:72–78). Mississippian culture in Louisiana, in contrast to its Plaquemine variant, is thus regarded as non-local or intrusive.

Chipped stone hoes, triangular projectile points, and ground stone artifacts generally characteristic of Mississippian culture are less common at sites in Louisiana, especially in the Delta and coastal region. Following local Coles Creek–Plaquemine tradition, tools were made of less durable, readily available materials, such as bone and shell. While Mississippian chiefdoms are associated with more elaborate, non-local artifacts made of stone, shell, and copper, often interred as burial goods at major mound centers (e.g., Knight and Steponaitis 1998:17–18; Pauketat 2004:84–93), the scarcity of such items has led researchers to conclude that contemporaneous communities in Louisiana were less complex, or removed from the Mississippian "climax" (Williams and Brain 1983:413). Intricately crafted goods bearing Mississippian symbolism and associated with the Southeastern Ceremonial Complex are less common, even on pottery and readily available materials such as shell (Jeter 2007; Kidder 2004b:557–558; Neuman 1984:281–283; cf. Galloway, ed. 1989; King, ed. 2007). Two small stone disk fragments from sites in Iberville and St. James parishes have been interpreted as "superficial or peripheral" ties to the Southeastern Ceremonial Complex (Weinstein 1987b:84). In comparison to Mississippian, Plaquemine has been defined by a deficit or lack of such ornate items (Jennings 1952:267).

More than earthen mounds or any class of artifact, Mississippian culture has been identified by shell-tempered ceramics. The presence of pulverized mussel shell as a tempering ingredient in ceramic vessels has long been associated with Mississippian culture, leading to assertions that the practice diffused southward into the LMV and westward along the Gulf Coast with other Mississippian traits (Haag 1971:31–33; Neuman 1984:275). Shell-tempered ceramics at the Transylvania site led David Hally (1972:606) to conclude that Mississippian culture was a relatively late introduction in northeast Louisiana, even as it developed from the local Plaquemine tradition. Mississippian shell-tempered ceramics are now known to date from much earlier in the Tensas Basin, with later, protohistoric Mississippian components in the Boeuf and Lower Ouachita basins to the west (Kidder 1990b:60–69, 1992c, 1993b). Recent work at the Lake Providence mound site (16EC6) indicates interactions between people in the Tensas Basin and Mississippian communities to the east and north as early as A.D. 1100. Douglas Wells and Richard Weinstein (2005, 2007) have identified shell-tempered pottery that originated in the American Bottom east of present-day Saint Louis, Missouri, between A.D. 1100 and 1250. These non-local ceramics suggest indirect interactions with the Mississippian polity of Cahokia, possibly directed by elite or high-status individuals at Lake Providence. Wells and Weinstein (2005:510, 2007:52, 61–63) argue for minimal Mississippian influence, however, and substantial continuity between local Coles Creek and Plaquemine traditions (cf. Kidder 1998a).

Shell-tempered wares appear later and are generally less common in south Louisiana, but they are found at sites in the Delta and along the coast, in the Florida Parishes north of Lake Pontchartrain, and in the Pearl River drainage (Hays 2000:83–91; Kelley et al. 2000:299–304; Livingood 2007; Rees and Livingood 2007; Shuman 2007). The presence or absence of shell-tempered ceramics at sites in the Delta has been used to distinguish Mississippian (Bayou Petre phase) from contemporaneous Plaquemine and earlier Coles Creek phases (Brown 1984:97–99; Kniffen 1936:412, 1938; McIntire 1958; Miller et al. 2000:343–348; Phillips 1970:951–953; Weinstein and Kelley 1992:37–40). Sim's Place and Buras are among the most prominent mound sites with Mississippian shell-tempered wares, although Mississippian components have also been identified at non-mound sites (Davis 1981:60–61, 1984:221–224; Davis and Giardino 1981; Gagliano and Weinstein 1979; Giardino 1985; Hays 1995:16–17; Mann 2006:44–52; Shuman 2007:101–103; Weinstein and Kelley 1992:378). Decorative designs on grog and shell-tempered ceramics are similar to those found at sites in the LMV to the north and the Mobile Bay region to the east (Figure 10.4). This has been interpreted as evidence of social interactions, trade, alliances, migrations, resource extraction, and a wide-ranging ceramic complex shared by different societies (Jeter and Williams 1989b:191–192; Kidder 2004b:555–556; Knight 1984:199–201; Weinstein 1987a).

Shell-tempered ceramics have also been found at sites around Vermilion

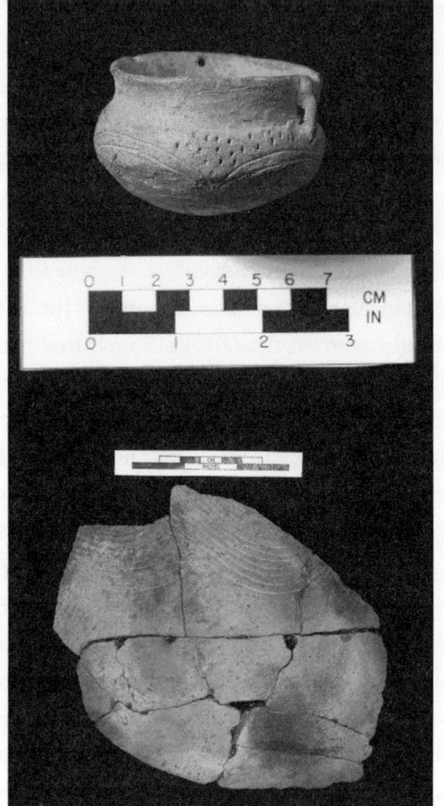

Fig. 10.4. Miniature Buras Incised pot (top) and partially reconstructed Winterville Incised vessel (bottom) from Sim's Place (16SC2). Photographs courtesy of Rob Mann (2006:45, 51, Figures 17 and 20a) and the Museum of Natural Science, Louisiana State University.

Bay in south-central Louisiana (Brown 1978b, 1980; Brown and Lambert-Brown 1979; Gagliano 1967:87, 102). The majority were recovered from Salt Mine Valley (16IB23) on Avery Island, with comparatively small amounts from other sites in the Petite Anse region (Figure 10.1; Brown 1979a, 1999b:138–140; Brown et al. 1979). The Mississippian component at Salt Mine Valley, which dates from around A.D. 1550 to 1650, is characterized by shell-tempered bowls and jars used in processing salt from saline springs. Salt was an important dietary supplement in agricultural societies such as Mississippian (Brown 1981). The shell-tempered ceramics from Salt Mine Valley are unusual for the region, indicating a non-local origin (Brown 1999b:140).

Recent studies suggest that shell tempering was not part of a uniform cultural package, but one aspect of more complex social interactions and practices dating from the Late Woodland period in the Ozark Mountains and Central Mississippi Valley (Feathers and Peacock 2008; Lafferty 2008; Pauketat 2001b:81–83; Sabo and Hilliard 2008). The appearance and use of shell tempering in the southern LMV was more variable than previously recognized, occurring in combination with other tempers and in otherwise non-Mississippian ceramics (Brown 1998a; Davis 1981; Davis and Giardino 1981; Kelley et al. 2000:299–304; Livingood 2007; Miller et al. 2000:305–361; Shuman 2007; Weinstein and Dumas 2008:210–215; Wells 2005). Correlation of ceramic temper with different cultures thus represents an often unrealistic "artificial dichotomy" that has tended to perpetuate notions of uniformity and disregard historical variation (Kidder 1998a:132, 2004:558). Temper selection and ceramic production reflect the decisions of potters, rather than a wholly intrusive or unvarying technological advancement. Further understanding of Plaquemine and Mississippian requires approaching such topics from the ground up, in terms of local communities and historical context.

Communities, People and Interaction

A better understanding of what Plaquemine and Mississippian represent, and the variable relationships between these archaeological cultures, depends largely on the scale of study (Kidder 2007c:199). Regional variation becomes increasingly apparent in moving from large-scale similarities and differences among cultural traditions to specific sites on a local level. Communities and people come into sharper focus when broad generalities—such as cultural diffusion, hybridization, and continuity—are rephrased as meaningful events and historical processes, from routine practices and innovations to social relations, alliances, and conflict (Pauketat 2000:19–21). Interaction among groups of people and communities can be discussed in terms of subsistence, exchange, and leadership, representing economic and political aspects of the Mississippi period in Louisiana. The economic and the political were interrelated and meaningful, constituting daily life in communities at the crossroads of Coles Creek, Plaquemine, and Mississippian.

Subsistence economy, or the foods people collect, produce, distribute and consume, is not merely a straightforward ecological adaptation, but an expression of culturally constructed foodways. The close association of maize agriculture with Mississippian culture, for instance, suggests that the production of food surpluses supported population growth and densely inhabited or nucleated settlements in fertile river valleys, which in turn allowed for the development of larger and more complex Mississippian polities (Smith 1978; Steponaitis

1986:388–389). Yet maize was introduced into the Southeast during the Middle Woodland period (A.D. 1–400), centuries before it was widely consumed or intensively grown (Fritz 1992, 1993:52–56; Smith 1992:274–276). Mississippian iconography and ideology were interwoven with representations of maize and agriculture, fertility symbolism less common among Plaquemine communities (Emerson 1997:207–223). In some instances, the social changes characterized as Mississippianization, or "becoming Mississippian," preceded or paralleled the intensification of maize agriculture (Muller 1997:226; Pauketat 2004:60). Mississippian polities were created through political consolidation, and were not inevitable products of maize agriculture or cultural diffusion (Pauketat 2000).

Maize has been identified at sites dating from the Mississippi period in Louisiana, in what have been described as Plaquemine and Mississippian contexts (e.g., Hays 1995:17; Miller et al. 2000:437–447; Roberts 2004:225, 2005:444–446, 484–489; Quimby 1957:133; Ryan and Wells 2007:129–135). While a sufficient food supply is a necessary prerequisite for densely populated, complex societies, ample evidence from Louisiana indicates that there were alternatives to agricultural intensification. Like shell-tempered ceramics, maize agriculture was not simply adopted as part of an inexorable Mississippian expansion. The domesticated plant was grown by communities in the LMV at different times and to varying degrees beginning in late Coles Creek times (Kidder 2002b:86). Maize appeared later in the southern part of the LMV and, once present, may have played a less prominent role in the subsistence economies of some communities (Fritz and Kidder 1993; Kidder 2004b:557; Kidder and Fritz 1993). This does not mean the development of complex societies was constrained by natural resource abundance in the LMV, although greater self-sufficiency in subsistence economy may have facilitated resistance to regional political consolidation.

Complex societies in the LMV developed independently of the potential food surpluses offered by agriculture, as indicated by densely inhabited sites and the monumental architecture of mounds and plazas. Botanical and faunal studies indicate both intensive and extensive use of wild plant foods such as acorn, pecan, hickory, and persimmon, along with deer, fish and plentiful aquatic resources (Davis 1987; Kidder 1992a, 1992b; Stevenson 1992). Seasonal harvesting of fish and shellfish in floodplain and coastal environments produced a consistent and reliable food surplus, augmenting wild plants and other fauna (Duhe 1981:36). Since at least the Middle Archaic period, subsistence economies that drew upon an abundance of wetland resources were more than sufficient for large communities to come together and engage in labor intensive activities, such as mound building (Byrd and Neuman 1978; Jackson 1991a; Jackson and Scott 2001; Saunders, Chapter 4 in this volume; Smith 1996). Maize became more important in some regions, such as the Tensas Basin, only after A.D. 1200 (Fritz and Kidder 1993). A wider range of mammals may have been hunted in some regions, with a relative decline in aquatic resources that are characteristic of Coles Creek subsistence (Davis 1987; Kelley 1992; Neuman 1984:162–163; Springer 1980). Although this appears to have been the case at Sim's Place, it is not evident at other sites, where fish, alligator, shellfish, and small mammals remained important throughout the Mississippi period (Coxe and Kelley 2004:239; Duhe 1981; Miller et al. 2000:394–436; Scott 2005:426–429; Smith 1995, 1996; Stevenson 1992).

Rejection of an earlier, mistaken assumption that Coles Creek mound construction was possible only through agriculture has led archaeologists to reexamine the development of Coles Creek inequality and complexity (cf. Dragoo 1976:20; Fritz and Kidder 1993:2; Kidder 1992a, 1992b; Roe and Schilling, Chapter 9 in this volume). Likewise, the general assertion that Plaquemine societies were variants of Mississippian culture, and therefore agricultural, deserves further examination (cf. Quimby 1951:132). Coastal Plaquemine communities were more similar to local Coles Creek than Mississippian in terms of self-sufficient subsistence economies, harvesting backswamp, marsh, and estuarine resources much as their ancestors had done for centuries (Byrd 1978, 1994; Byrd and Neuman 1978; Duhe 1977, 1981; Springer 1974, 1980). Inhabitants of mound centers and smaller communities on natural levees may have grown maize as a supplement to more traditional foods (Miller et al. 2000:437–446; Ryan and Wells 2007:130–135). This is not surprising, as foodways can be remarkably resistant to change and much of the low-lying Delta and coastal marsh is less suitable for agriculture than the natural levees of the alluvial plain. As in some Mississippian and earlier societies, maize may have been adopted as an unusual, ceremonial meal, appropriate for elite and ritual feasts (Johannessen 1993:75; Lopinot 1992, 1997:53–57).

The organization of subsistence economies and subsequent changes were not uniform or invariably representative of entire periods or cultures, but reflect culinary preferences, regional variations, and different social contexts of resource use (Jackson and Scott 1995). Archaeological and historical sources indicate that Plaquemine communities engaged in agriculture to varying degrees (Cutler 1965; Swanton 1911:73–76, 345). Others continued to fish, hunt, harvest shellfish, and collect wild plant foods. The transition to a subsistence economy emphasizing maize agriculture was not predetermined or merely environmentally constrained; it involved a host of other economic, political, and social factors. For example, the coordinated labor requirements of agriculture and the storage of agricultural surpluses, in contrast to fishing, hunting, and harvesting, may have posed unnecessary risks in contexts of recurrent warfare and regional conflicts. Among communities in the Delta and coastal zone, maize may have been regarded as impractical and largely unnecessary (cf. M. Webb 1982).

The self-sufficiency and apparent autonomy of local subsistence economies is paralleled by the seemingly insular qualities of Plaquemine interaction and exchange. The relative scarcity of non-local, exotic items has been a defining characteristic of Plaquemine. Since such highly valued items or prestige goods were often acquired over long distances and served as symbols of elite status, Plaquemine societies are thought to have been more parochial and relatively less complex than their Mississippian counterparts. Yet historical accounts of the Natchez, Chitimacha, and other LMV tribes describe these people as frequently interacting, socially stratified, and far from egalitarian (e.g., Brown 1998b; Neitzel 1997:58–85; Swanton 1911:45–181). Among the difficulties in dealing with complexity in archaeology is characterizing social interactions and change as a historical process, instead of fixed categories or an accomplished fact.

Archaeological evidence for extraregional interactions comes primarily from occurrences of supposedly non-local artifacts, particularly shell-tempered ceramics (e.g., Weinstein 1987a, 1987b; Weinstein and Dumas 2008; Wells and Weinstein 2007). The presence and absence of certain pottery types constitute archaeological indicators of Plaquemine and Mississippian cultures, leading to interpretations of generalized interactions and contact. Combinations of Mississippian and Plaquemine designs on mixtures of shell- and grog-tempered pastes calls into question such clear-cut distinctions. While clusters of sites comprise different phases, archaeological phases were not invariably associated with social, ethnic, or cultural boundaries. Rather than regarding shell-tempered ceramics as a benchmark for Mississippian culture, ceramic production and use can be viewed in relation to innovations, emulation, alliances, intermarriages, and exchanges of information and goods among communities (Pauketat 2001b:81–82). Potters were most likely women in the LMV and Mississippian Southeast, and they were referred to as such in early French accounts of Louisiana (Du Pratz 1975 [1774], in Swanton 1911:62, 303, 1946:549–555; Hudson 1976:388; Thomas 2001:44). The gender-specific organization of production within households has considerable antiquity in the Southeast and effected changes in ceramic technology, as well as resistance to change (Sassaman 1993:41, 2001).

Contrasting the evidence from northeast and south Louisiana, the historical development of communities was significantly different, and not only in terms of ceramics. Variations in ceramic assemblages reflect interregional exchanges and movements of people even before the Mississippi period. Around A.D. 1150–1200, residents of the Lake Providence mound site in the Tensas Basin made connections with people far upriver, in the vicinity of the great Mississippian city of Cahokia, perhaps through intermediaries in the Lower Yazoo Basin (Wells and Weinstein 2007:58, 62–64). Ceramic vessels were transported four hundred miles south, or approximately seven hundred miles by river, conceivably carried by traders, emissaries, or warriors. Such interregional exchanges may have involved intermarriages, alliances, or conferral of kinship, but certainly involved communication of practical and more esoteric knowledge. Descriptions of awe-inspiring places like Cahokia and Winterville were likely part of the dialogue. There subsequently was no gradual diffusion of shell-tempered ceramics or whole-scale adoption of classic Mississippian culture, but instead what appears to be emulation and measured implementation of new techniques and designs in the context of local ceramic traditions.

Related cultural changes can be understood by placing ceramic production in social context. As might be expected of intermarriages with women from distant lands, there was no uniform expansion of Mississippian culture into northeast Louisiana, but rather a loosening of previous restrictions on ceramic manufacture. Decisions within multi-generational households regarding ceramic production, including temper and decoration, became influenced by non-local as well as local social relations. This might be accounted for by a broadening of interregional economic ties and exchange. But acquisition of valued items over great distances, including exotic stone and Mississippian iconography, remained relatively minimal. The scarcity of non-local items suggests such extraregional economic relations may have been constrained by warfare, which would have nonetheless brought women into northeast Louisiana through conflicts and alliances, as captives and brides (Alt 2008:216–217; cf. Dye 1995). Warfare was common among historic tribes of the LMV and predated European contacts, trade relations, and colonial conflicts (Dye 2009:89–104, 141–166).

Succeeding changes in architecture, mound-and-plaza construction, and settlement patterns in northeast Louisiana in the centuries following A.D. 1200 indicate political competition and conflicts between communities, which were focused around large ceremonial centers such as Fitzhugh, Routh, and Transylvania, as well as smaller centers (Kidder 1994:152, 1998a:141–145; Wells 1997). The archaeological evidence suggests that political consolidation, which would have been directed by charismatic leaders and high-ranking families, did not succeed to the degree seen in the Lower Yazoo Basin. Short of simply equating mound size with degree of complexity, the political culture was organized differently.

Even at major mound centers, there is less evidence for Mississippian fertility symbolism and cosmology, represented more in the construction of mound-and-plaza complexes than in exotic prestige goods or lavish, elite burials. As in the privileged treatment of the Great Sun and nobles among the Natchez centuries later, status and authority may have revolved around kinship and social relations, ongoing struggles for regional dominance, and success in warfare (Brown 2007; Swanton 1911:100–157).

The relatively late intensification of maize agriculture in the southern LMV parallels the regional development of political culture, perhaps explaining why agriculture was not pursued centuries earlier, even though maize was known and occasionally eaten. Surplus food production and storage through agriculture may have been ineffective or unfeasible until sufficient political consolidation had resolved ongoing conflicts and restrained internal warfare. Political-religious leaders and aspirants would have meanwhile benefited from success in war and from restricting access to ancestral mortuary temples and ceremonial spaces, while providing lavish distributions of food. This would have introduced stylistically new, innovative, and exotic-looking wares into community rituals, including feasts and ceremonies in mound-and-plaza precincts.

Communities in south Louisiana experienced remarkably different histories in the five centuries after A.D. 1200. As mentioned previously, the relative scarcity of shell-tempered ceramics and non-local artifacts at Plaquemine sites has been interpreted as the limits of Mississippian culture, supporting arguments for continuity between Coles Creek and Plaquemine traditions (Kidder 1998a:143). From another perspective, local communities steadfastly resisted the political, economic, and ideological trends characterized as Mississippianization (Brown 1998c:657). Of relevance here is the minimal evidence for interregional exchange among communities from the Lower Red River and Catahoula Basin to the Delta west of Baton Rouge, including the Upper Terrebonne–Barataria and Atchafalaya basins. Cultural conservativism in such backswamp environments seems plausible, but well-developed water transport could have turned ecological constraints into efficient trade routes (Rees 2007). More likely, there was a deficit of extraregional alliances, extended social relations, and intermarriages, all of which might have served as conduits of traditional knowledge, technology, and trade goods, and which elsewhere promoted the uneven transference of non-local practices and beliefs. Residents of local communities with histories of self-sufficient foodways may have opposed foreign innovations and outlandish schemes, such as new ceramic styles and maize agriculture. Plaquemine mound centers in this region likewise seem conservative or behind the times, more closely resembling Coles Creek than Mississippian mound sites in layout and design. Social relations and alliances within a series of interrelated regional polities, likely antecedents of the seventeenth-century Chitimacha, may have constrained extraregional interactions and promoted resistance to Mississippianization.

The situation was different again in the eastern Delta, where Plaquemine communities participated first intermittently and then more fully after A.D. 1400 in the coastal interchange of objects, people, and ideas. Based on ceramic styles, these interactions were at least initially focused on the Mobile Bay region to the east, rather than upriver (Davis 1984; Knight 1984:199–201; Weinstein and Dumas 2008:210–214). The consolidation of a major Mississippian polity at Bottle Creek, in the Mobile–Tensaw Delta of south Alabama, may have served as an impetus for this interregional commerce beginning around A.D. 1250 (Brown, ed. 2003). Regardless, the eastern Delta became a crossroads for east-west social relations and exchange, as indicated by local and non-local designs on various combinations of grog- and shell-tempered ceramics (Weinstein and Dumas 2008:210–214). Mississippian styles and iconography were reinterpreted by local residents of the Delta through intermittent exchanges of containers of food, intermarriages, and emulation of unfamiliar manufacturing and decorative techniques. The variable changes in ceramics point toward broadening yet restrained social relations and exchange, rather than wholesale migrations or large-scale movements of people. The capabilities to undertake such interregional exchange easily and efficiently are supported by historical descriptions of large canoes and canoe flotillas on the Mississippi River, as well as by the archaeological recovery of such watercraft (Clayton et al. 1993:238, 245; Saltus and Pearson, Chapter 18 in this volume; Swanton 1911:66–67, 347).

Mississippian triangular arrow points, non-local stone with which to fashion these and other tools, and exotic craft goods remained minimal or absent at sites in the Delta, further indication of the limits of interregional exchange. Such limitations may have been social rather than ecological constraints, produced by relatively autonomous, competing polities of comparable size and authority. After A.D. 1200, maize agriculture supplemented long-established foodways. Yet local communities retained self-sufficient subsistence economies, as residents continued to hunt wild game and harvest fish, shellfish, fruits, and nuts. Political consolidation does not appear to have occurred on the scale seen in the Tensas Basin, although considerably less is known about large ceremonial centers, such as Magnolia Mound and Berwick. As in the Atchafalaya Basin to the west, the layout and design of mound centers was not significantly altered from late Coles Creek. Only a few ceremonial centers, such as Sim's Place and Buras, are known to have substantial mixtures of local Plaquemine and non-local Mississippian wares. Settlement patterns, political leadership, foodways, and related cultural practices appear otherwise resistant to change.

For residents of communities west of Atchafalaya Bay, Mississippian ideas and practices remained unfamiliar and remote until the closing centuries of the Mississippi period. As efficient water transportation was readily available, the protracted absence and sudden appearance of non-local Mississippian artifacts might best be understood as a locally unprecedented historical event. Sometime between A.D. 1550 and 1650, one or more groups of people moved into the area around Vermilion Bay. The new arrivals were Mississippians who produced salt from the saline springs at Avery Island, perhaps for long-distance trade (Brown 1981, 1999b). Based on dissimilarities with contemporaneous Plaquemine components in the surrounding region, as well as similarities with ceramics from upriver, Ian Brown (1999b:136–138) has suggested that the Petite Anse component at Salt Mine Valley represents a migration of people from the Lower Yazoo Basin of Mississippi. They may have been ancestors of the Tunica, Taensa, or Koroa, who are known to have traded salt.

Whether these Mississippians were welcomed or confronted by local Plaquemine residents is unknown. The Petite Anse region would be abandoned by Native Americans within the next century. Events transpired differently in northeast Louisiana and the Delta to the east, in what would become the central corridor of multi-ethnic colonial interactions and conflicts. At this point in the history of Louisiana, the arrival of foreigners from Europe and Africa takes center stage and eclipses both Plaquemine and Mississippian cultures. Around the time Mississippians arrived at Avery Island, survivors of the De Soto expedition retreated down the Mississippi River on their way to Mexico. The virulent diseases they and other early explorers unwittingly unleashed wiped out entire families, destroyed communities, forced survivors to relocate, and transformed a once densely inhabited landscape into a seemingly deserted wilderness. Catastrophic epidemics, warfare, and colonialism wrought havoc on native peoples, but their survival and continued resistance is demonstrated in alliances, migrations, sustained presence, and reuse of ancestral villages and mounds (Brain 1988; Brightman 2004; Galloway 2002; Giardino 1984a; Gregory 2004; Kidder 1993b; Kniffen et al. 1987; Rees 2007).

Conclusion

The end of the Mississippi period represents a turning point in Louisiana archaeology, when archaeological cultures are laid open to reveal historical processes and variation only indirectly hinted at in the archaeological record. One issue is becoming clearer. Native Americans traveled and interacted throughout the LMV and along the coast long before the arrival of Europeans. Conventional portrayals of the beginning of recorded history may imply otherwise, but the pre-Columbian Native American past was politically and economically dynamic, punctuated by conflicts and alliances, exchanges and intermarriages, population movements and decisive events. Historically known groups such as the Bayougoula, Chitimacha, Houma, Natchez, Taensa, and Tunica enter the documentary record at the end of this period, followed by the arrival of the Apalachee, Biloxi, Choctaw, Koasati (Coushatta), and other displaced tribal communities (Hunter 1990; Kniffen et al. 1987:44–105; McCrocklin 1990; Swanton 1911). Assessment of the modern-day cultural affiliations of sites and artifacts is hampered by erratic and biased documentation, the lack of archaeological information, and the biological and cultural crucible of contact. The painstaking identification, classification, and description of archaeological cultures in Louisiana have provided a general explanatory framework and culture history extending back over eight centuries. Such categories have served archaeologists well in piecing together narratives of a mostly undocumented Native American past. But as long as Plaquemine and Mississippian are viewed as bona fide Native American cultures, interaction and change tend to be construed on the same level.

Portraying Plaquemine culture as Mississippianized Coles Creek is at the very least problematic. The argument for continuity suggests that Plaquemine communities in present-day Louisiana sustained cultural practices and beliefs inherited from their Coles Creek ancestors. But continuity and outgrowth originally referred to an arbitrary archaeological chronology and not cultural development or evolution (Ford 1951:13; Quimby 1951:130–131). There is further inconsistency in defining Plaquemine as a variant of Mississippian culture and in distinguishing the two based primarily on the absence or presence of shell-tempered pottery (Kidder 1998a:131–132). Part of the problem is that current understanding of Plaquemine is still largely framed by the same culture historical approach, which led archaeologists to formulate the concept (Rees and Livingood 2007). Recent research in the Mississippian Southeast has looked beyond static cultural categories and has focused on actions and interactions of individuals and groups in producing culture (e.g., Pauketat 2007). These are among the major challenges of Plaquemine and Mississippian archaeology in Louisiana.

Whether viewed as a consequence of Mississippian influence or as an outgrowth of Coles Creek, debate over the origins of Plaquemine culture misses the point. James Ford (1951:13) offered a succinct appraisal and admonition for such "seekers after truth," in that he regarded these categories as arbitrary periods and "nothing more than convenient labels for short segments of a continually changing culture history." Archaeological cultures conceal considerable variation in Native American communities, from social and ethnic identities to interrelated political, economic, and ideological changes. Realization that the ancestors of people so distinct as the Natchez, Chitimacha, and Atakapa might all similarly be described as bearers of Plaquemine culture should raise serious concerns as to what other details might be overlooked. The significance of this issue relates not merely to how archaeologists describe and explain the past. It ultimately has to do with whether Louisiana history is thought to begin with the arrival of Europeans or to include the First Americans.

The archaeology of Louisiana is still young. Much remains to be done in order to unravel the conceptual knots of Plaquemine and Mississippian cultures. Divergent histories in northeast and south Louisiana were characterized by differences not only in ceramics and earthen mounds, but also by foodways, interregional exchange, warfare, alliances, intermarriages, and migration. Much more than a "poor cousin" downriver (Williams and Brain 1983:413), Plaquemine culture south of the Yazoo Basin was comprised of communities with different histories and perspectives on the Mississippian world and their relation to it (cf. Anderson 1997). Mississippianization has recently been redefined as a historical process in which social identities were renegotiated and authority was appropriated in local communities (Pauketat 2000:17–21, 2001b:86–88, 2004:119–144; cf. Phillips 1970:967). Plaquemine culture might likewise be reexamined as a process of community formation, social relations, and resistance. Increased understanding will come not only from the accrual of new data, but from using that information to critique and eventually move beyond long-established models of the past. The more detailed histories of Plaquemine and Mississippian, only gradually coming into focus through archaeological research, have yet to be written.

11

Caddo Communities of Northwest Louisiana

JEFFREY S. GIRARD

When first visited by French and Spanish explorers in the late seventeenth century, northwest Louisiana was the home of the Caddo people. Archaeological research has demonstrated continuity in Caddo artistic styles, economic features, settlement patterns, and other cultural traits back at least eight hundred years prior to that time (Figure 1.3). Although many changes took place, a basic cultural pattern emerged in the tenth century A.D. and persisted into the early nineteenth century in northwest Louisiana and surrounding areas. Caddo culture continues today with the people of the Caddo Nation of Oklahoma, descendants of the former residents of northwest Louisiana (Cast et al., Chapter 12 in this volume).

The term "Caddo" is used in several ways (Story 1978). Perhaps most commonly, it is an ethnographic phrase referring to the Kadohadacho, Hasinai, and several other groups who were living along the middle Red, Sabine, Neches, and Angelina rivers when first described by European writers (Swanton 1942). "Caddo" or "Caddoan" also constitutes a linguistic family that includes languages spoken by the ethnographic Caddo, as well as others who lived farther north along the Plains–Eastern Woodlands border (e.g., the Wichita, Pawnee, and Arikara; Chafe 1976). Archaeological studies refer to the "Caddo area" as a culture area that covers much of northwest Louisiana, northeast Texas, southeast Oklahoma, and southwest Arkansas.

As an archaeological expression, the Caddo area encompasses much of the physiographic province often referred to as the Trans-Mississippi South, or the region of mixed deciduous-conifer woodlands that extends west of the Mississippi River floodplain (Schambach 1998). Although boundaries of the Caddo area have not been defined in a precise manner, Louisiana Caddo groups concentrated along the Red River and its tributaries as far south as the Natchitoches area, and on the Sabine River and its eastern tributaries to the area of Toledo Bend Reservoir dam in southern Sabine Parish. The eastern extent is more difficult to discern. Caddo traits occur along all major tributaries of the Red River and continue to the upper reaches of the Bayou D'Arbonne drainage. The lower portions of Bayou D'Arbonne are culturally marginal areas, where archaeological traits exhibit similarities to both Caddo and Lower Mississippi Valley (LMV) cultures.

In this chapter, I focus on the manner in which the Caddos organized themselves across the landscape throughout the eight to nine centuries of their cultural dominance in northwestern Louisiana. I place particular emphasis on how recent archaeological studies have attempted to define past Caddo communities and the ways in which these communities were socially and economically interconnected.

The Landscape

Northwest Louisiana contains some of the oldest land surfaces in the state. The uplands are composed of marine deposits of Tertiary (Eocene to Miocene) age, which underwent uplifting, faulting, and erosion to produce a topography of rolling hills, narrow ridges with steep adjoining slopes, and drainages of varying size (Andersen 1960, 1993; Murray 1948; Russ 1975). Prior to extensive logging, the upland landscape was covered by mixed oak-pine forest interspersed with grassland prairies. Hardwoods were most abundant north and west of the modern city of Shreveport in the far northwest portion of the state.

A sharp environmental dichotomy exists between the uplands and the floodplain of the Red River, which cuts a diagonal swathe from the northwest corner into central Louisiana, where it diverts to the east and eventually joins the Mississippi River. In early historic times, dominant cypress-gum forests were interspersed with grassy floodplain prairies, which were most numerous to the north, in present-day Caddo and Bossier parishes. Natural levees bordering the active and relict channels of the river are the highest and best-drained landforms in the floodplain and were the primary locations of Caddo villages. Historic information suggests that floodplain and upland prairies were important areas of settlement for historic Caddo groups. It is not known whether the prairies are natural features or are former woodlands cleared by the Caddo people hundreds of years ago.

Constrained by resistant Tertiary deposits, the Red River floodplain has had a complex history of channel abandonment, migration, and reoccupation. At the end of the Pleistocene, the channel was entrenched at least 4 to 5 meters (13 to 16 ft) below its present elevation, and sediments deposited by the river have built up the adjoining land surfaces throughout the past 10,000 to 12,000 years (Pearson and Hunter 1993:31). Due to bank instability and a high sediment load, channel shifts occur frequently, and it has proven difficult to isolate and date specific depositional surfaces (cf. Saucier and Snead 1989). Channel migration and its possible effects on human settlement are discussed in several studies and remain critical topics for future research (e.g., Albertson and Dunbar 1993; Albertson et al. 1996; Autin 1997; Commonwealth Associates Inc. 1981; Girard 1997; Kelley and Coxe 1998; Lenzer 1980; Pearson and Hunter 1993).

Mounds Plantation and Early Caddo Communities

Several traits in the archaeological record that materialized in the tenth century A.D. mark the dawn of the Caddo cultural tradition in northwest Louisiana. One development was a considerable increase in the number of sites located within the floodplain of the Red River. Only a small number of identified floodplain sites, almost all located in northern Caddo and Bossier parishes, appear to relate to Late Woodland–period Fourche Maline occupations as defined by Schambach (1982a; 2001; 2002). One such settlement existed at the Mounds Plantation site (16CD12), located near the community of Dixie in Caddo Parish (Figure 11.1). Mounds Plantation apparently grew larger than other Fourche Maline settlements, becoming a place where regional festivities or ceremonies took place. Seven mounds eventually were constructed around a large plaza, with two or three others located on the peripheries (Figure 11.2). In 1959, amateur archaeologist Ralph McKinney partially excavated Mound 3, a small mound about 3 meters (9.8 ft) high and 36 meters (118 ft) in diameter. Mound 3 consisted of a midden capped by sediments and additional midden deposits. Clarence Webb recorded the mound strata during McKinney's fieldwork. He suggested that Mound 3 was built over the remains of a structure and became an area where cooking and ceremonial feasting occurred (Webb and McKinney 1975:120). Analysis of pottery recovered from the excavations suggests that these activities took place in the tenth or early eleventh centuries A.D.

The only other mound subject to excavation, Mound 5, is located on the eastern edge of the plaza. In 1959 and 1960, McKinney and Webb excavated several trenches into the mound's western half, revealing fourteen burial pits, several of which contained multiple individuals laid out in rows (Webb and McKinney 1975:Figure 4). Accompanying many of the graves, particularly a large central-shaft tomb that included twelve individuals, were items such as pottery vessels and pipes, finely crafted stone tools, ornaments of copper, wood, and bone, and split-cane matting. Two radiocarbon assays on samples taken from well-preserved logs that overlay the burials in the central-shaft tomb date to the late eleventh or early twelfth centuries. The burials in Mound 5 exhibit similarities to burials

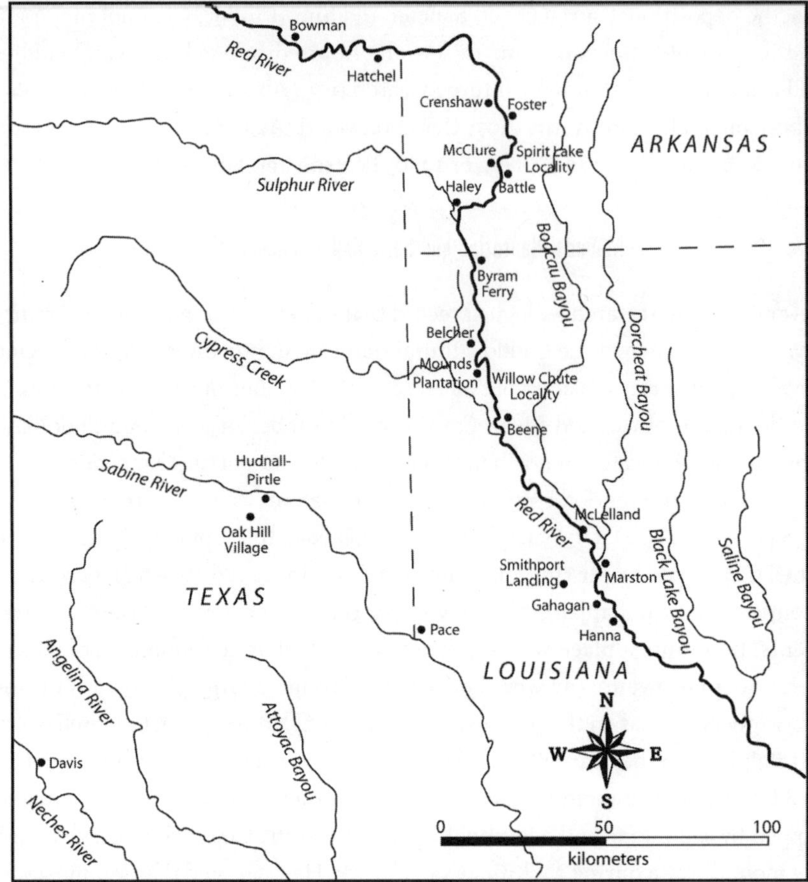

Fig. 11.1. Map of the southern Caddo area, showing locations of sites and localities discussed in the text.

at other roughly contemporaneous Caddo mound sites, such as George C. Davis (41CE19) in eastern Texas (Story 1997, 1998), Crenshaw (3MI6) in southwestern Arkansas (Schambach 1982b, 1997), and Gahagan (16RR1) in Red River Parish (Emerson and Girard 2004; Webb and Dodd 1939). The individuals buried at the mound centers were apparently community leaders, indicating that social hierarchies had developed within Caddo societies by the late eleventh century.

Considerable habitation debris is present on the surface of the Mounds Plantation site, suggesting that a substantial population resided there. Some of the smaller mounds might cap the remains of burned or dismantled structures. Archaeological sites identified in the limited surveys that have been conducted in adjacent areas appear to date primarily after the early thirteenth century,

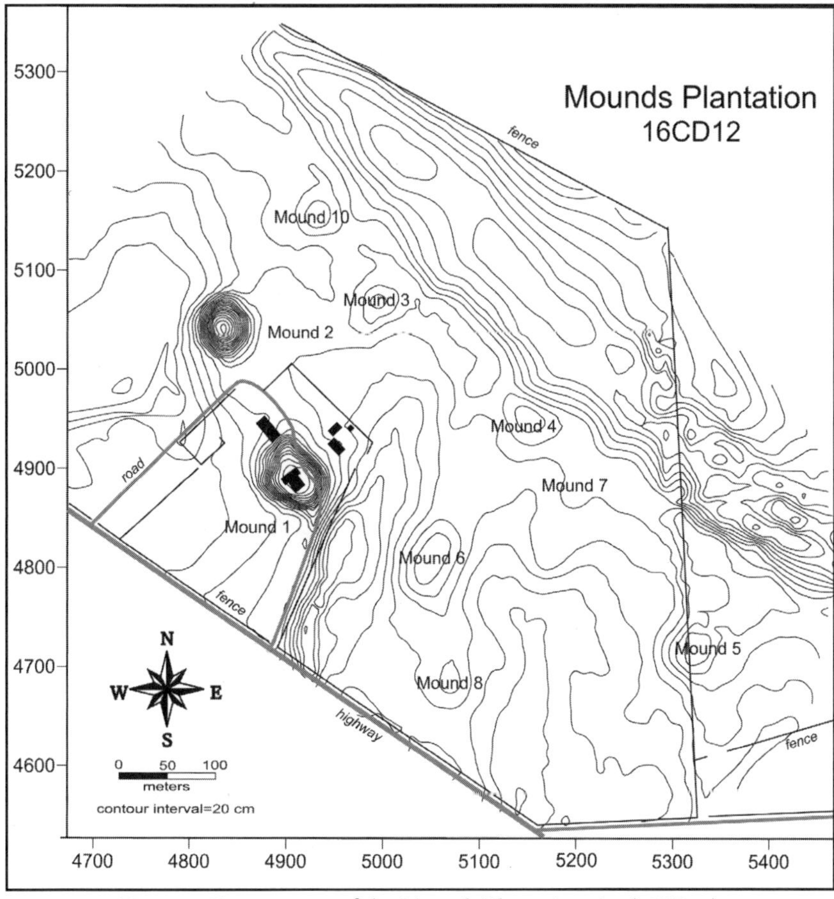

Fig. 11.2. Contour map of the Mounds Plantation site (16CD12).

when habitation at Mounds Plantation ceased (Girard 2005). Present evidence suggests that Caddo populations in the Red River floodplain of northwest Louisiana were aggregated into relatively few sites prior to about A.D. 1200. Mounds Plantation was, by far, the largest site and likely served as a central place for rituals and other important events, as well as a residential locus for leaders who maintained political authority over peripheral settlements. The number of outlying settlements appears to have increased substantially beginning in the late twelfth century, perhaps partly from dispersal of the residential population at Mounds Plantation. The site may have continued to be revered as a sacred center, but activities resulting in the deposition of significant numbers of artifacts ended. However, a few burials were placed in the upper sediments of Mounds 3 and 5 as late as the late sixteenth or early seventeenth centuries, shortly before European exploration (Webb and McKinney 1975).

The issue of Caddo origins has been subject to much discussion. Early research focused on finding how the earliest Caddo traits aligned temporally with chronological sequences in the LMV. It now appears that the first Caddo ceramics in northwest Louisiana were contemporary with middle Coles Creek pottery in the LMV, and radiocarbon dates from both regions indicate that this period falls between approximately A.D. 900 and 1050 (Girard 2004, Kidder 1990b). Slightly earlier dates have been suggested from research in eastern Texas (e.g., Perttula 1996; Story 2000). Controversies regarding the cultural antecedents to the Caddo remain unresolved. Webb argued that the Caddos emerged from ancestral Coles Creek–related groups (Webb and McKinney 1975; Webb and Gregory 1986; Webb 1982b). Schambach (1982a; 2002) sees a development from indigenous Fourche Maline populations with little or no influence from the Coles Creek area (Figure 1.3). Both positions infer a single "parent" culture that transformed into the Caddos, most likely in the Great Bend region of the Red River, with subsequent expansion into other portions of the Trans-Mississippi South.

It also is possible that the pre-Caddo (or Late Woodland period) Trans-Mississippi South was inhabited by multiple, small-scale, widely separated societies with few formal linkages. Some of these groups, including those at the Mounds Plantation site, became part of widespread early Mississippian trends involving the coalescence of formerly autonomous groups into larger regional-scale societies. A few lineages took on leadership roles and gained status, perhaps by hosting ceremonies at centers where multiple mounds surrounding plazas eventually were constructed. Several recent studies on the Mississippian Southeast have attempted to identify and understand the significance of the ceremonies likely to have been conducted at such centers, stressing the role of feasting in the establishment of regional polities and social hierarchies (e.g., Blitz 1993; Jackson and Scott 1995; Knight 2001; Pauketat et al. 2002). Large Early Caddo period centers developed at the Crenshaw site in southwest Arkansas (Durham and Davis 1975; Schambach 1982a, 1996), the Hudnall-Pirtle site (41RK4) in northeast Texas (Bruseth and Perttula 2006), and at Mounds Plantation in Caddo Parish (Webb and McKinney 1975). Somewhat smaller centers appeared on the southern periphery at the George C. Davis site in east Texas (Newell and Krieger 1949) and the Gahagan site in Red River Parish (Webb and Dodd 1939). Another small center may have existed at the James Pace site (16DS268) on the Sabine River, but this site appears to have been abandoned in the eleventh century, prior to major mound construction (Girard 1994a; Jensen 1968a; Story 1990). Relative

Fig. 11.3. Hodges Engraved carinated bowl (bottom) and Belcher Engraved bottle (top) from the Belcher site (16CD13).

to their contemporary Coles Creek neighbors in the LMV, Caddo centers were few and widely spaced across the expansive Caddo area (cf. Kidder 1998a, 1998b; Roe and Schilling, Chapter 9 in this volume).

One of the hallmark traits of Early Caddo culture was finely polished and engraved pottery, which likely served as one of several sumptuary goods circulated among or replicated by emerging leaders. Polished and engraved vessels are almost exclusively bottles and bowls, and they probably were used and displayed in ceremonies involving ritual consumption of food and beverages (Figure 11.3). Many of these vessels were buried, along with other status goods, in the graves of community leaders.

Recent research also has demonstrated that the Early Caddo period centers maintained contacts with the immense ceremonial and population center at Cahokia in southwestern Illinois (Emerson and Girard 2004; Emerson et al. 2003). Emerson and colleagues demonstrated that claystone effigy pipes recovered in elite burials at the Gahagan site were manufactured from a stone known as CBP Missouri flint clay from sources near St. Louis, Missouri. The effigies likely were manufactured at the Cahokia site in the early twelfth century and traded to the

Caddos shortly thereafter. Other items that point to interaction with emerging Mississippian elites include long-nosed god maskettes, spatulate stone celts, large "Gahagan" bifaces, and copper-covered ear ornaments. The presence of these items demonstrates direct contact between the southern Caddos and populations in the Cahokia region during the twelfth century (Emerson and Girard 2004:62–63). Although the nature of this contact is not known, Schambach (2002:112) suggests that similarities to the Mound 72 burials at Cahokia demonstrate that the distinctive Early Caddo–period elite burial pattern resulted from Caddo participation in the emerging Mississippian interaction sphere (Fowler et al. 1999). Despite evidence of contacts with Mississippian groups, both Perttula (1996:298) and Schambach (1996:40) have noted numerous differences between Caddo and classic Mississippian culture traits, and Caddo continuities with earlier Woodland-period traditions.

The Willow Chute Bayou Locality and Dispersed Floodplain Villages

Beginning around A.D. 1200, and lasting into the eighteenth century, many Caddos lived in widespread villages situated on natural levees in the Red River floodplain. These communities did not consist of compact aggregates of residences, but were dispersed for several kilometers along floodplain streams. Villages apparently consisted of multiple small clusters of houses and associated facilities, such as granaries, drying racks, and storage pits. A map made during the 1691–1692 expedition of Domingo Teran de los Rios, Governor of Coahuila, is an early historic depiction of one such village, which probably existed along the Red River in present-day northeast Texas, west of the city of Texarkana (Bolton 1970b; Swanton 1942: Plate 1). The Teran map shows twenty-five clusters of buildings or compounds that are separated by hedges or low embankments. The compounds are located on both sides of the Red River, with some apparently situated along abandoned course segments. Frank Schambach (1982b:7) has suggested that the entire village extended for at least 4 kilometers (2.5 mi) along the river. Recent research indicates that it might have extended as much as 9 kilometers (5.6 mi; Guccione and Hays 2008). One compound, located at the western end of the village, contains a mound with a structure on its summit, and Schambach notes the presence of a possible residence for a community leader to the east.

The Teran map presents a static picture of one village during the late seventeenth century. The degree to which the map reflects Caddo villages of other times and places is of considerable research interest. The Willow Chute Bayou locality, in present-day Bossier Parish, is the best example of a possible floodplain village in northwest Louisiana (Figure 11.1). The locality is on a spatial scale (approximately 12 km or 7.5 mi long) concordant with Caddo communities described in historic records (such as the Teran map) and with patterns found elsewhere, such as at the Spirit Lake locality in southwest Arkansas (Trubowitz 1984). The area contains numerous archaeological sites and is bounded by backswamps that have significant limitations for human habitation. Communication within the area would have been easy, as all sites are within a half-day walk along contiguous well-drained natural levees.

Most loci suitable for prehistoric settlement along Willow Chute currently are cultivated fields with excellent surface visibility. Sites consist of artifact scatters that range from 50 to 200 meters (165 to 655 feet) in extent along the natural levees bordering the stream. Over the span of almost a decade, Louis Baker, a local amateur archaeologist, made repeated surface collections, enabling the compilation of a large artifact database. Ceramics from Baker's collection, along with radiocarbon dates obtained during several subsurface investigations, indicate that the community first developed in the twelfth century and was abandoned by the middle of the fifteenth century (Girard 1997).

The permanent village along Willow Chute appears to have started at the north end of the stream at the Festervan site (16BO327), located across the Red River from Mounds Plantation. A deep test pit near the western edge of the site sampled a buried soil horizon approximately 1.2 meters (4 ft) below the present surface. The recovered pottery and a radiocarbon date on charcoal from this horizon indicate that the site was occupied between A.D. 700 and 900, just prior to the manufacture of significant amounts of distinctive Caddo pottery. The Festervan ceramic assemblage is not replicated elsewhere along Willow Chute and the site area is relatively extensive (about 12 hectares or 30 acres), suggesting that the population was aggregated at this one site prior to A.D. 1000. Expansion downstream appears to have taken place during the twelfth century A.D. Ceramic studies suggest that the community did not develop by a gradual movement from the Festervan site, but that it spread quickly across the entire locality into several core areas that grew through time. Some areas, particularly in the vicinity of the Vanceville mound (16BO7) and village (16BO168), have relatively high artifact densities and diverse pottery assemblages, and these areas probably were occupied throughout the history of the community.

At least three mounds eventually were constructed in the Willow Chute locality. The Vanceville Mound is located along the outer bend of a tight meander of Willow Chute Bayou. The site consists of a single conical mound approximately 2 meters (6.6 ft) tall and 25 meters (82 ft) in diameter, surrounded by an extensive midden deposit. Although the mound has not been excavated, a small test unit at the base suggested that artifacts are numerous within and beneath the mound fill. The recovered materials do not differ significantly from those found elsewhere along Willow Chute (Girard 1995), and it is unclear whether the presence of a mound at Vanceville is an indication of higher social status for the residents relative to their Willow Chute neighbors. The situation at the Swan Lake site (16BO11) appears to have been similar to Vanceville, with typical residential areas placed in close proximity to a single small mound (Girard 2007).

The Werner site (16BO8), located near the southern edge of the Willow Chute locality, differs considerably. The landowner leveled the mound during the early 1930s. When Clarence Webb visited the site in 1936, he noted that the mound had been approximately 38 meters (125 ft) in diameter and taller than the Vanceville Mound. The mound fill was red sandy loam, similar to the surrounding deposits, with no evidence of burials or other cultural features (Webb 1983:217). Local Boy Scouts, partially supervised by Webb, excavated the former mound area in 1958 and 1959. The investigations revealed a floor of "packed, level, red clay" with post molds and two ash pits. Most of the post molds were arranged in two concentric circles. The outer circle was approximately 24 meters (79 ft) in diameter, and the inner circle was approximately 14 meters (46 ft) in diameter. On the eastern side of the larger circle, the pattern bulged out to form what appeared to be an elaborate entrance. Although Webb considered the possibility that the outer ring represented a corral, probable roof and wall construction materials (burned small timbers, daub, and cane) were found along a portion of the arc, leading him to conclude that a large structure with an inner chamber was represented. Material culture associated with the remaining mound fill and underlying structure was atypical for the Willow Chute area. An unusually high percentage of engraved sherds was present, and the majority of these had highly polished surfaces with red and white pigments in the engraved lines. Chipped stone tools and chipping debris, common at other Willow Chute sites, were present only in small quantities. Numerous cut and perforated mussel shells (possibly ornaments) were recovered. The faunal assemblage was skewed to the presence of bones, particularly deer, which would have yielded choice meat cuts. Only sparse habitation debris was present in the immediate vicinity of the mound. These traits suggest that the structure beneath the Werner mound was not a typical habitation locus, but may have served as a meeting place for community leaders, or as a place of religious or ritual significance (Webb 1983:226–232). A radiocarbon date from one of the post molds indicates a mid-fifteenth-century date for the structure. Apparently, the mound was constructed to cover the remains of the structure—perhaps one of the last events that took place in the Willow Chute community.

Other dispersed villages likely existed in the Red River floodplain after ca. A.D. 1200. Scattered sites have been identified along Cowhide Bayou, Red Bayou, and Stumpy Bayou in north Caddo Parish (Girard 1994b, 1999; Webb 1959; Webb and McKinney 1975) and along Red Chute Bayou in southern Bossier Parish (Bennett 1982). Farther south are sites in Red River Parish, such as the Marston (16RR2), Hanna (16RR4), Charles Webb (16RR86), and Gahagan sites (Hunter et al. 2002; Thomas et al. 1980; Webb and Dodd 1939). However, surveys in these other areas have been too limited for the identification of the kind of contiguous site distributions evident along Willow Chute. Some Caddos may have resided in relatively isolated hamlets or farmsteads between village communities. These settlements probably consisted of individual or small clusters of households, with the inhabitants having relatively loose social and economic ties to the larger villages.

Changes in settlement patterns spanning the late twelfth and thirteenth centuries indicate social, economic, and political transformations that took place across the Caddo area. The Mounds Plantation site probably was converted from a substantial village, where feasting, elite residence, and mortuary ceremonies took place, into a sacred site, where activities resulting in artifact deposition may have been proscribed. Concurrently, dispersed floodplain villages like that along Willow Chute Bayou developed. These villages had one or more important communal structures, which occasionally were dismantled (perhaps ritually) and capped by mounds. Perttula and Rogers (2007:91) associate the scattering of Caddo people into new and more dispersed settlements in present-day eastern Texas as at least partly related to the intensification of maize agriculture. Communities likely became economically, as well as socially and politically, more autonomous. Unfortunately, with the exception of research at the Hanna site (Byrd 1980; Shea 1980), and the McLelland (16BO236) and Joe Clark (16BO237) sites (Gardner 1997; Weinand et al. 1997), subsistence data from northwest Louisiana Caddo sites are sparse.

Floodplain Households

Few investigations in Louisiana have been carried out on spatial scales that enable definition of individual houses and associated features. An exception is work carried out at the Hanna site in Red River Parish, where portions of several structures were identified (Thomas et al. 1980). The clearest picture comes from excavations at the McLelland and Joe Clark sites in southern Bossier Parish, where a small cluster of houses was identified, perhaps representing a farmstead not directly associated with a more extensive village (Kelley 1997). At the McLelland site, two circular house patterns and seven human burials were uncovered. As elsewhere in the Caddo area, the houses were constructed by placing posts in the ground. The holes dug for the posts, sometimes with remnants of the posts themselves, remained visible as stains in the ground. One of the houses at the McLelland site was 11 meters (36 ft) in diameter and had possible interior partitions, storage pits, and a central hearth. Three burials were placed within the structure. A child was apparently interred while the house was still occupied. Two adults were buried in the house area after the structure had been dismantled. A second structure, 12 meters (39 ft) in diameter, was present only 1 meter (3.3 ft) away from the first. It was not as well preserved because of damage to the deposits by modern levee construction. One burial was found in the area that postdates the structure. Scattered post holes, found on the north side of the structures, did not form distinct patterns and apparently represent ramadas, storage racks, or other exterior facilities made by placing posts in the ground.

The Joe Clark site was only about 200 meters (656 ft) away from the McLelland site. The Joe Clark site was not as well preserved, but post holes suggest that a single circular structure about 11 meters (36 ft) in diameter was present at the site. Both sites appear to date to the late seventeenth or early eighteenth centuries. They may have formed part of the Nakasas Caddo village identified during the expedition of Bienville in A.D. 1700 (McWilliams 1981).

Upland Communities

Lower portions of many of the tributary streams to the Red River were blocked by natural levees along the active channel, or by rafts comprised of fallen trees and debris (Alberston and Dunbar 1993; Bagur 2001; Humphreys 1984). Numerous habitation areas that may have formed small communities are situated on the lower portions of Tertiary ridges that overlook ephemeral lakes present in these areas. These sites are not located on highly productive agricultural lands, but are positioned in close proximity to both upland and bottomland resources. Although lake community subsistence resources might have been relatively stable, yields probably were low relative to agricultural production on the more fertile and extensive floodplain soils. No Caddo mounds are present in these areas, nor are there sites likely to represent distinctive centers or other communal areas. The lake areas undoubtedly were a valuable part of the overall late prehistoric economic system, but it is not known how they were linked socially or politically to the dispersed floodplain villages. It is possible that the lake communities had a degree of autonomy but maintained trade relationships with people in the floodplain, perhaps participating in their ceremonies and depending upon them for protection from enemies. It also is possible that sites along marginal lakes represent the intermittent use of these areas by the same people who resided in the floodplain communities. The lake areas may have been important for seasonal exploitation of lacustrine and upland resources, and as places of refuge during floods or times of conflict.

One example of a community situated along a marginal floodplain lake is the Smithport Landing site (16DS4). This site consists of several midden areas and a small cemetery situated on the lower slopes of a series of upland ridges overlooking the swampy bottomlands of Buffalo Bayou, near Smithport Lake in DeSoto Parish (Webb 1963). Artifacts were scattered over an area of 16 to 20 hectares (40 to 50 acres) on four distinct rises. Ceramic types indicate that the site was occupied from the Early Caddo period into the Middle Caddo period. Clarence Webb uncovered the burials of fourteen individuals apparently associated with nineteen ceramic vessels. The burials were shallow and individual burial pits could not be discerned, but Webb surmised that six different pits were present, with two or three individuals in some. Unlike the Early Caddo–period mound burials at Mounds Plantation and Gahagan, vessels accompanying the burials tended to be of utilitarian types. Only two engraved vessels, both Hickory Engraved bottles, were present.

Caddo archaeological sites also are present along the major upland streams in northwest Louisiana. Small upland settlements date back to the Woodland period in these areas. However, by the eleventh century, these small upland communities existed in a regional social environment where the more extensive floodplain villages were forming. Relationships between the dispersed floodplain villages and upland communities are not well understood, but some degree of interdependence, as well as conflict, likely existed. As with the marginal lake occupations, upland villages may have provided hunting products in exchange for agricultural or riverine goods. Cooperation for mutual defense and participation in religious and ceremonial events (including intermarriage) are other possible links. Social and economic tensions also may have existed due to such issues as differential power, political autonomy, and social pretentiousness. Because few upland sites have been investigated, little is known about these settlements. Communities consisting of dispersed residential areas, similar to those in floodplain environments, may have existed along some major upland tributaries. Relatively aggregated communities also may have been present, some of which may have developed into substantial size, similar to the Oak Hill village (41RK214), along the Sabine River in eastern Texas (Perttula and Rogers 2007). Although social and geographical boundaries probably were not rigid, it is possible that multiple communities were organized into larger "tribal" units (Gibson 2005). Residential mobility probably was greater than in the floodplain, and many sites might represent camps occupied temporarily during hunting expeditions. No major excavations have been conducted in upland settings. However, the number of recorded sites and information from local artifact collections clearly indicate that Caddo peoples regularly resided in the uplands of northwest Louisiana.

Protohistoric Changes to Caddo Settlement

Changes in settlement locations, including the abandonment of the Willow Chute locality, and the appearance of new pottery traits occurred during the fifteenth century. Although sample sizes are small, there appears to have been some movement closer to the active channel of the Red River, as exemplified by late sites such as Byram Ferry (16BO17), Belcher (16CD13), Beene Plantation (16BO19), McDade (16BO331), and McLelland/Joe Clark. Several sites that may date after the middle of the fifteenth century also have been identified along Bodcau and Dorcheat Bayous and their tributaries. In fact, some of the ceramic changes suggest increasing social connections between groups in the Red River and middle Ouachita River drainages (Kidder 1998b:134). It is not clear whether the changes are local phenomena or whether they are related to widespread transformations evident elsewhere in the Caddo area and southeastern United States.

Significant additions were made to the Belcher Mound during the sixteenth century and continuing into the middle seventeenth century, with elaborate mortuary ceremonialism involving placement of high status goods with certain individuals (Webb 1959). Schambach and Early (1982:119) have noted that almost all of the major mound groups in southwest Arkansas contain late burials. These groups include the Friday, Foster, and McClure sites (Moore 1912), all of which probably were abandoned by A.D. 1650, prior to sustained European contact (Perttula 1992:122). Continued use of mounds, however, is depicted in the 1691–1692 Teran map, which probably shows the Hatchel Mound (41BW3) and surrounding Hatchel-Mitchell-Moores archaeological complex in northeast Texas (Perttula 2005; Wedel 1978). Natchitoches Engraved pottery recovered from the Battle Mound site (3LA1) suggests that occupation extended into the early eighteenth century (Timothy Perttula, personal communication 2008).

Abandonment of the mound centers may have followed shortly after the practice of placing deceased leaders in mound shaft graves had been discontinued. Perttula (1992:227) argues that a general decrease in the number and complexity of settlements in the Red River floodplain occurred by the late seventeenth century. Remaining communities may have been more aggregated and widely spaced, a trend that continued when Caddo population levels fell precipitously after European colonization in the following century (see Perttula 1992, 1993, 2001, 2002). Despite population loss, the Caddos continued to exert considerable influence on historical developments in northwest Louisiana, until most Caddo groups left for Texas following the coerced signing of an 1835 treaty ceding a portion of their former territory to the United States (Carter 1995; Cast et al., Chapter 12 in this volume; Gregory 1973; Smith 1995).

Connections between Caddo Communities

The manner in which the Caddo people organized themselves across the landscape was based on social and political connections between communities, as well as the distribution of vital natural resources. Using records written by eighteenth-century Europeans who passed through or settled in the Caddo area, anthropologist John Swanton (1942) listed approximately twenty-five different Caddo "tribes" that formed three or more confederated groups, along with several that were relatively independent. The latter include the Nakasas and Yatasis, who lived in the Shreveport area during the late seventeenth and early eighteenth centuries, and the Adaes, who resided on the western side of the Red River floodplain in the area north and west of Natchitoches. Living in the floodplain along present Cane River, and perhaps on the adjoining uplands, were the Natchitoches and a smaller group called the Doustioni. The Caddo "tribes" probably were composed of multiple communities linked by kinship and other social and political ties. However, by the late eighteenth century, these entities were remnants of more expansive groups whose numbers had been diminished by disease and aggression from the expansion of European communities, as well as Native American groups such as the Osage and Chickasaw (Perttula 1992; 1993; Smith 1995).

Although it is not clear how stable these pan-communal groups were, or to what degree they held specific territories, it is likely that Caddo communities were linked into larger social and political entities prior to European contact. Archaeologists have used trait similarities, primarily decorative aspects on pottery, to isolate geographic areas that may represent past territories of groups similar to those identified by Swanton from historic records. Opinions differ regarding the degree to which these units are likely to coincide with past social or political entities. Units defined for northwest Louisiana (the Gahagan, Bossier, and Belcher phases) are mainly temporal divisions with vast spatial extents and are likely to be more inclusive than the historically defined social units.

It was not until the middle of the nineteenth century, when Caddo-speaking peoples resided together in Oklahoma, that the Caddo became clearly identified as a unified cultural group (Perttula 1993:92; Story 1978:51). In recent Caddo studies, there has been increased recognition of the considerable social diversity likely to have existed within the Caddo area (Perttula 1996; Story 1990). For example, Gibson (2005) attempted to link ceramic variation between sites classified within the Bossier phase to the presence of different social groups. Kelley's (2006:61–66) recent work at the Burnitt site (16SA204) demonstrated significant differences in sixteenth-century ceramic assemblages between the Sabine and Red River drainages, suggesting important social variation not distinguished by current cultural taxonomies.

Final Comment

The Caddo people flourished in northwest Louisiana for a span of at least eight centuries. Archaeological research enables us to monitor transformations in Caddo material culture and to use this information to track changes in how groups positioned themselves on the landscape. Ongoing studies are directed toward understanding Caddo culture within the broader social and political landscape of the late prehistoric and early historic Southeast. This chapter conveys some of the results of these efforts. Many aspects of past Caddo life in Louisiana and surrounding areas are left out, or only briefly touched upon in the brief summary presented here. For additional information, many excellent recent overviews are available, such as those by Carter (1995), Early (2000, 2004), Perttula (1992, 1996, 2002, 2004), and Smith (1995, 1998), as well as in the Tejas exhibit at the Texas Beyond History website (Texas Beyond History 2008).

12

The Caddo Nation, Archaeology, and NAGPRA

ROBERT CAST, BOBBY GONZALEZ,
AND TIMOTHY K. PERTTULA

The day we were to leave New York and come back home it was pouring down rain. The small cedar box had been wrapped in clear plastic so as not to get it wet and then placed in a Club Monaco shopping bag. The stunned faces of the airport security screeners said it all as the bag passed through the scanners at each airport checkpoint while supervisors read over our clearance paperwork and whispered in the ears of the security checkers. Bobby Gonzalez was bringing an ancestor back to the Caddo people—an ancestor who had been far removed and long forgotten until the Native American Graves Protection and Repatriation Act (NAGPRA) cleared the way for the Caddo to take control over what was originally theirs to begin with: the responsibility of properly caring for their deceased, as well as their objects of religious and cultural significance (Cast and Gonzalez 2005:3–4; PL 101–601; 104 Stat. 3048; 25 USC 3001 et esq.).

Bobby and the American Museum of Natural History (AMNH) staff had consulted about the proper care and packaging of the human remains before our arrival. Bobby prayed with the remains in an area that the AMNH had specifically set aside for such ceremonial purposes. The AMNH staff had called ahead to the Federal Transportation Security Administration and the airports to make them aware that we would be transporting human remains. They then provided each of us with the necessary paperwork to go through each checkpoint. Bobby had asked Nell Murphy of the AMNH staff if the remains could bypass the scanners at the airport. Nell explained that the policy had been different before September 11, 2001, but now even human remains that went through security checkpoints would need to be scanned.

Back in August 1997, the Caddo Nation of Oklahoma submitted a NAGPRA claim for a cranium that had been obtained by the AMNH in New York in 1877. Very little information was known about these remains, other than the fact that the museum had obtained a cranium as "either a purchase or a gift" from Charles

Colcock Jones, Jr. The cranium was described as having been found in a mound somewhere "in the vicinity of Shreveport" in Caddo or Bossier Parish, Louisiana (Robbins 2001:11043). Based on the presence of artificial cranial deformation, the museum dated these human remains between A.D. 800 and the contact period. Because of the cranial deformation, and in light of the archaeological investigations that had taken place in the past in Louisiana, the museum had determined the remains were culturally affiliated to the Caddo Nation.

Through consultation with the Caddo Nation and the Cultural Resources Office staff at the AMNH, a Notice of Inventory Completion was published for these human remains in the February 2001 *Federal Register* (Robbins 2001).

In June 2003, with financial assistance from the AMNH, the Caddo Nation Cultural Preservation Officers planned their visit to the museum. The primary purpose of the trip was to repatriate the skull of this Caddo person under the provisions of NAGPRA. The secondary purpose was to look at the ethnographic items culturally affiliated to the Caddo Nation and to consult further with the AMNH on these and any other collections we believed to be of significance. What we found during this consultation was another collection of artifacts and whole vessels taken from seventeen Caddo Indian graves in Cass County, Texas, and sold to the AMNH in 1900 by W. T. Scott. On a return trip to New York in 2004, working in conjunction with archaeological consultants Timothy K. Perttula and Rodney Bo Nelson, more funerary objects were discovered. The majority of these objects were in the W. T. Scott collection and came from several Caddo sites in southwestern Arkansas, although several were from the Shreveport vicinity.

Three Caddo vessels in the AMNH collections included two Keno Trailed, *var. Glendora,* bottles and a trailed-punctated bottle with a meandering negative-scroll motif, otherwise regularly executed with engraved lines on Hodges Engraved bottles (Figure 12.1). There is little doubt that these three vessels were recovered from a late seventeenth- to early eighteenth-century Caddo burial in northwestern Louisiana, most likely from the Beene Plantation site (16BO19). The site is adjacent to a relict channel of the Red River, on the river's east bank near Bossier City, Louisiana. It is likely that this site was occupied by the Yatasi Caddo from at least 1690 to ca. 1717 (Girard 2006:40, Chapter 11 in this volume). These artifacts were most likely associated with the human remains we had come to repatriate a year earlier. But that is another story (see Cast et al. 2006; Gonzalez et al. 2005:73; Perttula et al. 2005:109).

In retrospect, this Caddo person from Louisiana, whose skull was obtained by the museum in 1877 (only forty-two years after the Caddo had ceded their lands in Louisiana and eighteen years after they were forced out of the State of Texas),

Fig. 12.1. Keno Trailed *var. Glendora* bottle from the American Museum of Natural History collection, repatriated to the Caddo Nation.

had taken us on a whirlwind journey from the small town of Binger, Oklahoma (pop. 600), to New York, New York, and back again. We thought at the time that we were the ones, acting out of respect and tribal traditions, who were leading the way and doing something special by bringing this person's remains back home. But just maybe we were the ones being led.

Louisiana has always felt like home to the Caddo people, even though the Land Cession of 1835 forbade the Caddo from ever returning to the state "to live, settle, or establish themselves as a nation, tribe, or community of people within the same" (Kappler 1904). In 1935, a delegation of tribal members attended the state centennial celebration in Shreveport commemorating the 1835 Land Cession that had ceded their homelands to the United States (Figure 12.2). In 1955, another delegation attended a similar commemoration. As such, the Caddo people developed a new history within Louisiana, a state they knew held beneath its soil the remnants of their earlier history: many of the graves, sacred places, and traditional cultural properties of their ancestors.

The Caddo Nation of Oklahoma also has a more recent history of working closely with archaeologists, historians, and anthropologists in the State of Louisiana. In 1974, Hiram F. "Pete" Gregory invited members of the tribal government to attend the annual Caddo Conference, which was first held in 1946 (Gregory 1980:24–25). Tribal Chairman Medford Williams attended the conference that year. This was the first time that a Caddo tribal member had actually participated

Fig. 12.2. Delegation of Caddo Indians to the Shreveport Centennial Exposition, June 28 to July 1, 1935. Individuals identified as: 1. Ralph Murrow, 2. Chas. Parton Smith, 3. Mrs. Chas. P. Smith, 4. Mrs. Ben Carter, 5. Joe Johnson, 6. Ben Carter, 7. Alice Cussen, 8. Mrs. Chas. Adams, 9. Melva Jean Murrow, 10. Chas. Adams, Chief, 11. [?] Smith, 12. Helen Murrow, 13. Josephine Inkanish, 14. Harry Edge (2nd Chief), 15. Mrs. Harry Edge, 16. Mrs. Fritz Hendrix, 17. Mrs. Alfred Taylor, 18. Alfred Taylor, 19. Thos. Merle Keyes, Jr., 20. LeRoy Johnson, 21. Mrs. Ralph Murrow, 22. Thos. Keyes, Sr., 23. C. Ross Hume, 24. Fritz Hendrix, 25. Stanley Edge. Mrs. Thos. Keyes present, but not in the photograph. Photograph donated by Merle Keyes, courtesy of the Caddo Nation.

in the proceedings. Since that time, Caddo tribal members have continued to attend and participate in the conference, which is held each year in a different state within the Caddo people's homelands of Arkansas, Louisiana, Oklahoma, and Texas.

Mrs. Cecile Elkins Carter, Caddo tribal member, historian, and author of *Caddo Indians: Where We Come From* (Carter 1995), was greatly influenced by the work that archaeologists, anthropologists, ethnographers, and historians were doing in the homelands of the Caddo people. In 1993, she applied to the National Park Service for one of the first NAGPRA grants ever received by the Caddo Nation. This grant set in motion the future and sustained growth of more formal historic preservation practices for the Nation, and it was the foundation for the current Caddo Nation historic preservation program. In the mid-1990s, David Scholes became the next Director of the Cultural Preservation Office (CPO), and he continued with the repatriation efforts of the Caddo people.

In 1996, Stacey Halfmoon became the NAGPRA Coordinator and Historic Preservation Director for the Caddo Nation. In early 1997, the Caddo Nation received a grant from the National Park Service Tribal Historic Preservation Fund to formally establish a Tribal Historic Preservation Office (THPO). This office would participate and respond to federal Section 106 undertakings under the jurisdiction of the National Historic Preservation Act of 1966 (NHPA), both on and off tribal lands, working to establish formal government-to-government relationships with federal agencies under the NHPA, the Presidential Memorandum on "Government-to-Government Relations with Native American Tribal Governments" issued on April 29, 1994, and Executive Order 13175, "Consultation and Coordination with Indian Tribal Governments," issued on November 6, 2000.

In September 1997, Robert Cast was hired as the new Historic Preservation Officer for the Caddo Nation. He began contacting federal, state, and local agencies within the traditional homelands of the Caddo with news that a formal office was now in place and that the Caddo Nation was ready to begin consultations related to undertakings under Section 106 of the NHPA. This legislation requires that any federal agency take into account the effects of its activities on cultural resources prior to the expenditure of federal funds or the issuance of any federal license. Bobby Gonzalez, an ex-officio tribal council member, was hired as the new NAGPRA Coordinator in 2001 when Stacey Halfmoon accepted an internship with the Department of Defense in Washington, D.C.

In 2002, due to its continued involvement in historic preservation issues that matter to the Caddo people, the Caddo Nation of Oklahoma assumed the formal duties of the State Historic Preservation Office on its tribal lands, under Section 101(d) 2 of the NHPA. The Caddo Nation was the first among the thirty-nine tribal governments in Oklahoma to assume such responsibilities on tribal lands. With formal recognition of the THPO by the National Park Service came the responsibility of continuing the important preservation work that many others had put in motion years earlier.

Since that time, with the support of the Nation's tribal council and council chairpersons, the Cultural Preservation Office has been involved in a number of important projects directly related to Caddo archaeology and history within the State of Louisiana. The establishment of the Cane River National Heritage Area in Natchitoches, Louisiana, has made it possible for the tribe to receive grant funding to participate in a series of projects. One project dealt with the oral histories of the Caddo people concerning Natchitoches and the Cane River. Stories still told by the Caddo people call attention to the importance of these places. Another project, funded through the Cane River National Heritage Area grants program, was developed in partnership with our Repatriation Committee (a group of traditional practitioners and elders of the Caddo Nation), along with

Dr. Dayna Bowker Lee and Dr. Pete Gregory of Northwestern State University. The purpose of this project was to perform a "mounds tour" along the Red River in northwestern Louisiana. The participants visited mound sites sacred to the Caddo people, documenting the Repatriation Committee's responses to the tour, and their interpretations of these once-majestic places.

The committee was able to visit several important places relating to the Caddo people's long history in Louisiana. Mounds Plantation (16CD12), the Southern Compress site (16NA14), Drake's Salt Lick site (16NA11), Los Adaes (16NA16), Fort St. Jean Baptiste des Natchitoches (16NA68), and the Fish Hatchery site (16NA9) in Natchitoches were some of the places that were visited. More recently, the Caddo Nation Cultural Preservation Office completed a similar survey, visiting a number of the mound sites on the Louisiana Indian Mounds Trail, a state-designated driving trail that showcases some of the important cultural sites in northeast Louisiana. The late Dr. Thomas Eubanks, then the State Archaeologist for Louisiana, was instrumental in ensuring tribal participation and involvement in the development of the trail.

The Cultural Preservation Office also participated in the Freeman and Custis Bicentennial Symposium, which was organized by Louisiana State University at Shreveport in June 2006. The authors of this chapter presented a paper entitled "The First People of the Red River: The Caddo Before and After Freeman and Custis" (Perttula et al. 2008). Many Caddo tribal members attended the conference and set a precedent in establishing new relationships with professional biologists, historians, botanists, archaeologists, and scholars in many other fields. The symposium was a learning experience for the Caddo attendees, as well as for the public and professional participants.

In October 2006, the Caddo people participated in a similar symposium held at the Bossier Parish Library Historical Center. One of the highlights of this symposium was the opening exhibit of the McKinney Family Collection of Caddo artifacts from the Mounds Plantation site in northwestern Louisiana, subsequently housed at the Historical Center. Many of the tribal elders attended the symposium and were able to share stories about their connections to Louisiana and the artifacts represented in the collection. Several tribal members also put items on loan for the exhibit, such as traditional and historic Caddo shirts, dresses, and jewelry.

Why are so many of the previously mentioned places and items still sacred to the Caddo people? Some of these traditional Caddo cultural properties have been discussed elsewhere (Cast 2005). Why do the Caddo people feel the need to participate in these meetings and continue to be involved on a professional level with projects in Louisiana, far from the Caddo Nation tribal complex in the eroded, dusty red hills of Binger, Oklahoma? How can artifacts hundreds of years old, or older, still have significance to the Caddo people and, moreover, be considered sacred or traditional religious objects?

Among the misconceptions that a number of archaeologists have with tribal governments, and with tribal historic preservation programs in general, is that the work the archaeologists are doing does not really concern the tribe, that the tribe is not interested in archaeology per se, or that professional archaeology has very little to offer the tribal government and its people in an understandable or useful way. This reasoning, however, is part of a much bigger problem. How can archaeologists make their research and findings accessible and understandable to Native Americans, as well as to the general public? If there is no satisfactory answer to this question, then the pursuit of archaeology really becomes of no use to anyone except the archaeologists.

One way that archaeologists can inform the general public is by writing articles for a variety of newspapers, magazines, and journals, both locally and nationally, in support of public archaeology. They should provide information to a non-professional audience about the importance and relevance of archaeology. Another avenue currently being developed is to create internet websites with downloadable, educational curriculums for the general public to access, detailing the archaeological history of a state. For example, the Texas Beyond History website, developed with the participation of the Caddo Nation, features web pages outlining the history of the Caddo and could serve as a model for other states (Texas Beyond History 2008).

The best way that archaeologists can make their work and findings more understandable to a tribal government and its people is literally to know their audience. By building personal relationships with members of the Caddo Nation, a number of archaeologists working in the homelands of the Caddo people have been able both to share the results of their research and to obtain information important to their work. These relationships do not happen overnight, of course. For anyone interested in doing archaeology in the Caddo area, start now and take this advice: come meet the people first-hand and get to know them.

The potential benefits of such relationships are obvious. By working together with tribal nations, some of the research questions archaeologists ask may become better focused on the concerns of tribal people. Diabetes, for example, has taken a heavy toll in Indian Country. How might archaeologists provide information on the foodways and health of a tribal people's ancestors, and how might this information have an impact on present-day diet and health?

Spirituality is a very important and practical part of present-day Caddo people's everyday life. What kind of spirituality and religion did ancestors of the Caddo have? How might such religious practices show up in the archaeological record? These are among the many questions tribal elders have guided archaeologists to ask in their research.

No doubt, archaeologists and Caddo tribal members view "artifacts" very differently (Lippert 2006). By working together, however, each may be able to shed a little light on the past. "Indigenous archaeology" is a term that has been much discussed by tribal members and archaeologists, both of whom are trying to define exactly what it is (cf. Smith and Wobst, ed. 2005; Watkins 2000). We like to simply refer to it as "partnering up" for the benefit of everyone (Thomas 2005:xiii–xv).

Human Remains, Funerary Objects, Sacred Objects, Objects of Cultural Patrimony, and the Impacts of the Native American Graves Protection and Repatriation Act

Whenever archaeological projects are undertaken in the traditional homelands of the Caddo people, including northwest Louisiana but also beyond those modern boundaries, it should be understood that the Caddo Nation has an interest in the work. Those working in Caddo archaeology know that whenever there is ground disturbance, there is a chance of encountering human remains, burials, cemeteries, and funerary objects left behind by the Caddo people from ancient times to the late 1830s. In one real sense, NAGPRA has had very little to do with driving this concern. When NAGPRA was passed in 1990, it was intended to correct past injustices in the treatment of Native American skeletal remains, grave goods, and cultural patrimony, but its provisions applied specifically to federal agencies, federal lands, and federally funded museums and institutions (PL 101–601; 104 Stat. 3048; 25 USC 3001 et esq.). Burials, cemeteries, or funerary objects found on private or state lands are of no less importance to the Caddo people. Perhaps here is where archaeologists and Caddo people have very similar interests but very different concerns regarding the outcome of what happens to human remains and funerary objects.

Both Caddo tribal members and archaeologists want to see human remains and funerary objects documented to some extent. The Caddo Nation has taken the position that such discoveries should be treated like a crime scene. Human remains and associated objects must not be disturbed or removed from their original context in order to be properly documented. However, the disposition of the human remains and funerary objects are often troublesome when ascertaining jurisdiction, ownership, and, in some cases, cultural affiliation.

The Caddo Nation has become well-versed in the law, both state and federal, when it comes to the disposition of human remains and funerary objects. In 1991, the State of Louisiana passed the Unmarked Human Burial Sites Preservation Act, with the goal of protecting all unmarked burials, including human skeletal remains and funerary objects, from desecration, destruction, or commercial profit. This law pertains to unmarked Caddo burials and declares that "all human burial sites shall be accorded equal treatment, protection, and respect for human dignity without reference to ethnic origins, cultural backgrounds, or religious affiliations." (R.S. 8:671 et seq.). The Caddo tribal government has had to come to terms with inconsistencies between state burial laws, the interplay of these laws with NAGPRA in certain situations, and their traditional beliefs and ways of treating the remains of their ancestors (Gonzalez 2005). Because of the many discoveries of Caddo burials over the years, the Caddo Nation has been required to produce a number of uniform tenets in the form of a "reburial policy" regarding inadvertent discoveries of human remains and funerary objects, regardless of whether they are discovered on private, state, or federal lands.

Human remains and the objects placed with them should not be the property of an individual simply because he or she owns the land. The funerary objects placed in Caddo burials represent a very practical ritualism and, at the same time, a highly structured religious ceremony. Some of these rituals and ceremonies are manifested in the culture and practices of the present-day Caddo people (Gonzalez 2005:55–59).

Archaeologists should not excavate human remains and funerary objects of the Caddo people simply out of curiosity, or to add to some landowner's private collection. This is both irresponsible and unethical. If human remains or funerary objects are inadvertently discovered, the Caddo people will want these to remain buried in the same place they were originally interred, with as little further disturbance as possible. There will be times when the disturbance of human remains simply cannot be avoided, as sometimes happens with private, state and federal development projects. If disturbance cannot be avoided, then archaeological investigations should take place, with the stipulation that the human remains and funerary objects are to be reburied nearest to where they were originally encountered. Because of the disturbance, and as part of the traditional beliefs of the Caddo people, the Caddo Nation will ask a tribal representative—someone taught the traditional burial ceremonies of the Caddo—to be in attendance to perform a reburial of the individual and the associated items. As the Caddo traditional elders have said, "Once they were originally buried, all the ceremonies were done back at that time. We never expected to have to *rebury* our people."

In some rare cases, the Caddo Nation Repatriation Committee will allow analysis of human remains and funerary objects, but this is decided on a case-by-case basis. The researcher will need to meet with the committee and explain in detail the reasons for the study. Issues such as reburial and the study of human remains and funerary objects are usually worked out and determined in advance, either through a formalized written agreement between the Caddo Nation and the state, or the Caddo Nation and the individual landowner. As noted previously, NAGPRA has had very little to do with these long-standing, traditional concerns. In most cases, an area for reburial can be set aside on a property if human remains and funerary objects have to be removed from the original site. If this is not possible, then the preferred course of action is to have the human remains and funerary objects reburied at the tribal cemetery near Binger, Oklahoma.

NAGPRA does play a large role, however, in how the Caddo people have reburied culturally affiliated ancestors from federal lands, museums, and repositories holding collections that fall under its provisions. The Vicksburg District of the U.S. Army Corps of Engineers has established a reburial area for the Caddo people south of the Red River between Shreveport and Natchitoches, near Lock and Dam # 4. On February 24, 2000, a formal dedication and reburial ceremony took place there. Human remains and funerary objects from the Joe Clark (16BO237) and McLelland (16BO236) sites were reburied in a ceremony attended by personnel from the Vicksburg District of the U.S. Army Corps of Engineers, Caddo Nation officials, tribal members, state representatives, and archaeologists who worked on the project (Kelley 1997). Later, in September 2002, the Caddo reburied human remains from the Hanna site (16RR4), which had been held at the Smithsonian National Museum of Natural History. On May 8, 2002, the Caddo Nation and U.S. Army installation at Fort Polk signed a comprehensive NAGPRA agreement. This led to the reburial of human remains in January 2003, at the request of the Caddo Nation Repatriation Committee.

After consultations with the Vicksburg District U.S. Army Corps of Engineers, the State Archaeologist of Louisiana, and the Louisiana Division of Archaeology, on August 19, 2003, Caddo Nation representatives reburied human remains from the Conly site (16BI19) near Loggy Bayou on the Red River. These remains were eroding out of the channel-cut bank and in imminent peril due to increased flooding, water releases from Lake Bistineau, and looting activity along Loggy Bayou. The human remains were found to be the oldest known in the State of Louisiana, dating from between 7,500 and 8,000 years ago (Girard 2000a). Through consultations with the Caddo Nation and other tribal representatives, it was agreed that the human remains would be analyzed, and that after analysis, they would be reburied in a respectful manner. The area of reburial was stabilized to deter any further erosion or looting.

The Caddo Nation has also developed Treatment and Handling agreements with a number of museums and repositories that hold NAGPRA collections. These agreements have been developed for the specific care and handling of items, according to traditional concerns of the Caddo people. Part of the problem, under NAGPRA, is bringing together for reburial all of the human remains with the originally associated funerary objects. Human remains, associated funerary objects, and unassociated funerary objects excavated at the same time, from the same burial, may presently be held by three separate institutions. Unassociated funerary objects that are repatriated may be held in the Caddo Heritage Museum. Many of the collections have been repatriated on paper, but the Caddo Nation simply does not have the facilities to hold or house all of them. In the interim, or until actual repatriation, developing these types of agreements has at least allowed the Caddo Nation to provide more traditional methods for the treatment and handling of such items. The Caddo Nation currently has agreements with Northwestern State University in Natchitoches, the Sam Noble Oklahoma Museum of Natural History in Norman, the Arkansas Archeological Survey in Fayetteville, and the Texas Archeological Research Laboratory in Austin. There are two pending agreements under review with the Peabody Museum at Harvard University in Cambridge, Massachusetts, and Louisiana State University in Baton Rouge.

In 2008, the Fiftieth Caddo Conference was held in Natchitoches, Louisiana. As with other previous conferences, many Caddo tribal members participated. Papers were presented on Caddo archaeology, history and ethnography, and participants had many opportunities to visit with friends and colleagues. Unlike other conferences, this Caddo Conference was significant in that a group of Caddo people reburied human remains and funerary objects at the Natchitoches National Fish Hatchery, in a small area dedicated and set aside specifically for this purpose. These remains were from the Fish Hatchery site, a historic Caddo cemetery (Walker 1935).

Louisiana is a special place to the Caddo people. The citizens of Louisiana might be surprised at the extent to which the Caddo have continued to stay involved with their Louisiana homeland, and by what the Caddo are doing to preserve their cultural traditions. There is always much more work to be done. Research in Caddo archaeology and history, publications in newspapers, popular journals, and magazines, and educational media such as websites can help spread the news throughout the State of Louisiana that the Caddo are alive and well.

We have found that through "partnering up," we can accomplish more than we can on our own. In the past, researchers with selfish interests too often have used the Caddo to obtain information in the form of oral histories, stories, and interviews, and have subsequently published that information in books or articles, without informing or acknowledging those very people from whom they obtained the intellectual property. We hope that those days are over, and that anthropologists and archaeologists in particular realize the advantages of consulting and participating with the people behind the objects being studied.

We asked earlier, "Why do the Caddo people feel the need to participate in these meetings and continue to be involved on a professional level with projects in Louisiana, far from the Caddo Nation tribal complex in the eroded, dusty red hills of Binger, Oklahoma? How can artifacts hundreds of years old, or older, still have significance to the Caddo people and, moreover, be considered sacred or traditional religious objects?" These questions could be easily answered, but we would rather not do so here. Why not come to Binger, Oklahoma, and visit the Caddo Nation and its people to see their traditions firsthand? You are sure to find the answers there.

13

The Spanish in Northwest Louisiana, 1721–1773

GEORGE AVERY

The Spanish presence in northwest Louisiana begins with the establishment of the first mission for the Adaes Indians in A.D. 1717. No archaeological sites in northwest Louisiana have been associated with the Hernando de Soto expedition of A.D. 1539–1543, and pre-eighteenth-century European artifacts at American Indian sites cannot be exclusively attributed to the Spanish. In establishing a mission for the Adaes, the Spanish were reacting to the French trading post established among the Natchitoches Indians in 1713. A Spanish presidio and second mission would follow in 1721. When both were abandoned in 1773, the number of Adaeseños, or people associated with the presidio and mission, had grown to several hundred. The closing of the Los Adaes presidio and mission was prompted by the cession of all French land west of the Mississippi River to the Spanish in 1762, just prior to the end of the French and Indian War, also known as the Seven Years War. After 1762, most of modern-day Louisiana became a Spanish colony. In 1769, the Spanish governor of Louisiana appointed a local French trader, Athanase de Mézières, as lieutenant governor of Natchitoches. Northwest Louisiana remained under Spanish control until 1801 when the French took back the territory they ceded to the Spanish in 1762 in order to sell it to the Americans in 1803 as part of the Louisiana Purchase (Bolton 1970a, 1970b; Burton and Smith 2008; Byrd 2008; Castañeda 1936–1958).

The period from 1762 to 1801, known as the Spanish period in Louisiana, was a fascinating time characterized by the interaction of a variety of cultural groups in northwest Louisiana. These groups included Adaeseños, French Creoles, local and immigrant American Indian groups, enslaved people of African descent, and various other people of European descent. The history and archaeology of the Spanish period and early American period in northwest Louisiana include work by researchers associated with Northwestern State University, the National Park Service, and other universities, as well as by private contract archaeologists (see Commonwealth Associates, Inc. 1981; Espey Huston and Associates 1983; Girard 2002, 2003; Girard et al. 2008; Gregory 1973; Lee 1990; MacDonald et al. 2006; Mathews 1983; Morgan and Shatwell, ed. 2002; Pleasant and Pleasant 1990; Seale 1995). Present archaeological knowledge of the Spanish in northwest Louisiana is based primarily on investigations of Los Adaes. The Spanish and early American periods in northwest Louisiana deserve further consideration, but this chapter will specifically focus on the occupation of Los Adaes, which occurred from 1721 to 1773. This will provide a baseline of Spanish culture as it was introduced into northwest Louisiana and thereby serve as a starting point for future work dealing with cultural interaction in the later periods.

Los Adaes (16NA16) is located near Robeline, Louisiana, and is the archaeological remains of a Spanish fort, mission, and settlement (Figure 1.2). The fort was called *Nuestra Señora del Pilar de los Adaes*, and the mission was called *San Miguel de Cuellar de los Adaes*. Both the fort and mission were named after the Adaes, a local American Indian group whose name meant "a place along a stream" in the Caddoan language (Webb and Gregory 1986). Los Adaes served as the capital of the Spanish province of Texas from 1731 to 1770, and it was abandoned in 1773 (Gregory et al. 2004). Many of the people of Los Adaes returned to the area in the early 1800s, although it is likely that some never left. The descendants of the people of Los Adaes still live in the area today (Gregory 1983; Gregory et al. 2004).

Cultures in Contact: An Anthropological Perspective

Archaeologists are cultural anthropologists of the past. Just as cultural anthropologists learn about people by talking to them and observing their behavior, so too can archaeologists talk to the descendants of the people whose material culture they are excavating (see Echo-Hawk 2000; Mason 2000, 2006; Whitely 2002). Archaeologists who study the colonial period in North America can refer to the European documents from the time, in addition to the oral traditions of the descendent community (see Adams 1983; Beaudry, ed. 1988; Little, ed. 1992). Information from oral traditions and written documents is therefore used by archaeologists of the colonial period in northwest Louisiana, in addition to the information generated from excavations.

Anthropologists are particularly interested in what happens when people with different cultures come into contact with one another. Sometimes this contact is violent, resulting in either the destruction or dramatic alteration of social groups. Other times this contact is peaceful, and the different cultural groups accommodate one another's differences. Peaceful contact is often characterized by different cultural groups selecting certain attributes of one another and each incorporating those attributes into their own way of life. Anthropologists have learned that in situations of culture contact, all cultural groups involved will be affected to varying degrees. In colonial situations, both colonizer and colonized will adopt selected attributes from each other, and sometimes new cultural patterns emerge as people redefine themselves (see Cusick 1998; Loren 2000, 2001b). Archaeology can provide unique contributions beyond the historical documents to our understanding of what happens when people of different cultures come into contact with one another (see Deagan 1991), and northwest Louisiana provides a case where Spanish, French, American Indian, and African came into contact during the eighteenth century.

Los Adaes and Culture Contact in Northwest Louisiana

The Spanish people who came to northwest Louisiana in the early 1700s had already experienced over 150 years of contact with the American Indians of New Spain in what is now Mexico. The Spanish readily adopted the growing and consuming of maize as practiced by the American Indians, who, in turn, came to use many of the European implements made of iron and copper alloys. The Spanish, Africans, and American Indians also intermarried in New Spain. The percentage of peoples of mixed heritage in New Spain increased from 5 percent in the mid-1600s to 37 percent in the mid-1700s (Jaffery 2004:29). In northwest Louisiana, the material manifestation of this cultural mixing is evident in the presence of stone tools for grinding corn, as well as the words used to describe these tools. The American Indians of New Spain processed maize with grinding stones made of volcanic tuff. The Spanish adopted the stone grinding technology of the Nahuatl-speaking Indians of Mexico and used the terms *mano* and *metate* to describe the stone tools. *Mano* is the Spanish word for hand, since this tool is held in the hand, and *metate* is the Spanish version of the Nahuatl word *metatl,* which means quern or grinding stone. *Manos* and *metates* were still present, although not in use, in some households in northwest Louisiana in the mid-twentieth century (Gregory 1964). Numerous Nahuatl words have been identified as loan words in the Spanish that was still spoken in northwest Louisiana in the later twentieth century (Gregory 1996).

When the Marqués de Aguayo came to northwest Louisiana in 1721 with one hundred soldiers to establish a presidio and re-establish a mission in the area, he wanted to show a strong military presence to the French at Natchitoches, who had built a fort there by 1718. The French attacked the first mission for the Adaes Indians in 1719, only two years after the Spanish built it as a reaction to the French setting up a trading post among the Natchitoches Indians in 1713. The French attack on the first Spanish mission for the Adaes is sometimes referred to as the "Chicken War" by historians, as the only casualties were Spanish chickens (Chipman 1992:18–19). Even though the story of this attack is now told with some humor, the fear that the French were coming to invade Mexico—which was La Salle's intent in 1688 with his failed attempt on the Texas coast (see Bruseth and Turner 2005)—was sufficient to cause the Spanish to abandon the missions and presidio of east Texas and retreat to San Antonio.

The hundred Spanish soldiers brought by Aguayo to northwest Louisiana in 1721 were more than twice the number of French soldiers at Natchitoches, but at the same time, Aguayo did not want his presence to appear threatening to the American Indians in the area. Aguayo was aware that the Spanish missions in east Texas had failed in the 1690s largely as a result of the bad behavior of some of the soldiers toward the American Indian women in the area. In order to avoid or lessen such problems, Aguayo deliberately focused on recruiting married men, even if he had to recruit them from the jails. Thirty-one of the hundred soldiers at Los Adaes had families (Gregory et al. 2004). The Aguayo expedition also brought thousands of cattle, horses, pigs, sheep, and goats, along with other items of the Spanish colonial material culture of the time, including stone and metal tools and implements, and ceramic tableware. The site of the first mission for the Adaes was considered unsuitable for settlement, so the presidio and second mission for the Adaes were built roughly 1.5 miles to the east (Hadley et al. 1997:426–427).

After Aguayo established the presidio and mission at Los Adaes, the Spanish, French, and American Indian groups in the area lived in relative peace for the rest of the colonial period. There was no gold or silver to fight over, and the French treated the American Indians as equals. There was no attempt by the French to Christianize the American Indians, and there were no restrictions on what was traded, including firearms. The Spanish royal authority officially forbade the trade of guns to the American Indians in the early 1500s, and even though this prohibition was generally practiced, part of the reason was the "chronic shortage" of Spanish firearms and ammunition (Weber 1992:178). One governor at Los Adaes actually acquired French guns from Natchitoches to trade for horses, maize, and other items from the Bidai and Orcoquiza, who lived near the lower Trinity River in Texas (Bolton 1970a:336–337; cited in Weber 1992:429).

When the presidio and second mission for the Adaes were abandoned in 1773, it was not because of their military or religious shortcomings. The presidio had essentially failed its military inspection of 1767, which found, among other things, only two operable muskets for sixty soldiers. The inspection of the mission in the following year observed no Indian congregation. Even though Los Adaes had failed its inspections, it had succeeded in preventing the French from moving west of Natchitoches and in maintaining peaceful relations with the American Indians in the area (see Faulk 1965). After the end of the French and Indian War in 1763, Natchitoches came under the jurisdiction of the Spanish government, and Los Adaes was no longer needed. The presidio and mission were officially terminated, and in 1773, the non-military people of Los Adaes, or *Adaeseños*, were ordered to go to San Antonio, although some went east in defiance of the order. In 1779, some *Adaeseños* left San Antonio and eventually established a town at the old Spanish mission for the Nacogdoches Indians. The 1793 census for Nacogdoches, which used Spanish categories called *castas* to describe people, reveals the social complexity of those born at Los Adaes. The 1793 census included 22 *Españoles* (Spaniards), 55 *Mestizos* (Spanish and Indian), 19 *Coyotes* (Indian and *Mestizo*), 9 *Mulatos* (Spanish and African), 6 *Lobos* (Indian and *Mulato*), and 7 *Indios* (Indians) (Tjarks 1974:355). American Indian groups from Spanish colonial Texas represented in the Los Adaes population included Adaes, Bidai, Lipan Apache (Cannechi), and Tawakoni (Gregory 1983:54).

Archaeological Investigations at Los Adaes

Archaeological investigations at Los Adaes in the area of the presidio have uncovered portions of the presidio walls and the governor's house, as well as three structures and associated features outside the presidio walls. Limited testing at the mission indicated the possible presence of a burial pit, which is not surprising given the colonial custom of burying human remains in the floor of a church. The excavations of the presidio area directed by Hiram F. "Pete" Gregory (1983) in the late 1970s and early 1980s verified that Aguayo indeed built the presidio as planned (Figure 13.1). Many of the presidios on the northern frontier of New Spain had a design with four walls and two bastions for cannons, but the plans for the two presidios that bordered the French territory, Los Adaes and La Bahia (near the Texas coast), were more elaborate. Prior to archaeological excavations, some doubted that such elaborate presidios were even built. Excavations at Los Adaes revealed portions of two bastions and their connecting walls (Figure 13.1; Gregory et al. 2004), and excavations at La Bahia uncovered an even more elaborate presidio in the shape of a sixteen-pointed star (Bruseth et al. 2004). Therefore, archaeology has verified that both presidios were built according to the plans.

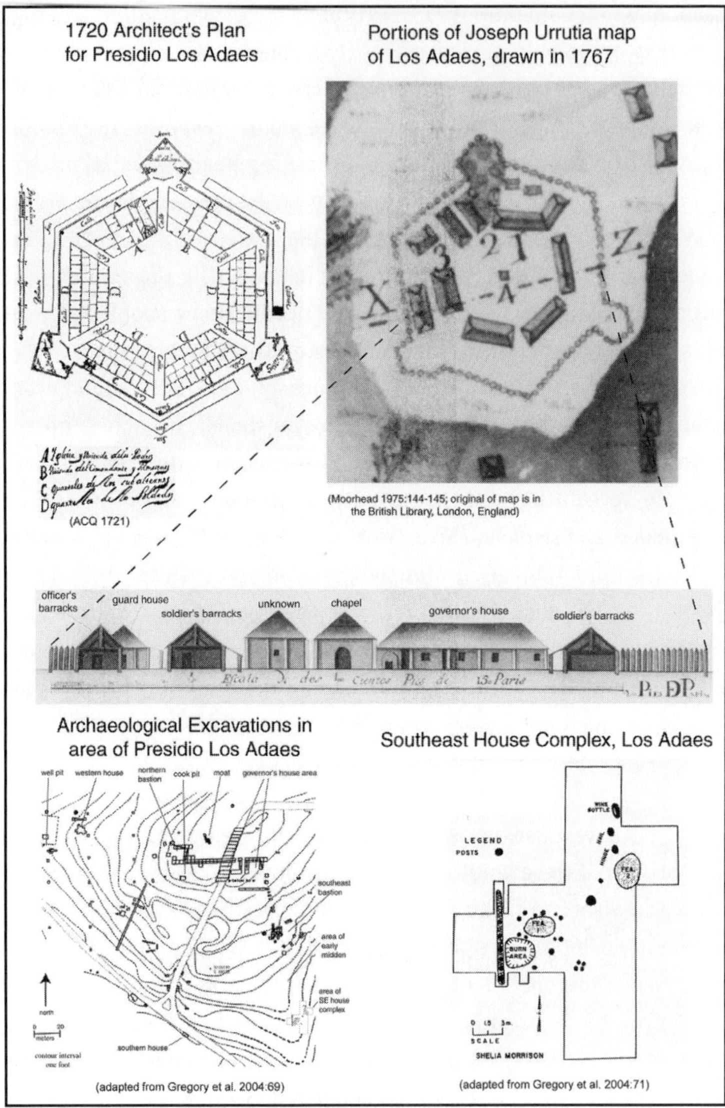

Fig. 13.1. Architect's plan, military inspector's drawing, and archaeological investigations of the Presidio area at Los Adaes (16NA16).

Two of the three structures excavated outside the presidio walls at Los Adaes were probably *jacal*-type or hut structures, consisting of depressed floor areas (probably from regular sweeping) and upright posts. Not all of the posts were placed in previously dug holes, as one of the probable *jacal*-type structures had no evidence of post molds or post holes. A French visitor to Los Adaes in 1768 described his stay in one of these *jacal*-type structures outside of the presidio as follows: "About three o'clock in the morning, however, we arrived at the hut of a baptized Indian, who took us kindly under his roof. . . . I went to sleep in the corner of his house, which by the bye, scarcely deserved that name, for the roof was only supported by a sort of paling, the greatest part of which had fallen to the ground from negligence and length of time. . . . The settlement of Adaes consists of about forty miserable houses, constructed with stakes driven into the ground" (Pagès 1793:48–50). The house excavated outside the southeastern bastion of the presidio is an interesting mix of architectural elements (Figure 13.1). The west wall is a wall trench with regularly spaced posts reminiscent of *poteaux en terre*, or post in the ground architecture, and a post at the bottom of Feature 1—a possible cooking pit—is similar to the building pattern of the American Indian people in the area, in which a central post supports the roof during the building of the house but is removed or burned after the roof is built. A large pit—Feature 2—was filled with trash, including many fragments of French tin-enameled pottery. French traders were reported to be living at Los Adaes, and this particular structure may have been associated with a French trader (Gregory et al. 2004:71–72).

The *jacal*-type structures outside the presidio at Los Adaes were in contrast to the more substantial structures within the presidio (Figure 13.1). These buildings, including a barracks, chapel, guardhouse, and governor's residence and storehouse, appear to be more French than Spanish in design. The roofs are a king-post construction, which is a Norman tradition, and the walls appear to be *poteaux en terre* construction (Gregory et al. 2004:69). The Joseph Urrutia map, parts of which are shown in Figure 13.1, was part of a military inspection at Los Adaes in 1767. All of the presidios of the northern frontier were inspected, and Los Adaes is unique with its wooden palisade and buildings with gabled roofs, in contrast to the stone or adobe walls and flat roofs of the other presidios (see Moorhead 1975:116–157).

Many of the examples of Spanish colonial material culture or artifacts recovered from Los Adaes reflect the cultural contact between the Spanish and others in Europe, Africa, Asia and the Americas. Tin-enameled pottery made in Mexico shows lacey elements (Figure 13.2a) similar to tin-enameled ware made in Spain, and the blue-on-white design (Figure 13.2b) was inspired by Asian porcelain (Deagan 1987:81, 84). The lacey pattern was at the end of its popularity by the time presidio Los Adaes was established in 1721, as archaeologists have determined that tin-enameled ware with the lacey pattern was made between 1650 and 1725 (Deagan 1987:82). French and British tin-enameled-ware fragments

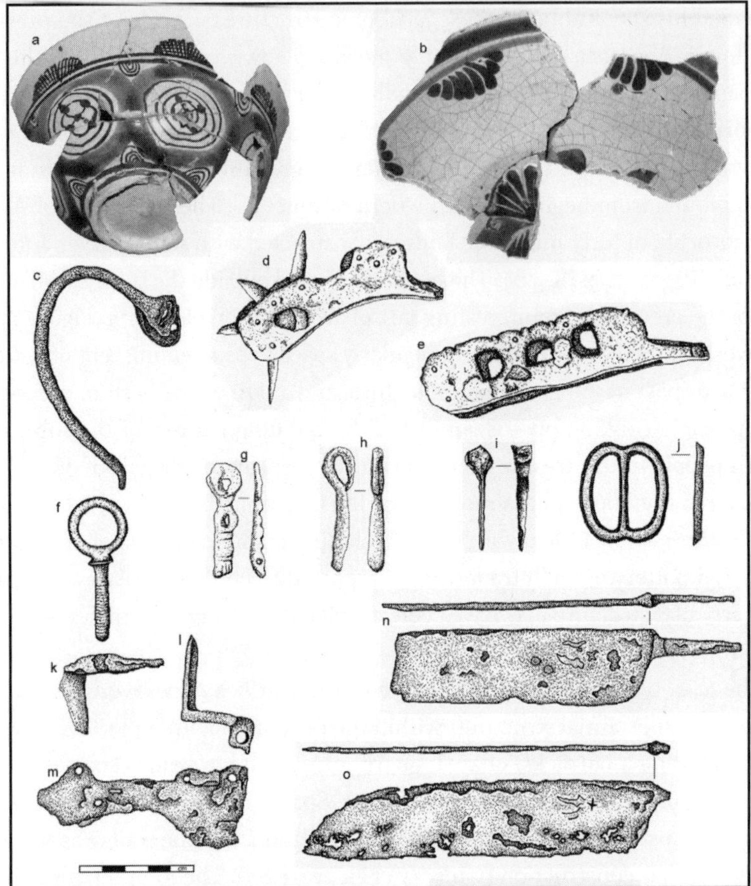

Fig. 13.2. Spanish colonial artifacts from Los Adaes (16NA16): a. Tin-enameled small bowl or cup made in Mexico; b. Tin-enameled brimmed bowl made in Mexico; c. Chocolate pot handle, cupreous metal; d. Spanish spur fragment, ferrous metal; e. Spanish spur fragment, ferrous metal; f. Vise screw for Spanish firearm lock; g. Higa or amulet, ferrous metal; h. Jingler, ferrous metal; i. Spanish horseshoe nail, ferrous metal; j. Spanish military buckle, cupreous metal; k–m. Spanish firearm lock fragments, ferrous metal; n–o. Spike tang knife blade fragments, ferrous metal. Illustrations by Melinda Parrie.

have been recovered from Los Adaes as well, accounting for over half of the total tin-enameled-ware sherds (Gregory et al. 2004). More French pottery fragments have been recovered from Los Adaes than any other site in northwestern Louisiana (Avery et al. 2007).

The Europeans all adopted hot drinks from other lands. The Spanish at Los

Adaes seem to have preferred chocolate, which was native to southern Mexico (see Coe and Coe 1996). Coffee, native to Africa, was being consumed at Natchitoches. The British seemed to have preferred tea, which was native to China. Chocolate is commonly listed in the account books of the Los Adaes soldiers (e.g., Bexar Archives Microfilm 1771). Several chocolate-pot handles have been recovered from Los Adaes (Figure 13.2c).

The Spanish were expert horsemen, and Spanish horse gear was much more ornate than either their French or British counterparts. The edge treatment on the rowel box from a Spanish spur is one such example (Figure 13.2e). Iron amulets (Figure 13.2g) and jinglers (Figure 13.2h) were hung from saddle aprons and spurs (see Mather 1983:80; Simmons and Turley 1980:110). The amulet is a stylized clenched fist called an *higa*, which is used to ward off the evil eye. *Higas* originated in the Mediterranean area and are common in Latin America today. They do not appear at Spanish colonial archaeological sites in the Americas until the later 1500s (Deagan 2002:95–96). *Higas* are not known among the descendent Spanish communities in northwest Louisiana today, although the tradition of the evil eye is still present. The Spanish horseshoe nail (Figure 13.2i) has a large head, which gives added traction. The Spanish ring bit offers an economy of movement to signal direction to the horse, although it is sometimes described as a "cruel" bit. This bit was brought by the Moors from North Africa to Spain, and the small rollers made of a copper alloy metal were intended to lessen the insult of the bit in the mouth of the horse (Blaine 1996:108).

Military artifacts are not common among the artifacts recovered from presidio Los Adaes, with the exception of gunflints, which were discarded when no longer serviceable. It is interesting that almost two-thirds of the ninety-four gunflints and gunflint fragments recovered from Los Adaes are the yellowish gray-brown flint commonly attributed to France. This is not surprising, as the French dominated the gunflint market. Both the British and Americans used mostly French gunflints during the American Revolution (Noël Hume 1991:220). Spanish gun locks of the early to mid-1700s were easily distinguished from French and British locks by the large loop at the top of the vise screw (Figure 13.2f), which tightened the upper and lower cock jaws to hold the gunflint (Figure 13.2k–m). The military buckle (Figure 13.2j) is a Spanish colonial strap buckle (Powell 2004). The Spanish and French military wore distinctive buttons during the colonial period. All six military buttons recovered from Los Adaes are French (Blaine and Avery 2005:27).

Most of the kitchen knife fragments (Figure 13.2n–o) recovered from Los Adaes have a straight cutting edge, curved back, and spike tang that would insert into a metal, bone, or wood handle. These are referred to as "beak point" knives, describing the way the curved back meets the straight cutting edge. This style of knife became popular in Europe during the mid-1600s. They were made in several European countries, including Spain, and also in Mexico (Simmons and Turley 1980:130).

Fragments of American Indian pottery, numbering almost 35,000, dominate the pottery collection from Los Adaes and comprise almost 90 percent of the total number of pottery fragments recovered from the site. Cooking, storage, and serving vessels are all represented. Some of the serving vessels represented are imitations of European forms, including brimmed bowls and plates. Most of the sherds have a plain or smoothed surface treatment. Only 10 percent have any surface markings or other treatments, such as slips, that might be described as a decoration. There is a trend in northwest Louisiana for the amount of surface markings on pottery to decrease through time during the colonial period, so that by the end of the 1700s, most of the American Indian pottery in the area was plain and without a slip (Gregory 2005). The reason for discontinuing surface markings on pottery may be related to why American Indians chose to put them there in the first place. Were they simply for aesthetic appeal, or was there some deeper symbolic or social meaning to them? Did the markings enhance the mechanical qualities in the use of the pottery vessels? Archaeologists know that these surface markings change through time and place, but the ultimate question as to why American Indians put surface markings on their pottery has not been definitively answered. It was probably related to a combination of variable aesthetic, symbolic, social, and technological factors.

Almost 25,000 fragments of animal bone have been recovered from Los Adaes. The great majority of these are fragments of cow bone and other domesticated animals, such as horse, pig, goat, and chicken. The most abundant wild mammal represented is deer, although elk, black-tailed jackrabbit, and Eastern chipmunk are also present. Five bird species, including wild turkey and Canada goose, are represented, as well as channel catfish, alligator gar, buffalo fish, box turtle, alligator snapping turtle, alligator, and bull frog (Gregory et al. 2004). The *jacal*-type structure located to the west of the presidio had a lot of deer bone, in contrast to the other structures, which had a predominance of cow bone. It has been suggested that for the Spanish, a diet with meat from domesticated animals was more prestigious than meat from wild animals (Parker 2003:218). The western *jacal* may have been occupied by people who were either of lower status or were not Spanish.

Plant remains are not as abundant in the archaeological collections from

Los Adaes. Unless plant fragments are burned or charred, they generally do not preserve in the acidic soils of northwest Louisiana. Plant remains recovered from Los Adaes include fragments of wood (pine, oak, maple, hickory, elm, cottonwood/willow, peach), hickory-nut shell, acorn meat, maize cob (12-row Eastern Complex), peach pits, and a watermelon seed (Dering 2001). The peach pits and peach tree wood fragment suggest that there were peach orchards in the immediate area, possibly in the northern bastion of the presidio. Peaches and watermelons are not native to the area, originating in China and Africa, respectively. Peaches were being grown by the Natchitoches Indians by the late 1600s, and the 1767–1768 inspection of the Spanish missions in the area reported that the *Tejas* or Hasinai Indians in modern-day east Texas had peach orchards (Swanton 1942:132–133). Watermelons were mentioned in the list of food items brought to the 1721 Aguayo expedition by the Nacono Indians near the Neches River, near modern-day Lufkin in east Texas (Hadley et al. 1997:417). A flower that blooms annually at Los Adaes is a living reminder of the Spanish presence there. Small orange lilies called copper lilies [*Habranthus tubispathus* (L'Her.) Traub] were brought by the Spanish to the province of Texas. These flowers are native to South America (Holmes and Wells 1980) and can be seen after a rain during the summer months at Los Adaes and other locations of the Spanish missions, including San Augustine and Nacogdoches, Texas. They are common in Natchitoches as well.

Summary of Current Research and Suggestions for the Future

The archaeological, ethnographic, and linguistic work of Hiram F. "Pete" Gregory (1964, 1973, 1983, 1996, 2005) has provided the anthropological foundation for our understanding of the Spanish in northwest Louisiana (see also Armistead and Gregory 1986; Gregory et al. 2004). Pete has guided numerous master's and doctoral theses related to Los Adaes (e.g., Berthelot 2001; Carlson 1994; Galán 2006; Lee 1986; Longoria 2007; Loren 1999) and also has served as a one-man brain trust for the development of two Los Adaes websites (Los Adaes Site Explorer 2005; Texas Beyond History 2007), as well as for the former Los Adaes Station Archaeology Program (Avery 1995–2005). The contributions of Jay C. Blaine (1996) to our understanding of Spanish colonial metal artifacts from Los Adaes and other sites in Texas and Oklahoma have been innumerable. In 2007, Jay was presented the Crabtree Award, which is given each year by the Society of American Archaeology to an outstanding avocational archaeologist. Recent studies of Spanish heritage in northwest Louisiana include Jason

Shatwell's (2004) undergraduate thesis comparing Los Adaes and Natchitoches, Dominica Dominguez Ramirez's (2004) master's thesis comparing identity manifestations of Adaeseños and Isleños, and Comfort Pratt's (2004) study focusing on the Spanish language in northwest Louisiana. Pratt's work built on Samuel Armistead's (1991) studies of the Spanish language in Louisiana. Recent work on Spanish presidios (Bense 2004) and missions (Graham 1998) has allowed a broader interpretation of the Spanish in northwest Louisiana during the time of Los Adaes, showing that the European–American Indian interaction that occurred in this area was quite rare on the frontier. The only other similar example appears to be that of presidio San Francisco's relations with the Russians and American Indians in northern California during the late 1700s and early 1800s (Blind et al. 2004).

There is much research to be done related to the eighteenth-century Spanish presence in northwest Louisiana. The records for the Los Adaes mission need to be found. The locations of Spanish ranches and Adaes habitation areas need to be determined, and this might be accomplished as a result of *El Camino Real de los Tejas* or the Royal Road to Texas being named a National Historic Trail. This trail connected Mexico City to Texas, with its easternmost destination being Los Adaes, the capital of Texas. A survey program conducted by James E. Corbin (1989) and Jeffrey M. Williams (2007) in east Texas has located numerous remnants of *El Camino Real de los Tejas*. Only the general location of the trail is known in northwest Louisiana (see L'Herrison 1981), but the results of the Corbin and Williams survey can provide topographic indicators for predicting with some precision where the trail was located. Once the trail and its offshoots are identified on the ground, it would simply be a matter of following the road cuts to find nearby archaeological sites.

There are a number of archaeological sites in northwest Louisiana that date from the late 1700s and early 1800s, in areas where historical documents have indicated the presence of people from the old settlement of Los Adaes (see Espey Huston and Associates 1983; Girard 2002, 2003; Girard et al. 2008; Gregory 1973; Pleasant and Pleasant 1990). Systematic surveying could locate additional sites related to Spanish occupation, both before and after 1773. The Sabine River is now the boundary between Louisiana and Texas, but during the eighteenth century it was just another river to cross in the province of Texas. Spanish colonial researchers in northwest Louisiana and northeast Texas have always been close, and it is important for this collaboration to continue in the future.

14

French Colonial Archaeology

ROB MANN

In A.D. 1682, René Robert Cavelier, sieur de La Salle, led a small party of Frenchmen and Native American men, women, and children down the Mississippi River in search of the Gulf of Mexico. On April 9, 1682, their canoes entered the open waters of the Gulf. On a small elevation overlooking the Gulf, the party unfurled banners and erected a cross. La Salle read a proclamation, claiming that he was taking "possession of this country of Louisiana" in the name of "Louis the Great, by Grace of God, King of France and Navarre" (Balesi 1992:56–58, 64–65n; Usner 1992:14). The entire proceeding was witnessed and recorded by the royal notary accompanying the expedition, officially ushering in the French colonial period (A.D. 1682–1763) of Louisiana history. For all La Salle's solemnity, however, it would be almost twenty years (1699) before the French returned to the mouth of the Mississippi River, and nearly another twenty years before the founding of New Orleans (1718), the most important French colonial settlement in *Louisiane* (see Dawdy and Matthews, Chapter 16 in this volume). While La Salle's ostensibly momentous ceremony at the mouth of the Mississippi is archaeologically invisible, the myriad colonial processes he set in motion irrevocably altered the material reality of daily life for the inhabitants of the French colony of *Louisiane*. The traces of this new materiality form the archaeological record of the French colonial period in Louisiana.

This chapter examines the archaeological manifestations of the French presence in the Lower Mississippi Valley (LMV) and the adjacent Gulf Coast, an area roughly coterminous with the territory known as *Basse Louisiane* or Lower Louisiana during the eighteenth century (Figure 14.1). Colonization is a messy business, and the French approach, it seems, was messier than most. To bring some order to what was in reality a dynamic and fluid social landscape, this summary of the archaeology of the French colonial period is organized around three categories: early fort sites, Native American sites, and concession/plantation

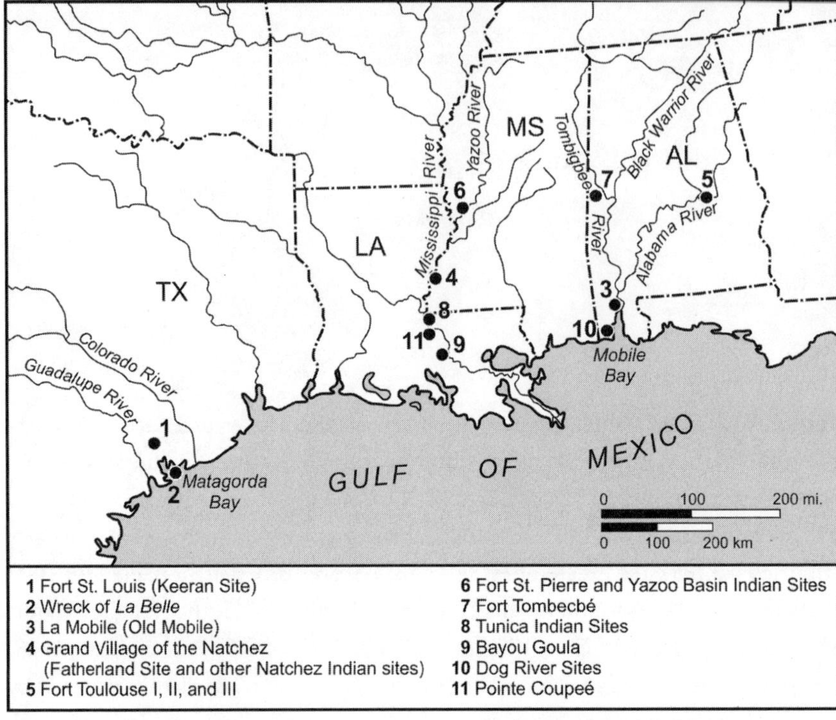

Fig. 14.1. Map showing locations of the major French colonial archaeological sites mentioned in the text. Map by Mary Lee Eggart.

sites. Of course, this runs the risk of artificially segregating the colonizers from the colonized. Each of these site types were places of cultural entanglement, where natives and newcomers (both free and enslaved) lived, toiled, traded, played, fought, and died together. It was at such places that the social processes of creolization took place. Much more archaeological research remains to be done if we are fully to understand the roots of these processes during this critical period of Louisiana history. This chapter concludes with an overview of current and future trends in the archaeology of French colonial *Louisiane*.

Early Forts

The nearly two-decade-long absence of the French from the LMV was not by design. In fact, La Salle himself planned to return as quickly as possible in order to establish a fort at the mouth of the Mississippi, to open up trade relations with

Native American groups along the river and convert them to Christianity, and to settle a permanent colony. If all went according to plan, La Salle also hoped to use the colony as a base for invading Spanish silver mines to the west (Bruseth and Turner 2005:3, 19).

But all did not go as planned. La Salle returned to France after his trip down the Mississippi. He sought and received the support of Louis XIV for his colony at the mouth of the Mississippi. He seemed on the verge of realizing his dreams of fortune and empire. In January 1685, he sailed into the Gulf of Mexico with three ships loaded with supplies, soldiers, and would-be colonists. The expedition overshot the mouth of the Mississippi, however, and from that point on the whole project descended into chaos. By 1687, La Salle was dead, assassinated by his own men in the Texas wilderness. Two of his four ships lay wrecked off the Texas coast. A third ship had abandoned the expedition and returned to France, while a fourth ship had been captured by Spanish privateers off the coast of Hispaniola (present-day Haiti and the Dominican Republic). La Salle's doomed settlement on the Texas coast, Fort St. Louis, would soon be overrun by the Karankawa, an indigenous coastal people who had initially befriended La Salle but began resisting the French colonists after French soldiers stole canoes and hides from one of their villages (Bruseth and Turner 2005:3–31).

La Salle's misbegotten colonial project left behind a rich archaeological record that has greatly informed our understanding of the earliest attempts to establish a permanent French presence in the Gulf Coast region. In the 1970s, Kathleen Gilmore (1973, 1984) interpreted the Keeran site (41VT4) in Victoria County, Texas, as being the site of La Salle's ill-fated Fort St. Louis. Gilmore's identification was confirmed in 1996 when eight French cannons—buried by the Spanish when they found the deserted settlement in 1689—were found at the Keeran site (Bruseth and Turner 2005:28). Since 1999, archaeologists with the Texas Historical Commission (THC) have been investigating the site and have found evidence of the French occupation of Fort St. Louis, as well as a later (1722) Spanish presidio built on the same site (Bruseth et al. 2004).

Importantly, Gilmore's early work at Fort St. Louis was also the impetus for a sustained and determined search for La Salle's two wrecked ships off the coast of Texas (Bruseth and Turner 2005:33). In 1995, archaeologists with the THC recovered artifacts and a magnificent brass cannon from La Salle's ship *La Belle,* which ran aground and sank during a winter storm in Matagorda Bay in 1686 (Bruseth and Turner 2005:5). Between 1996 and 1997, the wreck of *La Belle* was completely excavated. The project involved constructing a coffer dam around the wreck, which allowed archaeologists to excavate the vessel from the relatively dry bottom of Matagorda Bay (Bruseth 2005; Bruseth and Turner 2005). The hull was encapsulated by mud, resulting in the excellent preservation of the cargo stowed in the holds of the ship.

As a result of this unusually ambitious and complex archaeological investigation, over one million artifacts from the French colonial era were recovered, "giving us an unparalleled glimpse into what French immigrants thought they needed to start a colony in the seventeenth-century New World. The wreck itself is also a storehouse of information about seventeenth-century shipbuilding and about how the French provisioned transatlantic voyages" (Bruseth 2005:69). Conservation and analysis of *La Belle* and her contents is still ongoing, and detailed studies of various aspects of the wreck are certain to be published over the next few years (see Bruseth and Turner 2005:82–114).

La Salle's failed venture did not dissuade the French from their goal of colonizing the LMV. In 1699, a French expedition under the command of Pierre Le Moyne d'Iberville arrived on the Gulf Coast. Fresh from his exploits against the British in Newfoundland and Hudson's Bay, Iberville eagerly accepted an assignment from the French Minister of Marine, Louis Phélypeaux, comte de Pontchartrain, to check British and Spanish encroachment into the region. Iberville entered the mouth of the Mississippi River from the Gulf of Mexico in March 1699. He and a small party, which included a small group of Bayougoula Indian guides and Iberville's brother, Jean-Baptiste Le Moyne de Bienville, reconnoitered upriver looking for conclusive evidence that they had indeed found the Mississippi, and for high ground to establish a post from which the French could control the mouth of the river. When Iberville returned to his ships on the Gulf Coast, he set about fortifying this new French foothold by building Fort Maurepas on Biloxi Bay. Iberville left eighty men, including Bienville, under the command of M. de Sauvole at Fort Maurepas and sailed back to France to garner more support for a full-scale French colony on the Mississippi (T. S. McWilliams 1981:7). Blitz, Mann and Bellande (1995) summarize the archaeological efforts to locate the original site of Fort Maurepas near present-day Ocean Springs, Mississippi.

Iberville returned to Fort Maurepas in January 1700 and learned that in his absence Bienville had turned back an English ship that had ascended the Mississippi River some twenty-five or thirty leagues (T. S. McWilliams 1981:8; Jeter et al. 1986:79). This prompted Iberville to "take possession of the Mississippi by means of a small establishment for fear that if we do not do so, the English will make one" (quoted in Jeter et al. 1986:79). Construction of this "small establishment," known simply as the Fort de Mississippi (later called Fort de la Boulaye, see Jeter et al. 1986:80–82), began in February 1700 on the east bank of the river, about seventeen or eighteen leagues upriver from the Gulf. A Bayougoula Indian led Bienville to the spot, claiming to the French that it did not flood during high water (Jeter et al. 1986:85). The Fort de Mississippi never amounted to much and, despite the Bayougoula's assurances, the location was subject to frequent flooding. In December 1700, Father James Gravier arrived at the fort and described the setting: "There is neither fort, nor bastion, nor entrenchment, nor redoubt; all consists of a battery of six guns . . . and of five or six cabins. . . . The commandant M. De Bienville, has there a small and very neat house" (quoted in Jeter et al. 1986:86). The Fort de Mississippi was used primarily as a stopover for French travelers on the Mississippi and as a staging ground for French expeditions against native groups in the LMV (Jeter et al. 1986:87). The French had great difficulty keeping the Fort de Mississippi supplied, however, and in 1707, Bienville wrote to Pontchartrain that he ordered the fort to be abandoned "since I do not have enough men to guard it" and "because I have no ship's boat to send there to carry assistance" (quoted in Jeter et al. 1986:80).

The 1700–1707 Fort de Mississippi represented the first substantial French presence within the present-day State of Louisiana. As historian Maurice Ries (1936:841) has noted, the Fort de Mississippi "marked the turning-point between exploration and possession" of the LMV. There have been several attempts to locate the material remains of Fort de Mississippi, the most extensive being the search undertaken by Marvin Jeter and colleagues (Jeter et al. 1986:57–76). Utilizing historical documents and maps, as well as the results of previous, largely amateur investigations, they examined aerial photographs, conducted pedestrian surveys, subsurface auger tests, and proton magnetometer surveys in Plaquemines Parish near modern-day Phoenix, Louisiana. Although no direct evidence of the eighteenth-century fort could be identified, the project did record one new archaeological site, the Phoenix Cemetery (16PL146), which may contain an earlier component related to the occupation of the Fort de Mississippi (Jeter et al. 1986:11).

With the abandonment of the Fort de Mississippi, the French focused their colonial aspirations on the Gulf Coast proper. In 1702, the French had chosen a spot on high ground overlooking the Mobile River (now called Twenty-Seven Mile Bluff) for a new fort and settlement near the small villages of the Mobile Indians, one of the many *petites nations* that the French found inhabiting the Gulf Coast in the early eighteenth century (Waselkov 2002:4–5). Iberville named the post Fort Louis de Louisiane, and the settlement came to be known as La Mobile, after the Native Americans in whose midst the colony was located (T. S. McWilliams 1981:11). Fort Louis de Louisiane served as the administrative and military headquarters for French *Louisiane* from January 1702 until the middle of 1711 (Waselkov 2002:4).

In 1989, archaeologists with the University of South Alabama began an extensive field project to locate and excavate La Mobile (Old Mobile) and Fort Louis de Louisiane (Waselkov 2002). Over 15,000 shovel test pits were excavated and the soil screened through 1/4 inch (6.35 mm) mesh. Plotted artifact distributions suggested the locations of at least 55 structures on the site (Waselkov 2002:7). Nine of these structures have been confirmed through subsequent excavations, resulting in studies of the daily life and material realities of the early years of French colonization (Waselkov, ed. 2002). These include a revised classification for faience styles in French North America (Waselkov and Walthall 2002), an examination of French vernacular architectural styles (e.g., *poteaux sur sole, pieux en terre*) found on the site (Gums 2002), a refined glass bead chronology for French colonial and colonial-period Native American sites (including analysis of beads from three French colonial period Native American sites in Louisiana) (Smith 2002), and analyses of the floral and faunal remains recovered at Old Mobile (Clute and Waselkov 2002; Gremillion 2002).

Of the nine structures excavated at Old Mobile (1MB94), three are thought to be related to Fort de Louisiane, the exact location of which has so far remained elusive (Waselkov 2002:8–10). In her examination of these three structures, thought to have been occupied between ca. 1706 and 1708, Gums (2002) offers the first glimpse of the material life of French soldiers on the *Louisiane* frontier. Not surprisingly, both the material culture and architectural remains of these structures suggest the harsh conditions under which these French soldiers lived and labored.

Fort de Louisiane and the surrounding town proved to be poorly sited, and in the spring of 1711, Bienville, in charge of La Mobile after Iberville's departure from *Louisiane* in 1702, ordered the fort and settlement moved downstream to the head of the bay, the present-day site of Mobile, Alabama (Waselkov 2002:5). Around the same time, the French turned their attention to consolidating claims on the interior Southeast and LMV by establishing military and trading relations with the Native American societies of the region. On the Mississippi River, the French were anxious to check British encroachment from the east and to woo powerful native societies such as the Natchez into the French fold. A trading post was established at Natchez as early as 1714 (Elliott 1998). Following violent altercations between the French and Natchez in 1715, Bienville sent an officer and several soldiers to the region in 1716 to begin construction of Fort Rosalie des Natchez on the bluffs overlooking the Mississippi River (Elliott 1998).

As was the case throughout French North America, Fort Rosalie served as a check against rival colonial nations (especially the British) and as protection for local French traders and colonists. Contemporary reports suggest that Fort Rosalie was a simple palisaded redoubt manned by a small company of French soldiers (Hahn et al. 2005:32). Despite, or perhaps because of, the presence of Fort Rosalie, relations between the Natchez and the French remained tense throughout the 1720s. In 1729, anti-French factions of the Natchez rose up against the French soldiers at Fort Rosalie and the French colonists on surrounding concessions. Nearly three hundred soldiers and settlers were killed, and dozens of French women and children as well as African slaves were taken hostage (Giraud 1987:398). Fort Rosalie was razed, as were most of the structures on the concessions.

Panic spread throughout French *Louisiane*, but once the initial shock of the uprising had been absorbed, the French regrouped and moved against the Natchez, who built and occupied two forts of their own near Fort Rosalie and the French settlements. A combined force of French soldiers and militia and pro-French Choctaw warriors converged on Natchez in early 1730. Following a skirmish with the Choctaw, the Natchez retreated to their forts and the French laid siege to both. The French excavated a series of siege trenches in order to move their artillery into position. After several days of bombardment by the French and counter-attacks by the Natchez, the French were on the verge of quitting the field and retreating to the Mississippi when the Natchez in one of the forts raised a white flag (Hahn et al. 2005:41). The Natchez offered to release their captives if the French raised their siege and pulled back to the river. The French, low on ammunition and in poor spirits, agreed and dismantled their artillery batteries. The captives were turned over to the Choctaw, who ransomed most of them back to the French. The Natchez managed to slip out of their forts and cross the Mississippi over the next several days. The French, along with their native allies, would continue to pursue the Natchez over the next several months. The Natchez, for their part, harassed the French at every opportunity and struck at pro-French Native American groups as well. At Natchez, the French set about building a temporary fort and later rebuilt Fort Rosalie. It would remain a French outpost throughout the remainder of the French colonial period.

The Natchez wars of the first quarter of the eighteenth century marked a defining moment in the French colonization of the LMV. The Natchez had attempted to "cut off the French to a man" so "that then we will be able to prevent those who may come from the old French village [New Orleans] by the great water [Mississippi] ever to settle here" (Le Page Du Pratz, in Usner 1992:71). Instead, the Natchez, decimated by European diseases and demoralized by the death of several prominent leaders, were driven from their Grand Village homeland. The still nascent French presence and influence in the LMV was strengthened.

Several major archaeological investigations have been undertaken in the Natchez region, including at the Fatherland site (22AD501), the locality of the Grand Village of the Natchez (Brown 1985a; Neitzel 1983, 1997). The site of Fort Rosalie has not been archaeologically identified. Recent investigations along the Natchez Bluffs, however, have turned up artifacts and features that may be associated with the fort and its immediate environs (Hahn et al. 2005). At the Bicentennial Gardens site (22AD999), several wall trench features were encountered and interpreted as the remnants of a circular Native American (possibly Ofogoula) structure and three eighteenth-century French *pieux en terre* structures associated with the occupation of Fort Rosalie (Hahn et al. 2005:417–418). Evidence of the French military response to the Natchez uprising was found during excavations of the Fatherland site (Neitzel 1983). A portion of the trench built by the French during their 1730 siege of the two Natchez forts was encountered during excavations in the plaza area of the Grand Village of the Natchez (Neitzel 1983:46–56).

French colonial aspirations were not confined to the Mississippi. Around the same time the French moved to establish a presence among the Natchez, French attentions were also beginning to focus on the equally powerful and influential Caddoan peoples on the northwest peripheries of *Louisiane* (Usner 1992:30). In 1713, Louis Juchereau de St. Denis led a small contingent of French Canadians and Native Americans up the Red River to the Natchitoches, a division of the Caddoan confederacy. St. Denis set up a small post and opened trading relations with both local Native Americans and the Spanish, who were pushing into the Red River Valley from the west (Avery, Chapter 13 in this volume). The Spanish presence on their western flanks, though not seen as quite the same threat as British encroachments from the north and east, prompted the French to fortify their position on the Red River. In 1716, a sergeant and six soldiers were sent to the Natchitoches post, and Fort St. Jean Baptiste was built to garrison the French troops. By 1721, the force had grown to fifty soldiers (Morgan 2005:28–32). That same year, the Spanish built a fort, *Nuestra Señora del Pilar de los Adaes*, less than twenty miles from Fort St. Jean Baptiste. Unlike the contentious relations at Natchez, processes of creolization and ethnogenesis seemed to have predominated in the Red River Valley, as French, Caddo, and Spanish inhabitants seemed more interested in blurring social and political boundaries through a myriad of social, sexual, and economic relations (Avery 1997, Chapter 13 in this volume; Loren 2001a, 2001b, 2007).

Following the Natchez uprising of 1729, the French sought to shore up their often dilapidated military installations, and in 1735, St. Denis moved Fort St. Jean Baptiste from its original site to a new, higher location. The original site of the fort has since eroded into the Cane River (Jeffrey Girard, personal communication 2008). The new Fort St. Jean Baptiste was relocated on a ridgeline west of the Cane River in a setting less prone to flooding and erosion. Recent archaeological investigations of the American Cemetery (16NA67) site, located on the same ridgeline as the fort, recovered artifacts such as French faience and glass trade beads that are likely related to the post-1735 Fort St. Jean Baptiste occupation of the ridge (Morgan 2005; see also Emery 2004:175–179). No physical evidence of the fort itself was uncovered, and it seems likely that the fort site lies outside the boundaries of the American Cemetery site (Morgan 2005:139).

The archaeology of French colonial fort sites in present-day Louisiana is underdeveloped. The most extensive excavations of French forts have taken place well away from the colonial entrepôts on the Mississippi River and Gulf Coast. Forts Toulouse I, II, and III, established among the Alabama Indians near the head of the Alabama River at the confluence of the Coosa and Tallapoosa rivers in 1717 and rebuilt between 1749 and 1763, have been excavated by archaeologists since the 1960s (Sheldon et al. 2008; Waselkov 1989a). Fort St. Pierre was established in 1719 by the French on the Yazoo River to initiate trade relations with the northern neighbors of the Natchez (e.g., the Yazoo, Koroa, and Ofo) and to protect French concessions in the region (Usner 1992:29). Archaeological excavations undertaken by Harvard University's Lower Mississippi Survey (LMS) and the Mississippi Department of Archives and History between 1974 and 1977 revealed the plan of the fort, as well as a number of activity areas (Brown 1975, 1978c, 1979c, 1992). Fort Tombecbé was built by the French among the Choctaw on the Tombigbee River in 1736 during the French-Chickasaw wars of the 1730s (Usner 1992:81–87; Waselkov 1989b:58). Archaeological excavations of Fort Tombecbé took place in 1980 and 1981 (Waselkov 1989b:58–59). These studies have yielded large artifact assemblages and important information concerning the spatial layout of French forts in *Louisiane*, the use of French vernacular architecture within the forts, and the nature of French–Native American relations in the *Louisiane* hinterlands (Brown 1975, 1978c, 1979c, 1992; Waselkov 1989b:53–59). Within the limits of present-day Louisiana, the meandering of the Mississippi River has hindered archaeological exploration of French colonial-era fort sites. For example, excavations at Fort Saint Leon, a French fort built downriver from New Orleans in the late 1740s, were hampered by the fact that the site is located on the Mississippi River batture (the alluvial land between the river at low-water stage and the modern levee) and is only accessible during very dry periods (Gilmore and Noble 1983).

Native American Sites of the French Colonial Era

Unlike the dearth of information concerning French colonial fort sites in *Louisiane* in general and the LMV in particular, there is quite an extensive literature on Native American sites of the French colonial era. As the preceding account of early fortifications in colonial *Louisiane* indicates, the native inhabitants of the LMV and the interior Southeast were integral to French colonial settlement patterns and often dictated the terms of French colonization in the region (see DuVal 2006; Usner 1992). This is not to discount or underestimate the impact that epidemic diseases, internecine warfare, displacement, and enslavement wrought upon native societies by the coming of the French. It is merely to point out that Native Americans were active agents in multi-ethnic *Louisiane* during the eighteenth century (Galloway 1995; Hall 1992; Usner 1992). To privilege the European colonists as the only agents of change is otherwise ethnocentric and portrays native peoples as seemingly "without history" (Wolf 1982).

Archaeologists have long recognized the importance of colonial period Native American sites for constructing culture histories of the LMV (e.g., Ford 1936; Phillips et al. 1951; Williams 1967). These and many other archaeologists employed the Direct Historical Approach, a methodology which sought "to connect named Native tribes of the historic period with protohistoric and prehistoric archaeological remains, and this is generally held to be a simple matter of moving from the known to the unknown backward in time while moving at the same time from document to material artifact" (Galloway 2006:59; cf. Brain 1988:50–55). As a result of the application of the Direct Historical Approach in the Southeast and the LMV, considerable effort has gone into locating, recording, and excavating colonial period Native American sites (Brown 1990). Much of this effort has taken place in the vicinity of many of the fort sites described above. As noted earlier, French forts tended to be strategically located near important Native American villages and districts, which meant that those villages and districts were the ones most frequently described and charted by French colonial officials, military officers, surveyors, and missionaries. In turn, archaeologists applying the Direct Historic method have mined the colonial archives for documents and maps with information concerning the location of Native American village and ceremonial sites at the time of the French arrival (see Brown 1990). Archaeologists working in the colonial era have also long understood that Native American sites are the key to understanding the nature of French–Native American relations, as well as our ability to study long-term historical processes and the impact of European colonization on native societies.

On the Gulf Coast around Mobile Bay, archaeologists have relied upon indigenous pottery from colonial-period contexts to identify the ceramic traditions of the various *petites nations* (e.g., Cordell 2002; Silvia 2002; see Waselkov and Gums 2000:44–48). In addition to constructing ceramic chronologies, archaeologists are also starting to understand the nature of Native American relations with the French and their role in the economy of colonial *Louisiane* (Clute and Waselkov 2002; Gremillion 2002; Silvia 2002; Waselkov and Gums 2000:44–48). Diane Silvia (2002) excavated a small Native American house (1MB147) located just outside of the northwest boundary of Old Mobile that may have been occupied by members of more than one ethnic group (e.g., Apalachee and Mobilian). In addition to the rectangular structure, which consisted of small, closely spaced posts set in a shallow wall trench, an artifact-rich clay-extraction daub pit and a pit filled with marsh clams (*Rangia cuneata*) were also excavated (Silvia 2002:29–30). Artifacts recovered from the site included an array of eighteenth-century trade goods, such as glass beads, brass ornaments, white clay pipes, iron clasp knives, gun parts, and gunflints (Silvia 2002:30). Native material culture included a diverse ceramic assemblage, consisting of both local and immigrant (e.g., Apalachee) ware types, lithic artifacts knapped from locally available stone, and a red-filmed clay pipe made to imitate a red pipestone calumet (Silvia 2002:30). Faunal remains indicate traditional native dietary preferences to the exclusion of European-introduced domesticates (Clute and Waselkov 2002; Silvia 2002:30).

Possible Chato occupation areas were excavated at the Dog River site (1MB161, areas 2 and 6) (Waselkov and Gums 2000:184–189). The Chato were an immigrant group who sought refuge with the French on Mobile Bay in 1704 and 1705 following the destruction of their villages in northwest Florida by English colonists and their Creek allies (Waselkov and Gums 2000:30–31). By 1711, the Chato were living on the Dog River, where they formed close ties with the French colonists who had plantations on the river (Waselkov and Gums 2000:183). Area 2 of the Dog River site was marked by refuse pits, smudge pits, and post holes—though no native structures were clearly discernable (Waselkov and Gums 2000:184). Artifacts from Area 2 consisted primarily of Native American ceramics, including many types indicative of immigrant Florida groups. In contrast, European ceramics were scarce. Trade goods included glass beads, a glass pendant, copper kettle fragments, lead shot, and two gold beads. Additional native materials included ceramic calumet pipe fragments, chipped stone tools, and lithic debitage (Waselkov and Gums 2000:184). Waselkov and Gums (2000:189) concluded that the Chatos on Dog River "largely retained their own material culture and either had little use for or limited access to French trade goods. When trade did occur, their priority was to obtain French-made muskets, gunpowder, and lead shot . . . as well as glass beads and copper kettles."

Interior groups such as the Choctaw were more populous and powerful, both militarily and economically, than the *petites nations*. Because of their strategic importance to the French, they merited more attention in the colonial archives, providing ethnohistorians and archaeologists with a rich source of information concerning the Choctaw and their complex relationship with the French and other Native American groups (e.g., Galloway 1995, 2006:147–162; Usner 1992). Galloway (1995) provides a critical examination of both the historical and archaeological records pertaining to the ethnogenesis of the Choctaw, that is, their formation as a distinct ethnic group. Galloway (1995:10) notes that the archaeology of historic Choctaw sites is still poorly understood, despite decades of archaeological work in the region (see also Blitz 1985; Mooney 1997). The pioneering work of Henry B. Collins (1927b), James A. Ford (1936), George I. Quimby (1942), and William G. Haag (1953) established a connection between Chickachae Combed pottery and the historic Choctaw. Many historic "Choctaw" sites have been recorded based on the presence of this one artifact type (Blitz 1985:22–23; Galloway 1995:10; Mooney 1997:17; Voss and Blitz 1988:129–130). More recent studies have focused on historic Choctaw settlement patterns and on defining a more complete and inclusive ceramic complex for the late eighteenth- and early nineteenth-century Choctaw (Blitz 1985; Voss and Blitz 1988). Surveys conducted in the 1980s in the traditional Choctaw homeland investigated 75 archaeological sites, 39 of which had definite historic Choctaw components. Another 20 sites had probable Choctaw components (Voss and Blitz 1988:133). Still, there is a lack of information regarding Choctaw sites that clearly date to the French colonial period. European ceramics recovered from most historic-period Choctaw sites postdate 1770, and very few seem to have produced evidence of eighteenth-century French material culture such as faience (Mooney 1997; Voss and Blitz 1988:137).

The historic Choctaw appear to have much in common archaeologically with another powerful indigenous group in the LMV—the Natchez. Voss and Blitz (1988:137) assert that the Choctaw ceramic complex is morphologically and stylistically similar to the historic Natchez-phase ceramic complex (A.D. 1682–1729) and suggest that this similarity reflects "a common developmental relation, widespread sharing of ceramic styles by historic groups, or both." As noted above, the Natchez Bluffs area has been extensively investigated by archaeologists. Perhaps the most significant investigations have taken place at the Fatherland site. Early archaeological work at the site by Moreau B. Chambers and James Ford employed a Direct Historical Approach to determine that Fatherland was in fact the Grand Village of the Natchez, described and charted by various French officials, colonists, soldiers, surveyors, and missionaries in the early eighteenth century (Ford 1936:60; see also Brown 1990:230; Neitzel 1997).

Subsequent excavations at Fatherland in 1962 and 1972 were undertaken by Robert S. Neitzel, who also reported on and analyzed twenty-five burials recovered from the base of Mound C by Moreau in 1930 (Neitzel 1983, 1997; cf. Ford 1936:61–64). In 1962, Neitzel (1997:7) concentrated his excavations on Mounds B and C with the express purpose of archaeologically locating and identifying activities and events described in historical sources. Neitzel (1997:58–85) was able to convincingly identify the temple mound (Mound C), the Great Sun's house and mound (Mound B), and a burial (Burial 15) that may have been that of the Great Sun. Returning to the site in 1972, Neitzel (1983) focused on the plaza area of the Grand Village of the Natchez, which was buried under several feet of colluvial loess. The primary goal of the 1972 season was to locate structural remains and discern information concerning plaza architecture (Brown 1990:230). Neitzel's exacting field excavations and thorough reports provide a wealth of data concerning the material lives of the Natchez during the turbulent, penultimate period of their history. In addition to excellent descriptions of both the Native American and European materials recovered from the site, Neitzel's (1983, 1997) work documented changes in Natchez burial patterns and "contributed much to our knowledge of settlement patterns at this historic ceremonial center" (Brown 1990:230).

As important as the Fatherland excavations were, they did not address all the questions concerning Natchez lifeways in the protohistoric and colonial periods, especially Natchez responses to French colonization of the Natchez Bluffs (Brown 1985a:4). Since the 1970s, archaeologists associated with Harvard's LMS have been recording and excavating sites related to the protohistoric and colonial-era Natchez. Ian W. Brown, in particular, has investigated questions of cultural continuity and change among the Natchez during this tumultuous period of their history (e.g., Brown 1982b, 1985a). Brown (1985a) details the investigation of nine protohistoric-colonial Natchez sites. Brown's investigations sought to determine if historically documented differences in sociopolitical affiliations between different Natchez factions (i.e., pro-French or pro-British) could be discerned archaeologically. Furthermore, Brown (1985a:4) hoped to be able to discover archaeological evidence of the Natchez practice of "adopting peoples of diverse cultural groups." While Brown (1990:235) was unable to discern the sociopolitical affiliations of Natchez factions based on comparisons of artifact assemblages, he found that the archaeological record did show evidence of the Natchez's adoption of Mississippian groups from north of the Natchez homeland.

Ian Brown and the LMS have also investigated Native American sites of the late pre-colonial and French colonial periods in the Yazoo Basin (e.g., Brain 1988:196–263; Brown 1976, 1979c, 1983). Important sites there include Haynes Bluff, Portland, Lockguard, and Wrights Bluff. The latter two sites appear to be Yazoo Indian villages, which were occupied contemporaneously with Fort St. Pierre, the French colonial fort (1719–1729) located on the Yazoo River (Brown 1990:232). A looted burial at the Wrights Bluff site contained an array of colonial period artifacts, including gun parts from as many as seven guns, a screwdriver, a set of large cupreous, open-mouthed bells, a single white glass bead, several hand-wrought nails, and a catlinite pipe (Brown 1990:232). Brown (1990:232) has speculated that this important person may have been a gunsmith. At the Portland site, Brown (1976) excavated a series of partially overlapping trash pits that contained Native American pottery and lithics, as well as historic European artifacts, including iron axe heads, glass beads, white clay tobacco pipe stems (some of which may have been used as beads), vessel glass (including a projectile point knapped from a piece of clear glass), gunflints, lead balls and shot, gun parts, a "hawk-billed" knife blade fragment, copper and brass scraps, and a brass crucifix corpora (Brown 1976). Ethnohistorical and archaeological evidence led Brown (1976:6) to conclude that Portland was a "small Tunica hamlet" occupied between ca. 1698 and 1706 (see also Brain 1988:249–252).

Haynes Bluff, which may have originally had as many as seven earthen mounds, was recognized as having a historic component as early as 1908, when C. B. Moore excavated a burial with "small glass beads at the neck" from one of the smaller mounds (in Brain 1988:196). Though he conflated the pre-colonial and historic occupations, Ford (1936:108–111) used potsherds from the surface of the site to define a Tunica ceramic complex. He postulated that Haynes Bluff was the site of a combined Tunica-Yazoo-Koroa-Ofo settlement found by the French in the Yazoo Basin at the end of the seventeenth century (see also Brain 1988:199). When Jeffrey Brain and the LMS turned their attention to the Tunica, Haynes Bluff figured prominently in a larger project to trace the archaeology and history of the Tunica. Excavations at the site in 1974 were designed to "establish that Haynes Bluff was the focus of Tunica settlement on the Yazoo during the first years of the eighteenth century" (Brain 1988:204). French colonial trade goods recovered from burial, feature, and midden contexts demonstrated "flourishing" colonial-period occupation at the site. Although no "single definite Tunica context" could be discerned in this multi-ethnic settlement, a Tunica presence was confirmed by the presence of "obvious Tunica diagnostics" (Brain 1988:247).

Investigation of Tunica sites was undertaken by the LMS in the wake of the discovery of the Tunica Treasure (Brain 1979). The Tunica Treasure was a vast collection of French colonial-period European and Native American artifacts unearthed from mortuary contexts by a local collector on the Trudeau Plantation in West Feliciana Parish, Louisiana. Grave offerings from approximately one hundred looted burials included "dozens of firearms, scores of European ceramic vessels, hundreds of metal kettles, hundreds of thousands of glass beads, a vast assortment of tools, ornaments, and other miscellany, as well as a goodly representation of native artifacts" (Brain 1994:11). It is hard to overstate the importance of this collection, which may have never been adequately studied and described had it not been for the dedication and determination of Jeffrey Brain and the LMS (Brain 1979:2–32). It is an unparalleled collection of eighteenth-century French colonial and historic Native American material culture. Several detailed descriptive typologies and classifications of French colonial artifacts are included in Brain's (1979) report of the collection, including French colonial coarse earthenware vessels (Steponaitis 1979), glass beads, cast iron and cupreous kettles, cupreous trade bells (Brown 1979d), and gun parts (Hamilton 1979).

Once the collector identified Trudeau Plantation (16WF25) as the location of the Tunica Treasure, Brain (1988:65-90) and the LMS carried out excavations at the site in 1972, verifying the collection's provenience. The 1972 excavations uncovered both domestic debris (e.g., trash pits) and mortuary contexts, confirming that Trudeau was a Tunica village and cemetery dating from ca. A.D. 1731–1764. The LMS returned to Trudeau in 1980 and 1981. In 1980, the site was systematically surveyed in order to define the limits of the Tunica occupation and to locate artifact concentrations that might indicate occupational loci (Brain 1988:93). A geophysical survey of Trudeau was also undertaken in 1980. Several subsurface anomalies were detected and interpreted as possible cultural features (Brain 1988:105–110). These were investigated during the 1981 excavations. Significant findings included the burned remains of an eighteenth-century structure, possibly built using a combination of native and European construction techniques. This building may have served as either a chief's residence or a temple/charnel house (Brain 1988:115). Several more burials were uncovered, though many of them had been previously looted (Brain 1988:150–151).

Before the Tunica settled at Trudeau, they were living a few leagues above Tunica Bayou at the Portage de la Croix. The Tunica apparently arrived at the Portage de la Croix around 1706 and first settled there with the Houma, only to later chase them off and become the sole occupiers of this strategic location. The Portage de la Croix referred to the narrow neck of land between the ends of a large meander loop of the Mississippi. It was a major portage in the LMV (Brain 1988:152). With both large (Grand Tonicas) and smaller (Petits Tonicas) villages scattered over the area of the Portage de la Croix, the Tunica were able to control access to the Red River and the portage route on the Mississippi for much of the first quarter of the eighteenth century. This location was also ideal for the Tunica's continued participation in the trading of salt and other resources (Brain 1988:297). Caught up in the shifting and often contradictory alliances that were endemic to warfare in French colonial *Louisiane*, the Tunica at the Portage de Croix were attacked by visiting remnants of the Natchez in June 1731. Though they were ultimately able to fend off the Natchez, their chief was killed and their village destroyed in a battle that raged for days (Brain 1988:300). In the aftermath of the Natchez attack, the Tunica moved farther down the Mississippi to Trudeau.

While the main village (Grand Tonicas) at the Portage de la Croix has yet to be located archaeologically, two smaller sites—Angola Farm (16WF2) and Bloodhound Hill (16WF21)—have been discovered and investigated on the grounds of the Louisiana State Penitentiary (Angola). James Ford excavated ten colonial period burials at the Angola Farm site in 1934, which were reanalyzed by Brain in 1973 (Brain 1988:152–161). The burials consisted of nine adults and one infant, who was buried in a wooden chest along with a trade kettle and a French lead-glazed coarse earthenware jug (Brain 1988:153, 156–157). Interestingly, the adult males were well-equipped with European trade goods (e.g., flintlocks, musket balls, brass kettles, brass bells), while the adult females were interred with European ornaments (e.g., glass beads) and native pots. The artifacts suggest these burials date from the early eighteenth century, which corresponds with historical documents placing the Tunica in the area at that time (Brain 1988:161). The LMS returned to Angola Farm in 1975 but could not locate a village associated with the burials and Ford's surface collections (Brain 1988:161–162).

Bloodhound Hill, the second Tunica site in the Portage de la Croix area, was discovered when prison inmates uncovered two burials containing colonial-period artifacts. The LMS conducted excavations in 1977 at the Bloodhound site, which consists of two spatially discrete loci—Bloodhound Hill and the Terrace. The burials had been discovered on Bloodhound Hill, a sharp rise overlooking the gently sloping terrace. LMS excavations on Bloodhound Hill turned up an additional five burials in what Brain (1988:166) characterized as a "small cemetery, probably related to a minor satellite settlement." As at Angola Farm, the burials contained a mix of European trade goods (e.g., guns and gun parts, brass kettles, glass beads, brass bells, a seventeenth-century sword-rapier, copper-covered wooden buttons, copper bracelets, European pottery) and artifacts of native manufacture (e.g., pottery, chipped stone tools, shell ear pins, shell discs, and shell beads). The burial of a child (Burial 6) contained the greatest array and quantity of grave goods, including hundreds of glass beads, copper bracelets, brass bells, a marine shell necklace with a copper crucifix, a lead bale seal, iron folding knives, and a crushed Caddoan pot (Brain 1988:171–172).

Down below Bloodhound Hill, the LMS excavations revealed a 5- to 60-centimeter-thick (2 to 24 in) midden deposit, which was thought to represent the occupation of a small Tunica hamlet on the terrace sometime between ca. 1706 and 1731. Association of the terrace occupation with the Tunica (and hence the burials on the Hill) was established by the recovery of Native American pottery diagnostic of the early eighteenth-century Tunica (e.g., Winterville Incised, *vars. Angola* and *Tunica*, and Barton Incised, *vars. Trudeau* and *Portland*). Eighteenth-century European artifacts from the midden were dominated by gun parts and munitions, glass bottles, glass beads, and other items of adornment. Although numerous post holes were uncovered, no structural patterns were evident and no traces of native wall trenches were discerned. Nevertheless, numerous refuse pits, burned animal bone, daub, and other domestic debris indicate a sustained Tunica habitation on the terrace (Brain 1988:195).

While the Tunica are easily the best archaeologically known native inhabitants of colonial *Louisiane*, other colonial-period Native American sites have been investigated as well. Perhaps one of the most significant is the Bayou Goula site (16IV11) in Iberville Parish. The Bayougoula were first visited by Iberville during his 1699 reconnaissance up the Mississippi River. Their village, occupied jointly with the Mugulasha, was located on the west bank of the Mississippi. It was described in some detail by Iberville and Father Paul Du Ru in 1699 and 1700 (Usner 1992:21–24). In 1700, the Bayougoula turned on the Mugulasha, killing many. Six years later, the Taensa sought refuge with the Bayougoula after being forced from their villages around Lake St. Joseph. The Taensa, however, soon betrayed and rose up against the Bayougoula, killing many of them and burning their village (Fredlund 1982:19; Usner 1992:24).

The Bayou Goula site is located about twenty-five miles downstream from Baton Rouge. The site was excavated in 1940 and 1941 by Edwin B. Doran and Carlyle S. Smith under the auspices of the Louisiana State Archaeological

Survey, then under the direction of George I. Quimby. The site consisted of two low earthen mounds that were likely constructed either during the Coles Creek or Plaquemine period (Fredlund 1982:52). Stratified subsurface deposits consisted of an earlier (Coles Creek/Plaquemine) midden associated with the mounds, overlain by about one meter (3.3 ft) of mostly sterile water-lain silt (Fredlund 1982:52; Quimby 1957:105–106). The uppermost level consisted of the colonial-period midden and associated features. The Bayou Goula site report was published in 1957. Quimby (1957:102) considered the historic component of Bayou Goula to be the Bayougoula-Mugulasha village of ca. 1699–1706, though he acknowledged that other interpretations were possible and that the site was subsequently occupied by other native groups. More recent studies have questioned this affiliation, suggesting that the eighteenth-century component at the Bayou Goula site is more likely related to a French concession/settlement of ca. 1718–1740 (e.g., Brown 1977; Fredlund 1982; Giardino 1984a). Brown (1977), for example, noted that the shape of the excavated houses were more consistent with eighteenth-century French colonial structures. Glen Fredlund (1982) reanalyzed the artifact assemblage from the Bayou Goula site and reached the same conclusion. Both the documentary record and the complete artifact assemblage, which Quimby (1957) only partially analyzed and reported on, suggested to Fredlund (1982) that the habitational midden and features (e.g., structures, trenches, pits) at the Bayou Goula site were associated with the French concession established at the site in 1718 by Joseph Paris du Vernax and Étienne du Buisson. Both Fredlund (1982) and Brown (1977:203), however, concurred with Quimby (1957) that the intrusive burials at the site were "unquestionably historic Indian." This suggests the acculturation framework used by Quimby, Brown, and Fredlund is inadequate to address the fluid and multi-ethnic nature of colonization and settlement in French colonial *Louisiane* (Mann 2005; Mann and Loren 2000).

While it is possible that the Bayou Goula site is both the location of the ca. 1699–1706 Bayougoula-Mugulasha village and the ca. 1718–1740 du Vernax–du Buisson concession, Fredlund (1982) has put forth another candidate for the Bayougoula-Mugulasha village—Site 16IV134. Fredlund (1982:68–85) conducted a systematic surface survey of the site, excavating several auger holes and a single 1 by 1 meter unit. He also salvaged a historic burial, presumably Native American, that had been exposed in a recently excavated farm ditch. Associated grave goods included a crushed Fatherland Incised, *var. unspecified* bowl, a "large (2.5 cm) galena crystal," a cut quartz bead, and 242 glass beads, including several "gooseberry" beads (Brain 1979:106-Variety IVB1) that had been "painted" red (Fredlund 1982:72–75). The bulk of over 14,000 artifacts recovered from the site came from the surface survey. Native American ceramics and chipped stone were the most prevalent artifacts recovered, but a smattering of eighteenth-century European material culture (e.g., glass beads, gunflints, white clay pipes, tin-enameled ceramics) was found as well. Fredlund's (1982:70–72) limited excavations did reveal that intact subsurface deposits dating to the colonial period, including pits and post molds, are present on the site.

The Bayou Goula region was a nexus of settlement and activity during the French colonial period. Besides the Bayougoula and Mugulasha, the area was occupied at various times by the Taensa, Acolapissa, Tioux, Chitimacha, and Houma. French and African men, women, and children lived at colonial settlements such as the du Vernax–du Buisson concession. Additional archaeological research in this important area is clearly warranted.

Concession/Plantation Sites

If the founding of the Fort de Mississippi "marked the turning-point between exploration and possession" of *Louisiane* (Ries 1936:841), the transfer of the colony to John Law's Company of the Indies in 1717 marked a turning point from possession to settlement. In 1718, the non-indigenous population of *Louisiane* consisted of no more than 400 people scattered throughout the colony (Usner 1992:31). Over the next three years, 7,000 Europeans and 2,000 enslaved Africans would arrive in *Louisiane* (Usner 1992:32). Included in this number were 119 *concessionaires,* men who had been granted tracts of land (concessions) ranging in size from several hundred to several thousand acres (Usner 1992:32; Waselkov and Gums 2000:63). Turning these "speculative investments" into profit-making ventures required the *concessionaires* to develop their concessions, which usually meant the creation of plantations focused on the production of export crops, such as tobacco, corn, rice, and indigo (Waselkov and Gums 2000:63). In addition to the *concessionaires* (or their representatives) and their families, the concessions were inhabited by European *engages,* indentured servants usually contracted to serve the *concessionaires* for a period of three years, and enslaved Africans and Native Americans, who supplied the labor necessary to make the plantations productive (Usner 1992:32). At the end of the French colonial period, the population stood at approximately 4,000 Euroamericans, over 5,000 enslaved Africans and African Americans (as well as 100 enslaved Native Americans), 100 free persons of color, and perhaps as many as 30,000 Native Americans (Usner 1992:108, 115n).

Of the hundreds of concessions and plantations established in French *Louisiane,* only a handful have been documented archaeologically and even fewer have been the subject of extensive archaeological investigation (Waselkov and Gums 2000:93). In the Natchez region, for example, Frank (1982) used historical documents, maps, and extensive archaeological research conducted in the area (e.g., Brown 1985a; Neitzel 1983, 1997) to suggest that the French House site (22AD668) represents the White Earth Concession of 1720–1729. Frank's (1982:120–121) assessment is based, however, on a very scanty assemblage of eighteenth-century artifacts—three faience sherds, one sherd of Chinese porcelain, a single lead ball, and a single hand-wrought nail—recovered from "a road cut less than 3 meters square."

Though originally thought to be the site of the Bayougoula-Mugulasha village of ca. 1699–1706, excavations at the Bayou Goula site likely uncovered the remains of the early eighteenth-century du Vernax–du Buisson concession. Brown's (1977) and Fredlund's (1982) reanalyses of the Bayou Goula site features and material culture help to put the site into proper historical and archaeological context. The eight Bayougoula "dwellings" excavated at Bayou Goula (Quimby 1957:107–110), for example, were almost certainly European structures built in a French vernacular architectural tradition that used hand-hewn, vertical timbers held together with a sophisticated mortise-and-tenon system (Brown 1977). While Brown (1977:198) suggests that the structures at the Bayou Goula site were of *pièce sur pièce* (log on log; literally, piece on piece) construction, there are other possibilities, such as *poteaux sur sole* (posts on sill) construction (see Mann 2008a). Additional research on the European material culture recovered at Bayou Goula but not reported by Quimby (1957) may shed additional light on the nature of daily life at the du Vernax–du Buisson concession (cf. Fredlund 1982:60–67).

Recent research by Waselkov and Gums (2000) at the Dog River site on Mobile Bay is far and away the most extensive archaeological investigation of a French colonial concession, representing the Rochon Plantation of ca. 1725–1779. Several hundred cultural features, including midden deposits, palisade and wall trenches, post holes, refuse pits, and smudge pits were uncovered and excavated (Waselkov and Gums 2000:189–194). At least two French colonial *poteaux en terre* (posts in ground) structures were uncovered, one or both of which may have been occupied by enslaved Native Americans or Africans (Waselkov and Gums 2000:189–190). Exacting field methods and fine-scale recovery techniques, such as water screening and flotation, resulted in the recovery of approximately 170,000 artifacts. Detailed analyses of colonial-era European ceramics (including French coarse earthenwares and faience), faunal remains, and plant remains make it one of the most comprehensive examinations of colonial period artifacts from French *Louisiane* (Waselkov and Gums 2000:121–182). Perhaps even more significant is the possible discovery of material culture and structural remains relating to the enslaved Native Americans and/or Africans who toiled on the Rochon Plantation during the eighteenth century (Waselkov and Gums 2000:218–219).

Relatively little work has been done to locate and record the earliest French concessions and plantations along the Mississippi River. There were at least twelve settlements above and below New Orleans by 1726 (Usner 1992:48–49). Proximity to the Mississippi River, one of the most dynamic fluvial systems in the world, has unfortunately either destroyed or rendered many of them archaeologically invisible (Mann and Schilling 2004). Repeated flooding, alluviation, erosion, and river channel migration have impacted and altered the landscape of eighteenth-century *Louisiane*. Likewise, modern attempts to harness and rein in these natural processes have had the unforeseen consequence of destroying, burying, or otherwise obscuring many colonial-period sites in the LMV. Locating sites associated with French concessions consequently requires knowledge of both geomorphology and the historical record.

During his 1699 expedition up the Mississippi, Iberville came to a "creek 6 feet wide that runs out of the Myssysypy River. The Indians told me that, if I could get my longboats through it, I would shorten my journey by one day's travel" (R. G. McWilliams 1981:66). Though obstructed by a raft of logs and debris, Iberville and his men managed to portage their longboats through the small waterway and launch them back into the main channel of the Mississippi on the other side of this *pointe coupée*, or cut point. Within a few years, the Mississippi River migrated into this channel, cutting off an elongated point of land and leaving behind a twenty-two-mile-long ox-bow lake, later dubbed *la Fausse Riviere*, or False River. The west bank of the Mississippi River above False River became known as the *Côte de la Pointe Coupée*, or Pointe Coupée coast. A substantial French settlement sprung up along the Pointe Coupée coast during the eighteenth century.

The first documented evidence for a French settlement on the west bank of the Mississippi River along the Pointe Coupée coast comes from the 1727 census of Louisiana. In that year, 29 persons—18 men, 7 women, and 4 children—were living in what is today Pointe Coupee Parish (Costello 1999:21). A French garrison was located on the west bank at Pointe Coupée as early as 1722, but it seems that a permanent French military *poste* or fort was not established at Pointe Coupée until after the Natchez rebellion in 1729 (Giraud 1974:94). By 1731, the settlement consisted of 33 households populated by 37 white men, 25 white women, 7 *engagés* (laborers, presumably white men), 26 white children, 3 enslaved Native Americans, and 70 enslaved Africans (Costello 1999:23; Hall 1992:247). The

Fig. 14.2. Faience sherds from French Site 1 (16PC80).

community continued to grow throughout the eighteenth century. The 1745 census recorded a total of 689 people living at Pointe Coupée, including 260 Europeans, 391 African slaves, 20 Native American slaves, 15 mulatto slaves, and 3 free Native Americans (Costello 1999:27). As they had from the earliest days of the settlement, the French at Pointe Coupée also continued to trade for peltries secured by local Native American groups (Hall 1992:250; see Usner 1992). A ca. 1774 map drawn by George Gauld, British Admiralty Surveyor, shows two "Offagoula" Indian villages associated with the Pointe Coupée settlement, one at the top of the settlement almost directly opposite the "Tonica" (Tunica) village on the east bank, and the second about midway between the first village and the church. The Ofogoula or Ofo were a Siouan-speaking group and one of the *petites nations* who were closely allied with both the Tunica and the French throughout the eighteenth century (Kniffen et al. 1987:90; Swanton 1911:230).

In 2003, the Louisiana State University Regional Archaeology Program initiated a project to locate sites associated with the French colonial settlement at Pointe Coupée. Approximately fifteen acres along the Pointe Coupée coast were examined, using a variety of methodologies designed to maximize the chance of locating sites dating to the French colonial period. Only one site identified during the survey contained a component that dates to the French colonial occupation (Mann 2003a, 2008b). French Site 1 (16PC80) is located on the west bank of the Mississippi River, approximately one mile west of the community of Brooks. The site appears to have been originally established during the French colonial settlement of Pointe Coupée in the early to mid-eighteenth century. Diagnostic artifacts suggest it was continuously occupied throughout the colonial period and well into the postbellum period. Colonial-period artifacts were collected within each survey transect. Eighteenth- and early nineteenth-century artifacts include gunflints, white clay pipes, glass beads, and vessel glass (Mann 2003a). A large number of European ceramics, including French faience and coarse earthenwares, Chinese export porcelain, British slipware, white salt-glazed stoneware, creamware, pearlware, and whiteware were also recovered from the surface. The total faience assemblage consists of 191 sherds (Figure

14.2). Wares and decorated types of faience suggest that the site was initially settled between circa 1730 and 1740. The settlement grew from 33 households in 1731 to 48 farms in 1739 (Mann 2003a, 2008a).

Conclusions and Future Directions

There is still much to be learned about the daily material lives of the people who inhabited French colonial *Louisiane*. The archaeology of the French colonial period in the LMV is still largely underdeveloped. As the work at Pointe Coupée illustrates, there is a real need to document these all too rare cultural resources. A recent examination of the Louisiana Division of Archaeology's site files, for example, revealed that as of 2002, only 37 recorded archaeological sites in Louisiana have produced the tin-enameled ceramics that are characteristic of eighteenth-century occupations (Emery 2004). In the 22 parishes that comprise southeast Louisiana, the heart of French colonial *Louisiane*, 29 sites have produced tin-enameled ceramics. Probably less than half of these sites have components that predate 1760 (Emery 2004). Additional research is urgently needed on the early forts, Native American sites, and concessions/plantation sites described here, beginning with archaeological survey. The archaeology of slavery during the French colonial period is another issue in dire need of further exposition.

Encouragingly, the past few years have seen an upswing in the archaeology of the French colonial experience in the New World (e.g., Kelly 2004; Roy and Côté 2008; Scott 2008; Waselkov, ed. 2002). There has been a move away from studies that characterized much of the early work done on French colonial sites, in particular the "site-specific, descriptive, and essentially atheoretical—or, perhaps more precisely, lacking in explicit theoretical exposition" (Waselkov 1997:25). For instance, recent research has focused on the processes of creolization (e.g., Dawdy 2000a; Matthews 2001). In contrast to the relatively static concept of "acculturation," recent models emphasize the production of new cultural and ethnic identities forged in the daily practices of life, under larger political-economic constraints that were often beyond the control of individuals (see also Mann 2003b, 2007b, 2008a). Other avenues of inquiry remain to be developed. For example, few detailed archaeological examinations of gender and class relations in colonial *Louisiane* have yet to be undertaken (see Dawdy 2008). Given the relative scarcity of recorded French colonial-period sites, archaeologists should pursue every opportunity to systematically recover and investigate the material traces of life in French colonial *Louisiane*.

15

African American Archaeology

LAURIE A. WILKIE, PAUL FARNSWORTH, AND DAVID T. PALMER

Perhaps no arena of archaeological research in Louisiana has more potential to affect contemporary social change than the study of the African American past. As the flooding of New Orleans caused by Hurricane Katrina in 2005 and controversy over the Jena Six in 2006–2007 so clearly illustrated, racial inequalities and racism are an ongoing reality of life in Louisiana—a reality that many citizens and politicians would prefer to leave buried. With their ties both to the academy and to the public and private sectors, archaeologists are well-placed to illuminate the realities of racism as historically experienced by the enslaved and then free African American population of the state. Increasingly, archaeological research into African American Louisiana is doing just that (e.g., Babson 1990; Farnsworth 2000; Palmer 2005; Wilkie 2001a, 2001b, Wilkie and Bartoy 2000). The African American experience in Louisiana is also of relevance to audiences beyond the state. Louisiana, with its location in the Lower Mississippi Valley, was part of the "black belt" of the Deep South, where, first as enslaved and later as freed peoples, African American populations became concentrated, their labor used to support the massive sugar and cotton agriculture of the South (Hilliard 1972).

It is beyond the scope of this chapter to provide an exhaustive overview of all of the archaeological work on African American sites and material culture in Louisiana. Instead, we will provide a brief overview of the broad themes that are driving archaeological research on African American populations, as well as the great untapped potential for further research in the state. We will not discuss sites in New Orleans, since it is the focus of two other chapters in this volume (Chapters 16 and 17). Our emphasis will be on sites elsewhere in southeastern Louisiana, along the Mississippi River, where the greatest amount of research has been conducted.

Our discussion will focus upon two themes that pervade African Diaspora research in Louisiana: the effort to understand the African cultural origins of

Louisiana's black populace, and the nature of African Americans' responses to generations of racialized violence and segregation in Louisiana.

The Nature of the Record

Although African Americans comprised a sizeable proportion of the state's population, the sites associated with their pasts are especially vulnerable to erasure. Fields where slave quarters once stood are plowed under, and the swampy bottomlands and river edges where maroon and, later, freed people were often forced to live have become flooded or eroded away. The primarily black town of Bayou Sara, a thriving nineteenth- and early twentieth-century stop located on the Mississippi River down slope from the historically white town of St. Francisville, is an excellent example. Bayou Sara was flooded by the Army Corps of Engineers, while St. Francisville retains a rich archaeological record. Environmental racism, which continues to affect African Americans in the state, has also contributed to the destruction of sites linked to their history by disregarding their significance.

Historic preservation efforts have also, ironically, often contributed to this archaeological erasure. Plantation yard areas, where the planter's house, kitchen, and other associated buildings were located, are often the only areas that are preserved on vast plantation tracts. But the majority of the plantation's occupants and workers lived near the agricultural fields, where they created the planter's wealth. This biased preservation demonstrates a lack of regard for African Americans and their history, whether carried out with consciously racist intent or not. Popular historic sites, such as Oakley Plantation (Audubon State Commemorative Area, 16WF34) and Magnolia Mound Plantation (16EBR30) of the Baton Rouge park system, are prime examples of this phenomenon (Figure 1.2). Each historic site preserves a small part of the original plantation tract. Each interpretive center wished to represent the African American past in some way, and each achieved this goal by moving existing cabins from other locations, allowing the archaeology associated with those sites to be destroyed in the process. The two reconstructed cabins at Magnolia Mound were assembled out of four cabins moved from Riverlake Plantation (16PC63) in Pointe Coupee Parish. The antebellum cabins, which would otherwise have remained rotting in place, were protecting the associated archaeological site. While some salvage excavations were conducted before the cabins' removal, the sites were quickly plowed for sugarcane once they were removed (Farnsworth 1993a; Wilkie 1995). Planter's houses and associated buildings, in contrast, are usually preserved in place and are often the subject of long-term historical and archaeological research.

As a result of the bias towards understanding and preserving the histories of Louisiana's planter elite, the African American plantation spaces most likely to be archaeologically preserved are the homes of domestic servants and yard-based work spaces such as stables, smoke houses, planter houses and kitchens, and sometimes mills. Interestingly, while a number of planter kitchens have been excavated, these buildings are usually seen as a source of information about planter lifestyles. Little consideration is given to how the resulting assemblages may illuminate African American life (e.g., Burden and Castille 1981; Lane 1980; Kender 2000).

While numerous sites have been excavated over the last thirty years, African American archaeological information from the state remains largely unsynthesized. There are a number of reasons for this phenomenon. Development along the Mississippi River has been the impetus behind much of the archaeological work on African American sites, and much of the archaeology conducted on African American sites falls under the purview of cultural resource management (CRM). While much fine research on plantation life in the state has been conducted as part of environmental and CRM compliance work, the majority of CRM researchers working in Louisiana are not specialists in African American archaeology. CRM archaeologists are generally constrained by the demands of an applied field in their attempts to publish project results beyond limited-distribution compliance reports, with a few notable exceptions (e.g., Scott 2001; Yakubik and Méndez 1995). Additionally, there are few historical archaeologists based in Louisiana's universities, and few of those individuals regard Louisiana African Diaspora sites as their primary focus. As a consequence, much of the research in the academy is being conducted by graduate students, with their resulting masters' and doctoral theses providing the second major body of available literature. These caveats aside, past and present research on African American sites is providing new insights into the past lives of black families in Louisiana. Furthermore, there is great potential for future African American archaeological research in the state.

The African Basis of Louisiana Culture

Gwendolyn Midlo Hall's (1992, 2005) work has demonstrated that Louisiana was a major destination for many of the last enslaved Africans brought to North America. The first slave ships arrived in French Louisiana in A.D. 1719, bringing enslaved Africans who cultivated rice for the struggling colony. Many of these individuals hailed from an area of West Africa referred to in the slave trade as

Senegambia, in the present-day countries of Senegal and Gambia. These first Africans to arrive had common languages and, in many cases, shared beliefs.

While new shipments of Africans to the colony declined after 1731, shipments resumed when the Spanish took over the colony in 1763. Africans were brought from Senegambia, the Bights of Benin and Biafra (present-day Nigeria), and Central Africa in nearly equal proportions, leading to an African population that, while diverse, was large enough to support the maintenance of distinct ethnic identities (Hall 1992, 2005).

Michael Gomez (1998) has argued that the early nineteenth century was a period when enslaved Africans in the South were making the transition from self-identifying along African-ethnic lines to a racialized identity based upon a recognition of shared circumstance and skin color. In Louisiana, the influx of African slaves into the colony during the Spanish colonial period meant that there were African-born enslaved people in larger numbers than in other parts of the United States, a phenomenon Hall (1992:276–315) refers to as a "re-Africanization." There is consequently great potential for looking at how Africans expressed and transformed their traditions and values in Louisiana. To date, most of the available evidence points to continuities in religious and spiritual life, health practices, uses of house spaces, and cuisine.

While some archaeologists have moved away from looking at the role of African traditions among enslaved populations, instead favoring explorations of race, historians have been accumulating evidence for the endurance of African identities and traditions. These efforts help to counter the pervasive dismissal of African contributions to American cultural life. The dismissal of African cultural contributions is part of a systematic omission from national history and mythologies. It is as old as the nation and continues to be a reality in contemporary society. African American descendent communities are often very interested in learning what archaeology has to contribute to an understanding of their ancestors' cultural beliefs and traditions. As community partners, archaeologists are obligated to consider these interests as they evaluate the archaeological evidence (Brown 1997; Farnsworth 1993b; McDavid 2002; Wilkie 2001b; Wilkie and Bartoy 2000).

RELIGION AND SPIRITUAL PRACTICE

Louisiana has long been famous for its visible diasporic religions, produced from the forced relocation of African populations throughout the Americas. Marie Laveau used public displays of Voodoo ritual to enthrall and entice black and white customers alike to her antebellum New Orleans church and potion business. Lyle Saxon (Saxon et al. 1991), Robert Tallant (1946), Zora Neale Hurston (1990), B. A. Botkin (1945), and Robert Farris Thompson (1983) are among the folklorists, anthropologists, journalists, and art historians who have been fascinated by the African matrix that so clearly underlies Catholic and Protestant Christian practices in Louisiana. Africans who had already embraced Catholicism may have been among those brought to Louisiana from the Congo and Angola. Missionaries had been active in that region since at least the 1600s (Da Sorrento 1814). The large Senegambian presence in Louisiana meant that Africans brought not only indigenous religions and Christianity to Louisiana, but also Islam (Hall 1992:38). As groups intermixed, so would their religious beliefs, but in new and dynamic ways.

For some in Louisiana, the deities and spirits they brought from Africa remained recognizable over the course of generations and were worshiped as such. For others, the cosmologies of the past were lost completely or replaced, or else they became recognizable in fragmented ways in different ritual practices. "Hoodoo" refers to a generalized set of beliefs about ways to manipulate or protect oneself from the spiritual realm, and it has been commonplace in Louisiana, among both the black and white populace, to varying degrees. From an archaeological perspective, we can recognize materials that may have had related, ritualized meanings (Wilkie 1997).

Any number of materials recognizable as being used for their protective powers have been recovered from sites in Louisiana, the most abundant of these being pierced coins. Pierced coins have been found at Ashland–Belle Helene (16AN26), Oakley, Stonewall Plantation (16PC80), and Magnolia Mound (Burden and Gagliano 1977; Wilkie 1997; Yakubik and Méndez 1995). The ethnographic literature suggests that coins worn around the neck or ankle were commonly believed to have protective capabilities, the most important being the ability to turn aside curses. This practice has origins in West Africa. In the late 1700s, Thomas Winterbottom observed children in Sierra Leone wearing "a string of coral, beads, a dollar, or an English shilling" around the neck, ankles, or wrists, as the places on the body where "gris-gris" were worn (Winterbottom 1969:100). Sierra Leone was a common source of slaves fed into the Senegambian trade that supplied Africans to Louisiana. It is worth noting that "gris-gris" is one of the more common names still used to identify protective charms in Louisiana. Archaeological evidence has established that the practice of wearing coins dates from as early as the eighteenth century in Louisiana. A pierced Spanish coin with an illegible date was recovered from a deposit dating to the last quarter of the eighteenth century at Stonewall Plantation in Pointe Coupee Parish.

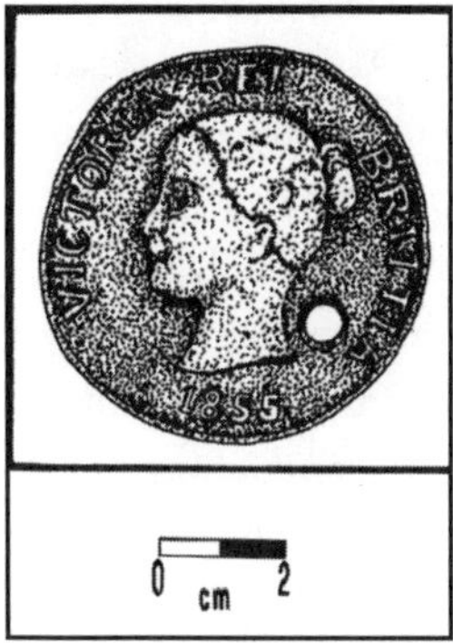

Fig. 15.1. Possible birth coin of Silvia Freeman (from Wilkie 2000:190, Figure 41).

Birth coins are one category of pierced coins. These coins, bearing the year of a child's birth, were worn around the neck for protection and general well-being. There is circumstantial evidence to suggest the birth coin of Silvia Freeman was recovered from the African American Freeman family's house at Oakley Plantation (Figure 15.1). This coin, a pierced Britannia penny, was found under the house and had apparently been lost through a sagging floor board. It bore a date of 1855, which was consistently recorded as the year of Freeman's birth (Wilkie 2000:189, 202). Winterbottom's descriptions of coins and beads worn around children's necks in Sierra Leone may be an African antecedent of the subsequent practice in Louisiana. A pierced 1793 Spanish *real* found in association with two black glass tubular beads from a nineteenth-century slave cabin at Ashland-Belle Helene plantation indicates that pierced coins were sometimes strung with other items (Yakubik and Méndez 1995:27).

Excavations at cabins and work spaces have revealed other items historically known to be incorporated into the practice of gris-gris: beads, cowry and other shells, rosaries and saint's medals, Native American objects, crystals, pins, buttons, seeds, and bones. Many of these objects, like the coins, appeared innocuous and were not necessarily recognized by planters as having roles or uses beyond their perceived everyday functions. Through the ritual uses of such mundane items, African Americans could subvert the efforts of planters to rob them of their cultural traditions and religious practices. No matter how remotely, these practices and objects connected them with previous generations, both in the Americas and Africa (Wilkie 1997).

Whatever their origins or meanings, these items are indicative of spiritual beliefs maintained through time. They also attest to an important lived reality for the enslaved, free Africans, and African Americans of Louisiana. The world was a dangerous place, where violence could and would be inflicted upon a body. The wearing of coins and other protective ritual devices, concealed from planters and other whites, represents one way in which African American families protected themselves and their children from the arbitrary violence, both physical and spiritual, that could characterize life in Louisiana.

The occurrence and role of Islam among enslaved Africans in Louisiana is also worth mentioning. While some scholars have remarked upon the presence of Islam among enslaved peoples, archaeologists have generally been reluctant to identify Muslim artifacts or deposits in the archaeological record. The presence of Islam among African Americans in Louisiana is suggested through possible evidence of dietary taboos.

At Whitney Plantation (16SJB11) in St. John the Baptist Parish, zooarchaeological analysis was conducted for the nineteenth-century planter's kitchen and manager's house (E. Roberts 2005) and the early nineteenth-century sugar mill (Farnsworth and Wilkie 2010). The assemblage of bones from the kitchen and manager's house contained a mixture of cow, pig, sheep/goat, wild animals, birds, and fish. The sugar mill assemblage, however, contained only cow remains. The harvest and grinding season was the most frantic time in sugar cultivation. Planters preferred to leave the sugarcane growing in the fields for as long as possible to increase its sugar content, but they risked losing the entire crop to frost damage. Sugarcane loses much of its sugar content shortly after cutting, and so it must be quickly brought to the mill. Closely spaced growing seasons added to the pressure to process the cane in a short time. As a result, sugar mills were run twenty-four hours a day during the season's peak. Enslaved mill workers ate and even took brief naps at the mill.

A list of slaves at Whitney Plantation from 1820 identifies the ethnicity of African-born persons. Of the 55 people listed, 18 are described as having been born in Africa. At least one-third of those people are described as Mandique, Bambara, or Timin (Temne), ethnicities with a high probability of being Muslim based on the prevalence of Islam in their region of origin at that time. While beef can be consumed by Muslims, there are religious restrictions prohibiting the consumption of pork. It is interesting to consider whether the exclusive consumption of beef by sugar-mill workers reflects the selection and serving of meat that would be acceptable to all workers, no matter their religious affiliation. In analyzing zooarchaeological remains at Stonewall Plantation, Michael Way (2007) found that the amount of beef consumed by the plantation's inhabitants declined through time. The opposite trend was found by Elizabeth Scott (2001) at nearby Nina Plantation (16PC62). At Stonewall, the earliest deposits date from the late 1700s, with the latest dating to the 1880s. Given the large influx of Senegambians to Louisiana during the late eighteenth century, Way hypothesized that changes in diet among the mixed population at the site represented declining Muslim dietary preferences among the enslaved people. The zooarchaeology of Africans and African Americans clearly deserves further investigation, as it can provide information on changing dietary practices, as well as health, ethnicity, and religion.

ARCHITECTURE AND YARD SPACES

John Michael Vlach (1986) demonstrated the African origin, via Haiti, of Louisiana's famous shotgun cabins. With a few notable exceptions, though, there has been little archaeological evidence of African architectural influences. In part, the colonial architecture of the French, making use of post-in-ground and post-in-beam supports, as well as mud daubing (*bousillage*), is not so different from the architectural traditions of the enslaved peoples who were brought from Africa (Corry 1807; Winterbottom 1969). Few early examples of slave housing have been found in Louisiana, but those that have been excavated demonstrate features not incompatible with African traditions. Early slave housing investigated at Nina Plantation and Orange Grove (16JE141) featured mud floors (Dawdy et al. 1997; Earth Search, Inc. 2009; Scott 2001; Yakubik et al. 1994). Orange Grove's cabin had a chimney made of crumbled brick and mud, reminiscent of the modified plaster and rubble construction found in African-Bahamian houses. As in Louisiana, Bahamian populations were drawn largely from Senegambia and Congo (Wilkie and Farnsworth 2005).

By the mid-nineteenth century, slave-quarter architecture in Louisiana, and much of the South, had become closely regulated. Agricultural journals directed at planters provided schematics for cabin designs that claimed to promote the health of enslaved peoples while also controlling their use of space (McKee 1992). These cabin designs continued to be used until the mid-twentieth century and are still a familiar sight in Louisiana. Raised on piers, the houses were often designed as "double pen" or duplex housing, which would serve two families. The houses often featured porches. The H-shaped chimney foundations of these houses are easily recognizable in plantation archaeology. On many plantations, the slave quarters were arranged in a linear fashion, with cabins facing one another across a plantation road. On sugar plantations, the mill was often located at the end of the row. This layout facilitated surveillance of the slave quarters by overseers. During the postbellum period, it facilitated easy access to African American living spaces for "bulldozers" (racist thugs) and others who would terrorize black families.

While the architecture and layout of buildings may have been imposed on them, African American enslaved and freed people sought to control the spaces surrounding their houses in ways that suited their own values, needs, and beliefs. The creation and maintenance of yard spaces as an extension of one's enclosed architectural space is well-documented throughout the African Diaspora (Mintz and Price 1976; Wilkie and Farnsworth 2005). The importance of house yards and compounds is drawn from African antecedents. Excavations at Oakley, Blythewood (16IV8), Alma (16PC76), Riverlake, and Ashland–Belle Helene plantations have all demonstrated evidence of yard activities to varying degrees (Palmer 2000, 2005; Wilkie 2000; Yakubik and Méndez 1995).

Enslaved people and tenants alike used fences to create a sense of ownership for their yard spaces. Block excavations at Oakley Plantation demonstrated that enslaved people and tenants swept their yards to maintain a hard, clean, dirt surface, causing garbage to accumulate at fence lines and immediately under the perimeter of the house. There was also some evidence that food preparation took place in the yards (Wilkie 2000). David Palmer (2000), in an ethnoarchaeological study of yard spaces at Riverlake and Alma plantations, found that tenants built elaborate fences and enclosures for penning animals and creating secure spaces in yards. Outer perimeter fences and inner fences closer to the houses served functional purposes, such as keeping animals out of gardens, but they also delineated space according to levels of intimacy with the occupants. A range of medicinal and food plants were raised in house gardens (Palmer 2000, 2005). Recent excavations at the slave hospital at L'Hermitage (16AN24) by Louisiana State University (LSU) graduate student Holly Tunkel may demonstrate whether any of these herbal medicines found their way into the plantation hospital. The yard areas provided spaces where enslaved and free people could express creativity, exercise autonomy over space, and develop resources to supplement their rations.

CUISINE

Extensive zooarchaeological analyses of African American diet have been conducted for Alma, Ashland-Belle Helene, Magnolia Mound, Nina, Riverlake, Stonewall, and Whitney plantations (Burden and Gagliano 1977; Palmer 2005; E. Roberts 2005; Scott 2001; Way 2007). These analyses demonstrate that enslaved peoples, and later tenants, quickly adapted to the locally available wild resources. Raccoon, opossum, squirrel, deer, turtle, alligator, water birds, and freshwater fish—particularly drum (gasper-goo), and catfish—became important supplements to meager slave rations.

Agricultural staples, particularly maize, would have been familiar even to people who had only recently arrived from Africa. American crops such as peanuts, potatoes, corn, squash, peppers, and tobacco had traveled quickly to Africa, and they were widely incorporated into the African diet. African crops such as okra, watermelon, sesame seeds, and sorghum likewise became well-established in the Americas (Carney 2001:381, 393–394; Farnsworth and Wilkie 2006). As the cooks for the planter classes, Africans and African Americans had a great deal of input and control over the development of Louisiana cuisine as consumed by black and white populations alike (Wilkie 2000:137–138, 142).

While there is great diversity in cooking traditions across West and Central Africa, there are also enough commonalities in style and mode of cooking to make some generalizations. At the time of the slave trade, most African cuisines were focused around one or two primary starches, which were pounded and cooked to create thick or even solid porridges. Taro, yams, rice, and sorghum were among some of the starches commonly used. Porridges were served with hot sauces, relishes, or stews. Meat was often used for flavoring rather than being the primary focus of the meal. Bones were often broken so that the marrow enriched the gravy of the stew. Thick iron and clay pots were most commonly used to slow-cook sauces in open areas (Lewicki and Johnson 1974). Popular Louisiana dishes such as gumbo, etouffee, jambalaya, okra stew, and greens flavored with saltback are culinary legacies of African cooks. Evidence of African cooking styles is archaeologically recognizable in planter table sets featuring soup plates and bowls, burned-out iron pots, and cracked animal long bones (Farnsworth and Wilkie 2006; Wilkie 2000:140–141).

There is evidence that Africans continued to use low-fired earthenware pots in their cooking. There is a small but consistent presence of these ceramics, sometimes referred to as Colono-Indian Ware or colonoware, recovered at plantation sites, including planter kitchens (Ferguson 1992:18–22). While there is no evidence that Africans produced such wares in Louisiana, it appears they did use Native American–produced ceramics. The remnants of these wares have often been misinterpreted as evidence of earlier Native American settlements. However, recent excavations at Stonewall Plantation demonstrated that Native American pots were found in association with French faiences and English earthenwares. Clay pots were found in multiple archaeological layers of a single pit and in association with European wares dating from the 1770s to the 1830s. The deposit represents the activities of white and black families at the plantation. So-called "prehistoric" ceramics were also found at the kitchens of Magnolia Mound and Nina plantations, as well as the quarters of Maitland Plantation (16CT176) (Burden and Gaglianao 1977; Ryan et al. 1997; Scott 2001). It seems likely these pots are not evidence of earlier, disturbed sites, but rather historic-period Native American ceramics. While African Americans apparently did not engage in large-scale production of ceramics at Stonewall, they do seem to have acquired and used Native American pots. These earthenware pots would have been the closest available substitute for African-style pots and would have facilitated slow-cooking at low temperatures (Ferguson 1992:105–106).

While this discussion is necessarily brief, we have demonstrated that there is an abundance of available archaeological evidence for considering African material life in colonial Louisiana. African influences extended in some instances well into the contemporary period. There is irony, then, in recognizing that while African traditions were shaping the rich cultural life of Louisiana, African-descended peoples were being politically and economically marginalized, or, worse, victimized by racialized violence. Just as the peoples of Africa succeeded in constructing African-influenced lifeways in Louisiana, they also succeeded in taking stands against the institutional racism of the state.

Standing Against Racism

Africans and African Americans have a long history of actively fighting racism and oppression in Louisiana. Slaves openly conspired against planter authority in Pointe Coupee in 1795, and they openly rebelled in St. John the Baptist Parish in 1811 (Hall 2005). During the Civil War, black soldiers were first allowed to fight against enslavement for the Union at Port Hudson, Louisiana. During Reconstruction, African Americans stepped forward at great personal risk to serve in the state government (Taylor 1974). African Americans opposed affronts to dignity using various means, including armed self-defense, throughout the early twentieth-century Jim Crow era and before the national civil rights movement (De Jong 2002). During the early civil rights era, Louisiana bus boycotts in Baton Rouge served as a model for boycotts in Selma and elsewhere. While these are dramatic examples of people of color striking out against social inequality, archaeology focused at the household level is beginning to explore the ways in which African American communities strove to circumvent the social, political, and economic inequities placed upon them.

The transition from slave to free labor led to the establishment of tenancy farming in the state, with sharecropping becoming the most insidious and common form of this arrangement. Under a sharecropping arrangement, farming families were provided housing, a parcel of land, mules, equipment, and other necessities for farming a crop. During the year, a family could purchase goods and supplies on credit from the plantation store. Debts were tallied throughout the year. When the crop came in, its value was compared with the accumulated debt of the family, and the account was "settled." Company stores were notorious for charging excessive rates for goods. Under this system, families were likely to begin each year in greater debt to the plantation (Conrad 1965). Upward mobility was possible only through two pathways: freeing oneself from the plantation tenancy system or gaining an education. Archaeological research at late nineteenth- and early twentieth-century African American sites demonstrates how families went about achieving these goals (e.g., Palmer 2005, 2006, 2007; Palmer and Juarez 2003; Wilkie 2000).

Achieving economic freedom required thrift, ingenuity, and the support of an extended African American community. Within plantations, families supplemented their diets by raising their own animals, hunting, fishing, and farming small garden plots. Postbellum deposits at Alma and Riverlake plantations include evidence that raccoon, opossum, catfish, drum, frogs, and turtles were being consumed by tenant families. At Oakley Plantation, domestic servant Silvia Freeman used her access to cash wages to purchase luxury items like cloth or tobacco for tenants on the plantation. In exchange, Freeman may have received home-canned foods. As a plantation cook, she would have had little time to develop her own yard area and produce such items (Wilkie 2000).

Black activists like Booker T. Washington recognized the importance of these informal economic networks and preached self-sufficiency to rural populations. In looking at the archaeological evidence from Alma and Riverlake plantations, Palmer (2005) found that tenant assemblages featured increased amounts of home-preserved foods through time, as represented in the occurrence of fruit sealers. He interpreted this as evidence that families were seeking new ways to minimize their debt to the plantation's management. The mason jars and other sealers presumably contained foodstuffs grown by tenants. As was the case at Oakley, different brands, sizes, and colors of fruit jars were recovered, suggesting that tenant families exchanged home-canned foods with one another. By trading preserves with one another, tenants could benefit from their neighbor's efforts as well as their own, with the end result being a possible expansion in the diversity of their diet. This would have been nutritionally more desirable than the limited dry and canned foodstuffs found in most plantation stores.

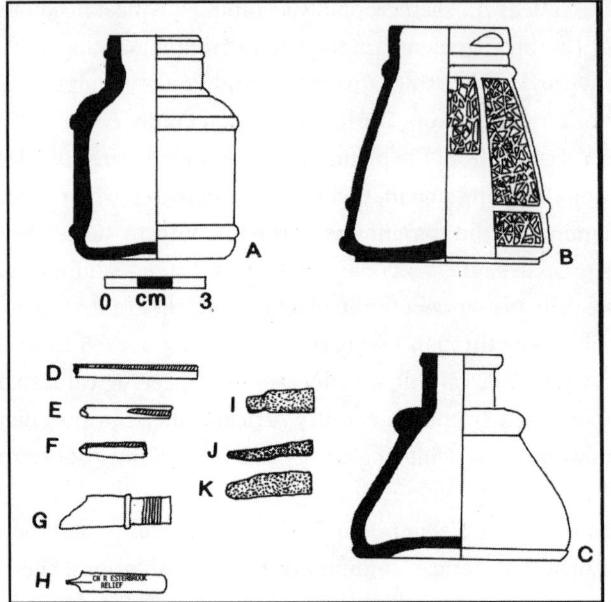

Fig. 15.2. Communications-related artifacts (from Wilkie 2000:214, Figure 43): a–c. Glass inkwells; d–k. Writing instruments.

In addition to economic freedom, escaping the cycle of plantation life required access to education. While education was legally denied to enslaved African Americans, freedom did little to improve their educational circumstances. Schools were underfunded, segregated, and scheduled to fit around the needs of the agricultural harvest. But African American communities found ways to enhance educational opportunities for their youth, often through the efforts of church groups. Churches ran schools for their communities and raised funds to supplement black teachers' salaries (Anderson 1988).

The importance of education to African American families is evident in the archaeological record. The Freeman house assemblage at Oakley, where the widowed Silvia Freeman raised five children, included pen nibs, pencil points, slate pencil fragments and inkwells (Figure 15.2). The nearby Scott house contained salvaged dry-cell battery graphites that had been reused as writing implements. Likewise, artifacts related to literacy were found at Alma and Riverlake plantations, as well as from the postbellum kitchen building at Whitney Plantation. Recent excavations by LSU graduate student Dena Struchtemeyer (2008) at an early twentieth-century African American school in Morganza, Louisiana, offer more insight into African American education. Among the archaeological finds was the discovery that students were receiving vocational education at the school, learning how to make St. Joe's bricks. Both concrete molds and completed bricks were recovered. Informants remembered school children making bricks at the school in the 1930s and 1940s, a date range consistent with the associated artifacts. The brick-making was likely part of the vocational training seen as appropriate for black students at that time, who even with an education would have limited employment opportunities.

Also recovered from the site were multiple examples of bullets and broken window glass (Struchtemeyer 2008:101, 107). Informants remembered a pair of crosses burned at the school (Kira Blaisdell Sloan, personal communication). Long before events like the Columbine and Virginia Tech massacres brought school violence to the attention of the white middle class, African American elementary school students faced the threat of racial violence in their schools.

Louisiana boasts a number of important historically black colleges, in particular Southern University, Dillard, and Xavier. While some excavations have taken place at Southern University (Maygarden et al. 1999), additional work at it and other black colleges would be particularly compelling. Politically engaged college students went into rural communities of Louisiana in the twentieth century, teaching new ideas about health and hygiene, new technologies, and promoting self-reliance. These and other educational sites deserve attention, especially if we hope to understand more fully African Americans' struggle against racism.

Conclusion

Although much of the African American archaeology in Louisiana has focused on the institution of the plantation, there remains tremendous opportunity to explore the entire breadth of the African American experience. Despite the heavy focus on plantations, this arena of research has not been exhausted. In particular, projects focusing on life experiences at plantations owned by free men or women of color (as free persons of African descent identified themselves during the antebellum period) would allow new insights into the complex racial dynamics of enslavement. Other new projects to be developed include archaeological investigations of African American life in towns and cities.

Still, much work remains. Fraternal lodges, community centers, dance halls, universities, and black-owned business districts all deserve archaeological consideration. There is also a wealth of previously excavated sites that merit reanalysis and reconsideration. Bill Haag's (1974) excavations at Catfish Town

(16EBR63) in Baton Rouge recovered materials from a historically black neighborhood, but these artifacts were not analyzed with an eye towards questions of race or ethnicity. Similarly, plantation work spaces, including mills and kitchens, were used by black laborers and should be accordingly examined. Finally, recent work by historians demonstrates the rich African cultural presence that lasted late into the Spanish colonial period in Louisiana. Archaeology has the potential to bring to light the triumphs and tragedies of the African American experience in Louisiana. In doing so, it offers a reflexive gaze upon life in the state today.

16

Colonial and Early Antebellum New Orleans

SHANNON LEE DAWDY AND CHRISTOPHER N. MATTHEWS

The history of New Orleans is quintessentially archaeological. The renowned richness of the city's cultural life is the result of multiple occupations and a cycle of building, destruction, and rebuilding. Archaeology has shown that the site known as New Orleans was occupied by Native Americans at least five hundred years ago, and that one group had an encampment on the very spot where the French cleared the river cane to set out a regular grid of streets—now called the Vieux Carré, or French Quarter (Dawdy, Gray et al. 2008). We can think of the period covered by this chapter as corresponding to three major stratigraphic levels in the colonizing of New Orleans—the French (A.D. 1718–1769), the Spanish (A.D. 1769–1803), and the early American (A.D. 1803–1825). The archaeological evidence collected in New Orleans over the past twenty-five years shows how New Orleans underwent tremendous demographic and economic changes with each wave of colonialism. Moreover, it reveals how strains of a unique creole culture not only persisted under rapidly changing conditions, but also flourished with new stimuli. Two themes that encapsulate this period of New Orleans history are colonization and creolization. The first represents forces of outside change that washed over the city, and the second represents local creativity and the continuity of evolving traditions.

When capitalized, "Creole" in Louisiana refers to the self-identification of people descended from the Louisiana colony's diverse early settlers, who came to be distinguished from their "American" neighbors in the nineteenth century primarily by being Francophone and Catholic (Tregle 1992). By the late nineteenth century, the term also came to be explicitly applied to local material practices, such as distinct architectural styles and cuisine. These local practices evolved out of the experiences and cultural diversity of the colonial and early American periods. When written in lower-case, anthropologists and archaeologists use the term "creole" more generally (and outside Louisiana) as a modifier denoting often unconscious social and material adaptations that led to the emergence of a new culture out of diverse donor populations under conditions of colonialism, a process referred to as creolization.

To date, approximately one hundred archaeological investigations have been conducted within New Orleans's city limits. The vast majority of them have been minor studies conducted to monitor federal construction projects or survey small, low-probability parcels on batture lands. But a growing number of projects, such as the studies reviewed here, have opened early New Orleans up to the discoveries that controlled, in-depth excavation can reveal. Given space limitations, we cannot offer a comprehensive survey of all the archaeological projects completed in New Orleans. We have instead selected a sample to discuss, based upon comparability according to contemporary archaeological standards, the presence of significant findings about the period prior to 1825, and, unavoidably, our own familiarity with the projects (For a more complete review of past projects in the French Quarter and New Orleans, see Dawdy, Gremillion et al. 2008; Pendley 1992; Godzinski et al. 2002).

The archaeological data speak particularly well to the domains of landscape and consumption, both of which reflect back upon social realities. By landscape we mean the social construction and occupation of a space for meaningful human interaction. Consumption refers to the creative acquisition and use of material objects for diverse, socially mediated purposes. In order to organize our discussion and demonstrate the ways in which archaeology is broadening our understanding of early New Orleans, we use landscape to illustrate changes experienced under colonization, and consumption to discuss the process of creolization.

Colonization, Landscape and Change

The French established New Orleans as a port and an urban capital to funnel goods and people in two directions—down through the vast Louisiana territory of the Mississippi drainage and up through the waters of the Gulf of Mexico. Under the French, Canadian pioneers and Caribbean buccaneers were soon followed by a large wave of African and European settlers, of whom approximately one-half (six thousand) survived the harsh conditions of passage and "seasoning" of their first year, to establish a way of life in the colony (Dawdy 2008, Usner 1992). A majority of the Africans were enslaved people from the Senegambia or Congo regions of Africa (Hall 1992; Wilkie et al., Chapter 15 in this volume). Many of the Europeans were indentured servants and convict laborers—or other groups considered undesirable by the French crown, such as German-speaking Protestants and wayward children of the nobility. By 1732, New Orleans was home to approximately 40 percent of the colonial population of a territory that extended for thousands of square miles. In most of this region, Native Americans comprised the overwhelming majority of the population, and their effects upon colonial society were significant, even in New Orleans (Dawdy 2008). The French crown had a laissez-faire attitude towards Louisiana after the initial enthusiasm of the 1710s and 1720s, so the colony's diverse population—and nowhere was it so diverse as New Orleans—was largely left to its own devices.

By the time Louis XV transferred Louisiana to his Spanish cousin in the 1760s, New Orleans was no longer a French outpost. It was a creole town with its own way of doing things. The Spanish period marks the next major stratigraphic layer in the city's history. Under the more active (and more bureaucratic) rule of Spanish administrators who took over in 1769, new waves of immigration occurred—small streams of people from the Canary Islands and other Spanish possessions, but more significantly from Acadia. In addition, it was under the Spanish that the agricultural sector of the colony's economy finally took off with the successful cultivation of sugar. The Spanish allowed new importations of enslaved Africans from a diverse range of slave ports on the West Coast of Africa, as well as from nearby ports in the Caribbean. By the 1790s, New Orleans was a boom town of sugar exports and slave imports. The crossroads market of New Orleans also attracted a growing number of English-speaking traders and businessmen, some arriving from the encroaching settlements of the Ohio Valley and British West Florida, and some arriving from the international waters of the Caribbean. Materially, New Orleans was fundamentally reshaped in this period (Figure 16.1). In addition to the economic and demographic changes that were occurring, the city suffered a disastrous fire in 1788, in which 80 percent of the town's buildings were damaged or destroyed. The population was just getting back on its feet when another fire hit in 1794, wiping away newly rebuilt structures in the center of the city, near the Place d'Armes (now Jackson Square). Spanish administrators wanted to avoid any more disasters of this nature and so dictated a new building code that required brick construction, slate roofs, and firewalls. Thus the architectural legacy of the "French" Quarter really comes from the Spanish period. The Spanish also invested in several public works and infrastructure improvements that changed daily life in the city—from building new hospitals and schools to establishing public markets. It was the Spanish who established the open-air structures along the levee known as the "French Market."

The last major stratigraphic level reviewed here is the American takeover of the city, which followed the Louisiana Purchase in the early antebellum period. The transformations of the 1800s and 1810s should be thought of as the third colonization of the territory. Though the United States purchased Louisiana from Napoleon in 1803 following a secret retrocession from Spain to France in

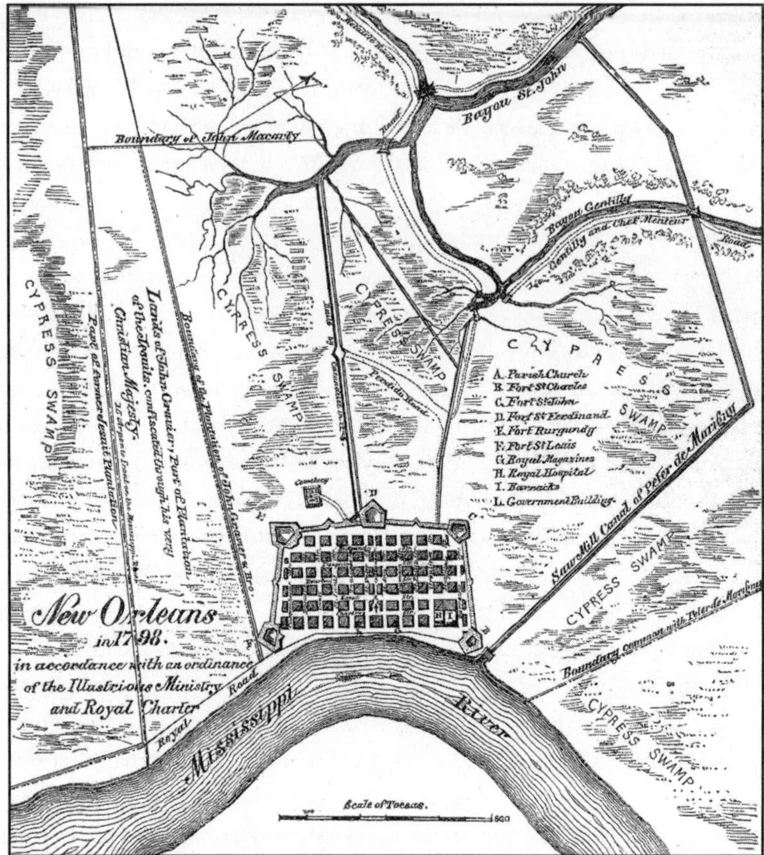

Fig. 16.1. "New Orleans in 1798 in accordance with an ordinance of the Illustrious Ministry and Royal Charter." From *Report on the Social Statistics of Cities,* compiled by George E. Waring, Jr., United States Census Office, Part II, 1886.

1801, France effectively held the territory for only a matter of months before the American transfer. In the early antebellum period, a cotton boom soon eclipsed the sugar boom, and a flood of boatmen and wheelers-and-dealers of all sorts entered the city. In less than two decades, the city tripled in both population and girth. During this period of intense development, "faubourgs," or suburbs, were created by subdividing plantations bordering the French Quarter in three directions (Marigny on the downriver side, Ste. Marie on the upriver side, and Tremé towards the lake; see Figure 16.2).

Each of these phases of colonization brought significant material shifts that are seen in the archaeological record, providing an understanding of the way in which global forces affected the everyday lives of early New Orleanians. Each

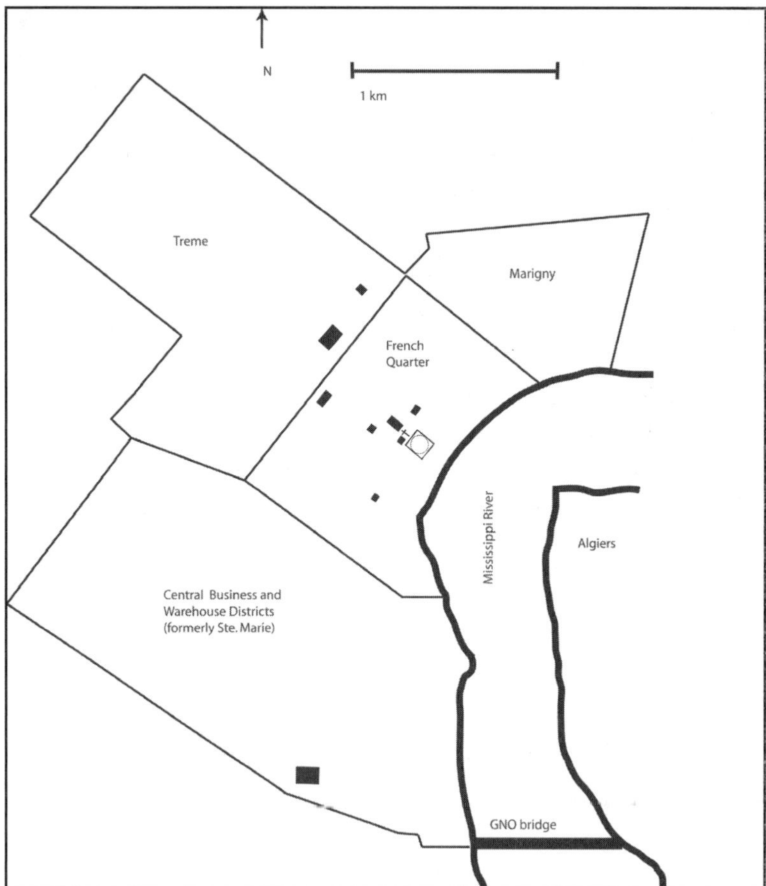

Fig. 16.2. Schematic map of early New Orleans neighborhoods and archaeological sites mentioned in the text. Map by Shannon Lee Dawdy.

episode heralded a new demographic landscape and a new economic reality. The development of the city can be marked not just in terms of scale, but in the kind of town it was in each of these periods. The landscape of New Orleans was significantly and uniquely altered as it underwent each phase of colonialism.

ROYAL MILITARY BARRACKS (16OR136)

Under the French, a devotion to a rigid, symmetrical urban design and a neglect of comfort for residents speaks to the original purpose of the town—to fulfill the King's glory and make a quick profit for his advisors. In 1991, Earth Search, Inc., excavated beneath the floor of a raised Creole cottage at 726–728 Toulouse Street in the French Quarter. A kitchen structure was discovered with clear evidence of having suffered a severe fire. Associated ceramics indicate this was probably the fire of 1788 (Yakubik and Franks 1997). Below this, excavators encountered the well-preserved remains of an even earlier structure (Yakubik and Dawdy 1996). Upright planks, a post, a sill trench, and a thin oyster-shell floor were clearly identifiable and datable to the French colonial period. Aligning the archaeological evidence with historic maps, these features were identified as the remains of a colonial barracks built ca. 1731. The deposits on the rough earth floor suggested that the soldiers lived in squalid and uncomfortable conditions. This project marked a watershed in the archaeology of French Quarter sites, demonstrating that a meticulous approach to the area's complex urban stratigraphy, combined with local preservation conditions, can result in identification of single events, such as the great fire of 1788, as well as an elucidation of daily life during New Orleans's earliest days. It was arguably the first archaeological study to make a significant contribution to our understanding of the French colonial period in the city.

ST. PETER STREET CEMETERY (16OR92)

In 1984, construction workers uncovered coffins and human bones on the site of a new condominium complex located on the edge of the French Quarter in the square bounded by St. Peter, Burgundy, North Rampart, and Toulouse streets. Historic maps and archival records demonstrate that this was the site of the city's first official cemetery, which had been established in the early 1720s. St. Peter's Cemetery, now erased from the landscape except for the part of it which remains buried, was a major landmark for locals in the colonial period until 1789, when it was replaced by St. Louis I Cemetery. Although no laws protected this accidental discovery, Douglas Owsley and Charles Orser from Louisiana State University were permitted to conduct salvage excavations. Twenty-nine skeletons were removed and eventually taken to the Smithsonian Institution for study. The analysis of these remains provides a fascinating picture of the racial make-up, diet, and physical conditions of New Orleans's population during the French colonial period (Owsley et al. 1985). One discovery was that people of African, European, and American Indian ancestry, as well as those of mixed ancestries, lay side by side in simple wood coffins. Segregation was not a strong factor in New Orleans's religious practices in the colonial period, a fact first suggested by archaeology and now backed by recent historical work (Clark 2007).

CONGO SQUARE (16OR47/48)

Although the Spanish did not invest heavily in Louisiana in terms of contributing immigrants from their homeland, they did invest significantly in the public infrastructure of the colony, an effect that was especially noticeable in New Orleans. In 1977–78, Richard Shenkel of the University of New Orleans (UNO) directed an excavation in Congo Square at the edge of the Tremé neighborhood (Shenkel and Chatelain 1979). The most significant find of this project was an intact portion of a moat and a footbridge associated with colonial Fort San Fernando. San Fernando was one of five forts located at pentagonal intersections of a rampart that once surrounded the French Quarter (thus giving Rampart Street its name; see Figure 16.1). In dozens of maps dating to the early eighteenth century, French administrators had drawn their intent to fortify the town against other imperial powers and Indians, but the walls and bastions were never built. One of the last French governors of the colony was thrown into the Bastille when he could not account for the money set aside for this purpose, although construction was finally underway by 1761. One of the first things the Spanish did when they arrived was to complete construction of the long-anticipated ramparts. Although archaeologists knew about the fort from historical documentation, excavation revealed that the fortified walls were interrupted with multiple (and remarkably well-preserved) wooden bridges along their length. These bridges suggest that traffic flowed freely across the walls and that the fortifications seem to have served a largely symbolic purpose—to impress upon the locals the military power of the new Spanish administration.

Spain's first appointed governor of Louisiana faced a revolt by New Orleans residents in 1768. They sent him packing for Havana and operated as a sovereign government for several months until the Spanish invaded with a large force and placed the leaders of the revolt before a firing squad. Archaeological investigation indicates that the walls and forts that surrounded the heart of the city symbolized Spanish dominion without stemming the economic flows of the city. The area of Fort San Fernando was located near Bayou Road, a key artery connecting plantations to the city. Enslaved plantation workers (Africans, Native Americans, and their descendents) were allowed to come to town to sell produce and livestock, as well as handicrafts. After the fort was torn down in 1803 and the enslaved were barred from the public markets under the American regime, the area became a public square best known as a social and religious meeting place for Africans and Afro-Creoles on Sunday afternoons. In the early antebellum period, the deepening separation between white and black lives and the growing population of the enslaved are visible in the creation of the city's first public space identified as "black"—Congo Square.

CABILDO (16OR129)

Since 1721, the lot flanking the upriver side of St. Louis Cathedral on the central town square had been set aside for government use. Up until its transfer to the Louisiana State Museum in the mid-twentieth century, the site housed at various times a police station, a civil prison, a military prison, the Superior Council chamber, the Cabildo (town hall or colonial capital building), jailers' quarters, a firehouse, and an arsenal (Yakubik and Franks 1997:32). These functions were contained in a complex of buildings and small courtyards that underwent building, demolition, fire damage, and remodeling for over two hundred years.

Excavations conducted by Earth Search, Inc., in 1990 helped establish the building sequence at the site (Yakubik and Franks 1997). Excavation in the rear courtyard was at the location of the former civil prison. Below-ground architectural features consisted of the lower walls and foundation of the 1730 jail, a 1790 brick floor, a late nineteenth-century foundation of a small shed structure, and the remains of a corridor addition. The richest artifact-bearing feature was a midden deposit dating to ca. 1800–1840 that had accumulated on the prison floor. This deposit, full of rat bones, vividly confirmed historical accounts describing the fetid condition of the prison, even suggesting the accounts were understated. Another finding was that the prisoners were involved in the manufacture of bone buttons, evidenced by the discovery of numerous bone button blanks in the prison yard. Forced labor and squalid conditions characterized the early American period in the prison, suggesting that although the city was growing wealthy, conditions for the underclass that made up the majority of the prisoner population may have actually deteriorated rather than improved.

MAGINNIS COTTON MILL/DUPLESSIS PLANTATION (16OR144)

Now lying in New Orleans's Warehouse District, the Duplessis Plantation was on the outskirts of the city when it was established in 1765. The site was occupied by a series of well-known Creole families up until the area's urbanization in the 1820s. Over the course of this time, the indigo plantation's property was subdivided and sold off, while the main house became an elite suburban residence. In 1997, the Greater New Orleans Archaeology Program (GNOAP) of the College of Urban and Public Affairs at UNO undertook excavations at the Maginnis Cotton

Mill, which now lies over the site of the plantation house (Dawdy and Ibáñez 1997). Excavations revealed the well-preserved walls and floor of the main house, with associated midden deposits dating from the early Spanish colonial period through the late nineteenth century. The findings suggest one of the sources for the architectural style of New Orleans's Garden District, with its colonnaded porches and Greek Revival details. These houses were not simply emulating the great houses of nearby plantations. They were trying to compete with the elegant survivals of the faubourg's plantation past.

The plantation's fields were converted to lush gardens as American influence emphasized the front of the house for display of the occupant's wealth, taste, and standing (Dawdy 2000b). As the streets were subdivided, houses that once proudly faced the river became crowded by imitators and scrutinized by intimate street traffic. Archaeological findings suggest that along with this new scale and style of urban architecture, an aesthetic of ostentatious display took hold in the early American period. The house was redesigned in the early American period according to the latest style. Trying to maintain the status she had held in the colonial period, the owner of the property, a widow of plantation wealth, drove herself into bankruptcy trying to keep up with the new expectations for crystal glasses, gilt furnishings, and fine imported liquors, evidence of which was found in the archaeological strata associated with her occupation. Her artifact assemblage included ivory dominoes (often used in games of chance), examples of proprietary wine bottles stamped with the appellation of her husband's family estate in Bordeaux (Saint-Julien Medoc), and refined white-bodied wares and porcelains that represent a considerably greater household expenditure in conspicuous entertainment compared to other occupations at the site (Dawdy 2000a). Interpretation of the Duplessis house illuminates the ways in which the American colonization transformed New Orleans's landscape and affected the consumption habits of Creole elites.

Creolization, Consumption and Continuity

At the same time that Louisiana's three waves of colonization were radically altering the landscape of New Orleans, a process of adaptation and creolization was occurring in economic and social terms, as members of the city's always-diversifying population adjusted to the local environment and to one another. In many ways, the colonial and antebellum periods in New Orleans present a counterpoint to mainstream colonial American history. This difference results from a combination of forces that enabled early New Orleanians to incorporate foreign influences while sustaining productive social relations and meaningful consumption practices. These adaptations helped them maintain cultural practices that could withstand continuous external threats and major geopolitical changes. The syncopated rhythm of continuity and change were features of a unique Creole consciousness that people developed while living in the city. This consciousness helps to explain a variety of material forms—such as ceramics, houses, and food—that demonstrate simultaneous and sometimes conflicting cultural influences (Dawdy 2000a). The mélange and reconciliation of New Orleans's multiple ethnic roots—rather than the choice of one over another—can be understood as an expression of a Creole mode of living and thinking. The archaeological remains tell the story of New Orleanians' struggle to construct a stable way of life in a place that was constantly bombarded by forces of change. Thus, the other side of the story is not how an Indian town became an Afro-French one or how a French town became an American one. Rather, it is how everyone in New Orleans eventually becomes Creole.

THE ST. AUGUSTINE SITE (16OR148)

The St. Augustine site, located in the Tremé section of the city, is the site of an early industrial plantation house. From 1720 until 1810, the site was at the center of a brickyard and tilery built by the Company of Indies, which directed the Louisiana colony from 1717 to 1731. The Company of Indies actively sought the improvement of the colony through agriculture and industry. This plantation served these efforts. After 1731, the former works supervisor, Charles Antoine de Morand, obtained the plantation, continuing its operation until his death in 1756. It then passed into the hands of women in the Moreau family and, through marriage, to Claude Tremé, for whom the surrounding Faubourg Tremé is named (Figure 16.2).

The quality of life at the brickworks is poorly documented for any of its inhabitants, though one mention of Morand is telling. Not following suit with many others who had improved their social status in the colony through the creation of wealth, the "chevalier de Morand requested that the Company have regard to his birth [i.e., his noble status] even though he lived like a commoner" (Giraud 1987: 312). This quotation suggests that life at the brickworks, and in early colonial New Orleans more generally, challenged Old World social hierarchies. One effect of this was the loosening of social mores guiding the behavior of people at varied ranks, who strategically redefined their position to take advantage of the isolated setting in which the new creole society was developing.

Fig. 16.3. Native American ceramics from Madame John's Legacy (16OR51). Photograph by Shannon Lee Dawdy.

This is an important context for understanding the social organization of the site in the colonial period and the ways in which new identities were forged. Given limited surviving documentation (especially during the time of Morand [1731–1756]), archaeology provides an important context for understanding the process of creolization.

Initial testing at the St. Augustine site was performed by the GNOAP in 1999 (Matthews 1999). One of the most interesting findings was a large amount of Native American pottery found in colonial-era deposits. While not unique (other sites in the city have produced native ceramics, including the Cabildo, Madam John's Legacy, and the Rising Sun Hotel site, discussed in this chapter), the St. Augustine site has one of the largest and most varied collections (typified by those shown in Figure 16.3). The site's stratified deposits represent several different occupation periods stretching from the site's first use in the 1720s through a mid-nineteenth century occupation associated with the use of the site by the Sisters of the Presentation, and later the Sisters of Mount Carmel, who lived at the site and ran a school for free girls of color.

The earliest deposits are marked by an absence of Native American pottery. These deposits are few and relate to efforts to construct a landscape for building the manor house. However, this finding contrasts with that found in the early French colonial settlement at Mobile, Alabama. The French founding of Mobile dates to the period of the initial French colonization of the Lower Mississippi Valley in the 1690s, thus predating New Orleans, but later occupations of Mobile are comparable. Archaeologists Gregory Waselkov (1991) and Diane Silvia (1998) have shown that in the early period at Mobile, Native American ceramics included a number of Colono or copy wares—native-produced ceramics made in European vessel forms (see also Waselkov and Sylvia 1995). These vessels stopped being made and were replaced in the archaeological record at Mobile by traditional native vessel forms after the French decline in the region in the 1730s. While the absence of ceramics in the earliest deposits at the St. Augustine site is not definitive evidence, the fact that none of the Native American–made wares found at the site are copy vessels suggests a different dynamic to the Native American–settler relationship in early New Orleans as compared to Mobile.

A historical conjuncture helps to explain this discrepancy. The event occurred in 1729, when the European settlements near present-day Natchez, Mississippi, were destroyed by Natchez Indians in cooperation with captive Africans. Over two hundred settlers were killed, more than one-eighth of the entire European population living along the Mississippi River at the time. Governor Bienville, who had been recalled to France at the time of the attack, explained it as the result of a policy that cut back on exchange between the French settlers and the surrounding native population. This new policy viewed these exchanges in purely economic terms. As such, they were judged to be costly and non-productive (McGowan 1976, Usner 1998). This attempt to "rationalize" Louisiana's economy cut key Indian allies of the French out of a loop of cultural relations that had come to define politics in southeastern North America.

The earliest deposits at the St. Augustine site contain no Native American ceramics, but it is very likely that the rich middle phase deposits, which contain a large number of them, date to the post-1729 era. Following the Natchez rebellion, the French strategy changed dramatically. Most significant was the abandonment of the colony by the Company of Indies and a subsequent period of localization. Under these conditions, an increase in the use of traditionally made Native American pottery at the St. Augustine site and elsewhere makes sense. As Bienville and others acknowledged in reference to the role of the Indian trade in general, these pots, their contents, and similar trade goods served as signs of the intercultural exchange that helped sustain peace within the region. A vessel analysis of the colonial-period sherds from the St. Augustine site shows that while all Native American–made vessels were open bowls and similar storage and serving forms, these forms were also found among the European-made ceramics. This means that the Native American–made vessels were functionally redundant. Analysis also indicates that the vessels were well-curated and lightly used. Their primary function therefore appears not to have been food storage and preparation but rather decoration or display. As such, they may have served to symbolize peaceful and productive relations that were enacted through gift exchanges between trading partners living on two sides of a politically dangerous cultural divide in the eighteenth century.

The last phase of deposits from the St. Augustine site date to the Americanization era, when the site was incorporated into the city as part of the Faubourg Tremé and became a Catholic mother house and school for free girls of color. There are no Native American–made ceramics in these deposits at all. This is hardly surprising, given that the transformations to the site involved its articulation with a growing urban center after 1800. However, this only fails to surprise if we situate Native Americans solely as forest inhabitants, an inaccurate assumption given their presence in the city as traders during the previous century. Their absence from the archaeological record is also notable since Native Americans remained a common part of New Orleans's urban landscape as itinerant traders in the markets. There was even an "Indian" market house built on the Bayou Road in the city during the early American period (Usner 1998). Just as a native presence was symbolized in the Native American pots found in colonial households, the absence of heirloom pots in the subsequent period symbolizes the removal of their symbolic and political authority in the city's development. No longer were Native American ways of life, such as gift exchange, a part of mainstream New Orleans culture. Nor were the threat of Indian attacks or the protection of Indian alliances key factors in political life. With Americanization, Native Americans not only became outnumbered for the first time, but they also became outsiders in their own territory or, as they were once described, "fragments of an erratic race" (cited in Usner 1998:118–19).

In the colonial period, Native American ceramics were part of New Orleans culture and New Orleans was part Indian. The Native American incorporation of the French into their gift-exchange system is one example of creolization. The process, however, had changed by the American period, taking on a new connotation that tied being Indian to segregational notions of race.

MADAME JOHN'S LEGACY (16OR51)

A National Historic Landmark, the standing structure known as Madame John's Legacy is a well-known stop on today's walking tours of New Orleans. Located on Dumaine Street in the French Quarter, this "French Indies"–style house is a rare representative of the architecture that typified the town in the French colonial period. Already a landmark in the 1880s, its lore grew when George Washington

Cable chose it for the setting of an imaginative story that gave it its name. For the entire French period, the site was owned by a French woman named Elizabeth Real, who operated an inn there with the help of her two ship-captain husbands (the first was also an Indian trader who was killed in the Natchez Rebellion). In the Spanish period, the site was occupied by a well-known smuggler, followed by the captain of the Spanish regiment and his daughters. In the early American period, it passed into the family of Louisiana's first American governor (Dawdy 1998).

Excavations at the site by Richard Shenkel (1972) and later by Shannon Dawdy (1998) uncovered evidence of the 1788 fire and the house's reconstruction that same year. Dawdy's excavations in the rear courtyard included a spectacularly well-preserved trash pit dating to the 1788 fire. It contained the household's burned contents, a much larger and more representative sample of material possessions than archaeologists usually collect, as well as food-preparation remains dating to some months prior to the fire. Artifacts included a smoke-stained set of creamware plates and bowls, bone buttons from burned clothing, and a large amount of animal bone. Below and above this trash pit were deposits associated with the French colonial and early American occupations.

As at the St. Augustine site, Madame John's Legacy produced a surprisingly large number of Native American pots, in a diversity of sizes, types, and decorations (Figure 16.3). The largest sample dates to the 1788 fire, suggesting that in the Spanish period Indian diplomatic ties, and perhaps even Native American aesthetics, were still very much a force in local culture. The deposits from this same feature also contained a very large number of British ceramics. Trade with the British and Americans was tightly regulated, and many items were outright banned by the Spanish. However, the results from investigations of this site and others suggests that the late colonial economy of New Orleans was a healthy one—thanks in large part to smuggling.

The fact that the house passed from one smuggler's family (François Marin) to another's (Rene Beluche) is not all that remarkable when one considers the evidence that smuggling was a primary source of consumer goods in eighteenth-century New Orleans. Governor's wives and army captains, as well as merchants and slaves who traveled between town and plantation, were all implicated in the contraband trade. According to official ledger books, the export economy of New Orleans prior to the sugar boom of the 1790s was abysmal, but Madame Real had the means to purchase gilt mirrors and multiple sets of fine china from the proceeds of her husbands' intercoastal trade and from her hospitality to traders arriving from other (often outlawed) ports (Dawdy 1998). Smuggling activity in and around New Orleans continued relatively unabated during the three periods of colonization. By creating wealth that was dependent upon intimate local connections, smuggling assisted in the creation of a tight-knit and socially conservative Creole community (Dawdy 2008). New members of the community were adopted through the farflung Caribbean connections that this trade encouraged—from places like Cartagena, Vera Cruz, and the west coast of Cuba. These traders from many nations spoke a common language of economic independence from European domination. To avoid sanctions, members of this community needed to trust one another, often across divisions of language, race, and class. This economy, like the frontier gift exchange between the French and the Indians, was a way in which the circulation of goods created conditions of creolization.

Among the favorite things smuggled into New Orleans were luxury foods, including fine white flour and French red wine. Food and diet are another source of information about people's daily lives in New Orleans that reflect the process of creolization. Elizabeth Scott's analysis of the faunal remains from Madame John's Legacy, the Maginnis site, and the St. Augustine site (discussed above) confirms that French colonial residents used a wide variety of species in their environment, especially compared to British contemporaries (Scott and Dawdy 2010). However, as with the evidence from Native American pottery, the deposits from later Spanish and antebellum levels yielded evidence of a diet even richer in wild game and fish than in the early French period. This suggests Native American influence on local foodways taking hold, with the creole generations coming of age in the mid eighteenth century and with the movement of Native Americans into the city following the Natchez Rebellion. Further, this creole diet was fairly conservative well into the antebellum period, despite the growth of commercial food markets in the urban center. A wide selection of wild game and fish, therefore, appears to be an established feature of New Orleans Creole cuisine by the 1780s, although no restaurants or cookbooks of that genre were to appear for another hundred years.

Wild species identified in the faunal collections include swamp rabbit, ducks, passenger pigeon, turtles, and several kinds of fish. At the St. Augustine site, deer, opossum, turtles, and fish accounted for 15.7 percent of the estimated meat weight. While one might think that the more rural location of the St. Augustine Plantation would result in much greater use of wild resources than the urban site, this does not seem to have been the case. The evidence suggests that many wild birds and fish (and probably the rabbits) were available in New Orleans through markets or self-provisioning by households. Archival research and analysis of pottery also suggests that Native American ingredients were being incorporated into traditional French and African dishes. Archaeobotanical evidence from these same sites demonstrated the very early incorporation and late retention of Native American plant crops, such as an early form of Dent corn and *Nicotiana rustica*, a strong Native American species of tobacco that may be one source of Louisiana's novelty, perique tobacco (Dawdy et al. 2002).

The diet of these three diverse households (an inn and middle-class residence, a plantation with enslaved workers, and an elite suburban residence) were more similar than different. One further surprise is that Americanization did not bring a major shift in what New Orleanians were eating in the early antebellum period. Food consumption is another cultural vector for creolization, which is particularly helpful in illustrating the syncopated two-step of its cycle. Initially, Native American, European, and African ingredients were selected and recombined. This produced a new (though not unchanging) Creole cooking tradition. Anglo-American immigrants then adopted the local Creole food culture in an act of assimilation. The reasons that they more willingly adopted this facet of local Creole culture than others relates to issues of gender and race. In the early antebellum period, the vast majority of English-speaking immigrants were white males, while the vast majority of the cooks were women and/or enslaved Afro-Louisianans. Resisting Creole food would have meant taking over the aprons and pots of the kitchen, which probably held no interest for the masculine entrepreneurs of the boomtown era. They allowed cooking to remain a female, black, and/or Creole domain.

RISING SUN HOTEL (16OR225)

In 2004–2005, Shannon Lee Dawdy and Earth Search, Inc., jointly conducted an excavation at the planned site of a new building for the Historic New Orleans Collection (Dawdy, Gray et al. 2008). Located near the corner of Conti and Chartres Street in the French Quarter, this site had several occupations that were well-documented by archival or archaeological sources, and in several cases by a combination of the two. They included a protohistoric Native American encampment, a French colonial garden, a Spanish colonial structure (burned in 1794), a guesthouse or inn run by a widow from 1796 to 1809 (where William Clark of the Lewis and Clark expedition lived for a time), an early nineteenth-century coffeehouse and hotel, and a hotel and tavern combination in a wooden frame structure, named the Rising Sun Hotel, which operated briefly before burning to the ground in 1822. A large number of cosmetic rouge pots of French manufacture were found in the 1822 fire level, leading to speculation that this hotel may have been the brothel of folk-song fame.

While it may be impossible for archaeology to answer such a loaded question, the long occupation of this site does provide evidence of a very old and enduring hospitality tradition in New Orleans. This was another means by which creolization occurred through practices of consumption. The inns, boarding houses, and hotels of New Orleans offered Creole culture for sale in the form of food and the aesthetics of domestic interiors, if not in more personal attentions. By 1818, visitor Benjamin LaTrobe was already dazzled by the juxtaposition of the familiar and the exotic in the city's households and markets. While not as self-consciously mannered as latter-day marketing to tourists, the hospitality components at Madame John's Legacy and at the Rising Sun Hotel sites demonstrate a certain conservatism in ceramic forms and in French imports—such as Bordeaux wine and French cosmetics—that may have been chosen to please visitors.

The zooarchaeological analysis of food remains from the hospitality components of the site indicate a diversity of fish, wild birds and ducks, and other game in the French and Spanish period, but a switch to large inexpensive cuts of beef, pork, and mutton/goat during the early American period, with a surprising absence of fish (deFrance and Cannarozzi 2009). During the later, more upscale hotel occupation (the Conti Verandah Hotel, ca. 1825–1887), however, wild game in the form of deer, rabbit, and fish return as staples in the hospitality fare, perhaps as ingredients of the new Creole cuisine that emerged as a marketable form for tourists and local connoisseurs in the mid-nineteenth century through cookbooks and restaurants. The recognizable "Frenchness" and "Creolité" of New Orleans are not simply products of its history. They are consumable constructions of its history (Dawdy and Weyhing 2008). Creolization and consumption are both ways of defining what "home" is. Together, they define a charming hospitality, which is why so many guests over the generations have "gone native" and made New Orleans their home.

Conclusion

In the historic period, New Orleans was colonized three times—by the French, by the Spanish, and by the Americans. Each phase brought tremendous demographic and economic changes that transformed the landscape of the city. At the same time, by the second generation of settlement, the city had developed a remarkably stable local culture that was built out of elements of its Indian-, African-, and French-descended residents. Patterns of consumption in Native American pottery, in food, in smuggled luxuries, and in French imports demonstrate some of the powerful material dimensions of creolization.

While we have here used landscape to discuss change and colonization, and consumption to discuss continuity and creolization, the alignment between these forms of archaeological data and the phenomena we have described are not fixed. Other combinations are possible and likely. Certain elements of the landscape have, in fact, been virtually impervious to change and may be credited to creole conservatism, such as the post-1790s architecture of the French Quarter, or the layout of the confusing radial street grid of New Orleans, which corresponds to the boundaries of old French plantations. The memory of these privileged Creole spaces is preserved in the names of neighborhoods such as "Marigny" and "Bouligny." Consumption may be a more obvious source of change-through-assimilation rather than continuity-through-creolization. Native Americans readily adopted not only the functional items of European manufacture, such as guns and knives, but also cloth and beads. Pursuit of these goods then drew them deeper into economic exchanges with Europeans that forever altered their way of life. And the consumption of sugar radically transformed the ecology of southeastern Louisiana.

Given the complexity of the city's stratigraphic past, the archaeology of early New Orleans has only scratched the surface of what can be learned from the material evidence of daily life. The projects reviewed here have laid the foundation of a major new comprehensive research program to investigate the city's colonial past. This five-year effort began in 2008 with a season of excavation in the garden directly behind St. Louis Cathedral (Dawdy, Gremillion et al. 2008). The early results from this site (called St. Antoine's Garden, 16OR443) confirm in rich detail many of the preliminary sketches produced by earlier work. A high concentration (approximately 50 percent) of Native American pottery, in addition to native-made smoking pipes and chert hide scrapers, attests to the exchanges among French Louisiana's diverse population. Analysis of the archaeobotanical and faunal remains provides evidence of a ready adoption of wild local resources. And a pre-1722 hut that appears to be made of woven palmetto walls and square-hewn timbers may be our earliest example yet of creole architecture in Louisiana. As their research goes forward, archaeologists hope to tackle other questions, such as the material effects of African slavery in the creolization process, in collaborative practices such as gardening and cuisine; the role of religious institutions in daily life; and how public spaces were used under evolving rules about race and class.

17

Immigration and Urbanization in New Orleans

D. RYAN GRAY AND JILL-KAREN YAKUBIK

The city of New Orleans grew rapidly after the Louisiana Purchase (A.D. 1803), from a sometimes neglected colonial backwater of approximately 8,000 residents to a booming port metropolis of nearly 175,000 by A.D. 1860. As it gained in importance as an entrepôt for goods exported from the rich Mississippi River Valley, settlers from throughout the United States moved into the city seeking to make their fortunes. These ranged from the rough-hewn "Kaintuck" boatmen, who transported wares downriver by flatboat to New Orleans and then legendarily populated the barrooms, billiard halls, and gambling dives of the riverfront and backswamp, to the wealthy businessmen who dealt in the import and export of plantation commodities. Soon afterwards, poor European immigrants, particularly those of Irish and German origin, also poured into the city. While these antebellum years are often considered the "golden age" of New Orleans (and are marketed as such to this day), the realities of life for the urban poor, for working-class immigrants, for African American slaves, and even for New Orleans's large population of *gens de couleur libre* (free persons of color) were not idyllic. Immigrants and the urban poor lived and worked in oppressive conditions, often on the swampy margins of the city, where they were susceptible to epidemics of yellow fever and other endemic diseases. Much of the wealth of the city, stemming from trade in sugar and cotton, was built from the labor of enslaved African Americans. Although urban slaves may have fared somewhat better than those on plantations, they also lived in a world where they had no reliable legal rights, and they or their family members could be sold at any time. Even the African American *gens de couleur libre* elite saw their position eroded throughout the 1850s, as their own rights were increasingly circumscribed.

The city continued to grow through the years of postwar Reconstruction, Jim Crow racial segregation, and into the modern era, reaching its peak population of over 600,000 in 1960. In the late 1800s and early 1900s, new groups of European immigrants arrived, especially from Italy and Eastern Europe. The

African American population increased as well, as freedmen left plantations and came to the city to start new lives. To accommodate this growth, residences were converted into boarding houses and tenements, families took in lodgers to make ends meet, and environmentally marginal or low-lying wetlands were developed (Colten 2005:16–76; Lewis 2003). Health and sanitation continued to be issues that plagued the city, eventually culminating in large-scale slum-clearance projects beginning in the late 1930s. Social and racial relations in the city were turbulent and occasionally marked by violence, including the race riots of 1866 and 1900, the so-called "Battle of Liberty Place" of 1874, the lynching of Italian prisoners in 1891, and intermittent labor conflicts in the docks, rail yards, and breweries.

A great deal of historical research on New Orleans has focused on the growth and development of ethnic enclaves and bounded neighborhoods, which has brought much-needed attention to the role of diverse ethnic groups in shaping the modern city (e.g., Blassingame 1973; Campanella 2006; Korn 1969; Lewis 2003; Nau 1958; Niehaus 1965). Differences in ethnicity and race certainly structured the social lives of the city's residents. Nevertheless, these varied lives were inextricably linked. Recent archaeological projects in New Orleans have allowed us to examine the formation and maintenance of distinct ethnic identities in the city, even while increasing our understanding of the commonalities in the experiences of these diverse groups. Such topics are more relevant than ever since August 29, 2005, in the destructive wake of Hurricane Katrina. For the urban poor, whose stories are often neglected in historical accounts, archaeology provides a unique source of evidence about their daily lives.

Archaeology of Nineteenth-Century New Orleans: Foundations

Until quite recently, a great deal of the most intensive archaeological work in New Orleans was focused primarily in or around the Vieux Carré, with a corresponding emphasis on the colonial period (see Dawdy and Matthews, Chapter 16 in this volume). Nevertheless, many of those projects identified substantial nineteenth-century components, including a series of excavations at the Hermann-Grima House (16OR45) on St. Louis Street (Beavers and Lamb 1993; Beavers et al. 1988, 1990; Lamb and Beavers 1983; Lamb et al. 1985; Shenkel 1977), excavations at the Congo Square and Jazz Complex sites (16OR47 and 16OR48) in the Faubourg Tremé (Shenkel et al. 1979), and investigations at the Gallier House (16OR46) on Royal Street (Hudson 1972). The utility of some of the reports of these investigations is hampered by occasionally idiosyncratic analytical techniques and methodologies, particularly with regard to reporting of ceramic wares, and little interpretive context for the later materials recovered. Several of these projects shared common themes, such as the identification of archaeological markers of ethnic difference and/or socioeconomic status.

Probably the best reported of the projects in the vicinity of the French Quarter dating from this period was a series of test excavations at lots near the corner of Esplanade and N. Rampart Streets (Castille et al. 1982). Excavations at the New Orleans Post Office site (16OR63) examined two historic house lots. The first was a residential compound typical of the antebellum slaveholding South, consisting of a primary residence and yard with a servants' quarters and/or kitchen, storerooms, stables, and other outbuildings. The second consisted of the location of a more modest residence. The goals of the excavations were to compare the two lots in order to investigate the layout of urban compounds, to compare social and status differences (particularly since the second lot was the antebellum residence of a free person of color), to examine the material aspects of urban slavery, and to document economic networks represented in the material assemblage. While the excavations were able to refine a middle-class urban residential pattern, the lack of contemporaneous, dense feature deposits between the two lots made further comparisons difficult. It was also noted that an artifact pattern for urban slavery would be difficult to identify because most relevant urban deposits probably represent a mixture of materials associated with slaves and owners (Castille et al. 1982:1/3–1/7, 6/1–6/5).

Other projects around the city have also increased the body of available data for the study of nineteenth- and early twentieth-century New Orleans (Figure 17.1). Excavations at Algiers Point on the West Bank of the Mississippi River were hampered by a deficiency of documentary information, but they nonetheless produced assemblages that could be related to working-class and middle-class occupations (Goodwin et al. 1984:179–195). Research at the New Orleans General Hospital site (16OR69) in the Lower Garden District focused on what had been the location of a suburban plantation's sugar house, which was later converted into an orphanage dormitory. However, the majority of materials from the site dated to the subsequent (post-1866) development of modest residences on that city block. While analysis of material from the site produced insight into refuse disposal patterns, lack of a detailed contextual history for the late nineteenth-century occupation of the block hampered further interpretation (Goodwin and Yakubik 1982:83–96, 180–187). Finally, a series of test excavations in the Holy Cross Historic District, although not as horizontally extensive as some of the others outlined here, demonstrated the usefulness of computer-

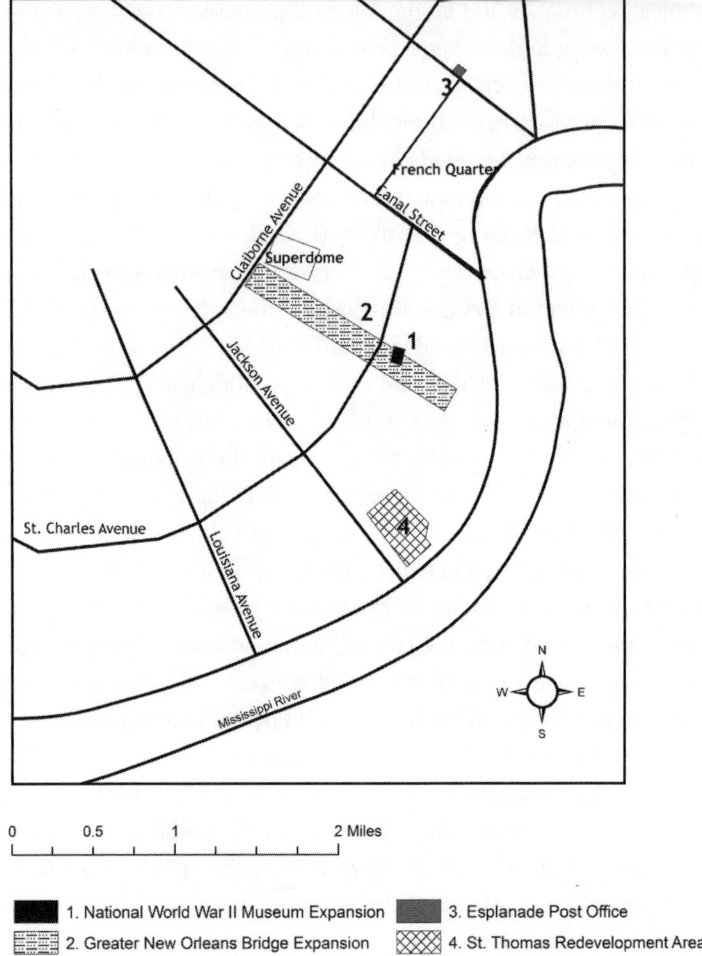

Fig. 17.1. Locations of selected New Orleans projects discussed in the text.

aided-design (CAD) overlays of historic and modern maps in targeting specific areas of urban lots for testing (Franks et al. 1991; Yakubik and Franks 1992).

The most intensive and fully reported archaeological investigations of nineteenth-century urban New Orleans were those undertaken in conjunction with the Greater New Orleans Bridge No. 2 expansion. During this project, a total of fourteen city squares were tested, with detailed historical research complementing targeted excavations. Objectives of the project included further refinement of the urban residential unit defined at the Esplanade and N. Rampart site, the examination of social and economic variation among residential units (particularly with respect to immigrant households), and the investigation of the commercial and industrial use of the batture (the land between the river and the levee) in the project area (Castille et al. 1986:1/1–2/7; see Dargo 1975:74–101 on the batture controversy). The wealth of artifactual material that was recovered demonstrated more than ever the complexities of working with urban assemblages. For example, while attempts to define broad consumption patterns based upon ethnicity (particularly with regards to Irish, German, and Italian households) or socioeconomic class (as defined by occupation and/or nativity) were occasionally compelling when applied within specific artifact groups, the results would often appear contradictory when employed more widely (Castille et al. 1986:7/9–7/23; cf. Davoli 1998). Nevertheless, the corpus of data provided by these investigations continues to be an invaluable source for research and comparison.

Recent Archaeological Investigations in New Orleans

Following the development of post-processual archaeology since the 1980s, recent urban historical archaeology has embraced an interpretive approach, in which the meanings of material remains are based upon discrete contexts rather than placement in broad or predictable patterns (Hodder 1986; e.g., Praetzellis and Praetzellis, ed. 2004; Praetzellis, ed. 2004). In the modern era, even as capitalism provided an ideological backdrop for the growth of American cities, various forms of social identity and inequality were contested, negotiated, reproduced, or rejected (Orser 2007:57–59). As evidence of consumption practices that are intimately connected to social relations in capitalist society, the archaeological record is uniquely suited to critically examine the diverse experiences of a city's population, particularly with regard to the urban poor and other groups who are not otherwise well-represented in the historical record (Leone 1995; Leone et al. 1987; Mullins 2004). Increased numbers of large, urban archaeological projects have been typically undertaken by private cultural resource management (CRM) firms in response to the requirements specified in Section 106 of the National Historic Preservation Act (see Byrd and Neuman, Chapter 2 in this volume). These projects have incorporated elements of an interpretive, contextual approach in order to better understand the numerous strategies by which identities were negotiated in a society structured by capitalism and, in the case of post-emancipation New Orleans, Jim Crow segregation.

A great deal of recent archaeological work has resulted from the redevelopment of many of the city's major public housing projects. This has stemmed in part from discoveries in the summer of 1999 at the Iberville Housing Project, just outside of the modern French Quarter. During maintenance work on underground utilities alongside a building, observers reported seeing large amounts of bone and cultural materials in construction back dirt. Archaeologists were called to the scene because of the proximity of the site to St. Louis Cemetery No. 1, the oldest extant cemetery in the city, and fears that human burials might have been disturbed. While none of the bone was human, intact archaeological deposits from historic house lots on City Square 130 (16OR180) were recorded just outside the footprint of the existing structure. The Iberville Housing Project was constructed around 1940, practically obliterating all of the above-ground architectural remnants of New Orleans's Storyville, one of the nation's most notorious red-light districts. While archaeological remains associated with this era (1898–1917) garnered the most publicity (e.g., Gray 2003; Powell 2002), the majority of the materials dated to the antebellum period, when newly subdivided lots had rapidly filled with a mixture of Creole tradesmen, free persons of color, and European immigrants (Gray et al. 2003). One striking aspect of the assemblage was the age of its earliest deposits. These appeared to date to the very beginning of the nineteenth century, when the block in question was part of the nominally undeveloped City Commons area. This suggests that official historical records, in portraying a neat and orderly development of the city, actually obscure the growth on its fringes, where the urban poor were pushed into environmentally marginal areas. As the city continued to develop, such areas became the interstices where issues of space, ownership, and social relations were contested, and are still contested today (Gray 2004, 2009a).

In the fall of 2000, the Housing Authority of New Orleans (HANO) began the demolition of the St. Thomas Housing Project adjacent to the Lower Garden District, as part of a massive Hope VI redevelopment that would replace dilapidated public housing with mixed-income residences (Figure 17.1). Based on the work at the Iberville Housing Project, it was anticipated that archaeological deposits would be disturbed during redevelopment. Archaeologists worked with developers and contractors to identify, test, and monitor especially sensitive areas for the presence of historically significant cultural remains. Eventually, five city blocks were selected for intensive excavations: City Square 102 (16OR153), City Square 70 (16OR163), City Square 39 (16OR159), City Square 32 (16OR170), and City Square 33 (16OR177). City Square 102 was the location of the St. Joseph Orphan Asylum, a Catholic orphanage founded in response to the yellow fever epidemic of 1853. City Squares 70 and 39 were mixed-use residential and commercial blocks, and City Square 32 was located along Adele Street, often cited as the original Irish Channel of New Orleans (Campanella 2006:227–230, Saxon et al. 1991:50–75). Finally, City Square 33 was selected because of the age of the recovered materials. Early urban deposits there were preserved beneath fill that was associated with the construction of a cotton warehouse in the 1850s.

To date, the best reported of the investigated blocks is City Square 70 (16OR163), the block historically bounded by Annunciation, St. Mary, Chippewa, and Felicity Streets (Gray 2005, Gray, Maygarden, Weed et al. 2010). Attention was initially drawn to the block by a preliminary analysis of historical documents conducted by Fifield and Bethea (1999), which was subsequently expanded. Although a number of structural features and sheet-midden deposits were excavated in Square 70, three privy (or outhouse) pits with artifact-rich, temporally-discrete fill provided the best archaeological samples from the block. Each deposit and assemblage was associated with a household from which it likely originated, including that of a middle-class Irish family from the 1880s, a Jewish clothing merchant and his son, an attorney from the early 1900s, and an African American laborer from the 1920s. The various residents provide both an indication of the diversity of the neighborhood in this period and suggest demographic changes on the block over time. These assemblages are discussed more extensively below.

The assemblage from Square 33 (16OR177), a block fronting Tchoupitoulas Street, was quite different. A cotton warehouse complex, the Pelican Cotton Press, was built on the block in 1854. Layers of fill associated with its construction preserved earlier archaeological remains, which apparently dated from the development of the block between the 1820s and the 1850s, when it was part of the rapidly urbanizing community of Lafayette (not to be confused with the modern city of the same name; see Briede 1937). Lafayette city directories show the corner lot, where excavations were focused, as the location of a billiard hall and "coffee house," a euphemism for a tavern by the 1840s. Despite difficult working conditions, a large number of features were excavated, including a brick patio, building footings, a trash pit filled with wine bottle and tumbler fragments, and a well. Large quantities of decorated pearlware type tablewares and jugs were recovered, along with additional fragments of wine bottles, animal bone, and pipe stems and bowls, including two with Masonic motifs. In contrast with other urban sites, practically no artifacts associated with children occurred at the site, further substantiating its association with the barrooms and flophouses populated by transient boatmen flocking to the city in the antebellum years (Gray 2004; Gray, Maygarden, Orton et al. 2010).

During the investigation of the St. Joseph Orphan Asylum (16OR153), a well, a privy, building footings, trash pits, and other features associated with the orphanage were excavated. The orphanage remained in operation up until the 1930s, and two former residents were interviewed as part of the investigation, providing additional perspective on the project. Large numbers of fragments from nearly identical sets of porcelain plates and annular ironstone bowls suggested the institutional character of life at the site. A collection of unmatched buttons attested to the fact that most of the orphans' clothing consisted of hand-me-downs donated by neighborhood residents, as confirmed by the informants. Religious figurines and medals, lice combs, toothbrushes, dolls, and marbles further suggested the details of day-to-day life in the orphanage. Further analysis of large quantities of faunal remains from the well and privy will undoubtedly provide information on diet and health at the orphanage (Gray 2002; Gray, Maygarden, Smith et al. 2010).

A number of other large-scale urban projects have been undertaken in the years since Hurricane Katrina. A series of excavations conducted in conjunction with the expansion of the National World War II Museum in downtown New Orleans incorporated detailed demographic research to inform interpretations of materials representing a broad spectrum of the city's inhabitants (Maygarden et al. 2005). A privy and barrel well associated with a home belonging to Joseph Maybin (1795–1876), the founder of New Orleans's first Presbyterian church, contained hundreds of ceramic vessels, glass containers, and personal items, including chess pieces, letterpress printing type, and a set of dentures (Gray 2006; Pokrant et al. 2010). The changing character of the neighborhood was demonstrated by a diverse array of features, which were associated with wealthy antebellum slaveholding merchants, consumptive Irish carpenters, first- and second-generation immigrants crowded into boarding houses, and a small Norwegian enclave centered on a seaman's chapel. Perhaps most unique are excavations focusing on a laundry operated by a Chinese immigrant who lived and worked at the site from 1889 to nearly 1920. Artifact analyses and historical research have provided new perspectives on the relationship of material culture to the formation of a distinctly Chinese-American ethnicity in the American South (Gray 2009b; Gray, Maygarden, Eppler et al. 2010).

This discussion is by no means exhaustive. Other projects, while primarily focused on earlier site components, have recovered significant cultural remains dating to later periods (Dawdy and Matthews, Chapter 16 in this volume; e.g., Dawdy and Ibanez 1997). The controversial demolition of more public housing following Hurricane Katrina initiated even more large-scale investigations (Gray,

Godzinski et al. 2008; Godzinski and Gray 2008). Still other projects have been initiated ad hoc, for the specific purposes of testing or evaluation. Some of these have significantly added to the corpus of knowledge about archaeological deposits in the city (e.g., Godzinski et al. 2002; Hardy et al. 2002; Lee et al. 1997), and many more CRM projects are building on this body of data.

People in the Past: Immigration, Labor, and Consumption

While a detailed discussion of all these projects is beyond the scope of this chapter, further discussion of the lots investigated at St. Thomas Square 70 will illustrate how recent archaeological projects are incorporating detailed historical research in order to better explore the ways in which the ideological structures of capitalism and racial segregation affected the social lives of people in New Orleans. The material record can help to identify the myriad strategies with which individuals and groups negotiated, contested, conformed to, and transformed these ideologies in their daily practices.

In 1861, Zachary Bruenn, a Prussian-born Jewish clothing merchant, purchased a lot within Square 70 at 111 to 113 St. Mary Street. Bruenn proceeded to build a large, two-story double residence with wraparound galleries on the property. Initially, he rented one side of this property to an Irish drayman (a wagon driver) and his family for extra income. Later, as Bruenn's fortunes improved, he bought adjacent homes to use as rentals, and his family came to occupy the entire residence. Bruenn resided at this home until his death in 1912 at the age of ninety. His son Bernard, a successful attorney who also lived at what is now 729-731 St. Mary Street, died from a stroke only four years later. The younger Bruenn was known for his liberalism and sympathy to Republican causes, even while working in cooperation with the local Democratic Party (Fortier 1914:72–74). After 1916, Zachary Bruenn's daughter retained possession of the house and rented it out. By 1920, it was occupied by a Russian grocer and his family on one side and an Irish fireman with his wife and child on the other.

Much of the footprint of the Bruenn house was obliterated by one of the buildings from the 1939 housing project. However, some features associated with the rear yard of the property were preserved. These included a brick-lined privy shaft with a smoothly plastered interior surface. Excavation of this feature provided the best artifactual sample for the household. The privy was apparently cleaned regularly while in active use by the family, as required by an often-ignored city ordinance. A distinctive layer of sandy fill at the bottom of the feature appeared to be associated with a house-cleaning episode, probably

Fig. 17.2. Selection of artifacts from the Bruenn household assemblage, including snuff bottles (upper left) and chamber pot with Classical motif (center).

from the time of Bernard's death rather than Zachary's, as indicated by the presence of a 1913 penny. A number of ceramic vessels were associated with this fill, including soap dishes, a wash pitcher, a Rockingham mixing bowl, porcelain tableware, and a tall manganese-glazed redware vase with a scalloped rim. A gilt and transfer-printed chamber pot decorated with a classical motif is probably the most striking vessel in the ceramic assemblage. Also worth mentioning are two Victorian English majolica seashell sauce dishes, possibly related to an aquarium listed in Bernard Bruenn's succession inventory (Fifield and Bethea 1999). The glassware from the privy was dominated by intact snuff bottles, of which at least eight were recovered, although schnapps bottles, a bottle of Doctor Pesholdt's German Bitters, and a number of elaborate glass tablewares were also present (Figure 17.2). The faunal assemblage from the feature was perhaps even more distinctive. It consisted predominantly of birds (including chicken, turkey, duck, and goose) and fish (trout and other unidentifiable species), instead of the more common large domesticated mammals. The faunal remains may suggest a kosher dietary pattern, despite the presence of crab claws (as the consumption of shellfish would have been prohibited).

Even more intriguing was a single deposit occurring on top of the artifact-laden sand associated with the previously described cleaning episode. This deposit consisted of a piece of slate covered in fish scales, small fish bone fragments, and fragments of egg shell. This grouping of materials is consistent with the *se'udat havra'ah* (Hebrew for "community meal"), the traditional Jewish feast of mourning. This meal generally takes place soon after a loved one's funeral and includes food items symbolically associated with life and fertility, particularly eggs and lentils. Fish are considered the only appropriate meat to serve with this meal, as the consumption of meat from most domesticated animals is associated with celebration rather than mourning. While the ethnobotanical remains from this feature have not yet been analyzed, they could provide additional support for this interpretation. The cleaning episode represented by the feature fill, and the remains of this meal on top of it, might be seen as evidence of a series of events connected to the death of Bernard Bruenn, perhaps carried out by his sister. While the recovered materials seem to indicate an association with Jewish cultural traditions, there are also signs of tension in the household. As noted earlier, crab is forbidden by Jewish dietary law. In addition, a ceramic crucifix suggests a non-Jewish resident in the Bruenn household or someone who was perhaps not averse to possessing the trappings of Christianity. Such findings must be placed in the social context of the Jewish community in New Orleans during this period.

The Jewish community in New Orleans played a strong and influential role in the city, and individuals such as the philanthropist Judah Touro were greatly respected (Korn 1969). Nevertheless, with increased prevalence during the late nineteenth and early twentieth centuries, Jews were excluded from clubs and organizations maintained by the city's elite, even while an influx of Orthodox Eastern European Jews fostered class heterogeneity within the existing community (Campanella 2006:266–270; Gill 1997:177–178). Bernard Bruenn himself was a Freemason. While policies regarding the religious affiliations of members varied widely from lodge to lodge at that time, the assemblage hints that Bernard Bruenn may have sought to draw attention away from his heritage in his business and political contacts, even while privately maintaining some Jewish traditions. While the information presently available from the archaeological record is tentative at best, it does suggest some of the tensions and ambiguities that existed for a successful Jewish family living in a discriminatory society.

Just a few doors down from the home of the Bruenn family, on St. Mary Street, a row of small brick cottages was constructed by the 1850s. These cottages were occupied by a crowded and shifting array of renters. In 1880, the residents consisted mainly of first-generation Irish and German immigrants and their extended families. Most of the men are listed in the census simply as laborers, and many of the women are listed as washerwomen or domestic servants. By 1920, this particular row of cottages was inhabited almost exclusively by African American families, even while other portions of the block remained ethnically diverse. The occupations listed for the residents of the row present an interesting cross-section of working-class New Orleans, including a grocery warehouseman, laborers in a molasses factory, a pickle works, and a bedspring factory, cotton mill workers, a pecan huller, a cook, and two longshoremen (one of whom, James Samuels, was racially identified as black, but was listed as being of Portuguese and Palestinian extraction).

A single privy associated with this row of cottages was identified and excavated. It appears to have been filled with trash sometime around 1920, based on the latest dated artifacts. Because of the rapid turnover of renters in most of these residences, the household with which the assemblage from the privy was associated cannot be determined with complete certainty. However, the most likely candidate is George Tiles, a twenty-four-year-old Alabama-born black longshoreman. He and his wife, a maid, shared the tiny cottage with Louis Burns, a twenty-four-year-old chauffeur. Burns's wife, Ethel, was employed as a washerwoman. As representatives of the black working class at the beginning of the twentieth century, families like the Tileses and the Burnses found themselves in a nearly untenable position. Riverfront commerce, particularly as it related to the timely shipping of cotton, continued to be the cornerstone of New Orleans's economy after the Civil War. During times of prosperity, when there was plenty of work on the docks, black and white cotton screwmen, longshoremen, teamsters, draymen, and other dockworkers cooperated with each other in an unprecedented manner. This is best expressed in the biracial Cotton Men's Executive Council of the 1880s and the Dock and Cotton Council of the early 1900s. Sometimes these unions could wield power even beyond the docks, as in 1907, when they joined brewery workers in a strike. As the Jim Crow policies of racial segregation surged, however, racist opposition to social equality was used by business leaders to create schisms in the biracial labor movement. Black workers increasingly found themselves in the position of either accepting the lower wages offered by employers, or negotiating in conjunction with white unions but still finding themselves relegated to the more menial and lower-paying jobs (Arnesen 1994; Rosenberg 1988). The area including City Square 70, with its close proximity to the docks, racially mixed demographics, and large population of dockworkers, is often mentioned in historic accounts of labor activities of the period.

A rich artifactual record was recovered from the privy, including numerous ceramic and glass vessels. Fragments of nearly one hundred ceramic vessels were recovered, mostly ironstone, porcelaineous stoneware, and porcelain tablewares. Matched vessels were scarce, and decorations varied widely. The assemblage was noteworthy in the presence of substantial numbers of outdated wares—for example, an ironstone plate manufactured by England's Turner, Goddard, and Company between 1867 and 1874. Such variety and curation of ceramic wares has been noted in other urban African American assemblages as evidence of an economic strategy of thrift (e.g., Warner 1998). An equally wide range of glass container forms was identified, including a variety of nationally marketed patent medicines, proprietary bottles from local druggists, liquor bottles, storage jars, ink bottles, condiment containers, goblets, and tumblers. Many other artifacts were recovered from the trash deposit, including irrigation syringes, toothbrushes, pipe bowls (including one decorated with what may be a design associated with a fraternal order or benevolent association), jewelry, rosary beads, harmonica reed plates, and a number of examples of the Victorian bric-a-brac discussed at length by Mullins (1999). All of these things together suggest a household that was very much a part of consumer life in the city. The presence of pistol bullets in the assemblage may reflect a more pragmatic approach to survival and self-defense in the often racially charged atmosphere of the time. Small quantities of bone from deer and wood duck suggest that hunting augmented the food supply from local markets. Fish provided a further source of nourishment, as indicated by bones from catfish, jack, and sheepshead.

Another privy from a residence on St. Mary Street was partially preserved beneath the foundation of a St. Thomas Housing Project building. The privy was filled soon after 1884, based upon the date on a coin from the fill. The majority of the households in the vicinity in 1880 were comprised of working-class Irish-American families. This privy may have been associated with a rental property at 109 St. Mary, which was occupied by carpenter Leon Cummings in 1891. A number of bottles, ceramic vessels, objects relating to health and hygiene, toys, and personal items (including a rosary, a bottle filled with a collection of buttons, and a watch fob with a benevolent society seal) were recovered from the privy during a salvage excavation of intact portions of the feature. Although this privy appears to have been filled at least thirty years before the one associated with the African American residence, many of the ceramic wares were virtually indistinguishable, including identical Rockingham pitchers and ironstone vessels with the same flow black-printed sailing ship pattern. Domestic mammals, such as cow, pig, and sheep/goat, were represented in the faunal assemblage, along with chicken, turkey, and less common species like duck, goose, frog, and turtle. Freshwater catfish bones were numerous, and freshwater drum, red and black drum, and sea catfish also were present. Non-food animals were common as well, as multiple litters of puppies and kittens were identified.

Overall, the assemblage from the privy associated with Irish laborers had a great deal in common with the one associated with African American workers deposited approximately thirty years later. Both revealed a willingness to supplement diet with a wide range of animals, at least some of which could have been obtained outside of the regular market economy, through hunting and fishing. Such strategies could have helped alleviate food shortages in times of economic adversity, such as seasonal fluctuations in the availability of dock jobs. Ceramic wares in each of these assemblages were quite distinct from the fashionable wares occurring in the Bruenn assemblage. Snuff bottles, common in the Bruenn assemblage, were absent from the other features, where pipes were common. While each of the artifact assemblages is interesting by itself, it is in comparing these three very different households that we can better understand how such individuals made up the unique and changing city that is New Orleans.

Conclusions

Events beginning with the landfall of Hurricane Katrina in August 2005 have dramatically altered the city of New Orleans. Many today have looked at the development of the city and pointed to its smaller historical footprint, confined to the higher ground of natural levees, as a model for the New Orleans of the future. Others see such proposals as a means by which large segments of the population, especially the poor and the middle class, will be separated from their past and disenfranchised in the future (e.g., Marable and Clark, ed. 2008; Steinberg and Shields, ed. 2008). In a sense, these people are victims of the city's former prosperity, when its rapid growth forced development into environmentally marginal lands, the former backswamps and marshes (Colten 2005). However, this pattern of growth was neither inevitable nor natural. It was economically and ideologically structured by capitalism and the racist social policies of segregation. If the city is to regain prosperity, it must find a way to equitably reestablish its residents, the people whose labor keeps the city functioning and whose cultures create its unique character.

What then, is the place of archaeology in post-Katrina New Orleans? In a pragmatic sense, the influx of federally funded projects, the massive planned redevelopments of housing throughout the city, and scores of private developments following suit will provide new and unique opportunities to do archaeology in the city. For instance, an archaeological project resulting from work on a Federal Emergency Management Agency (FEMA) trailer site may already be rewriting the history of the New Orleans area prior to European settlement (Gray, Eppler et al. 2008). More discoveries such as these will undoubtedly follow.

However, archaeology is also in a unique position with respect to the people of the city, and it has a fundamental responsibility to the public. Archaeology allows access to the daily experiences of individuals in the past in a tangible manner, unlike static documents such as census records and city directories. Such personal and concrete connections can help a community better understand its own sense of place, its own historicity. Moreover, by exposing the dynamics of race, place, and poverty, and the power relations in which the daily lives of people were enmeshed, archaeology offers a critique of social inequalities. At a time when people are still being displaced from their neighborhoods and their traditions, archaeology provides one way of reminding residents that they are part of the history of New Orleans. The decisions they make today will determine its future.

18

Underwater Archaeology

ALLEN R. SALTUS, JR., AND CHARLES E. PEARSON

The underwater archaeology of Louisiana is unique, a reflection of the state's distinctive geography, geology, and history. There is the long coastline along the Gulf of Mexico and a dominance of water on the landscape in the southern part of the state, both of which have made travel by boat a necessity and prescribed an economy closely associated with watercraft. Elsewhere in Louisiana, although water is less prevalent than in the south, rivers and streams have served as important routes of travel and commerce since prehistoric times. The importance of watercraft in Louisiana is reflected in the state's history and in the large numbers of vessels of all types and sizes, as well as in the docks, landings, boat-building yards, and other related facilities that are still seen today. The French and, to a lesser extent, Spanish heritages of Louisiana mean that the cultural traditions associated with the building and use of watercraft are distinctive relative to most other areas of the United States. Aspects of Louisiana's geology also have a direct relationship to the occurrence of underwater archaeological sites in the state. In the Delta region of south Louisiana, subsidence is an ongoing natural process and, as a result, untold numbers of deltaic landforms, and the archaeological sites located on them, have sunk below the present ground surface and are now covered by marsh or water. Further, the rise of the sea level over the past 18,000 years or so has submerged archaeological sites that were located on the once dry areas of the Gulf of Mexico's outer continental shelf (OCS), located offshore of Louisiana. The state's long and intensive history of boat use, plus the natural processes of subsidence and sea-level rise, have produced an unknown but large number of underwater properties, many of which exist today as archaeological sites.

This chapter considers these sunken watercraft, submerged terrestrial sites, and other classes of underwater remains within Louisiana. This is an extensive topic, encompassing a wide variety of sites and essentially the entire period of human occupation of the state. In many ways, the topic "underwater archaeology" is equivalent to "terrestrial archaeology," meaning that only the very broadest treatment is possible here. This chapter represents a first effort. The topic

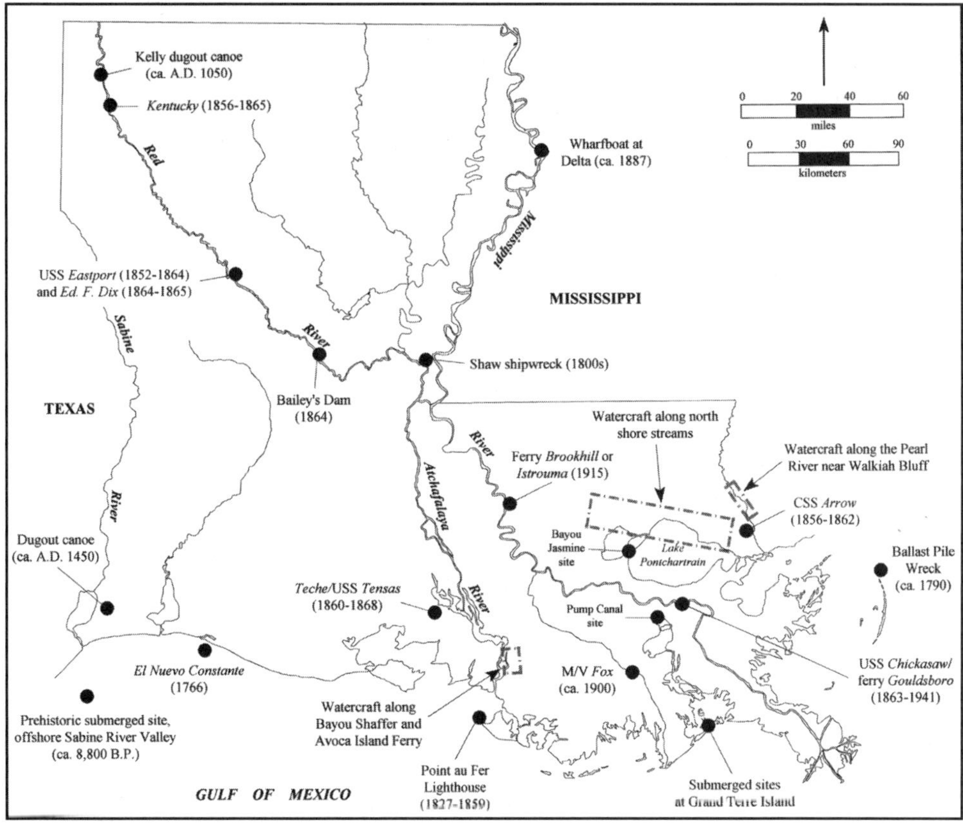

Fig. 18.1. Map showing the locations of selected underwater sites discussed in the text. Dates of origin, loss, or estimated age of sites are provided if known.

of underwater archaeology is not considered in Robert Neuman's (1984) *An Introduction to Louisiana Archaeology*, the only previous book-length overview of Louisiana archaeology, and no synthesis of underwater archaeology in the state has ever been published. We examine the topic by first looking at the nature of underwater archaeology in Louisiana in terms of its history and research orientation. We then turn to a consideration of the objects of interest to underwater archaeologists. Finally, we briefly mention some of the more prominent and interesting underwater archaeological sites recorded in the state (see Figure 18.1 for the locations of most of the sites discussed).

The history of professional underwater archaeology in Louisiana is short, despite the great importance of watercraft and water-related activities in the history of the state. Interestingly, subsided terrestrial sites—and not shipwrecks—seem to have received the earliest attention from professionals within the state. In the 1930s, Fred Kniffen (1936), then a young professor at Louisiana State

University, took cores at subsided sites in the coastal area to gather information on subsidence rates. It was not until the 1970s that professional research on other classes of underwater sites in the state began, and most of this early work consisted of historical overviews or remote-sensing surveys to identify submerged shipwrecks and other cultural remains. These early studies included a 1973 magnetometer survey of a large portion of the Red River by the Gulf South Research Institute (1975), which located over 250 magnetic "anomalies" or targets, some of which were believed to represent sunken historic vessels. Other studies were compilations of historically reported vessel losses along the Lower Mississippi River that recorded several hundred wrecks (Detro et al. 1979; Gulf South Research Institute 1973). In 1976, the Gulf South Research Institute (1976) reported on the discovery of a buried vessel (16CO51) near the Mississippi River and the community of Shaw, Louisiana. Tentatively identified as a nineteenth-century Mississippi River flatboat, this may represent the earliest reported professional examination of a wreck site in Louisiana. In 1975, Robert Neuman (1975) reported on his work at the Bayou Jasmine site (16SJB2) in St. John the Baptist Parish, a subsided prehistoric site dating to as early as 800 B.C. The Bayou Jasmine site is not entirely underwater, but it is mostly below sea level and is permanently wet, as are many subsided sites in the state.

The first significant amount of archaeological research on a historic shipwreck did not occur until 1980–1981, with the excavation of the eighteenth-century Spanish ship *El Nuevo Constante* (16CM112), located in the Gulf of Mexico off Cameron Parish (Pearson et al. 1981; Pearson and Hoffman 1995). It was not until 1990 that Louisiana published a management plan for submerged cultural resources. This plan includes general information on the status of underwater sites in the state and provides broad guidance relative to pertinent research topics (Terrell 1990).

The brief history of underwater research in the state is reflected in the fact that as of September 2007, the Louisiana Division of Archaeology site files listed only ninety sites as "shipwrecks." This small number is somewhat misleading, because several of these sites represent locales containing a number of sunken vessels. Even so, the number of reported underwater sites in Louisiana is small relative to the number of shipwrecks and other types of submerged sites that are believed to exist (Clune and Wheeler 1991).

The reasons for the lack of research on underwater sites in Louisiana are many, although a major one is certainly the inhospitable working conditions found at most underwater sites. Louisiana's waters are typically sediment-laden and dark. Visibility underwater is poor to nonexistent. Additionally, on larger rivers, the current is often so strong that diving is hazardous or impossible. Another reason is the expense involved in conducting underwater archaeology, a factor that is inflated by the very difficult diving conditions that often exist. Similarly, the archaeological study of subsided terrestrial sites that might now be buried and submerged requires specialized and time-consuming techniques. It also appears that a lack of knowledge about the underwater resources of Louisiana and a misconception of their relative importance have contributed to the minimal amount of research. The lack of knowledge is related, in part, to the almost complete absence of published works on the state's underwater archaeological sites. The misconception about the importance of underwater sites in Louisiana seems to be held by the public at large, as well as by the professional community. Public interest and excitement in shipwrecks is stirred when treasure or exotic goods are found, and even the professional community seems to take a greater interest in a shipwreck if it produces treasure or is associated with an important historical event. In Louisiana, many of the reported and known wrecks represent mundane, everyday working vessels that have elicited little or only short-lived interest, despite the fact that they often represent types of watercraft that are important in the history of the state, or about which we know very little.

By and large, research in underwater archaeology in Louisiana today is driven by two factors. One is the array of federal regulations and laws related to cultural resource management (CRM). The other is associated with developments and advancements in remote sensing technologies. Most of the underwater archaeology now occurring in the state is funded by federal agencies, particularly the U.S. Army Corps of Engineers, and reflects agency compliance with various cultural resource and environmental laws. State and local governments and private industry, particularly the oil and gas industry, also fund underwater studies in compliance with these laws and regulations. The fact that most underwater archaeology in Louisiana is related to CRM work does not mean it is bereft of research value or entirely atheoretical. These studies are typically guided by tacit if not explicitly stated research goals, and often synthesize sets of historical, geological, and archaeological data into useful narratives on some aspect of Louisiana history or archaeology.

Much of the work resulting from these CRM studies consists of preliminary remote-sensing surveys of specified project areas. This brings into play the second important factor driving research in underwater archaeology in Louisiana: remote-sensing technology. The development and refinement of instruments such as magnetometers, side-scan sonars, subbottom profilers, and, more recently, multi-beam systems have made survey of marine and riverine settings

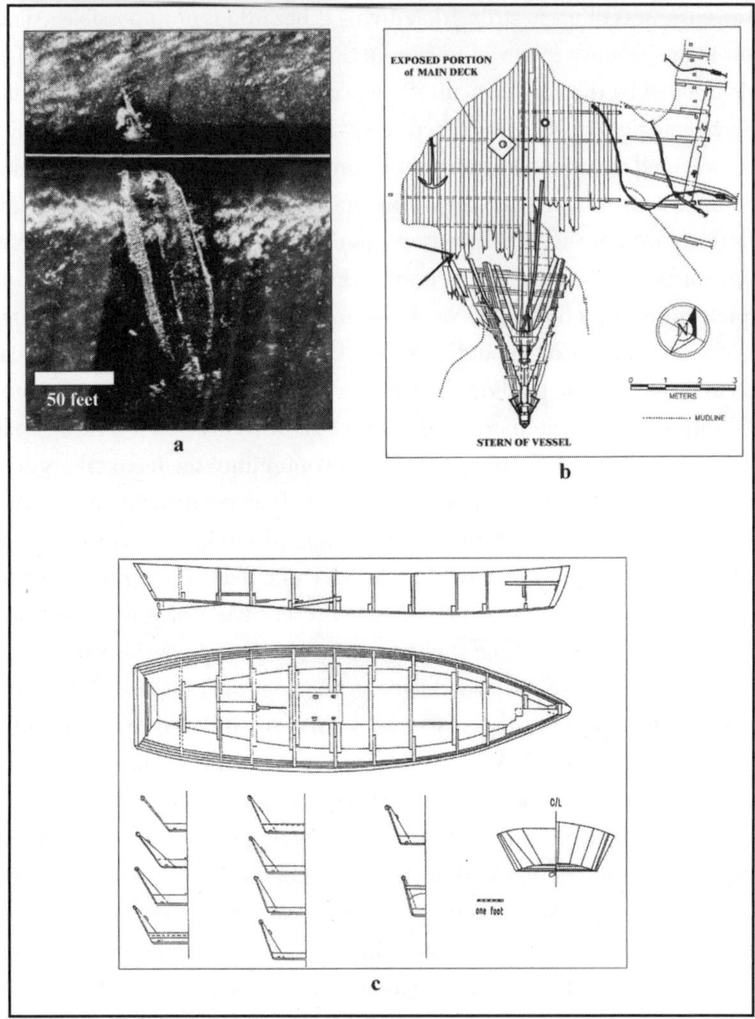

Fig. 18.2. Images of Louisiana archaeology underwater: a. Side-scan sonar image of an unidentified shipwreck offshore of Grand Isle, Louisiana. Image courtesy of T. Baker Smith, Inc.; b. Plan drawing of the exposed stern of the sidewheel steamboat *Kentucky* on the Red River in Bossier Parish (from Goodwin and Seidel 2004:Figure 50); c. Plans of an early twentieth-century cypress skiff found at the Adams Place site along Bayou Shaffer in St. Mary Parish (from Pearson and Saltus 1991:Figure 52).

not only possible, but also efficient and productive. Coupled with the precise placement available through Global Positioning System (GPS), these remote-sensing instruments permit intensive coverage of large areas, often making water survey more efficient than terrestrial survey (Figure 18.2a). The strategies and instrumentation used in remote-sensing surveys throughout Louisiana are now pretty much standardized. These strategies have developed over the years as technological advancements have occurred and as our understanding of underwater cultural resources has grown. To a large degree, remote-sensing surveys conducted in the state have been influenced by the requirements first established in the early 1970s for the offshore oil industry by the Minerals Management Service (MMS) in the U.S. Department of the Interior.

Remote-sensing surveys have dominated underwater research in the state, as reflected in the fact that 49 of 57 cultural resource reports on file at the Louisiana Division of Archaeology dealing with underwater archaeology (as of September 2007), relate principally to remote-sensing survey work (Philip Rivet, personal communication 2007). Much more costly and time-consuming are the follow-up efforts involved in examining objects identified during these surveys and in conducting underwater testing or excavation. As noted previously, the often prohibitive cost is one reason why so little excavation has been conducted on underwater sites. Avoidance is generally the desired option of the agency involved in the work.

There has been very little research in underwater archaeology in Louisiana that is not related to CRM requirements. Among the few examples of independent, directed research have been the series of studies of several rivers draining into Lake Pontchartrain conducted by Allen Saltus (1985, 1986, 1988, 1992a) in the 1980s and early 1990s. These studies were funded by National Park Service grants awarded through the Louisiana Division of Archaeology and involved remote-sensing surveys and diver evaluation of identified "targets," coupled with historical research, in order to inventory submerged resources along waterways in the Florida Parishes. Some important findings came out of these studies that have implications for underwater research elsewhere in the state. Of the approximately 150 watercraft documented in these surveys, a surprising number were extremely well preserved, and many were almost entirely intact. Further, the discovered watercraft encompassed almost every type of vessel known to have operated on these rivers in the historic period, and included nineteenth-century sailing barges and sloops as well as more recent skiffs and work barges. In addition, it was found that vessel remains were not randomly distributed, nor were they closely associated with navigation hazards. Rather, they were concentrated at former landings and settlements, where many of the vessels had been abandoned as derelicts. These findings, pertaining to a variety of types of well-preserved vessels concentrated at former landings and docking areas, have been duplicated in studies conducted along other waterways in Louisiana (e.g., Krause et al. 2004; Pearson and Saltus 1991, 1996).

These underwater cultural resource studies (principally remote-sensing surveys), and the handful of pure research projects conducted in Louisiana, have certainly expanded our knowledge of underwater archaeology in the state and have contributed to a broader understanding of maritime archaeology and history. Unfortunately, the vast majority of this information is presented only in CRM reports submitted to agencies, the so-called "gray literature" that has a very limited distribution. While this literature is accessible to the serious scholar, relatively little has been published and made more broadly available to either the professional community or the general public. The published materials on underwater archaeology in the state apparently include just one book, about the wreck of the eighteenth-century Spanish merchantman *El Nuevo Constante* (Pearson and Hoffman 1995), although Kane (2004) has drawn upon the CRM literature in his recent archaeological and historical examination of western river steamboats. The remaining body of published literature on underwater archaeology in Louisiana consists of a handful of articles in professional journals (Birchett and Pearson 1996; Pearson 2000a, 2001; Pearson and Floyd 1982; Saltus 1990, 1992b, 1999a, 2000) and a few brochures printed by state and federal agencies (Pearson and Birchett 2003; Pearson and Hoffman 1998). Irion and Ball (2001) have written on the nineteenth-century wrecks of the steamers *Josephine* and *New York*, both of which lie in the Gulf of Mexico just outside of Louisiana state waters. Additionally, a few articles have been published on subsided or submerged terrestrial sites, including the Bayou Jasmine site and the Morton Shell Mound (16IB3) on Weeks Island (Neuman 1977b:10–18, 1984:119–121, 198–204).

Offsetting this meager corpus of published literature is a considerable body of source material in other disciplines that is pertinent to research in underwater archaeology. Of particular relevance is the tremendous amount of material that bears on the history of navigation and riverine and maritime economy within Louisiana. This includes published works as well as archival documents. These are too numerous to discuss here, but they include several recently published studies dealing with steamboat navigation on specific Louisiana waterways (Bagur 2001; Block 2003; Bradshaw 2001; Brasseaux and Fontenot 2004; Brock and Joiner 1999) and several works on vernacular watercraft in the state (Brassieur 1993, 2007; Comeaux 1985; Knipmeyer 1976). Also important to underwater research in Louisiana are several classic studies on river steamboat history, construction, and archaeology, as presented by Bates (1968, 1996), Hunter (1949), Norman (1942), and Petsche (1974). In addition, there are several published listings of steamboat losses, including many within Louisiana (e.g., Mitchell 1975; Way 1994; Way and Rutter 1990). These and other sources are indispensable to anyone conducting underwater research in the state.

Vessels of various types constitute the most obvious class of underwater archaeological site in Louisiana. These range from prehistoric dugout canoes to twentieth-century vessels and in between, including eighteenth-century sailing ships, nineteenth-century steamboats, and small folk or vernacular craft, like bateaus and skiffs. Considering the great range of vessel types represented in the known archaeological record in Louisiana, the term "watercraft" better represents these types of remains, as not all sunken vessels are "shipwrecks" in the true sense of the word.

The scope of underwater archaeological sites within the state extends well beyond watercraft. The various types of structures associated with landings and docking areas also represent underwater sites, although these are often ignored as such. Other types of man-made structures, such as facilities associated with water mills, dams, and even fish weirs, although not numerous, constitute additional submerged sites. As mentioned earlier, submerged terrestrial sites are another category of underwater cultural resources. These are especially prevalent in the offshore and deltaic regions of the state, where once higher land has subsided or been flooded by the rising sea level, leaving these landforms and the archaeological sites on them buried or submerged beneath marsh and water. All of these types of sites are expressive of the state's archaeological past and the subject of underwater archaeology.

One question of interest concerns the total number of underwater sites that exist within the state today. The recording of these resources as archaeological sites is related to a complex set of phenomena, including the original number of sites in existence, the physical characteristics of individual sites, events associated with loss (in the case of watercraft) or submergence (in the case of terrestrial sites), the natural processes that have impacted the sites since sinking or submergence, and the preservation potential inherent at the location of each site. Several studies have specifically addressed the possible numbers of underwater sites that might exist within particular areas of the state. Drawing on historical accounts of vessel losses, Detro, Davis, and Middleton (1979) identified 700 wrecks in the Mississippi River between Baton Rouge and the river's mouth. Pearson and colleagues recorded 1,800 vessel losses within the boundaries of the New Orleans District, U.S. Army Corps of Engineers, representing essentially the southern one-third of the state (Pearson, Castille et al. 1989). Pearson and Wells (1999) identified 364 losses along the course of the Red River within the state. Birchett, Pearson, and Castille (2001) identified 295 reported vessel losses within the Atchafalaya Basin.

These studies demonstrate that large numbers of historic vessel losses have occurred within Louisiana, but the findings of each are limited in terms of the connection to the actual archaeological record of shipwrecks. This is particularly evident from the bias in historical accounts toward large commercial vessels, military ships, or those lost in spectacular accidents. Typically ignored in these accounts are losses of non-commercial watercraft, such as the small vernacular craft so common throughout the state, and mundane, everyday vessels, such as barges. The few systematic surveys conducted along Louisiana waterways have demonstrated that these smaller and more common watercraft actually comprise the largest proportion of the archaeological remains in existence (Flayharty and Muller 1983; Pearson and Saltus 1991; Saltus 1985, 1986, 1988, 1992a; Stout 1992). These studies further demonstrate that abandoned vessels occur in considerable numbers in the archaeological record, yet they are rarely reported in historical accounts. Saltus's sample surveys of waterways in the Florida Parishes identified nine to ten times more watercraft wrecks than were reported in the historical literature. His research, and that of others, has amply demonstrated that the historical record of vessel use within a specific area is a better predictor of the archaeological record than the historical record of vessel losses.

Even more difficult to quantify is the total number of submerged terrestrial sites that might exist within the state, although all lines of evidence indicate that it is large. Many partially exposed prehistoric shell middens and earthen mounds are known from now-subsided landforms in the deltaic region of the state, and completely buried or submerged examples also exist, although only a few of these have been examined archaeologically (e.g., Jones et al. 1994; Neuman 1977b). An intensive survey of much of the exposed natural levee of a single subdelta feature off Bayou Lafourche in Lafourche Parish recorded 93 Native American sites on about 4,500 acres of land (Pearson, Guevin et al. 1989). Many subdeltas of similar size and age now exist as partially or completely subsided features in the coastal sections of the state and some, if not most, likely contain similar site densities.

The preservation potential for underwater sites in Louisiana varies, but throughout much of the state it is good. This is particularly true for south Louisiana, where watercraft can become submerged and quickly buried by fine-grained sediments (i.e., silts and clays), producing a protective, low-oxygen environment that inhibits rot and deterioration. Although burial can aid in the preservation of sunken boats, preservation can be good even when boats are just submerged. Of the approximately 150 watercraft documented in the Florida Parishes by Saltus, few were buried by sediment, but a large number were found to be virtually intact, including several nineteenth-century sailing sloops, schooners, and barges, as well as smaller vernacular watercraft. Preservation was enhanced if a sunken vessel remained entirely submerged. When periodically exposed to air, as during periods of low water, the exposed portions of watercraft tend to deteriorate rapidly.

On larger rivers, especially where waterside development has been extensive over the years, the preservation potential is typically lower because vessels have been purposefully removed or accidentally damaged by development. The good state of preservation of sunken vessels is commonly surprising even along these areas, however, as in the case of New Orleans, where several partially intact watercraft have been discovered sunk along the heavily developed riverfront (Krause et al. 2004). Among these vessels is the Civil War gunboat USS *Chickasaw*, built in 1863 and converted in 1880 into the railroad transfer ferry *Gouldsboro*. The *Gouldsboro* worked at New Orleans until she was abandoned in 1941. A large portion of her hull appears to exist intact, sixty-six years after her abandonment (Krause et al. 2004; Way 1994:193).

In some instances a meandering channel will shift away from a wreck, burying it with sediment that aids its preservation, but often leaving the wreck some distance from the river. This has occurred in the case of three Civil War–era boats on the Red River: the steamboat *Kentucky* (Goodwin and Seidel 2004), the ironclad gunboat USS *Eastport*, and the sidewheeler *Ed. F. Dix* (Pearson and Birchett 2001). Archaeological excavations indicate that the hulls of all of these vessels appear to be largely intact, even though each was subjected to the full force of the Red River for some period of time before being buried.

Despite conventional wisdom, the remains of even large vessels can exist in waterways that have been cleared and dredged to aid navigation, as is often the case in Louisiana. The term "removed" is used by agencies, such as the U. S. Army Corps of Engineers, in reference to clearing the remains of a wreck from a waterway. However, this term typically means the removal of a sunken vessel only to the extent that it no longer constitutes a hazard to navigation. It does not necessarily mean that an entire sunken vessel was removed. In fact, reports exist of the same wreck being "removed" several times over the course of many years. The steamer *New Falls City* was scuttled on the Red River in 1864 and reportedly "removed" in 1880, 1890, and 1893. Yet some parts of the vessel were still present in 1897 (Pearson and Wells 1999:201). Those portions of a wreck that lie outside or beneath the designated navigable channel are commonly left behind. This phenomenon is amply demonstrated in the recent discovery of the complete lower hull of a 95-foot-long sidewheel steamboat lying buried in the bottom of Bayou Teche at the city of New Iberia—in spite of the fact that Bayou Teche has been "cleared" of boat wrecks and other types of obstructions several times since the 1870s. This wreck is thought to be that of the steamboat *Teche*, formerly the Civil War gunboat USS *Tensas*, which sank in Bayou Teche in 1868 (Pearson et al. 2007). This wreck, designated the New Iberia Shipwreck (16IB80), is now listed on the National Register of Historic Places.

Subsided terrestrial sites are similarly preserved through burial, although exposure to open water and the effects of erosion can be deleterious to these sites. Sites that remain submerged and do not undergo alternating wet and dry conditions often appear to have exceptional preservation, even when under only several feet of water.

Underwater Archaeological Sites in Louisiana

The following sections provide a brief overview of the types of underwater sites that exist in Louisiana, using specific examples that tell us something about the prehistoric or historic past. Space permits only brief statements about individual sites. References are provided, however, for readers interested in additional information.

SUBMERGED TERRESTRIAL SITES

As has been noted, Louisiana is somewhat unique in having large numbers of submerged terrestrial sites, although very few have been examined. These sites occur through two different processes, one involving submergence as a result of the rising sea level and the other involving burial and/or submergence through subsidence, or the slow sinking of the land. It is believed that large numbers of prehistoric sites were established on what is now the OCS during the period of lower sea level that existed prior to about 5,000 years ago. These sites now lie under the waters of the Gulf of Mexico, having been covered by the rising sea level. Since the early 1970s, the MMS has required remote-sensing surveys to identify now-submerged landforms that might contain prehistoric sites potentially affected by oil and gas production in federal waters of the OCS. Some of these federal surveys have extended into Louisiana state waters, and a small number have been specifically required in state waters, especially along pipeline right-of-ways.

Many submerged "high probability" landforms have been identified in these surveys, but no submerged prehistoric sites have been positively identified in Louisiana state waters in the Gulf of Mexico, which extend three miles out from the coast. However, a possible prehistoric shell midden has been identified on the OCS, adjacent to the now-submerged offshore portion of the Sabine River Valley, just outside of state waters. This site consists of organic deposits containing various types of burned bone and a possible marsh clam (*Rangia cuneata*) midden. It lies at about 60 feet beneath present sea level, covered by 40 feet of water and 20 feet of modern marine sediment. Radiocarbon dates suggest this cultural deposit dates to around 8800 B.P. (Pearson, Weinstein et al. 1989:8–9). It is expected that other prehistoric sites exist in similar river valley settings off the coast of Louisiana and elsewhere, where they have been preserved and protected from the erosive impacts of rising sea level.

Subsided sites are archaeological sites typically formed in a deltaic coastal zone. In these environments, surface landforms such as natural levees slowly sink due to the compaction of underlying sediments. As they settle, existing surfaces are covered by the deposition of additional sediments. Subsided sites can remain buried beneath overlying sediments, or they can be exposed and/or submerged if the overlying deposits are subjected to processes of erosion, as commonly occurs in coastal Louisiana. A large number of partially subsided prehistoric sites are known in coastal Louisiana. These might be best classified as "wet sites," because their surfaces lie beneath the water table and are constantly saturated, rather than being fully submerged, as at true underwater sites. Examples of completely subsided prehistoric sites certainly exist, however, and some of these now lie beneath bodies of water that have expanded and eroded away the overlying sediments. Very few of these inundated, subsided sites have been examined in the state. One that has been partially examined is an early-nineteenth-century settlement associated with the pirate Jean Lafitte at the western end of Grand Terre Island in coastal Louisiana. Due to a combination of subsidence and rising sea level, the site (16JE128) is now beneath a foot or so of water, and some portions are buried by a blanket of sediment deposited since the 1820s. The remains of features associated with the settlement can be seen today in the shallow water, including brick house piers, artifact scatters, and a barrel well. Other well-preserved features presumably lie buried beneath the sediment blanketing the site. Many other subsided prehistoric wet sites lie beneath marsh rather than open water. Only a very small number of these sites have been examined by archaeologists. Among these are the previously mentioned Bayou Jasmine site and the Pump Canal site (16SC27), located adjacent to Lake Cataouatche in St. Charles Parish. The Pump Canal site contains stratified midden deposits that extend from slightly above the level of the lake to a depth of about 1.6 meters (5.3 ft) below sea level (Jones et al. 1994). Preservation of organic materials such as bone, fiber, and wood at subsided sites tends to be excellent due to their constant saturation.

PREHISTORIC WATERCRAFT

Native Americans have inhabited Louisiana for the past 12,000 years, and during much of this time they must have used watercraft of some type. Dugout canoes were the principal type used prehistorically, but how far back into antiquity their use goes is unknown. A number of dugout canoes have been found in Louisiana, but few have been studied in any detail or reliably dated. It is consequently unknown how many are Native American watercraft and how many are dugouts made by settlers, or pirogues as they were known by the French.

Among the Native American canoes that have been dated is the Kelly Dugout Canoe (16CD169), recovered from the eroding bank of the Red River near the community of Dixie in Caddo Parish. This almost complete canoe measures 31 feet long, about 2 feet wide, and is carved from a single cypress log (Van Osdell 1984). Two radiocarbon dates were obtained on wood samples from the canoe, one at A.D. 1065 +/- 70 (UGA-5294) and the other at A.D. 1005 +/- 65 (UGA-5295). These dates suggest that the canoe may be associated with Caddo culture of northwest Louisiana (see Girard, Chapter 11 in this volume). A smaller, 12-foot-long canoe found at Fluker's Bluff on the Amite River in St. Helena Parish produced a radiocarbon date of A.D. 1222 (LSU Nuclear Science Laboratory, Sample 70 002), although there is some question about the accuracy of this date (Pearson, Castille et al. 1989). McGimsey reported a dugout recovered from the coastal marshes of Cameron Parish, east of Sabine Lake (16CM147; McGimsey et al. 2000:86). This canoe was formed from a cypress log. The two remaining fragments measure 21 feet long and almost 3 feet wide. A radiocarbon date of A.D. 1490 was obtained on wood from this canoe. A partial dugout canoe from Lake Salvador in St. Charles Parish, measuring a little over 27 feet long, yielded three radiocarbon dates ranging between A.D. 1540 and A.D. 1650 (16SC49; Louisiana Geological Survey, Samples 3.141, 3.142 and 3.145). The latter two canoes are thought to be of Native American origin. Another dugout (16ST190), not radiocarbon dated, was found along Wilson Slough between the east and west branches of the Pearl River near Walkiah Bluff. It has bear claw decorations on both sides of both ends and also appears to be of Native American origin.

UNDERWATER SITES OF THE COLONIAL PERIOD

Relatively few underwater sites of the colonial period (circa A.D. 1699 to 1803) have been reported in Louisiana, although a great variety and number of watercraft operated on the state's waters during this period. In addition, waterside facilities associated with these vessels were numerous. The watercraft of the period included pirogues and bateaus that transported cargoes throughout the state and traveled the Mississippi River in large convoys during the French period, sailing vessels of many types, as well as flatboats and keelboats. A small number of pirogues have been found in Louisiana that might date to the colonial period, but none have been confirmed.

The three-masted frigate *El Nuevo Constante,* which was lost off the coast of present-day Cameron Parish in 1766, is the only colonial period shipwreck in the state to receive intensive study. *El Nuevo Constante,* a British-built ship, was sailing from Veracruz, Mexico, to Spain as a member of the New Spain fleet when she was driven ashore by a hurricane. Excavations of the wreck recovered a variety of well-preserved cargo items, including several thousand pounds of copper, the dyes cochineal, annatto, and indigo, and a variety of ceramics made in Mexico for export. A small quantity of gold and silver was also found, presumably being illegally smuggled out of New Spain. The lower hull of this 125-foot-long ship was largely intact and yielded a considerable amount of information on eighteenth-century ship construction. In combination with intensive historical research, the archaeology provides a unique and more comprehensive view of the ships and cargoes involved in the eighteenth-century Spanish colonial trade (Pearson and Hoffman 1995).

At least one other possible colonial period wreck has been reported. This is the Ballast Pile Wreck, located in state waters off the northern Chandeleur Islands in St. Bernard Parish. This site, which was investigated by Texas A&M University in 1989, consists of a pile of stone ballast containing a few pottery sherds and lead artifacts, plus six iron cannons. Markings on three of the cannons indicate that they were cast in Sweden between 1771 and 1784 (Garrison et al. 1989). Neither the identity of this vessel nor the events of its loss are known.

NINETEENTH-CENTURY SITES

A number of underwater archaeological sites dating to the nineteenth century have been examined in Louisiana. Most of these are watercraft wrecks and include Civil War–era gunboats and steamboats, as well as common working vessels, such as schooners, sloops, and barges. After 1812, steamboats became a common mode of travel and transport in the United States and large numbers of them traveled Louisiana's rivers and coastal waters. Kane (2004) has discussed several of the steamboat wrecks studied in Louisiana. Among those that have been excavated are two Civil War gunboats, the Union ironclad USS

Eastport (16GR33) and the Confederate gunboat CSS *Arrow* (16ST99). The large, 280-foot-long *Eastport* was scuttled on the Red River in 1864 when low water prevented her escape with the rest of the Union fleet during the ill-fated Red River campaign. In 1989, a magnetometer survey discovered the wreck adjacent to the Red River near the town of Montgomery in Grant Parish. Cores revealed that the wreck was buried beneath about 35 feet of river sediment. In 1995, excavations were undertaken to verify that the buried remains were indeed the *Eastport.* This examination required the excavation of a large 300-foot-square hole above the wreck, which was allowed to fill with water where diving could take place. The work revealed that a large portion of the hull and armored casemate of the *Eastport* are still extant. Most interesting was the discovery of another steamboat wreck lying directly on top of the *Eastport.* This was the sidewheel steamboat *Ed. F. Dix*, which struck and sank on top of the wreck of the *Eastport* in May 1865 while carrying Union troops up the Red River. Excavations of the *Ed. F. Dix* recovered Civil War–era food containers, such as barrels and boxes, and information was gathered on the vessel's construction (Birchett and Pearson 1996; Pearson and Birchett 2001).

The Confederate gunboat *Arrow* was a sidewheel coastal steamer that was converted into a gunboat at New Orleans in 1861. After the fall of New Orleans in the spring of 1862, the *Arrow* was taken to the West Pearl River and scuttled. The wreck became buried beneath a sand bar, preserving the remains, until being reexposed in the 1970s. Excavations of the *Arrow* collected a considerable amount of information on the steamer's construction and machinery. A variety of ship's fittings were recovered, as well as a 32-pounder canister and round shot used in the vessel's single gun (Pearson 2000a; Pearson and Saltus 1996).

Another Civil War–era steamboat discovered on the Red River is the sidewheeler *Kentucky.* The *Kentucky* sank in 1865 while traveling down the Red River carrying approximately 900 paroled Confederate veterans who had recently surrendered at Shreveport. Many of those onboard died in the sinking, but the exact number is unknown; estimates range from as few as 50 to as many as 200 (Goodwin and Seidel 2004:149). Like the USS *Eastport* and *Ed. F. Dix*, the *Kentucky* was buried beneath river sediment as the Red River shifted away from the location of the wreck. A considerable amount of information on the construction of the *Kentucky* was collected during the archaeological investigation, in addition to historical information on the vessel and the events of its loss (Figure 18.2b) (Goodwin and Seidel 2004).

Other nineteenth-century steamboat wrecks that have been examined in Louisiana include the sidewheel steamboat in Bayou Teche mentioned earlier, believed to be the remains of a steamboat known as the *Teche*. It was built in Cincinnati, Ohio, in 1860 and sank in 1868 (Pearson et al. 2007). In addition, a structural and historical study was undertaken of a wooden vessel found on the bank of the Mississippi River at Baton Rouge. This vessel is thought to be either the *Brookhill* or the *Istrouma*, two ferryboats that sank in a hurricane in 1915 (Earth Search, Inc. 1997).

The remains of over 150 non-steamboat watercraft have been reported in Louisiana, although few have been studied in detail. Among those that have is the M/V *Fox*, a small lugger-like boat found on shore in Larose, Louisiana. Research on the *Fox* consisted of an intensive structural and historical study that incorporated oral interviews with local informants (Goodwin et al. 1984). This research determined that the *Fox* was built in the 1870s, was used as a commercial cargo carrier, and was a type known locally as a *pointu les deux*. Remote-sensing survey and limited diver inspection recorded a well-preserved wooden wreck in Lake Pontchartrain off New Orleans. This vessel is believed to be a nineteenth-century sailing barge or schooner that measures about 120 feet long and 20 feet wide (Stout 1985). The remains of a smaller schooner were discovered entirely buried in the bottom of the Pearl River, across from the community of Logtown, Mississippi. A brief examination of the vessel indicated that almost the entire hull is preserved and measures 52 feet long and 21 feet wide. The schooner is unidentified, but it is thought to be one of the many schooners that sailed between New Orleans and the communities on the north shore of Lake Pontchartrain during the nineteenth century (Pearson and Saltus 1996:87–90). The Logtown schooner is important because it represents one of just a handful of schooner wrecks known out of the hundreds of lake schooners built, none of which have been studied in any appreciable detail.

In 1994, the hull of a partially buried, 142-foot-long wooden boat was discovered on the west bank of the Mississippi River near the community of Delta in Madison Parish, Louisiana (Hahn et al. 1994). Archaeological and historical research suggests that this vessel is the abandoned remains of the wharfboat operated by the Delta Wharf Boat & Transfer Company between about 1874 and 1887. Wharfboats served as floating docks and were either purposefully built or modified from old steamboat hulls. Again, as with so many of the wrecks that have been examined in Louisiana, wharfboats represent common work vessels about which very little was written in contemporary accounts.

A large number of nineteenth- and some twentieth-century watercraft were located by Saltus in his several studies of waterways in Louisiana's Florida Parishes. These craft fall into several watercraft groups, including dugout pirogues, plank pirogues, skiffs, punts, rafts, barges, launches, sloops, schooners, sailing barges, and one keelboat–barge. These resources are important because they represent the most common and numerous classes of watercraft operating in nineteenth-century Louisiana. Most are everyday, mundane watercraft that were constructed by local builders relying on experience and "eye" estimates, not on drawn plans. Because so little was written about the construction or use of these vessels in contemporary accounts, most of what we know about them comes from their physical remains. In almost every instance, the examination of these boats has produced unique information on construction techniques or technology.

The recently discovered Mardi Gras Shipwreck (16GM01) is another early nineteenth-century or possibly late eighteenth-century shipwreck. This wreck lies in the Gulf of Mexico in 4,000 feet of water. Although it rests outside of state waters, it is of interest in terms of its mode of discovery and examination. The wreck is believed to be that of a two-masted schooner, found during an MMS-required remote-sensing survey for a pipeline. In 2007, Texas A&M University conducted a study of the site. Because of the great depth, this study had to be done entirely with a remotely operated vehicle (ROV). The ROV made detailed photographs of the wreck site and recovered some artifacts. The study revealed that the remains of the vessel and the artifacts have been extremely well-preserved in deep-water conditions (Ford et al. 2008). This suggests that other wrecks in comparable settings, including areas within Louisiana state waters, may be similarly well-preserved and can be discovered and examined with available technology.

While a variety of nineteenth-century watercraft have been found and examined, many classes of boats known to have been common in nineteenth-century Louisiana are missing from the presently known archaeological record. These include keelboats and large bateaus, cargo vessels that existed in relatively large numbers on Louisiana waters during the first three decades of the nineteenth century. Archaeological research on some of the vessels of the nineteenth century is supplemented by a considerable amount of historical information, including contemporary primary documents and secondary literature. This information often makes it possible to track the life history of individual vessels identified in the archaeological record.

A small number of non-watercraft underwater sites dating to the nineteenth century have been examined in Louisiana. These include entities such as lighthouses, mill sites, and submerged features associated with coastal communities. Underwater components of several lighthouses have been documented. These include the remains of the Pass Manchac Light in Lake Pontchartrain, the Trinity Shoal Light located offshore from Vermilion Parish, which dates from 1871 to 1873 (El Darragi and Saltus 2003), and structural features associated with the former Point au Fer Lighthouse (16TR257), which operated from 1827 to 1859 at the entrance to Atchafalaya Bay (Pearson 1992). One of the features at the Point au Fer Lighthouse, initially described by its discoverers as a "treasure vault" associated with the pirate Jean Lafitte, turned out to be a structure associated with the lighthouse's water supply. As noted previously, a portion of what is presumed to be Jean Lafitte's settlement has been found in shallow water at the western end of Grand Terre Island, as have structural elements associated with nearby Fort Livingston (16JE49; Godzinski et al. 2001). Allen Saltus (1999b) investigated submerged portions of several water mill sites in St. Tammany, Vernon, and Washington parishes. The Civil War–era Bailey's Dam (16RA90), in the Red River between Alexandria and Pineville in Rapides Parish, is one of the more unusual underwater sites in the state. This dam was quickly built by Union forces in the spring of 1864 to raise the level of the river in order to free the Union gunboat fleet, which was trapped by low water above Alexandria. Archaeological work on the remains of Bailey's Dam demonstrated that the construction closely followed the few contemporary plans of the structure (Smith and Castille 1986).

TWENTIETH-CENTURY SITES

Most of the twentieth-century underwater sites examined in Louisiana consist of smaller vernacular craft or everyday work vessels such as barges. The remains of several twentieth-century vessels that lay on dry land when discovered have been recorded and, while not strictly underwater sites, several are noted here. Pearson and Saltus (1991) recorded the remains of a number of locally built small craft along waterways in the Lower Atchafalaya Basin. These include the remains of nine complete or almost complete watercraft at the Adams Place site (16SMY55) on Bayou Shaffer, a few miles south of Morgan City. Some of these boats were submerged and completely buried adjacent to the bank. Others were derelict remains that had been pulled up the bank and abandoned. These boats include one motorized Lafitte skiff, formerly used for shrimping, three skiffs, one "flat" made from plywood, a plywood duck boat, a pirogue made from cypress planks, a bateau, and one unidentified boat that was deeply buried in the bayou. The skiffs, the bateau, and the unidentified boat were all made from cypress planks and are believed to date to the first quarter of the twentieth century (Figure 18.2c). The other boats are more recent in age. The Adams Place site is particularly important because it yielded the remains of an entire assemblage of boats, reflecting a range of water-related activities undertaken by the inhabitants of the site throughout most of its period of occupation, from the mid-nineteenth century to the early 1970s. Each boat was constructed and used for a specific task or narrow range of tasks associated with critical economic pursuits, such as shrimping, fishing, hunting, and trapping.

The Adams Place site mirrors the phenomena noted earlier by Saltus in the Florida Parishes, in that most of the boats appeared to be abandonments and many were extremely well-preserved. In fact, one early twentieth-century cypress skiff that had been completely submerged and buried at the Adams Place site still floated after it was excavated. Other boats found along and near Bayou Shaffer both compliment and expand on the assemblage found at the Adams Place site. These include several additional early to mid-twentieth-century cypress skiffs, a large rectangular wooden barge measuring 117 feet long and 26 feet wide, and a small, keeled vessel believed to be a sailing lugger or sloop (Pearson and Saltus 1991). The barge contained a small quantity of coal and was presumably involved in transporting this material to one of the many sugarhouses that once existed in the area. These two vessels could date as early as the mid-nineteenth century, but they represent types used well into the twentieth century. On Avoca Island, immediately east of Bayou Shaffer, the remains of the Avoca Island Ferry (16SMY122) have been studied in detail (Cramer et al. 2007). This small, 56-foot-long wooden ferry operated between 1939 and 1945 and is representative of the many similar ferries that were once necessities of travel in this region of Louisiana. The partial remains of another small, wooden barge-like boat, possibly a ferry dating to the nineteenth century, were discovered in the 1980s during the construction of the floodwall at Morgan City (Goodwin and Selby 1984). These ferries have almost entirely disappeared in the past several decades, enhancing the historical significance of any newly discovered archaeological examples.

A similar assemblage of vessels has been recorded along a short stretch of the Lower Pearl River near Walkiah Bluff, Mississippi. Some of these boats lie on the Louisiana side of the river, others on the Mississippi side. Among the vessels recorded were a 30-foot long, chain-driven, sternwheel launch made from cypress, a small wooden skiff, a Corps of Engineers snagboat named *Pearl 2*, a wooden pontoon barge used to raise sinkers, a wooden work barge formerly used as a logging ferry, and a small, unidentified vessel, possibly a fish car used by commercial fisherman to hold their catch. A small log raft or crib was also found, consisting of eight large pine logs that had been attached together for floating downriver to a sawmill (Pearson 2000b, 2001). As at Bayou Shaffer, these watercraft are best viewed as an assemblage of types used during the first half of the twentieth century. In this instance, most of the watercraft can be associated with the lumber industry that thrived on the Pearl River in the late nineteenth and early twentieth centuries. The sternwheel launch may have been used to handle the large log rafts that were floated on the river. The snagboat *Pearl 2*, which was built in 1893 and sank in 1902, was involved principally in clearing the river to accommodate the timber industry. The log crib, a somewhat unusual watercraft, represents water-related paraphernalia associated with the lumber industry. The sinker barge dates to the 1950s or later, after the timber industry had disappeared from the Pearl River. It was built and used specifically to raise sunken logs lost from the rafts and cribs that were floated down the river in earlier years.

As noted, many of the twentieth-century vessels recorded in Louisiana are vernacular craft that reflect local boat-building traditions. The archaeological examples are particularly important because these traditions have largely disappeared, and their expression is now principally found in the physical remains of the boats. These archaeological remains also provide information about the two major cultural traditions associated with boat building in Louisiana, the Anglo tradition that spread from the east, and the French tradition. Anglo-American builders typically employed what was known as "thwart ship," or cross planking on the bottom of small boats, while the French tradition more often used bottom planks that extended the length of the boat, and which were supported by internal frames. These cultural differences are reflected in the skiff from the Pearl River, which has a bottom made of planks running across the width of the boat, while every one of the several skiffs recorded along Bayou Shaffer, in the heart of French Louisiana, have planks running the length of the boat (Pearson 2001; Pearson and Saltus 1991).

Although a variety of twentieth-century boats have been recorded as archaeological sites in Louisiana, as with nineteenth-century watercraft there are classes that are lacking. For example, no archaeological examples of sailing luggers have been reported, even though these boats were used in large numbers in the state's coastal waters during the late nineteenth and twentieth centuries.

Summary and Conclusions

This chapter provides only a brief overview of underwater archaeology in Louisiana. An effort has been made to emphasize those factors that presently drive underwater archaeological research in the state, to identify the types of sites that are known or expected to exist, and to highlight some of the underwater discoveries that have been made. As discussed, independently directed research on underwater sites in the state is rare. Most underwater research is conducted because of federal requirements, to fulfill the goals of CRM. As a result, the U.S. Army Corps of Engineers has been responsible for funding most of the underwater archaeology in the state. The results of this research have been largely confined to limited-distribution CRM reports. Very little has been published with a wider public audience in mind.

It has also been noted that the preservation of underwater sites in Louisiana is often very good. However, in recent years some unique factors present dangers to these now-preserved sites, especially in the coastal zone of the state. In most areas, the Louisiana coast is eroding at a rapid rate, and submerged boats, subsided terrestrial sites, and other archaeological features are becoming exposed to the forces of erosion and waves. No studies have been conducted to specifically assess the nature or intensity of the impact of coastal erosion on submerged archaeological sites, but it must be significant in some instances.

Recent activities related to the devastation caused by hurricanes Katrina and Rita in 2005 had an impact on the archaeological record of underwater sites in the state. One aspect of the cleanup in the aftermath of these hurricanes has been the removal of many sunken boats from the state's waterways. One firm alone reported removing as many as 600 vessels. While some of these represent recent vessels lost in the hurricanes, others were apparently much older. In one case, it was reported that the removed vessel had been abandoned for at least eighty years (Buskey 2007). It is unknown how many of these boats were historically significant. Many were locally built wooden vessels, representing local, often family boat-building traditions that are now ended, having been superseded by commercial builders. These types of unique watercraft will never be built again in Louisiana. Those that were removed and taken to landfills as hurricane debris represent a significant loss to an important cultural heritage.

The techniques for finding and examining underwater sites in Louisiana have been reasonably well-established. These techniques take into account the generally poor and often dangerous conditions found in most of the waters of the state, especially for conducting archaeology. Generally, this research involves some type of remote-sensing survey, coupled with background research that establishes the historic settlement and navigation history of a particular area. Additionally, background research on the natural setting and geologic history is conducted to assess issues such as changes in stream or shoreline morphology and the potential for preservation. Defining the geological history of a locale is particularly important on actively meandering streams, where the modern river channel may be a great distance from where it was one hundred or more years ago. Excavation techniques have to be tailored to each site and usually involve working in almost zero-visibility conditions, meaning that excavation and recording of underwater sites tends to be tedious and time-consuming.

Underwater archaeological sites in Louisiana represent a repository of the state's maritime heritage. Some of the watercraft that have been studied represent "national" types, such as steamboats and large sailing vessels, that reflect Louisiana's ties to and interaction with the wider world in terms of both the construction and uses of watercraft. However, the majority of submerged watercraft that have been discovered consist of small, locally or regionally made boats that reflect the state's distinctive cultural heritage and its specific maritime and riverine economies. These include a number of skiffs, a few sailing vessels, and other types—such as the M/V *Fox* and the Avoca Island Ferry—that can be truly considered vernacular watercraft, as well as regionally built vessels, such as the snag boat *Pearl 2*, which played specific economic roles. For both types of watercraft, but especially the locally and regionally built ones, the almost complete lack of construction plans or detailed contemporary descriptions enhances the importance of archaeological examples. What we know about such watercraft comes principally from their physical remains.

Directions for future research in underwater archaeology are suggested by previous studies. While detailed studies of individual sites contribute to our understanding of events of the past, the examination of complete assemblages of watercraft in specific settings has great appeal. Studies in the Florida Parishes, along Bayou Shaffer, and along the Lower Pearl River have begun the process of viewing entire maritime or riverine landscapes. These studies have examined groups of watercraft within the context of their environmental and historical settings, enhancing our understanding of the cultural background involved in the building and use of classes of watercraft through time. The simple fact that many sunken watercraft represent purposeful abandonments, at or near their place of use, enhances their utility for interpreting local or regional history. Changes in the assemblage of watercraft over time can be viewed as reflections of changes in other cultural phenomena (e.g., economy, technology, ethnicity of boat builders), as well as changes in environmental setting. The various watercraft found along the Lower Pearl River, for example, when considered as a group or assemblage of objects, underscore this point. These vessels can be placed within the historical context of the logging industry which played such an important role in the region through the nineteenth and early twentieth centuries. Each of the watercraft served a distinctive function within this economic sphere (Pearson 2000b). That all of these vessels dated prior to the mid-twentieth century underscores the importance of logging along the Pearl River and its disappearance as inland timber resources were depleted.

Remote-sensing technologies now make studies of entire segments of waterways feasible. The contextual landscape or assemblage studies discussed here are possible when remote-sensing survey is coupled with the physical examination of identified submerged vessels, as well as bank-line facilities and structures, and a consideration of local economic and settlement history. This contextual, anthropological approach should be pursued, as it promises to advance underwater archaeological research beyond the more limited "time-capsule" approach so prevalent in the field today.

References

Abrams, Cynthia L., Steven D. Smith, Mark D. Groover, Ramona M. Grunden, Jill S. Quattlebaum, and Christopher O. Clement

1995 *Exploring Fort Polk: Results of an 8,027-Acre Survey in the Main Fort and Peason Ridge Portions of the Fort Polk Military Reservation, Vernon and Natchitoches Parishes, Louisiana.* South Carolina Institute of Archaeology and Anthropology, Cultural Resources Division. University of South Carolina, Columbia. U.S. Army Joint Readiness Training Center, Fort Polk, and National Park Service, Southeast Regional Office, Atlanta.

Adams, William H.

1983 Ethnoarchaeology as a Merging of Historical Archaeology and Oral History. *North American Archaeologist* 4(4):293–305.

Adovasio, J. M., J. D. Gunn, J. Donahue, and R. Stuckenrath

1978 Meadowcroft Rockshelter, 1977: An Overview. *American Antiquity* 43(4):632–651.

Albertson, Paul E., and Joseph B. Dunbar

1993 *Geomorphic Investigation of Shreveport to Daingerfield Navigation Project.* Technical Report GL-93-31. U.S. Army Engineer Waterways Experiment Station. U.S. Army Corps of Engineers, Vicksburg District.

Albertson, Paul E., Maureen K. Corcoran, Whitney Autin, John Kruger, and Theresa Foster

1996 *Geomorphic Investigation of the Great Bend Region.* U.S. Army Engineer Waterways Experiment Station. U.S. Army Corps of Engineers, Vicksburg District.

Allain, Larry, Malcolm Vidrine, Vicki Grafe, Charles Allen, and Steve Johnson

1999 *Paradise Lost? The Coastal Prairie of Louisiana and Texas.* U.S. Fish and Wildlife Service and the U.S. Geological Survey. Brochure available online at: library.fws.gov/pubs/paradise_lost.pdf

Alt, Susan

2008 Unwilling Immigrants: Culture, Change, and the "Other" in Mississippian Societies. In *Invisible Citizens: Captives and Their Consequences,* edited by Catherine M. Cameron, pp. 205–222. University of Utah Press, Salt Lake City.

Andersen, Harold V.

1960 *Geology of Sabine Parish.* Geological Bulletin No. 34. Department of Conservation, Louisiana Geological Survey, Baton Rouge.

1993 *Geology of Natchitoches Parish*. Geological Bulletin No. 44. Louisiana Geological Survey, Baton Rouge.

Anderson, David G.

1990 The Paleoindian Colonization of Eastern North America: A View from the Southeastern United States. In *Early Paleoindian Economies of Eastern North America*, edited by Kenneth B. Tankersley and Barry L. Isaac, pp. 163–216. Research in Economic Anthropology, Supplement 5. JAI Press, Greenwich, Connecticut.

1991 Examining Prehistoric Settlement Distribution in Eastern North America. *Archaeology of Eastern North America* 19:1–22.

1994 *The Savannah River Chiefdoms: Political Change in the Late Prehistoric Southeast.* University of Alabama Press, Tuscaloosa.

1996 Models of Paleoindian and Early Archaic Settlement in the Lower Southeast. In *The Paleoindian and Early Archaic Southeast*, edited by David G. Anderson and Kenneth E. Sassaman, pp. 29–57. University of Alabama Press, Tuscaloosa.

1997 The Role of Cahokia in the Evolution of Southeastern Mississippian Society. In *Cahokia: Domination and Ideology in the Mississippian World,* edited by Timothy R. Pauketat and Thomas E. Emerson, pp. 248–268. University of Nebraska Press, Lincoln.

2004 Paleoindian Occupations in the Southeastern United States. In *New Perspectives on the First Americans,* edited by B. T. Lepper and R. Bonnichsen, pp. 119–128. Center for the Study of the First Americans. Texas A&M University Press, College Station.

Anderson, David G., and Michael K. Faught

1998 The Distribution of Fluted Paleoindian Projectile Points: Update 1998. *Archaeology of Eastern North America* 26:163–187.

2000 Paleoindian Artifact Distributions: Evidence and Implications. *Antiquity* 74:507–513.

Anderson, David G., and J. Christopher Gillam

2000 Paleoindian Colonization of the Americas: Implications from an Examination of Physiography, Demography, and Artifact Distribution. *American Antiquity* 65(1):43–66.

Anderson, David G., and Glen T. Hanson

1988 Early Archaic Settlement in the Southeastern United States: A Case Study from the Savannah River Valley. *American Antiquity* 53(2):262–286.

Anderson, David G., Joe W. Joseph, Mary Beth Reed, and Steven D. Smith

1997 *Fort Polk Preservation Plan, Prehistory and History in Western Louisiana: A Technical Synthesis of Cultural Resource Investigations at Fort Polk.* National Park Service, Southeast Archeological Center. Tallahassee, Florida. U.S. Army Joint Readiness Training Center, Fort Polk, Louisiana.

Anderson, David G., and Robert C. Mainfort, Jr. (editors)

2002 *The Woodland Southeast.* University of Alabama Press, Tuscaloosa.

Anderson, David G., Lisa D. O'Steen, and Kenneth E. Sassaman

1996 Environmental and Chronological Considerations. In *The Paleoindian and Early Archaic Southeast,* edited by David G. Anderson and Kenneth E. Sassaman, pp. 3–15. University of Alabama Press, Tuscaloosa.

Anderson, David G., Michael Russo, and Kenneth E. Sassaman

2007 Mid-Holocene Cultural Dynamics in Southeastern North America. In *Climate Change and Cultural Dynamics: A Global Perspective on Mid-Holocene Transitions,* edited by D. G. Anderson, K. A. Maasch, and D. H. Sandweiss, pp. 457–490. Elsevier, New York.

Anderson, David G., and Kenneth E. Sassaman

1996 Modeling Paleoindian and Early Archaic Settlement in the Southeast: A Historical Perspective. In *The Paleoindian and Early Archaic Southeast,* edited by David G. Anderson and Kenneth E. Sassaman, pp. 16–28.University of Alabama Press, Tuscaloosa.

2004 Early and Middle Holocene Periods, 9500 to 3750 B.C. In *Handbook of North American Indians,* Vol. 14: *Southeast,* edited by Raymond D. Fogelson, pp. 87–100. Smithsonian Institution Press, Washington, D.C.

Anderson, David G., and Kenneth E. Sassaman (editors)

1996 *The Paleoindian and Early Archaic Southeast.* University of Alabama Press, Tuscaloosa.

Anderson, David G., and Steven D. Smith

2003 *Archaeology, History, and Predictive Modeling: Research at Fort Polk, 1972–2002.* University of Alabama Press, Tuscaloosa.

Anderson, James D.

1988 *The Education of Blacks in the South, 1860–1935.* University of North Carolina Press, Chapel Hill.

Archivo Colegio Querétero (ACQ)

1721 Concerning the Transfer of Missions from the Río San Marcos to the Area of the Río San Antonio, including Plans of the Presidio de los Adaes. ACQ Reel 9, Frames 1639–1647. Old Spanish Missions Historical Research Library, Our Lady of the Lake University. San Antonio, Texas. Original document from Archivo Colegio Querétero, Mexico.

Arco, Lee J., Katherine A. Adelsberger, Ling-yu Hung, and Tristram R. Kidder

2006 Alluvial Geoarchaeology of a Middle Archaic Mound Complex in the Lower Mississippi Valley, U.S.A. *Geoarchaeology* 21(6):591–614.

Armistead, Samuel

1991 Tres Dialectos Españoles de Louisiana. *Lingüística Española Actual* 13:279–301.

Armistead, Samuel, and Hiram R. Gregory

1986 French Loan Words in the Spanish Dialect of Sabine and Natchitoches Parishes. *Louisiana Folklife* 10:121–130.

Arnesen, Eric

1994 *Waterfront Workers of New Orleans: Race, Class, and Politics, 1863–1923.* University of Illinois Press, Urbana.

Aten, Lawrence E.

1983 *Indians of the Upper Texas Coast.* Academic Press, New York.

Aten, Lawrence E., and Charles N. Bollich

2002 *Late Holocene Settlement in the Taylor Bayou Drainage Basin: Test Excavations at the Gaulding Site (41JF27), Jefferson County, Texas.* Studies in Archeology No. 40. Texas Archeological Research Laboratory, University of Texas at Austin. Special Publication No. 4, Texas Archeological Society.

Autin, Whitney J.

1997 Geological Correlation of Surficial Deposits at Willow Chute, Lower Red River Valley, Bossier Parish, Louisiana. Appendix I in *Regional Archaeology Program, Management Unit 1: Eighth Annual Report,* by Jeffrey S. Girard, pp. 90–100. Report on file with the Louisiana Division of Archaeology, Department of Culture, Recreation, and Tourism, Baton Rouge.

Autin, Whitney J., Scott F. Burns, Bobby J. Miller, Roger T. Saucier, and John I. Snead

1991 Quaternary Geology of the Lower Mississippi Valley. In *Quaternary Nonglacial Geology: Conterminous U.S.,* edited by R. B. Morrison, pp. 547–582. The Geology of North America, Vol. K-2. Geological Society of America, Boulder.

Autin, Whitney J., Richard P. McCulloh, and A. Todd Davison

1986 Quaternary Geology of Avery Island, Louisiana. *Transactions, Gulf Coast Association of Geological Societies* 36:379–390.

Avery, George

1995–2005 Annual Reports of the Los Adaes Station Archaeology Program. Reports on file with the Louisiana Division of Archaeology, Department of Culture, Recreation, and Tourism, Baton Rouge.

1997 More Friend than Foe: Eighteenth-Century Spanish, French, and Caddoan Interaction at Los Adaes, a Capital of Texas Located in Northwestern Louisiana. *Louisiana Archaeology* 22(1995):163–193.

Avery, George, H. F. Gregory, Jason Emery, and Jeffrey Girard

2007 French Faience in Northwest Louisiana. In *French Colonial Pottery: A Conference,* edited by George Avery, pp. 411–470. Northwestern State University Press, Natchitoches.

Babson, David

1990 The Archaeology of Racism and Ethnicity on Southern Plantations. *Historical Archaeology* 24(4):20–28.

Bagur, Jacques D.

2001 *A History of Navigation on Cypress Bayou and the Lakes.* University of North Texas Press, Denton.

Baker, Charles M.

1982 A Brief Study of the Arkansas Novaculite Quarries. In *Fancy Hill: Archaeological Studies in the Southern Ouachita Mountains*, edited by Ann M. Early and W. Fredrick Limp, pp. 307–334. Research Series No. 16. Arkansas Archeological Survey, Fayetteville.

Balesi, Charles J.

1992 *The Time of the French in the Heart of North America, 1673–1818.* Alliance Française, Chicago.

Barker, Alex W.

1992 *An Archaeological Survey of the Western Margin of the Upper Tensas Basin, Louisiana: Final Report.* Museum of Anthropology, University of Michigan, Ann Arbor. Report prepared for the Louisiana Division of Archaeology, Department of Culture, Recreation, and Tourism, Baton Rouge.

1993 Settled on Complexity: Defining and Debating Social Complexity in the Lower Mississippi Valley. Paper presented at the 58th Annual Meeting of the Society for American Archaeology, St. Louis.

1999 Chiefdoms and the Economics of Perversity. Unpublished Ph.D. dissertation, Department of Anthropology, University of Michigan, Ann Arbor.

Barker, Alex W., and Timothy R. Pauketat (editors)

1992 *Lords of the Southeast: Social Inequality and the Native Elites of Southeastern North America.* Archeological Papers of the American Anthropological Association No. 3. Washington, D.C.

Barnett, James F., Jr.

2007 *The Natchez Indians: A History to 1735.* University Press of Mississippi, Jackson.

Barry, John M.

1997 *Rising Tide: The Great Mississippi Flood of 1927 and How It Changed America.* Simon and Schuster, New York.

Bates, Alan L.

1968 *The Western Rivers Steamboat Cyclopœdium or American Riverboat Structure & Detail Salted with Lore.* Hustle Press, Leonia, New Jersey.

1996 *The Western Rivers Engineroom Cyclopœdium.* Cyclopœdium Press, Louisville, Kentucky.

Beaudry, Mary C. (editor)

1988 *Documentary Archaeology in the New World.* Cambridge University Press, Cambridge.

Beavers, Richard C.

1979 Radiometric Dating Samples—Coquilles Site. *Louisiana Archaeological Society Newsletter* 6:12–18.

Beavers, Richard C., and Teresia R. Lamb

1993 *Hermann-Grima Historic House, New Orleans, Louisiana: Ironing Room and Mystery Building Archaeological Testing.* Research Report No. 18. Archaeological and Cultural Research Program, Department of Anthropology, University of New Orleans. Report on file with the Louisiana Division of Archaeology, Department of Culture, Recreation, and Tourism, Baton Rouge.

Beavers, Richard C, Teresia R. Lamb, and John R. Greene

1988 *Hermann-Grima Historic House, East Alleyway Excavation, New Orleans, Louisiana.* Research Report No. 14. Archaeological and Cultural Research Program, Department of Anthropology, University of New Orleans.

1990 *Hermann-Grima Historic House Wine Room Excavations, New Orleans, Louisiana.* Archaeological and Cultural Research Program, Department of Anthropology, University of New Orleans.

Belmont, John S.

1967 The Cultural Sequence at the Greenhouse Site, Louisiana. *Southeastern Archaeological Conference Bulletin* 6:27–35.

1980 *Goldmine (16RI13): Preliminary Report on the 1980 Season.* Submitted to the Louisiana Division of Archaeology, Department of Culture, Recreation, and Tourism, Baton Rouge.

1983 Appendix D: Faunal Remains, D.1 Analysis of the Bone and Shell. In *Excavations at the Lake George Site, Yazoo County, Mississippi, 1958–1960,* by Stephen Williams and Jeffrey P. Brain, pp. 451–469. Papers of the Peabody Museum of Archaeology and Ethnology Vol. 74. Harvard University, Cambridge.

1984 The Troyville Concept and the Gold Mine Site. *Louisiana Archaeology* 9(1982):65–98.

1985 A Reconnaissance of the Boeuf Basin, Louisiana. *Louisiana Archaeology* 10(1983):271–284.

Belmont, John S., and Stephen Williams

1981 Painted Pottery Horizons in the Southern Lower Mississippi Valley. In *Traces of Prehistory, Papers in Honor of William G. Haag,* edited by F. H. West and R. W. Neuman, pp. 19–42. Geoscience and Man 22. Louisiana State University, Baton Rouge.

Bennett, W. J., Jr.

1982 *Archeological Investigations within the Bayou Bodcau and Tributaries Project Area, Louisiana.* Report No. 21. Archeological Assessments, Inc., Nashville, Arkansas. U.S. Army Corps of Engineers, Little Rock District.

Bense, Judith A.

1994 *Archaeology of the Southeastern United States, Paleoindian to World War I.* Academic Press, New York.

2004 Introduction: Presidios of the North American Spanish Borderlands. *Historical Archaeology* 38(3):1–5.

Berkhofer, Jr., Robert F.

1978 *The White Man's Indian: Images of the American Indian from Columbus to the Present.* Random House, New York.

Berthelot, Raymond Octave

2001 A Comparison of the Archaeological and Documentary Evidence Relating to the Material Culture from Nuestra Señora del Pilar de Los Adaes, an Eighteenth-Century Spanish Colonial Frontier Presidio. Unpublished M.A. thesis, Department of History, Louisiana State University, Baton Rouge.

Bexar Archives Microfilm

1771 Book of Accounts of the Troops of Los Adaes detached in Béxar, January 1, 1771, to December 31, 1771. 225 pp. Microfilm Roll 10, frames 0760–0823. Cammie Henry Research Center, Northwestern State University, Natchitoches.

Beyer, George E.

1896 The Mounds of Louisiana. *Publications of the Louisiana Historical Society* 1(4):12–32.

1899 Investigations of Some Shell-Mounds in Calcasieu Parish. *Publications of the Louisiana Historical Society* 2(2):16–23.

Binford, Lewis R.

1965 Archaeological Systematics and the Study of Cultural Process. *American Antiquity* 31(2):203–210.

1968 Some Comments on Historical versus Processual Archaeology. *Southwestern Journal of Anthropology* 24(3):267–275.

1980 Willow Smoke and Dogs' Tails: Hunter-Gatherer Settlement Systems and Archaeological Site Formation. *American Antiquity* 45(1):4–20.

Biolsi, Thomas, and Larry Zimmerman (editors)

1997 *Indians and Anthropologists: Vine Deloria, Jr., and the Critique of Anthropology.* University of Arizona Press, Tucson.

Birchett, Thomas C. C., and Charles E. Pearson

1996 The Search for the Wreck of the USS *Eastport* and *Edward F. Dix.* In *Underwater Archaeology*, edited by Stephen R. James, Jr., and Camille Stanley, pp. 88–93. Society for Historical Archaeology, Uniontown, Pennsylvania.

Birchett, Thomas C. C., Charles E. Pearson, and George J. Castille

2001 *Historic Navigation and Shipwreck Study, Lower Atchafalaya Basin, Re-evaluation Study, South Central Louisiana.* Coastal Environments, Inc., Baton Rouge. U.S. Army Corps of Engineers, New Orleans District.

Bitgood, Mark J.

1989 *The Baytown Period in the Upper Tensas Basin.* Lower Mississippi Survey Bulletin 12. Peabody Museum, Harvard University, Cambridge.

Blaine, Jay C.

1996 Conservation and Identification of Metal Artifacts from Los Adaes. *Southern Studies* 7(1):97–119.

Blaine, Jay C., and George Avery

2005 *Los Adaes Station Archaeology Program. Metal Artifacts.* Report on file with the

Louisiana Division of Archaeology, Department of Culture, Recreation, and Tourism, Baton Rouge.

Blassingame, John W.

1973 *Black New Orleans: 1860–1880*. University of Chicago Press, Chicago.

Blind, Eric Blandan, Barbara L. Voss, Sannie Kenton Osborn, and Leo R. Barker

2004 El Presidio de San Francisco: At the Edge of Empire. *Historical Archaeology* 38(3):135–149.

Blitz, John H.

1985 *An Archaeological Study of the Mississippi Choctaw Indians*. Archaeological Report No. 16. Mississippi Department of Archives and History, Jackson.

1993 Big Pots for Big Shots: Feasting and Storage in a Mississippian Community. *American Antiquity* 58(1):80–96.

Blitz, John H., and Patrick Livingood

2004 Sociopolitical Implications of Mississippian Mound Volume. *American Antiquity* 69(2):291–301.

Blitz, John H., and C. Baxter Mann

2000 *Fisherfolk, Farmers, and Frenchmen: Archaeological Explorations on the Mississippi Gulf Coast*. Archaeological Report No. 30. Mississippi Department of Archives and History, Jackson.

Blitz, John H., C. Baxter Mann, and Ray L. Bellande

1995 Fort Maurepas and Vieux Biloxi: Search and Research. *Mississippi Archaeology* 30(1):23–58.

Block, William T.

2003 Early River Boats of Southwest Louisiana. W. T. Block, Jr., Papers, Collection No. 191, Box 1, Folder 1. Archives and Special Collections Department, Frazar Memorial Library, McNeese State University. Lake Charles, Louisiana. Available online at www.wtblock.com/wtblockjr/.

Bolton, Herbert E.

1970a *Athanase de Mézières and the Louisiana-Texas Frontier, 1768–1780*. Reprint by Kraus Reprint Co., New York. Originally published 1914, Arthur H. Clark Co., Cleveland.

1970b *Texas in the Middle Eighteenth Century: Studies in Spanish Colonial History and Administration*. Reprint by University of Texas Press, Austin. Originally published 1915, University of California Press, Berkeley.

Bonnichsen, Robson, Bradley T. Lepper, Dennis J. Stanford, and Michael R. Waters (editors)

2006 *Paleoamerican Origins: Beyond Clovis*. Texas A&M University Press, College Station.

Borremans, Nina T., and Craig D. Shaak

1986 A Preliminary Report on Investigations of Sponge Spicules in Florida "Chalky" Paste Pottery. In *Ceramic Notes No. 3: Papers in Ceramic Analysis*, edited by Prudence Rice, pp. 125–132. Occasional Publications of the Ceramic Technology Laboratory. Florida State Museum, Gainesville.

Botkin, Benjamin A. (editor)

1945 *Lay My Burden Down: A Folk History of Slavery.* University of Chicago Press, Chicago.

Brackenridge, Henry M.

1814 *Views of Louisiana; Together with a Journal of a Voyage up the Missouri River, in 1811.* Cramer, Spear, and Eichbaum, Pittsburgh, Pennsylvania.

Bousman, C. Britt, Barry W. Baker, and Anne C. Kerr

2004 Paleoindian Archeology in Texas. In *The Prehistory of Texas,* edited by Timothy K. Perttula, pp. 15–97. Texas A&M University Press, College Station.

Bradshaw, Jim

2001 *100 Years on the River: The Chotin Family and Their Boats.* Louisiana Life Series 11, Center for Louisiana Studies, University of Louisiana at Lafayette.

Brain, Jeffrey P.

1969 Winterville: A Case Study of Prehistoric Culture Contact in the Lower Mississippi Valley. Ph.D. dissertation, Department of Anthropology, Yale University, New Haven.

1978 Late Prehistoric Settlement Patterning in the Yazoo Basin and Natchez Bluffs Regions of the Lower Mississippi Valley. In *Mississippian Settlement Patterns,* edited by Bruce Smith, pp. 331–368. Academic Press, New York.

1979 *Tunica Treasure.* Papers of the Peabody Museum of Archaeology and Ethnology Vol. 71. Harvard University, Cambridge.

1988 *Tunica Archaeology.* Papers of the Peabody Museum of Archaeology and Ethnology Vol. 78. Harvard University, Cambridge.

1989 *Winterville: Late Prehistoric Culture Contact in the Lower Mississippi Valley.* Archaeological Report No. 23. Mississippi Department of Archives and History, Jackson.

1991 Cahokia from the Southern Periphery. In *New Perspectives on Cahokia: Views from the Periphery,* edited by J. B. Stoltman, pp. 93–100. Monographs in World Archaeology 2. Prehistory Press, Madison, Wisconsin.

1994 *On the Tunica Trail.* Third edition. Anthropological Study No. 1. Louisiana Archaeological Survey and Antiquities Commission, Department of Culture, Recreation, and Tourism, Baton Rouge.

Brain, Jeffrey P., and Philip Phillips

1996 *Shell Gorgets: Styles of the Late Prehistoric and Protohistoric Southeast.* Peabody Museum Press, Cambridge.

Brasher, Ted J.

1973 An Investigation of Some Central Functions of Poverty Point. Unpublished M.A. thesis, Northwestern State University, Natchitoches.

Brasseaux, Carl A. (editor)

1996 *A Refuge for All Ages: Immigration in Louisiana History.* Louisiana Purchase Bicentennial Series in Louisiana History Vol. 10. Center for Louisiana Studies, University of Southwestern Louisiana, Lafayette.

Brasseaux, Carl, and Keith P. Fontenot

2004 *Steamboats on Louisiana's Bayous: A History and Directory.* Louisiana State University Press, Baton Rouge.

Brassieur, C. Ray

1983 Appendix III: Analyses of Cultural Material Recovered by Peason Ridge Surveys. In *U.S.L. Fort Polk Archaeological Survey and Cultural Resources Management Program,* Vol. I, edited by A. Frank Servello, pp. 241–328. University of Southwestern Louisiana, Lafayette.

1993 The Louisiana Lugger: Lessons from Living Tradition. In *The European Origins of the Small Watercraft of the United States and Canada, Proceedings of the 19th Annual Museum Small Craft Association Meeting,* edited by Joseph T. Butler, Jr., pp. 51–68. Center for Traditional Louisiana Boat Building, Nicholls State University and the Museum Small Craft Association, Thibodaux, Louisiana.

2007 Atchafalaya Basin Boats and Boat Builders, In *Inherit the Atchafalaya,* by Greg Guirard and C. Ray Brassieur, pp. 52–58. Center for Louisiana Studies, University of Louisiana at Lafayette.

Briede, Kathryn

1937 A History of the City of Lafayette. *Louisiana Historical Quarterly* 20(4):895–964.

Brightman, Robert A.

2004 Chitimacha. In *Handbook of North American Indians,* Vol. 14: *Southeast,* edited by Raymond D. Fogelson, pp. 642–652. Smithsonian Institution Press, Washington, D.C.

Brock, Erik J., and Gary D. Joiner

1999 *Red River Steamboats.* Arcadia Publishing, Mount Pleasant, South Carolina.

Brown, David O.

1982 Chemical Analysis of Ceramics and Lithics from the Eagle Hill II Site. In *Eagle Hill: A Late Quaternary Upland Site in Western Louisiana,* by Joel D. Gunn and David O. Brown, pp. 163–179. Special Report 12. Center for Archaeological Research, University of Texas at San Antonio.

Brown, Ian W.

1975 Excavations at Fort St. Pierre. *Conference on Historic Site Archaeology Papers, 1974* 9:60–85.

1976 The Portland Site (22-M-12), An Early Eighteenth-Century Historic Indian Site in Warren County, Mississippi. *Mississippi Archaeology* 11(1):2–11.

1977 A Reexamination of the Houses at the Bayou Goula Site, Iberville Parish, Louisiana. *Louisiana Archaeology* 3(1976):193–205.

1978a *James Alfred Ford: The Man and His Works.* Special Publication No. 4, Southeastern Archaeological Conference. Memphis, Tennessee.

1978b Archaeology on Avery Island, 1978. *Louisiana Archaeological Society Newsletter* 5(4):9–11.

1978c Artifact Patterning and Activity Areas: The Evidence from Fort St. Pierre, Mississippi. *Conference on Historic Site Archaeology Papers, 1977* 12:309–321.

1979a Archaeological Investigations at Salt Mine Valley (35-I-5). *Petite Anse Project Research Notes* 8. Lower Mississippi Survey, Peabody Museum. Harvard University, Cambridge.

1979b *Certain Coastal Settlement Pattern Changes in the Petite Anse Region of Southwest Louisiana.* Peabody Museum, Harvard University, Cambridge. Report on file with the Louisiana Division of Archaeology, Department of Culture, Recreation, and Tourism, Baton Rouge.

1979c *Early Eighteenth-Century French-Indian Culture Contact in the Yazoo Bluffs Region of the Lower Mississippi Valley.* Ph.D. dissertation, Department of Anthropology, Brown University, Providence, Rhode Island.

1979d Bells. In *Tunica Treasure,* by Jeffery P. Brain, pp.197–205. Papers of the Peabody Museum of Archaeology and Ethnology Vol. 71. Harvard University, Cambridge.

1980 Archaeological Investigations on Avery Island, Louisiana, 1978. *Southeastern Archaeological Conference Bulletin* 22:110–118.

1981 *The Role of Salt in Eastern North American Prehistory.* Anthropological Study No. 3. Louisiana Archaeological Survey and Antiquities Commission, Department of Culture, Recreation, and Tourism, Baton Rouge.

1982a *The Southeastern Check Stamped Pottery Tradition: A View from Louisiana.* Midcontinental Journal of Archaeology Special Paper 4. Kent State University Press, Kent, Ohio.

1982b An Archaeological Study of Culture Contact and Change in the Natchez Bluffs Region. In *La Salle and His Legacy: Frenchmen and Indians in the Lower Mississippi Valley,* edited by Patricia K. Galloway, pp. 176–193. University Press of Mississippi, Jackson.

1983 Plaquemine Culture Houses in the Natchez Bluffs Region, Mississippi: Excavations at the Lookout Site. *Mississippi Archaeology* 18(1):14–26.

1984 Late Prehistory in Coastal Louisiana: The Coles Creek Period. In *Perspectives on Gulf Coast Prehistory,* edited by Dave D. Davis, pp. 94–124. Ripley P. Bullen Monographs in Anthropology and History No. 5. University Press of Florida, Gainesville.

1985a *Natchez Indian Archaeology: Culture Change and Stability in the Lower Mississippi Valley.* Archaeological Report No. 15. Mississippi Department of Archives and History, Jackson.

1985b Plaquemine Architectural Patterns in the Natchez Bluffs and Surrounding Regions of the Lower Mississippi Valley. *Midcontinental Journal of Archaeology* 10(2):251–305.

1987 Afterword—The Morgan Site in Regional Perspective. In *Excavations at Morgan: A Coles Creek Mound Complex in Coastal Louisiana,* edited by R. Fuller and D. Fuller, pp. 155–164. Lower Mississippi Survey Bulletin 11. Peabody Museum, Harvard University. Cambridge.

1990 Historic Indians of the Lower Mississippi Valley: An Archaeologist's View. In *Towns and Temples along the Mississippi,* edited by David H. Dye and Cheryl A. Cox, pp. 227–238. University of Alabama Press, Tuscaloosa.

1992 Certain Aspects of French-Indian Interaction in Lower *Louisiane.* In *Calumet and Fleur-de-lys: Archaeology of Indian and French Contact in the Midcontinent,* edited by John A. Walthall and Thomas E. Emerson, pp.17–34. Smithsonian Institution Press, Washington, D.C.

1998a *Decorated Pottery of the Lower Mississippi Valley: A Sorting Manual.* Mississippi Department of Archives and History, Jackson.

1998b The Eighteenth-Century Natchez Chiefdom. In *The Natchez District in the Old, Old South,* edited by Vincas P. Steponaitis, pp. 49–65. Southern Research Report No. 11. Academic Affairs Library, Center for the Study of the American South, University of North Carolina, Chapel Hill.

1998c Plaquemine Culture. In *Archaeology of Prehistoric Native America: An Encyclopedia,* edited by Guy Gibbon, pp. 657–659. Garland Publishing, Inc., New York.

1999a In the Land of Salt and Tabasco: Archaeology of Coastal Louisiana. Manuscript on file with the Gulf Coast Survey, Alabama Museum of Natural History, Tuscaloosa, and Avery Island Inc., Avery Island, Louisiana.

1999b Salt Manufacture and Trade from the Perspective of Avery Island, Louisiana. *Midcontinental Journal of Archaeology* 24(2):113–151.

2007 Plaquemine Culture in the Natchez Bluffs Region of Mississippi. In *Plaquemine Archaeology,* edited by Mark A. Rees and Patrick C. Livingood, pp. 145–160. University of Alabama Press, Tuscaloosa.

Brown, Ian W. (editor)

2003 *Bottle Creek: A Pensacola Culture Site in South Alabama.* University of Alabama Press, Tuscaloosa.

Brown, Ian W., Richard S. Fuller, and Nancy Lambert-Brown

1979 Site Survey in the Petite Anse Region, Southwest Coast, Louisiana. *Petite Anse Project Research Notes* 11. Lower Mississippi Survey, Peabody Museum. Harvard University, Cambridge.

Brown, Ian W., and Nancy Lambert-Brown

1978 Lower Mississippi Survey Petite Anse Project. *Petite Anse Project Research Notes* 5. Lower Mississippi Survey, Peabody Museum. Harvard University, Cambridge.

1979 The Mississippian Ceramics from Salt Mine Valley (33-I-5). *Petite Anse Project Research Notes* 10. Lower Mississippi Survey, Peabody Museum. Harvard University, Cambridge.

Brown, Kenneth L.

1997 Some Thoughts on Archaeology and Public Responsibility. *African-American Archaeology* 18:6–7.

Bruseth, James E.

1980 Intrasite Structure at the Claiborne Site. In Caddoan and Poverty Point Archaeology: Essays in Honor of Clarence Hungerford Webb, edited by Jon L. Gibson. *Louisiana Archaeology* 6(1979):283–318.

1991 Poverty Point Development as Seen at the Cedarland and Claiborne Sites, Southern Mississippi. In *The Poverty Point Culture: Local Manifestations, Subsistence Practices, and Trade Networks,* edited by Kathleen M. Byrd, pp. 7–25. Geoscience and Man 29. Louisiana State University, Baton Rouge.

2005 The Shipwreck of La Salle's *La Belle.* In *Unlocking the Past: Historical Archaeology in North America,* edited by Lu Ann De Cunzo and John H. Jameson, pp. 68–71. University Press of Florida, Gainesville.

Bruseth, James E., Jeffery J. Durst, Tiffany Osburn, Kathleen Gilmore, Kay Hindes, Nancy Reese, Barbara Meisner, and Mike Davis

2004 A Clash of Two Cultures: Presidio La Bahía on the Texas Coast as a Deterrent to French Incursion. In Presidios of the North American Spanish Borderlands, edited by Judith A. Bense. *Historical Archaeology* 38(3):78–93.

Bruseth, James E., and Timothy K. Perttula

2006 Archeological Investigations at the Hudnall-Pirtle Site (41RK4), An Early Caddo Mound Center in Northeast Texas. *Caddo Archeology Journal* 15:57–158.

Bruseth, James E., and Toni S. Turner

2005 *From a Watery Grave: The Discovery and Excavation of La Salle's Shipwreck,* La Belle. Texas A&M University Press, College Station.

Bullen, Ripley P.

1972 The Orange Period of Peninsular Florida. In *Fiber Tempered Pottery in the Southeastern United States and Northern Columbia: Its Origins, Context, and Significance,* edited by Ripley P. Bullen and James B. Stoltman, pp. 9–33. FAS Publications No. 6. Florida Anthropological Society, Gainesville.

1974 The Origins of the Gulf Tradition as Seen from Florida. *Florida Anthropologist* 27(2):77–88.

Burden, Eileen K., and George Castille

1981 *Archaeological Testing of Portions of Magnolia Mound Plantation, East Baton Rouge Parish, Louisiana.* Coastal Environments, Inc., Baton Rouge. Louisiana Division of Archaeology, Department of Culture, Recreation, and Tourism, Baton Rouge.

Burden, Eileen K., and Sherwood M. Gagliano.

1977 *Archaeological Excavation at Magnolia Mound: A Search for the 1830 Kitchen.* Report on file with the Louisiana Division of Archaeology, Department of Culture, Recreation, and Tourism, Baton Rouge.

Burke, Allison

2002 The Panther Lake Phase of the Tchefuncte Culture. Paper presented at the 59th Southeastern Archaeological Conference, Biloxi, Mississippi.

Burton, H. Sophie, and F. Todd Smith

2008 *Colonial Natchitoches: A Creole Community on the Louisiana-Texas Frontier.* Texas A&M University Press, College Station.

Bushnell, David I.

1935 The Manahoac Tribes in Virginia, 1608. *Smithsonian Miscellaneous Collections.* Vol. 94, No. 8. Washington, D.C.

Buskey, Nikki

2007 Crews Clearing Abandoned Boats from Area Bayous. *The Courier*, August 15, 2007. Houma, Louisiana. Online at: www.houmatoday.com/article/20070815/NEWS/708150318

Butler, Brian M., and Paul D. Welch (editors)

2006 *Leadership and Polity in Mississippian Society.* Occasional Paper No. 33. Center for Archaeological Investigations, Southern Illinois University, Carbondale.

Byrd, Kathleen M.

1974 Tchefuncte Subsistence Patterns: Morton Shell Mound, Iberia Parish, Louisiana. Unpublished M.A. thesis, Department of Geography and Anthropology, Louisiana State University, Baton Rouge.

1978 Zooarchaeological Analyses of Material from Certain Sites along Bayous Chene, Shaffer, and the Lower Atchafalaya River. In *Archaeological Survey of the Lower Atchafalaya Region, South Central Louisiana,* by Jon L. Gibson, pp. 216–224. Center for Archaeological Studies Report No. 5. University of Southwestern Louisiana, Lafayette. U.S. Army Corps of Engineers, New Orleans District.

1980 Zooarchaeological Analysis of the Hanna Site: An Alto Focus Occupation in Louisiana. In The Hanna Site: An Alto Focus Village in Red River Parish. *Louisiana Archaeology* 5(1978):235–265.

1994 Tchefuncte Subsistence Practices at the Morton Shell Mound, Iberia Parish, Louisiana. *Louisiana Archaeology* 16(1989):1–128.

2008 *Colonial Natchitoches: Outpost of Empires.* Xlibris Corporation, Bloomington.

Byrd, Kathleen M., and Robert W. Neuman

1978 Archaeological Data Relative to Prehistoric Subsistence in the Lower Mississippi River Alluvial Valley. In *Man and Environment in the Lower Mississippi Valley,* edited by Sam B. Hilliard, pp. 9–21. Geoscience and Man 29. Louisiana State University, Baton Rouge.

Caldwell, Joseph A.

1958 *Trend and Tradition in the Prehistory of the Eastern United States.* Memoir No. 88. American Anthropological Association, Menasha, Wisconsin.

Campanella, Richard

2006 *Geographies of New Orleans: Urban Fabrics before the Storm.* Center for Louisiana Studies, University of Louisiana at Lafayette.

Campbell, L. Janice, and Carol S. Weed

1986 *Cultural Resource Investigations in the Proposed Multipurpose Range Complex Area, Fort Polk, Vernon Parish, Louisiana.* Two vols. New World Research, Inc., Report of Investigations 85–6. Pollock, Louisiana. National Park Service, Archeological Services Branch. Atlanta, Georgia.

Campbell, L. Janice, James R. Morehead, and A. Frank Servello

1990 *Data Recovery at 16VN791: A Multicomponent Prehistoric Site in the Birds Creek Drainage, Fort Polk Military Reservation, Fort Polk, Louisiana.* Report of Investigations No. 188. New World Research, Inc., Fort Walton Beach, Florida.

Cannon, Michael D., and David J. Meltzer

2004 Early Paleoindian Foraging: Examining the Faunal Evidence for Large Mammal Specialization and Regional Variability in Prey Choice. *Quaternary Science Reviews* 23:1955–1987.

Carlson, Shawn Bonath

1994 Texas Beyond the Periphery: An Archaeological Study of the Spanish Missions during the 18th Century. Unpublished Ph.D. dissertation, Department of Anthropology, Texas A&M University, College Station.

Carney, Judith A.

2001 African Rice in the Columbian Exchange. *Journal of African History* 42(3): 377–396.

Carpenter, W. M.

1838 Interesting Fossils Found in Louisiana. *American Journal of Science and Arts* 34(1):201–203.

Carr, Philip J., and Lee H. Stewart

2004 Poverty Point Chipped Stone Tool Raw Materials: Inferring Social and Economic Strategies. In *Signs of Power: The Rise of Cultural Complexity in the Southeast,* edited by Jon L. Gibson and Philip J. Carr, pp. 129–145. University of Alabama Press, Tuscaloosa.

Carter, Cecile E.

1995 *Caddo Indians: Where We Come From.* University of Oklahoma Press, Norman.

Cast, Robert

2005 Perspectives: The Caddo Tribe of Oklahoma. In *Assessment of Properties of Traditional Religious and Cultural Importance to the Signatory Tribes of the Native American Historical Initiative: Reconnecting to the Lands of the Louisiana Army National Guard,* edited by David W. Morgan, pp. 129–136. Cultural Resource Office, Northwestern State University, Natchitoches.

Cast, Robert, and Bobby Gonzalez

2005 Introduction: A Rediscovering of Caddo Heritage. In *A Rediscovering of Caddo Heritage: The W. T. Scott Collection at the American Museum of Natural His-*

tory and Other Caddo Collections from Arkansas and Louisiana, by B. Gonzalez, R. Cast, T. K. Perttula, and B. Nelson, pp. 1–5. Caddo Nation of Oklahoma, Historic Preservation Program, Binger.

Cast, Robert, T. K. Perttula, B. Gonzalez, and B. Nelson

2006 A Rediscovery of Caddo Heritage. *Archaeologies: The Journal of the World Archaeological Congress* 2(1):45–51.

Castañeda, Carlos E.

1915–1936 *Our Catholic Heritage in Texas, 1519–1936*. Seven vols. Von Boeckman Jones Company, Austin, Texas.

Castille, George J., Douglas D. Bryant, Joan M. Exnicios, William D. Reeves, and Susan D. deFrance

1986 *Urban Archaeology in Old New Orleans: Historical and Archaeological Investigations within the Greater New Orleans Bridge No. 2 Right-of-Way*. Coastal Environments, Inc., Baton Rouge. Submitted to the Louisiana Department of Transportation and Development, Baton Rouge.

Castille, George J., David B. Kelley, Sally K. Reeves, and Charles E. Pearson

1982 *Archaeological Excavations at Esplanade Avenue and North Rampart Street, New Orleans, Louisiana*. Coastal Environments, Inc., Baton Rouge. Submitted to the National Park Service, Southwest Region, Santa Fe.

Chafe, Wallace

1976 *The Caddoan, Iroquoian, and Siouan Languages*. Mouton, The Hague.

Chipman, Donald E.

1992 *Spanish Texas, 1519–1821*. University of Texas Press, Austin.

Clark, Emily

2007 *Masterless Mistresses: The New Orleans Ursulines and the Development of a New World Society, 1727–1834*. University of North Carolina Press, Chapel Hill.

Clark, John E.

2004a Surrounding the Sacred: Geometry and Design of Early Mound Groups as Function and Meaning. In *Signs of Power: The Rise of Cultural Complexity in the Southeast*, edited by Jon L. Gibson and Philip J. Carr, pp. 162–213. University of Alabama Press, Tuscaloosa.

2004b Mesoamerica Goes Public: Early Ceremonial Centers, Leaders, and Communities. In *Mesoamerican Archaeology*, edited by Julia Hendon and Rosemary Joyce, pp. 43–72. Blackwell Publishing, Malden, Massachusetts.

2006 The Advent of Mesoamerica's Cosmos. Paper presented at the 71st Annual Meeting of the Society for American Archaeology, San Juan, Puerto Rico.

Clark, John E., Jon L. Gibson, and James A. Zeidler

2010 First Towns in the Americas: Searching for Agriculture, Population Growth, and Other Enabling Conditions. In *Becoming Villagers*, edited by M. Bandy and J. Fox. Amerind Studies in Archaeology. University of Arizona Press, Tucson, in press.

Clausen, C. J., A. D. Cohen, C. Emiliani, J. A. Holman, and J. J. Stipp

1979 Little Salt Spring, Florida: A Unique Underwater Site. *Science* 203(4381):609–614.

Clayton, Lawrence A., Vernon J. Knight, Jr., and Edward C. Moore (editors)

1993 *The De Soto Chronicles: The Expedition of Hernando de Soto to North America in 1539–1543.* Two vols. University of Alabama Press, Tuscaloosa.

Clune, John, and Karla W. Wheeler (compilers)

1991 *A Database of Louisiana Shipwrecks.* On file with the Louisiana Division of Archaeology, Department of Culture, Recreation, and Tourism, Baton Rouge.

Clute, Janet R., and Gregory A. Waselkov

2002 Faunal Remains from Old Mobile. In French Colonial Studies at Old Mobile: Selected Studies, edited by Gregory A. Waselkov. *Historical Archaeology* 36(1):129–134.

Cobb, Charles R.

2003 Mississippian Chiefdoms: How Complex? *Annual Review of Anthropology* 26:63–84.

2005 Archaeology and the "Savage Slot": Displacement and Emplacement in the Premodern World. *American Anthropologist* 107(4):563–574.

Cobb, Charles R., and Michael S. Nassaney

2002 Domesticating Self and Society in the Woodland Southeast. In *The Woodland Southeast,* edited by David G. Anderson and Robert C. Mainfort, Jr., pp. 525–539. University of Alabama Press, Tuscaloosa.

Coe, Sophie D., and Michael D. Coe

1996 *The True History of Chocolate.* Thames and Hudson, London.

Collins, Henry B., Jr.

1927a Archaeological Work in Louisiana and Mississippi. In Explorations and Fieldwork of the Smithsonian Institution in 1926. *Smithsonian Miscellaneous Collections* 78(7):200–207. Washington, D.C.

1927b Potsherds from Choctaw Village Sites in Mississippi. *Journal of the Washington Academy of Sciences* 17:259–263.

Collins, Michael B.

2007 Discerning Clovis Subsistence from Stone Artifacts and Site Distributions on the Southern Plains Periphery. In *Foragers of the Terminal Pleistocene in North America,* edited by Renee B. Walker and Boyce N. Driskell, pp. 59–87. University of Nebraska Press, Lincoln.

Colten, Craig E.

2005 *An Unnatural Metropolis: Wresting New Orleans from Nature.* Louisiana State University Press, Baton Rouge.

Comeaux, Malcolm

1985 Folk Boats of Louisiana. In *Louisiana Folklife: A Guide to the State,* edited by Nicholas R. Spitzer, pp. 161–178. Louisiana Folklife Program, Division of the Arts, Baton Rouge.

Commonwealth Associates, Inc.

1981 *A Cultural Resources Survey of the Red River Waterway from Shreveport to the Mississippi River.* Two vols. Report No. 2021. Commonwealth Associates, Inc., Jackson. U.S. Army Corps of Engineers, New Orleans District.

Conn, Steven

2004 *History's Shadow: Native Americans and Historical Consciousness in the Nineteenth Century.* University of Chicago Press, Chicago.

Conn, Thomas L.

1976 The Utilization of Chert at the Poverty Point Site. Unpublished M.A. thesis, Department of Geography and Anthropology, Louisiana State University, Baton Rouge.

Connaway, John M.

1982 The Keenan Bead Cache: Lawrence County, Mississippi. *Louisiana Archaeology* 8(1981):57–71.

Connaway, John M., Samuel O. Brookes, and Samuel O. McGahey

1977 *The Denton Site: A Middle Archaic Occupation in the Northern Yazoo Basin, Mississippi.* Archaeological Report No. 4. Mississippi Department of Archives and History, Jackson.

Connaway, John M., Samuel O. McGahey, Clarence H. Webb, and Roger T. Saucier

1977 *Teoc Creek: A Poverty Point Site in Carroll County, Mississippi.* Archaeological Report No. 3. Mississippi Department of Archives and History, Jackson.

Connolly, Robert

2003 The 1980–1982 Excavations on the Northwest Ridge 1 at the Poverty Point Site. *Louisiana Archaeology* 25(1998).

Conrad, David Eugene

1965 *The Forgotten Farmers: The Story of Sharecroppers in the New Deal.* University of Illinois Press, Urbana.

Corbin, James E.

1989 Retracing the *Camino de los Tejas* from the Trinity River to Los Adaes: New Insights into East Texas History. In *A Texas Legacy: The Old San Antonio Road and the Caminos Reales, A Tricentennial History, 1691–1991,* edited by A. Joachim McGraw, John W. Clark, Jr., and Elizabeth A. Robbins, pp. 191–223. Texas State Department of Highways and Public Transportation, Austin.

Cordell, Ann S.

2002 Continuity and Change in Apalachee Pottery Manufacture. In French Colonial Studies at Old Mobile: Selected Studies, edited by Gregory A. Waselkov. *Historical Archaeology* 36(1):36–54.

Corry, Joseph

1807 *Observations upon the Windward Coast of Africa: The Religion, Character, Customs, etc., of the Natives.* G. and W. Nicol, London.

Costello, Brian J.

1999 *A History of Pointe Coupee Parish, Louisiana.* New Roads Printing, New Roads, Louisiana.

Costin, Cathy Lynne

2001 Craft Production Systems. In *Archaeology at the Millennium: A Sourcebook,* edited by Gary M. Feinman and T. Douglas Price, pp. 273–327. Kluwer Academic/Plenum Publishers, New York.

Cotter, John L.

1991 Update on Natchez Man. *American Antiquity* 56(1):36–39.

Coxe, Carey L., and David B. Kelley

2004 Faunal Remains. In *Data-Recovery Excavations at the Hedgeland Site (16CT19), Catahoula Parish, Louisiana,* edited by Joanne Ryan, pp. 227–239. Coastal Environments, Inc., Baton Rouge. U.S. Army Corps of Engineers, Vicksburg District.

Cramer, Jeramé J., Charles E. Pearson, and David B. Kelley

2007 *Cultural Resources Investigation, Avoca Island Diversion Project, St. Mary and Terrebonne Parishes, Louisiana.* Coastal Environments, Inc., Baton Rouge. U.S. Army Corps of Engineers, New Orleans District.

Crawford, Jessica

2003 Archaic Effigy Beads: A New Look at Some Old Beads. Unpublished M.A. thesis, Department of Anthropology, University of Mississippi, Oxford.

Crumley, Carole L.

1994 Historical Ecology: A Multidimensional Ecological Orientation. In *Historical Ecology: Cultural Knowledge and Changing Landscapes,* edited by Carole L. Crumley, pp. 1–16. School of American Research Press, Santa Fe.

Cummings, Linda Scott

2006 Box 9.3, Poverty Point Objects. In *Ancient Starch Research,* edited by Robin Torrence and Huw Barton, pp. 182–184. Left Coast Press, Walnut Creek, California.

Cusick, James G.

1998 *Studies in Culture Contact. Interaction, Culture Change, and Archaeology.* Occasional Paper No. 25. Center for Archaeological Investigations, Southern Illinois University, Carbondale.

Cusick, James G., Todd McMakin, Shannon Dawdy, and Jill-Karen Yakubik

1995 *Cultural Resources Documentation Black River Bridge at Jonesville JCT. LA 3037 to LA 565, Catahoula and Concordia Parishes Route LA-U.S. 84.* Earth Search, Inc., New Orleans. Louisiana Department of Transportation and Development, Baton Rouge.

Cutler, Hugh C.

1965 Appendix 3: Plant Remains from the Grand Village of the Natchez. In *Archeology of the Fatherland Site: The Grand Village of the Natchez,* by Robert S. Neitzel, p. 102. Anthropological Papers of the American Museum of Natural History Vol. 51, Pt. 1. American Museum of Natural History, New York.

Daniel, I. Randolf., Jr.

2001 Stone Raw Material Availability and Early Archaic Settlement in the Southeastern United States. *American Antiquity* 66(2):237–266.

Dargo, George

1975 *Jefferson's Louisiana: Politics and the Clash of Legal Traditions.* Harvard University Press, Cambridge.

Da Sorrento, Jerom Merolla

1814 A Voyage to Congo and Several Other Countries in Southern Africa, in a *General Collection of the Best and Most Interesting Voyages and Travels in All Parts of the World,* edited by John Pinkerton, pp. 195–336. Longman, Hurst, Rees, Orme, and Borwn, London.

Davis, Dave D.

1981 Ceramic Classification and Temporal Discrimination: A Consideration of Later Prehistoric Stylistic Change in the Mississippi River Delta. *Midcontinental Journal of Archaeology* 6(1):55–89.

1984 Protohistoric Cultural Interaction along the Northern Gulf Coast. In *Perspectives on Gulf Coast Prehistory,* edited by Dave D. Davis, pp. 216–231. Ripley P. Bullen Monographs in Anthropology and History No. 5. University Press of Florida, Gainesville.

1987 Comparative Aspects of Late Prehistoric Faunal Ecology at the Sims Site. *Louisiana Archaeology* 11(1984):111–138.

Davis, Dave D., and Marco J. Giardino

1981 Some Notes Concerning Mississippian Period Ceramics in the Mississippi River Delta. *Louisiana Archaeology* 7(1980):53–66.

Davis, Dave D., Marco J. Giardino, Vickie Carpenter, and Ken Jones

1982 *Archaeological Survey of Grand Bayou, St. Charles Parish, Louisiana.* On file with the Louisiana Division of Archaeology, Department of Culture, Recreation, and Tourism, Baton Rouge.

Davis, Norman

2005 Celestial Alignments at the Marksville Site. In *The William G. Haag Honorary Symposium,* edited by Paul Farnsworth, Charles H. McNutt, and Stephen Williams, pp. 64–94. Occasional Paper 26. Anthropological Research Center, University of Memphis.

Davoli, Elizabeth

1998 Patent Medicines: Ethnic or Socio-Economic Indicators? Paper presented at the 1st Annual South Central Historical Archaeology Conference, Jackson, Mississippi.

Dawdy, Shannon Lee

1998 *Madame John's Legacy (16OR51) Revisited: A Closer Look at the Archaeology of Colonial New Orleans.* Greater New Orleans Archaeology Program, College of Urban and Public Affairs, University of New Orleans. Submitted to the Friends of the Cabildo.

2000a Understanding Cultural Change through the Vernacular: Creolization in Louisiana. *Historical Archaeology* 34(3):107–123.

2000b Ethnicity in the Urban Landscape: The Archaeology of Creole New Orleans. In *Archaeology of Southern Urban Landscapes,* edited by Amy Young, pp. 127–149. University of Alabama Press, Tuscaloosa.

2008 *Building the Devil's Empire: French Colonial New Orleans.* University of Chicago Press, Chicago.

Dawdy, Shannon Lee, Ryan Gray, Rebecca Graff, and Jill-Karen Yakubik

2008 *Archaeological Investigations at the Rising Sun Hotel Site (16OR225), New Orleans, Louisiana*, Vol. 1. Earth Search, Inc., New Orleans. Submitted to The Historic New Orleans Collection.

Dawdy, Shannon Lee, Kristen Gremillion, Susan Mulholland, and Jason Ramsey

2008 *Archaeological Investigations at St. Anthony's Garden (16OR443), New Orleans, Louisiana.* Vol. 1, *2008 Fieldwork and Archaeobotanical Results.* Department of Anthropology, University of Chicago. Submitted to the St. Louis Cathedral, New Orleans.

Dawdy, Shannon Lee, and Juana L. C. Ibáñez

1997 *Beneath the Surface of New Orleans's Warehouse District: Archaeological Investigations at the Maginnis Cotton Mill (16OR144).* Greater New Orleans Archaeology Program, College of Urban and Public Affairs, University of New Orleans. Submitted to the Cotton Mill Limited Partnership.

Dawdy, Shannon Lee, Christopher N. Matthews, Elizabeth M. Scott, and Gayle J. Fritz

2002 *Greater New Orleans Archaeology Program End of Federal Fiscal Year Report, 2001–2002.* Greater New Orleans Archaeology Program, College of Urban and Public Affairs, University of New Orleans. On file with the Louisiana Division of Archaeology, Department of Culture, Recreation, and Tourism, Baton Rouge.

Dawdy, Shannon Lee, and Richard Weyhing

2008 Beneath the Rising Sun: 'Frenchness' and the Archaeology of Desire. *International Journal of Historical Archaeology* 11(3):270–387.

Dawdy, Shannon Lee, Jill-Karen Yakubik, and Herschel Franks

1997 *Archaeological Investigations at Orange Grove Plantation (16JE141).* Earth Search, Inc., New Orleans. Cytec Industries, Westwego, Louisiana.

Deagan, Kathleen

1987 *Artifacts of the Spanish Colonies of Florida and the Caribbean, 1500–1800.* Vol. 1: *Ceramics, Glassware, and Beads.* Smithsonian Institution Press, Washington, D.C.

1991 Historical Archaeology's Contributions to Our Understanding of Early America. In *Historical Archaeology in Global Perspective,* edited by Lisa Falk, pp. 97–112. Smithsonian Institution Press, Washington, D.C.

2002 *Artifacts of the Spanish Colonies of Florida and the Caribbean, 1500–1800.* Vol. 2: *Portable and Personal Possessions.* Smithsonian Institution Press, Washington, D.C.

Debusschere, K., B. J. Miller, and A. F. Ramenofsky

1989 A Geoarchaeological Reconstruction of Cowpen Slough, A Late Archaic Site in East Central Louisiana. *Geoarchaeology* 4:251–270.

Deetz, James

1983 Scientific Humanism and Humanistic Science: A Plea for Paradigmatic Pluralism in Historical Archaeology. In *Historical Archaeology of the Eastern United States: Papers from the R. J. Russell Symposium*, edited by Robert W. Neuman, pp. 27–34. Geoscience and Man 23. Louisiana State University, Baton Rouge.

deFrance, Susan D., and Nicole Cannarozzi

2009 *Faunal Remains from the Rising Sun Hotel Site (16OR225), New Orleans, Louisiana.* Department of Anthropology, University of Florida, Gainesville. Submitted to the Department of Anthropology, University of Chicago.

De Hon, Rene A., Paul A. Washington, Lloyd N. Glawe, Leonard M. Young, and Eric A. Morehead

2001 Formation of Northern Louisiana Ironstones. *Gulf Coast Association of Geological Societies Transactions* 51:55–61.

De Jong, Greta

2002 *A Different Day: African American Struggles for Justice in Rural Louisiana, 1900–1970.* University of North Carolina Press, Chapel Hill.

Delcourt, Paul A., and Hazel R. Delcourt

1987 *Long Term Forest Dynamics of the Temperate Zone: A Case Study of Late-Quaternary Forests in Eastern North America.* Springer-Verlag, New York.

Dering, Philip

2001 Los Adaes Botanical Analysis, 2000–2001 Project Year. In *Los Adaes Station Archaeology Program, 2001 Annual Report*, by George Avery, pp. 142–148. Report on file with the Louisiana Division of Archaeology, Department of Culture, Recreation, and Tourism, Baton Rouge.

Detro, Randall A., Donald W. Davis, and Francine Middleton

1979 *Mississippi River Ship and Boat Sinkings from the Delta to Baton Rouge, 1814 to 1979.* Nicholls State University, Thibodeaux, Louisiana. U.S. Army Corps of Engineers, New Orleans District.

Dillehay, Thomas D.

1989 *Monte Verde: A Late Pleistocene Settlement in Chile.* Vol. 1, *Paleoenvironment and Site Context.* Smithsonian Institution Press, Washington, D.C.

1997 *Monte Verde: A Late Pleistocene Settlement in Chile.* Vol. 2, *The Archaeological Context and Interpretation.* Smithsonian Institution Press, Washington, D.C.

2000 *The Settlement of the Americas: A New Prehistory.* Basic Books, New York.

Dincauze, Dena F.

2000 *Environmental Archaeology: Principles and Practice.* Cambridge University Press, Cambridge.

Domning, Daryl P.

1969 A List, Bibliography, and Index of the Fossil Vertebrates of Louisiana and Mississippi. *Transactions–Gulf Coast Association of Geological Societies* 19:385–422.

Dongoske, Kurt E., Mark Aldenderfer, and Karen Doehner (editors)

2000 *Working Together: Native Americans and Archaeologists.* Society for American Archaeology, Washington, D.C.

Downs, Lauren E.

2004 Plaquemine Culture Structures in the Natchez Bluffs: Architectural Grammar at the Mound 3 Summit Locale, the Anna Site, Adams County, Mississippi. Unpublished M.A. thesis, Department of Anthropology, University of Alabama, Tuscaloosa.

Dragoo, Don W.

1976 Some Aspects of Eastern North American Prehistory: A Review of 1975. *American Antiquity* 41(1):3–27.

Duffield, Lathel F.

1963 The Wolfshead Site: An Archaic-Neo-American Site in San Augustine County, Texas. *Bulletin of the Texas Archaeological Society* 34:83–141.

Duhe, Brian J.

1977 Preliminary Evidence of Seasonal Fishing Activity at Bayou Jasmine. *Louisiana Archaeology* 3(1976):33–74.

1981 A Study of Prehistoric Coles Creek–Plaquemine Cultural and Technological Adaptations in the Upper Barataria Basin. *Southeastern Archaeological Conference Bulletin* 24:34–37.

Dunbar, James S., Michael K. Faught, and S. David Webb

1988 Page/Ladson (8Je591): An Underwater Paleoindian Site in Northwestern Florida. *Florida Anthropologist* 41(4):442–452.

Dunbar, James S., and Pamela K. Vojnovski

2007 Early Floridians and Late Megamammals: Some Technological and Dietary Evidence from Four North Florida Paleoindian Sites. In *Foragers of the Terminal Pleistocene in North America,* edited by Renee B. Walker and Boyce N. Driskell, pp. 167–202. University of Nebraska Press, Lincoln.

Du Pratz, Le Page

1975 [1774] *The History of Louisiana.* Translated and edited by Joseph G. Tregle, Jr. Louisiana Bicentennial Reprint Series, Louisiana State University Press, Baton Rouge.

Durham, James H., and Michael K. Davis

1975 Report on Burials Found at Crenshaw Mound "C," Miller County, Arkansas. *Bulletin of the Oklahoma Anthropological Society* 23:1–90.

DuVal, Kathleen

2006 Interconnectedness and Diversity in "French Louisiana." In *Powhatan's Man-*

tle: Indians in the Colonial Southeast. Rev. ed., edited by Gregory A. Waselkov, Peter H. Wood, and Tom Hatley, pp. 133–162. University of Nebraska Press, Lincoln.

Dye, David H.

1995 Feasting with the Enemy: Mississippian Warfare and Prestige-Goods Circulation. In *Native American Interactions: Multiscalar Analyses and Interpretations in the Eastern Woodlands,* edited by M. S. Nassaney and K. E. Sassaman, pp. 289–316. University of Tennessee Press, Knoxville.

2009 *War Paths, Peace Paths: An Archaeology of Cooperation and Conflict in Native Eastern North America.* Alta Mira Press, Lanham, Maryland.

Early, Ann M.

2000 The Caddos of the Trans-Mississippi South. In *Indians of the Greater Southeast,* edited by B. G. McEwan, pp. 122–141. University Press of Florida, Gainesville.

2004 Prehistory of the Western Interior after 500 B.C. In *Handbook of North American Indians.* Vol. 14, *Southeast,* edited by R.B. Fogelson, pp. 560–573. Smithsonian Institution Press, Washington, D.C.

Earth Search, Inc.

1997 *Documentation of the Remains of a Historic Boat, Baton Rouge Front, Mississippi River Levees, East Baton Rouge Parish, Louisiana.* Earth Search, Inc., New Orleans. U.S. Army Corps of Engineers, New Orleans District.

2009 Outreach Website for Orange Grove, online at: www.earth-search.com/

Echo-Hawk, Roger C.

2000 Ancient History in the New World: Integrating Oral Traditions and the Archaeological Record. *American Antiquity* 65(2):267–290.

El Darragi, S. Dean, and Allen R. Saltus, Jr.

2003 *Archaeological and Hazard Report Block 90, Vermilion Area.* Cochran Technologies, Inc., Houston. Submitted to Spinnaker Exploration Company, Houston, Texas.

Elliot, Jack D., Jr.

1998 *The Fort of Natchez and the Colonial Origins of Mississippi.* Eastern National Parks and Monument Association, Fort Washington, Pennsylvania.

Ellis, Christopher J., Albert C. Goodyear, Dan F. Morse, and Kenneth B. Tankersley

1998 Archaeology of the Pleistocene-Holocene Transition in Eastern North America. In As the World Warmed: Human Adaptations Across the Pleistocene-Holocene Boundary, edited by B. V. Eriksen and L. G. Straus. *Quaternary International* 49/50:151–166.

Emerson, Thomas E.

1997 Cahokian Elite Ideology and the Mississippian Cosmos. In *Cahokia: Domination and Ideology in the Mississippian World,* edited by T. R. Pauketat and T. E. Emerson, pp. 190–228. University of Nebraska Press, Lincoln.

Emerson, Thomas E., and Jeffrey S. Girard

2004 Dating Gahagan and Its Implications for Understanding Cahokia-Caddo Interactions. *Southeastern Archaeology* 23(1):57–64.

Emerson, Thomas E., Randall E. Hughes, Mary R. Hynes, and Sarah U. Wisseman

2003 The Sourcing of and Interpretation of Cahokia-Style Figurines in the Trans-Mississippi South and Southeast. *American Antiquity* 68(2):287–313.

Emerson, Thomas E., Randy Hughes, S. Wisseman, Jon L. Gibson, and Ned J. Jenkins

2006 A Preliminary Analysis of Steatite Quarry Sourcing Using PIMA Technology. Paper presented at the 63rd Southeastern Archaeological Conference, Little Rock, Arkansas.

Emerson, Thomas E., and R. Barry Lewis (editors)

1991 *Cahokia and the Hinterlands: Middle Mississippian Cultures of the Midwest.* University of Illinois Press, Urbana.

Emerson, Thomas E., and Dale McElrath

2001 Interpreting Discontinuity and Historical Process in Midcontinential Late Archaic and Early Woodland Societies. In *The Archaeology of Traditions: Agency and History before and after Columbus,* edited by T. R. Pauketat, pp. 195–217. University Press of Florida, Gainesville.

Emery, Jason A.

2004 What Do Tin-Enameled Ceramics Tell Us? Explorations of Socio-Economic Status through the Archaeological Record in Eighteenth-Century Louisiana: 1700–1790. Unpublished M.A. thesis, Department of Geography and Anthropology, Louisiana State University, Baton Rouge.

Espey, Huston and Associates, Inc.

1983 *The Archaeological Investigation of the Louis Procello Site, 16DS212, De Soto Parish, Louisiana.* Espey, Huston, and Associates, Inc., Austin, Texas. Prepared for Southwestern Electric Power Company, Shreveport.

Ethridge, Robbie

2006 Creating the Shatter Zone: Indian Slave Traders and the Collapse of the Southeastern Chiefdoms. In *Light on the Path: The Anthropology and History of the Southeastern Indians,* edited by Thomas J. Pluckhahn and Robbie Ethridge, pp. 207–218. University of Alabama Press, Tuscaloosa.

Evans, Amanda M., Robert J. Floyd, and Matthew E. Keith

2007 Identifying Offshore Prehistoric Sites from Remote Sensing Data: Preliminary Site Investigation in the Gulf of Mexico. Paper presented at the 72nd Annual Meeting of the Society for American Archaeology, Austin.

Evans, Clifford

1968 James Alfred Ford, 1911–1968. *American Anthropologist* 70(6):1161–1167.

Fagan, Brian M.

2000 *The Little Ice Age: How Climate Made History, 1300–1850.* Basic Books, New York.

2004 *The Long Summer: How Climate Changed Civilization.* Basic Books, New York.

Farnsworth, Paul

1993a Current Research, Louisiana: Riverlake Plantation. *Society for Historical Archaeology Newsletter* 26(3):27–28.

1993b "What Is the Use of Plantation Archaeology?" No Use At All, If No One Else Is Listening! *Historical Archaeology* 27(1):114–116.

2000 Brutality or Benevolence in Plantation Archaeology. *Journal of International Historical Archaeology* 4(2):145–158.

Farnsworth, Paul, and Laurie A. Wilkie

2006 Fish and Grits: Southern, African, and British Influences in Bahamian Foodways. In *Caribbean and Southern: Transnational Perspectives on the U.S. South,* edited by Helen A. Regis, pp. 34–72. Southern Anthropological Society Proceedings, No. 38. University of Georgia Press, Athens.

2010 Excavations at the Sugar Mill of Whitney Plantation, St. John the Baptist Parish, Louisiana, in preparation.

Faught, Michael K.

2004 The Underwater Archaeology of Paleolandscapes, Apalachee Bay, Florida. *American Antiquity* 69(2):275–289.

Faulk, Odie B.

1965 *A Successful Failure. The Saga of Texas: 1519–1810.* Steck-Vaughn Company, Austin.

Feathers, James K., and Evan Peacock

2008 Origins and Spread of Shell-Tempered Ceramics in the Eastern Woodlands: Conceptual and Methodological Frameworks for Analysis. *Southeastern Archaeology* 27(2):286–293.

Ferguson, Leland

1992 *Uncommon Ground: Archaeology and Early African America, 1650–1800.* Smithsonian Institution Press, Washington, D.C.

Ferring, Reid C.

2001 *The Archaeology and Paleoecology of the Aubrey Clovis Site (41DN479), Denton County, Texas.* Center for Environmental Archaeology, Department of Geography, University of North Texas, Denton.

Fiedel, Stuart J.

2007 Quacks in the Ice: Waterfowl, Paleoindians, and the Discovery of America. In *Foragers of the Terminal Pleistocene in North America,* edited by Renee B. Walker and Boyce N. Driskell, pp. 1–14. University of Nebraska Press, Lincoln.

Fifield, Rick, and Judy Bethea

1999 *St. Thomas Public Housing Project, St. Thomas Hope VI Revitalization, Section 106 Approval, Archaeology Review, Preliminary Information.* Submitted to Historic Restoration, Inc., New Orleans.

Firestone, R. B., A. West, J. P. Kennett, L. Becker, T. E. Bunch, Z. S. Revay, P. H. Schultz, T. Belgya, D. J. Kennett, J. M. Erlandson, O. J. Dickenson, A. C. Goodyear, R. S. Harris, G. A. Howard, J. B. Kloosterman, P. Lechler, P. A. Mayewski, J. Montgomery, R. Poreda, T. Darrah, S. S. Que Hee, A. R. Smith, A. Stich, W. Topping, J. H. Wittke, and W. S. Wolbach

2007 Evidence for an Extraterrestrial Impact 12,900 Years Ago that Contributed to the Megafaunal Extinctions and the Younger Dryas Cooling. *Proceedings of the National Academy of Sciences* 104(41):16016–16021.

Fisk, Harold N.

1944 *Geological Investigation of the Alluvial Valley of the Lower Mississippi River.* U.S. Army Corps of Engineers, Mississippi River Commission, Vicksburg.

Flayharty, Robert A., and John W. Muller

1983 *Cultural Resources Investigations of a Portion of Bayou Grand Caillou, Terrebonne Parish, Louisiana.* Planning Division, U.S. Army Corps of Engineers, New Orleans District.

Fogleman, James A.

1991 The Avoyelles–St. Landry Area of South-Central Louisiana in Poverty Point Times. In *The Poverty Point Culture: Local Manifestations, Subsistence Practices, and Trade Networks,* edited by K. Byrd, pp. 89–94. Geoscience and Man 29. Louisiana State University, Baton Rouge.

Foner, Eric

2002 *Who Owns History? Rethinking the Past in a Changing World.* Hill and Wang, New York.

Ford, Ben, Amy Borgens, William Bryant, Dawn Marshall, Peter Hitchcock, Cesar Arias, and Donny Hamilton

2008 *Archaeological Excavation of the Mardi Gras Shipwreck (16GM01), Gulf of Mexico Continental Slope.* Department of Oceanography and Center for Maritime Archaeology and Conservation, Texas A&M University, College Station. OCS Report 2008-037. Minerals Management Service, Gulf of Mexico OCS Region, U.S. Department of the Interior, New Orleans.

Ford, James A.

1935a An Introduction to Louisiana Archaeology. *Louisiana Conservation Review* 4(5):8–11.

1935b *Ceramic Decoration Sequence at an Old Indian Village Site Near Sicily Island, Louisiana.* Anthropological Study No. 1. Department of Conservation, Louisiana Geological Survey, New Orleans.

1935c Outline of Louisiana and Mississippi Pottery Horizons. *Louisiana Conservation Review* 4(6):33–38.

1936 *Analysis of Indian Village Site Collections from Louisiana and Mississippi.* Anthropological Study No. 2. Department of Conservation, Louisiana Geological Survey, New Orleans.

1938 A Chronological Method Applicable to the Southeast. *American Antiquity* 3(3):260–264.

1951 *Greenhouse: A Troyville–Coles Creek Period Site in Avoyelles Parish, Louisiana.* Anthropological Papers of the American Museum of Natural History Vol. 44, Pt. 1. American Museum of Natural History, New York.

1952 *Measurements of Some Prehistoric Design Developments in the Southeastern States.* Anthropological Papers of the American Museum of Natural History Vol. 44, Pt. 3. American Museum of Natural History, New York.

1954 On the Concept of Types: The Type Concept Revisited. *American Anthropologist* 56(1):42–57.

1955 The Puzzle of Poverty Point. *Natural History* 64:466–472.

1963 *Hopewell Culture Burial Mounds near Helena, Arkansas.* Anthropological Papers of the American Museum of Natural History Vol. 50, Pt. 1. American Museum of Natural History, New York.

Ford, James A., Philip Phillips, and William G. Haag

1955 *The Jaketown Site in West-Central Mississippi.* Anthropological Papers of the American Museum of Natural History Vol. 45, Pt. 1. American Museum of Natural History, New York.

Ford, James A., and George I. Quimby, Jr.

1945 *The Tchefuncte Culture: An Early Occupation of the Lower Mississippi Valley.* Memoir No. 2. Society for American Archaeology, Menasha, Wisconsin.

Ford, James A., and Clarence H. Webb

1956 *Poverty Point: A Late Archaic Site in Louisiana.* Anthropological Papers of the American Museum of Natural History Vol. 46, Pt. 1. American Museum of Natural History, New York.

Ford, James A., and Gordon Willey

1940 *Crooks Site: A Marksville Period Burial Mound in LaSalle Parish, Louisiana.* Anthropological Study No. 3. Department of Conservation, Louisiana Geological Survey, New Orleans.

1941 An Interpretation of the Prehistory of the Eastern United States. *American Anthropologist* 43(3):325–363.

Ford, Janet

1990 The Tchula Connection: Early Woodland Culture and Burial Mounds in North Mississippi. *Southeastern Archaeology* 9(2):103–115.

Forshey, Caleb Goldsmith

1845 Description of Some Artificial Mounds on Prairie Jefferson, Louisiana. *American Journal of Science and Arts* 49, Art. 4, pp. 38–42. New Haven.

Fortier, Alcée

1914 *Louisiana:Comprising Sketches of Parishes, Towns, Events, Institutions, and Persons, Arranged in Cyclopedic Form, Vol. III.* Century Historical Association, Madison, Wisconsin.

Fowke, Gerard

1927 Archaeological Work in Louisiana. *Smithsonian Miscellaneous Collections* 78(7):254–259. Washington, D.C.

1928 Archaeological Investigations—II. *44th Annual Report of the Bureau of American Ethnology, 1926–27*, pp. 399–540. Smithsonian Institution, Washington, D.C.

Fowler, Don D.

2000 Archaeology and the Law. In *Topics in Cultural Resource Law*, edited by Donald Forsyth Craib, pp. 1–8. Society for American Archaeology, Washington, D.C.

Fowler, Melvin L., Jerome Rose, Barbara Vander Leest, and Steven R. Ahler

1999 *The Mound 72 Area: Dedicated and Sacred Space in Early Cahokia*. Reports of Investigations No. 54. Illinois State Museum Society, Springfield.

Frank, Joseph V.

1982 The French House Site 22AD668: The White Earth Concession (1720–1729). *Louisiana Archaeology* 8(1981):109–128.

Franks, Herschel A., J. Mossa, Jill-Karen Yakubik, E. Weiss, J. Treffinger, and D. Gatzke

1991 *A Research Design for Archaeological Investigations and Architectural Evaluations within the Proposed Upper Site, New Lock and Connecting Channels, Inner Harbor Navigation Canal, New Orleans, Louisiana*. Earth Search, Inc., New Orleans. U.S. Army Corps of Engineers, New Orleans District.

Fredlund, Glen G.

1982 Where Did the Bayougoula Dance; Why Do They Sing No More: A Reexamination of the Archaeology of the Bayou Goula Area, Iberville Parish, Louisiana. Unpublished M.A. thesis, Department of Geography and Anthropology, Louisiana State University, Baton Rouge.

Freudenburg, William R., Robert Gramling, Shirley Laska, and Kai Erikson

2009 *Catastrophe in the Making: The Engineering of Katrina and the Disasters of Tomorrow*. Island Press, Washington, D.C.

Fritz, Gayle J.

1990 Multiple Pathways to Farming in Precontact Eastern North America. *Journal of World Prehistory* 4(4):387–435.

1992 "Newer," "Better" Maize and the Mississippian Emergence: A Critique of Prime Mover Explanations. In *Late Prehistoric Agriculture: Observations from the Midwest*, edited by W. I. Woods, pp. 19–43. Studies in Illinois Archaeology No. 8. Illinois Historic Preservation Agency, Springfield.

1993 Early and Middle Woodland Period Paleoethnobotany. In *Foraging and Farming in the Eastern Woodlands*, edited by C. Margaret Scarry, pp. 39–56. University Press of Florida, Gainesville.

1994 Coles Creek and Plaquemine Landscapes. Paper presented at the 51st Southeastern Archaeological Conference, Lexington, Kentucky.

1997 *Archaeological Plant Remains from the Birds Creek Site (16CT416), Catahoula, Parish*. Washington University, St. Louis.

Fritz, Gayle J., and Tristram R. Kidder

1993 Recent Investigations into Prehistoric Agriculture in the Lower Mississippi Valley. *Southeastern Archaeology* 12(1):1–14.

Fullen, Stephen

2005 Temporal Trends in Tchula Period Pottery in Louisiana. Unpublished M.A. thesis, Department of Geography and Anthropology, Louisiana State University, Baton Rouge.

Fuller, Richard S.

1998 Indian Pottery and Cultural Chronology of the Mobile-Tensaw Basin and Alabama Coast. *Journal of Alabama Archaeology* 44(1–2):1–51.

Fuller, Richard S., and Diane S. Fuller

1987 *Excavations at Morgan: A Coles Creek Period Mound Complex in Coastal Louisiana.* Lower Mississippi Survey Bulletin 11. Peabody Museum, Harvard University, Cambridge.

Gagliano, Sherwood M.

1963 A Survey of Preceramic Occupations in Portions of South Louisiana and South Mississippi. *Florida Anthropologist* 16(4):105–132.

1967 *Occupation Sequence at Avery Island.* Coastal Studies Series No. 22. Louisiana State University Press, Baton Rouge.

1970 *Archaeological and Geological Studies at Avery Island, 1968–1970: Progress Report.* Coastal Studies Institute, Louisiana State University, Baton Rouge.

1977 *Cultural Resources Evaluation of the Northern Gulf of Mexico Continental Shelf.* Vol. 1: *Prehistoric Cultural Resource Potential.* Coastal Environments, Inc., Baton Rouge. National Park Service, U.S. Department of the Interior.

1984 Geoarchaeology of the Northern Gulf Shore. In *Perspectives on Gulf Coast Prehistory,* edited by Dave D. Davis, pp. 1–40. Ripley P. Bullen Monographs in Anthropology and History No. 5. University Press of Florida, Gainesville.

Gagliano, Sherwood M., and Hiram F. Gregory, Jr.

1965 A Preliminary Survey of Paleoindian Points from Louisiana. *Louisiana Studies* 4(1):62–77.

Gagliano, Sherwood M., Charles E. Pearson, Richard A. Weinstein, Diane E. Wiseman, and Christopher M. McClendon

1982 *Sedimentary Studies of Prehistoric Archaeological Sites. Criteria for the Identification of Submerged Archaeological Sites of the Northern Gulf of Mexico Continental Shelf.* Preservation Planning Series. Coastal Environments, Inc., Baton Rouge.

Gagliano, Sherwood M., and Clarence H. Webb

1970 Archaic and Poverty Point Transition at the Pearl River Mouth. *Southeastern Archaeological Conference Bulletin* 12:42–72.

Gagliano, Sherwood M., and Richard A. Weinstein

1979 Appendix A. The Buras Mounds: A Lower Mississippi River Delta Mound

Group, Plaquemines Parish, Louisiana. In *A Cultural Resources Survey of the Empire to the Gulf of Mexico Waterway,* by Sherwood M. Gagliano, pp. A1–A33. Coastal Environments, Inc., Baton Rouge. U.S. Army Corps of Engineers, New Orleans District.

Galán, Francis X.

2006 *Last Soldiers, First Pioneers: The Los Adaes Border Community on the Louisiana-Texas Frontier, 1721–1779.* Ph.D. dissertation, Department of History, Southern Methodist University, Dallas.

Galloway, Patricia

1995 *Choctaw Genesis, 1500–1700.* University of Nebraska Press, Lincoln.

2002 Colonial Period Transformations in the Mississippi Valley: Disintegration, Alliance, Confederation, Playoff. In *The Transformation of the Southeastern Indians, 1540–1760,* edited by Robbie Ethridge and Charles Hudson, pp. 225–248. University Press of Mississippi, Jackson.

2006 *Practicing Ethnohistory: Mining Archives, Hearing Testimony, and Constructing Narrative.* University of Nebraska Press, Lincoln.

Galloway, Patricia (editor)

1989 *The Southeastern Ceremonial Complex: Artifacts and Analysis.* University of Nebraska Press, Lincoln.

Gardner, Paul S.

1997 Plant Remains. In *Two Caddoan Farmsteads in the Red River Valley,* edited by D. B. Kelley, pp. 109–120. Research Series No. 51. Arkansas Archeological Survey, Fayetteville.

Garrison, Ervan G., Charles P. Giammona, James Jobling, Anthony R. Tripp, Eri N. Weinstein, and Gary A. Wolff

1989 *An Eighteenth-Century Ballast Pile Site, Chandeleur Islands, Louisiana: An Instrumental and Archaeological Study.* Texas A&M Research Foundation, College Station. OCS Study MMS 89–0092. Minerals Management Service, Gulf of Mexico OCS Region, U.S. Department of the Interior, New Orleans.

Gatschet, Albert S.

1883 The Shetimasha Indians of St. Mary's Parish, Southern Louisiana. *Transactions of the Anthropological Society of Washington* 2:148–159.

Gertjejansen, Doyle J., and J. Richard Shenkel

1983 Laboratory Simulation of Tchefuncte Period Ceramic Vessels from the Pontchartrain Basin. *Southeastern Archaeology* 2(1): 37–63.

Giardino, Marco J.

1984a Documentary Evidence for the Location of Historic Indian Villages in the Mississippi Delta. In *Perspectives on Gulf Coast Prehistory,* edited by Dave D. Davis, pp. 232–257. Ripley P. Bullen Monographs in Anthropology and History No. 5. University Press of Florida, Gainesville.

1984b Temporal Frameworks: Archaeological Components and Burial Styles: The

Human Osteology of the Mt. Nebo Site in North Louisiana. *Louisiana Archaeology* 9(1982):99–126.

1985 Ceramic Attribute Analysis and Ethnic Group Composition: An Example from Southeastern Louisiana. Unpublished Ph.D. dissertation, Department of Anthropology, Tulane University, New Orleans.

Gibson, Jon L.

1968a Cad Mound: A Stone Bead Locus in East Central Louisiana. *Bulletin of the Texas Archaeological Society* 38:1–17.

1968b Russell Landing: A North Louisiana Phase of the Tchefuncte Period. Unpublished M.A. thesis, Department of Geography and Anthropology, Louisiana State University, Baton Rouge.

1969 The Nature of Southern Hopewell. *Southeastern Archaeological Conference Bulletin* 11:58–66.

1970 The Hopewellian Phenomenon in the Lower Mississippi Valley. *Louisiana Studies* 9(3):176–192.

1973 Social Systems at Poverty Point: An Analysis of Intersite and Intrasite Variability. Unpublished Ph.D. dissertation, Department of Anthropology, Southern Methodist University, Dallas.

1974a Poverty Point, the First North American Chiefdom. *Archaeology* 27(2): 96–105.

1974b The Tchefuncte Culture in the Bayou Vermilion Basin, South Central Louisiana: A Developmental Case Study. *Bulletin of the Texas Archeological Society* 45:67–95.

1976 *Archaeological Survey of Bayou Teche, Vermilion River, and Freshwater Bayou, South Central Louisiana.* Center for Archaeological Studies Report No. 2. University of Southwestern Louisiana, Lafayette.

1979 Poverty Point Trade in South Central Louisiana: An Illustration from Beau Rivage. *Louisiana Archaeology* 4(1977):91–116.

1984a Old Creek, A Troyville Period Ossuary in LaSalle Parish, Louisiana: Reflections after a Quarter Century. *Louisiana Archaeology* 9(1982):127–204.

1984b The Troyville-Baytown Issue. *Louisiana Archaeology* 9(1982):31–64.

1985a Mounds on the Ouachita. *Louisiana Archaeology* 10(1983):171–270.

1985b Ouachita Prehistory. *Louisiana Archaeology* 10(1983):319–335.

1987 The Poverty Point Earthworks Reconsidered. *Mississippi Archaeology* 22(2):14–31.

1989 *Digging on the Dock of the Bay(ou): The 1988 Excavations at Poverty Point.* Center for Archaeological Studies Report No. 8. University of Southwestern Louisiana, Lafayette.

1990 *Archaeological Survey of the Mid-Teche Ridge, South Louisiana: From Bayou Gerimond to Bayou Portage Guidry.* Center for Archaeological Studies. University of Southwestern Louisiana, Lafayette. National Park Service, U.S. Department of the Interior.

1991 Catahoula—An Amphibious Poverty Point Period Manifestation in Eastern Louisiana. In *The Poverty Point Culture: Local Manifestations, Subsistence Practices, and Trade Networks,* edited by Kathleen M. Byrd, pp. 61–87. Geoscience and Man 29. Louisiana State University, Baton Rouge.

1992 Clarence H. Webb (1902–1992). *Louisiana Archaeology* 19:5–43.

1993 Beyond the Peripheries: A Cultural Resources Survey of a Tract of Land Adjoining the Poverty Point Site in West Carroll Parish, Louisiana. Manuscript on file at Poverty Point State Historic Site, Epps, Louisiana.

1994a Before Their Time? Early Mounds in the Lower Mississippi Valley. *Southeastern Archaeology* 13(2):162–186.

1994b Empirical Characterization of Exchange Systems in Lower Mississippi Valley Prehistory. In *Prehistoric Exchange Systems in North America,* edited by Timothy G. Baugh and Jonathon E. Ericson, pp. 127–175. Plenum Press, New York.

1994c Over the Mountain and Across the Sea: Regional Poverty Point Exchange. In Exchange in the Lower Mississippi Valley and Contiguous Areas in 1100 B.C., edited by Jon L. Gibson. *Louisiana Archaeology* 17(1990):251–299.

1995 Things That Count: Mean Vertical Position and Poverty Point Archaeology. In "An' Stuff Like That There": In Appreciation of William G. Haag, edited by Jon L. Gibson, Robert W. Neuman, and Richard A. Weinstein. *Louisiana Archaeology* 18(1991):61–83.

1996a *Ancient Earthworks of the Ouachita Valley in Louisiana.* Technical Reports No. 5. Southeast Archeological Center, Tallahassee.

1996b Poverty Point and Greater Southeastern Prehistory: The Culture That Did Not Fit. In *Archaeology of the Mid-Holocene Southeast,* edited by Kenneth E. Sassaman and David G. Anderson, pp. 288–305. University Press of Florida, Gainesville.

1996c The Orvis Scott Site: A Poverty Point Component on Joes Bayou, East Carroll Parish, Louisiana. *Midcontinental Journal of Archaeology* 21(1):1–48.

1998a Elements and Organization of Poverty Point Political Economy: High Water Fish, Exotic Rocks, and Sacred Earth. In *Research in Economic Anthropology* 19, edited by Barry L. Issac, pp. 291–340. JAI Press, Stamford, Connecticut.

1998b Broken Circles, Owl Monsters, and Black Earth Midden: Separating Sacred and Secular at Poverty Point. In *Ancient Earthen Enclosures of the Eastern Woodlands,* edited by Robert C. Mainfort, Jr., and Lynne P. Sullivan, pp. 17–30. University Press of Florida, Gainesville.

1998c Tchefuncte Culture. In *Archaeology of Prehistoric Native America: An Encyclopedia,* edited by Guy Gibbon, pp. 831–832. Garland Publishing, New York.

1999 Swamp Exchange and the Walled Mart: Poverty Point's Rock Business. In *Raw Materials and Exchange in the Mid-South,* edited by Evan Peacock and Samuel O. Brookes, pp. 57–63. Archaeological Report No. 29. Mississippi Department of Archives and History, Jackson.

2000 *The Ancient Mounds of Poverty Point, Place of Rings.* University Press of Florida, Gainesville.

2001 The Chicken or the Egg B.C.: Building Progression at Poverty Point, Louisiana. Paper presented at the 27th Annual Meeting of the Louisiana Archaeological Society, Natchitoches.

2002 Behold, the Wonderful Work of Our Hands: Poverty Point History and Sociality, Part I. Paper presented at the 59th Southeastern Archaeological Conference, Biloxi, Mississippi.

2004a The Power of Beneficent Obligation in First Mound-Building Societies. In *Signs of Power: The Rise of Cultural Complexity in the Southeast,* edited by Jon L. Gibson and Philip J. Carr, pp. 254–269. University of Alabama Press, Tuscaloosa.

2004b Makers of Fine Items: Craft Specialization at Poverty Point. Paper presented to A Poverty Point Gathering, The Enigma of the Specialist, Poverty Point, Louisiana.

2005 Bossier Tribes, Caddo in North Louisiana's Pineywoods. *Caddoan Archeology Journal* 14:93–118.

2006 Navels of the Earth: Sedentism in Early Mound-Building Cultures in the Lower Mississippi Valley. In Sedentism in Non-Agricultural Societies, edited by Yvonne Marshall. *World Archaeology* 38(2):311–329.

2007 "Formed from the Earth at That Place": The Material Side of Community at Poverty Point. *American Antiquity* 72(3):509–523.

Gibson, Jon L. (editor)

1984 *Louisiana Archaeology and the Society: Celebration of a Decade of Achievement.* Special Publication No. 2. Louisiana Archaeological Society, Lafayette.

Gibson, Jon L., and Philip J. Carr (editors)

2004 *Signs of Power: The Rise of Cultural Complexity in the Southeast.* University of Alabama Press, Tuscaloosa.

Gibson, Jon L., and David L. Griffing

1994 Only a Stone's Throw Away: Exchange in the Poverty Point Hinterland. In Exchange in the Lower Mississippi Valley and Contiguous Areas in 1100 B.C., edited by Jon L. Gibson. *Louisiana Archaeology* 17(1990):207–250.

Gibson, Jon L., Paul A. LaHaye, Christie M. Hardy, and James H. Mathews

2003 *Before Wal-Mart: History and Agency at the Fannin Genin Site (16SL185), St. Landry Parish, South-Central Louisiana.* University of Louisiana at Lafayette and Carved Trowel Archaeology, Ltd. Submitted to Carter-Burgess, Inc. and St. Landry Parish Economic Industrial Development District, Opelousas, Louisiana.

Gibson, Jon L., and Layton J. Miller

1973 *The Trappey Mastodon.* Anthropology Research Series No. 27. University of Southwestern Louisiana, Lafayette.

Gibson, Jon L., and J. Richard Shenkel

1988 Louisiana Earthworks: Middle Woodland and Predecessors. In *Middle Woodland Settlement and Ceremonialism in the Mid-South and Lower Mississippi Valley: Proceedings of the 1984 Mid-South Archaeological Conference, Pinson Mounds, Tennessee—June, 1984*, edited by Robert C. Mainfort, Jr., pp. 7–18. Archaeological Report No. 22. Mississippi Department of Archives and History, Jackson.

Gill, James

1997 *Lords of Misrule: Mardi Gras and the Politics of Race in New Orleans.* University Press of Mississippi, Jackson.

Gillam, J. Christopher

1999 Paleoindian Settlement in Northeastern Arkansas. In *Arkansas Archaeology: Essays in Honor of Dan and Phyllis Morse*, edited by R. C. Mainfort and M. D. Jeter, pp. 99–118. University of Arkansas Press, Fayetteville.

Gillespie, Susan D., and Deborah L. Nichols (editors)

2003 *Archaeology Is Anthropology.* Archeological Papers of the American Anthropological Association No. 13. Arlington, Virginia.

Gilmore, Kathleen

1973 *The Keeran Site: The Probable Site of La Salle's Fort St. Louis in Texas.* Office of the State Archaeologist Report 24. Texas Historical Commission, Austin.

1984 La Salle's Fort St. Louis in Texas. *Bulletin of the Texas Archaeological Society* 55:61–72.

Gilmore, Kathleen and Vergil E. Noble

1983 *Archaeological Testing at Fort St. Leon, Plaquemines Parish, Louisiana.* Contributions in Archaeology 2. Institute of Applied Sciences, North Texas State University, Denton.

Girard, Jeffrey S.

1994a Investigations at the James Pace Site (16DS268), DeSoto Parish, Louisiana. *Caddoan Archeology Newsletter* 5(1):8–16.

1994b *Regional Archaeology Program, Management Unit I: Sixth Annual Report.* Northwestern State University, Natchitoches, Louisiana. Report on file with the Louisiana Division of Archaeology, Department of Culture, Recreation, and Tourism, Baton Rouge.

1995 *Regional Archaeology Program, Management Unit 1: Seventh Annual Report.* Northwestern State University, Natchitoches, Louisiana. Report on file with the Louisiana Division of Archaeology, Department of Culture, Recreation, and Tourism, Baton Rouge.

1997 Caddoan Settlement in the Red River Floodplain: Perspectives from the Willow Chute Bayou Area, Bossier Parish, Louisiana. *Louisiana Archaeology* 22(1995):143–162.

1999 *Regional Archaeology Program, Management Unit 1: Tenth Annual Report.* Northwestern State University, Natchitoches, Louisiana. Report on file with the Louisiana Division of Archaeology, Department of Culture, Recreation, and Tourism, Baton Rouge.

2000a *Regional Archaeology Program Management Unit 1: Eleventh Annual Report.* Northwestern State University, Natchitoches, Louisiana. Report on file with the Louisiana Division of Archaeology, Department of Culture, Recreation, and Tourism, Baton Rouge.

2000b Excavations at the Fredericks Site (16NA2), Natchitoches Parish, Louisiana. *Louisiana Archaeology* 24(1997):1–106.

2001 *Regional Archaeology Program Management Unit 1: Twelfth Annual Report.* Northwestern State University, Natchitoches, Louisiana. Report on file with the Louisiana Division of Archaeology, Department of Culture, Recreation, and Tourism, Baton Rouge.

2002 *Regional Archaeology Program Management Unit 1: Thirteenth Annual Report.* Northwestern State University, Natchitoches, Louisiana. Report on file with the Louisiana Division of Archaeology, Department of Culture, Recreation, and Tourism, Baton Rouge.

2003 *Regional Archaeology Program Management Unit 1: Fourteenth Annual Report.* Northwestern State University, Natchitoches, Louisiana. Report on file with the Louisiana Division of Archaeology, Department of Culture, Recreation, and Tourism, Baton Rouge.

2004 Coles Creek–Early Caddo Interaction on the Southeastern Periphery of the Caddo Area. Paper presented at the 46th Annual Caddo Conference, Northwestern State University, Natchitoches.

2005 *Regional Archaeology Program, Management Unit 1: Sixteenth Annual Report.* Northwestern State University, Natchitoches, Louisiana. Report on file with the Louisiana Division of Archaeology, Department of Culture, Recreation, and Tourism, Baton Rouge.

2006 *Regional Archaeology Program Management Unit 1: Seventeenth Annual Report.* Northwestern State University, Natchitoches, Louisiana. Report on file with the Louisiana Division of Archaeology, Department of Culture, Recreation, and Tourism, Baton Rouge.

2007 *Regional Archaeology Program, Management Unit 1: Eighteenth Annual Report.* Northwestern State University, Natchitoches, Louisiana. Report on file with the Louisiana Division of Archaeology, Department of Culture, Recreation, and Tourism, Baton Rouge.

Girard, Jeffrey S., Robert C. Vogel, and H. Edwin Jackson

2008 History and Archaeology of the Pierre Robleau Household and Bayou Pierre Community: Perspectives on Rural Society and Economy in Northwest Louisiana at the Time of the Freeman and Custis Expedition. In *Freeman and Custis Red River Expedition of 1806: Two Hundred Years Later,* edited by L. M. Hardy, pp. 147–180. Bulletin of the Museum of Life Sciences No. 14, Louisiana State University, Shreveport.

Giraud, Marcel

1974 *A History of French Louisiana*. Vol. 1: *The Reign of Louis XIV, 1698–1715*, translated by Joseph C. Lambert. Louisiana State University Press, Baton Rouge.

1987 *A History of French Louisiana*, Vol. 5: *The Company of the Indies, 1723–1731*, translated by Brian Pearce. Louisiana State University Press, Baton Rouge.

Glassie, Henry

1999 *Material Culture*. Indiana University Press, Bloomington.

Godzinski, Michael, and D. Ryan Gray

2008 *Research Design for Phase III Cultural Resources Investigations at the C. J. Peete Housing Complex, New Orleans, Louisiana*. Earth Search, Inc., New Orleans. Prepared for the Housing Authority of New Orleans.

Godzinski, Michael, Benjamin D. Maygarden, Allen R. Saltus, Jr., Paul Heinrich, Ryan Gray, Eads Poitevent, Jeffrey Clary, Jill-Karen Yakubik, Barry South, and Rhonda Smith

2001 *Cultural Resource Investigations on Grand Terre Island, Jefferson Parish, Louisiana*. Earth Search, Inc., New Orleans. U.S. Army Corps of Engineers, New Orleans District.

Godzinski, Michael, Benjamin D. Maygarden, Jeffrey Treffinger, Heather Apollonio, Bethany Bingham, Wendy Bosma, Jeffery Clary, Danny Ryan Gray, Gail Lazarus, Kathryn B. Lintott, Kerriann Marden, Sara Orton, Eads Poitevent IV, Rhonda L. Smith, Barry South, Mary Elizabeth Weed, Ellen Wilmer, and Jill-Karen Yakubik

2002 *Cultural Resources Evaluation, Desire Streetcar Line*. Earth Search, Inc., New Orleans. On file with the Louisiana Division of Archaeology, Department of Culture, Recreation, and Tourism, Baton Rouge.

Goldsmith, Sarah Sue

2003 *Nations Within: The Four Sovereign Tribes of Louisiana*. Louisiana State University Press, Baton Rouge.

Gomez, Michael

1998 *Exchanging Our Country Marks: The Transformation of African Identities in the Colonial and Antebellum South*. University of North Carolina Press, Chapel Hill.

Gonzalez, B.

2005 Caddo Tribal Religious Burial Ceremonies: Beyond Archaeology. In *A Rediscovering of Caddo Heritage: The W. T. Scott Collection at the American Museum of Natural History and Other Caddo Collections from Arkansas and Louisiana*, by B. Gonzalez, R. Cast, T. K. Perttula, and B. Nelson, pp. 55–59. Caddo Nation of Oklahoma, Historic Preservation Program, Binger.

Gonzalez, B., R. Cast, T. K. Perttula, and B. Nelson

2005 *A Rediscovering of Caddo Heritage: The W. T. Scott Collection at the American Museum of Natural History and Other Caddo Collections from Arkansas and Louisiana.* Caddo Nation of Oklahoma, Historic Preservation Program, Binger.

Goodwin, R. Christopher, and John L. Seidel

2004 *Phase II and Phase III Archeological Investigations of the Shipwreck* Kentucky *(Site 16BO358) at Eagle Bend, Pool 5 Red River Waterway, Bossier Parish, Louisiana.* R. Christopher Goodwin and Associates, Inc., New Orleans. U.S. Army Corps of Engineers, New Orleans District.

Goodwin, R. Christopher, and Galloway W. Selby

1984 *Historical Archeology of the Morgan City Floodwall Boat.* R. Christopher Goodwin and Associates, Inc., New Orleans. U.S. Army Corps of Engineers, New Orleans District.

Goodwin, R. Christopher, Galloway W. Selby, and Laura A. Landry

1984 *Evaluation of the National Register Eligibility of the M/V Fox, an Historic Boat in Lafourche Parish, Louisiana.* R. Christopher Goodwin and Associates, Inc., New Orleans. U.S. Army Corps of Engineers, New Orleans District.

Goodwin, R. Christopher, and Jill-Karen Yakubik

1982 *Data Recovery at the New Orleans General Hospital Site (16OR69).* R. Christopher Goodwin and Associates, Inc., New Orleans. On file with the Louisiana Division of Archaeology, Department of Culture, Recreation, and Tourism, Baton Rouge.

Goodwin, R. Christopher, Jill-Karen Yakubik, and Peter A. Gendel

1984 *Archaeological Data Recovery at Algiers Point.* R. Christopher Goodwin and Associates, Inc., New Orleans. U.S. Army Corps of Engineers, New Orleans District.

Goodyear, Albert C.

1974 *The Brand Site: A Techno-Functional Study of a Dalton Site in Northeast Arkansas.* Research Series No. 7. Arkansas Archeological Survey, Fayetteville.

1982 The Chronological Position of the Dalton Horizon in the Southeastern United States. *American Antiquity* 47(2):382–395.

2006 Evidence of Pre-Clovis Sites in the Eastern United States. In *Paleoamerican Origins: Beyond Clovis,* edited by Robson Bonnichsen, Bradley T. Lepper, Dennis J. Stanford, and Michael R. Waters, pp. 103–112. Texas A&M University Press, College Station.

Graham, Elizabeth

1998 Mission Archaeology. *Annual Review of Anthropology* 27:25–62.

Gray, D. Ryan

2002 Archaeological Excavations at the St. Joseph's Orphan Asylum and in the Irish Channel. Paper presented at the Irish Channel Roots XI Symposium, St. Alphonsus Arts and Cultural Center, New Orleans.

2003 "A Scarlet World": Archaeology in New Orleans' Storyville District. Paper presented at the National Meeting of the Archaeological Institute of America, New Orleans.

2004 "Gonna Move to the Outskirts of Town": Archaeology and Historic Development on the Edge of New Orleans. Paper presented at the Annual Meeting of the Society for Historical Archaeology Conference on Historical and Underwater Archaeology, St. Louis.

2005 Creating Community from a Divided Past: Archaeology in New Orleans' St. Thomas Housing Project. Paper presented at the 2004–2005 South Central Historical Archaeology Conference, Selma.

2006 From Ruin to Respectability in Old New Orleans: Recent Archaeology in the French Quarter and Warehouse District. Paper presented at Loyola University, sponsored by the Archaeological Institute of America and Louisiana Landmarks Society.

2009a "Taming Amorphous Urbanism": Disorder, Informal Development, and the Urban Poor in New Orleans. Paper presented in the Archaeologies of Poverty Symposium at the Society for Historical Archaeology Conference on Historical and Underwater Archaeology, Toronto.

2009b The Material Dimensions of Public and Private Practice: Archaeology of a Chinese Laundry in New Orleans. Unpublished M.A. thesis, Department of Anthropology, University of Chicago, Illinois.

Gray, D. Ryan, Howard Earnest, Benjamin Maygarden, and Jill-Karen Yakubik

2003 *Archaeological Monitoring and Test Excavations at City Square 130 (16OR180) in the Iberville Housing Project, New Orleans, Louisiana.* Earth Search, Inc., New Orleans.

Gray, D. Ryan, Kimberly Eppler, Aubra Lee, Dayna Lee, Benjamin Maygarden, Justine McKnight, Rhonda Smith, and Jill-Karen Yakubik

2008 *Archaeological Data Recovery, Federal Emergency Management Agency (FEMA) Temporary Housing, Kingsley House Project Area (16OR221), New Orleans, Orleans Parish, Louisiana.* 3 vols. Earth Search, Inc., New Orleans. U.S. Army Corps of Engineers, New Orleans District.

Gray, D. Ryan, Michael Godzinski, Dayna Lee, and Jill-Karen Yakubik

2008 *Research Design for Phase III Cultural Resources Investigations at the Lafitte Housing Complex, New Orleans, Louisiana.* Earth Search, Inc., New Orleans. Housing Authority of New Orleans.

Gray, D. Ryan, Benjamin Maygarden, Kimberly Eppler, Harriet Swift, and Jill-Karen Yakubik

2010 *Archaeological Investigations at City Squares 158 and 159 for the National World War II Museum Expansion, New Orleans, Louisiana.* Earth Search, Inc., New Orleans, in preparation.

Gray, D. Ryan, Benjamin Maygarden, Sara Orton, Rhonda Smith, Erin Sneddon, and Jill-Karen Yakubik

2010 *Archaeological Data Recovery at City Square 33 (16OR177), New Orleans, Louisiana.* Earth Search, Inc., New Orleans, in preparation.

Gray, D. Ryan, Benjamin Maygarden, Rhonda Smith, Mary Elizabeth Weed, and Jill-Karen Yakubik

2010 *Archaeological Data Recovery at the St. Joseph Orphan Asylum (16OR153), New Orleans, Louisiana.* Earth Search, Inc., New Orleans, in preparation.

Gray, D. Ryan, Benjamin Maygarden, Mary Elizabeth Weed, and Jill-Karen Yakubik

2010 *"Time Flies, It Waits For No One . . .": Archaeological Data Recovery at City Square 70 (16OR163) in the St. Thomas Housing Project, New Orleans, Louisiana.* Earth Search, Inc., New Orleans, in preparation.

Grayson, Donald K.

2006 Late Pleistocene Faunal Extinctions. In *Handbook of North American Indians.*, Vol. 3: *Environment, Origins, and Population,* edited by Douglas H. Ubelaker, pp. 208–218. Smithsonian Institution Press, Washington, D.C.

Grayson, Donald K., and David J. Meltzer

2002 Clovis Hunting and Large Mammal Extinction: A Critical Review of the Evidence. *Journal of World Prehistory* 16(4):313–359.

2003 A Requiem for North American Overkill. *Journal of Archaeological Science* 30:585–593.

2004 North American Overkill Continued? *Journal of Archaeological Science* 31: 133–136.

Greengo, Robert E.

1964 *Issaquena: An Archaeological Phase in the Yazoo Basin of the Lower Mississippi Valley.* Memoir No. 18. Society for American Archaeology, Salt Lake City, Utah.

Greenwell, Dale

1984 The Mississippi Gulf Coast. In *Perspectives on Gulf Coast Prehistory,* edited by Dave D. Davis, pp. 125–155. Ripley P. Bullen Monographs in Anthropology and History No. 5. University Press of Florida, Gainesville.

Gregory, Hiram F., Jr.

1964 Metates: Reminders of the Spanish in Natchitoches. *Louisiana Studies* 2: 153–154.

1969 Plaquemine Period Sites in the Catahoula Basin: A Cultural Microcosm in East-Central Louisiana. *Louisiana Studies* 8:111–134.

1973 Eighteenth-Century Caddoan Archaeology: A Study in Models and Interpretation. Unpublished Ph.D. dissertation, Department of Anthropology, Southern Methodist University, Dallas.

1980 The Doctor and Caddology: Dr. Clarence H. Webb's Contributions to Caddo Archaeology. *Louisiana Archeology* 6(1979):19–28.

1983 Los Adaes: The Archaeology of an Ethnic Enclave. In *Historical Archaeology of the Eastern United States: Papers from the R.J. Russell Symposium,* edited by

Robert W. Neuman, pp. 53–57. Geoscience and Man 23. Louisiana State University, Baton Rouge.

1991 Terral Lewis: Recapitulation. In *The Poverty Point Culture, Local Manifestations, Subsistence Practices, and Trade Networks,* edited by Kathleen M. Byrd, pp. 121–127. Geoscience and Man 29. Louisiana State University, Baton Rouge.

1992 The Louisiana Tribes: Entering Hard Times. In *Indians in the Southeastern United States in the Late 20th Century,* edited by J. Anthony Paredes, pp. 162–182. University of Alabama Press, Tuscaloosa.

1996 Adaesaño: A Nahuatl Lexicon from Natchitoches and Sabine Parishes, Louisiana. *Southern Studies* 7(1):89–96.

2004 Survival and Maintenance among Louisiana Tribes. In *Handbook of North American Indians.,* Vol. 14: *Southeast,* edited by Raymond D. Fogelson, pp. 653–658. Smithsonian Institution Press, Washington, D.C.

2005 *Los Adaes (16NA16) Native American Ceramics.* Report on file with the Louisiana Division of Archaeology, Department of Culture, Recreation, and Tourism, Baton Rouge.

Gregory, Hiram F., Jr., George Avery, Aubra L. Lee, and Jay C. Blaine

2004 Presidio Los Adaes: Spanish, French, and Caddoan Interaction on the Northern Frontier. *Historical Archaeology* 38(3):65–77.

Gregory, Hiram F., Jr., Lester C. Davis, and Donald G. Hunter

1970 The Terral Lewis Site: A Poverty Point Activity Facies in Madison Parish, Louisiana. *Southeastern Archaeological Conference Bulletin* 12:35–46.

Gregory, Hiram. F., Jr., Clint Pine, William S. Baker, Jr., Aubra Lee, Reinaldo Barnes, and George A. Stokes

1987 *A Survey of Catahoula Basin, 1987.* Northwestern State University, Natchitoches. Report on file with the Louisiana Division of Archaeology, Department of Culture, Recreation, and Tourism, Baton Rouge.

Gremillion, Kristen J.

1996 The Paleoethnobotanical Record for the Mid-Holocene Southeast. In *Archaeology of the Mid-Holocene Southeast,* edited by Kenneth E. Sassaman and David G. Anderson, pp. 99–114. University Press of Florida, Gainesville.

2002 Archaeobotany at Old Mobile. In French Colonial Studies at Old Mobile: Selected Studies, edited by Gregory A. Waselkov. *Historical Archaeology* 36(1):117–128.

2004 Seed Processing and the Origins of Food Production in Eastern North America. *American Antiquity* 69:215–234.

2006 Southeast Plants. In *Handbook of North American Indians.,* Vol. 3: *Environment, Origins, and Population,* edited by Douglas H. Ubelaker, pp. 388–395. Smithsonian Institution Press, Washington, D.C.

Griffin, James B.

1946 Culture Change and Continuity in Eastern United States. In *Man in Northeast-*

ern North America, edited by F. Johnson, pp. 37–95. Papers of the Robert S. Peabody Foundation for Archaeology 3. Andover, Massachusetts.

1952 Culture Periods in Eastern United States Archeology. In *Archeology of Eastern United States,* edited by J. B. Griffin, pp. 352–364. University of Chicago Press, Chicago.

1966 Mesoamerica and the Eastern United States in Prehistoric Times. In *Handbook of Middle American Indians.*, Vol. 4: *Archaeological Frontiers and External Connections,* edited by Gordon F. Ekholm and Gordon R. Willey, pp. 111–131. Robert Wauchope, general editor. University of Texas Press, Austin.

1967 Eastern North American Archaeology: A Summary. *Science* 156(3772):175–191.

1985 Changing Concepts of the Prehistoric Mississippian Cultures of the Eastern United States. In *Alabama and the Borderlands: From Prehistory to Statehood,* edited by Reid R. Badger and Lawrence A. Clayton, pp. 40–63. University of Alabama Press, Tuscaloosa.

1990 Comments on the Late Prehistoric Societies in the Southeast. In *Towns and Temples along the Mississippi,* edited by David H. Dye and Cheryl A. Cox, pp. 5–15. University of Alabama Press, Tuscaloosa.

Griffing, David L.

1990 Surface Surveys of the Insley Site, Franklin Parish, Louisiana. *Louisiana Archaeology* 12(1985):219–240.

Guccione, Margaret J., and Philip Hays

2008 Geomorphology, Sedimentology, and Vegetation History Along the Red River Floodplain, Bowie County, Texas. In *Integrated Cultural Resources Investigations for the Bowie County Levee Realignment Project, Bowie County, Texas and Little River County, Arkansas,* by Scott A. Sundermeyer, John T. Penman, and Timothy K. Perttula, pp. 109–166. Miscellaneous Reports, Report of Investigations No. 29. LopezGarcia Group, Dallas.

Guderjan, Thomas H., and James R. Morehead

1981 Big Brushy: A Stratified Multiple Component Site at Fort Polk, Louisiana. *Louisiana Archaeology* 7(1980):1–29.

Gulf South Research Institute (GSRI)

1973 *Environmental Inventory for the Mississippi River—Cairo, Illinois, to Venice, Louisiana.* Gulf South Research Institute, Baton Rouge. U.S. Army Corps of Engineers, Vicksburg District.

1975 *Environmental Analysis—Red River Waterway, Louisiana, Texas, Arkansas, and Oklahoma.* Vols. 1–7. Gulf South Research Institute, Baton Rouge. U.S. Army Corps of Engineers, New Orleans District.

1976 *Archeological Salvage Investigations of Riverboat at Shaw, Louisiana.* Gulf South Research Institute, Baton Rouge. Louisiana Archaeological Survey and Antiquities Commission, and the Department of Culture, Recreation, and Tourism, Baton Rouge.

Gums, Bonnie L.

2002 Earthfast (*Pieux en Terre*) Structures at Old Mobile. In French Colonial Studies at Old Mobile: Selected Studies, edited by Gregory A. Waselkov. *Historical Archaeology* 36(1):13–25.

Gunn, Joel D.

1984 Points from Peason Ridge and Nearby Areas. In *Occupation and Settlement in the Uplands of Western Louisiana*, by Joel D. Gunn and Anne C. Kerr, pp. 135–147. Special Report 17. Center for Archaeological Research, University of Texas at San Antonio.

Gunn, Joel D., and David O. Brown

1982 *Eagle Hill: A Late Quaternary Upland Site in Western Louisiana*. Special Report 12. Center for Archaeological Research, University of Texas at San Antonio.

Gunn, Joel D., and Anne C. Kerr

1984 *Occupation and Settlement in the Uplands of Western Louisiana*. Special Report 17. Center for Archaeological Research, University of Texas at San Antonio.

Haag, William G.

1953 Choctaw Archaeology. *Southeastern Archaeological Conference Newsletter* 3:25–28.

1965 Louisiana in North American Prehistory. *Louisiana Studies* 4(3):279–323.

1971 *Louisiana in North American Prehistory*. Mélanges No. 1. Museum of Geoscience. Louisiana State University, Baton Rouge.

1974 *The Archaeology of the Baton Rouge Civic Center Area*. Report on file with the Louisiana Division of Archaeology, Department of Culture, Recreation, and Tourism, Baton Rouge.

1978 A Prehistory of the Lower Mississippi Valley. In *Man and Environment in the Lower Mississippi Valley*, edited by S. B. Hilliard, pp. 1–8. Geoscience and Man 19. Louisiana State University, Baton Rouge.

1990 Excavations at the Poverty Point Site: 1972–1975. In Recent Research at the Poverty Point Site, edited by Kathleen M. Byrd. *Louisiana Archaeology* 13(1986):1–36.

Hadley, Diana, Thomas H. Naylor, and Mardith K. Schuetz-Miller (editors)

1997 *The Presidio and Militia on the Northern Frontier of New Spain*. Vol. 2, Pt. 2: *The Central Corridor and the Texas Corridor, 1700–1765*. University of Arizona Press, Tucson.

Hahn, Thurston H. G., III, Allen R. Saltus, Jr., and Stephen R. James, Jr.

1994 *Delta Landing: Historical and Archaeological Investigations of Three Sunken Watercraft at Delta, Madison Parish, Louisiana*. Coastal Environments, Inc., Baton Rouge. U.S. Army Corps of Engineers, Vicksburg District.

Hahn, Thurston H. G., III, Douglas Wells, and Joanne Ryan

2005 *5,000 Years of Life and Death along the Natchez Bluffs: Archaeological and Historical Inventory and Reporting for Reaches 6 and 7 of the Natchez Bluffs Stability*

Study and the Orleans Street Disposal Area, Adams County, Mississippi. Coastal Environments, Inc., Baton Rouge. U.S. Army Corps of Engineers, Vicksburg District.

Hall, Gwendolyn Midlo

1992 *Africans in Colonial Louisiana: The Development of Afro-Creole Culture in the Eighteenth Century.* Louisiana State University Press, Baton Rouge.

2005 *Slavery and African Ethnicities in the Americas.* University of North Carolina Press, Chapel Hill.

Hall, Martin, and Stephen W. Silliman (editors)

2006 *Historical Archaeology.* Blackwell Publishing, Malden, Massachusetts.

Hally, David J.

1972 The Plaquemine and Mississippian Occupations of the Upper Tensas Basin, Louisiana. Unpublished Ph.D. dissertation, Department of Anthropology, Harvard University, Cambridge.

Hamilton, Fran E.

1999 Southeastern Archaic Mounds: Examples of Elaboration in a Temporally Fluctuating Environment? *Journal of Anthropological Archaeology* 18(3):344–355.

Hamilton, T. M.

1979 Guns, Gunflints, Balls, and Shot. In *Tunica Treasure,* by Jeffery P. Brain, pp. 206–216. Papers of the Peabody Museum of Archaeology and Ethnology Vol. 71. Harvard University, Cambridge.

Handley, Martin, Brandi Carrier, Nathanael Heller, Susan Barrett Smith, Shane Poche, Jill Langenberg, and William Athens

2006 *Monitoring of a Proposed Fire Protection Program Waterline Replacement Project, Jonesville, Catahoula Parish, Louisiana.* R. Christopher Goodwin and Associates, Inc., New Orleans. Report on file with the Louisiana Division of Archaeology, Department of Culture, Recreation, and Tourism, Baton Rouge.

Hardy, Meredith D., John E. Cornelison, Jr., Tammy D. Cooper, and Jeff Jones

2002 *Archaeological Monitoring and Data Recovery for the Reconstruction of Building IV, 419 Rue Decatur, Vieux Carre, New Orleans, Louisiana.* Prepared for the Southeast Archeological Center, National Park Service, Tallahassee, Florida.

Harmon, Anna M., and Jerome C. Rose

1989 Bioarcheology of the Louisiana and Arkansas Study Area. In *Archeology and Bioarcheology of the Lower Mississippi Valley and Trans-Mississippi South in Arkansas and Louisiana,* edited by M. D. Jeter, J. C. Rose, G. I. Williams, Jr., and A. C. Harmon, pp. 323–354. Research Series No. 37. Arkansas Archeological Survey, Fayetteville.

Hartman, Chester W., and Gregory D. Squires

2006 *There Is No Such Thing as a Natural Disaster: Race, Class, and Hurricane Katrina.* Routledge, New York.

Hayden, Brian

2001 Fabulous Feasts: A Prolegomenon to the Importance of Feasting. In *Feasts: Archaeological and Ethnographic Perspectives on Food, Politics, and Power*, edited by Michael Dietler and Brian Hayden, pp. 23–64. Smithsonian Institution Press, Washington, D.C.

Haynes, Gary (editor)

2009 *American Megafaunal Extinctions at the End of the Pleistocene*. Springer, New York.

Hays, Christopher

1995 *1995 Annual Report for Management Units IV and V, Regional Archaeology Program, Museum of Natural Science, Louisiana State University*. Report on file with the Louisiana Division of Archaeology, Department of Culture, Recreation, and Tourism, Baton Rouge.

2000 *2000 Annual Report for Management Units IV and V, Regional Archaeology Program, Museum of Natural Science, Louisiana State University*. Report on file with the Louisiana Division of Archaeology, Department of Culture, Recreation, and Tourism, Baton Rouge.

Hays, Christopher T., and Richard A. Weinstein

1999 Perspectives on Tchefuncte Cultural Chronology: A View from the Bayou Jasmine Site, St. John the Baptist Parish, Louisiana. *Louisiana Archaeology* 23(1996):49–89.

2004 Early Pottery at Poverty Point: Origins and Functions. In *Early Pottery: Technology, Function, Style, and Interaction in the Lower Southeast*, edited by Rebecca Saunders and Christopher T. Hays, pp. 150–168. University of Alabama Press, Tuscaloosa.

Hegmon, Michelle

2003 Setting Theoretical Egos Aside: Issues and Theory in North American Archaeology. *American Antiquity* 68(2):213–243.

Heinrich, Paul V.

1983 Addenda 1: Lithic Resources of Sabine and Vernon Parishes. In *U.S.L. Fort Polk Archaeological Survey and Cultural Resources Management Program*, Vol. 1, edited by A. Frank Servello, pp. 552–554. University of Southwestern Louisiana, Lafayette.

1987 Lithic Resources of Western Louisiana. *Louisiana Archaeology* 11(1984):165–190.

Hemmings, C. Andrew

2004 *The Organic Clovis: A Single Continent-Wide Cultural Adaptation*. Unpublished Ph.D. dissertation, Department of Anthropology, University of Florida, Gainesville.

Hemmings, E. Thomas

1982 *Human Adaptation in the Grand Marais Lowland: Intensive Archaeological Survey and Testing in the Felsenthal Navigation Pool, Ouachita and Saline Rivers,*

Southern Arkansas. Research Series No. 17, Arkansas Archeological Survey, Fayetteville.

Hester, Thomas R., Michael B. Collins, Dee Ann Story, Ellen S. Turner, Paul Tanner, Kenneth M. Brown, Larry D. Banks, Dennis Stanford, and Russell J. Long

1992 Paleoindian Archaeology at McFaddin Beach, Texas. *Current Research in the Pleistocene* 9:20–22.

Heyden, Doris

1981 Caves, Gods, and Myths: World-View and Planning in Teotihuacan. In *Mesoamerican Sites and World Views*, edited by Elizabeth P. Benson, pp. 1–39. Research Library and Collections, Dumbarton Oaks, Washington, D.C.

Hicks, Dan, and Mary C. Beaudry (editors)

2006 *The Cambridge Companion to Historical Archaeology*. Cambridge University Press, Cambridge.

Hill, Christopher L.

2006a Geological Framework and Glaciation of the Central Area. In *Handbook of North American Indians.*, Vol. 3: *Environment, Origins, and Population*, edited by Douglas H. Ubelaker, pp. 67–80. Smithsonian Institution Press, Washington, D.C.

2006b Geological Framework and Glaciation of the Eastern Area. In *Handbook of North American Indians.*, Vol. 3: *Environment, Origins, and Population*, edited by Douglas H. Ubelaker, pp. 81–98. Smithsonian Institution Press, Washington, D.C.

2006c Geological Framework and Glaciation of the Western Area. In *Handbook of North American Indians.*, Vol. 3: *Environment, Origins, and Population*, edited by Douglas H. Ubelaker, pp. 47–60. Smithsonian Institution Press, Washington, D.C.

Hilliard, Samuel B.

1972 *Hog Meat and Hoecake: Food Supply in the Old South, 1840–1860*. Southern Illinois University Press, Carbondale.

Hillman, Mitchell M.

1990a Paleoindian Settlement on the Macon Ridge, Northeastern Louisiana. *Louisiana Archaeology* 12(1985):203–218.

1990b The 1985 Test Excavation of the "Dock" Area of Poverty Point. In Recent Research at the Poverty Point Site, edited by Kathleen M. Byrd. *Louisiana Archaeology* 13(1986):133–149.

Hodder, Ian

1985 Postprocessual Archaeology. *Advances in Archaeological Method and Theory* 8:1–26.

1986 *Reading the Past: Current Approaches to Interpretation in Archaeology*. Cambridge University Press, Cambridge.

1991 Interpretive Archaeology and Its Role. *American Antiquity* 56(1):7–18.

Holland-Lilly, Mimi

1996 Batesville Mounds: Recent Investigations at a Middle Woodland Site. *Mississippi Archaeology* 31(1):40–55.

Hollenbach, Kandace D.

2007 Gathering in the Late Paleoindian Period: Archaeobotanical Remains from Dust Cave, Alabama. In *Foragers of the Terminal Pleistocene in North America,* edited by Renee B. Walker and Boyce N. Driskell, pp. 132–147. University of Nebraska Press, Lincoln.

Holmes, W. C., and Christopher J. Wells

1980 The Distribution of *habranthus tubispathus* (L'Her.) *traub* in South America and North America—Texas and Louisiana. *Sida* 8(4):328–333.

Holmes, William H.

1886 *Ancient Pottery of the Mississippi Valley.* Fourth Annual Report of the Bureau of American Ethnology, 1882–1883, pp. 361–436. Government Printing Office, Washington, D.C.

1903 *Aboriginal Pottery of the Eastern United States.* Twentieth Annual Report of the Bureau of American Ethnology, 1898–1899. Government Printing Office, Washington, D.C.

Homburg, Jeffrey

1992 Archaeological Investigations at the L.S.U. Campus Mounds Site. *Louisiana Archaeology* 15(1988):31–204.

House, John H.

1982 *Powell Canal: Baytown Period Occupation on Bayou Macon in Southeast Arkansas.* Research Series 19. Arkansas Archeological Survey, Fayetteville.

Hrdlička, Aleš

1909 Report on an Additional Collection of Skeletal Remains from Arkansas and Louisiana. *Journal of the Academy of Natural Sciences of Philadelphia* 14: 171–249.

Hudson, Charles

1976 *The Southeastern Indians.* University of Tennessee Press, Knoxville.

Hudson, Jack C.

1972 *Gallier House Complex (16OR46), Part I: Gallier House; Part II: Warehouse Area.* Submitted to the Ella West Freeman Foundation, New Orleans.

Humphreys, H. D.

1984 The "Great Raft" of the Red River. In *North Louisiana.*, Vol. 1: *To 1865—Essays on the Region and Its History,* edited by B. H. Gilley, pp. 73–91. McGinty Trust Fund Publications, Ruston, Louisiana.

Hunter, Donald G.

1990 The Apalachee on Red River, 1763–1834: An Ethnohistory and Summary of Archaeological Testing at the Zimmerman Hill Site, Rapides Parish, Louisiana. *Louisiana Archaeology* 12(1985):7–127.

Hunter, Donald G., and William S. Baker, Jr.

1979 Excavations in the Atkins Midden at the Troyville Site, Catahoula Parish, Louisiana. *Louisiana Archaeology* 4(1977):21–51.

Hunter, Donald G., Gayle J. Fritz, Whitney J. Autin, and Kam-biu Liu

1995 *Manifest East: Cultural Resources Investigations along Portions of Louisiana Highway 8, Catahoula Parish, Louisiana.* Coastal Environments, Inc., Baton Rouge. Louisiana Department of Transportation and Development, Baton Rouge.

Hunter, Donald G., K. L. Orr, J. M. Compton, and J. M. Abraham

2003 *Historic Archaeology on the Batture: Data Recovery at Sites 16AN69 and 16AN70, Ascension Parish, Louisiana.* Coastal Environments, Inc., Baton Rouge. U.S. Army Corps of Engineers, New Orleans District.

Hunter, Donald G., Charles E. Pearson, Josetta LeBoeuf, and David B. Kelley

2002 *Cultural Resources Evaluations of the T. C. Bearden (16NA494), Rambin Wreck (16NA495), and Charles Webb (16RR86) Archaeological Sites, Located along Red River in Natchitoches and Red River Parishes, Louisiana.* Coastal Environments, Inc., Baton Rouge. U.S. Army Corps of Engineers, Vicksburg District.

Hunter, Louis C.

1949 *Steamboats on Western Rivers: An Economic and Technological History.* Harvard University Press, Cambridge.

Hurston, Zora Neale

1990 *Mules and Men.* Reprint by Harper and Row, New York. Originally published 1935, J. B. Lippincott, Philadelphia.

Hutchings, Wallace Karl

1997 *The Paleoindian Fluted Point: Dart or Spear Armature? The Identification of Paleoindian Delivery Technology through Analysis of Lithic Fracture Velocity.* Unpublished Ph.D. dissertation, Department of Archaeology, Simon Fraser University, Vancouver, Canada.

Irion, Jack B., and David A. Ball

2001 The *New York* and the *Josephine:* Two Steamships of the Charles Morgan Line. *International Journal of Nautical Archaeology* 30(1):48–56.

Jackson, H. Edwin

1986 Sedentism and Hunter-Gatherer Adaptations in the Lower Mississippi Valley: Subsistence Strategies during the Poverty Point Period. Unpublished Ph.D. dissertation, Department of Anthropology, University of Michigan, Ann Arbor.

1989 Poverty Point Adaptive Systems in the Lower Mississippi Valley: Subsistence Remains from the J. W. Copes Site. *North American Archaeologist* 10(3): 173–204.

1991a Bottomland Resources and Exploitation Strategies during the Poverty Point Period: Implications of the Archaeological Record from the J. W. Copes Site. In *The Poverty Point Culture, Local Manifestations, Subsistence Practices, and Trade Networks,* edited by Kathleen M. Byrd, pp. 131–157. Geoscience and Man 29. Louisiana State University, Baton Rouge.

1991b The Trade Fair in Hunter-Gatherer Interaction: The Role of Inter-Societal Trade in the Evolution of Poverty Point Culture. In *Between Bands and States: Sedentism, Subsistence, and Interaction in Small Scale Societies,* edited by Susan A. Gregg, pp. 265–286. Occasional Paper No. 9. Southern Illinois University, Carbondale.

1999 Vertebrate Fauna from 16AV1. In *Marksville (16AV1), Lake Anacoco, and the Chenier Plain, Regional Archaeology Program, Management Unit III, 1998/1999 Annual Report,* by Charles R. McGimsey, H. Edwin Jackson, Katherine M. Roberts, and James Hebert, pp. 82–92. Report on file with the Louisiana Division of Archaeology, Department of Culture, Recreation, and Tourism, Baton Rouge.

Jackson, H. Edwin, and Marvin D. Jeter

1991 Late Archaic Settlement and Poverty Point Connections in the Lowlands of Southeast Arkansas: An Initial Assessment. *Mississippi Archaeology* 26(2): 33–55.

1994 Preceramic Earthworks in Arkansas: A Report on the Poverty Point Period Lake Enterprise Mound (3AS379). *Southeastern Archaeology* 13(2):153–162.

Jackson, H. Edwin, and Susan L. Scott

1995 The Faunal Record of the Southeastern Elite: The Implications of Economy, Social Relations, and Ideology. *Southeastern Archaeology* 14(2):103–119.

2000 Vertebrate Fauna from 16AV25. In *Archaeology of the Marksville Period: Explorations of Southwest Louisiana Prehistory, Regional Archaeology Program, Management Unit III, 1999/2000 Annual Report,* by Charles R. McGimsey, Katherine M. Roberts, H. Edwin Jackson, Katherine M. Roberts and Susan L. Scott, pp. 52–63. Report on file with the Louisiana Division of Archaeology, Department of Culture, Recreation, and Tourism. Baton Rouge.

2001 Archaic Faunal Utilization in the Louisiana Bottomlands. *Southeastern Archaeology* 20(2):187–196.

2002 Woodland Faunal Exploitation in the Midsouth. In *The Woodland Southeast,* edited by David G. Anderson and Robert C. Mainfort, Jr., pp. 461–482. University of Alabama Press, Tuscaloosa.

Jaffery, Nora E.

2004 *False Mystics: Deviant Orthodoxy in Colonial Mexico.* University of Nebraska Press, Lincoln.

Jenkins, Ned J., David H. Dye, and John A. Walthall

1986 Early Ceramic Development in the Coastal Plain. In *Early Woodland Archaeology,* edited by Kenneth B. Farnsworth and Thomas E. Emerson, pp. 546–563. Center for American Archaeology Press, Kampsville, Illinois.

Jenkins, Ned J., and Richard A. Krause

1986 *The Tombigbee Watershed in Southeastern Prehistory.* University of Alabama Press, Tuscaloosa.

Jennings, Jesse D.

1952 Prehistory of the Lower Mississippi Valley. In *Archaeology of Eastern United States*, edited by J. B. Griffin, pp. 256–271. University of Chicago Press, Chicago.

Jennings, Thomas A.

2007 San Patrice Technology and Mobility across the Plains-Woodland Border. Unpublished M.A. thesis, Department of Anthropology, University of Oklahoma, Norman. Online at the Paleoindian Database of the Americas: pidba.utk.edu/main.htm

2008a San Patrice: An Example of Late Paleoindian Adaptive Versatility in South-Central North America. *American Antiquity* 73(3):539–559.

2008b *San Patrice Technology and Mobility across the Plains-Woodland Border.* Memoir No. 12. Oklahoma Anthropological Society, Norman.

Jensen, Harald P.

1968a *Archeological Investigations in the Toledo Bend Reservoir: 1966–1967.* Archeological Salvage Project, Southern Methodist University, Dallas.

1968b Coral Snake Mound [X16SA48]. *Bulletin of the Texas Archaeological Society* 39:9–44.

Jeter, Marvin D.

2002 From Prehistory through Protohistory to Ethnohistory in and near the Northern Lower Mississippi Valley. In *The Transformation of the Southeastern Indians, 1540–1760*, edited by Robbie Ethridge and Charles Hudson, pp. 177–223. University Press of Mississippi, Jackson.

2007 The Outer Limits of Plaquemine Culture: A View from the Northerly Borderlands. In *Plaquemine Archaeology*, edited by Mark A. Rees and Patrick C. Livingood, pp. 161–195. University of Alabama Press, Tuscaloosa.

Jeter, Marvin D., R. Christopher Goodwin, Herschel A. Franks, Eric Poplin, Carol A. Poplin, Jill-Karen Yakubik, Peter A. Gendel, Jeffery Treffinger, Jack Hill, and Wayne Grip

1986 *Archaeological Research to Locate and Identify the French "Fort on the Mississippi" 16PL27 (1700–1707), Plaquemines Parish, Louisiana.* R. Christopher Goodwin and Associates, Inc., New Orleans. U.S. Army Corps of Engineers, New Orleans District.

Jeter, Marvin D., and H. Edwin Jackson

1994 Poverty Point Extraction and Exchange: The Arkansas Lithic Connections. In Exchange in the Lower Mississippi Valley and Contiguous Areas in 1100 B.C., edited by Jon L. Gibson. *Louisiana Archaeology* 17(1990):133–206.

Jeter, Marvin D., Jerome C. Rose, G. Ishmael Williams, Jr., and Anna M. Harmon

1989 *Archeology and Bioarcheology of the Lower Mississippi Valley and Trans-Mississippi South in Arkansas and Louisiana.* Research Series No. 37. Arkansas Archeological Survey, Fayetteville.

Jeter, Marvin D., and Robert J. Scott, Jr.

2008 Keo, Quartz Crystals, Carets, Et Cetcra: Southerly Plum Bayou vs. Northerly Coles Creek Cultural Elements. *The Arkansas Archeologist* 47:43–82.

Jeter, Marvin D., and G. Ishmael Williams, Jr.

1989a Ceramic-Using Cultures, 600 B.C.–A.D. 1000. In *Archeology and Bioarcheology of the Lower Mississippi Valley and Trans-Mississippi South in Arkansas and Louisiana,* by Marvin D. Jeter, Jerome C. Rose, G. Ishmael Williams, Jr., and Anna M. Harmon, pp. 111–170. Research Series No. 37. Arkansas Archeological Survey, Fayetteville.

1989b Late Prehistoric Cultures, A.D. 1000–1500. In *Archeology and Bioarcheology of the Lower Mississippi Valley and Trans-Mississippi South in Arkansas and Louisiana,* by Marvin D. Jeter, Jerome C. Rose, G. Ishmael Williams, Jr., and Anna M. Harmon, pp. 171–220. Research Series No. 37. Arkansas Archeological Survey, Fayetteville.

1989c Lithic Horizons and Early Cultures. In *Archeology and Bioarcheology of the Lower Mississippi Valley and Trans-Mississippi South in Arkansas and Louisiana,* by Marvin D. Jeter, Jerome C. Rose, G. Ishmael Williams, Jr., and Anna M. Harmon, pp. 71–110. Research Series No. 37. Arkansas Archeological Survey, Fayetteville.

Jewell, Edwin L. (editor)

1873 *Jewell's Crescent City Illustrated. The Commercial, Social, Political and General History of New Orleans, including Biographical Sketches of its Distinguished Citizens.* E. L. Jewell, New Orleans.

Johannessen, Sissel

1993 Farmers of the Late Woodland. In *Foraging and Farming in the Eastern Woodlands,* edited by C. Margaret Scarry, pp. 39–56. University Press of Florida, Gainesville.

Johnson, Eileen M.

1987 *Lubbock Lake: Late Quaternary Studies on the Southern High Plains.* Texas A&M University Press, College Station.

Johnson, Jay K.

1980 Poverty Point Period Social Organization in the Yazoo Basin, Mississippi: A Preliminary Consideration. In Caddoan and Poverty Point Archaeology: Essays in Honor of Clarence Hungerford Webb, edited by Jon L. Gibson. *Louisiana Archaeology* 6(1979):251–281.

2000 Beads, Microdrills, Bifaces, and Blades from Watson Brake. *Southeastern Archaeology* 19(2):95–104.

Johnson, Jay K., Gena M. Aleo, Rodney T. Stuart, and John Sullivan

2002 *The 1996 Excavations at the Batesville Mounds: A Woodland Period Platform Mound Complex in Northwest Mississippi.* Archaeological Report No. 32. Mississippi Department of Archives and History, Jackson.

Jones, Dennis, and Carl Kuttruff

1994 *Prehistoric Earthen Enclosures and the Marksville Site: Results of 1993 Archaeological Investigations.* Report on file with the Louisiana Division of Archaeology, Department of Culture, Recreation, and Tourism, Baton Rouge.

1998 Prehistoric Enclosures in Louisiana and the Marksville Site. In *Ancient Earthen Enclosures of the Eastern Woodlands,* edited by Robert C. Mainfort, Jr., and Lynne P. Sullivan, pp. 31–56. University Press of Florida. Gainesville.

Jones, Dennis, Rob Mann, and Rebecca Saunders

2009 The Toncrey Mound Site: Vanishing Evidence of Mississippian Connections on the Louisiana Gulf Coast. Paper presented at the 66th Southeastern Archaeological Conference, Mobile, Alabama.

Jones, Dennis, and Malcolm K. Shuman

1987 *Archaeological Atlas and Report of Prehistoric Indian Mounds in Louisiana.*, Vol. 1: *Ascension, Iberville, Point Coupee, St. James, and West Baton Rouge Parishes.* Museum of Geoscience, Louisiana State University. Report on file with the Louisiana Division of Archaeology, Department of Culture, Recreation, and Tourism, Baton Rouge.

Jones, Kenneth R., Herschel A. Franks, and Tristram R. Kidder

1994 *Cultural Resources Survey and Testing for Davis Pond Freshwater Diversion, St. Charles Parish, Louisiana.* 2 vols. Earth Search, Inc., New Orleans. U.S. Army Corps of Engineers, New Orleans District.

Jones, Reca

1985 Archaeological Investigations in the Ouachita River Valley, Bayou Bartholomew to Riverton, Louisiana. *Louisiana Archaeology* 10(1983):103–169.

Justice, Noel D.

1987 *Stone Age Spear and Arrow Points of the Midcontinental and Eastern United States: A Modern Survey and Reference.* Indiana University Press, Bloomington.

Kane, Adam L.

2004 *The Western River Steamboat.* Texas A&M University Press, College Station.

Kappler, Charles J.

1904 *Indian Affairs: Laws and Treaties,*, Vol. 2: *Treaties.* Government Printing Office, Washington, D.C.

Kassabaum, Megan C.

2007 Looking Beyond the Obvious: Identifying Patterns in Coles Creek Mortuary Data. Unpublished M.A. thesis, Department of Anthropology, University of North Carolina, Chapel Hill.

Keller, John E.

1981 *The Catahoula Cur Site: A Transitional Archaic Occupation in Grant Parish, Louisiana.* USDA Forest Service, Kisatchie National Forest, Pineville.

1983 *Kisatchie National Forest Cultural Resources Overview,* edited by David M. Johnson. USDA Forest Service, Kisatchie National Forest, Pineville.

Kelley, David B.

1992 Coles Creek Period Faunal Exploitation in the Ouachita River Valley of Southern Arkansas. *Midcontinental Journal of Archaeology* 17(2):227–264.

Kelley, David B. (editor)

1997 *Two Caddoan Farmsteads in the Red River Valley: The Archeology of the McLelland and Joe Clark Sites.* Research Series No. 51. Arkansas Archeological Survey, Fayetteville.

2006 *The Burnitt Site: A Late Caddoan Occupation in the Uplands of the Sabine River Basin in Louisiana.* Coastal Environments, Inc., Baton Rouge. Louisiana Department of Transportation and Development, Baton Rouge.

Kelley, David B., and Carey L. Coxe

1998 *Cultural Resources Survey of Levee Rehabilitation/Restoration Areas along the Red River between Fulton, Arkansas, and the Louisiana State Line: Items 4,5, and 9.* Coastal Environments Inc., Baton Rouge. U.S. Army Corps of Engineers, Vicksburg District.

Kelley, David B., Douglas C. Wells, Dana B. Lee, Richard A. Weinstein, and Josette LeBoeuf

2000 *Cultural Resources Evaluation of the Lower Atchafalaya Backwater Area, South Louisiana.* Coastal Environments, Inc., Baton Rouge. U.S. Army Corps of Engineers, New Orleans District.

Kelly, Kenneth G. (editor)

2004 Historical Archaeology in the French Caribbean. Special Issue No. 1. *Journal of Caribbean Archaeology.*

Kelly, Robert L., and Mary M. Prasciunas

2007 Did the Ancestors of Native Americans Cause Animal Extinctions in Late-Pleistocene North America? And Does It Matter If They Did? In *Native Americans and the Environment: Perspectives on the Ecological Indian,* edited by Michael E. Harkin and David R. Lewis, pp. 95–122. University of Nebraska Press, Lincoln.

Kelly, Robert L., and L. C. Todd

1988 Coming into the Country: Early Paleoindian Hunting and Mobility. *American Antiquity* 53(2):231–244.

Kelton, Paul

2007 *Epidemics and Enslavement: Biological Catastrophe in the Native Southeast, 1492–1715.* University of Nebraska Press, Lincoln.

Kender, Carolyn M.

2000 Analysis of Ceramics Excavated from the Kitchen of the Edward Douglass White State Historic Site (16LF38), Lafourche Parish, Louisiana. Unpublished M.A. thesis, Department of Geography and Anthropology, Louisiana State University, Baton Rouge.

Kidder, Tristram R.

1986 *Final Report on Archaeological Test Excavations in the Central Boeuf Basin, Louisiana, 1985.* Lower Mississippi Survey Bulletin 10. Peabody Museum, Harvard University, Cambridge.

1990a *Final Report on the 1989 Archaeological Investigations at the Osceola (16TE2) and Reno Brake (16TE93) Sites, Tensas Parish, Louisiana.* Archaeological Report 1. Center for Archaeology, Tulane University, New Orleans.

1990b Ceramic Chronology and Culture History of the Southern Ouachita River Basin: Coles Creek to the Early Historic Period. *Midcontinental Journal of Archaeology* 15(1):51–99.

1991 New Directions in Poverty Point Settlement Archaeology: An Example for Northeast Louisiana. In *The Poverty Point Culture: Local Manifestations, Subsistence Practices, and Trade Networks,* edited by Kathleen M. Byrd, pp. 27–50. Geoscience and Man 29. Louisiana State University, Baton Rouge.

1992a Coles Creek Period Social Organization and Evolution in Northeast Louisiana. In *Lords of the Southeast: Social Inequality and the Native Elites of Southeastern North America,* edited by Alex W. Barker and Timothy R. Pauketat, pp. 145–162. Archeological Papers of the American Anthropological Association No. 3. Washington, D.C.

1992b Timing and Consequences of the Introduction of Maize Agriculture in the Lower Mississippi Valley. *North American Archaeology* 13(1):15–41.

1992c Excavations at the Jordon Site (16MO1), Morehouse Parish, Louisiana. *Southeastern Archaeology* 11(2):109–131.

1993a *1992 Archaeological Test Excavations in Tensas Parish, Louisiana.* Archaeological Report 2, Center for Archaeology, Tulane University, New Orleans.

1993b The Glendora Phase: Protohistoric–Early Historic Culture Dynamics on the Lower Ouachita River. In *Archaeology of Eastern North America: Papers in Honor of Stephen Williams,* edited by J. B. Stoltman, pp. 231–260. Archaeological Report No. 25. Mississippi Department of Archives and History, Jackson.

1994 Matheny: A Multicomponent Site on Bayou Bartholomew, Northeast Louisiana. *Midcontinental Journal of Archaeology* 19(2):137–169.

1995 *Archaeological Data Recovery at 16JE218, Jefferson Parish, Louisiana.* Earth Search, Inc., New Orleans. U.S. Army Corps of Engineers, New Orleans District.

1996 Perspectives on the Geoarchaeology of the Lower Mississippi Valley. *Engineering Geology* 45:305–323.

1998a Mississippi Period Mound Groups and Communities in the Lower Mississippi Valley. In *Mississippian Towns and Sacred Spaces: Searching for an Architectural Grammar,* edited by R. Barry Lewis and Charles Stout, pp. 123–150. University of Alabama Press, Tuscaloosa.

1998b Rethinking Caddoan–Lower Mississippi Valley Interaction. In *The Native History of the Caddo: Their Place in Southeastern Archeology and Ethnohistory,* edited by T. K. Perttula and J. E. Bruseth, pp. 129–143. Studies in Archeology No. 30. Texas Archeological Research Laboratory, University of Texas at Austin.

1998c The Rat That Ate Louisiana: Aspects of Historical Ecology in the Mississippi River Delta. In *Advances in Historical Ecology,* edited by William Balee, pp. 141–168. Columbia University Press, New York.

2002a Mapping Poverty Point. *American Antiquity* 67(1):89–101.

2002b Woodland Period Archaeology of the Lower Mississippi Valley. In *The Woodland Southeast,* edited by David G. Anderson and Robert C. Mainfort, Jr., pp. 66–90. University of Alabama Press, Tuscaloosa.

2004a Plazas as Architecture: An Example from the Raffman Site, Northeast Louisiana. *American Antiquity* 69(3):514–532.

2004b Prehistory of the Lower Mississippi Valley After 800 B.C. In *Handbook of North American Indians.,* Vol. 14: *Southeast,* edited by Raymond D. Fogelson, pp. 545–559. Smithsonian Institution Press, Washington, D.C.

2006 Climate Change and the Archaic to Woodland Transition (3000–2500 Cal B.P.) in the Mississippi River Basin. *American Antiquity* 71(2):195–231.

2007a A New History of Poverty Point. Paper presented at the 71st Annual Meeting of the Society for American Archaeology, San Juan.

2007b Early Woodland in the Upper Tensas Basin, Northeast Louisiana. Manuscript on file, Department of Anthropology, Washington University, St. Louis.

2007c Contemplating Plaquemine Culture. In *Plaquemine Archaeology,* edited by Mark A. Rees and Patrick C. Livingood, pp. 196–205. University of Alabama Press, Tuscaloosa.

Kidder, Tristam R., Katherine A. Adelsberger, Lee J. Arco, and Timothy M. Schilling

2008 Basin-Scale Reconstruction of the Geological Context of Human Settlement: An Example from the Lower Mississippi Valley, USA. *Quaternary Science Reviews* 27(11–12):1250–1270.

Kidder, Tristram R., and David A. Barondess

1982 A Proposed Bone Tool Classification: A Case Study from Southeast Louisiana. *Louisiana Archaeology* 8(1981):87–108.

Kidder, Tristram R., and Gayle J. Fritz

1993 Subsistence and Social Change in the Lower Mississippi Valley: The Reno Brake and Osceola Sites, Louisiana. *Journal of Field Archaeology* 20(3):281–297.

Kidder, Tristram R., Anthony L. Ortmann, and Lee J. Arco

2008 Poverty Point and the Archaeology of Singularity. *The SAA Archaeological Record* 8(5):9–12.

Kidder, Tristram R., and Lori M. Roe

2007 Early Woodland Settlements in the Upper Tensas Basin, Northeast Louisiana. Manuscript on file, Department of Anthropology, Washington University, St. Louis.

Kidder, Tristram R., and Kenneth E. Sassaman

2009 The View from the Southeast. In *Archaic Societies: Diversity and Complexity across the Midcontinent,* edited by Thomas E. Emerson, Dale L. McElrath, and Andrew C. Fortier, pp. 667–696. State University of New York Press, Albany.

Kidder, Tristram R., and Douglas C. Wells

1994 Baytown Period Social Organization and Evolution in the Lower Mississippi Valley. Manuscript on file, Center for Archaeology, Department of Anthropology, Tulane University, New Orleans.

King, Adam (editor)

2007 *Southeastern Ceremonial Complex: Chronology, Content, Context.* University of Alabama Press, Tuscaloosa.

King, Thomas F.

1987 Prehistory and Beyond: The Place of Archaeology. In *The American Mosaic: Preserving a Nation's Heritage,* edited by Robert E. Stipe and Antoinette J. Lee, pp. 236–264. US/ICOMOS, Washington, D.C.

Klinger, Timothy C., Steven M. Imhoff, and Richard P. Kandare

1992 *Marie Saline: Data Recovery at 3AS329, Flesenthal National Wildlife Refuge Ashley County, Arkansas.* Report 92–25. Historic Preservation Associates, Fayetteville.

Kniffen, Fred B.

1936 Preliminary Report of the Indian Mounds and Middens of Plaquemines and St. Bernard Parishes. In *Reports on the Geology of Plaquemines and St. Bernard Parishes,* pp. 407–422. Bulletin No. 8. Louisiana Geological Survey, Department of Conservation, New Orleans.

1938 Indian Mounds of Iberville Parish. In *Reports on the Geology of Iberville and Ascension Parishes,* pp. 189–207. Bulletin No. 13. Louisiana Geological Survey, Department of Conservation, New Orleans.

Kniffen, Fred B., Hiram F. Gregory, and George A. Stokes

1987 *The Historic Indian Tribes of Louisiana: From 1542 to the Present.* Louisiana State University Press, Baton Rouge.

Knight, Vernon J., Jr.

1984 Late Prehistoric Adaptation in the Mobile Bay Region. In *Perspectives on Gulf Coast Prehistory,* edited by Dave D. Davis, pp. 198–215. Ripley P. Bullen Monographs in Anthropology and History No. 5. University Press of Florida, Gainesville.

1990 Social Organization and the Evolution of Hierarchy in Southeastern Chiefdoms. *Journal of Anthropological Research* 46(1):1–23.

2001 Feasting and the Emergence of Platform Mound Ceremonialism in Eastern North America. In *Feasts: Archaeological and Ethnographic Perspectives on Food, Politics, and Power,* edited by Michael Dietler and Brian Hayden, pp. 311–333. Smithsonian Institution Press, Washington, D.C.

Knight, Vernon J., Jr., and Vincas P. Steponaitis

1998 A New History of Moundville. In *Archaeology of the Moundville Chiefdom,* edited by V. J. Knight, Jr., and V. P. Steponaitis, pp. 1–25. Smithsonian Institution Press, Washington, D.C.

Knight, Vernon J., Jr., and Vincas P. Steponaitis (editors)

1998 *Archaeology of the Moundville Chiefdom.* Smithsonian Institution Press, Washington, D.C.

Knipmeyer, William P.

1976 Folk Boats of Eastern French Louisiana. In *American Folklife,* edited by Don Yoder, pp. 105–149. University of Texas Press, Austin.

Korn, Bertram Wallace

1969 *The Early Jews of New Orleans.* American Jewish Historical Society, Waltham, Massachusetts.

Krause, Kari, Katy Coyle, Sam Turner, J. B. Pelletier, Jeremy Pincoske, David George, William P. Athens, and R. C. Goodwin

2004 *Cultural Resources Survey and Archeological Inventory of the Proposed Carrollton Revetment Project, Orleans Parish, Louisiana, Phase 1.* Volume 1. R. Christopher Goodwin and Associates, Inc., New Orleans. U.S. Army Corps of Engineers, New Orleans District.

Kukla, Jon

2003 *A Wilderness So Immense: The Louisiana Purchase and the Destiny of America.* Alfred A. Knopf, New York.

Kuttruff, Carl, Michael J. O'Brien, and R. Lee Lyman

1997 The 1933 Excavations at the Marksville Site by Frank M. Setzler and James A. Ford. Paper presented at the 54th Southeastern Archaeological Conference, Baton Rouge, Louisiana.

Lafferty, Robert H., III

2008 The Diffusion of Shell-Tempered Pottery into the Baytown Area of the Northern Lower Mississippi Valley. *Southeastern Archaeology* 27(2):172–192.

Lamb, Mary T.

1983 Boudreaux Site (16TE53), Jefferson Parish, Louisiana: Marksville Settlement Patterning. Unpublished M.A. thesis, Department of Anthropology, University of Florida, Gainesville.

Lamb, Teresia R., and Richard C. Beavers

1983 *Archaeology of the Stableyard Complex, Hermann-Grima House, New Orleans, Louisiana.* Research Report No. 7. Archaeological and Cultural Research Program, Department of Anthropology, University of New Orleans. Christian Women's Exchange, New Orleans.

Lamb, Teresia R., Richard C. Beavers, and John R. Greene

1985 *Hermann-Grima Historic House, New Orleans, Louisiana, Courtyard Restoration Project.* Archaeological and Cultural Research Program, Department of Anthropology, University of New Orleans. Coastal Associates, Inc., New Orleans.

Lane, Sheri Dixon

1980 *An Archaeological Study of the Magnolia Mound Plantation House.* Report on file with the Louisiana Division of Archaeology, Department of Culture, Recreation, and Tourism, Baton Rouge.

Lapham, Heather A.

2006 Southeast Animals. In *Handbook of North American Indians.*, Vol. 3: *Environment, Origins, and Population,* edited by Douglas H. Ubelaker, pp. 396–404. Smithsonian Institution Press, Washington, D.C.

Lasley, Scott E.

1983 Particle Induced X-Ray Emission (PIXE) Analysis of Trade Items from Poverty Point, Louisiana. Unpublished senior honors thesis, Department of Physics, University of Southwestern Louisiana, Lafayette.

Lee, Aubra L.

1986 Floral and Faunal Analyses of House Remains at Los Adaes, Natchitoches Parish, Louisiana. Unpublished M.A. thesis, Department of Social Sciences, Northwestern State University, Natchitoches.

1990 Fusils, Paint, and Pelts: An Examination of Natchitoches-Based Indian Trade in the Spanish Period, 1766–1791. Unpublished M.A. thesis, Department of Social Sciences, Northwestern State University, Natchitoches.

2006a Gregory, Gibson, and Hunter: Batting Clean Up Is Not So Bad. Paper presented at the 33rd Annual Meeting of the Louisiana Archaeological Society, Monroe.

2006b Troyville: Embankment and Riverbank Excavations. *Louisiana Archaeological Society Newsletter* 34:5–8.

2007 Update on Recent Archaeological Work at Troyville. Paper presented for the 20th Annual Louisiana Archaeology Week, Jonesville.

Lee, Aubra L., Jennae Biddescombe, David Harlan, Catherine Nolan, Rhonda Smith, and Jill-Karen Yakubik

2010 *Archaeological Data Recovery and Monitoring at the Troyville Mound Site (16CT7).* Earth Search, Inc., New Orleans. Louisiana Department of Transportation and Development, Baton Rouge, in preparation.

Lee, Aubra L., Rhonda Lee Smith, Jill-Karen Yakubik, Tristram R. Kidder, Ruben Saenz II, Benjamin Maygarden, Gayle Fritz, and Roger T. Saucier

1997 *Archaeological Data Recovery at the Birds Creek Site (16CT416), Catahoula Parish, Louisiana.* Earth Search, Inc., New Orleans. Louisiana Department of Transportation and Development, Baton Rouge.

Lee, Aubra L., and Jill-Karen Yakubik

2003 *A Research Design for Archaeological Data Recovery and Monitoring at the Troyville Mounds Site (16CT7).* Earth Search, Inc., New Orleans. Louisiana Department of Transportation and Development, Baton Rouge.

Lee, Aubra L., Jill-Karen Yakubik, Rhonda L. Smith, Melissa Braud, and Benjamin D. Maygarden

1997 *Archaeological Investigations at the Villa Meilleur (16OR142).* Earth Search, Inc., New Orleans. Report on file with the Louisiana Division of Archaeology, Department of Culture, Recreation, and Tourism, Baton Rouge.

Lehmann, Geoffrey R.

1982 *The Jaketown Site: Surface Collections from a Poverty Point Regional Center in the Yazoo Basin, Mississippi.* Archaeological Report No. 9. Mississippi Department of Archives and History, Jackson.

Leidy, Joseph

1866 Remarks. *Proceedings of the Academy of Natural Sciences of Philadelphia* 18:109.

Lenzer, John P.

1980 Geology and Geomorphology. In The Hanna Site: An Alto Focus Village in Red River Parish. *Louisiana Archaeology* 5(1978):45–70.

Leone, Mark

1995 A Historical Archaeology of Capitalism. *American Anthropologist* 97(2):251–266.

Leone, Mark, Parker Potter, and Paul Shackel

1987 Toward a Critical Archaeology. *Current Anthropology* 28(3):283–301.

Lepper, Bradley T., and Robert E. Funk

2006 Paleo-Indian: East. In *Handbook of North American Indians.*, Vol. 3: *Environment, Origins, and Population,* edited by Douglas H. Ubelaker, pp. 171–193. Smithsonian Institution Press, Washington, D.C.

Lewicki, Tadeusz, and Marion Johnson

1974 *West African Food in the Middle Ages according to Arabic Sources.* Cambridge University Press, Cambridge.

Lewis, Barbara L.

1991 Analysis of Pathologies Present in the Tchefuncte Indian Skeletal Collection. Unpublished M.A. thesis, Department of Geography and Anthropology, Louisiana State University, Baton Rouge.

1994 Treponematosis and Lyme Borreliosis Connections: Explanation for Tchefuncte Disease Syndromes? *American Journal of Physical Anthropology* 93(4):455–474.

1997 Tchefuncte Use of Animal Bone with Inferences for Tchefuncte Culture, Ritual, and Animal Cosmologies. *Louisiana Archaeology* 22(1995):31–70.

Lewis, Peirce

2003 *New Orleans: The Making of an Urban Landscape.* 2nd ed. Center for American Places, Santa Fe, New Mexico, and Staunton, Virginia.

Lewis, R. Barry

2000 Sea-Level Rise and Subsidence Effects on Gulf Coast Archaeological Site Distributions. *American Antiquity* 65(3):525–541.

Lewis, R. Barry, and C. Stout (editors)

1998 *Mississippian Towns and Sacred Spaces: Searching for an Architectural Grammar.* University of Alabama Press, Tuscaloosa.

L'Herrison, Lawrence E., Jr.

1981 The Evolution of the Texas Road and the Subsequent Settlement Occupancy of the Adjacent Strip of Northwestern Louisiana, 1528–1824. Unpublished M.A. thesis, Department of Geography, Louisiana State University, Baton Rouge.

Lightfoot, Kent G.

1995 Culture Contact Studies: Redefining the Relationship Between Prehistoric and Historical Archaeology. *American Antiquity* 60(2)199–217.

Lindauer, Owen, and John H. Blitz

1997 Higher Ground: The Archaeology of North American Platform Mounds. *Journal of Archaeological Research* 5(2):169–207.

Lippert, Dorothy

2006 Building a Bridge to Cross a Thousand Years. *American Indian Quarterly* 30 (3–4):431–440.

Listi, Ginesse

2007 Bioarchaeological Analysis of Diet and Nutrition During the Coles Creek Period in the Lower Mississippi Valley. Unpublished Ph.D. dissertation, Department of Anthropology, Tulane University, New Orleans.

Little, Barbara J. (editor)

1992 *Text-Aided Archaeology.* CRC Press, Boca Raton, Florida.

Livingood, Patrick C.

2007 Plaquemine Recipes: Using Computer-Assisted Petrographic Analysis to Investigate Plaquemine Ceramic Recipes. In *Plaquemine Archaeology,* edited by Mark A. Rees and Patrick C. Livingood, pp. 108–126. University of Alabama Press, Tuscaloosa.

Loewen, James W.

1999 *Lies across America: What Our Historic Sites Get Wrong,* Simon and Schuster, New York.

Longoria, Linda Dale

2007 Chinese Porcelain in the Missions and Presidios of Eighteenth-Century Spanish Texas. Unpublished M.A. thesis, Department of Anthropology, University of Texas at San Antonio.

Lopinot, Neal H.

1992 Spatial and Temporal Variability in Mississippian Subsistence: The Archaeobotanical Record. In *Late Prehistoric Agriculture: Observations from the Midwest,* edited by W. I. Woods, pp. 44–94. Studies in Illinois Archaeology No. 8. Illinois Historic Preservation Agency, Springfield.

1997 Cahokian Food Production Reconsidered. In *Cahokia: Domination and Ideology* in the Mississippian World*, edited by T. R. Pauketat and T. E. Emerson, pp. 52–68. University of Nebraska Press, Lincoln.

Lopinot, Neal H., Jack H. Ray, and Michael D. Conner (editors)

1998 *The 1997 Excavations at the Big Eddy Site (23CE426) in Southwest Missouri.* Special Publication No. 2. Center for Archaeological Research, Southwest Missouri State University, Springfield.

2000 *The 1999 Excavations at the Big Eddy Site (23CE426).* Special Publication No. 3. Center for Archaeological Research, Southwest Missouri State University, Springfield.

Loren, Diana DiPaolo

1999 Creating Social Distinction: Articulating Colonial Policies and Practices along the Eighteenth-Century Louisiana/Texas Frontier. Unpublished Ph.D. dissertation, Department of Anthropology, State University of New York, Binghamton.

2000 The Intersections of Colonial Policy and Colonial Practice: Creolization on the Eighteenth-Century Louisiana/Texas Frontier. *Historical Archaeology* 34(3):85–98.

2001a Manipulating Bodies and Emerging Traditions at the Los Adaes Presidio. In *The Archaeology of Traditions: Agency and History before and after Columbus*, edited by Timothy R. Pauketat, pp. 58–76. University Press of Florida, Gainesville.

2001b Social Skins: Orthodoxies and Practices of Dressing in the Early Colonial Lower Mississippi Valley. *Journal of Social Archaeology* 1(2):172–189.

2007 Corporeal Concerns: Eighteenth-Century Casta Paintings and Colonial Paintings and Colonial Bodies in Spanish Texas. In Between Art and Artifact, edited by Diana DiPaolo Loren and Uzi Baram. *Historical Archaeology* 41(1):23–36.

Lorenz, Karl G.

1997 A Re-Examination of Natchez Sociopolitical Complexity: a View from the Grand Village and Beyond. *Southeastern Archaeology* 16(2):97–112.

Los Adaes Site Explorer

2005 Los Adaes Site Explorer Website. Louisiana Division of Archaeology, Department of Culture, Recreation, and Tourism, Baton Rouge. Online at: www.crt.state.la.us/siteexplorer/

Louisiana Division of Archaeology (LDA)

2000 *Ancient Mound Sites of Louisiana.* Brochure prepared by the Louisiana Division of Archaeology, Office of Cultural Development, Department of Culture, Recreation, and Tourism, Baton Rouge.

2009 Website of the Louisiana Division of Archaeology, Office of Cultural Development, Department of Culture, Recreation, and Tourism, Baton Rouge. Online at: www.crt.state.la.us/archaeology/

Louisiana Division of Historic Preservation

2009 Website of the Louisiana Division of Historic Preservation, Office of Cultural Development, Department of Culture, Recreation, and Tourism, Baton Rouge. Online at: www.crt.state.la.us/hp/

Lubar, Steven, and W. David Kingery (editors)

1993 *History from Things: Essays on Material Culture.* Smithsonian Institution Press, Washington, D.C.

Lyman, R. Lee, Michael J. O'Brien, and Robert C. Dunnell

1997 *The Rise and Fall of Culture History.* Plenum Press, New York.

Lyon, Edwin A.

1996 *A New Deal for Southeastern Archaeology.* University of Alabama Press, Tuscaloosa.

MacDonald, Kevin C., David W. Morgan, and Fiona J. L. Handley

2006 The Cane River African Diaspora Archaeological Project: Prospectus and Initial Results. In *African Re-Genesis: Confronting Social Issues in the Diaspora,* edited by J. B. Haviser and K. C. MacDonald, pp. 123–144. UCL Press, London.

Mainfort, Robert C., Jr.

1999 Late Period Phases in the Central Mississippi Valley: A Multivariate Approach. In *Arkansas Archaeology: Essays in Honor of Dan and Phyllis Morse,* edited by R. C. Mainfort, Jr., and M. D. Jeter, pp. 143–167. University of Arkansas Press, Fayetteville.

Mainfort, Robert C., Jr., and Marvin D. Jeter (editors)

1999 *Arkansas Archaeology: Essays in Honor of Dan and Phyllis Morse.* University of Arkansas Press, Fayetteville.

Mann, Rob

2002 *2002 Annual Report for Management Units IV and V, Regional Archaeology Program, Museum of Natural Science, Louisiana State University.* Report on file with the Louisiana Division of Archaeology, Department of Culture, Recreation, and Tourism, Baton Rouge.

2003a *2003 Annual Report for Management Units IV and V, Regional Archaeology Program, Museum of Natural Science, Louisiana State University.* Report on file with the Louisiana Division of Archaeology, Department of Culture, Recreation, and Tourism, Baton Rouge.

2003b Colonizing the Colonizers: Canadien Fur Traders and Fur Trade Society in the Great Lakes Region, 1763–1850. Unpublished Ph.D. dissertation, Department of Anthropology, State University of New York, Binghamton.

2005 Intruding on the Past: The Reuse of Ancient Earthen Mounds by Native Americans. *Southeastern Archaeology* 24(1):1–10.

2006 *2006 Annual Report for Management Units IV and V, Regional Archaeology Program, Museum of Natural Science, Louisiana State University.* Report on file with the Louisiana Division of Archaeology, Department of Culture, Recreation, and Tourism, Baton Rouge.

2007a 2007 *Annual Report for Management Units IV and V, Regional Archaeology Program, Museum of Natural Science, Louisiana State University.* Report on file with the Louisiana Division of Archaeology, Department of Culture, Recreation, and Tourism, Baton Rouge.

2007b "True Portraitures of the Indians, and of Their Own Peculiar Conceits of Dress": Discourses of Dress and Identity in the Great Lakes, 1830–1850. In Between Art and Artifact, edited by Diana DiPaolo Loren and Uzi Baram. *Historical Archaeology* 41(1):37–52.

2008a From Ethnogenesis to Ethnic Segmentation in the Wabash Valley: Constructing Identity and Houses in Great Lakes Fur Trade Society. In The Archaeology of French Colonial and Post-Colonial Settlements, edited by Elizabeth Scott. *International Journal of Historical Archaeology* 12(4):319–337.

2008b Pointe Coupée: Recent Archaeological Investigations at an Eighteenth-Century Colonial Settlement in French *Louisiane.* In Rêves d'Amériques: Regard sur l'archéologie de la Nouvelle-France/Dreams of the Americas: Overview of New France Archaeology, edited by Christian Roy and Hélène Côté, pp. 127–140. *Archéologiques,* Hors série 2, AAQ, Québec.

Mann, Rob, and Diana DiPaolo Loren

2000 Practical Negotiations: Making Social Landscapes at Bayou Goula. Paper presented at the 57th Southeastern Archaeological Conference, Macon, Georgia.

Mann, Rob, and Timothy Schilling

2004 Looking for the French in French *Louisiane:* Preliminary Results of the Pointe Coupée Survey Project. Paper presented at the 37th Annual Society for Historical Archaeology Conference on Historical and Underwater Archaeology, St. Louis.

Manuel, Joseph O., Jr.

1979 A Radiocarbon Date From the Hornsby Site—16SH21. *Louisiana Archaeological Society Newsletter* 6(1):18–19.

Marable, Manning, and Kristen Clarke (editors)

2008 *Seeking Higher Ground: The Hurricane Katrina Crisis, Race, and Public Policy Reader.* Palgrave, Macmillan, New York.

Marckese, Thomas A.

1993 A Clovis Point Found at Cote Blanche Island. *Louisiana Archaeology* 20: 165–167.

1995 Three Fluted Points from South Central Louisiana. *Current Research in the Pleistocene* 12:32–33.

Mariaca, Maria T.

1988 Late Marksville/Early Baytown Period Subsistence Economy: Analysis of

Three Faunal Assemblages from Northeastern Louisiana. Unpublished M.A. thesis, Department of Archaeology, Boston University, Boston.

Martin, Paul S.

1967 Prehistoric Overkill. In *Pleistocene Extinctions: The Search for a Cause*, edited by P. S. Martin and H. E. Wright, Jr., pp. 75–120. Yale University Press, New Haven.

1984 Prehistoric Overkill: The Global Model. In *Quaternary Extinctions*, edited by P. S. Martin and G. Klein, pp. 354–403. University of Arizona Press, Tucson.

Mason, Ronald J.

2000 Archaeology and Native American Oral Traditions. *American Antiquity* 65(2):239–266.

2006 *Inconstant Companions: Archaeology and North American Indian Oral Traditions.* University of Alabama Press, Tuscaloosa.

Mather, Christine (editor)

1983 *Colonial Frontiers: Art and Life in Spanish New Mexico. The Fred Harvey Collection.* Ancient City Press, Santa Fe.

Mathews, James H.

1983 Analysis of Ceramics from Three Eighteenth- and Nineteenth-Century Sites in the Locale of Natchitoches, Louisiana. Unpublished M.A. thesis, Department of History, Social Sciences, and Social Work, Northwestern State University, Natchitoches.

Mathews, James H., Joseph Meyer, James R. Morehead, L. Janice Campbell, and Prentice M. Thomas, Jr.

1997 *Fort Polk 27: The Results of a Twenty-Seventh Program of Site Testing at Ten Sites, Fort Polk Military Reservation, Vernon Parish, Louisiana.* Report of Investigations No. 336. Prentice Thomas and Associates, Inc., Fort Walton Beach, Florida.

Matthews, Christopher N.

1999 *Management Report of Excavations at the St. Augustine Site (16OR148), 1999.* Greater New Orleans Archaeology Program. Report on file with the Louisiana Division of Archaeology, Department of Culture, Recreation, and Tourism, Baton Rouge.

2001 Political Economy and Race: Comparative Archaeologies of Annapolis and New Orleans in the Eighteenth Century. In *Race and the Archaeology of Identity*, edited by Charles E. Orser, Jr., pp.71–87. University of Utah Press, Salt Lake City.

Maygarden, Benjamin D., D. Ryan Gray, and Jill-Karen Yakubik

2005 *Historical and Cartographic Background Research, National D-Day Museum Expansion, Archaeological Mitigation Plan, New Orleans, Louisiana.* Earth Search, Inc., New Orleans. Report on file with the Louisiana Division of Archaeology, Department of Culture, Recreation, and Tourism, Baton Rouge.

Maygarden, Benjamin D., Aubra Lee, Jill-Karen Yakubik, and Pauline Barrow

1999 *Historical Research and Archaeological Survey of the Historic Portion of Southern University, Baton Rouge, East Baton Rouge Parish.* Earth Search, Inc., New Orleans. Report on file with the Louisiana Division of Archaeology, Department of Culture, Recreation, and Tourism, Baton Rouge.

McAvoy, J. M., and L. D. McAvoy

1997 *Archaeological Investigations of Site 44SX202, Cactus Hill, Sussex County, Virginia.* Research Report No. 8. Virginia Department of Historic Resources, Richmond.

McCrocklin, Claude

1990 The Red River Coushatta Indian Villages of Northwest Louisiana, 1790–1835. *Louisiana Archaeology* 12(1985):129–178.

McDavid, Carol

2002 Archaeologies That Hurt, Descendants That Matter: A Pragmatic Approach to Collaboration in the Public Interpretation of African-American Archaeology. *World Archaeology* 34(2):303–314.

McGahey, Samuel O.

1996 Paleoindian and Early Archaic Data from Mississippi. In *The Paleoindian and Early Archaic Southeast,* edited by D. G. Anderson and K. E. Sassaman, pp. 354–384. University of Alabama Press, Tuscaloosa.

2000 *Mississippi Projectile Point Guide.* Archaeological Report No. 31. Mississippi Department of Archives and History, Jackson.

McGimsey, Charles R.

2001 *The Rings of Marksville and Other Stories of Southwest Louisiana History, Regional Archaeology Program, Management Unit III, 2000/2001 Annual Report.* Department of Sociology and Anthropology, University of Louisiana at Lafayette. Report on file with the Louisiana Division of Archaeology, Department of Culture, Recreation, and Tourism, Baton Rouge.

2003a *The Morton Shell Mound Project and Other Stories of Southwest Louisiana History, Regional Archaeology Program, Management Unit III, 2002/2003 Annual Report.* Department of Sociology and Anthropology, University of Louisiana at Lafayette. Report on file with the Louisiana Division of Archaeology, Department of Culture, Recreation, and Tourism, Baton Rouge.

2003b The Rings of Marksville. *Southeastern Archaeology* 22(1):47–62.

2003c Dating the Lac St. Agnes Mound (16AV26). *Louisiana Archaeological Society Newsletter* 30:12–13.

2004 *The Gold Mine Site (16RI13): An AD 825 Ossuary in Northeast Louisiana, Regional Archaeology Program, Management Unit III, 2003/2004 Annual Report.* Department of Sociology and Anthropology, University of Louisiana at Lafayette. Report on file with the Louisiana Division of Archaeology, Department of Culture, Recreation, and Tourism, Baton Rouge.

2005 An Exploration into Archaeology's Past: The 1926 Expedition of Henry B. Collins, Jr., in Louisiana. *Louisiana Archaeology* 26(1999):17–54.

McGimsey, Charles R., H. Edwin Jackson, Katherine M. Roberts, and James Hebert

1999 *Marksville (16AV1), Lake Anacoco, and the Chenier Plain, Regional Archaeology Program, Management Unit III, 1998/1999 Annual Report.* Department of Sociology and Anthropology, University of Louisiana at Lafayette. Report on file with the Louisiana Division of Archaeology, Department of Culture, Recreation, and Tourism, Baton Rouge.

McGimsey, Charles R., and Katherine M. Roberts

2000 Reconsidering the Marksville Site (16AV1) Paleoethnobotany. In *Archaeology of the Marksville Period: Explorations of Southwest Louisiana Prehistory, Regional Archaeology Program, Management Unit III, 1999/2000 Annual Report,* by Charles R. McGimsey, Katherine M. Roberts, H. Edwin Jackson, and Susan L. Scott, pp. 67–78. Department of Sociology and Anthropology, University of Louisiana at Lafayette. Report on file with the Louisiana Division of Archaeology, Department of Culture, Recreation, and Tourism, Baton Rouge.

McGimsey, Charles R., Katherine M. Roberts, H. Edwin Jackson, and Michael L. Hargrave

2005 Marksville Then and Now: 75 Years of Digging. *Louisiana Archaeology* 26(1999):75–98.

McGimsey, Charles R., Katherine M. Roberts, H. Edwin Jackson, and Susan L. Scott

2000 *Archaeology of the Marksville Period: Explorations of Southwest Louisiana Prehistory, Regional Archaeology Program, Management Unit III, 1999/2000 Annual Report.* Department of Sociology and Anthropology, University of Louisiana at Lafayette. Report on file with the Louisiana Division of Archaeology, Department of Culture, Recreation, and Tourism, Baton Rouge.

McGimsey, Charles R., and Josette van der Koogh

2001 *Louisiana's Archaeological Radiometric Database.* Special Publication No. 3, Louisiana Archaeological Society, Baton Rouge.

McGowan, James T.

1976 Creation of a Slave Society: Louisiana Plantations in the Eighteenth Century. Unpublished Ph.D. dissertation, Department of History, University of Rochester, New York.

McIntire, William G.

1958 *Prehistoric Indian Settlements of the Changing Mississippi River Delta.* Louisiana State University Press, Baton Rouge.

McKee, Larry

1992 The Ideals and Realities Behind the Design and Use of Nineteenth-Century Virginia Slave Cabins. In *The Art and Mystery of Historical Archaeology: Essays in Honor of James Deetz,* edited by A. E. Yentsch and M. C. Beaudry, pp. 195–214. CRC Press, Boca Raton.

McNiven, Ian J., and Lynette Russell

2005 *Appropriated Pasts: Indigenous Peoples and the Colonial Culture of Archaeology.* AltaMira, Lanham, Maryland.

McNutt, Charles H.

2008 Late Mississippian Phases in the Central Mississippi Valley: A Commentary. *Southeastern Archaeology* 27(1):122–143.

McNutt, Charles H. (editor)

1996 *Prehistory of the Central Mississippi Valley.* University of Alabama Press, Tuscaloosa.

McWilliams, Richebourge G. (translator and editor)

1981 *Iberville's Gulf Journals.* University of Alabama Press, Tuscaloosa.

McWilliams, Tennant S.

1981 Introduction. In *Iberville's Gulf Journals,* translated and edited by Richebourge G. McWilliams, pp. 1–16. University of Alabama Press, Tuscaloosa.

Melançon, Mark A.

1999 Seriation of Certain Tchefuncte Ceramic Decoration Styles in Avoyelles, Lafayette, St. Landry, and St. Martin Parishes, Louisiana. *Louisiana Archaeology* 23(1996):37–47.

Meltzer, David J.

2004 Peopling of North America. In *The Quaternary Period in the United States,* edited by Alan R. Gillespie, Stephen C. Porter, and Brian F. Atwater, pp. 539–563. Elsevier, New York.

2005 The Seventy-Year Itch: Controversies over Human Antiquity and Their Resolution. *Journal of Anthropological Research* 61(4):433–468.

2006 History of Research on the Paleoindian. In *Handbook of North American Indians.,* Vol. 3: *Environment, Origins, and Population,* edited by Douglas H. Ubelaker, pp. 110–128. Smithsonian Institution Press, Washington, D.C.

2009 *First Peoples in a New World: Colonizing Ice Age America.* University of California Press, Berkeley.

Meyer, Joseph, James R. Morehead, L. Janice Campbell, James H. Mathews, and Prentice M. Thomas, Jr.

1996 *Fort Polk 24: The Results of a Twenty-Fourth Program of Site Testing at Ten Sites, Fort Polk Military Reservation, Vernon Parish, Louisiana.* Report of Investigations No. 326. Prentice Thomas and Associates, Inc., Fort Walton Beach, Florida.

Meyer, Joseph, James R. Morehead, James H. Mathews, Prentice M. Thomas, Jr., and L. Janice Campbell

1996 *Fort Polk 18: The Results of an Eighteenth Program of Site Testing at Ten Sites, Fort Polk Military Reservation, Vernon Parish, Louisiana.* Report of Investigations No. 272. Prentice Thomas and Associates, Inc., Fort Walton Beach, Florida.

Miller, Cinder Griffin, R. Christopher Goodwin, Glenn Walter, T. R. Kidder, Marie Danforth, Roger T. Saucier, John Jones, William Hayden, Allen Green, Angele Montana, Nathanael Heller, Charlene Keck, Michele Williams, and Dave D. Davis

2000 *Phase III Data Recovery Excavations at Site 16LF66, The Discovery Site, A Site Identified Within the Discovery Producer Services LLC Larose Gas Processing Plant in Lafourche Parish, Louisiana.* R. Christopher Goodwin and Associates, Inc., New Orleans. Discovery Gas Transmission LLC, St. Rose, Louisiana.

Mintz, Sidney, and Richard Price

1976 *The Birth of African American Culture: An Anthropological Perspective.* Beacon Press, Boston.

Mitchell, C. Bradford (editor)

1975 *Merchant Steam Vessels of the United States, 1790–1868 (The Lytle-Holdcamper List).* The Steamship Historical Society of America, Staten Island, New York.

Mooney, Timothy Paul

1997 *Many Choctaw Standing: An Archaeological Study of Culture Change in the Early Historic Period.* Archaeological Report No. 27. Mississippi Department of Archives and History, Jackson.

Moore, Clarence B.

1909 Antiquities of the Ouachita. *Journal of the Academy of Natural Sciences of Philadelphia* 14:7–170.

1910 Antiquities of the St. Francis, White, and Black Rivers, Arkansas. *Journal of the Academy of Natural Sciences of Philadelphia* 14:253–364.

1912 Some Aboriginal Sites on Red River. *Journal of the Academy of Natural Sciences of Philadelphia* 14(4):481–644.

1913 Some Aboriginal Sites in Louisiana and in Arkansas: Atchafalaya River, Lake Larto, Tensas River, Bayou Maçon, and Bayou D'Arbonne in Louisiana; Saline River in Arkansas. *Journal of the Academy of Natural Sciences of Philadelphia* 16:5–99.

Moorhead, Max L.

1975 *The Presidio: Bastion of the Spanish Borderlands.* University of Oklahoma Press, Norman.

Morehead, James R.

1980 Lithic Analysis. In *Oak Island Archaeology: Prehistoric Estuarine Adaptations in the Mississippi River Delta,* by J. Richard Shenkel, pp. 148–287. Archaeological and Cultural Research Program, University of New Orleans. Jean Lafitte National Historical Park, New Orleans. National Park Service, U.S. Department of the Interior.

Morehead, James R., L. Janice Campbell, James H. Mathews, Philip D. Bourgeois, Jr., Carrie Williams, and Prentice M. Thomas, Jr.

2002 *Fort Polk 50: The Results of a Fiftieth Program of Site Testing at Ten Sites, Fort*

Polk Military Reservation, Vernon Parish, Louisiana. Report of Investigations No. 630. Prentice Thomas and Associates, Inc., Fort Walton Beach, Florida.

Morehead, James R., L. Janice Campbell, James H. Mathews, Joseph Meyer, and Prentice M. Thomas, Jr.

1996 *Fort Polk 22: The Results of a Twenty-Second Program of Site Testing at Ten Sites, Fort Polk Military Reservation, Vernon Parish, Louisiana.* Report of Investigations No. 302. Prentice Thomas and Associates, Inc., Fort Walton Beach, Florida.

Morehead, James R., L. Janice Campbell, James H. Mathews, Prentice M. Thomas, Jr., and Carrie Williams

2007 *Fort Polk 60: The Results of the Sixtieth Program of Site Testing at Ten Sites, Fort Polk Military Reservation, Vernon Parish, Louisiana.* Report of Investigations No. 1060. Prentice Thomas and Associates, Inc., Fort Walton Beach, Florida.

Morehead, James R., L. Janice Campbell, Prentice M. Thomas, Jr., James H. Mathews, and Joseph Meyer

1995 *Fort Polk 13: The Results of a Thirteenth Program of Site Testing at Ten Sites, Fort Polk Military Reservation, Vernon Parish, Louisiana.* Report of Investigations No. 252. Prentice Thomas and Associates, Inc., Fort Walton Beach, Florida.

Morehead, James R., James H. Mathews, L. Janice Campbell, A. Frank Servello, and Prentice M. Thomas, Jr.

2007 *Fort Polk 59: The Results of the Fifty-Ninth Program of Site Testing at Ten Sites, Fort Polk Military Reservation, Vernon Parish, Louisiana.* Report of Investigations No. 777. Prentice Thomas and Associates, Inc., Fort Walton Beach, Florida.

Morehead, James R., Prentice M. Thomas, Jr., L. Janice Campbell, James H. Mathews, and Joseph Meyer

1995 *Fort Polk 12: The Results of a Twelfth Program of Site Testing at Ten Sites, Fort Polk Military Reservation, Vernon Parish, Louisiana.* Report of Investigations No. 249. Prentice Thomas and Associates, Inc., Fort Walton Beach, Florida.

Morgan, David W.

2005 *Phase II Archaeological Investigations at the American Cemetery (16NA67), Natchitoches Parish, Louisiana.* Cultural Resources Office, Northwestern State University, Natchitoches.

Morgan, Nancy I. M., and Justin Shatwell (editors)

2002 *Archaeology, Interpretation, and Management in Cane River National Heritage Area: Symposium Proceedings from the 35th Annual Conference of the Society for Historical Archaeology, January 8–12, 2002, Mobile, Alabama.* Cane River Creole National Heritage Area, Natchitoches.

Morse, Dan F.

1997 *Sloan: A Paleoindian Dalton Cemetery in Arkansas.* Smithsonian Institution Press, Washington, D.C.

Morse, Dan F., David G. Anderson, and Albert C. Goodyear
1996 The Pleistocene-Holocene Transition in the Eastern United States. In *Humans at the End of the Ice Age: The Archaeology of the Pleistocene-Holocene Transition,* edited by L. G. Straus, B. V. Eriksen, J. M. Erlandson and D. R. Yesner, pp. 319–338. Plenum, New York.

Morse, Dan F., and Phyllis A. Morse
1983 *Archaeology of the Central Mississippi Valley.* Academic Press, New York.

Muller, Jon
1997 *Mississippian Political Economy.* Plenum Press, New York.

Mullins, Paul
1999 *Race and Affluence: An Archaeology of African America and Consumer Culture.* Kluwer Academic/Plenum Publishers, New York.
2004 Ideology, Power, and Capitalism: The Historical Archaeology of Consumption. In *A Companion to Social Archaeology,* edited by Lynn Meskell and Robert Preucel, pp. 195–211. Blackwell Publishing, Malden, Massachusetts.

Murray, Grover E.
1948 *Geology of DeSoto and Red River Parishes.* Geological Bulletin No. 25. Department of Conservation, Louisiana Geological Survey, Baton Rouge.

Nassaney, Michael S.
1992 Communal Societies and the Emergence of Elites in the Prehistoric American Southeast. In *Lords of the Southeast: Social Inequality and the Native Elites of Southeastern North America,* edited by A. Barker and T. Pauketat, pp. 111–143. Archeological Papers of the American Anthropological Association No. 3. Washington, D.C.

Nassaney, Michael S., and Charles R. Cobb
1991 Patterns and Processes of Late Woodland Development in the Greater Southeastern United States. In *Stability, Transformation, and Variation: The Late Woodland Southeast,* edited by M. S. Nassaney and C. R. Cobb, pp. 285–322. Plenum Press, New York.

Nassaney, Michael S., and Kendra Pyle
1999 The Adoption of the Bow and Arrow in Eastern North America: A View from Central Arkansas. *American Antiquity* 64(2):243–263.

National Trust for Historic Preservation
1999 *With Heritage So Rich.* Preservation Books, Washington, D.C. Originally published in 1966, Random House, New York.

Nau, John Fredrick
1958 *The German People of New Orleans, 1850–1900.* E. J. Brill, Leiden.

Neitzel, Robert S.
1964 The Natchez Grand Village. *Florida Anthropologist* 17(2):63–66.
1983 *The Grand Village of the Natchez Revisited: Excavations at the Fatherland Site, Adams County, Mississippi, 1972.* Archaeological Report No. 12. Mississippi Department of Archives and History, Jackson.

1997 *Archaeology of the Fatherland Site: The Grand Village of the Natchez.* Archaeological Report 28. Mississippi Department of Archives and History, Jackson. Originally published 1965, Anthropological Papers of the American Museum of Natural History Vol. 51, Pt. 1. American Museum of Natural History, New York.

Neuman, Robert W.

1975 *Archaeological Salvage Excavations at the Bayou Jasmine Site, Saint John the Baptist Parish, Louisiana, 1975.* Report on file with the Louisiana Division of Archaeology, Department of Culture, Recreation, and Tourism, Baton Rouge.

1977a *An Archaeological Assessment of Coastal Louisiana.* Mélanges No. 11. Museum of Geoscience, Louisiana State University, Baton Rouge.

1977b Archaeological Techniques in the Louisiana Coastal Region. *Louisiana Archaeology* 3(1976):1–21.

1984 *An Introduction to Louisiana Archaeology.* Louisiana State University Press, Baton Rouge.

1985 *Report on the Soil Core Borings Conducted at the Campus Mounds Site (16EBR6) East Baton Rouge Parish, Louisiana.* Museum of Geoscience Technical Report. Louisiana State University, Baton Rouge.

2002 Louisiana Archaeology: A Selective History. In *Histories of Southeastern Archaeology,* edited by Shannon Tushingham, Jane Hill, and Charles H. McNutt, pp. 88–98. University of Alabama Press, Tuscaloosa.

Neuman, Robert W., and Nancy W. Hawkins

1982 *Louisiana Prehistory.* Anthropological Study No. 6. Louisiana Department of Culture, Recreation, and Tourism, Baton Rouge.

1993 *Louisiana Prehistory.* 2nd ed. Anthropological Study No. 6. Louisiana Archaeological Survey and Antiquities Commission, Department of Culture, Recreation, and Tourism, Baton Rouge.

Neuman, Robert W., and A. Frank Servello

1976 *Atchafalaya Basin Archaeological Survey.* Department of Geography and Anthropology, School of Geoscience, Louisiana State University, Baton Rouge. U.S. Army Corps of Engineers, New Orleans District.

Neuman, Robert W., and Lanier A. Simmons

1969 *A Bibliography Relative to Indians of the State of Louisiana.* Anthropological Study No. 4. Department of Conservation, Louisiana Geological Survey, Baton Rouge.

Newcomb, William W., Jr.

2004 Atakapans and Neighboring Groups. In *Handbook of North American Indians.,* Vol. 14: *Southeast,* edited by Raymond D. Fogelson, pp. 659–663. Smithsonian Institution Press, Washington, D.C.

Newell, H. Perry, and Alex D. Krieger

1949 *The George C. Davis Site, Cherokee County, Texas.* Memoir No. 5. Society for American Archaeology, Menasha, Wisconsin.

Niehaus, Earl

1965 *The Irish in New Orleans.* Louisiana State University Press, Baton Rouge.

Noël Hume, Ivor

1991 *A Guide to Artifacts of Colonial America.* Vintage Books, New York. Originally published 1969, Alfred A. Knopf, New York.

Norman, N. Philip

1942 The Red River of the South: Historical Aspects Pertaining to the Navigation of This River, with a Tabulated List of Steamboats, Steamboat Masters, and Way Landings. *Louisiana Historical Quarterly* 25:397–533.

O'Brien, Michael J., and Robert C. Dunnell (editors)

1998 *Changing Perspectives on the Archaeology of the Central Mississippi Valley.* University of Alabama Press, Tuscaloosa.

O'Brien, Michael J., and W. Raymond Wood

1998 *The Prehistory of Missouri.* University of Missouri Press, Columbia.

Orser, Charles E., Jr.

1998 The Archaeology of the African Diaspora. *Annual Review of Anthropology* 27:63–82.

2001 The Anthropology in American Historical Archaeology. *American Anthropologist* 103(3):621–632.

2007 *The Archaeology of Race and Racialization in Historic America.* University Press of Florida, Gainesville.

Orser, Charles E., Jr. (editor)

1996 *Images of the Recent Past: Readings in Historical Archaeology.* AltaMira Press, Lanham, Maryland.

Ortmann, Anthony L.

2003 *Project 2/01: Results of the 2001 and 2002 Field Seasons at Poverty Point.* Report on file with the Louisiana Division of Archaeology, Department of Culture, Recreation, and Tourism, Baton Rouge.

2005 *Project 2/01: Results of the 2001 and 2002 Field Seasons at Poverty Point.* Report on file with the Louisiana Division of Archaeology, Department of Culture, Recreation, and Tourism, Baton Rouge, and Poverty Point State Historic Site, Epps, Louisiana.

2010 Placing the Poverty Point Mounds in Their Temporal Context. *American Antiquity* 75(3): 657–678.

Owsley, Douglas W., Charles E. Orser, Jr., Robert Montgomery, and Claudia C. Holland

1985 *An Archaeological and Physical Anthropological Study of the First Cemetery in New Orleans.* Department of Geography and Anthropology, Louisiana State University. Report on file with the Louisiana Division of Archaeology, Department of Culture, Recreation, and Tourism, Baton Rouge.

OxCal 3.10

2009 Oxford Radiocarbon Accelerator Unit Research Laboratory for Archaeology. Electronic database online at: c14.arch.ox.ac.uk.

Pagès, Pierre Marie François de

1793 *Travels Round the World, in the Years 1767, 1768, 1769, 1770, and 1771*. Translated from the French. J. Murray, London.

Palmer, David T.

2000 Artifacts and Culture: A Diachronic Investigation of the Lives of African-Americans at Blythewood Sugar Plantation, Louisiana. Unpublished M.A. thesis, Department of Geography and Anthropology, Louisiana State University, Baton Rouge.

2005 "Counterpunch the Devil with the Word": African American Daily Life at Alma and Riverlake Plantations, Louisiana, 1870–1940. Unpublished Ph.D. dissertation, Department of Anthropology, University of California, Berkeley.

2006 Archaeology of African American Life at Alma and Riverlake Sugar Plantation, Louisiana, c. 1870–1940. Poster presented at the 39th Annual Society for Historical Archaeology Conference on Historical and Underwater Archaeology, Sacramento.

2007 Foodways and the Maintenance and Assertion of Dignity by African American Workers at Alma and Riverlake Sugar Plantations, Louisiana, 1870–1940. Paper presented at the 40th Annual Society for Historical Archaeology Conference on Historical and Underwater Archaeology, Williamsburg, Virginia.

Palmer, David T., and Chelsey A. Juarez

2003 Faunal Diversity, Economic Strategy, and Cultural Preferences at Alma and Riverlake Plantations, Louisiana: Preliminary Results. Poster presented at the 36th Annual Meeting of the Society for Historical Archaeology Conference on Historical and Underwater Archaeology, Providence, Rhode Island.

Parker, Catherine

2003 Zooarchaeological Remains. In *Presidio Santa María de Galve: A Struggle for Survival in Colonial Spanish Pensacola*, edited by Judith A. Bense, pp. 210–228. University Press of Florida, Gainesville.

Patten, Bob

2007a Graphical Astronomy at Poverty Point. Electronic document online at: www.stonedagger.com/PovertyPoint.html.

2007b Taking Measure of the Maya World. Unpublished manuscript. Lakewood, Colorado.

Patterson, Thomas C.

1994 Toward a Properly Historical Ecology. In *Historical Ecology: Cultural Knowledge and Changing Landscapes*, edited by Carole L. Crumley, pp. 223–237. School of American Research Press, Santa Fe.

Pauketat, Timothy R.

1987 A Functional Consideration of a Mississippian Domestic Vessel Assemblage. *Southeastern Archaeology* 6(1):1–15.

1998 Refiguring the Archaeology of Greater Cahokia. *Journal of Archaeological Research* 6(1):45–89.

2000 Politicization and Community in the Pre-Columbian Mississippi Valley. In *The Archaeology of Communities: A New World Perspective,* edited by Marcello A. Canuto and Jason Yaeger, pp. 16–43. Routledge, New York.

2001a A New Tradition in Archaeology. In *The Archaeology of Traditions: Agency and History Before and After Columbus,* edited by T. R. Pauketat, pp. 1–16. University Press of Florida, Gainesville.

2001b Practice and History in Archaeology: An Emerging Paradigm. *Anthropological Theory* 1(1):73–98.

2004 *Ancient Cahokia and the Mississippians.* Cambridge University Press, New York.

2007 *Chiefdoms and Other Archaeological Delusions.* AltaMira Press, Lanham, Maryland.

Pauketat, Timothy R., and Thomas E. Emerson (editors)

1997 *Cahokia: Domination and Ideology in the Mississippian World.* University of Nebraska Press, Lincoln.

Pauketat, Timothy R., Lucretia S. Kelly, Gayle J. Fritz, Neal H. Lopinot, Scott Elias, and Eve Hargrave

2002 The Residues of Feasting and Public Ritual at Early Cahokia. *American Antiquity* 67(2): 257–279.

Pauketat, Timothy R., and Diana DiPaolo Loren

2005 Alternative Histories and North American Archaeology. In *North American Archaeology,* edited by Timothy R. Pauketat and Diana DiPaolo Loren, pp. 1–29. Blackwell Publishing, Malden, Massachusetts.

Payne, Claudine

1994 Mississippian Capitals: An Archaeological Investigation of Precolumbian Political Structure. Unpublished Ph.D. dissertation, Department of Anthropology, University of Florida, Gainesville.

Peacock, Evan, Philip J. Carr, Sarah E. Price, John Underwood, William L. Kingery, and Michael Lilly

2010 Confirmation of an Archaic-Period Mound in Southwest Mississippi. *Southeastern Archaeology,* in press.

Pearce, Roy Harvey

1988 *Savagism and Civilization: A Study of the Indian and the American Mind.* University of California Press, Berkeley.

Pearson, Charles E.

1992 *Examination of a Purported "Treasure Vault" in South Louisiana (The Point Au Fer Lighthouse Site, 16TR257).* Coastal Environments, Inc., Baton Rouge. Report on file with the Louisiana Division of Archaeology, Department of Culture, Recreation, and Tourism, Baton Rouge.

2000a The Archaeology of the Confederate Gunboat *Arrow. Louisiana Archaeology* 24(1997):107–144.

2000b *Cultural Resources Investigations of Several Watercraft Sites Located along the Pearl River in the Vicinity of Walkiah Bluff, Mississippi and Louisiana.* Coastal Environments, Inc., Baton Rouge. U.S. Army Corps of Engineers, Vicksburg District.

2001 Underwater Archaeology Along the Lower Pearl River, Mississippi and Louisiana. *Mississippi Archaeology* 36(2):67–100.

Pearson, Charles E., and Thomas C. C. Birchett

2001 *The History and Archaeology of Two Civil War Steamboats: The Ironclad Gunboat U.S.S. Eastport and the Steamer Ed. F. Dix.* Coastal Environments, Inc., Baton Rouge. U.S. Army Corps of Engineers, Vicksburg District.

2003 *Two Civil War Steamboat Wrecks on Red River: The History and Archaeology of the Ironclad U.S.S. Eastport and the Steamer Ed. F. Dix.* Coastal Environments, Inc., Baton Rouge. U.S. Army Corps of Engineers, Vicksburg District.

Pearson, Charles E., Eileen K. Burden, Sherwood M. Gagliano, Paul E. Hoffman, Allen R. Saltus, and William H. Spencer

1981 *El Nuevo Constante: Investigation of an Eighteenth-Century Spanish Shipwreck off the Louisiana Coast.* Anthropological Study No. 4. Louisiana Archaeological Survey and Antiquities Commission, Department of Culture, Recreation, and Tourism, Baton Rouge.

Pearson, Charles. E., George J. Castille, Donald Davis, Thomas Redard, and Allen R. Saltus, Jr.

1989 *A History of Waterborne Commerce and Transportation within the U.S. Army Corps of Engineers New Orleans District and an Inventory of Known Underwater Cultural Resources.* Coastal Environments, Inc., Baton Rouge. U.S. Army Corps of Engineers, New Orleans District.

Pearson, Charles E., and Robert Floyd

1982 Side-Scan Sonar Record of an Eighteenth-Century Spanish Merchant Vessel in the Gulf of Mexico. *International Journal of Nautical Archaeology and Underwater Exploration* 11(1):62–63.

Pearson, Charles E., Bryan L. Guevin, and Sally K. Reeves

1989 *A Tongue of Land near La Fourche: The Archaeology and History of Golden Ranch Plantation, Lafourche Parish, Louisiana.* Coastal Environments, Inc., Baton Rouge. Gheens Foundation, Louisville, and the Louisiana Division of Archaeology, Department of Culture, Recreation, and Tourism, Baton Rouge.

Pearson, Charles E., and Paul E. Hoffman

1995 *The Last Voyage of El Nuevo Constante: The Wreck and Recovery of an Eighteenth-Century Spanish Ship Off the Louisiana Coast.* Louisiana State University Press, Baton Rouge.

1998 *El Nuevo Constante: Investigations of an Eighteenth-Century Spanish Shipwreck off the Louisiana Coast.* 2nd ed. Anthropological Study No. 4. Louisiana Archaeological Survey and Antiquities Commission, Department of Culture, Recreation, and Tourism, Baton Rouge.

Pearson, Charles E., and Donald G. Hunter

1993 Geoarchaeology of the Red River Valley. In *Quaternary Geology and Geoarchaeology of the Lower Red River Valley*, edited by W. J. Autin and J. Snead, pp. 25–43. Friends of the Pleistocene, South Central Cell, 11th Annual Field Conference, Alexandria, Louisiana.

Pearson, Charles E., David B. Kelley, Richard A. Weinstein, and Sherwood M. Gagliano

1986 *Archaeological Investigations on the Outer Continental Shelf: A Study within the Sabine River Valley, Offshore Louisiana and Texas.* Coastal Environments, Inc., Baton Rouge. OCS Study 86–0119. Minerals Management Service, Gulf of Mexico OCS Region, U.S. Department of the Interior, New Orleans.

Pearson, Charles E., Becky Owens, and Allen R. Saltus, Jr.

2007 *Cultural Resource Testing, Mapping, and Determination of Historical Significance of the New Iberia Shipwreck (16IB80), Iberia Parish, Louisiana.* Coastal Environments, Inc., Baton Rouge. Louisiana Department of Wildlife and Fisheries, Baton Rouge.

Pearson, Charles E., and Allen R. Saltus, Jr.

1991 *Remote-Sensing Survey of the Atchafalaya Basin Main Channel, Atchafalaya Channel Training Project, Sts. Martin and Mary Parishes, Louisiana.* Coastal Environments, Inc., Baton Rouge. U.S. Army Corps of Engineers, New Orleans District.

1996 *Underwater Archaeology on the Lower Pearl and West Pearl Rivers, Louisiana and Mississippi: The Examination of 11 Target Areas and Excavation of the Gunboat CSS* Arrow. Coastal Environments, Inc., Baton Rouge. U.S. Army Corps of Engineers, Vicksburg District.

Pearson, Charles E., Richard A. Weinstein, and David B. Kelley

1989 Evaluation of Prehistoric Site Preservation on the Outer Continental Shelf: The Sabine River Area, Offshore Texas and Louisiana. In *Underwater Archaeology Proceedings from the Society for Historical Archaeology Conference*, edited by J. Barto Arnold III, pp. 6–11. Society for Historical Archaeology, Baltimore.

Pearson, Charles E., and Tom Wells

1999 *Steamboats on Red River: A History of Waterborne Commerce and an Assessment of Steamboat Losses along the Red River, Louisiana and Arkansas.* Coastal Environments, Inc., Baton Rouge. U.S. Army Corps of Engineers, Vicksburg District.

Peebles, Christopher S., and Susan M. Kus

1977 Some Archaeological Correlates of Ranked Societies. *American Antiquity* 42(3):421–448.

Pendley, Bettie

1992 A Framework for Implementing a Comprehensive Archaeological Program in New Orleans, Louisiana. Unpublished M.A. thesis, College of Urban and Public Affairs, University of New Orleans, Louisiana.

Peregrine, Peter N.

1996 *Archaeology of the Mississippian Culture: A Research Guide*. Garland, New York.

Perrault, Stephanie L., and Richard A. Weinstein

1994 *National Register Eligibility Testing at the Sarah Peralta Site, East Baton Rouge Parish, Louisiana*. Coastal Environments, Inc., Baton Rouge. On file with the Louisiana Division of Archaeology, Department of Culture, Recreation, and Tourism, Baton Rouge.

Perttula, Timothy K.

1992 *"The Caddo Nation": Archaeological and Ethnohistoric Perspectives*. University of Texas Press, Austin.

1993 Kee-Oh-Na-Wan'-Wah: The Effects of European Contact on the Caddoan Indians of Texas, Louisiana, Arkansas, and Oklahoma. In *Ethnohistory and Archaeology: Approaches to Postcontact Change in the Americas*, edited by J. D. Rogers and S. M. Wilson, pp. 89–109. Plenum Press, New York.

1996 Caddoan Area Archaeology since 1990. *Journal of Archaeological Research* 4(4):295–348.

2001 "The Great Kingdom of the Tejas": The Life and Times of Caddo Peoples in Texas between ca. 1530–1859. *Bulletin of the Texas Archeological Society* 72:73–89.

2002 Caddoan Area Protohistory and Archaeology. In *Between Contacts and Colonies: Archaeological Perspectives on the Protohistoric Southeast*, edited by C. B. Wesson and M. A. Rees, pp. 49–66. University of Alabama Press, Tuscaloosa.

2004 The Prehistoric and Caddoan Archeology of the Northeast Texas Piney Woods. In *The Prehistory of Texas*, edited by T. K. Perttula, pp. 370–407. Texas A&M University Press, College Station.

2005 1938–1939 WPA Excavations at the Hatchel Site (41BW3) on the Red River in Bowie County, Texas. *Southeastern Archaeology* 24(2):180–198.

Perttula, Timothy K. (editor)

2004 *The Prehistory of Texas*. Texas A&M University Press, College Station.

Perttula, Timothy K., D. B. Lee, and R. Cast

2008 The First People of the Red River: The Caddo before and after Freeman and Custis. In *Freeman and Custis Red River Expedition of 1806: Two Hundred Years Later*, edited by L. M. Hardy, pp. 81–110. Bulletin of the Museum of Life Sciences No. 14. Museum of Life Sciences, Louisiana State University in Shreveport.

Perttula, Timothy K., B. Nelson, and R. L. Cast

2005 American Museum of Natural History Collections from the Vicinity of Shreveport, Louisiana. In *A Rediscovering of Caddo Heritage: The W. T. Scott Collection at the American Museum of Natural History and Other Caddo Collections from Arkansas and Louisiana*, by B. Gonzalez, R. Cast, T. K. Perttula, and

B. Nelson, pp. 107–111. Caddo Nation of Oklahoma, Historic Preservation Program, Binger.

Perttula, Timothy K., and Robert Rogers

2007 The Evolution of a Caddo Community in Northeastern Texas: The Oak Hill Village Site (41RK214), Rusk County, Texas. *American Antiquity* 72(1):71–94.

Petsche, Jerome E.

1974 *The Steamboat Bertrand: History, Excavation, and Architecture.* Publications in Archeology 11. National Park Service, U.S. Department of the Interior, Washington, D.C.

Phillips, Philip

1939 Introduction to the Archaeology of the Mississippi Valley. Unpublished Ph.D. dissertation, Department of Anthropology, Harvard University, Cambridge.

1970 *Archaeological Survey in the Lower Yazoo Basin, Mississippi, 1949–1955.* Papers of the Peabody Museum of Archaeology and Ethnology Vol. 60, Pts. 1 and 2. Harvard University, Cambridge.

Phillips, Philip, James A. Ford, and James B. Griffin

1951 *Archaeological Survey in the Lower Mississippi Alluvial Valley, 1940–1947.* Papers of the Peabody Museum of American Archaeology and Ethnology Vol. 25. Harvard University, Cambridge.

Pleasant, Randall L., and Darryl O. Pleasant

1990 The Adaes Village: A Nineteenth-Century Mestizo Village in Northwest Louisiana. Paper presented at the Caddo Conference, Northwestern State University, Natchitoches.

Pokrant, Marie, D. Ryan Gray, Benjamin Maygarden, Angele Montana, and Jill-Karen Yakubik

2010 *Archaeological Investigations at 923 Magazine Street (16OR211), New Orleans, Louisiana.* Earth Search, Inc., New Orleans. Report on file with the Louisiana Division of Archaeology, Department of Culture, Recreation, and Tourism, Baton Rouge.

Powell, Eric A.

2002 Tales from Storyville: Digging the "Sporting Life" in Old New Orleans. *Archaeology Magazine* 55(6):26–31.

Powell, John T.

2004 Military Artifacts of Spanish Florida, 1539–1821: An Internet Museum. Electronic document online at: www.artifacts.org/

Praetzellis, Adrian, and Mary Praetzellis (editors)

2004 *Putting the "There" There: Historical Archaeologies of West Oakland.* Anthropological Studies Center, Sonoma State University, California.

Praetzellis, Mary (editor)

2004 *SF-80 Bayshore Viaduct Seismic Retrofit Projects Report on Construction Monitoring, Geoarchaeology, and Technical and Interpretive Studies for Historical Archaeology.* Anthropological Studies Center, Sonoma State University, California.

Pratt, Comfort

2004 *El Español del Noroeste de Luisiana. Pervivencia de un Dialecto Amenazado.* Editorial Verbum, Madrid.

Prewitt, Elton R.

1995 Distributions of Typed Projectile Points in Texas. *Bulletin of the Texas Archeological Society* 66:83–174.

Quimby, George I.

1942 The Natchezan Culture Type. *American Antiquity* 7(3):255–275.

1951 *The Medora Site, West Baton Rouge Parish, Louisiana.* Anthropological Series 24(2). Field Museum of Natural History, Chicago.

1957 *The Bayou Goula Site, Iberville Parish, Louisiana.* Fieldiana: Anthropology 47(2). Chicago Natural History Museum, Chicago.

Rafferty, Janet

2002 Woodland Period Settlement Patterning in the Northern Gulf Coastal Plain of Alabama, Mississippi, and Tennessee. In *The Woodland Southeast,* edited by David G. Anderson and Robert C. Mainfort, pp. 204–227. University of Alabama Press, Tuscaloosa.

Raisor, Michelle, and D. Gentry Steele

2001 Documentation of Human Remains from the Conly Site (16BI1). In *Regional Archaeology Program, Management Unit 1: Twelfth Annual Report,* edited by J. S. Girard, pp. 78–86. Report on file with the Louisiana Division of Archaeology, Department of Culture, Recreation, and Tourism, Baton Rouge.

Ramenofsky, Ann F.

1991 Investigating Settlement Strategies at Cowpen Slough, A Late Archaic–Poverty Point Site in Louisiana. In *The Poverty Point Culture: Local Manifestations, Subsistence Practices, and Trade Networks,* edited by K. Byrd, pp. 156–172. Geoscience and Man 29. Louisiana State University, Baton Rouge.

Ramenofsky, Ann F., and Ann Marie Mires

1985 The Archaeology of Cowpen Slough, 16CT147. Report on file with the Louisiana Division of Archaeology, Department of Culture, Recreation, and Tourism, Baton Rouge.

Ramirez, Dominica Dominguez

2004 Travels in Louisiana: Journeys into Ethnicity and Heritage by Two Hispanic Groups. Unpublished M.A. thesis, Department of Geography and Anthropology, Louisiana State University, Baton Rouge.

Raphael, Ray

2004 *Founding Myths: Stories That Hide Our Patriotic Past.* New Press, New York.

Rapp, George, and Christopher L. Hill

2006 *Geoarchaeology: The Earth-Science Approach to Archaeological Interpretation.* 2nd ed. Yale University Press, New Haven.

Read, William A.

1927 *Louisiana Place-Names of Indian Origin.* Louisiana State University, Baton Rouge.

Redfield, Alden

1971 Dalton Forms from the Lower Mississippi Alluvial Valley. *Southeastern Archaeological Conference Bulletin* 13:98–107.

Rees, Mark A.

2001 Historical Science or Silence? Toward a Historical Anthropology of Mississippian Political Culture. In *The Archaeology of Traditions: The Southeast before and after Columbus,* edited by Timothy R. Pauketat, pp. 121–140. University Press of Florida, Gainesville.

2007 Plaquemine Mounds of the Western Atchafalaya Basin. In *Plaquemine Archaeology,* edited by Mark A. Rees and Patrick C. Livingood, pp. 66–93. University of Alabama Press, Tuscaloosa.

2008 From Grand Dérangement to Acadiana: History and Identity in the Landscape of South Louisiana. *International Journal of Historical Archaeology* 12(4):338–359.

Rees, Mark A., and Patrick C. Livingood

2007 Introduction and Historical Overview. In *Plaquemine Archaeology,* edited by Mark A. Rees and Patrick C. Livingood, pp. 1–19. University of Alabama Press, Tuscaloosa.

Rees, Mark A., and Patrick C. Livingood (editors)

2007 *Plaquemine Archaeology.* University of Alabama Press, Tuscaloosa.

Reuss, Martin

2004 *Designing the Bayous: The Control of Water in the Atchafalaya Basin, 1800–1995.* Texas A&M University Press, College Station.

Rice, Linda L.

1981 The Vertebrate Paleontology of Late Pleistocene (Rancholabrean) Mammalian Sites of Louisiana. Unpublished M.S. thesis, Department of Geology, Louisiana State University, Baton Rouge.

Richter, Daniel K.

2001 *Facing East from Indian Country: A Native History of Early America.* Harvard University Press, Cambridge.

Rick, T. C., J. M. Erlandson, and R. L. Velanoweth

2001 Paleocoastal Marine Fishing on the Pacific Coast of the Americas: Perspectives from Daisy Cave, California. *American Antiquity* 66(4):595–613.

Ricklis, Robert A.

2004 The Archeology of the Native American Occupation of Southeast Texas. In *The Prehistory of Texas,* edited by Timothy K. Perttula, pp. 181–204. Texas A&M University Press, College Station.

Ricklis, Robert A., and Richard A. Weinstein

2005 Sea-Level Rise and Fluctuation on the Central Texas Coast: Exploring Cultural-Ecological Correlates. In *Gulf Coast Archaeology: The Southeastern United States and Mexico,* edited by Nancy Marie White, pp. 108–154. University Press of Florida, Gainesville.

Ries, Maurice

1936 The Mississippi Fort, Called Fort de la Boulaye. *Louisiana Historical Quarterly* 19:829–899.

Ring, Diane M.

1986 Evaluation of the Hegwood Bayou Phase as a Late Marksville Period Phase in the Northern Boeuf Basin, Louisiana. Unpublished A.B. thesis, Department of Anthropology, Harvard University, Cambridge.

Rivet, Philip G.

1973 Tchefuncte Ceramic Typology: A Reappraisal. Unpublished M.A. thesis, Department of Geography and Anthropology, Louisiana State University, Baton Rouge.

Robbins, John

2001 Notice of Inventory Completion for Native American Human Remains and Associated Funerary Objects in the Possession of the American Museum of Natural History, New York, New York. *Federal Register* Vol. 66, No. 35 (February 21, 2001: 11042–11043. Online GPO access at: www.gpoaccess.gov/fr/

Roberts, Erika

2005 Digging Through Discarded Identity: Archaeological Investigations around the Kitchen and the Overseer's House at Whitney Plantation, Louisiana. Unpublished M.A. thesis, Department of Geography and Anthropology, Louisiana State University, Baton Rouge.

Roberts, Katherine M.

1999 Marksville Paleoethnobotanical Remains. In *Marksville (16AV1), Lake Anacoco, and the Chenier Plain: Explorations of Southwest Louisiana Prehistory, Regional Archaeological Program, Management Unit III, 1998/1999 Annual Report,* by Charles R. McGimsey, H. Edwin Jackson, Katherine M. Roberts, and James Hebert, pp. 72–81. Department of Sociology and Anthropology, University of Louisiana at Lafayette. Report on file with the Louisiana Division of Archaeology, Department of Culture, Recreation, and Tourism, Baton Rouge.

2000 Baptiste Site Archaeobotany. In *Archaeology of the Marksville Period: Explorations of Southwest Louisiana Prehistory, Regional Archaeology Program, Management Unit III, 1999/2000 Annual Report,* by Charles R. McGimsey, Katherine M. Roberts, H. Edwin Jackson, and Susan L. Scott, pp. 48–51. Department of Sociology and Anthropology, University of Louisiana at Lafayette. Report on file with the Louisiana Division of Archaeology, Department of Culture, Recreation, and Tourism, Baton Rouge.

2004 Plant Remains. In *Data Recovery Excavations at the Hedgeland Site (16CT19), Catahoula Parish, Louisiana,* edited by J. Ryan, pp. 207–226. Coastal Environments, Inc., Baton Rouge. U.S. Army Corps of Engineers, Vicksburg District.

2005 Plant Remains. In *Lake Providence: A Terminal Coles Creek Culture Mound Center, East Carroll Parish, Louisiana,* edited by R. A. Weinstein, pp. 431–489.

Coastal Environments, Inc., Baton Rouge. U.S. Army Corps of Engineers, Vicksburg District.

2006 Seasonality, Optimal Foraging, and Prehistoric Plant Food Production in the Lower Mississippi in the Tensas Basin, Northeast Louisiana. Unpublished Ph.D. dissertation, Department of Anthropology, Washington University in St. Louis.

Roe, Lori M.

2007 Coles Creek Antecedents of Plaquemine Mound Construction: Evidence from the Raffman Site. In *Plaquemine Archaeology*, edited by Mark A. Rees and Patrick C. Livingood, pp. 20–37. University of Alabama Press, Tuscaloosa.

2008 Questioning Coles Creek Hierarchy. Paper presented at the 65th Southeastern Archaeological Conference, Charlotte, North Carolina.

Rogers, R. A., L. A. Rogers, R. S. Hoffmann, and L. D. Martin

1991 Native American Biological Diversity and the Biogeographic Influence of Ice Age Refugia. *Journal of Biogeography* 18(6):623–630.

Rogers, J. Daniel, and Bruce D. Smith (editors)

1995 *Mississippian Communities and Households.* University of Alabama Press, Tuscaloosa.

Rolingson, Martha A.

1990 The Toltec Mounds Site: A Ceremonial Center in the Arkansas River Lowland. In *The Mississippian Emergence*, edited by Bruce D. Smith, pp. 27–49. Smithsonian Institution Press, Washington, D.C.

2002 Plum Bayou Culture of the Arkansas–White River Basin. In *The Woodland Southeast*, edited by David G. Anderson and Robert C. Mainfort, Jr., pp. 44–65. University of Alabama Press, Tuscaloosa.

Rolingson, Martha A., and J. Michael Howard

1997 Igneous Lithics of Central Arkansas: Identification, Sources, and Artifact Distribution. *Southeastern Archaeology* 16(1):33–50.

Rose, Jerome C., and Anna M. Harmon

1989 Bioarcheology of the Louisiana and Arkansas Study Area. In *Archeology and Bioarcheology of the Lower Mississippi Valley and Trans-Mississippi South in Arkansas and Louisiana*, by Marvin D. Jeter, Jerome C. Rose, G. Ishmael Williams, Jr., and Anna M. Harmon, pp. 323–354. Research Series No. 37. Arkansas Archeological Survey, Fayetteville.

Rosenberg, Daniel

1988 *New Orleans Dockworkers: Race, Labor, and Unionism, 1892–1923.* State University of New York Press, Albany.

Roy, Christian, and Hélène Côté (editors)

2008 Rêves d'Amériques: Regard sur l'archéologie de la Nouvelle-France / Dreams of the Americas: Overview of New France Archaeology. *Archéologiques*, Hors série 2, AAQ, Québec.

Russ, David P.

1975 The Quaternary Geomorphology of the Lower Red River Valley, Louisiana. Unpublished Ph.D. dissertation, Department of Geosciences, Pennsylvania State University, College Park.

Russo, Michael

1993 *1993 Annual Report for Management Unit 3, Regional Archaeology Program.* Department of Sociology and Anthropology, University of Southwestern Louisiana. Report on file with the Louisiana Division of Archaeology, Department of Culture, Recreation, and Tourism, Baton Rouge.

1994a A Brief Introduction to the Study of Archaic Mounds in the Southeast. *Southeastern Archaeology* 13(2):89–93.

1994b Why We Don't Believe in Archaic Ceremonial Mounds and Why We Should: The Case from Florida. *Southeastern Archaeology* 13(2):93–108.

1996 Southeastern Archaic Mounds. In *Archaeology of the Mid-Holocene Southeast,* edited by Kenneth E. Sassaman and David G. Anderson, pp. 259–287. University Press of Florida, Gainesville.

Russo, Michael, and James Fogleman

1996 Stelly Mounds (16SL1): an Archaic Mound Complex. *Louisiana Archaeology* 21(1994):127–158.

Ryan, Joanne

2004 Ceramic Analysis. In *Data Recovery Excavations at the Hedgeland site (16CT19), Catahoula Parish, Louisiana,* edited by Joanne Ryan, pp. 89–159. Coastal Environments, Inc., Baton Rouge. U.S. Army Corps of Engineers, Vicksburg District.

Ryan, Joanne (editor)

2004 *Data Recovery Excavations at the Hedgeland Site (16CT19), Catahoula Parish, Louisiana.* Coastal Environments, Inc., Baton Rouge. U.S. Army Corps of Engineers, Vicksburg District.

Ryan, Joanne, Charles E. Pearson, Thurston H. G. Hahn III, Elizabeth L. Davoli, and Carey L. Cox

1997 *Phase II and III Historical and Archaeological Investigations of Maitland Plantation (16CT176), Catahoula Parish, Louisiana.* Coastal Environments, Inc., Baton Rouge. U.S. Army Corps of Engineers, Vicksburg District.

Ryan, Joanne, and Douglas C. Wells

2007 *Phase III Data-Recovery Excavations at 16IV94 and 16IV109, Iberville Parish, Louisiana.* Coastal Environments, Inc. Baton Rouge. Providence Engineering, Baton Rouge.

Ryan, Thomas M.

1975 Semisubterranean Structures and Their Spatial Distribution at the Marksville Site (16AV1). *Proceedings of the 31st Southeastern Archaeological Conference* 18:215–225.

Sabo, George, and Jerry E. Hilliard

2008 Woodland Period Shell-Tempered Pottery in the Central Arkansas Ozarks. *Southeastern Archaeology* 27(2):164–171.

Saltus, Allen R., Jr.

1985 *Submerged Cultural Resource Investigation of the Maurepas Basin with Intensive Surveys at Warsaw Landing, Blood River and Springfield Area, Natalbany River, Louisiana.* Center for Regional Studies, Southeastern Louisiana University, Hammond. U.S. Department of the Interior and the Louisiana Division of Archaeology, Department of Culture, Recreation, and Tourism, Baton Rouge.

1986 *Submerged Cultural Resources Investigation of the Western Portion of the Maurepas Basin with Intensive Underwater Surveys at Hoo Shoo Too Landing, 16EBR60, Colyell Bay, Catfish Landing, and at the Mouth of Bayou Chene Blanc.* Center for Regional Studies, Southeastern Louisiana University, Hammond. U.S. Department of the Interior and the Louisiana Division of Archaeology, Department of Culture, Recreation, and Tourism, Baton Rouge.

1988 *Submerged Cultural Resources Investigation of Various Waterways of Lake Pontchartrain's North Shore.* Center for Regional Studies, Southeastern Louisiana University, Hammond. U.S. Department of the Interior and the Louisiana Division of Archaeology, Department of Culture, Recreation, and Tourism, Baton Rouge.

1990 Watercraft Remains in the Central Gulf Coast Riverine Environment. In *Southeastern Louisiana Historical Papers,* Vol. 14, edited by Joy Jackson, pp. 25–38. Center for Regional Studies, Southeastern Louisiana University, Hammond.

1992a *Submerged Cultural Resources Investigation of a Portion of the Tchefuncte River, SRM 2.0 to SRM 3.5.* Center for Regional Studies, Southeastern Louisiana University, Hammond. U.S. Department of the Interior and the Louisiana Division of Archaeology, Department of Culture, Recreation, and Tourism, Baton Rouge.

1992b Research Significance of Local Riverine Watercraft. In *The European Origins of the Small Watercraft of the United States and Canada,* edited by Joseph T. Butler, Jr., pp. 42–50. Proceedings of the 19th Annual Museum Small Watercraft Association Meeting. Thibodaux, Louisiana.

1999a Historic and Archaeological Resources Value of Abandoned Watercraft in Inland Waters. In *Archaeonautica, Construction Navale Maritime et Fluvial, Approaches Archéologique, Historique et Ethnologique,* edited by Patrice Pomey and Eric Riet, pp. 187–192. Éditions CNRS, Paris.

1999b 16VN2481, The Swain's Mill Site. In *Fort Polk 38: The Results of a Thirty-Eighth Program of Site Testing at Ten Sites, Fort Polk Military Reservation, Vernon Parish, Louisiana,* by Prentice M. Thomas, Jr., Paul LaHaye, Chris Parrish, James R. Morehead, James H. Mathews, L. Janice Campbell and Allen R. Saltus, Jr., pp. 143–181. Prentice Thomas and Associates, Inc., Fort Walton Beach, Florida.

2000 Watercraft Assemblages in Inland Waters. In *Down the River to the Sea*, edited by Jerzy Litwin, pp. 187–192. Eighth International Symposium on Boat and Ship Archaeology, Gdansk, Poland.

Sassaman, Kenneth E.

1993 *Early Pottery in the Southeast: Tradition and Innovation in Cooking Technology.* University of Alabama Press, Tuscaloosa.

2001 Hunter-Gatherers and Traditions of Resistance. In *The Archaeology of Traditions: The Southeast before and after Columbus*, edited by Timothy R. Pauketat, pp. 218–236. University Press of Florida, Gainesville.

2004 Common Origins and Divergent Histories in Early Pottery Traditions of the American Southeast. In *Early Pottery: Technology, Function, Style, and Interaction in the Lower Southeast*, edited by Rebecca Saunders and Christopher T. Hays, pp. 23–39. University of Alabama Press, Tuscaloosa.

2005 Poverty Point as Structure, Event, Process. *Journal of Archaeological Method and Theory* 12(4):335–364.

Sassaman, Kenneth E., and Michael J. Heckenberger

2004 Crossing the Symbolic Rubicon in the Southeast. In *Signs of Power: The Rise of Cultural Complexity in the Southeast*, edited by Jon L. Gibson and Philip J. Carr, pp. 214–233. University of Alabama Press, Tuscaloosa.

Saucier, Roger T.

1963 *Recent Geomorphic History of the Pontchartrain Basin, Louisiana*. Contribution No. 63-2. Coastal Studies Institute, Louisiana State University, Baton Rouge.

1974 *Quaternary Geology of the Lower Mississippi Valley*. Research Series No. 6. Arkansas Archeological Survey, Fayetteville.

1981 Current Thinking on Riverine Processes and Geologic History as Related to Human Settlement in the Southeast. In *Traces of Prehistory: Papers in Honor of William G. Haag*, edited by Frederick H. West and Robert W. Neuman, pp. 7–18. Geoscience and Man 22. Louisiana State University, Baton Rouge.

1990 The Geomorphic Context of the Osceola Site, Tensas Parish, Louisiana. In *Final Report on the 1989 Archaeological Investigations at the Osceola (16TE2) and Reno Brake (16TE93) Sites, Tensas Parish, Louisiana*, edited by T. R. Kidder, pp. 108–146. Archaeological Report 1. Center for Archaeology, Tulane University, New Orleans.

1994a *Geomorphology and Quaternary Geologic History of the Lower Mississippi Valley.* 2 vols. U.S. Army Engineer Waterways Experiment Station, Vicksburg.

1994b The Paleoenvironmental Setting of Northeast Louisiana during the Paleoindian Period. *Louisiana Archaeology* 16(1989):129–146.

Saucier, Roger T., and J. I. Snead (compilers)

1989 Quaternary Geology of the Lower Mississippi Valley. In *Quaternary Non-Glacial Geology: Conterminous United States*, edited by R. B. Morrison. The Geological Society of America, Boulder.

Saunders, Joe W.

1994 *1994 Annual Report for Management Unit 2.* College of Pure and Applied Sciences, Department of Geosciences, Northeast Louisiana University, Monroe. Report on file with the Louisiana Division of Archaeology, Department of Culture, Recreation, and Tourism, Baton Rouge.

1998 *1998 Annual Report for Management Unit 2.* College of Pure and Applied Sciences, Department of Geosciences, Northeast Louisiana University, Monroe. Report on file with the Louisiana Division of Archaeology, Department of Culture, Recreation, and Tourism, Baton Rouge.

1999 *1999 Annual Report for Management Unit 2.* College of Pure and Applied Sciences, Department of Geosciences, Northeast Louisiana University, Monroe. Report on file with the Louisiana Division of Archaeology, Department of Culture, Recreation, and Tourism, Baton Rouge.

2000 *2000 Annual Report for Management Unit 2.* College of Pure and Applied Sciences, Department of Geosciences, University of Louisiana at Monroe. Report on file with the Louisiana Division of Archaeology, Department of Culture, Recreation, and Tourism, Baton Rouge.

2001 *2001 Annual Report for Management Unit 2.* College of Pure and Applied Sciences, Department of Geosciences, University of Louisiana at Monroe. Report on file with the Louisiana Division of Archaeology, Department of Culture, Recreation, and Tourism, Baton Rouge.

2010 Late Archaic? What the Hell Happened to the Middle Archaic. In *Trend and Tradition, With Some Turmoil: What Happened to the Southeastern Archaic,* edited by David Hurst Thomas and Matthew C. Sanger. American Museum of Natural History, New York, in press.

Saunders, Joe W., and Thurman Allen

1994 Hedgepeth Mounds, An Archaic Mound Complex in North-Central Louisiana. *American Antiquity* 59(3):471–489.

1997 The Archaic Period. *Louisiana Archaeology* 22(1995):1–30.

Saunders, Joe W., Thurman Allen, Reca Jones, and Gloria Swoveland

2000 Caney Mounds (16CT5). *Louisiana Archaeological Society Newsletter* 27: 14–21.

Saunders, Joe W., Thurman Allen, Dennis LaBatt, Reca Jones, and David Griffing

2001 An Assessment of the Antiquity of Lower Jackson Mound. *Southeastern Archaeology* 20(1):67–77.

Saunders, Joe W., Thurman Allen, and Roger T. Saucier

1994 Four Archaic? Mound Complexes in Northeast Louisiana. *Southeastern Archaeology* 13(2):134–153.

Saunders, Joe W., and Reca B. Jones

2003 *2003 Annual Report for Management Unit 2.* Regional Archaeology Program, Department of Geosciences, University of Louisiana at Monroe. Report on file with the Louisiana Division of Archaeology, Department of Culture, Recreation, and Tourism, Baton Rouge.

2004 *2004 Annual Report for Management Unit 2*. Regional Archaeology Program, Department of Geosciences, University of Louisiana at Monroe. Report on file with the Louisiana Division of Archaeology, Department of Culture, Recreation, and Tourism, Baton Rouge.

Saunders, Joe W., Reca B. Jones, and Thurman Allen

2005 *2005 Annual Report for Management Unit 2*. Regional Archaeology Program, Department of Geosciences, University of Louisiana at Monroe. Report on file with the Louisiana Division of Archaeology, Department of Culture, Recreation, and Tourism, Baton Rouge.

2006 *2006 Annual Report for Management Unit 2*. Regional Archaeology Program, Department of Geosciences, University of Louisiana at Monroe. Report on file with the Louisiana Division of Archaeology, Department of Culture, Recreation, and Tourism, Baton Rouge.

2007 *2007 Annual Report for Management Unit 2*. Regional Archaeology Program, Department of Geosciences, University of Louisiana at Monroe. Report on file with the Louisiana Division of Archaeology, Department of Culture, Recreation, and Tourism, Baton Rouge.

Saunders, Joe W., Rolfe D. Mandel, C. Garth Sampson, Charles M. Allen, E. Thurman Allen, Daniel A. Bush, James K. Feathers, Kristen J. Gremillion, C. T. Hallmark, H. Edwin Jackson, Jay K. Johnson, Reca Jones, Roger T. Saucier, Gary L. Stringer, and Malcolm Vidrine

2005 Watson Brake, A Middle Archaic Mound Complex in Northeast Louisiana. *American Antiquity* 70(4):631–668.

Saunders, Joe W., Rolfe D. Mandel, Roger T. Saucier, E. Thurman Allen, C. T. Hallmark, Jay K. Johnson, Edwin H. Jackson, Charles M. Allen, Gary L. Stringer, Douglas S. Frink, James K. Feathers, Stephen Williams, Kristen J. Gremillion, Malcolm F. Vidrine, and Reca Jones

1997 A Mound Complex in Louisiana at 5400–5000 Years B.P. *Science* 277(5333):1796–1799.

Saunders, Joe W., Robert W. Neuman, and Thurman Allen

2009 Recent Investigations at the Belmont Mound (16SJ1). *Louisiana Archaeology* 28(2001):78–91.

Saunders, Rebecca

1994 The Case for Archaic Mound Sites in Southeastern Louisiana. *Southeastern Archaeology* 13(2):118–134.

1997 Stylistic Influences on the Gulf Coastal Plain: New Evidence from Paddle Stamped Pottery in Louisiana. *Louisiana Archaeology* 22(1995):93–123.

Saunders, Rebecca, and Christopher T. Hays

2004 Introduction: Themes in Early Pottery Research. In *Early Pottery: Technol-*

ogy, Function, Style, and Interaction in the Lower Southeast*, edited by Rebecca Saunders and Christopher T. Hays, pp. 1–22. University of Alabama Press, Tuscaloosa.

Saunders, Rebecca, and James B. Stoltman

1999 A Multidimensional Consideration of Complicated Stamped Ceramic Production in Southern Louisiana. *Southeastern Archaeology* 18(1):1–23.

Saxon, Lyle, Edward Dreyer, and Robert Tallant (compilers)

1991 *Gumbo Ya-Ya: A Collection of Louisiana Folk Tales*. Reprint by Pelican Publishing Company, Gretna, Louisiana. Originally published 1945, Houghton Mifflin, Boston.

Scarry, John F. (editor)

1996 *Political Structure and Change in the Prehistoric Southeastern United States*. University Press of Florida, Gainesville.

Schambach, Frank F.

1970 Pre-Caddoan Cultures in the Trans-Mississippi South: A Beginning Sequence. Unpublished Ph.D. dissertation, Department of Anthropology, Harvard University, Cambridge.

1982a An Outline of Fourche Maline Culture in Southwest Arkansas. In *Arkansas Archeology in Review*, edited by Neal Trubowitz and Marvin D. Jeter, pp. 132–197. Research Series No. 15, Arkansas Archeological Survey, Fayetteville.

1982b The Archeology of the Great Bend Region in Arkansas. In *Contributions to the Archeology of the Great Bend Region*, edited by F. F. Schambach and F. Rackerby, pp. 1–11. Research Series No. 22, Arkansas Archeological Survey, Fayetteville.

1996 Mounds, Embankments, and Ceremonialism in the Trans-Mississippi South. In *Mounds, Embankments, and Ceremonialism in the Midsouth*, edited by R. C. Mainfort and R. Walling, pp. 36–43. Research Series No. 46, Arkansas Archeological Survey, Fayetteville.

1997 The Development of the Burial Mound Tradition in the Caddo Area. *Journal of Northeast Texas Archaeology* 9:53–72.

1998 *Pre-Caddoan Cultures in the Trans-Mississippi South*. Research Series No. 53. Arkansas Archeological Survey, Fayetteville.

2001 Fourche Maline and Its Neighbors: Observations on an Important Woodland Period Culture of the Trans-Mississippi South. *The Arkansas Archeologist* 40:21–50.

2002 Fourche Maline: A Woodland Period Culture of the Trans-Mississippi South. In *The Woodland Southeast*, edited by D. G. Anderson and R. C. Mainfort, Jr., pp. 91–112. University of Alabama Press, Tuscaloosa.

Schambach, Frank, and Ann M. Early

1982 Southwest Arkansas. In *A State Plan for the Conservation of Archeological Resources in Arkansas*, edited by H. A. Davis, pp. SW1–SW149. Research Series No. 21, Arkansas Archeological Survey, Fayetteville.

Schilling, Timothy M.

2004 Excavations at the Bayou Grande Cheniere Mounds (16PL159): A Coles Creek Period Mound Complex. Unpublished M.A. thesis, Department of Geography and Anthropology, Louisiana State University, Baton Rouge.

2006 Recent Investigations at the Mott Mounds (16FR11). Paper presented at the 63rd Southeastern Archaeological Conference, Little Rock, Arkansas.

Schortman, Edward M., and Patricia A. Urban

2004 Modeling the Roles of Craft Production in Ancient Political Economies. *Journal of Archaeological Research* 12:185–226.

Schuldenrein, Joseph

1996 Geoarchaeology and the Mid-Holocene Landscape History of the Greater Southeast. In *Archaeology of the Mid-Holocene Southeast,* edited by Kenneth E. Sassaman and David G. Anderson, pp. 3–27. University Press of Florida, Gainesville.

Scott, Elizabeth

2001 Food and Social Relations at Nina Plantation. *American Anthropologist* 103(3):671–691.

Scott, Elizabeth (editor)

2008 The Archaeology of French Colonial and Post-Colonial Settlements. *International Journal of Historical Archaeology* 12(4).

Scott, Elizabeth M., and Shannon Lee Dawdy

2010 Colonial and Creole Diets in Eighteenth-Century New Orleans. In *French Colonial Archaeology: A View from the South,* edited by K. Kelly and M. Hardy. University Press of Florida, Gainesville, in press.

Scott, Susan L.

2005 Vertebrate Fauna. In *Lake Providence: A Terminal Coles Creek Culture Mound Center, East Carroll Parish, Louisiana,* edited by R. A. Weinstein, pp. 411–430. Coastal Environments, Inc., Baton Rouge. U.S. Army Corps of Engineers, Vicksburg District.

Scott, Susan L., and H. Edwin Jackson

2000 Analysis of the Vertebrate Fauna. In *Regional Archaeology Management Unit 1: Eleventh Annual Report,* edited by Jeffrey S. Girard, pp. 50–57. Northwestern State University, Natchitoches, Louisiana. Report on file with the Louisiana Division of Archaeology, Department of Culture, Recreation, and Tourism, Baton Rouge.

Seale, Richard

1995 From French Village to American Town: The Development of Natchitoches, Louisiana, 1788–1818. Unpublished M.A. thesis, Department of History, Social Sciences, and Social Work, Northwestern State University, Natchitoches.

Sears, William H.

1964 The Southeastern United States. In *Prehistoric Man in the New World,* edited by J. D. Jennings and E. Norbeck, pp. 259–287. University of Chicago Press, Chicago.

Servello, A. Frank, and Thomas H. Bianchi

1983 Geomorphology and Cultural Stratigraphy of the Eagle Hill Area of Peason Ridge. In *U.S.L. Fort Polk Archaeological Survey and Cultural Resources Management Program,* Vol. 1, edited by A. Frank Servello, pp. 377–566. University of Southwestern Louisiana, Lafayette. U.S. Army Corps of Engineers, Fort Worth District.

Servello, A. Frank, James R. Morehead, James H. Mathews, L. Janice Campbell, and Prentice M. Thomas, Jr.

2004 *Fort Polk 57: The Results of the Fifty-Seventh Program of Site Testing at Ten Sites, Fort Polk Military Reservation, Vernon Parish, Louisiana.* Report of Investigations No. 775. Prentice Thomas and Associates, Inc., Fort Walton Beach, Florida.

Setzler, Frank M.

1933a Hopewell Type Pottery from Louisiana. *Journal of the Washington Academy of Sciences* 23:149–153.

1933b Pottery of the Hopewell Type from Louisiana. *Proceedings of the United States National Museum* 82:1–21.

Shackel, Paul A.

2001a Introduction: Contested Memories and the Making of the American Landscape. In *Myth, Memory, and the Making of the American Landscape,* edited by Paul A. Shackel, pp. 1–16. University Press of Florida, Gainesville.

2001b Public Memory and the Search for Power in American Historical Archaeology. *American Anthropologist* 103(3):655–670.

Shatwell, Jason

2004 A Tale of Two Forts: The Family, Economic, and Cultural Ties between Presidio Nuestra Señora del Pilar de Los Adaes and Fort St. Jean Baptiste. Unpublished Scholar's College thesis, Northwestern State University, Natchitoches.

Shea, Andrea

1980 Analysis of Plant Remains from the Hanna Site. In The Hanna Site: An Alto Focus Village in Red River Parish. *Louisiana Archaeology* 5(1978):273–285.

Sheffield, Mason West

2003 Archaic Faunal Exploitation in the Lower Mississippi Valley: Analysis of Faunal Remains from Plum Creek Archaic (16OU89). Unpublished M.A. thesis, Department of Anthropology and Sociology, University of Southern Mississippi, Hattiesburg.

Sheldon, Craig T., Jr., Ned J. Jenkins, and Gregory A. Waselkov

2008 French Habitations at the Alabama Post, ca. 1720–1763. In Rêves d'Amériques:

Regard sur l'archéologie de la Nouvelle-France/Dreams of the Americas: Overview of New France Archaeology, edited by Christian Roy and Hélène Côté, pp. 112–126. *Archéologiques,* Hors série 2, AAQ, Québec.

Shenkel, J. Richard

1972 Archaeological Investigation of Madame John's Legacy, 1971. Manuscript on file, Louisiana State Museum, Baton Rouge.

1974 Big Oak and Little Oak Islands, Excavations and Interpretations. *Louisiana Archaeology* 1:37–65.

1977 *Archaeological Investigations at the Hermann-Grima House.* Christian Women's Exchange, New Orleans.

1980 *Oak Island Archaeology: Prehistoric Estuarine Adaptations in the Mississippi River Delta.* Archaeological and Cultural Research Program, University of New Orleans. National Park Service, U.S. Department of the Interior, and Jean Lafitte National Historical Park, New Orleans.

1984a An Early Marksville Burial Component in Southeastern Louisiana. *Midcontinental Journal of Archaeology* 9(1):105–134.

1984b Early Woodland in Coastal Louisiana. In *Perspectives on Gulf Coast Prehistory,* edited by Dave D. Davis, pp. 41–71. Ripley P. Bullen Monographs in Anthropology and History No. 5. University Press of Florida, Gainesville.

1986 An Additional Comment on Volume Calculations and a Comparison of Formulae Using Several Southeastern Mounds. *Midcontinental Journal of Archaeology* 11(2):201–220.

Shenkel, J. Richard, and George Holley

1975 A Tchefuncte House. *Southeastern Archaeological Conference Bulletin* 18:226–242.

Shenkel, J. Richard, R. Sauder, and E. R. Chatelain

1979 *Archaeology of the Jazz Complex and Beauregard (Congo) Square, Louis Armstrong Park, New Orleans, Louisiana.* University of New Orleans. Submitted to the City of New Orleans.

Shetrone, Henry C.

1930 *The Mound-Builders.* D. Appleton and Company, New York.

Shuman, Malcolm K.

2007 Transitional Coles Creek–Plaquemine Relationships on Northwest Lake Salvador, St. Charles Parish, Louisiana. In *Plaquemine Archaeology,* edited by Mark A. Rees and Patrick C. Livingood, pp. 94–107. University of Alabama Press, Tuscaloosa.

Shuman, Malcolm K., Dennis Jones, Ben Goodwin, and Marco Giardino

1999 New Data on Two Prehistoric Mound Sites on the Ouachita River in Catahoula Parish, Louisiana. *Louisiana Archaeological Society Newsletter* 26:13–18.

Silvia, Diane E.

2002 Native American and French Cultural Dynamics on the Gulf Coast. In French

Colonial Studies at Old Mobile: Selected Studies, edited by Gregory A. Waselkov. *Historical Archaeology* 36(1):26–35.

Simmons, Marc, and Frank Turley

1980 *Southwestern Colonial Ironwork: The Spanish Blacksmithing Tradition from Texas to California*. Museum of New Mexico Press, Santa Fe.

Simms, Alexander, Kurt Lambeck, Anthony Purcell, John B. Anderson, and Antonio B. Rodriguez

2007 Sea-Level History of the Gulf of Mexico since the Last Glacial Maximum with Implications for the Melting History of the Laurentide Ice Sheet. *Quaternary Science Reviews* 26(7–8):920–940.

Sims, Douglas C., and John M. Connaway

2000 Updated Chronometric Database for Mississippi. *Mississippi Archaeology* 35(2):208–269.

Small, J. F.

1966 Additional Information on Poverty Point Baked Clay Objects. *Florida Anthropologist* 19 (2–3):65–67.

Smith, Brent W.

1981 The Late Archaic–Poverty Point Steatite Trade Network in the Lower Mississippi Valley: Some Preliminary Observations. *Florida Anthropologist* 34: 20–25.

Smith, Bruce D.

1978 Variation in Mississippian Settlement Patterns. In *Mississippian Settlement Patterns*, edited by B. D. Smith, pp. 479–503. Academic Press, New York.

1984 Mississippian Expansion: Tracing the Historical Development of an Explanatory Model. *Southeastern Archaeology* 3(1):13–32.

1985 Mississippian Patterns of Subsistence and Settlement. In *Alabama and the Borderlands: From Prehistory to Statehood*, edited by R. R. Badger and L. A. Clayton, pp. 64–80. University of Alabama Press, Tuscaloosa.

1986 The Archaeology of the Southeastern United States: From Dalton to de Soto, 10,500–500 B.P. In *Advances in World Archaeology*, Vol. 5, edited by F. Wendorf and A. Close, pp. 1–92. Academic Press, New York.

1992 *Rivers of Change: Essays on Early Agriculture in Eastern North America*. Smithsonian Institution Press, Washington, D.C.

Smith, Bruce D. (editor)

1978 *Mississippian Settlement Patterns*. Academic Press, New York.

1990 *The Mississippian Emergence*. Smithsonian Institution Press, Washington, D.C.

Smith, Claire, and H. Martin Wobst (editors)

2005 *Indigenous Archaeologies: Decolonizing Theory and Practice*. Routledge, London.

Smith, F. Todd

1995 *The Caddo Indians: Tribes at the Convergence of Empires, 1542–1854*. Texas A&M University Press, College Station.

1998 The Political History of the Caddo Indians, 1686–1874. In *The Native History of the Caddo: Their Place in Southeastern Archeology and Ethnohistory*, edited by T. K. Perttula and J. E. Bruseth, pp. 175–181. Studies in Archeology No. 30. Texas Archeological Research Laboratory, University of Texas at Austin.

Smith, Lawson M., Joseph B. Dunbar, and Louis D. Britsch

1986 *Geomorphological Investigation of the Atchafalaya Basin, Area West, Atchafalaya Delta, and Terrebonne Marsh*, Vol. 1. Technical Report GL-86-3. Department of the Army Waterways Experimental Station, U.S. Army Corps of Engineers, Vicksburg District.

Smith, Marvin T.

2002 Eighteenth-Century Glass Beads in the French Colonial Trade. In French Colonial Studies at Old Mobile: Selected Studies, edited by Gregory A. Waselkov. *Historical Archaeology* 36(1):55–61.

Smith, Rhonda L.

1995 Vertebrate Faunal Identifications from the Bayou des Familles Site. In *Archeological Data Recovery at 16JE218, Jefferson Parish, Louisiana*. U.S. Army Corps of Engineers, New Orleans District.

1996 Vertebrate Subsistence in Southeastern Louisiana Between A.D. 700 and 1500. Unpublished M.A. thesis, Department of Anthropology, University of Georgia, Athens.

Smith, Steven D., and George J. Castille

1986 *Bailey's Dam*. Anthropological Study No. 8. Louisiana Archaeological Survey and Antiquities Commission, Department of Culture, Recreation, and Tourism, Baton Rouge.

Smith, Steven D., Philip G. Rivet, Kathleen M. Byrd, and Nancy W. Hawkins

1983 *Louisiana's Comprehensive Archaeological Plan*. Louisiana Division of Archaeology, Department of Culture, Recreation, and Tourism, Baton Rouge.

Spaulding, Albert C.

1953 Statistical Techniques for the Discovery of Artifact Types. *American Antiquity* 18(4):305–313.

Springer, James

1974 The Bruly St. Martin Site and Its Implications for Coastal Settlement in Louisiana. *Louisiana Archaeology* 1:75–82.

1980 An Analysis of Prehistoric Food Remains from the Bruly St. Martin Site, Louisiana, with a Comparative Discussion of Mississippi Valley Faunal Studies. *Midcontinental Journal of Archaeology* 5(2):193–223.

Squier, Ephraim G., and Edwin H. Davis

1848 *Ancient Monuments of the Mississippi Valley*. Smithsonian Contributions to Knowledge Vol. 1. Smithsonian Institution, Washington, D.C.

Stafford, Thomas, Russell Graham, Ernest Lundelius, Holmes Semken, Greg McDonald, and John Southon

2005 14C-Chronostratigraphy of Late Pleistocene Megafauna Extinctions in Relation to Human Presence in the New World. Paper presented at the Clovis in the Southeast Conference, Columbia, South Carolina.

Steinberg, Phil, and Rob Shields (editors)

2008 *What Is a City? Rethinking the Urban after Hurricane Katrina.* University of Georgia Press, Athens.

Steponaitis, Vincas P.

1978 Location Theory and Complex Chiefdoms: A Mississippian Example. In *Mississippian Settlement Patterns,* edited by Bruce D. Smith, pp. 417–53. Academic Press, New York.

1979 Lead-Glazed Earthenwares. In *Tunica Treasure,* by Jeffery P. Brain, pp. 44–73. Papers of the Peabody Museum of Archaeology and Ethnology Vol. 71. Harvard University, Cambridge.

1986 Prehistoric Archaeology in the Southeastern United States, 1970–1985. *Annual Review of Anthropology* 15:363–404.

Stevenson, Joe

1992 Zooarchaeology of the Kleinpeter Site. Unpublished M.A. thesis, Department of Geography and Anthropology, Louisiana State University, Baton Rouge.

Stoltman, James B.

2004 Did Poverty Pointers Make Pots? In *Early Pottery: Technology, Function, Style, and Interaction in the Lower Southeast,* edited by Rebecca Saunders and Christopher T. Hays, pp. 210–222. University of Alabama Press, Tuscaloosa.

Story, Dee Ann

1978 Some Comments on Anthropological Studies Concerning the Caddo. In *Texas Archeology: Essays Honoring R. King Harris,* edited by K. D. House, pp. 46–68. Southern Methodist University Press, Dallas.

1990 Cultural History of the Native Americans. In *The Archeology and Bioarcheology of the Gulf Coastal Plain,* by D. A. Story, J. A. Guy, B. A. Burnett, M. D. Freeman, J. C. Rose, D. G. Steele, B. W. Olive, and K. J. Reinhard, pp. 163–366. Research Series No. 38, Arkansas Archeological Survey, Fayetteville.

1997 1968–1970 Archeological Investigations at the George C. Davis Site, Cherokee County, Texas. *Bulletin of the Texas Archeological Society* 68:1–113.

1998 The George C. Davis Site: Glimpses into Early Caddoan Symbolism and Ideology. In *The Native History of the Caddo: Their Place in Southeastern Archeology and Ethnohistory,* edited by T. K. Perttula and J. E. Bruseth, pp. 9–43. Studies in Archeology No. 30. Texas Archeological Research Laboratory, University of Texas at Austin.

2000 Introduction. In *The George C. Davis Site, Cherokee County, Texas,* by H. P. Newell and A. D. Krieger, pp. 1–31. 2nd ed. Society for American Archaeology, Washington, D.C.

Stout, Michael E.

1985 *Remote Sensing Investigation of the Citrus Lakefront Levee Mobilization Sites, Lake Pontchartrain and Vicinity Hurricane Protection Project, Orleans Parish, Louisiana.* U.S. Army Corps of Engineers, New Orleans District.

1992 *A Reconnaissance Survey of Derelict Boats on Bayou DuLarge, Terrebonne Parish, Louisiana.* U.S. Army Corps of Engineers, New Orleans District.

Strickland-Olsen, Mary, Jenna Tedrick Kuttruff, and Carl Kuttruff

1999 Archaic Fiber Perishables from Avery Island: Analysis and Conservation of Louisiana¹s Oldest Dated Textiles. *Louisiana Archaeology* 23(1996):91–128.

Stright, Melanie J.

1986 Human Occupation of the Continental Shelf during the Late Pleistocene/Early Holocene: Methods for Site Location. *Geoarchaeology* 1(4):347–364.

1999 Spatial Data Analysis of Artifacts Redeposited by Coastal Erosion: A Case Study of McFaddin Beach, Texas. Unpublished Ph.D. dissertation, Department of Anthropology, American University, Washington, D.C.

Stright, Melanie J., Eileen M. Lear, and James F. Bennett

1999 *Spatial Data Analysis of Artifacts Redeposited by Coastal Erosion: A Case Study of McFaddin Beach, Texas.* 2 vols. OCS Study MMS 99–0068. Minerals Management Service, U.S. Department of the Interior. Herndon, Virginia.

Struchtemeyer, Dena L.

2008 Separate But Equal? The Archaeology of an Early Twentieth-Century African American School. Unpublished M.A. thesis, Department of Geography and Anthropology, Louisiana State University, Baton Rouge.

Struiver, Minze, Paula J. Reimer, Edouard Bard, J. Warren Beck, G. S. Burr, Konrad A. Hughen, Bernd Kromer, Gerry McCormac, Johannes van der Plicht, and Mark Spurk

1998 INTCAL98 Radiocarbon Age Calibration, 24,000–0 cal BP. *Radiocarbon* 40(3):1041–1083.

Sturtevant, William C.

1966 Anthropology, History, and Ethnohistory. *Ethnohistory* 13:1–51.

Styles, Bonnie W., and Walter E. Klippel

1996 Mid-Holocene Faunal Exploration in the Southeastern United States. In *Archaeology of the Mid-Holocene Southeast,* edited by Kenneth E Sassaman and David G. Anderson, pp. 115–133. University Press of Florida, Gainesville.

Swanson, Betsy

1991 *Terre Haute de Barataria: An Historic Upland on an Old River Distributary Overtaken by Forest in the Barataria Unit of the Jean Lafitte National Historical Park and Preserve.* Jefferson Parish Historical Commission, Harahan.

Swanton, John R.

1911 *Indian Tribes of the Lower Mississippi Valley and Adjacent Coast of the Gulf of Mexico.* Bureau of American Ethnology Bulletin 43. Smithsonian Institution, Washington, D.C.

1928 *Social Organization and Social Usages of the Indians of the Creek Confederacy.* Bureau of American Ethnology Forty-Second Annual Report, 1924–1925. Smithsonian Institution, Washington, D.C.

1931 *Source Material for the Social and Ceremonial Life of the Choctaw Indians.* Bureau of American Ethnology Bulletin 103. Smithsonian Institution, Washington, D.C.

1942 *Source Material on the History and Ethnology of the Caddo Indians.* Bureau of American Ethnology Bulletin 132. Smithsonian Institution, Washington, D.C.

1946 *The Indians of the Southeastern United States.* Bureau of American Ethnology Bulletin 137. Smithsonian Institution, Washington, D.C.

Swidler, Nina, Kurt Dongoske, Roger Anyon, and Alan Downer (editors)

1997 *Native Americans and Archaeologists: Stepping Stones to Common Ground.* AltaMira Press, Walnut Creek, California.

Sylvia, Diane E.

1998 Indian and French Interaction in Colonial Louisiana during the Early Eighteenth Century. Unpublished Ph.D. dissertation, Department of Anthropology, Tulane University, New Orleans.

Tallant, Robert

1946 *Voodoo in New Orleans.* Pelican Publishing Company, Gretna, Louisiana.

Taylor, Joe Gray

1974 *Louisiana Reconstructed, 1863–1877.* Louisiana State University Press, Baton Rouge.

Taylor, Walter W.

1964 Tethered Nomadism and Water Territoriality: An Hypothesis. *Actas y Memorias del XXXV Congreso Internacionale Americanistas* 2:197–203.

1983 *A Study of Archeology.* Southern Illinois University, Carbondale. Originally published 1948 as Memoir No. 69 of the American Anthropological Association.

Terrell, Bruce G.

1990 *Louisiana Submerged Cultural Resource Management Plan.* Louisiana Division of Archaeology, Office of Cultural Development, Department of Culture, Recreation, and Tourism, Baton Rouge.

Texas Beyond History

2007 Los Adaes. Electronic document online at: www.texasbeyondhistory.net/adaes/index.html

2008 Texas Beyond History website: www.texasbeyondhistory.net

Thomas, Cyrus

1894 *Report on the Mound Explorations of the Bureau of Ethnology.* Bureau of American Ethnology Twelfth Annual Report. Smithsonian Institution, Washington, D.C.

Thomas, D. H.

2005 Foreword: Some Personal Thoughts on "Partnering Up." In *A Rediscovering of Caddo Heritage: The W. T. Scott Collection at the American Museum of Natural History and Other Caddo Collections from Arkansas and Louisiana,* by B. Gonzalez, R. Cast, T. K. Perttula, and B. Nelson, pp. xiii–xv Caddo Nation of Oklahoma, Historic Preservation Program, Binger.

Thomas, Larissa

2001 The Gender Division of Labor in Mississippian Households: Its Role in Shaping Production for Exchange. In *Archaeological Studies of Gender in the Southeastern United States,* edited by Jane M. Eastman and Christopher B. Rodning, pp. 27–56. University Press of Florida, Gainesville.

Thomas, Prentice M., Jr., and L. Janice Campbell

1978 *A Multicomponent Site on the Happyville Bend of Little River: 16LA37—The Whatley Site.* Report of Investigations No. 11. New World Research, Inc., Pollock, Louisiana.

1991 The Elliot's Point Complex: New Data Regarding the Localized Poverty Point Expression on the Northwest Florida Gulf Coast, 2000 B.C.–500 B.C. In *The Poverty Point Culture: Local Manifestations, Subsistence Practices, and Trade Networks,* edited by Kathleen M. Byrd, pp. 103–119. Geoscience and Man 29. Louisiana State University, Baton Rouge.

Thomas, Prentice M., Jr., and L. Janice Campbell (editors)

1978 *The Peripheries of Poverty Point.* Report of Investigations No. 12. New World Research, Inc., Pollock, Louisiana.

Thomas, Prentice M., Jr., L. Janice Campbell, and Steven R. Ahler

1980 The Hanna Site: An Alto Focus Village in Red River Parish. *Louisiana Archaeology* 5(1978).

Thompson, Robert Farris

1983 *Flash of the Spirit: African and Afro-American Art and Philosophy.* Random House, New York.

Tidwell, Mike

2003 *Bayou Farewell: The Rich Life and Tragic Death of Louisiana's Cajun Coast.* Random House, New York.

Tjarks, Alicia V.

1974 Comparative Demographic Analysis of Texas, 1777–1793. *Southwestern Historical Quarterly* 77(3):291–338.

Toth, Alan

1974 *Archaeology and Ceramics at the Marksville Site.* Anthropological Papers 56. Museum of Anthropology. University of Michigan, Ann Arbor.

1979a The Marksville Connection. In *Hopewell Archaeology: The Chillicothe Conference,* edited by David S. Brose and N'omi Greber, pp. 188–199. Kent State University Press, Kent, Ohio.

1979b *The Lake St. Agnes Site: A Multi-Component Occupation of Avoyelles Parish, Louisiana.* Mélanges No.13. Museum of Geoscience, Louisiana State University, Baton Rouge.

1988 *Early Marksville Phases in the Lower Mississippi Valley: A Study of Culture Contact Dynamics.* Archaeological Report No. 21. Originally published in 1977. Mississippi Department of Archives and History, Jackson.

Tregle, Joseph G.

1992 Creoles and Americans. In *Creole New Orleans: Race and Americanization,* edited by Arnold R. Hirsch and Joseph Logsdon, pp. 131–188. Louisiana State University Press, Baton Rouge.

Trigger, Bruce G.

1985 *Archaeology as Historical Science.* Monograph 14. Department of Ancient Indian History, Culture, and Archaeology, Banaras Hindu University, Varanasi, India.

1991 Distinguished Lecture in Archaeology: Constraint and Freedom—A New Synthesis for Archaeological Explanation. *American Anthropologist* 93(3): 551–569.

2006 *A History of Archaeological Thought,* 2nd ed. Cambridge University Press, Cambridge.

Trouillot, Michel-Rolph

1995 *Silencing the Past: Power and the Production of History.* Beacon Press, Boston.

Trubowitz, Neal L.

1984 Introduction to the Cedar Grove Project. In *Cedar Grove: An Interdisciplinary Investigation of a Late Caddo Farmstead in the Red River Valley,* edited by N. L. Trubowitz, pp. 1–7. Research Series No. 23. Arkansas Archeological Survey, Fayetteville.

Turner, Ellen Sue, and Thomas R. Hester

1999 *A Field Guide to Stone Artifacts of Texas Indians.* Gulf Publishing, Lanham, Maryland.

United Nations Educational, Scientific, and Cultural Organization (UNESCO)

2009 World Heritage Centre. Website of the United Nations Educational, Scientific and Cultural Organization online at: whc.unesco.org/

Usner, Daniel H., Jr.

1992 *Indians, Settlers, and Slaves in a Frontier Exchange Economy: The Lower Mississippi Valley before 1783.* University of North Carolina Press, Chapel Hill.

1998 *American Indians in the Lower Mississippi Valley: Social and Economic Histories.* University of Nebraska Press, Lincoln.

Van Heerden, Ivor L., and Mike Bryan

2006 *The Storm: What Went Wrong and Why during Hurricane Katrina: The Inside Story from One Louisiana Scientist.* Viking, New York.

Van Osdell, Mary A.

1984 A Bygone Era Resurrected in Wood. *Forests & People* 34(1):18–21.

VanPool, Christine S. and Todd L. VanPool

1999 The Scientific Nature of Postprocessualism. *American Antiquity* 64(1):33–53.

Vasbinder, Fiona H.

2005 King George Island Mounds Site (16LV22): A Late Archaic Mound Complex along the Lower Amite River. Unpublished M.A. thesis, Department of Geography and Anthropology, Louisiana State University, Baton Rouge.

Veatch, Arthur C.

1899a Special Report No. 2: The Shreveport Area. In *A Preliminary Report on the Geology of Louisiana,* edited by Gilbert D. Harris and Arthur C. Veatch, pp. 152–208. Louisiana State University and A. and M. College, Baton Rouge.

1899b Special Report No. 3: The Five Islands. In *A Preliminary Report on the Geology of Louisiana,* edited by Gilbert D. Harris and Arthur C. Veatch, pp. 213–262. Louisiana State University and A. and M. College, Baton Rouge.

1902a Special Report No. II: The Salines of North Louisiana. In *A Report on the Geology of Louisiana,* edited by Gilbert D. Harris, Arthur C. Veatch, and Jov. A. A. Pacheco, pp. 47–100. Louisiana State University and A. and M. College, Baton Rouge.

1902b Special Report No. IV: Notes on the Geology along the Ouachita. In *A Report on the Geology of Louisiana,* edited by Gilbert D. Harris, Arthur C. Veatch and Jov. A. A. Pacheco, pp. 153–172. Louisiana State University and A. and M. College, Baton Rouge.

Vescelius, Gary S.

1957 Mound 2 at Marksville. *American Antiquity* 22(4):416–420.

Vlach, John Michael

1986 The Shot Gun House: An African Architectural Legacy. In *Common Places: Readings in American Vernacular Architecture,* edited by D. Upton and J. M. Vlach, pp. 58–78. University of Georgia Press, Athens.

Voss, Jerome A., and John H. Blitz

1988 Archaeological Investigations in the Choctaw Homeland. *American Antiquity* 53(1):125–145.

Walker, H. Jesse, and James L. Coleman

1987 Atlantic and Gulf Coastal Province. In *Geomorphic Systems of North America,* edited by William L. Graf, pp. 51–110. Centennial Special Volume 2. Geological Society of America, Boulder.

Walker, Renee B.

2007 Hunting in the Late Paleoindian Period: Faunal Remains from Dust Cave, Alabama. In *Foragers of the Terminal Pleistocene in North America,* edited by Renee B. Walker and Boyce N. Driskell, pp. 99–115. University of Nebraska Press, Lincoln.

Walker, Renee B., and Boyce N. Driskell (editors)

2007 *Foragers of the Terminal Pleistocene in North America.* University of Nebraska Press, Lincoln.

Walker, Winslow M.

1932 A Reconnaissance of Northern Louisiana Mounds. In *Explorations and Field-Work of the Smithsonian Institution in 1931*, pp. 169–174. Smithsonian Institution, Washington, D.C.

1933 Trailing the Moundbuilders of the Mississippi Valley. In *Explorations and Field-Work of the Smithsonian Institution in 1932*, pp. 77–80. Smithsonian Institution, Washington, D.C.

1934 A Variety of Caddo Pottery from Louisiana. *Journal of the Washington Academy of Sciences* 24(2):99–104.

1935 A Caddo Burial Site at Natchitoches, Louisiana. *Smithsonian Miscellaneous Collections* 94(14). Washington, D.C.

1936 *The Troyville Mounds, Catahoula Parish, Louisiana.* Bureau of American Ethnology Bulletin 113. Smithsonian Institution, Washington, D.C.

Walthall, John A., Clarence H. Webb, Steven H. Stow, and Sharon I. Goad

1982 Galena Analysis and Poverty Point Trade. *Midcontinental Journal of Archaeology* 7(1):133–148.

Ward, Heather D.

1998 The Paleobotanical Record of the Poverty Point Culture: Implications of Past and Current Research. *Southeastern Archaeology* 17(2):166–173.

Waring, George E., Jr. (compiler)

1886 *Report on the Social Statistics of Cities, Part II.* United States Census Office, Government Printing Office, Washington, D.C.

Warner, Mark S.

1998 "The Best There Is of Us": Ceramics and Status in African American Annapolis. In *Annapolis Pasts: Historical Archaeology in Annapolis, Maryland*, edited by Paul Shackel, Paul Mullins, and Mark Warner, pp.190–212. University of Tennessee Press, Knoxville.

Waselkov, Gregory A.

1989a Introduction: Recent Archaeological and Historical Research. In *Fort Toulouse: The French Outpost at the Alabamas on the Coosa*, by Daniel H. Thomas, pp. vi–xlii. University of Alabama Press, Tuscaloosa.

1989b A Summary of French Colonial Archaeology in Eastern "Louisiane." *Mississippi Archaeology* 24(2):53–69.

1991 *Archaeology at the French-Colonial Site of Old Mobile (Phase I, 1989–91).* Anthropological Monograph 1. University of South Alabama, Mobile.

1997 *The Archaeology of French Colonial North America.* English-French ed. Guides to Historical Archaeological Literature No. 5. Society for Historical Archaeology, Rockville, Maryland.

2002 French Colonial Archaeology at Old Mobile: An Introduction. In French Colonial Studies at Old Mobile: Selected Studies, edited by Gregory A. Waselkov. *Historical Archaeology* 36(1):3–12.

Waselkov, Gregory A. (editor)

2002 French Colonial Studies at Old Mobile: Selected Studies. *Historical Archaeology* 36(1).

Waselkov, Gregory A., and Bonnie L. Gums

2000 *Plantation Archaeology at Rivière aux Chiens, ca. 1725–1848.* Center for Archaeological Studies, University of South Alabama, Mobile.

Waselkov, Gregory A., and Diane E. Sylvia

1995 *Final Archaeological Data Recovery at the Dog River Site, 1MB161 (ALDOT Project BRS-BRM-7500(10)), Mobile County, Alabama.* Center for Archaeological Studies, University of South Alabama, Mobile.

Waselkov, Gregory A., and John A. Walthall

2002 Faience Styles in French Colonial North America: A Revised Classification. In French Colonial Archaeology at Old Mobile: Selected Studies, edited by Gregory A. Waselkov. *Historical Archaeology* 36(1):62–78.

Waters, Michael R., and Thomas W. Stafford

2007 Redefining the Age of Clovis: Implications for the Peopling of the Americas. Science 315(5815):1122–1126.

Watkins, Joe

2000 *Indigenous Archaeology: American Indian Values and Scientific Practice.* AltaMira Press, Lanham, Maryland.

Way, Frederick, Jr.

1994 *Way's Packet Directory, 1848–1994.* Ohio University Press, Athens.

Way, Frederick, Jr., and Joseph W. Rutter

1990 *Way's Steam Towboat Directory.* Ohio University Press, Athens.

Way, Michael A.

2007 "Turtles All the Way Down": Foodways at a Point Coupee Louisiana Plantation. Unpublished senior honors thesis, Department of Anthropology, University of California, Berkeley.

Weaver, Elizabeth C.

1963 Technological Analysis of Prehistoric Lower Mississippi Ceramic Materials: A Preliminary Report. *American Antiquity* 29(1):49–56.

Webb, Clarence H.

1944 Stone Vessels from a Northeast Louisiana Site. *American Antiquity* 9(4): 386–394.

1946 Two Unusual Types of Chipped Stone Artifacts from Northwest Louisiana. *Bulletin of the Texas Archeological and Paleontological Society* 17:9–17.

1948 Evidences of Pre-Pottery Cultures in Louisiana. *American Antiquity* 13(3):227–232.

1959 *The Belcher Mound: A Stratified Caddoan Site in Caddo Parish, Louisiana.* Memoir No. 16. Society for American Archaeology, Salt Lake City, Utah.

1963 The Smithport Landing Site: An Alto Focus Component in DeSoto Parish, Louisiana. *Bulletin of the Texas Archeological Society* 32:143–187.

1965 The Paleo-Indian Era: Distribution of Finds, Louisiana. *Southeastern Archaeological Conference Bulletin* 2:4–6.

1968 The Extent and Content of Poverty Point Culture. *American Antiquity* 33(3):297–321.

1970 Settlement Patterns in the Poverty Point Complex. *Southeastern Archaeological Conference Bulletin* 12:3–12.

1977 *The Poverty Point Culture.* Geoscience and Man 17. Louisiana State University, Baton Rouge.

1981 *Stone Points and Tools of Northwestern Louisiana.* Special Publication No. 1. Louisiana Archaeological Society, Baton Rouge.

1982a *The Poverty Point Culture.* Geoscience and Man 17. Revised 2nd ed. Louisiana State University, Baton Rouge.

1982b Peer Review. In *Arkansas Archeology in Review,* edited by N. L. Trubowitz and M. D. Jeter, pp. 361–366. Research Series No. 15. Arkansas Archeological Survey, Fayetteville.

1983 The Bossier Focus Revisited: Montgomery I, Werner and Other Unicomponent Sites. In *Southeastern Natives and Their Pasts: Papers Honoring Dr. Robert E. Bell,* edited by Don G. Wyckoff and Jack L. Hofman, pp. 183–240. Oklahoma Archeological Survey Studies in Oklahoma's Past No. 11, and Cross Timbers Heritage Association Contribution No. 2. Oklahoma Archeological Survey, Norman.

2000 *Stone Points and Tools of Northwestern Louisiana.* 2nd ed. Special Publication No. 1. Louisiana Archaeological Society, Baton Rouge.

Webb, Clarence H., and H. Monroe Dodd, Jr.

1939 Further Excavations of the Gahagan Mound: Connections with a Florida Culture. *Bulletin of the Texas Archeological and Paleontological Society* 11:92–126.

Webb, Clarence H., and Brian J. Duhe

1984 The Louisiana Archaeological Society's First Decade, 1974–1984. In *Louisiana Archaeology and the Society: Celebration of a Decade of Achievement,* edited by Jon L. Gibson, pp. 55–87. Special Publication No. 2. Louisiana Archaeological Society, Lafayette.

Webb, Clarence H., and Hiram F. Gregory

1986 *The Caddo Indians of Louisiana.* 2nd ed. Anthropological Study No. 2. Louisiana Archaeological Survey and Antiquities Commission, Department of Culture, Recreation, and Tourism, Baton Rouge.

Webb, Clarence H., and Ralph McKinney

1975 Mounds Plantation (16CD12), Caddo Parish, Louisiana. *Louisiana Archaeology* 2:39–127.

Webb, Clarence H., Joel L. Shiner, and E. Wayne Roberts

1971 The John Pearce Site (16CD56): A San Patrice Site in Caddo Parish, Louisiana. *Bulletin of the Texas Archeological Society* 42:1–49.

Webb, Malcolm C.

1982 The Neutral Calorie? On the Maintenance of Ranked Societies in the "Agriculturally Deficient" Environment of Gulf Coastal Louisiana. *Louisiana Archaeology* 8(1981):1–19.

Weber, David J.

1992 *The Spanish Frontier in North America.* Yale University Press, New Haven.

Wedel, Mildred M.

1978 *La Harpe's 1719 Post on Red River and Nearby Caddo Settlements.* Bulletin 30. Texas Memorial Museum, Austin.

Weinand, Daniel C., Elizabeth J. Reitz, David B. Kelley, and Melissa Braud

1997 Vertebrate Fauna and Freshwater Mussels. In *Two Caddoan Farmsteads in the Red River Valley,* edited by David B. Kelley, pp. 97–108. Research Series No. 51, Arkansas Archeological Survey, Fayetteville.

Weinstein, Richard A.

1986 Tchefuncte Occupation in the Lower Mississippi Delta and Adjacent Coastal Zone. In *The Tchula Period in the Mid-South and Lower Mississippi Valley: Proceedings of the 1982 Mid-South Archaeological Conference,* edited by David H. Dye and Ronald C. Brister, pp. 102–127. Archaeological Report No. 17. Mississippi Department of Archives and History, Jackson.

1987a Development and Regional Variation of Plaquemine Culture in South Louisiana. In *Emergent Mississippian: Proceedings of the Sixth Mid-South Archaeological Conference,* edited by Richard A. Marshall, pp. 85–106. Occasional Paper No. 87–01. Cobb Institute of Archaeology, Mississippi State University, Mississippi State.

1987b The Rosedale and Shellhill Discs: "Southern Cult" Evidence from Southeastern Louisiana. *Louisiana Archaeology* 11(1984):65–88.

1995 The Tchula Period in the Lower Mississippi Valley and Adjacent Coastal Zone: A Brief Summary. In "An' Stuff Like That There": In Appreciation of William G. Haag, edited by Jon L. Gibson, Robert W. Neuman, and Richard A. Weinstein. *Louisiana Archaeology* 18(1991):153–187.

1996 Archaeological Investigations at the Lee Site, East Baton Rouge Parish, Louisiana. *Louisiana Archaeology* 21(1994):1–55.

Weinstein, Richard A. (editor)

2005 *Lake Providence: A Terminal Coles Creek Culture Mound Center, East Carroll Parish, Louisiana.* 2 vols. Coastal Environments, Inc., Baton Rouge. U.S. Army Corps of Engineers, Vicksburg District.

Weinstein, Richard A., and Ashley A. Dumas

2008 The Spread of Shell-Tempered Ceramics along the Northern Coast of the Gulf of Mexico. *Southeastern Archaeology* 27(2):202–221.

Weinstein, Richard A., and David B. Kelley

1992 *Cultural Resources Investigations in the Terrebonne Marsh, South-Central Louisiana*. Coastal Environments, Inc., Baton Rouge. U.S. Army Corps of Engineers, New Orleans District.

Weinstein, Richard A., David B. Kelley, and Joe W. Saunders (editors)

2003 *The Louisiana and Arkansas Expeditions of Clarence Bloomfield Moore*. University of Alabama Press, Tuscaloosa.

Weinstein, Richard A., and Philip G. Rivet

1978 *Beau Mire: A Late Tchula Period Site of the Tchefuncte Culture, Ascension Parish, Louisiana*. Anthropological Report No. 1. Louisiana Archaeological Survey and Antiquities Commission, Department of Culture, Recreation, and Tourism, Baton Rouge.

Welch, Paul D.

2006 *Archaeology at Shiloh Indian Mounds, 1899–1999*. University of Alabama Press, Tuscaloosa.

Wells, Douglas C.

1997 Political Competition and Site Placement: Late Prehistoric Settlement in the Tensas Basin of Northeast Louisiana. *Louisiana Archaeology* 22(1995):71–91.

1998 *The Early Coles Creek Period and the Evolution of Social Inequality in the Lower Mississippi Valley*. Unpublished Ph.D. dissertation, Department of Anthropology, Tulane University, New Orleans.

2001 *Cultural Resources Evaluation of the Upper Atchafalaya Backwater Area, Iberville and Pointe Coupee Parishes, South Louisiana*. Coastal Environments, Inc., Baton Rouge. U.S. Army Corps of Engineers, New Orleans District.

2005 Aboriginal Ceramics. In *Lake Providence: A Terminal Coles Creek Culture Mound Center, East Carroll Parish, Louisiana*, edited by R. A. Weinstein, pp. 311–390. Coastal Environments, Inc., Baton Rouge. U.S. Army Corps of Engineers, Vicksburg District.

Wells, Douglas C., and Richard A. Weinstein

2005 The Preston Phase in Regional Context. In *Lake Providence: A Terminal Coles Creek Culture Mound Center, East Carroll Parish, Louisiana*, edited by R. A. Weinstein, pp. 491–511. Coastal Environments, Inc., Baton Rouge. U.S. Army Corps of Engineers, Vicksburg District.

2007 Extraregional Contact and Cultural Interaction at the Coles Creek–Plaquemine Transition: Recent Data from the Lake Providence Mounds, East Carroll Parish, Louisiana. In *Plaquemine Archaeology*, edited by Mark A. Rees and Patrick C. Livingood, pp. 38–65. University of Alabama Press, Tuscaloosa.

Wesson, Cameron B., and Mark A. Rees

2002 Protohistory and Archaeology: An Overview. In *Between Contacts and Colonies: Archaeological Perspectives on the Protohistoric Southeast*, edited by C. B. Wesson and M. A. Rees, pp. 1–11. University of Alabama Press, Tuscaloosa.

Wheat, Joe Ben

1979 *The Jurgens Site.* Memoir No. 15. Plains Anthropologist, Lincoln, Nebraska.

White, David R. M.

1998 *"Cultural Gumbo"? An Ethnographic Overview of Louisiana's Mississippi River Delta and Selected Adjacent Areas.* Applied Cultural Dynamics, Santa Fe. Jean Lafitte National Historical Park and Preserve, New Orleans.

White, Nancy Marie

2005 Prehistoric Connections around the Gulf Coast. In *Gulf Coast Archaeology: The Southeastern United States and Mexico,* edited by Nancy Marie White, pp. 1–55. University Press of Florida, Gainesville.

White, Nancy Marie (editor)

2005 *Gulf Coast Archaeology: The Southeastern United States and Mexico.* University Press of Florida, Gainesville.

White, Nancy Marie, and Richard A. Weinstein

2008 The Mexican Connection and the Far West of the U.S. Southeast. *American Antiquity* 73(2):227–277.

White, Richard

1991 *The Middle Ground: Indians, Empires, and Republics in the Great Lakes Region, 1650–1815.* Cambridge University Press, Cambridge.

Whitely, Peter M.

2002 Archaeology and Oral Tradition: The Scientific Importance of Dialogue. *American Antiquity* 67(3):405–415.

Wilkie, Laurie A.

1995 Plantation Archaeology: Where Past and Present Can Collide. *African American Archaeology* 13. Available online at: www.diaspora.uiuc.edu/aaanewsletter/newsletter13.html.

1997 Secret and Sacred: Contextualizing the Artifacts of African American Magic and Religion. *Historical Archaeology* 31(4):81–106.

2000 *Creating Freedom: Material Culture and African American Identity at Oakley Plantation, Louisiana, 1840–1950.* Louisiana State University Press, Baton Rouge.

2001a Race, Identity, and Habermas' Lifeworld. In *Race and the Archaeology of Identity,* edited by Charles E. Orser, Jr., pp. 108–124. University of Utah Press, Salt Lake City.

2001b Black Sharecroppers and White Frat Boys: Living Communities and the Construction of Their Archaeological Pasts. In *The Archaeology of the Contemporary Past,* edited by Victor Buchli and Gavin Lucas, pp. 108–118. Routledge, London.

Wilkie, Laurie A., and Kevin M. Bartoy

2000 A Critical Archaeology Revisited. *Current Anthropology* 41(5): 747–778.

Wilkie, Laurie A., and Paul Farnsworth

2005 *Sampling Many Pots: An Archaeology of Memory and Tradition at a Bahamian Plantation.* University Press of Florida, Gainesville.

Willey, Gordon R.

1953 A Pattern of Diffusion-Acculturation. *Southwestern Journal of Anthropology* 9(4):369–384.

1966 *An Introduction to American Archaeology.*, Vol. 1: *North and Middle America.* Prentice-Hall, Englewood Cliffs, New Jersey.

1969 James Alfred Ford, 1911–1968. *American Antiquity* 34(1):62–71.

Willey, Gordon R., and Philip Phillips

1958 *Method and Theory in American Archaeology.* University of Chicago Press, Chicago.

Willey, Gordon R., and Jeremy A. Sabloff

1993 *A History of American Archaeology.* 3rd ed. Freeman, New York.

Williams, Jeffrey M.

2007 GIS Aided Archaeological Research of El Camino Real de los Tejas, with Focus on the Landscape and River Crossings along El Camino Carretera. Unpublished M.A. thesis, Department of Forestry, Stephen F. Austin State University, Nacogdoches.

Williams, Stephen

1956 Settlement Patterns in the Lower Mississippi Valley. In *Prehistoric Settlement Patterns in the New World,* edited by Gordon R. Willey, pp. 52–62. Viking Fund Publications in Anthropology No. 23. Wenner-Gren Foundation for Anthropological Research, New York.

1963 The Eastern United States. In *The National Survey of Historic Sites and Buildings, Themes II and III: Early Indian Farmers and Village Communities,* edited by William G. Haag, pp. 267–325. National Park Service, U.S. Department of the Interior, Washington, D.C.

1967 On the Location of the Historic Taensa Villages. *Conference on Historic Sites Archaeology Papers 1965–1966* 1:3–13.

Williams, Stephen, and Jeffrey P. Brain

1983 *Excavations at the Lake George Site, Yazoo County, Mississippi, 1958–1960.* Papers of the Peabody Museum of Archaeology and Ethnology Vol. 74. Harvard University, Cambridge.

Wilson, James

1998 *The Earth Shall Weep: A History of Native America.* Grove Press, New York.

Wilson, Joseph T., Nicholas R. Spitzer, Ray Brassieur, Michael Caron, Jeffrey Mark Golliher, H. F. Gregory, C. Paige Gutierrez, Janice Pierce, and Robert R. Rathburn

1979 *Mississippi Delta Ethnographic Overview.* Report prepared for the National Park Service by the National Council for the Traditional Arts. National Park Service, Washington, D.C.

Winterbottom, Thomas M.

1969 *An Account of the Native Africans in the Neighborhood of Sierra Leone, to which is*

Added an Account of the Present State of Medicine among Them. 2 vols. 2nd rev. ed. Cass, London. Originally published in 1803, C. Whittingham, London.

Wiseman, Diana E., Richard A. Weinstein, and Kathleen G. McCloskey

1979 *Cultural Resources Survey of the Mississippi River–Gulf Outlet, Orleans and St. Bernard Parishes, Louisiana.* Coastal Environments, Inc., Baton Rouge. U.S. Army Corps of Engineers, New Orleans District.

Wolf, Eric R.

1982 *Europe and the People without History.* University of California Press, Berkeley.

Wright, Herbert E., Jr.

2006 Climate and Biota of Eastern North America. In *Handbook of North American Indians.*, Vol. 3: *Environment, Origins, and Population,* edited by Douglas H. Ubelaker, pp. 99–109. Smithsonian Institution Press, Washington, D.C.

Wylie, Alison

2002 *Thinking from Things: Essays in the Philosophy of Archaeology.* University of California Press, Berkeley.

Yakubik, Jill-Karen, and Shannon Lee Dawdy

1996 *Archaeological Investigations at the Durel Cottage (16OR136).* Earth Search, Inc., New Orleans. Historic New Orleans Collection.

Yakubik, Jill-Karen, and Herschel A. Franks

1992 *Archaeological Survey and Testing in the Holy Cross Historic District, New Orleans, Louisiana.* Earth Search, Inc., New Orleans. U.S. Army Corps of Engineers, New Orleans District.

1997 *Archaeological Investigations at the Site of the Cabildo, New Orleans, Louisiana.* Earth Search, Inc., New Orleans. Louisiana State Museum, New Orleans.

Yakubik, Jill-Karen, Carrie A. Leven, Kenneth R. Jones, Benjamin Maygarden, Shannon Dawdy, Donna K. Stone, James Cusick, Catheren Jones, Rosalinda Méndez, Herschel A. Franks, and Tara Bond

1994 *Archaeological Data Recovery at Ashland–Belle Helene Plantation (16AN26), Ascension Parish, Louisiana.* Earth Search, Inc., New Orleans. Report on file with the Louisiana Division of Archaeology, Department of Culture, Recreation, and Tourism, Baton Rouge.

Yakubik, Jill-Karen, and Rosalinda Méndez

1995 *Beyond the Great House: Archaeology at Ashland–Belle Helene Plantation.* Discovering Louisiana Archaeology Series Vol. 1. Louisiana Department of Culture, Recreation, and Tourism, Baton Rouge. Electronic document available online at: www.crt.state.la.us/archaeology/virtualbooks/GREATHOU/MTGH.HTM

Yodis, Elaine G., Craig E. Colten, and David C. Johnson

2003 *Geography of Louisiana.* McGraw Hill, Boston.

Zinn, Howard

2003 *A People's History of the United States: 1492–Present.* Harper Collins, New York.

Contributors

George Avery, Ph.D., Department of Social and Cultural Analysis, Stephen F. Austin State University, Nacogdoches, Texas.

Ian W. Brown, Ph.D., Department of Anthropology, University of Alabama, Tuscaloosa.

Kathleen M. Byrd, Ph.D., Northwestern State University of Louisiana, Natchitoches (retired).

Robert Cast, Caddo Nation Cultural Preservation Office, Binger, Oklahoma.

Shannon Lee Dawdy, Ph.D., Department of Anthropology, University of Chicago, Illinois.

Paul Farnsworth, Ph.D., William Self Associates, Inc., Orinda, California.

Jon L. Gibson, Ph.D., Lake Claiborne, Louisiana.

Jeffrey S. Girard, M.A., School of Social Sciences, Northwestern State University of Louisiana, Natchitoches.

Bobby Gonzalez, Caddo Nation Cultural Preservation Office, Binger, Oklahoma.

D. Ryan Gray, M.A., Earth Search, Inc., New Orleans.

Christopher T. Hays, Ph.D., University of Wisconsin, Washington County, West Bend.

Aubra L. Lee, Ph.D., Earth Search, Inc., New Orleans.

Rob Mann, Ph.D., Department of Geography and Anthropology, Louisiana State University, Baton Rouge.

Christopher N. Matthews, Ph.D., Center for Public Archaeology and Department of Anthropology, Hofstra University, Hempstead, New York.

Charles R. McGimsey, Ph.D., RPA, Louisiana Division of Archaeology, Baton Rouge.

Robert W. Neuman, M.A., Louisiana State University (retired). Natchitoches, Louisiana.

David T. Palmer, Ph.D., RPA, Department of Sociology and Anthropology, University of Louisiana at Lafayette.

Charles E. Pearson, Ph.D., Coastal Environments, Inc., Baton Rouge.

Timothy K. Perttula, Ph.D., Archeological & Environmental Consultants, LLC., Austin, Texas.

Mark A. Rees, Ph.D., Department of Sociology and Anthropology, University of Louisiana at Lafayette.

LORI M. ROE, PH.D., Murray State University, Murray, Kentucky.

ALLEN R. SALTUS, JR., M.S., Archaeological Research, Inc., Jackson, Louisiana.

JOE W. SAUNDERS, PH.D., Department of Geosciences, University of Louisiana at Monroe.

TIMOTHY M. SCHILLING, PH.D. expected 2010, Department of Anthropology, Washington University, St. Louis, Missouri.

RICHARD A. WEINSTEIN, M.A., Coastal Environments, Inc., Baton Rouge.

LAURIE A. WILKIE, PH.D., Department of Anthropology, University of California, Berkeley.

JILL-KAREN YAKUBIK, PH.D., Earth Search, Inc., New Orleans.

Index

Index of Sites